A Book Of

DISCRETE STRUCTURE AND GRAPH THEORY

FOR

SEMESTER – III

SECOND YEAR (S.E.) DEGREE COURSE IN
COMPUTER ENGINEERING AND INFORMATION TECHNOLOGY

STRICTLY AS PER NEW REVISED SYLLABUS OF
NORTH MAHARASHTRA UNIVERSITY, JALGAON
EFFECTIVE FROM JUNE – 2013-2014

Dr. LATHA K. IYER
M. Sc., Ph. D.
Department of Mathematics
Maharashtra Institute of Technology,
PUNE.

Dr. NEETA D. KANKANE
B. Sc. (Gold Medalist),
M. Sc. (Gold Medalist) Ph. D.
Department of Mathematics
Maharashtra Institute of Technology,
PUNE.

N3018

DISCRETE STRUCTURE AND GRAPH THEORY (COMP./I.T.) (S.E. NMU)   ISBN 978-93-83525-46-1

Second Edition : July 2015

© : **Authors**

The text of this publication, or any part thereof, should not be reproduced or transmitted in any form or stored in any computer storage system or device for distribution including photocopy, recording, taping or information retrieval system or reproduced on any disc, tape, perforated media or other information storage device etc., without the written permission of Authors with whom the rights are reserved. Breach of this condition is liable for legal action.

Every effort has been made to avoid errors or omissions in this publication. In spite of this, errors may have crept in. Any mistake, error or discrepancy so noted and shall be brought to our notice shall be taken care of in the next edition. It is notified that neither the publisher nor the authors or seller shall be responsible for any damage or loss of action to any one, of any kind, in any manner, therefrom.

Published By :
NIRALI PRAKASHAN
Abhyudaya Pragati, 1312, Shivaji Nagar,
Off J.M. Road, PUNE – 411005
Tel - (020) 25512336/37/39, Fax - (020) 25511379
Email : niralipune@pragationline.com

Printed By :
REPRO INDIA LTD.
50/2 TTC MIDC Industrial Area,
MAHAPE
Navi Mumbai

☞ DISTRIBUTION CENTRES

PUNE

Nirali Prakashan : 119, Budhwar Peth, Jogeshwari Mandir Lane, Pune 411002, Maharashtra
Tel : (020) 2445 2044, 66022708, Fax : (020) 2445 1538
Email : bookorder@pragationline.com, niralilocal@pragationline.com

Nirali Prakashan : S. No. 28/27, Dhyari, Near Pari Company, Pune 411041
Tel : (020) 24690204 Fax : (020) 24690316
Email : dhyari@pragationline.com, bookorder@pragationline.com

MUMBAI

Nirali Prakashan : 385, S.V.P. Road, Rasdhara Co-op. Hsg. Society Ltd.,
Girgaum, Mumbai 400004, Maharashtra
Tel : (022) 2385 6339 / 2386 9976, Fax : (022) 2386 9976
Email : niralimumbai@pragationline.com

☞ DISTRIBUTION BRANCHES

JALGAON

Nirali Prakashan : 34, V. V. Golani Market, Navi Peth, Jalgaon 425001,
Maharashtra, Tel : (0257) 222 0395, Mob : 94234 91860

KOLHAPUR

Nirali Prakashan : New Mahadvar Road, Kedar Plaza, 1st Floor Opp. IDBI Bank
Kolhapur 416 012, Maharashtra. Mob : 9850046155

NAGPUR

Pratibha Book Distributors : Above Maratha Mandir, Shop No. 3, First Floor,
Rani Jhanshi Square, Sitabuldi, Nagpur 440012, Maharashtra
Tel : (0712) 254 7129

DELHI

Nirali Prakashan : 4593/21, Basement, Aggarwal Lane 15, Ansari Road, Daryaganj
Near Times of India Building, New Delhi 110002
Mob : 08505972553

BENGALURU

Pragati Book House : House No. 1, Sanjeevappa Lane, Avenue Road Cross,
Opp. Rice Church, Bengaluru – 560002.
Tel : (080) 64513344, 64513355,Mob : 9880582331, 9845021552
Email:bharatsavla@yahoo.com

CHENNAI

Pragati Books : 9/1, Montieth Road, Behind Taas Mahal, Egmore,
Chennai 600008 Tamil Nadu, Tel : (044) 6518 3535,
Mob : 94440 01782 / 98450 21552 / 98805 82331,
Email : bharatsavla@yahoo.com

niralipune@pragationline.com | www.pragationline.com

Also find us on   www.facebook.com/niralibooks

PREFACE

Many of the applications in present days technological **scenario** involve the use of computers in the development of Discrete Systems. In order to understand and study the structure of Discrete Systems, the knowledge of Discrete Mathematics is essential. This subject is included as a course "**Discrete Structures and Graph Theory**" in the second year curriculum of Computer Engineering and Information Technology Courses of North Maharashtra University, Jalgaon. From the current academic year 2013-14.

Chapter 1 deals with Propositional Calculus or Logic. Logic is the cornerstone of Discrete Structures, as many of the concepts developed are based on logical reasoning. To the computer technologist, logic is essential in the design of software and program verification.

In **Chapter 2**, we discuss Sets and Their Properties. Sets are the building blocks using which the other structures are built, namely groups and graphs. Hence it is essential to understand sets in order to have a clear understanding of more complicated structures.

In **Chapter 3** deals with some elementary counting techniques involving permutations and combinations. These techniques are then applied to discrete probability theory.

In **Chapter 4**, the concept of Relations, Digraphs and Lattices is studied in detail. Relations are used in data structures and job scheduling problems.

In **Chapter 5**, various types of functions and their properties, Pigeon-Hole Principle are discussed. Many concepts in computer science are conveniently stated in the language of functions.

In **Chapter 6**, special types of functions such as Discrete Numeric Functions, Generating Functions and Recurrence Relations are elaborately discussed. These functions are of special importance in software development.

In **Chapter 7**, we deals with the analysis of algorithms. In this chapter, we discuss different types of algorithms such as largest number; sorting, bubble sort divide and conquer binary search, Strassens matrix multiplication and time, complexity of algorithm. Many interesting problems such as completely of problems. tractable and intractable problems.

Chapter 8, deals with connectivity of graphs which is the central theme of graph theory. In this chapter, the famous "Konigsberg Seven Bridges Problem", from which the Theory of Graphs originated and some other important problems connected with Hamiltonian and Eulerian circuits are studied. Many interesting problems such as Three Utilities Problem, Odd Party Problem, Travelling Salesman Problem etc. are also discussed in this chpater.

In **Chapter 9**, we develop the theory of trees and their properties. Main applications of trees are in network analysis, data structures and files.

In **Chapter 10**, we introduce some special algebraic structures like semi groups, groups, rings and fields. In this chapter, we also discuss coding theory which is one of the most important application of algebraic structures. In particular, cyclic codes generated by polynomial rings are also discussed.

In **Chapter 11**, we introduce Boolean algebra, Boolean function and expression. In this chapter, we also discuss the number system and interconvertion of number system.

The subject of Discrete Structures is more conceptual rather than mathematical. Hence care has been taken to introduce the student to various concepts gradually. Each concept is followed by examples so that the student will have a firm grasp of the concept. Pains have been taken to present the topic in a lucid and comprehensive manner. A large number of problems including those of previous examination papers have been solved. It is therefore expected that the student will greatly benefit from this book.

We convey our sincere thanks to **Dr. M. Y. Gokhale**, Professor and Head, Department of Mathematics, MIT, Pune for his warm encouragement and support.

We also express our sincere thanks to **Shri. Dineshbhai Furia** and **Shri. Jignesh Furia**, for bringing out this book in time limit.

Special thanks are due to **Shri. M. P. Munde** and his entire team for efficiently carrying out the printing and publication of this work.

We are thankful to Mr. Santosh Bare for DTP and Mrs. **Anagha Kaware** for Proof Reading.

A book of this nature and scope is likely to contain some unintentional ommissions and errors. We would therefore highly appreciate any useful suggestions and corrections from the reader.

3rd **September 2013**　　　　　　　　　　　　　　　　　　　　　　　　Dr. LATHA K. IYER
Pune　　　　　　　　　　　　　　　　　　　　　　　　　　　　　　　　　Dr. NEETA D. KANKANE

SYLLABUS

UNIT I

Propositions, Sets, Probability

Propositions, compound proposition, basic logical operations, truth tables, tautology, contradiction quantifiers : universal and existential quantifiers, set theory : set, combinations of sets, mathematical induction principle, cardinality of finite sets, rule of sum, rule of product, permutations, combinations, discrete probability. **(8 Hrs.)**

UNIT II

Relation : Definition, properties of binary relations, equivalence relations and partitions, partial ordering relations and lattice, chains and antichains, transitive closure and Warshall's algorithm.

Function : Functions, definition, composition of functions, types of functions, recursive functions, Pigeonhole principle. **(8 Hrs.)**

UNIT III

Recurrence Relation : Recurrence relation, linear recurrence relations with constant coefficients, homogenous solutions, particular solutions, total solutions, solution by the method of generating functions.

Analysis of algorithms : Introduction, largest number algorithm, sorting algorithms : bubble sort, divide and conquer algorithms : binary search algorithm, strassens matrix multiplication, time complexity of algorithms, complexity of problems, tractable and intractable problems. **(8 Hrs.)**

UNIT IV

Graphs : Basic terminology, multigraphs and weighted graph, paths and circuits, Dijkstra's shortest path algorithms, Euler and Hamiltonian paths and circuits, factors of a graph, planner graph.

Trees : Trees rooted trees, path length in rooted trees, prefix code, binary search trees, spanning trees and cut set, minimum spanning trees, Kruskal's and prism algorithms for minimum spanning tree. **(8 Hrs.)**

UNIT V

Algebraic system : Semigroup, subsemigroup, monoid submonid, groups, Abelian group, subgroups, isomorphism, automorphism, homomorphism, ring, integral domain, field.

Boolean algebra : Lattice and algebraic systems, principle of duality, basic properties of lattice defined by lattices, distributive and complemented lattices, Boolean lattices and Boolean algebras, Boolean functions and Boolean expressions, number system and interconversion of number systems. **(8 Hrs.)**

❑❑❑

CONTENTS

Unit - I

1. Logic and Proofs	1.1 – 1.58
2. Theory of Sets	2.1 – 2.50
3. Permutations, Combinations and Discrete Probability	3.1 – 3.68

Unit - II

4. Relations	4.1 – 4.78
5. Functions	5.1 – 5.36

Unit - III

6. Recurrence Relations	6.1 – 6.32
7. Analysis of Algorithms	7.1 – 7.30
8. Graph Theory	8.1 – 8.114

Unit - IV

9. Trees	9.1 – 9.74

Unit - V

10. Groups and Rings	10.1 – 10.54

Unit - VI

11. Boolean Algebras	11.1 – 11.28
University Question Paper (March 2015)	P.1 – P.2

•••

Unit 1

Chapter 1: LOGIC AND PROOFS

SYLLABUS:
- Propositions, compound proposition, basic logical operations, truth tables, tautology, contradiction. Quantifiers : Universal and existential quantifiers, Set theory : Set, Combinations of sets, Mathematical induction principle, Cardinality of finite sets, Rule of sum, Rule of product, Permutations, Combinations, Discrete probability.

OBJECTIVES:
- To study the basic principles of logical reasoning.
- To learn various methods of proof, to construct arguments and test their validity.

UTILITY:
- Basically to develop skills in logical reasoning.
- In the design of computer hardware and software.

KEY CONCEPTS:
- Statement form.
- Logical connectives: Conjunction, Disjunction, Negation, Conditional and Bi-conditional.
- Normal forms.
- Argument.
- Methods of proofs.
- Quantifiers.

1.0 Introduction

Logic is central to the theme of Discrete Structures. A discrete structure is defined by a **set of axioms**. Properties of the structure are then derived from the axioms as theorems. These theorems are proved using valid rules of reasoning. The science of logic provides rules by which one can determine whether any particular proof (argument) is valid or not. These rules should be framed in a language which is precise and unambiguous. An ordinary language is unsuitable for this purpose, since languages are prone to be misinterpreted or misconstrued. For example consider the statement "He tries to study hard" and "He tries hard to study". A mere shuffling of the words, changes the entire meaning. To avoid such mistakes, a formal language is developed using symbols. A set of well defined rules is also built to perform. This is Symbolic Logic or Propositional Calculus. A 'calculus' is a set of rules for calculating with symbols. In Differential Calculus we do calculations on functions. In propositional calculus, we do calculations on propositions, with well-defined symbols, to determine the truth or falsehood of compound propositions.

The "formalism" in Symbolic Logic is well suited to be programmed on the computer. Computer programs are themselves "formal proofs", so that their construction and verification closely resemble logical manipulation. Logic plays a major role in formal hardware and software, verification of proofs and in the theory of programming languages.

1.1 Propositions (Statements)

1.1.1 Definition

A **proposition** or **statement** is a declarative sentence which is either true or false, but not both.

Examples:
  (i)   There are seven days in a week.
  (ii) $2 + 2 = 5$.
  (iii) The earth is flat.
  (iv) The equation $x^2 + x + 1 = 0$ has no real root.
  (v)   It will rain tomorrow.

Examples (i) and (iv) are true statements, whereas statements (ii) and (iii) are obviously false. In the case of example (v), although its truth value cannot be predicted at this point of time, it can be definitely determined in the future (i.e. tomorrow). Hence it is also a statement.

The following are, however, examples of sentences which are not propositions.
  (i) $x + 3 = 5$.
  (ii) Bring that book!
  (iii) When is your interview?
  (iv) What a beautiful painting!
  (v)   **This statement is false.**

Example (i) is not a statement, since its truth value depends on the value of x. If $x = 2$, the sentence is true; if $x \neq 2$, the sentence is false. It is in fact a propositional function.

Examples (ii), (iii), (iv) are not declarative sentences; one is a command, the other is a question while the third is an exclamation. Hence these are not statements.

Example (v), although a declarative sentence cannot be assigned a truth value, it is neither true nor false. Hence it is also not a proposition.

1.1.2 Notation

The statements in Examples 1.1.1 are sentences, which cannot be further split or broken down into simpler sentences. Such statements are called **primary, primitive** or **atomic** statements.

We denote primary statements by the lower case letters p, q, r ......

In Mathematics, we have the concept of real or complex variable. Similarly in logic, we have the concept of **propositional variable** or **statement variable**. We denote statement variables also by the same symbols p, q, r. This dual use of the same symbols to denote either a definite statement, called a **constant**, or an arbitrary statement called a **variable**, should not cause any confusion, as its use will be clear from the context.

(Note that when 'p' is used as a statement variable, it has **no** truth value and hence is not a statement. It should be replaced only by a statement and then its truth value can be determined --). For example, we may replace p by a true statement "2 + 3 = 5" or by a false statement "3 + 3 = 5".

1.2 Logical Connectives

It is possible to form new and rather complicated statements from the primary statements by using certain connecting words, with whose usage; we are already familiar in the English language. These statements are called **Compound Statements.**

In our everyday use of the English language, we use the words "not", "and", "or", "but", "while" etc., to connect two or more statements. However, these connectives, being quite flexible in their usage, lead to inexact and ambiguous interpretations. Hence we shall borrow only some of these connectives, redefine and symbolize them, to suit our purpose.

1.2.1 Negation

> The negation of a statement is formed either by introducing the word "not" at a proper place or by prefixing the statement with the phrase "It is not the case that".

If "p" denotes a statement, then negation of p is denoted by "∼ p" (or $\bar{p}$). If the truth value of p is true, then the truth value of ∼ p is false. If the truth value of p is false, then the truth value of ∼ p is true. Consider the following examples:

(i) If p is the statement "I am going for a walk", ∼ p is the statement "I am not going for a walk" or "It is not the case that I am going for a walk".

(ii) If q is the statement "3 is not a prime number", ∼ q is the statement "3 is a prime number".

1.2.2 Conjunction ("And")

> If p and q are the statements, the compound statement "p and q" is called as the conjunction of p and q; and is denoted by **p ∧ q.**

Examples:

(i) Let us consider the statements

        p : The sun is shining.
        q : The birds are singing.

Then p ∧ q is the statement" The sun is shining and the birds are singing."

(ii)   Let   p : 2 is a prime number.
            q : Ram is an intelligent boy.

Then p ∧ q is the statement "2 is a prime number and Ram is an intelligent boy."

This statement is perfectly acceptable in logic, although it makes no sense in our everyday language, as we cannot see the connection between the two statements.

The words "but" and "while" are treated as equivalent words to "and".

Consider the following examples:

(iii) Translate into symbolic form the statement
      Amar is poor but happy.

Solution: Let, p : Amar is poor.
                    q : Amar is happy.

Then the given statement in the symbolic form is p ∧ q.

(iv) Translate into symbolic form the statement
We watch television while we have dinner.

Solution: Let, p : We watch television.
                    q : We have dinner.

Then the given statement in the symbolic form is p ∧ q.

1.2.3 Disjunction ("or")

> If p and q are statements, then the compound statement "p or q" is called as the disjunction of p and q, and is denoted by **p ∨ q.**

Examples:

(i) There is an error in the program or the data is wrong.
            Let p : There is an error in the program.
                q : The data is wrong.
            Then p ∨ q : There is an error in the program or the data is wrong.

In the above example, the connective "or" is used in the **inclusive** sense, i.e. at least one possibility exists or even both the possibilities exist.

Consider the next example.

(ii) Either I will read a book or go to sleep.
            Let p : I will read a book.
                q : I will go to sleep.
            Then p ∨ q : I will read a book or go to sleep.

In everyday language as this example demonstrates the connective "or" is used in the **exclusive sense,** i.e. either one or the other activity can happen, but not both.

In logic, the symbol ' ∨ ' is used in the inclusive sense only; where we wish to specify that "exclusive or" is to be used, we use a new symbol "$\bar{\vee}$".

Hence in the above example, the more correct notation is **p $\bar{\vee}$ q.**

Normally in our everyday language, the relation "or" is used between two statements, which have some kind of relationship between them. In logic, this is not necessary, as the following example demonstrates.

(iii) Let p : It is raining today.
             q : Aarti is an intelligent girl.
Then   p ∨ q : It is raining today and Aarti is an intelligent girl.

This Statement makes perfect sense in logic, though not in English

1.2.4 Conditional ("If ...... then")

If p and q are statements, the compound statement "If p then q", denoted by **p→ q** is called a conditional statement or implication.

p is called the **antecedent** or hypothesis, while q is called the **consequent**.

The **converse** of p → q is the conditional q → p, and the **contrapositive** of p → q is the conditional ~ q → ~ p.

Examples:

(i)   Let   p : Hari works hard.
                q : Hari will pass the exam.
       Then p → q : If Hari works hard, then he will pass the exam.

(ii) Give the converse and contrapositive of the conditional
    If it rains, then I carry an umbrella.

Solution: Let p : It rains.
                    q : I carry an umbrella.

Converse of p → q is

       q → p : If I carry an umbrella, then it rains.

Contrapositive of p → q is

   ~ q → ~ p : **If I do not carry an umbrella, then it does not rain.**

In ordinary usage, the conditional statement may not always have the form "If ... then". While putting the statement into symbolic form, we have to interpret the statement correctly. Consider the following examples.

(iii) Write in symbolic form the statement:
    Farmers will face hardship if the dry spell continues.

Solution: Let, p : Farmers will face hardship.
q : The dry spell continues.
Then q → p is the correct symbolic representation of the given statement.

(iv) Write in symbolic form the statement:
Rahul's father will buy him a computer only if he passes the exam, with distinction.
Solution: Let, p : Rahul's father will buy him a computer.
q : Rahul passes the exam with distinction.
Then p → q is the correct symbolic version of the statement.

(v) Write in symbolic form the statement:
A sufficient condition for a function to be continuous is that the function is differentiable.
Solution: Let, p : The function is differentiable.
q : The function is continuous.
The statement has to be interpreted as p is sufficient for q or in other words p implies q.
Hence the correct solution is p → q.

(vi) Put into symbolic form the statement:
A necessary condition for a candidate to get admission is to pass the entrance exam.
Solution: Let, p : A candidate gets admission.
q : The candidate has passed the entrance exam.
In this example, the statement q is necessary for p. Hence p → q is the required symbolic form.

(vii) Put into symbolic form the statement:
Unless I reach the station on time, I will miss the train.
Solution: Let, p : I reach the station on time.
q : I will miss the train.
Then ~ p → q is the required symbolic form.

> Hence it is **IMPORTANT** to **REMEMBER** that the statement forms
>   If p, then q,
>   q if p,
>   p only if q,
>   p is sufficient for q,
>   q is necessary for p.
>   All are **EQUIVALENT** to the statement form p → q.

1.2.5 Biconditional ("If and only if")

If p and q are statements, the compound statement "p if and only if q", denoted by **p ↔ q**, is called a bi-conditional statement.
Often "if and only if" is shortened as "iff".
p ↔ q is also read as
"If p then q, and conversely".
Many of the theorems in Mathematics are of the type "if and only if".

Examples:
(i) An integer is even if and only if it is divisible by 2.
(ii) A right angled triangle is isosceles if and only if the other two angles are equal to forty five degrees.
(iii) Two lines are parallel if and only if they have the same slope.

1.3 Propositional or Statement Form

We know what a statement variable is (refer to article 1.1.2). Using the logical connectives defined above, we can construct or form an expression, involving the statement variables.
The following are examples of statement forms:
(i) $\sim (p \vee q) \to p$
(ii) $(p \to q) \leftrightarrow (p \wedge \sim q)$
(iii) $((p \wedge q) \vee (p \wedge \sim r)) \to ((p \wedge r) \vee q)$

One can thus construct any number of complicated statement forms, from the statement variables by using the logical connectives.

A **statement form has no fixed truth value.** It is only when the statement variables in a form, are **assigned** definite truth values, that we obtain the truth value of the statement form.
Hence the truth value of a statement **assumes** the truth value "true" or the truth value "false", depending on the truth values assigned to the statement variables, appearing in the statement form.
We denote by 'T' the truth value true, and 'F' by 'F' the truth value false.
In circuit logic, 'T' is denoted by '1' and 'F' by '0'.

SOLVED EXAMPLES

Example 1: Using the following statements:
        p : Mohan is rich
        q : Mohan is happy

write the following statements in symbolic form.
(i) Mohan is rich but unhappy.
(ii) Mohan is poor but happy.
(iii) Mohan is neither rich nor happy.
(iv) Mohan is poor or he is both rich and unhappy.

Solution:
(i) $p \wedge \sim q$
(ii) $\sim p \wedge q$
(iii) $\sim (p \vee q)$ or $\sim p \wedge \sim q$
(iv) $\sim p \vee (p \wedge \sim q)$.

Example 2: Using the following statements:
p : Rajani is tall
q : Rajani is beautiful

write the following statements in symbolic form.
(i) Rajani is tall and beautiful.
(ii) Rajani is tall but not beautiful.
(iii) It is false that Rajani is short or beautiful.
(iv) Rajani is tall or Rajani is short and beautiful.

Solution:
(i) $p \wedge q$
(ii) $p \wedge \sim q$
(iii) $\sim (\sim p \vee q)$
(iv) $p \vee (\sim p \wedge q)$.

Example 3: Using the following statements:
p : I will study discrete structures
q : I will go to a movie
r : I am in a good mood

write the following statements in symbolic form.
(i) If I am not in a good mood, then I will go to a movie.
(ii) I will not go to a movie and I will study discrete structures.
(iii) I will go to a movie only if I will not study discrete structures.
(iv) If I will not study discrete structures, then I am not in a good mood.

Solution:
(i) $\sim r \to q$
(ii) $\sim q \wedge p$
(iii) $q \to \sim p$
(iv) $\sim p \to \sim r$

Example 4: Write the following statements in symbolic form:
  (i) Indians will win the world-cup if their fielding improves.
  (ii) If I am not in a good mood or I am not busy, then I will go for a movie.
  (iii) If you know Object Oriented Programming and Oracle, then you will get a job.
  (iv) I will score good marks in the exam if and only if I study hard.

Solution:
(i) Let, p : Indians will win the world-cup.
          q : Their fielding improves.
  Then $q \to p$ **is the required form.**
(ii) Let, p : I am in a good mood.
           q : I am busy.
           r : I will go for a movie.
  Then $(\sim p \vee \sim q) \to r$.
(iii) Let, p : You know Object Oriented Programming.
            q : You know Oracle.
            r : You will get a job.
  Then $p \wedge q \to r$ is the required symbolic form.
(iv) Let p : I will score good marks in the exam.
          q : I study hard.
  Then $p \leftrightarrow q$ is the required symbolic form.

Example 5: Put the following statements into symbolic form:
  (i) Whenever weather is nice, then only we will have a picnic.
  (ii) If either Anil takes Mathematics or Aparna takes Biology, then Deepa will take Chemistry.
  (iii) Program is readable only if it is well structured.
  (iv) Unless he studies, he will fail in the examination.

Solution:
(i) Let, p : Weather is nice.
          q : We will have a picnic.
  The statement is equivalent to "we will have a picnic only if the weather is nice".

Chp 1 | 1.9

Hence q → p is the required form.

(ii) Let,   p : Anil takes Mathematics.
              q : Aparna takes Biology.
              r : Deepa will take Chemistry.
Then (p ∨ q) → r is the required form.

(iii) Let,   p : Program is readable.
              q : Program is well structured.
Then p → q is the required form.

(iv) Let,   p : He studies.
              q : He will fail in the examination.

The statement is equivalent to the statement "If he does not study, then he will fail in the examination".

Hence ~ p → q is the required form.

Example 6: To describe the various restaurants in the city, let p denote the statement "the food is good", q the statement "the service is good" and r the statement "the rating is three-star". Write the following statements in symbolic form: **(May 93)**

(i) Either the food is good or service is good, or both.

(ii) Either the food is good or service is good, but not both.

(iii) The food is good while the service is poor.

(iv) It is not the case that both the food is good and the rating is three-star.

(v) If both the food and service are good, then the rating is three-star.

(vi) It is not true that a three-star rating always means good food and good service.

Solution:

(i) As "∨" means "inclusive or", the statement required is p ∨ q.

(ii) We have to use "exclusive or" i.e. "$\bar{\vee}$". Hence the statement is p $\bar{\vee}$ q.

     Equivalently the statement is also p ∧ $\bar{q}$ ∨ $\bar{p}$ ∧ q.

(iii) "While" is interpreted as "and". Hence the statement is p ∧ ~ q.

(iv) "It is not the case" implies negation. Hence the statement is ~ (p ∧ r).

(v) The statement is (p ∧ q) → r.

(vi) Here we have negation of implication. Hence the statement is ~ (r → (p ∧ q)).

Example 7: Using the following propositions:

p : I am bored
q : I am waiting for one hour
r : There is no bus

translate the following into English.
(i) $(q \vee r) \rightarrow p$
(ii) $\sim q \rightarrow \sim p$
(iii) $(q \rightarrow p) \vee (r \rightarrow p)$

Solution:
(i) If I am waiting for one hour or there is no bus, then I get bored.
(ii) If I am not waiting for one hour, then I am not bored.
(iii) If I am waiting for one hour then I am bored, or if there is no bus, then I am bored.

Example 8: Write the logical negation of the following statements in the symbolic form:
(i) Gopal is intelligent and rich.
(ii) Gopal is intelligent but not rich.
(iii) Gopal is either intelligent or rich.

Solution: Let
p : Gopal is intelligent.
q : Gopal is rich.

(i) $\sim (p \wedge q)$ which is equivalent to $\sim p \vee \sim q$.
(ii) $\sim (p \wedge \sim q)$ which is equivalent to $\sim p \vee q$.
(iii) $\sim (p \vee q)$ which is equivalent to $\sim p \wedge \sim q$.

Example 9: Translate the following statements into symbolic form:
If the utility cost goes up or the request for additional funding is desired, then a new computer will be purchased if and only if we can show that the current computing facilities are indeed not adequate.

Solution: Let p : The utility cost goes up.
q : The request for additional funding is desired.
r : A new computer will be purchased.
s : We can show that the current computing facilities are indeed adequate.

Then $(p \vee q) \rightarrow (r \times \sim s)$.

Example 10: Consider the following advertisement for a game:
(i) There are three statements in this advertisement.
(ii) Two of them are not true.

(iii) The average increase in IQ scores of people who learn this game is more than 20 points.

Is the statement (iii) true? Justify your answer.

Solution:

Let us suppose statement (iii) is false. Statement (i) is true since there are actually three statements in the advertisement. This leaves us with statement (ii). Statement (ii) cannot be true, since if it so, we shall have only one statement which is false, which contradicts statement (ii) itself. Hence statement (ii) is false, which means that there are actually two statements which are true. Hence statement (iii) cannot be false. It has to be a true statement.)

Example 11: Write the following statements in symbolic form:
- (i) The sun is bright and humidity is not high.
- (ii) It is already 9.00 a.m., I should start my job.
- (iii) If the requirement of Computer Engineers is increased, then more seats will be offered by University and more computers will be purchased by the University Computer Department if the rates are competitive

Solution: (i) Let p : The sun is bright,
q : Humidity of high.

Then the given statement in symbolic form is: $p \wedge \sim q$.

(ii) Let r : It is already 9.00 a.m.,
s : I should start my job.

Then the statement in symbolic form is: $r \wedge s$.

(iii) Let p : The requirement of Computer Engineers is increased,
q : More seats will be offered by University,
r : More computers will be purchased by the University Computer, Department
s : The rates are competitive.

Then the given statement in symbolic form is: $p \rightarrow (q \wedge (s \rightarrow r))$

EXERCISE - 1.1

1. Let p denote the statement, "The material is interesting", and q denote the statement, "The exercises are challenging", and r denote the statement, "The course is enjoyable".

   Write the following statements in symbolic form:
   - (i) The material is interesting and the exercises are challenging.
   - (ii) The material is uninteresting, the exercises are not challenging and the course is not enjoyable.

(iii) If the material is not interesting and the exercises are not challenging, then the course is not enjoyable.
(iv) The material is interesting means the exercises are challenging and conversely.
(v) Either the material is interesting, or the exercises are challenging, but not both.

2. Let the propositions   p: Gopal is tall.
   q: Gopal is handsome.

Write the following sentences in symbolic form, using p, q and appropriate connectives.
(i) Gopal is tall and handsome.
(ii) Gopal is tall but not handsome.
(iii) It is false that Gopal is short or handsome.
(iv) Gopal is neither tall nor handsome.
(v) Gopal is tall means he is also handsome.
(vi) It is not true that Gopal is short or not handsome.

3. Write the following statements in symbolic form:
(i) The sun is bright and humidity is not high.
(ii) If I finish my homework before dinner and it does not rain, then I will go to the ball game.
(iii) If you do not see me tomorrow, it means I have gone to Chicago.

4. Let 'p' be the proposition "high speed driving is dangerous" and 'q' be the proposition "Rajesh was a wise man."
Write down the meaning of the following propositions:
(i) $p \wedge q$
(ii) $\sim p \wedge q$
(iii) $\sim (p \wedge q)$
(iv) $(p \wedge q) \vee (\sim p \wedge \sim q)$
(v) $(p \vee q) \wedge \sim (p \wedge q)$.

5. Write the following compound statements in symbolic form:
(i) It is humid and cloudy, or it is raining, but at the same time it is false that it is both humid and raining.
(ii) Being able to type is sufficient to learn word processing.
(iii) If Manisha is not sick, then if she goes to the picnic, she will have a good time.
(iv) I can study only if I am not tired or hungry.

6. State the converse and contrapositive of each of the following statements:
(i) If it rains, I am not going to the city.
(ii) I can't complete the task if I don't get help.
(iii) I will come only if I am not too busy.
(iv) If you complete this job, you can take a holiday.

7. Express the following statements in propositional form:
(i) There are many clouds in the sky but it did not rain.

(ii) I will get first class if and only if I study well and score above 80 in Mathematics.
(iii) Computers are cheap but softwares are costly.
(iv) It is very hot and humid or Ramesh is having heart problem.
(v) In small restaurants the food in good and service is poor.
(vi) If I finish my submission before 5.00 in the evening and it is not very hot, I will go and play a game of hockey.

8. Write the following statements in symbolic form:
   (i) The sun is bright and humidity is not high.
   (ii) It is already 11.00 a.m., I should start my job.
   (iii) If the requirement of computer engineers increased, then more seats will be offered by University and more computers will be purchased by University Computer Department if the rates are competitive.

9. Negate each of the statement:
   (i) If there is a riot, then someone is killed.
   (ii) It is day light and all the people are arisen.

10. Use p : Today is Monday
        q : The grass is wet
        r : The dish ran away with the spoon,
    to write an English sentence that corresponds to each of the following:
    (1) ~ r ∧ q
    (2) ~ q ∨ r
    (3) ~ (p ∨ q)
    (4) p ∨ ~ r

11. The following statements are given. Write their converse and contrapositive statements.
    (i) If he is considerate of others, then a man is a gentleman.
    (ii) If a steel root is stretched, then it has been heated.

1.4 Truth Tables

> A table giving all possible truth values of a statement form, corresponding to the truth values assigned to its variables, is called a truth table.

If a statement form consists of two distinct variables, the table will contain $2^2 = 4$ values. If it consists of three distinct variables, it will contain 2^3 values. In general, if a statement form contains n distinct variables, then the table will contain 2^n values.

Let us consider first, the truth tables of the basic statement forms ~ p, p ∧ q, p ∨ q, p → q and p ↔ q.

Table 1.1

P	~p
T	F
F	T

Table 1.2

p	q	p ∧ q
T	T	T
T	F	F
F	T	F
F	F	F

Table 1.3

p	Q	p ∨ q
T	T	T
T	F	T
F	T	T
F	F	F

Table 1.4

p	q	p → q
T	T	T
F	T	T
T	F	F
F	F	T

Table 1.5

p	Q	p ↔ q
T	T	T
F	T	F
T	F	F
F	F	T

Note the following important points:

(i) As shown in Table 1.2 p ∧ q has truth value T if and only if both p and q have truth values T.

(ii) As shown in Table 1.3 p ∨ q has truth value F only when both p and q have truth values F. Otherwise, it has truth value T.

(iii) As shown in Table 1.4 p → q has truth value F only when p has truth value T and q has truth value F. If p has truth value F, p → q has truth value T, whatever may be the truth value of q.

(iv) p ↔ q has truth value T only when both have the same truth values.

Truth table for "Exclusive or".

Recall that p $\bar{\vee}$ q implies either p or q is true but not **both**. Hence we have:

Table 1.6

p	q	p $\bar{\vee}$ q
T	T	F
T	F	T
F	T	T
F	F	F

SOLVED EXAMPLES

Example 1: Construct the truth tables for the following statement forms:

(i) (~ p ∨ q) → q

(ii) ~ (p ∧ q) ∨ (p × q)

(iii) $(\sim p \to r) \wedge (p \times q)$
(iv) $((\sim p \wedge q) \vee (q \wedge r)) \to r$

Solution:

(i)

P	q	~p	~p ∨ q	(~p ∨ q) → q
T	T	F	T	T
T	F	F	F	T
F	T	T	T	T
F	F	T	T	F

(ii)

P	q	p ∧ q	~(p ∧ q)	p × q	~(p ∧ q) ∨ (p × q)
T	T	T	F	T	T
T	F	F	T	F	T
F	T	F	T	F	T
F	F	F	T	T	T

(iii)

P	q	r	~p	~p → r	p × q	(~p → r) ∧ (p × q)
T	T	T	F	T	T	T
T	T	F	F	T	T	T
T	F	T	F	T	F	F
T	F	F	F	T	F	F
F	T	T	T	T	F	F
F	T	F	T	F	F	F
F	F	T	T	T	T	T
F	F	F	T	F	T	F

(iv)

P	q	r	~p	~p ∧ q	q ∧ r
T	T	T	F	F	T
T	T	F	F	F	F
T	F	T	F	F	F
T	F	F	F	F	F
F	T	T	T	T	T
F	T	F	T	T	F
F	F	T	T	F	F
F	F	F	T	F	F

(~p ∧ q) ∨ (q ∧ r)	((~p ∧ q) ∨ (q ∧ r)) → r
T	T
F	T
F	T
F	T
T	T
T	F
F	T
F	T

Example 2: If p → q is false, determine the truth value of (~ (p ∧ q)) → q.
Solution: p → q has truth value F only when p has truth value T and q has truth value F. Now, we have

P	Q	p ∧ q	~ (p ∧ q)	(~ (p ∧ q)) → q
T	F	F	T	F

Hence the truth value of (~ (p ∧ q)) → q is false.

Example 3: If p and q are false propositions, find the truth value of (p ∨ q) ∧ (~ p ∨ ~ q).
Solution:

p	Q	p ∨ q	~ p	~ q	~ p ∨ ~ q	(p ∨ q) ∧ (~ p ∨ ~ q)
F	F	F	T	T	T	F

Example 4: If p → q is true, can we determine the truth value of ~ p ∨ (p → q)? Explain your answer.
Solution: Since p → q is true, we have to consider the following possible truth values of p and q.

P	Q	~ p	p → q	~ p ∨ (p → q)
T	T	F	T	T
F	T	T	T	T
F	F	T	T	T

Yes, it is possible to determine the truth value of ~ p ∨ (p → q) and it is T.

Example 5: Given the truth values of p and q as T and that of r and s as F, find the truth values of the following:
    (i) p ∨ (q ∧ r)   (ii) p → (r ∧ s)   (iii) (p ∧ (q ∧ r)) ∨ ~ ((p ∨ q) ∧ (r ∨ s)).
Solution: (i)

P	Q	r	(q ∧ r)	p ∨ (q ∧ r)
T	T	F	F	T

(ii)

P	R	s	r ∧ s	p → (r ∧ s)
T	F	F	F	F

(iii)

P	Q	r	q ∧ r	p ∧ (q ∧ r)
T	T	F	F	F

p ∨ q	r ∨ s	(p ∨ q) ∧ (r ∨ s)	~ ((p ∨ q) ∧ (r ∨ s))	(p ∧ (q ∧ r)) ∨ ~ ((p ∨ q) ∧ (r ∨ s))
T	F	F	T	T

Some interesting problems framed on the biconditional p ↔ q are given below.

Example 6: An island has two tribes of natives. Any native from the first tribe always tells the truth, while any native from the other tribe always lies. We arrive at the island and ask a native if there is gold on the island. He answers, "There is gold on the island if and only if I always tell the truth". Which tribe is he from? Is there gold on the island?

Solution: We cannot determine the tribe from which the native is. However, we can determine if there is gold on the island.

Let, p : He always tells the truth.
q : There is gold on the island.

Then the native's answer is q ↔ p. or equivalently p ↔ q. We shall consider the following two cases.

Case I: The native always tells the truth. Then in this case, the truth table for p × q (↔) is

p	q	p ↔ q
T	T	T

Since p ↔ q is T and p is T, then q has to be T. Hence in this case, there is gold on the island. Now consider, case II.

Case II: The native always lies. In this case, the truth table for p ↔ q is

p	q	p ↔ q
F	T	F

Since p ↔ q is F and p is also F, then q must be T.
Hence in this case also, we find that there is gold on the island.

Example 7: A certain country is inhabited only by people who either always tells the truth or always tells lies, and who will respond to questions only with a "yes" or a "no". A tourist comes to a fork in the road, where one branch leads to the capital and the other does not. There is no sign indicating which branch to take, but there is an inhabitant, Mr. Z, standing at the fork. What single question should the tourist ask him to determine which branch to take?

Solution: Let p : "Mr. Z always tells the truth".

q : "The left-hand branch leads to the capital".

Let A : p ↔ q.

Then the single question which the tourist should ask Mr. Z is, Is "A" true?
We shall consider two cases.

Case I: Mr. Z always speaks the truth. Consider the following table:

P	q	p ↔ q	Answer of Mr. Z
T	T	T	Yes
T	F	F	No

Hence when Mr. Z says "Yes", q is T, i.e. the left-hand branch leads to the capital.
Now let us consider, case II.

Case II: Mr. Z always tells lies.
Consider the truth table:

p	q	p ↔ q	Answer of Mr. Z
F	T	F	Yes
F	F	T	No

If Mr. Z answers "Yes", in this case also q being T, the tourist will take the left-hand branch leading to the capital.

Example 8: Given that the value of $p \to q$ is false, determine the truth value of $(\sim p \vee \sim q) \to q$.

Solution: Consider the truth table.

p	Q	p → q	~ p	~ q	~ p ∨ ~ q	(~ p ∨ ~ q) → q
T	F	F	F	T	T	F

Example 9: Given that the value of $p \to q$ is true, can you determine the value of $\sim p \vee (p \leftrightarrow q)$?

Solution: Consider the truth table

Q	Q	p → q	~ p	p ↔ q	~ p ∨ (p ↔ q)
T	T	T	F	T	T
F	T	T	T	F	T
F	F	T	T	T	T

1.5 Tautology

We have seen how to construct the truth table of various statement forms. The last column in the truth table gives the truth values of the statement form for all possible assignment of truth values to its variables.

1.5.1 Definitions

A statement form is called a Tautology, if it always assumes the truth value 'T' irrespective of the truth values assigned to its variables.

A statement form is called a **contradiction** if it always assumes the truth value 'F' irrespective of the truth values assigned to its variables.

A statement form which is neither a tautology nor a contradiction is called a **contingency.**

Examples:

(i) $p \vee \sim p$ is a tautology ; $p \wedge \sim p$ is a contradiction.

Solution: Consider the truth table:

P	~p	p ∨ ~p	p ∧ ~p
T	F	T	F
F	T	T	F

(ii) $p \rightarrow p$ is a tautology.

Solution:

P	p	p → p
T	T	T
F	F	T

SOLVED EXAMPLES

Example 1: Construct truth tables to determine whether each of the following is a tautology, a contingency or a contradiction.

   (i) $p \rightarrow (q \rightarrow p)$
   (ii) $(p \wedge q) \wedge \sim (p \vee q)$
   (iii) $(p \wedge q) \rightarrow p$
   (iv) $(p \rightarrow q) \leftrightarrow (q \vee \sim p)$
   (v) $(p \wedge (\sim p \vee q)) \wedge \sim q$

Solution:

(i) Consider the truth table:

P	q	q → p	p → (q → p)
T	T	T	T
T	F	T	T
F	T	F	T
F	F	T	T

Hence p → (q → p) is a tautology.

(ii) Consider the truth table:

p	Q	p ∧ q	p ∨ q	~ (p ∨ q)	(p ∧ q) ∧ ~ (p ∨ q)
T	T	T	T	F	F
F	T	F	T	F	F
T	F	F	T	F	F
F	F	F	F	T	F

Hence (p ∧ q) ∧ ~ (p ∨ q) is a contradiction.

(iii)

P	q	p ∧ q	(p ∧ q) → p
T	T	T	T
F	T	F	T
T	F	F	T
F	F	F	T

Hence (p ∧ q) → p is a tautology.

(iv) Consider the truth table:

p	Q	~ p	(p → q)	(q ∨ ~ p)	(p → q) ↔ (q ∨ ~ p)
T	T	F	T	T	T
T	F	F	F	F	T
F	T	T	T	T	T
F	F	T	T	T	T

Hence (p → q) ↔ (q ∨ ~ p) is a tautology.

(v) Consider the truth table:

p	Q	~ p	(~ p ∨ q)	p ∧ (~ p ∨ q)	~ q	(p ∧ (~ p ∨ q)) ∧ ~ q
T	T	F	T	T	F	F
T	F	F	F	F	T	F
F	T	T	T	F	F	F
F	F	T	T	F	T	F

Hence (p ∧ (~ p ∨ q)) ∧ ~ q is a contradiction.

Example 2: Show that $(p \land (p \to q)) \to q$ is a tautology, without using truth table.

Solution: We have only to show that wherever $p \land (p \to q)$ is true, q is also true, since in the other cases $(p \land (p \to q)) \to q$ is anyway true.

Now $p \land (p \to q)$ is T implies p is T and $p \to q$ is T. These together means that q is T.

Hence the required form is a tautology.

Example 3: Show that $(p \to q) \land \sim q \to \sim p$ is a tautology.

Solution: We need only to show that $p \to q$ and $\sim q$ both true imply $\sim p$ is true.

Since truth value of $\sim q$ is T, truth value of q is F. Since $p \to q$ is true, this means that p is false, i.e. truth value of $\sim p$ is T. Hence the proof.

1.6 Equivalence of Statement Forms

The concept of equivalence of statement forms is similar to the concept of equality of algebraic expressions in mathematics.

Definition:

> Two statement forms are **logically equivalent** if both have the **same** truth values, whatever may be the truth values assigned to the statement variables, occurring in both the forms.

In other words, if we consider the truth tables for both the statement forms, the final columns in both the tables should be identical.

Examples:

1. p and $p \land p$ are logically equivalent (**Idempotence**)

Solution: Consider the truth table:

p	$p \land p$
T	T
F	F

Since the truth tables for p and $p \to p$ are identical, it follows that p and $p \to p$ are logically equivalent.

2. The following are some basic logically equivalent forms. Proofs are left as exercises for the students.

   (i) $p \land q$ and $q \land p$ are logically equivalent. (ii) $p \lor q$ and $q \lor p$ are logically equivalent.
   (iii) p and $\sim (\sim p)$ are logically equivalent.

3. p → q and ~ q → ~ p are logically equivalent. **(Contrapositive)**
Solution:

P	Q	p → q	~ q	~ p	~ q → ~ p
T	T	T	F	F	T
T	F	F	T	F	F
F	T	T	F	T	T
F	F	T	T	T	T

Note that the columns for p → q and ~ q → ~ p are identical.
Hence p → q and ~ q → ~ p are logically equivalent forms.
The logical equivalence proved above is very often practiced in everyday language.
Consider the two statements "He will pass if he works hard" and "If he does not work hard, he will not pass the exam". Both these statements obviously convey the same meaning.

4. p ∧ (q ∨ r) and (p ∧ q) ∨ (p ∧ r) are logically equivalent. **(Distributivity)**
Solution: Consider the following truth tables:

(a)

P	Q	r	(q ∨ r)	p ∧ (q ∨ r)
T	T	T	T	T
T	T	F	T	T
T	F	T	T	T
T	F	F	F	F
F	T	T	T	F
F	T	F	T	F
F	F	T	T	F
F	F	F	F	F

(b)

P	q	R	(p ∧ q)	(p ∧ r)	(p ∧ q) ∨ (p ∧ r)
T	T	T	T	T	T
T	T	F	T	F	T
T	F	T	F	T	T
T	F	F	F	F	F
F	T	T	F	F	F
F	T	F	F	F	F
F	F	T	F	F	F
F	F	F	F	F	F

The last columns in both (a) and (b) are identical. Hence the two forms are logically equivalent.

5. $p \vee (q \wedge r)$ and $(p \vee q) \wedge (p \vee r)$ are logically equivalent. Proof is similar to (4) and is left as an exercise.

6. $\sim (p \wedge q)$ and $\sim p \vee \sim q$ are logically equivalent **(De Morgan's laws)**

Solution: Consider the following truth tables:

P	Q	p ∧ q	~ (p ∧ q)
T	T	T	F
T	F	F	T
F	T	F	T
F	F	F	T

P	q	~ p	~ q	~ p ∨ ~ q
T	T	F	F	F
T	F	F	T	T
F	T	T	F	T
F	F	T	T	T

The last columns in both the tables are identical. Hence $\sim (p \wedge q)$ and $\sim p \vee \sim q$ are logically equivalent.

7. $\sim (p \vee q)$ and $\sim p \wedge \sim q$ are logically equivalent. Proof is left as an exercise.

Examples:

The following examples on logical equivalence show that the conditional can be replaced by the connectives $\sim$ and $\vee$.

8. $p \rightarrow q$ and $\sim p \vee q$ are logically equivalent **(Elimination of conditional)**.

Solution:

P	q	p → q	~ p	~ p ∨ q
T	T	T	F	T
T	F	F	F	F
F	T	T	T	T
F	F	T	T	T

Similarly, we have the next example, in which the biconditional can also be eliminated.

9. $p \leftrightarrow q$ is logically equivalent to $(p \rightarrow q) \wedge (q \rightarrow p)$ which in turn is logically equivalent to $(\sim p \vee q) \wedge (\sim q \vee p)$.

Proof is left as an exercise to the students.

Notation: Hereafter we shall denote logical equivalence by the symbol '≡' modifying the equal sign '=' in Mathematics.

The following is a list of some important equivalences (many of which have been already proved), called as **identities**.

1.7 Logical Identities

1.	$p \equiv p \vee p$	Idempotence of $\vee$
2.	$p \equiv p \wedge p$	Idempotence of $\vee$
3.	$p \vee q \equiv q \vee p$	Commutativity of $\vee$
4.	$p \wedge q \equiv q \wedge p$	Commutativity of $\wedge$
5.	$p \vee (q \vee r) \equiv (p \vee q) \vee r$	Associativity of $\vee$
6.	$p \wedge (q \wedge r) \equiv (p \wedge q) \wedge r$	Associativity of $\wedge$
7.	$p \wedge (q \vee r) \equiv (p \wedge q) \vee (p \wedge r)$	Distributivity of $\wedge$ over $\vee$
8.	$p \vee (q \wedge r) \equiv (p \vee q) \wedge (p \vee r)$	Distributivity of $\vee$ over $\wedge$
9.	$p \equiv \sim(\sim p)$	Double negation
10.	$\sim(p \vee q) \equiv \sim p \wedge \sim q$	De Morgan's laws
11.	$\sim(p \wedge q) \equiv \sim p \wedge \sim q$	De Morgan's laws
12.	$p \vee \sim p \equiv$ Tautology	
13.	$p \wedge \sim p \equiv$ Contradiction	
14.	$p \vee (p \wedge q) \equiv p$	Absorption laws
15.	$p \wedge (p \vee q) \equiv p$	Absorption laws

Students are advised to work out the proofs of the Absorption laws, as an exercise.
The following theorem relates logical equivalence and a tautology.

1.8 Theorem

Let **A** and **B** be two statement forms. Then **A** is logically equivalent to **B** if and only if **A** $\leftrightarrow$ **B** is a tautology.

Proof:

Let **A** and **B** be logically equivalent.
Then **A** and **B** assume the **same** truth values for any assignment of truth values to the statement variables in **A** and **B**.
Hence either both **A** and **B** are true or both are false.
Therefore **A** $\leftrightarrow$ **B** is a tautology.
Conversely if **A** $\leftrightarrow$ **B** is a tautology, it means that wherever **A** is true, **B** is **true** (and conversely), and wherever **A** is false, **B** is also false (and conversely).
Therefore **A** and **B** are logically equivalent.

1.9 Normal Forms

One of the main problems in logic is to determine whether a given statement form is a tautology or a contradiction. Constructing truth tables for this purpose may not always be practical (even with the help of a computer), especially where the statement form may contain a large number of variables or has a complicated structure. Hence it is necessary to consider alternate methods, such as reducing the statement form to so called **normal forms.**

1. Disjunctive Normal Form (dnf):

A conjunction of statement variables and (or) their negations is called as a **fundamental conjunction.** (It is also called as a **min term**).

For example, p, $\sim p$, $\sim p \wedge q$, $p \wedge q$, $p \wedge \sim p \wedge q$ are fundamental conjunctions.

We know that $p \wedge \sim p$ is always false. Hence if a fundamental conjunction contains at least one pair of factors, in which one is the negation of the other, it will be false.

A statement form which consists of a **disjunction** of **fundamental conjunctions**, is called a **disjunctive normal** form (abbreviated as dnf).

Examples of dnf:

(i) $(p \wedge q) \vee \sim q$
(ii) $(\sim p \wedge q) \vee (p \wedge q) \vee q$
(iii) $(p \wedge q \wedge r) \vee (p \wedge \sim r) \vee (q \wedge r)$
(iv) $(p \wedge \sim q) \vee (p \wedge r)$
(v) $(p \wedge q \wedge r) \vee \sim r$

In the following illustrative examples, we will reduce the given statement form to dnf, by using logical equivalence.

Examples:

1. Obtain the dnf of the form $(p \rightarrow q) \wedge (\sim p \wedge q)$.

Solution: $p \rightarrow q \equiv \sim p \vee q$ (Elimination of biconditional)

Hence
$(p \rightarrow q) \wedge (\sim p \wedge q)$
$\equiv (\sim p \vee q) \wedge (\sim p \wedge q)$
$\equiv (\sim p \wedge \sim p \wedge q) \vee (q \wedge \sim p \wedge q)$
$\equiv (\sim p \wedge q) \vee (q \wedge \sim p)$

(by using the distributive laws, idempotence laws and commutative laws).

2. Obtain the dnf of $(p \wedge (p \rightarrow q)) \rightarrow q$

Solution: $(p \wedge (p \rightarrow q)) \rightarrow q$
$\equiv \sim (p \wedge (\sim p \vee q)) \vee q$
$\equiv \sim p \vee \sim (\sim p \vee q) \vee q$
$\equiv \sim p \vee (p \wedge \sim q) \vee q$

3. Obtain the dnf of the form $\sim (p \to (q \wedge r))$.

Solution: $\sim (p \to (q \wedge r))$

$\equiv \sim (\sim p \vee (q \wedge r))$
$\equiv \sim (\sim p \vee (q \wedge r))$
$\equiv \sim (\sim p) \wedge \sim (q \wedge r)$ (De Morgan's Laws)
$\equiv p \wedge (\sim q \vee \sim r)$ (Idempotent laws and De Morgan's laws)
$\equiv (p \wedge \sim q) \vee (p \wedge \sim r)$.

2. Conjunctive Normal Form (cnf):

> A disjunction of statement variables and (or) their negations is called a **fundamental disjunction or maxterm.**

For example, p, $\sim p$, $\sim p \vee q$, $p \vee q$, $p \vee \sim p \vee q$ are fundamental disjunctions.

We know that $p \vee \sim p$ is always true. Hence if a fundamental disjunction contains at least one pair of factors, in which one is the negation of the other, it will be true ($p \vee \sim p \vee q$ is logically equivalent to a tautology).

> A statement form which consists of a **conjunction** of **fundamental disjunctions**, is called a **conjunctive normal form** (abbreviated as cnf).

Note that a cnf is a tautology if and only if every fundamental disjunction contained in it is a tautology.

Examples of cnf:

(i) $p \wedge q$
(ii) $\sim p \wedge (p \vee q)$
(iii) $(p \vee q \vee r) \wedge (\sim p \vee r)$

The following examples illustrate the procedure to obtain cnf of a given statement form, without using truth tables.

Examples: (i) Obtain the cnf of the form $(\sim p \to r) \wedge (p \leftrightarrow q)$.

Solution: $(\sim p \to r) \wedge (p \leftrightarrow q)$

$\equiv (\sim p \to r) \wedge ((p \to q) \wedge (q \to p))$
$\equiv (\sim (\sim p) \vee r) \wedge ((\sim p \vee q) \wedge (\sim q \vee p))$
$\equiv (p \vee r) \wedge (\sim p \vee q) \wedge (\sim q \vee p)$

(ii) Obtain the cnf of the form $(p \wedge q) \vee (\sim p \wedge q \wedge r)$.

Solution: $(p \wedge q) \vee (\sim p \wedge q \wedge r)$

$\equiv (p \vee (\sim p \wedge q \wedge r)) \wedge (q \vee (\sim p \wedge q \wedge r))$ (Distributive law)
$\equiv ((p \vee \sim p) \wedge (p \vee q) \wedge (p \vee r)) \wedge ((q \vee \sim p) \wedge (q \vee q) \wedge (q \vee r))$
$\equiv (p \vee q) \wedge (p \vee r) \wedge (q \vee \sim p) \wedge q \wedge (q \vee r)$.

3. Truth Table Method (to find dnf):

Let **P** be a statement form containing n variables $p_1, p_2, ..., p_n$. We obtain its dnf from the truth table as follows. For each row in which P assumes value T, form the conjunction $p_1 \wedge p_2 \wedge ... \wedge \sim p_k \wedge ... \wedge p_n$ where we take p_k if there is T in the k-th position in the row and $\sim p_k$ if there is F in that position. Such a term is called a minterm. The disjunction of the minterms is the dnf of the given form.

Examples:

1. Find the dnf of the form $(\sim p \rightarrow r) \wedge (p \times q)$.

Solution: Consider the truth table.

P	q	r	~p	~p → r	p ↔ q	(~p → r) ∧ (p ↔ q)
T	T	T	F	T	T	T
T	T	F	F	T	T	T
T	F	T	F	T	F	F
T	F	F	F	T	F	F
F	T	T	T	T	F	F
F	T	F	T	F	F	F
F	F	T	T	T	T	T
F	F	F	T	F	T	F

Consider the rows of p, q, r in which T appears in the **last column.**
Then the required dnf is $(p \wedge q \wedge r) \vee (p \wedge q \wedge \sim r) \vee (\sim p \wedge \sim q \wedge r)$.

---

2. The statement form f (p, q, r) is given by the following table. Find its dnf.

p	q	r	f (p, q, r)
F	F	F	T
F	F	T	F
F	T	F	T
F	T	T	F
T	F	F	T
T	F	T	F
T	T	F	F
T	T	T	T

Then the required dnf is $(\sim p \wedge \sim q \wedge \sim r) \vee (\sim p \wedge q \wedge \sim r) \vee (p \wedge \sim q \wedge \sim r) \vee (p \wedge q \wedge r)$.

SOLVED EXAMPLES

Example 1: Prove that the following formulae are logically equivalent and show that the operator "Exclusive or" is symmetric.

(i) $p \veebar q$ and $q \veebar p$.

(ii) $(p \veebar q) \veebar r$ and $p \veebar (q \veebar r)$.

Solution: (i) Consider the truth tables.

p	q	p $\bar{\vee}$ q	q $\bar{\vee}$ p
T	T	F	F
T	F	T	T
F	T	T	T
F	F	F	F

Hence "Exclusive or" is a symmetric operator and also the two formulae are logically equivalent.

(ii) Consider the truth tables.

p	q	r	(p $\bar{\vee}$ q)	(p $\bar{\vee}$ q) $\bar{\vee}$ r	(q $\bar{\vee}$ r)	q $\bar{\vee}$ (q $\bar{\vee}$ r)
T	T	T	F	T	F	T
T	T	F	F	F	T	F
T	F	T	T	F	T	F
T	F	F	T	T	F	T
F	T	T	T	F	F	F
F	T	F	T	T	T	T
F	F	T	F	T	T	T
F	F	F	F	F	F	F

The columns for (p $\bar{\vee}$ q) $\bar{\vee}$ r and p $\bar{\vee}$ (q $\bar{\vee}$ r) are identical.
Hence the formulae are logically identical.

Example 2: Eliminating conditional and biconditional, find the logical equivalent forms of

(i) $(\bar{q} \to \bar{p}) \to (p \to q)$

(ii) $p \leftrightarrow (\bar{p} \vee \bar{q})$

   (Note that $\bar{q}$ is ~ q)

Solution: (i) $\bar{q} \to \bar{p} \equiv (\bar{\bar{q}} \vee \bar{p}) = q \vee \bar{p}$

$p \to q \equiv (\bar{p} \vee q)$

∴ $(\bar{q} \to \bar{p}) \to (p \to q)$

$\equiv (q \vee \bar{p}) \to (\bar{p} \vee q)$.

Let $q \vee \bar{p} \equiv s$ and $\bar{p} \vee q \equiv t$

then we have $s \to t \equiv (\bar{s} \vee t)$

$\bar{s} \equiv \overline{(q \vee \bar{p})} \equiv \bar{q} \wedge \bar{\bar{p}}$ (by De Morgan's law)

$\equiv \bar{q} \wedge p$.

$\therefore \quad \bar{s} \vee t \equiv (\bar{q} \wedge p) \vee (\bar{p} \vee q)$

$\equiv (\bar{q} \vee \bar{p} \vee q) \wedge (p \vee \bar{p} \vee q)$ (by Distributive law)

$\equiv ((q \vee \bar{q}) \vee \bar{p}) \wedge ((p \vee \bar{p}) \vee q)$

$\equiv (T \vee \bar{p}) \wedge (T \vee q)$

$\equiv T \wedge T \equiv T.$

$\therefore$ The given form is logically equivalent to a tautology.

(ii) $\qquad p \leftrightarrow (\bar{p} \vee \bar{q})$

$\equiv (p \rightarrow (\bar{p} \vee \bar{q})) \wedge ((\bar{p} \vee \bar{q}) \rightarrow p)$

$\equiv (\bar{p} \vee (\bar{p} \vee \bar{q})) \wedge (\overline{(\bar{p} \vee \bar{q})} \vee p)$

$\equiv ((\bar{p} \vee \bar{p}) \vee \bar{q}) \wedge ((\bar{\bar{p}} \wedge \bar{\bar{q}}) \vee p)$

$\equiv (\bar{p} \vee \bar{q}) \wedge ((p \wedge q) \vee p)$

$\equiv (\bar{p} \wedge ((p \wedge q) \vee p)) \vee (\bar{q} \wedge ((p \wedge q) \vee p))$

$\equiv (\bar{p} \wedge p \wedge q) \vee (\bar{p} \wedge p) \vee (\bar{q} \wedge p \wedge q) \vee (\bar{q} \wedge p)$

$\equiv (c \wedge q) \vee c \vee (c \wedge p) \vee (\bar{q} \wedge p)$

$\equiv c \vee c \vee c \vee \bar{q} \wedge p$

$\equiv p \wedge \bar{q}$

Example 3: Eliminating conditional and biconditional, find logical equivalent forms of

(i) $(p \leftrightarrow (q \vee r)) \rightarrow \bar{p}$
(ii) $((p \rightarrow q) \rightarrow q) \rightarrow p$

Solution: (i) Here we shall solve the problems, by using the truth table method, i.e. finding a form in dnf which is logically equivalent to the given form.

p	q	r	$\bar{p}$	$(q \vee r)$	$p \times (q \vee r)$	$(p \times (q \vee r)) \rightarrow \bar{p}$
T	T	T	F	T	T	F
T	T	F	F	T	T	F
T	F	T	F	T	T	F
T	F	F	F	F	F	T
F	T	T	T	T	F	T
F	T	F	T	T	F	T
F	F	T	T	T	F	T
F	F	F	T	F	F	T

Consider only the values of p, q, r corresponding to T in the last column of the truth table.

Then the logically equivalent form is

$$(p \wedge \bar{q} \wedge \bar{r}) \vee (\bar{p} \wedge q \wedge r) \vee (\bar{p} \wedge q \wedge \bar{r}) \vee (\bar{p} \wedge \bar{q} \wedge r) \vee (\bar{p} \wedge \bar{q} \wedge \bar{r})$$

(ii) $((p \to q) \to q) \to p$

Solution:

p	q	p → q	(p → q) → q	((p → q) → q) → p
T	T	T	T	T
T	F	F	T	T
F	T	T	T	F
F	F	T	F	T

The logically equivalent form is $(p \wedge q) \vee (p \wedge \bar{q}) \vee (\bar{p} \wedge \bar{q})$

Example 4: Prove that $p \to (q \to r)$ and $(p \wedge r) \to \bar{q}$ are logically equivalent.

Solution:

p	Q	r	$\bar{q}$	$\bar{r}$	(q → r) p → (q → r)	(p ∧ r̄)	(p ∧ r̄) → q̄
T	T	T	F	F	T	F	T
T	T	F	F	T	F	T	F
T	F	T	T	F	T	F	T
T	F	F	T	T	T	T	T
F	T	T	F	F	T	F	T
F	T	F	F	T	T	F	T
F	F	T	T	F	T	F	T
F	F	F	T	T	T	F	T

The marked columns are identical. Hence the two forms are logically equivalent.

Example 5: There are two restaurants next to each other. One has a sign that says "Good food is not cheap" and the other has a sign that says "Cheap food is not good". Are the signs saying the same thing?

Solution: We shall show that the two statements are logically equivalent.

Let,   p : Food is good.
       q : Food is cheap.

Then the symbolic form of "Good food is not cheap" is $p \to \sim q$ and symbolic form of "Cheap food is not good" is $q \to \sim p$.

Now $p \to \sim q$ and $q \to \sim p$ are logically equivalent. Consider the truth table.

p	q	~p	~q	p → ~q	q → ~p
T	T	F	F	F	F
T	F	F	T	T	T
F	T	T	F	T	T
F	F	T	T	T	T

Both the marked columns are identical. Hence the two forms are logically equivalent.

Example 6: Show that $p \vee q$ and $(p \vee q) \wedge \sim (p \wedge q)$ are logically equivalent.

Solution: Consider the truth tables.

P	q	$p \veebar q$	$p \vee q$	$p \wedge q$	$\sim (p \wedge q)$	$(p \vee q) \wedge \sim (p \wedge q)$
T	T	F	T	T	F	F
T	F	T	T	F	T	T
F	T	T	T	F	T	T
F	F	F	F	F	T	F

Since the marked columns are identical $(p \veebar q)$ and $(p \vee q) \wedge \sim (p \wedge q)$ are logically equivalent.

Example 7: Obtain the disjunctive normal form of
(i) $(p \rightarrow q) \wedge (\sim p \wedge q)$,
(ii) $(p \wedge (p \rightarrow q)) \rightarrow q$.

Solution: (i) $p \rightarrow q$ is logically equivalent to $\sim p \vee q$

$\therefore \quad (p \rightarrow q) \wedge (\sim p \wedge q) \equiv (\sim p \vee q) \wedge (\sim p \wedge q)$
$\equiv (\sim p \wedge \sim p \wedge q) \vee (q \wedge \sim p \wedge q)$
$\equiv (\sim p \wedge q) \vee (q \wedge \sim p)$.

(ii) $(p \wedge (p \rightarrow q)) \rightarrow q \equiv \sim (p \wedge (\sim p \vee q)) \vee q$
$\equiv \sim p \vee \sim (\sim p \vee q) \vee q$
$\equiv \sim p \vee (p \wedge \sim q) \vee q$

Example 8: Show that the following statement is tautological:
$(p \wedge (p \rightarrow q)) \rightarrow q$

Solution: $(p \wedge (p \rightarrow q)) \rightarrow q \equiv \sim (p \wedge (\sim p \vee q)) \vee q$
$\equiv (\sim p \vee \sim (\sim p \vee q)) \vee q$
$\equiv (\sim p \vee (p \wedge \sim q)) \vee q$
$\equiv (\sim p \vee \sim q) \vee q$
$\equiv \sim p \vee T \equiv T$.

Example 9: Obtain the conjunctive normal form and disjunctive normal form of the following formulae given below:
(i) $p \wedge (p \rightarrow q)$
(ii) $\sim (p \vee q) \leftrightarrow (p \wedge q)$

Solution:
(i) $\quad p \wedge (p \rightarrow q) \equiv p \wedge (\sim p \vee q)$ – cnf
$p \wedge (\sim p \vee q) \equiv (p \wedge \sim p) \vee (p \wedge q)$
$\equiv F \vee (p \wedge q)$
$\equiv (p \wedge q)$ – dnf. (a single conjunct)

(ii) $\sim (p \vee q) \rightleftarrows (p \wedge q)$
$\equiv (\sim \sim (p \vee q) \vee (p \wedge q)) \wedge (\sim (p \wedge q) \vee \sim (p \vee q))$
$\equiv ((p \vee q) \vee (p \wedge q)) \wedge ((\sim p \vee \sim q) \vee (\sim p \wedge \sim q))$
$\equiv (p \vee q) \wedge ((\sim p \vee \sim q \vee \sim p) \wedge (\sim p \vee \sim q \vee \sim q))$
$\equiv (p \vee q) \wedge (\sim p \vee \sim q) \wedge (\sim p \vee \sim q)$
$\equiv (p \vee q) \wedge (\sim p \vee \sim q)$ – cnf

Further,
$(p \vee q) \wedge (\sim p \vee \sim q) \equiv ((p \vee q) \wedge \sim p) \vee ((p \vee q) \wedge \sim q)$
$\equiv (p \wedge \sim p) \vee (q \wedge \sim p) \vee ((p \wedge \sim q) \vee (q \wedge \sim q))$
$\equiv F \vee (q \wedge \sim p) \vee (p \wedge \sim q) \vee F$
$\equiv (q \wedge \sim p) \vee (p \wedge \sim q)$ – dnf.

Example 10: Find the conjunctive normal form and disjunctive normal form for the following:

(i) $(p \vee \bar{q}) \rightarrow q$

(ii) $p \leftrightarrow (\bar{p} \vee \bar{q})$

Solution:

(i) $(p \vee \bar{q}) \rightarrow q \equiv \overline{(p \vee \bar{q})} \vee q$
$\equiv (\bar{p} \wedge \bar{\bar{q}}) \vee q$
$\equiv (\bar{p} \wedge q) \vee q$ – dnf

$(\bar{p} \wedge q) \vee q \equiv (\bar{p} \vee q) \wedge (q \vee q)$
$\equiv (\sim p \vee q) \wedge q$ – cnf.

(ii) $p \times (\bar{p} \vee \bar{q}) \equiv (\bar{p} \vee (\bar{p} \vee \bar{q})) \wedge (\overline{(\bar{p} \vee \bar{q})} \vee p)$
$\equiv (\bar{p} \vee \bar{p} \vee \bar{q}) \wedge ((\bar{\bar{p}} \wedge \bar{\bar{q}}) \vee p)$
$\equiv (\bar{p} \vee \bar{q}) \wedge (p \vee p) \wedge (q \vee p)$
$\equiv (\bar{p} \vee \bar{q}) \wedge p \wedge (q \vee p)$ – cnf
$\equiv ((\bar{p} \wedge p) \vee (\bar{q} \wedge p)) \wedge (q \vee p)$
$\equiv (F \vee (\bar{q} \wedge p)) \wedge (q \vee p)$
$\equiv (\bar{q} \wedge p) \wedge (q \vee p)$
$\equiv (\bar{q} \wedge p \wedge q) \vee (\bar{q} \wedge p \wedge p)$
$\equiv (F \wedge p) \vee (\bar{q} \wedge p)$
$\equiv F \vee (\bar{q} \wedge p)$
$\equiv (\bar{q} \wedge p)$ – dnf   (Single conjunct)

Example 11: Find the conjunctive and disjunctive normal forms for the following without using truth table.

(i) $(p \to q) \wedge (q \to p)$

(ii) $((p \wedge (p \to q)) \to q)$

Solution: (i) $(p \to q) \wedge (q \to p) \equiv (\sim p \vee q) \wedge (\sim q \vee p)$ ... (cnf)

Further, using the distributive law on the above cnf, we have,

$((\sim p \vee q) \wedge \sim q) \vee ((\sim p \vee q) \wedge p) = (\sim p \wedge \sim q) \vee (q \wedge \sim q) \vee (\sim p \wedge p) \vee (q \wedge p)$

$\hspace{6cm} = (\sim p \wedge \sim q) \vee (q \wedge p) \to$ dnf

$\hspace{8cm} (\because p \wedge \sim p \equiv q \wedge \sim q)$

(ii) Solution in 7 (ii).

Example 12: If p and q are false propositions, state whether $(p \vee q) \wedge (\sim p \vee \sim q)$ is true or false. Verify.

Solution: The statement is false. Consider the truth table.

P	Q	~p	~q	p ∨ q	~p ∨ ~q	(p ∨ q) ∧ (~p ∨ ~q)
F	F	T	T	F	T	F

Example 13: Show that (i) $(p \wedge (\sim p \vee q)) \vee (q \wedge \sim (p \wedge q))$ is equivalent to q.

(ii) $((p \vee \sim q) \wedge (\sim p \vee \sim q)) \vee q$ is a tautology.

Solution: (i) $p \wedge (\sim p \vee q) \equiv (p \wedge \sim p) \vee (p \wedge q)$

$\hspace{4cm} \equiv c \vee (p \wedge q) \equiv p \wedge q$

Similarly, $\quad q \wedge \sim (p \wedge q) \equiv q \wedge (\sim p \vee \sim q)$

$\hspace{4cm} \equiv (q \wedge \sim p) \vee (q \wedge \sim q) \equiv (q \wedge \sim p) \vee c$

$\hspace{4cm} \equiv q \wedge \sim p$

Here, $\quad (p \wedge (\sim p \vee q)) \vee (q \wedge \sim (p \wedge q))$

$\hspace{4cm} \equiv (p \wedge q) \vee (q \wedge \sim p) \equiv (p \vee \sim p) \wedge q$

$\hspace{4cm} \equiv T \wedge q \equiv q$

(iii) $((p \vee \sim q) \wedge (\sim p \vee \sim q)) \vee q$

$\hspace{4cm} \equiv (p \vee \sim q \vee q) \wedge (\sim p \vee \sim q \vee q)$

$\hspace{4cm} \equiv (p \vee T) \wedge (\sim p \vee T)$

$\hspace{4cm} \equiv T \wedge T \equiv T$

Example 14: Obtain cnf of each of the following:

(i) $p \wedge (p \to q)$

(ii) $\sim (p \vee q) \leftrightarrow (p \wedge q)$

(iii) $q \vee (p \wedge \sim q) \vee (\sim p \wedge \sim q)$

Solution: (i) $p \wedge (p \to q) \equiv (p \wedge (\sim p \vee q))$

$\hspace{4cm} \equiv (p \wedge \sim p) \vee (p \wedge q)$

$\hspace{4cm} \equiv c \vee (p \wedge q)$

$\hspace{4cm} \equiv (p \wedge q)$ – cnf

(ii) Solved Ex. 9

(iii) $q \vee (p \wedge \sim q) \vee (\sim p \wedge \sim q)$
$$\equiv ((q \vee p) \wedge (q \vee \sim q)) \vee (\sim p \wedge \sim q)$$
$$\equiv (q \vee p) \wedge T \vee (\sim p \wedge \sim q)$$
$$\equiv (q \vee p) \vee (\sim p \wedge \sim q)$$
$$\equiv (q \vee p \vee \sim p) \wedge (q \wedge p \vee \sim q)$$
$$\equiv (q \vee T) \wedge (p \vee q \vee \sim q)$$
$$\equiv T \wedge (p \vee T) \equiv T \wedge T$$
$$\equiv T \equiv (p \vee \sim p) - \text{cnf (single disjunct)}$$

1.10 Logical Implication

Let **A** and **B** be two statement forms. Then **A** logically implies **B**, denoted by $A \Rightarrow B$ if $A \rightarrow B$ is a tautology.

In other words, whenever **A** is true, **B** should be true.
The following are some basic examples of logical implication.

Examples 15:
(i) $p \wedge p \Rightarrow p$, $p \vee p \Rightarrow p$.
(ii) $p \wedge q \Rightarrow p$, $p \wedge q \Rightarrow q$.
(iii) $p \Rightarrow p \vee q$, $q \Rightarrow p \vee q$.

SOLVED EXAMPLES

Example 16: Show that $(p \wedge q) \Rightarrow (p \rightarrow q)$
Solution: Consider the truth table

p	q	p ∧ q	p → q	(p ∧ q) → (p → q)
T	T	T	T	T
T	F	F	F	T
F	T	F	T	T
F	F	F	T	T

Hence $(p \wedge q) \Rightarrow (p \rightarrow q)$.

Example 17: Show that $(p \rightarrow q) \Rightarrow p \rightarrow (p \wedge q)$ without constructing truth table.
Solution:
We have to show that if $p \rightarrow q$ is true, then so is $p \rightarrow (p \wedge q)$.

Suppose this is not the case.
Then this means that $p \to (p \wedge q)$ has truth value F, i.e. p is T and $p \wedge q$ is F.
This can happen only when q is F.
But if q is F, then so is p, since we assume $p \to q$ is T.
This contradicts the truth value of p which is T.
Hence $p \to (p \wedge q)$ is true. Hence, this is the logical implication.)

Example 18: Prove that $(p \to (q \to r)) \Rightarrow ((p \to q) \to (p \to r))$.
Solution: Consider the truth table:

p	Q	r	$q \to r$	$p \to (q \to r)$	$p \to q$	$p \to r$	$((p \to q) \to (p \to r))$
T	T	T	T	T	T	T	T
T	F	T	T	T	F	T	T
T	T	F	F	F	T	F	F
T	F	F	T	T	F	F	T
F	T	T	T	T	T	T	T
F	F	T	T	T	T	T	T
F	T	F	F	T	T	T	T
F	F	F	T	T	T	T	T

Since the given statement forms have the same truth values, each logically implies the other, i.e. they are in fact equivalent forms.

EXERCISE - 1.2

1. Show that the truth values of the following forms are independent of their components:
   (i) $(p \wedge (p \to q)) \to q$
   (ii) $(p \leftrightarrow q) \leftrightarrow ((p \wedge q) \vee (\sim p \wedge \sim q))$
2. Determine which of the forms given below are tautologies, contradictions or neither.
   (i) $(p \to \sim p) \to \sim p$
   (ii) $(p \to (q \to r)) \to ((p \to q) \to (p \to r))$
   (iii) $(p \vee q) \wedge \sim p \to q$
   (iv) $(p \to q) \wedge (q \to r) \to (p \to r)$
   (v) $(p \wedge q) \leftrightarrow p$.
3. Show that $p \to (q \to r)$ and $p \to (\sim q \vee r)$ are logically equivalent.
4. Show that $p \leftrightarrow q$ and $(p \wedge q) \vee (\sim p \wedge \sim q)$ are logically equivalent.
5. Find the dnf of $(q \to p) \wedge (\sim p \wedge q)$.
6. Find the dnf of $(p \to (q \wedge r)) \wedge (\sim p \to (\sim p \wedge \sim r))$ by truth table method.
7. Obtain cnf of (i) $(\sim p \to r) \wedge (p \to q)$, (ii) $(p \wedge q) \vee (\sim p \wedge q \wedge r)$
8. Obtain dnf of: (i) $(p \to q) \wedge (\sim p \wedge q)$, (ii) $(p \wedge (p \to q)) \to q$.

9. Show that $(p \to (q \to r))$ logically imply $(p \to q) \to (p \to r)$.
10. Without constructing truth tables, show that
    (i) $(p \to q) \to q \Rightarrow p \vee q$
    (ii) $(p \wedge q) \Rightarrow (p \to q)$
11. (i) Show that: $(p \wedge (p \to q)) \to q$.
    (ii) $(p \to q) \wedge \sim q \to \sim p$ are tautologies, without using truth table.
12. Obtain the conjunctive and disjunctive normal forms.
    (i) $p \wedge (p \to q)$
    (ii) $(p \vee \sim q) \to q$
13. Show that the following statements are tautological.
    (i) $(p \wedge (p \to q)) \to q$
    (ii) $(p \to q) \leftrightarrow (q \vee \sim p)$
14. Find the dnf of:
    (i) $(p \to q) \wedge (\sim p \wedge q)$
    (ii) $(p \to (q \wedge r)) \wedge (\sim p \to (\sim p \wedge \sim r))$ by truth table method.
15. A computer has been built to answer any yes or no question but it has been programmed either to answer all questions truthfully or to give incorrect answers to all questions. If we wish to find out whether Fermat's last Theorem is true, what question should we put to the computer, so that it will give a correct answer.

1.11 Methods of Proof

Whenever an assertion is made, which is claimed to be true, one has to state an argument, which establishes the truth of the assertion.

In Mathematics, we prove theorems; a theorem being a mathematical assertion which is shown to be true. A proof consists of a sequence of statements. Some of these statements may be axioms (universal truths), some may be previously proved theorems and other statements may be hypothesis (assumed to be true). To construct a proof, we need to derive new assertions from existing ones. This is done using Rules of **Inference.** Before we discuss some of these rules of inference, let us formally define a **valid argument**.

Definition:

A valid argument is a finite sequence of statements $p_1, p_2, \ldots, p_n$, called as **premises** together with a statement C called the **conclusion** such that $p_1 \wedge p_2 \wedge \ldots \wedge p_n \to C$ is a tautology.

This concept is used in the following methods.

1. Modus Ponens (Law of Detachment):
This rule is presented in the following form

$$\frac{\begin{array}{c} p \to q \\ p \end{array}}{\therefore q}$$

The assertions above the horizontal line are called premises (or hypothesis).
The assertion below the line is called the conclusion.
This rule constitutes a valid argument since $(p \wedge (p \to q)) \to q$ is a tautology.

Example: If Suresh gets a first class, he will get a job easily. Suresh gets a first class. Therefore he will get a job easily.

Let,   p : Suresh gets a first class.
       q : Suresh will get a job easily.

Then the premises are $p \to q$ and p; the conclusion is q.
The inferential form is thus

$$\frac{\begin{array}{c} p \\ p \to q \end{array}}{\therefore q}$$

Hence this form of argument is valid.

---

2. Modus tollens (Law of contraposition):
This rule is presented in the following form

$$\frac{\begin{array}{c} p \to q \\ \sim q \end{array}}{\therefore \sim p}$$

This argument is valid since $(p \to q) \wedge \sim q \to \sim p$ is a tautology.

Example: If Suresh gets a first class, he will get a job. Suresh does not get a job. Therefore Suresh does not get a first class.

Let,   p : Suresh gets a first class.
       q : Suresh gets a job.

Then the inferential form is

$$\frac{\begin{array}{c} p \to q \\ \sim q \end{array}}{\therefore \sim p}$$

Hence the above argument is valid.

3. Disjunctive Syllogism: The rule of inference is presented in the form

$$p \lor q$$
$$\sim p$$
$$\therefore q$$

Note that $(p \lor q) \land \sim p \to q$ is a tautology ($\sim p$ is T, $p \lor q$ is T implies q is T)

Example: Either it is raining or it is windy. It is not raining. Therefore it is windy.

Let,   p : It is raining.
       q : It is windy.

Then the inferential form is

$$p \lor q$$
$$\sim p$$
$$\therefore q$$

Hence the argument is valid.

4. Hypothetical syllogism: Rule is in the form

$$p \to q$$
$$q \to r$$
$$\therefore p \to r$$

Note that $(p \to q) \land (q \to r) \to (p \to r)$ is a tautology.
Hence the above argument is a valid argument.

Example: If Suresh studies hard, he will obtain a first class. If he obtains a first class, he will get a good job. Therefore if Suresh studies hard, he will get a good job.

Let,   p : Suresh studies hard.
       q : He obtains a first class.
       r : He will get a good job.

Hence the inferential form is

$$p \to q$$
$$q \to r$$
$$\therefore p \to r$$

Hence the argument is valid.

SOLVED EXAMPLES

Example 1: Determine whether the following is a valid argument:
If Geeta goes to class, she is on time.
But Geeta is late.
She will therefore miss class.

Solution: Let, p : Geeta goes to class.
q : Geeta is on time.

The rule of inference is

$$p \to q$$
$$\sim q$$
$$\overline{\therefore \sim p}$$

This is the law of contraposition or Modus tollens. Hence the argument is valid.

Example 2: I am happy if my program runs. A necessary condition for the program to run is it should be error free. I am not happy. Therefore the program is not error free.

Solution: Let, p : I am happy.
q : My program runs.
r : It should be error free.

Then the argument is

$$q \to p$$
$$q \to r$$
$$\sim p$$
$$\overline{\therefore \sim r}$$

Consider the following assignment of truth values to p, q, r. Let the truth values of p, q, r be F, F, T respectively. Then $q \to p$ is T, $q \to r$ is T and $\sim p$ is T. But the conclusion $\sim r$ is F. Hence the above argument is invalid.

Example 3: If today is Tuesday, then there is a test in Computer Science or in Discrete Mathematics. If the Discrete Mathematics professor is sick, there will be no test in Discrete Mathematics. Today is Tuesday and the professor of Discrete Mathematics is sick. Hence there will be a test in Computer Science.

Solution: Let p : Today is Tuesday.
q : There is a test in Computer Science.
r : There is a test in Discrete Mathematics.
s : Discrete Mathematics professor is sick.

Argument is

$$p \to (q \vee r)$$
$$s \to \sim r$$
$$\underline{p \wedge s}$$
$$\therefore q$$

Wherever $p \to (q \vee r)$, $s \to \sim r$, $p \wedge s$ are true, q is also true. This is because $p \wedge s$ is T implies p is T, s is T. s is T implies $\sim r$ is T, $\therefore$ r is F.
$\therefore \quad p \to (q \vee r)$ is T implies q is T.
Hence the argument is valid.

Example 4: Ramesh is studying ORACLE or he is not studying JAVA. If Ramesh is studying JAVA, then he is not studying ORACLE. Therefore he is studying ORACLE.
Write the above statement in symbolic form and test the validity of the argument using laws of logic.
Solution: Let, p: Ramesh is studying ORACLE.
q: Ramesh is studying JAVA.
Argument is

$$p \vee \sim q$$
$$\underline{q \to \sim p}$$
$$\therefore \quad p$$

Argument is invalid, since consider the following assignment of truth values to p and q. Let the truth values of p and q be both F respectively. Then $p \vee \sim q$ has truth value T and $q \to \sim p$ has truth value T. Hence for validity of the argument p should have truth value T, which is not the case.

Example 5: Show that the following premises are inconsistent.
  (i)   If Jack misses many classes through illness, then he fails high school.
  (ii) If Jack fails high school, then he is uneducated.
  (iii) If Jack reads a lot of books, then he is not uneducated.
  (iv) If Jack misses many classes through illness, then he reads a lot of books.

Solution: Let
  p : Jack misses many classes through illness
  q : Jack fails high school
  r : Jack is uneducated
  s : Jack reads a lot of books.

Then the premises are:

$$p \to q,$$
$$q \to r,$$
$$s \to \sim r,$$
$$p \to s.$$

Consider the following assignment of truth values to p, q, r and s.

p	q	r	s
T	T	T	F

Then $\quad p \to q$ is T,
$\quad\quad\quad q \to r$ is T,
$\quad\quad\quad s \to \sim r$ is T.
ut $\quad\quad p \to s$ is F.
Hence, the premises are inconsistent.

Example 6: Determine the validity of the argument given:

$\quad\quad S_1$: If I like Mathematics then I will study
$\quad\quad S_2$: Either I will study or I will fail
$\therefore\quad S$: If I fail then I do not like Mathematics

Solution: Let,
$\quad\quad p$: I like Mathematics
$\quad\quad q$: I will study
$\quad\quad r$: I will fail.
$\quad\quad S_1 : p \to q$
$\quad\quad S_2 : q \vee r$
$\quad\quad S : r \to \sim p$

For validity, $S_1 \wedge S_2$ should logically imply S.

Assign the truth values T, T, T to p, q, r respectively. Then S_1 is T, S_2 is T but S is false. Hence, the argument is invalid.

Example 7: Test the validity of the argument: If a person is poor, he is unhappy. If a person is unhappy, he dies young, therefore poor person dies young.

Solution: Let
$\quad\quad p$: Person is poor
$\quad\quad q$: Person is unhappy
$\quad\quad r$: Person dies young

In symbolic form the argument is:
$\quad\quad S_1 : p \to q,$
$\quad\quad S_2 : q \to r,$
$\quad\quad S : p \to r$

The above argument is the value of **Hypothetical Syllogism**. Hence it is valid.

Alternatively, let $p \to r$ be F, then p is T and r is F. If $p \to q$ is T, then q is T. But $q \to r$ is F. Hence, conclusion is false implies one of the premises is false. Therefore the argument is valid.

Example 8: Determine whether the argument given is valid or not.
If I try hard and I have talent, then I will become a musician. If I become a musician, then I will be happy.
Therefore, if I will not be happy, then I did not try hard or I do not have talent.

Solution: Let
- p : I try hard
- q : I have talent
- r : I will become a musician
- s : I will be happy

The argument is then put in symbolic form as:

$$S_1 : (p \wedge q) \to r$$
$$S_2 : r \to s$$
$$\therefore S : \sim s \to \sim p \vee \sim q$$

Suppose argument is invalid. This means that for some assignment of truth values, S_1 is T, S_2 is T, but S is F. S will have truth value F is $\sim s$ is T, and $\sim p \vee \sim q$ is F, i.e. s is F, p is T and q is T. Since we have assumed S_2 to be true, the truth values of r and s are both F. since S_1 is also, by assumption, true, r is F implies either p or q is F. This is a contradiction, since by assumption both p and q are T.
The given argument is valid.

1.12 Predicates

Consider the following sentences:
(i) "x is tall and handsome".
(ii) "x + 3 = 5" (iii) "x + y ≥ 10".

These sentences are not propositions, since they do not have any truth value. However, if values are assigned to the variables, each of them becomes a proposition, which is either true or false. For example, the above sentences can be converted into
(i) "He is tall and handsome".
(ii) "2 + 3 = 5" (true statement)
(iii) "2 + 5 ≥ 10" (false statement)

Hence we have the following definition.

Definition:

> An assertion that contains one or more variables is called a **predicate**; its truth value is predicated after assigning truth values to its variables.

A predicate P containing n variables $x_1, x_2, \ldots, x_n$ is called an **n-place** predicate.
Examples (i) and (ii) are one-place predicates while Example (iii) is a 2-place predicate.

> If we want to specify the variables in a predicate, we denote the predicate by $P(x_1, x_2, \ldots x_n)$. Each variable x_i is also called as an **argument**.

For example,
- (i) "x is a city in India" is denoted by P (x).
- (ii) "x is the father of y" is denoted by P (x, y).
- (iii) "x + y ≥ z" is denoted by P (x, y, z).

> The values which the variables may assume constitute a collection or (a) set called as the **universe of discourse.**

When we specify a value for a variable appearing in a predicate, we **bind** that variable.

A predicate becomes a proposition only when all its variables are bound.

Consider the following examples:

(i) P (x): x + 3 = 5.

Let the universe of discourse be the set of all integers. Binding x by putting x = – 1, we get a false proposition. Binding x by putting x = 2, we get a true proposition.

(ii) P (x, y): x + y = 10. Let the universe of discourse be the set of natural numbers.

Putting x = 1, we get the one-place predicate P (1, y): 1 + y = 10. Further setting y = 10, we obtain the proposition P (1, 9) which is true. However, if we set y = 10, P (1, 10) is a false proposition. In each case, we have bound both the variables (x by 1, y by 9 and y by 10).

A second method of binding individual variables in a predicate is by **quantification** of the variable.

1.12.1 Universal Quantifier

> If P(x) is a predicate with the individual variable x as an argument, then the assertion "For all x, P(x)" which is interpreted as "For all values of x, the assertion P(x) is true", is a statement in which the variable x is said to be **universally quantified.**
>
> We denote the phrase "For all" by ∀, called the **universal quantifier.** The meaning of ∀ is "for all" or "For every" or "For each".
>
> If P(x) is true for every possible value of x, then ∀ **x P(x)** is true; otherwise ∀ x P(x) is false.

Example: Let P(x) be the predicate "x ≥ 0"; where x is any positive integer. Then the proposition ∀ x P(x) is true. However, if x is any real number, then ∀ x P(x) is a false proposition.

1.12.2 Existential Quantifier

> Suppose for the predicate P(x), ∀ x P(x) is false, but there exists at least one value of x for which P(x) is true, then we say that in this proposition, x is bound by **existential quantification.**
>
> We denote the words "there exists" by the symbol ∃.
>
> Then the notation ∃ **x P(x)** means "there exists a value of x (in the universe of discourse) for which P(x) is true."

Example: Let P(x) be the predicate "x + 3 = 5" and let the universe of discourse be the set of all integers. Then the proposition $\exists x\, P(x)$ is true (by setting x = 2) but $\forall x\, P(x)$ is false.

Let P (x, y) be a two-place predicate, then

$\exists x\, \forall y\, P(x, y)$ is the proposition "There exists a value of x such that for all values of y, P(x, y) is true".

$\forall y\, \exists x\, P(x, y)$ is the proposition "For each value of y, there exists an x such that P(x, y) is true."

$\exists x\, \exists y\, P(x, y)$ is the proposition "There exist a value of x and a value of y such that P (x, y) is true."

$\forall x\, \forall y\, P(x, y)$ is the proposition "For all values of x and y, P(x, y) is true".

Example: Consider the universe as the set of all integers: Let P(x, y) denote the predicate x + y = 10.

(i) Then the symbolic statement $\forall x\, \exists y\, P(x, y)$ is interpreted as "For every integer x, there exists an integer y such that x + y = 10 (i.e. y = 10 – x)".

(ii) Now consider the statement $\exists y\, \forall x\, P(x, y)$. This statement is read as "there exists an integer y so that for all integers x, x + y = 10". This statement is of course false.

(iii) The statement $\exists x\, \exists y\, P(x, y)$ is read as "there exist integers x and y such that x + y = 10". This is a true statement.

1.12.3 Negation of a Quantified Statement

Consider the statement $\forall x\, P(x)$. Its negation is "it is not the case that for all x, P(x) is true". This means that for some x = a, P(a) is not true, or in other words there exists an x such that ~P(x) is true. Hence $\forall x\, P(x)$ is logically equivalent to $\exists x\, [\sim P(x)]$.

Example: Consider the example" All the invited guests were present for the dinner.
The negation is: "All the invited guests were not present for the dinner, equivalently".
Some guests were not present for the dinner, i.e. $\exists x\, (\sim P(x))$; where,

        x : x is a guest
        P(x) : x was present for the dinner.

Example: Consider the statement "There is a student in this class, who is not familiar with C programming". The negation of the above statement is "All students in this class are familiar with C programming".

Hence symbolically, $\exists x\, (\sim P(x))$ and $\forall x\, (P(x))$ are logically equivalent.
We summarize these results in the following table.

Statement	Negation
$\forall x\, (P(x))$	$\exists x\, (\sim P(x))$
$\exists x\, (\sim P(x))$	$\forall x\, (P(x))$
$\forall x\, (\sim P(x))$	$\exists x\, (P(x))$
$\exists x\, P(x)$	$\forall x\, (\sim P(x))$

1.13 Rules of Inference for Predicates

In this section, we consider rules of inference, to test the validity of arguments, involving predicates, similar to those we considered for arguments involving propositions.

We have the famous lines:

"All men are mortal,

Socrates is a man.

Therefore Socrates is mortal".

This is a universally quantified statement, about an attribute or property that is of mortality, over the universe of men. The argument is that Socrates, being a member of the set, satisfies the attribute.

This form of argument is called as **universal instantiation**, as we are taking a particular instance of a general (universal statement).

The above type of statement can be formulated in symbolic language as:

$$\frac{\forall x\, P(x)}{\therefore P(a)}$$

where x is an element of the universe, P(x) the attribute of x and a, a particular member of the universe.

Next, we have a second type of statement, as illustrated by the following example:

2 is a square-free integer. Therefore, there are integers, that are square free.

In symbolic form, we can express the above statement as:

$$\frac{P(a)}{\therefore \exists x\, P(x)}$$

Such a type of statement is called as **Existential generalization** that is making a general statement, from a particular instance.

The rule of universal instantiation leads to the following rules:

1. Universal Modus Ponens:	$\forall x\, (P(x) \rightarrow Q(x))$ $\underline{P(a)}$ $\therefore Q(a)$
2. Universal Modus Tollens:	$\forall x,\, (P(x) \rightarrow Q(x))$ $\underline{\sim Q(a)}$ $\therefore \sim P(a)$

SOLVED EXAMPLES

Example 1: All law-abiding citizens obey the traffic rules.
Mr. Joshi is a law-abiding citizen. Therefore he obeys the traffic rules.
Translate into symbolic language, we have,

$$\forall x \, (L(x) \rightarrow T(x))$$
$$\underline{L(a)}$$
$$\therefore T(a)$$

where the universe of discourse is citizens, $L(x) \equiv$ x is a law-abiding citizen,
$T(x) \equiv$ x obeys the traffic rules.

Example 2: All the first year students know C-programming Manisha is a first year student. Therefore, Manisha knows C-programming.
In symbolic form, the statements:

$$\forall x \, (C(x) \rightarrow P(x))$$
$$\underline{C(a)}$$
$$\therefore P(a)$$

Example 3: All cats like milk. Timmy does not like milk. Therefore, Timmy is not a cat.
Symbolically,

$$\forall x \, (C(x) \rightarrow M(x))$$
$$\underline{\sim M(a)}$$
$$\therefore \sim C(a)$$

Apart from these standard forms, we test the validity of quantified forms of argument, along similar lines as we did in the case of propositional arguments.

Example 4: Determine the validity of the following argument:

- S_1 : All my friends are musicians
- S_2 : John is my friend.
- S_3 : None of my neighbours are musicians.
- S : John is not my neighbour.

Solution: Let the universe of discourse be the set of people.

Let,
- $F(x)$: x is my friend
- $M(x)$: x is a musician
- $N(x)$: x is my neighbour

Then argument in symbolic form is

- S_1 : $\forall x \, (F(x) \rightarrow M(x))$
- S_2 : $F(a)$ (a = John)
- S_3 : $\forall x \, (N(x) \rightarrow \sim M(x))$
- $\therefore S$: $\sim N(a)$

Suppose ~ N(a) has value F, i.e. N(a) is T. Since S_3 is T, we must have ~ M(a) is T or M(a) is F. But S_1 is T, hence we must have F(a) to be false, but this is a contradiction. Hence, if S is false, either of S_1 or S_3 should be false. Hence argument is valid.

Example 5: Babies are illogical. Nobody is despised who can manage a crocodile. Illogical persona is despised. Therefore, babies cannot manage crocodiles.

Solution: Let a be the domain of people.

Let
- B(x) : x is a baby.
- L(x) : x is logical
- D(x) : x is despised.
- C(x) : x can manage a crocodile.

Statement is as follows:

S_1 : $\forall x [B(x) \rightarrow \sim L(x)]$
S_2 : $\forall x [C(x) \rightarrow \sim D(x)]$
S_3 : $\forall x [\sim L(x) \rightarrow D(x)]$

S ∴ $\forall x [B(x) \rightarrow \sim C(x)]$

Suppose $\forall x [B(x) \rightarrow C(x)]$ is F.

This means $\exists x = a$, such that ∴ B(a) is T and ~ C(a) is F, i.e. C(a) is T. For S_2 to be T, this means that ~ D(a) is T or D(a) is F. For S_3 to be T, this mean that ~ L(a) is F or L(a) is T. But then B(a) is F, a contradiction. Hence argument is valid.

Example 6: Suppose the universe of discourse is the set of integers. Let P (x, y) be the predicate x – y = 0. Indicate which of the propositions are true and which are false.

(i) P (2, 3)
(ii) P (3, 3)
(iii) $\forall x \exists y$ P (x, y)
(iv) $\exists x \forall y$ P (y, x)

Solution:

(i) P (2, 3) is false.
(ii) P (3, 3) is true.
(iii) For each value of x, set y = x. i.e. if x = 0, y = 0, if x = 1, y = 1 etc.
Then P (x, y) is true.
Hence $\forall x \exists y$ P (x, y) is true.
(iv) In this case, there should be a specific value $x = x_0$ such that P (y, x_0) is true, no matter what the value of y is. This means $x_0 - y = 0$ for any value of y, obviously false.

Example 7: Transcribe the following into logical notation. Let the universe of discourse be the real numbers.

(i) For any value of x, x^2 is non-negative.
(ii) For every value of x, there is some value of y such that x · y = 1.

(iii) There are positive values of x and y such that $x \cdot y > 0$.
(iv) There is a value of x such that if y is positive, then $x + y$ is negative.
(v) For every value of x, there is some value of y such that $x - y = 1$.

Solution:
(i) $\forall x \, [x^2 \geq 0]$
(ii) $\forall x \, \exists y \, [x \cdot y = 1]$
(iii) $\exists x \, \exists y \, [(x > 0) \land (y > 0) \land (x \cdot y > 0)]$
(iv) $\exists x \, \forall y \, [(y > 0) \to (x + y < 0)]$
(v) $\forall x \, \exists y \, [x - y = 1]$.

Example 8: Negate the following in such a way that the symbol ~ does not appear outside the square brackets.
(i) $\forall x \, [x^2 \geq 0]$
(ii) $\exists x \, [x \cdot 2 = 1]$
(iii) $\forall x \, \exists y \, [x + y = 1]$
(iv) $\forall x \, \forall y \, [(x > y) \to (x^2 > y^2)]$.

Solution:
(i) Negation of the statement is "There is a value of x such that $x^2 < 0$".
   Hence Negation of the statement in logical notation is $\exists x \, [x^2 < 0]$.
(ii) Negation is "For all values of x, $x \cdot 2 \neq 1$".
   Hence the required form is $\forall x \, [x \cdot 2 \neq 1]$.
(iii) Negation is "There is a value of x such that for all values of y, $x + y \neq 1$". Hence the required form is $\exists x \, \forall y \, [x + y \neq 1]$.

Example 9: Write the following statements in symbolic form, using quantifiers.
(i) All students have taken a course in communication skills.
(ii) There is a girl student in the class who is also a sports person.
(iii) Some students are intelligent, but not hardworking.

Solution:
(i) Let P(x): Student x has taken a course in communication skills.
   Then the statement can be written as $\forall x \, P(x)$.
(ii) Let   P(x) : x is a student
             Q(x) : x is a girl
             R(x) : x is a sports person.
   The statement is interpreted as x is a student, x is a girl and x is a sports person.
   Hence this statement can be written as $\exists x \, [P(x) \land Q(x) \land R(x)]$.
(iii) There exists an x such that x is intelligent, but x is not hardworking. Here in symbolic form the statement is $\exists x \, [P(x) \land \sim Q(x)]$.

Chp 1 | 1.49

Example 10: For the universe of all integers, let P(x), Q(x), R(x), S(x) and T(x) be the following statements:

$$P(x) : x > 0$$
$$Q(x) : x \text{ is even}$$
$$R(x) : x \text{ is a perfect square}$$
$$S(x) : x \text{ is divisible by 4}$$
$$T(x) : x \text{ is divisible by 5.}$$

Write the following statements in symbolic form:
  (i) At least one integer is even.
  (ii) There exists a positive integer that is even.
  (iii) If x is even, then x is not divisible by 5.
  (iv) No even integer is divisible by 5.
  (v) There exists an even integer divisible by 5.
  (vi) If x is even and x is a perfect square, then x is divisible by 4.

Solution:
  (i) $\exists Q(x)$
  (ii) $\exists x \, [P(x) \wedge Q(x)]$
  (iii) $\forall x \, [Q(x) \rightarrow \sim T(x)]$
  (iv) $\forall x \, [Q(x) \rightarrow \sim T(x)]$
  (v) $\exists x \, [Q(x) \wedge T(x)]$
  (vi) $\forall x \, [Q(x) \wedge R(x) \rightarrow S(x)]$.

In the above example, determine the truth table of each statement.
Solution: (i), (ii), (iv) and (vi) are true statements. Statements (iii) and (v) are false.

Example 11: Rewrite the following statements using quantifier variables and predicate symbols.
  (i) All birds can fly.
  (ii) Not all birds can fly.
  (iii) Some men are genius.
  (iv) Some numbers are not rational.
  (v) There is a student who likes Mathematics but not Geography.
  (vi) Each integer is either even or odd.

Solution: (i) Let $\quad$ B(x) : x is a bird.
$\quad\quad\quad\quad\quad\quad\quad\quad$ F(x) : x can fly.
Then the statement can be written as: $\forall x \, [B(x) \rightarrow F(x)]$.
  (ii) $\exists x \, [B(x) \wedge \sim F(x)]$ or equivalently $\sim [\forall x \, (B(x) \rightarrow F(x))]$.
  (iii) $\quad\quad\quad\quad\quad\quad$ M(x) : x is a man
$\quad\quad\quad\quad\quad\quad\quad\quad$ G(x) : x is a genius.

Statement is interpreted as $\exists x\,[M(x) \wedge G(x)]$.

(iv) $N(x)$:   x is a number
                         $R(x)$:   x is rational

Statement is in symbolic form, $\exists x\,[N(x) \wedge \sim R(x)]$ or equivalently $\sim [\forall x\,(N(x) \rightarrow R(x))]$

(v) $S(x)$:   x is a student
                          $M(x)$:   x likes Mathematics
                          $G(x)$:   x likes Geography

Statement is: $\exists x\,[S(x) \wedge M(x) \wedge \sim G(x)]$.

(vi) $I(x)$:   x is an integer.
                          $E(x)$:   x is even
                          $O(x)$:   x is odd.

Statement in symbolic form: $\forall x\,[I(x) \rightarrow E(x) \vee O(x)]$.

Example 12: Negate each of the following statements:
    (i) $\forall x,\ |x| = x$
    (ii) $\exists x,\ x^2 = x$.

Solution: (i) $\exists x,\ |x| \neq x$,   (ii) $\forall x,\ x^2 \neq x$.

Example 13: Determine the truth value of each of the statement and negate every statement.
    (i) $\exists x,\ x + 2 = x$.
    (ii) $\forall x,\ x + 1 > x$.

Solution: (i) F, $\forall x,\ x + 2 \neq x$,   (ii) T, $\exists x,\ x + 1 \leq x$.

1.14 Techniques of Theorem Proving

The properties of quantifiers that we have studied in the previous section, help us to evolve techniques for theorem proving. The word theorem at once reminds us of some of the most famous theorems in mathematics such as Pythagoras Theorem, Binomial Theorem etc.

> A theorem is nothing but an exercise in logical reasoning or argument. It consists of two distinct parts - hypothesis and conclusion. Hypothesis is a set of statements, which if true, implies the conclusion. Hence a theorem is usually in the form of a conditional or biconditional statement form.

Example 1: If a function is differentiable, then it is continuous.

Example 2: For real numbers x, y; $x^2 = y^2 \leftrightarrow x = \pm y$.

However, there are also many theorems, which are not strictly in the form of conditional or biconditional.

Example 3: $\sqrt{2}$ is an irrational number.

Example 4: Every positive integer is a product of prime numbers.

In what follows, we shall consider some typical examples, which illustrate some of the techniques of theorem proving.

> An important principle applied in theorem proving is the **Rule of universal specification**, which states that if P(x) is a statement for a given universe, and if $\forall x\, P(x)$ is true, then P(a) is true for each a in the universe.

The following example illustrates this idea.

    All men are mortal.

    Socrates is a man.

    Therefore Socrates is mortal.

In the above argument, if

$$P(x) : x \text{ is a man}$$
$$Q(x) : x \text{ is mortal,}$$

then let s represent the particular person Socrates, then the argument in symbolic form is

$$\forall x\, [P(x) \rightarrow Q(x)]$$
$$\underline{P(s)}$$
$$\therefore Q(s)$$

Observe that in the above example we have used the rule of universal specification in conjunction with Modus Ponens (or the rule of detachment).

Another example in similar vein. All integers are rational numbers.

π is not a rational number. Therefore π is not an integer.

In symbolic form, we present the argument as:

Let, $P(x)$: x is an integer

            $Q(x)$: x is a rational number.

Let a represent π.

Then the argument is $\forall x, (P(x) \rightarrow Q(x))$

$$\underline{\sim Q(a)}$$
$$\therefore \sim P(a)$$

In the above argument we have combined the rule of universal specification together with Modus Tollens, and hence the argument is valid.

Let us now turn our attention to some theorems in mathematics.

Theorem 1:	If n is divisible by 6, then n² is divisible by 4.
Proof:	Since n is divisible by 6, it is divisible by 2, 2 being a factor of 6. **Hence n² is divisible by 4.**

Theorem 2:	Let n be an integer. Prove that $7n^2 + 5n - 4$ is even.
Proof:	We consider the following cases.
Case I:	n is even. Since the product of an even integer and any integer is even, $7n^2$ and $5n$ are even. Hence, $7n^2 + 5n - 4$ is even.
Case II:	n is odd. The product of odd integers is odd and sum of two odd integers is even. Hence $7n^2 + 5n$ is even and since sum of even integers being even, $7n^2 + 5n - 4$ is even.

Theorem 3:	If $n^2 + 1 = 2m$, for integers m, n; then m is the sum of squares of two integers.
Proof:	Since $n^2 + 1 = 2m$, this implies that $n^2 + 1$ is even. Hence n^2 must be odd, which in turn implies that n is odd. Let $n = 2k + 1$ for an integer k. Then $n^2 + 1 = (2k + 1)^2 + 1 = 2m$, i.e. $4k^2 + 4k + 1 = 2m$ Hence, $m = 2k^2 + 2k + 1 = (k + 1)^2 + k^2$. Thus the theorem is proved.

The above examples are illustrations of **Direct proofs**. However, in many cases, a direct proof is rather difficult; hence an indirect approach of proving the **contrapositive** yields the result immediately. Recall that by contrapositive method we mean that instead of proving "P → Q" is true, its logical equivalence "~ Q → ~ P" is proved to be true.

Theorem 4:	If l is a non-zero rational number, and m is an irrational number, then lm is irrational.
Proof:	Let, P: l is a non-zero rational number Q:lm is irrational We prove the contrapositive, i.e. "~ Q → ~ P" is true. Suppose lm is not irrational; then lm is rational.

	Hence, we can express lm as lm = $\frac{a}{b}$, where a ≠ 0, b ≠ 0. Further l being non-zero rational, l = $\frac{c}{d}$, c ≠ 0, d ≠ 0. Hence, lm = $\frac{a}{b}$ gives m = $\frac{a}{lb}$ = $\frac{ad}{bc}$, where ad ≠ 0, bc ≠ 0. But this contradicts the fact that m is irrational. Hence "∼ Q → ∼ P" is true, i.e. "P → Q" is true.

Theorem 5:	For all positive real numbers x, y, if the product xy is greater than 49, then x > 7 or y > 7.
Proof:	Consider the negation of the conclusion, x > 7 or y > 7, that is, suppose 0 < x ≤ 7 and 0 < y ≤ 7. This would imply that 0 < x·y ≤ 7.7 = 49. Hence the product does not exceed 49.

Similar to the method of indirect proof is the method of contradiction. This is illustrated in the following examples.

Theorem 6:	There are infinitely many prime numbers.
Proof:	Let us assume the contrary. Hence let $p_1, p_2, ..., p_n$ be exhaustive list of all prime numbers, n in number. Let $p_1 < p_2 < ... < p_n$. Consider P = $p_1 p_2 ... p_n$ + 1 P is not a prime number since P > p_i ∀ 1 ≤ i ≤ n. Hence P must have prime factors. Let p_k be a prime factor of P. Then p_k divides (P − $p_1 p_2 ... p_n$), i.e. p_k divides 1, which is absurd. Hence p_k is not any one of the p_i's listed. This means that there are infinitely many prime numbers.

Another beautiful theorem is the following.

Theorem 7:	$\sqrt{2}$ is an irrational number.
Proof:	Suppose $\sqrt{2}$ is not an irrational number.

> Then $\sqrt{2}$ is a rational number.
> Hence we can express $\sqrt{2}$ as $\sqrt{2}$ = p/q, where p and q are positive integers, having no common factor except 1.
> Squaring we obtain $2 = p^2/q^2$.
> Hence $p^2 = 2q^2$. This implies that p^2 is even and hence p is also even. Hence p^2 contains a factor of 4.
> Since $q^2 = p^2/2$, q^2 is even and therefore q should also be even.
> Since p and q are both even, they have a common factor 2, which contradicts our assumption that p and q have a common factor other than 1.
> Hence $\sqrt{2}$ cannot be rational number, it is irrational.

Proof of another important theorem (real numbers are uncountable) is based on the same principle – proof by contradiction, and will be discussed in the chapter on sets.

Often we have to deal with statements in mathematics, which have to be proved or disproved. To disprove a given statement, all that we have to do is to produce a counter example. Here are few illustrations.

SOLVED EXAMPLES

Example 1: Prove or disprove $n^2 + 41n + 41$ is a prime number for every integer n.

Solution: If n = 1, expression = 43 and for n = 2, it is 47, both being prime numbers. However, this by no means imply that the number is prime for all n. Consider n = 41. Then $41^2 + 41 + 41 = 41 \times 43$. Hence, n = 41 is a counter example.

Example 2: Prove or disprove: If a and b are irrational, then a^b is also irrational.

Solution: Proof: Counter example:

Consider, $e^{\pm \log 2} = 2 \text{ or } \frac{1}{2}$

Example 3: Let A and B be two matrices, with product AB valid, then AB = 0 → A = 0 or B = 0.

Solution: Counter example:

Let,
$$A = \begin{pmatrix} 0 & 1 \\ 0 & 0 \end{pmatrix}, \quad B = \begin{pmatrix} 1 & 1 \\ 0 & 0 \end{pmatrix}$$

then
$$AB = \begin{pmatrix} 0 & 1 \\ 0 & 0 \end{pmatrix} \begin{pmatrix} 1 & 1 \\ 0 & 0 \end{pmatrix} = \begin{pmatrix} 0 & 0 \\ 0 & 0 \end{pmatrix}$$

EXERCISE - 1.3

Determine the validity of the following arguments:

1. If I like computer science, then I will study.
   Either I don't study or I pass computer science.
   If I don't graduate, it means that I did not pass computer science.
   Therefore, if I like computer science, then I will graduate.

2. If I stay up late, watching T.V., then I will be late next morning.
   I did not stay up late.
   Therefore, I am not late the next morning.

3. If I study, then I will pass.
   If I do not go to a movie, then I will study.
   I passed.
   Therefore, I did not go to a movie.

4. If Ram's computer program is correct, then he will be able to complete his assignment in almost 2 hours.
   It takes Ram over two hours to complete his assignment.
   Therefore Ram's computer program is not correct.

5. If I drive to work, then I will arrive tired. I do not drive to work. Therefore I will not arrive tried.

6. I will become famous or I will not become a writer. I will become a writer. Therefore, I will become famous.

7. If I work, I cannot study either I work, or I pass Mathematics. I passed Mathematics. Therefore, I studied.

8. If 3 is a prime number, then 2 does not divide 5. Either 4 is not even or 2 divides 5. But 4 is even. Therefore, 3 is not a prime number.

9. All integers are rational numbers. The real numbers π is not a rational number. Therefore, π is not an integer.

10. No human beings are quadrupeds. All men are human beings. Therefore, no man is a quadruped.

11. In a heterogeneous group of students, there are some who are freshers, some seniors and some are already graduates. There are students who are specialising in Mathematics or Physics or Computer science (a student can specialise in only one). Considering the above description, write the following statements using quantifiers.
    (i) There is a senior student, who is not specialising in Mathematics.
    (ii) No graduate student specialises in Physics.
    (iii) Some graduate students are neither taking Mathematics nor Physics.
    (iv) Every senior student in the group is specialising in Mathematics or Computer Science.

12. Write each of the following in terms of quantifiers:
    (i) Every integer is either odd or even.
    (ii) There are no even prime numbers.
    (iii) The sum of two odd integers is even.
    (iv) All prime numbers are not odd.
13. Let P(x, y) denote the sentence "x divides y", where the universe for both x and y comprises all integers. Determine the truth value of
    (i) $\forall y \exists x P(x, y)$. (ii) $\exists y \forall x P(x, y)$.
    (iii) $\forall x \forall y [(P(x, y) \land P(y, x)) \rightarrow (x = y)]$
14. Let P(x, y, z) be the predicate $x \cdot y = z$. Transcribe each of the following into English.
    (i) P(z, 3, x)   (ii) $\forall x \exists y P(x, y, 1)$ (iii) $\forall x P(x, 1, x)$ (iv) $\exists y \exists x P(x, y, x)$
15. Let the universe of discourse be the set of real numbers. Transcribe the following into an English sentence and indicate which are true and which are false.
    (i) $\exists x [x^2 = 2]$ (ii) $\exists x \forall y [x + y = y]$ (iii) $\exists y \exists z \forall x [x \cdot y = z]$
    (iv) $\exists z \forall x \forall y [x \cdot y = z]$
16. Negate each of the following in such a way so that the symbol ~ does not appear before a quantifier.
    (i) $\exists x \forall y [x > y]$ (ii) $\forall y \exists x [x^2 = y]$ (iii) $\forall x \forall y [(y > 0) \rightarrow (x \cdot y > 0)]$
17. Give a direct proof of the following:
    (i) For all integers m and n, if both m and n are even, then m + n is even.
    (ii) For all integers if both m and n are even, then mn is even.
18. Give an indirect proof of the following:
    (i) If $x + y \geq 100$, then $x \geq 50$ or $y \geq 50$.
    (ii) If n^2 is odd, then n is odd.
19. Prove by contradiction the following:
    If the average of four different integers is 9, then at least one number should be greater than 10.
20. Prove that if x is an irrational number, then 1 − x is also irrational.
21. Prove that if two lines are each perpendicular to a third line, in the plane, then the two lines are parallel.

Points to Remember

- A **proposition or statement** is a declarative sentence which is either true or false, but not both.
- Combining primary statements using certain connecting words like "not", "and", "or", "but", "while" etc is called **Compound Statements.**
- The **negation** of a statement is formed either by introducing the word "not" at a proper place or by prefixing the statement with the phrase "It is not the case that".
- If p and q are the statements, the compound statement "p and q" is called as the **conjunction** of p and q; and is denoted by $p \land q$.

- If p and q are statements, then the compound statement "p or q" is called as the **disjunction** of p and q, and is denoted by p ∨ q.
- If p and q are statements, the compound statement "If p then q", (is) denoted by **p → q** (which) is called a **conditional statement** or **implication.**
- If p and q are statements, the compound statement "p if and only if q", denoted by **p ↔ q**, is called a **bi-conditional statement.**
- A table giving all possible truth values of a statement form, corresponding to the truth values assigned to its variables, is called a **truth table**.
- A statement form is called a **Tautology** if it always assumes the truth value 'T' irrespective of the truth values assigned to its variables.
- A statement form is called a **contradiction** if it always assumes the truth value 'F' irrespective of the truth values assigned to its variables.
- A statement form which is neither a tautology nor a contradiction is called a **contingency.**
- Two statement forms are **logically equivalent** if both have the same truth values, whatever may be the truth values assigned to the statement variables, occurring in both the forms.
- A conjunction of statement variables and (or) their negations is called as a **fundamental conjunction.** (It is also called as a **min term).**
- A statement form which consists of a **disjunction** of **fundamental conjunctions**, is called a **disjunctive normal** form (abbreviated as dnf).
- A disjunction of statement variables and (or) their negations is called a **fundamental disjunction or maxterm.**
- A statement form which consists of a **conjunction** of **fundamental disjunctions**, is called a **conjunctive normal form** (abbreviated as cnf).
- An assertion that contains one or more variables is called a **predicate;** its truth value is predicated after assigning truth values to its variables. If we want to specify the variables in a predicate, we denote the predicate by $P(x_1, x_2, \ldots x_n)$. Each variable x_i is also called as an **argument.**
- The values which the variables may assume constitute a collection or (a) set called as the **universe of discourse.**
- If P(x) is a predicate with the individual variable x as an argument, then the assertion "For all x, P(x)" which is interpreted as "For all values of x, the assertion P(x) is true", is a statement in which the variable x is said to be **universally quantified.**
- A theorem is nothing but an exercise in logical reasoning or argument. It consists of two distinct parts - hypothesis and conclusion. Hypothesis is a set of statements, which if true, implies the conclusion. Hence a theorem is usually in the form of a conditional or biconditional statement form.

Chapter 2: Theory of Sets

SYLLABUS:
- **Relations :** Definition, Properties of binary relations, Equivalence relations and partitions, Partial ordering relations and lattice, chains and antichains, Transitive closure and Warshall's algorithm.
- **Function :** Functions, Definitions, Composition of functions, Types of function, Recursive functions, Pigeonhole principle.

OBJECTIVES:
- Notion of set and its properties are the necessary prerequisites for the student to understand more complicated structures.
- To learn the set theory approach for solving problems on counting.

UTILITY:
- As a basic tool to study various discrete structures such as graphs, groups and rings.
- In problems related to combinatorics.

KEY CONCEPTS:
- Subset, universal set, empty set.
- Set operations: Union, Intersection, Complementation.
- Power set.
- Principle of Inclusion – Exclusion.
- Mathematical Induction.

2.0 Introduction

Set is a fundamental concept in the theory of Discrete Structures. Any algebraic structure, be it a 'group' or 'graph', has its 'underlying structure'. Hence, one ought to have a clear understanding of the term **set.**

The theory of sets was first introduced by the German Mathematician G. Cantor (1845 – 1918), who defined a set simply as a collection of objects. Later, contradictions or *paradoxes* were discovered in the definition. We have the famous *Russell's Paradox*, due to Bertrand Russell. Russell asked the following question.

Suppose the universe of discourse in **the set of all sets,** and let S be a set, whose objects are sets, **which are not members of themselves,** then is S a member of itself? If S is not a member of itself, then by the condition imposed on S, S should belong to itself. On the other hand, if S does not belong to itself, then S should be a member of itself, as per the definition. This is the paradox.

The discovery of the paradoxes, however, did not mean that Cantor's original work characterised as 'naive set theory' was to be abandoned. It was found that by suitably redefining the universe of discourse, the paradoxes could be circumvented. Thus, evolved a theory, which ranks today as one of the most important areas of Modern Mathematics.

In the ensuing discussion, we shall adopt the modified version of Cantor's theory. For each separate situation, we shall define a universal set and within its framework, the set under discussion will be a collection of objects, the objects being also members of the universal set.

2.1 Sets

2.1.1 Definition

A set is a **collection of** objects.

An object in the collection is called an **element** or member of the set.

The term **class** is also used to denote a set.

A set may contain **finite** number of elements or **infinite** number of elements.

A set is called an **empty set** or a **null set** if it contains no element. An empty set is denoted by the letter ϕ.

Examples:
(i) The set of letters forming the word 'PASCAL', is a finite set, whose elements are the five **distinct** letters of the word.
(ii) The set of all telephone numbers in the directory. This is also a finite, though a large, set.
(iii) The set of persons in a moving queue. This is also a finite set, but difficult to list, due to the constant flux (At any instant of time, people are entering as well as leaving the queue).
(iv) The set of whole (natural) numbers greater than 10. This is an infinite set, but the elements in the set can be listed, i.e. 11, 12, 13, ...
(v) The set of all points in the plane. This is also an infinite set, but the elements cannot be listed, as the points are 'dense' not 'discrete.'
(vi) The set consisting of a circle, the number 5, a tree and Bill Gates.
This example shows that the elements in a set can be totally different in character, they need not have a common characteristic.
(vii) The set of real roots of the equation $x^2 + 1 = 0$. This is obviously an empty set.

2.1.2 Notations

A set is generally denoted by capital letters A, B, C, ..., X, Y, Z.
Elements of the set are denoted by small letters a, b, c, ..., x, y, z.
If x is an element of the set A, we express this fact by writing

$$'x \in A'$$ ($\in$ means 'belongs to')

If x is not an element of A, we write

$$'x \notin A'$$

There are various ways of describing a set.

(a) **Listing Method:** In this method, the elements are listed within braces.
   e.g.   (i) A = {pencil, byte, 5}
             (ii) B = {2, 4, 6, 8, ... }
(b) **Statement Form:** A statement describing the set, especially where the elements share a common characteristic. e.g.
   (i) The set of all equilateral triangles.
   (ii) The set of all Prime Ministers of India.
(c) **Set-Builder Notation:** It is not always possible or convenient to describe a set by the Listing method or the Statement form. A more concise or compact way of describing the set is to specify the property shared by all the elements of the set. This property is denoted by P(x), where P is a statement concerning an element x of the set. The set is then simply written as
   {x | P(x)} where the braces { } denote the clause " the set of ", and the slash or stroke | denotes "such that" (read as ". A is the set of all x such that x is greater than 10").
   Examples: (i) A = {x | x > 10}
                      (ii) B = {x | x is real and $x^8 - 5x^4 + 4 = 0$}.

2.1.3 Some Special Sets (Number Sets)

The following sets occur frequently in our discussion. We give below the standard notations used to denote these sets.

N	–	the set of all natural numbers {1, 2, 3, ... }.
Z	–	the set of all integers {...... – 2, –1, 0, 1, 2, ... }.
Z^+	–	the set of all positive integers {0, 1, 2, ... }.
Q	–	the set of rational numbers.
Q^+	–	the set of non-negative rational numbers.
$\mathbb{R}$	–	the set of real numbers.
$\mathbb{C}$	–	the set of complex numbers.

2.2 Subsets

2.2.1 Definition

*If every element of a set A is also an element of a set B, then we say A is a **subset** of B, or A is **contained** in B. This is denoted by writing 'A $\subseteq$ B'. This can be also denoted by 'B $\supseteq$ A'*

If A is not a subset of B, this is indicated by writing 'A $\not\subseteq$ B'.

Examples:
   (i)   N $\subseteq$ Z^+ $\subseteq$ Z $\subseteq$ Q $\subseteq$ $\mathbb{R}$ $\subseteq$ $\mathbb{C}$

(ii)   A = {1, 3, 6},   B = {−1, 1, 2, 3, 4, 6}
            C = {1, 2, 3}

Then   A ⊆ B,
But   A ⊆ C

It is clear from the definition that **Every set is a subset of itself. The empty set is a subset of any set.**

2.2.2 Universal Set

*If all sets, considered during a **specific discussion** are subsets of a given set, then this set is called as the **Universal Set**, and is denoted by 'U'.*

Hence, the universal set is a relative concept dependent on the specific discussion. Therefore, it is also referred to as the **universe of discourse**.

2.2.3 Equality of Sets

Two sets A and B are equal if A is a subset of B and B is also a subset of A, i.e. A ⊆ B and B ⊆ A implies A = B.

Examples:
(i) If   A = {BASIC, COBOL, FORTRAN}
      and B = {FORTRAN, COBOL, BASIC}
      then A = B.

(ii) If   A = $\{x \mid x^2 + 1 = 0\}$
      and B = $\{i, -i\}$ $(i = \sqrt{-1})$
      then A = B

2.2.4 Important Remark

A set itself can be an element of some other set. Hence, one should be able to clearly distinguish between an element of a set and subset of a set.

Examples:
1. Let A = {a, b, {a, b}, {{a, b}}}.
   Identify each of the following statements as true or false. Justify your answers.
   (a) a ∈ A, (b) {a} ∈ A, (c) {a, b} ∈ A (d) {{a, b}} ⊆ A, (e) {a, b} ⊆ A (f) {a, {b}} ⊆ A.

Solution:
   (a) True, as a is an element of A.
   (b) False, as {a} is not an element but a subset of A.
   (c) True, as {a, b} is an element of A, listed third in the set.
   (d) True, as a subset containing the single element {a, b} of A.
   (e) True, as the subset containing the elements a, b of A.
   (f) False, as {b} is not an element of A.

2. Determine whether each of the following statements is true for arbitrary sets A, B, C. Justify your answers.
   (a) If $A \in B$ and $B \subseteq C$, then $A \in C$
   (b) If $A \in B$ and $B \subseteq C$, then $A \subseteq C$.
   (c) If $A \subseteq B$ and $B \in C$, then $A \in C$.
   (d) If $A \subseteq B$ and $B \in C$, then $A \subseteq C$.

Solution: (a) True, as A being an element of B, it should also belong to C as B is a subset of C.
   (b) False, as A is not a subset but an element of B.
   (c) False. Consider $A = \{a\}$, $B = \{a, b\}$, $C = \{\{a, b\}\}$.
   (d) False. Consider the same example as in (c).

2.3 Venn Diagrams

A Venn diagram (named after the British logician John Venn) is a pictorial depiction of a set. A rectangle represents the universal set. The interior of the rectangle represents the elements in the set. A circle drawn within the rectangle depicts an arbitrary set. It is not compulsory to show an arbitrary set, always by a circle. An oval shaped or elliptical curve could also be drawn to represent a set. In fact any closed curve of any shape can be used to depict a set.

Venn Diagram

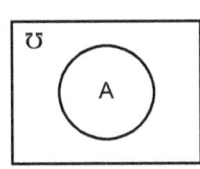

Fig. 2.1

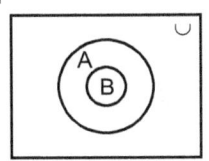

$B \subset A$

Fig. 2.2

2.4 Set Operations

We shall now define various set operations, which will combine the given sets to yield new sets. These operations are analogous to the algebraic operations of addition, multiplication of numbers.

2.4.1 Complement of a Set

Let A be a given set. **Complement** of A, denoted by $\overline{A}$ is defined as

$$\overline{A} = \{x \mid x \notin A\}$$

Examples:

(i) If $A = \{x \mid x \text{ is a real number and } x \leq 7\}$, then
$\overline{A} = \{x \mid x \text{ is a real number and } x > 7\}$
where the universal set $\overline{U} = R$.

(ii) If $U = N = \{1, 2, 3, 4, 5, ...\}$
and $E = \{2, 4, 6, ...\}$
then $\overline{E} = \{1, 3, 5, ...\}$

Note that $\overline{\phi} = U$
and $\overline{U} = \phi$

2.4.2 Union of Sets

> The union of two sets A and B is the set consisting of all elements which are in A, or in B, or in both sets A and B. It is denoted by $A \cup B$.

In the set – builder notation,
$$A \cup B = \{x \mid x \in A \text{ or } x \in B\}.$$

Examples:

(i) If $A = \{2, 4, 6, 8, 10\}$
$B = \{1, 2, 6, 8, 12, 15\}$
then $A \cup B = \{1, 2, 4, 6, 8, 10, 12, 15\}$.

(ii) If $A = \{n \mid n \in N, 4 < n < 12\}$
$B = \{n \mid n \in N, 8 < n < 15\}$
then $A \cup B = \{5, 6, 7, 8, 9, 10, 11, 12, 13, 14\}$.

(iii) If $A = \{\phi\}$
$B = \{a, \phi, \{\phi\}\}$
then $A \cup B = \{\phi, a, \{\phi\}\}$
$= B$.

This is because $A \subseteq B$

Note that for any set A $\quad A \cup \phi = A$
$A \cup U = U$
$A \cup \overline{A} = U$.

2.4.3 Intersection of Sets

The intersection of two sets A and B, denoted by $A \cap B$ is the set consisting of elements which are in A **as well as** in B.
Thus, $A \cap B = \{x \mid x \in A \text{ and } x \in B\}$
→ If $A \cap B = \phi$, the sets are said to be **disjoint**.

Examples:

(i) If $A = \{a, b, c, g\}$
$B = \{d, e, f, g\}$
then $A \cap B = \{g\}$.

(ii) If $A = \{n \mid n \in N, 4 < n < 12\}$
$B = \{n \mid n \in N, 5 < n < 10\}$
then $A \cap B = \{6, 7, 8, 9\} = B$.

(iii) If $A = \{\phi\}$
$B = \{a, \phi, \{\phi\}\}$
then $A \cap B = \{\phi\} = A$.

Note that for any set
$A \cap \phi = \phi$
$A \cap U = A$
$A \cap \overline{A} = \phi$.

2.4.4 Difference of Sets (Relative Complement)

Let A and B be any two sets.
The difference A − B is the set defined as
$A - B = \{x \mid x \in A \text{ and } x \notin B\}$ is the (relative) complement of B in A.
Similarly,
$B - A = \{x \mid x \in B \text{ and } x \notin A\}$ is the complement of A in B.

Examples:

(i) If $A = \{1, 2, 3, \ldots, 10\}$
$B = \{1, 3, 5, \ldots 9\}$
then $A - B = \{2, 4, 6, 8, 10\}$
$B - A = \phi$.

(ii) If $A = \{a, b, \{a, c\}, \phi\}$
$A - \{a, b\} = \{\{a, c\}, \phi\}$
$\{a, c\} - A = \{c\}$.

2.4.5 Properties of Difference

Let A and B be any two sets.

Then (i) $\bar{A} = U - A$
(ii) $A - A = \phi$

(iii) $A - \bar{A} = A$, $\bar{A} - A = \bar{A}$
(iv) $A - \phi = A$

(v) $A - B = A \cap \bar{B}$
(vi) $A - B = B - A$ if and only if $A = B$
(vii) $A - B = A$ if and only if $A \cap B = \phi$
(viii) $A - B = \phi$ if and only if $A \subseteq B$.

Proofs of the properties (i) to (v) are immediate consequences of the definition. We shall prove the remaining properties.

(vi) If $A = B$, then $A - B = \phi = B - A$ by (ii). Conversely let $A - B = B - A$. Let $x \in A$. Assume $x \notin B$, then x should be in $A - B$. But since $A - B = B - A$, it follows that $x \in B - A$ which means $x \in B$, a contradiction. Hence, x should be an element of B. Therefore, $A \subseteq B$. Similarly we can prove $B \subseteq A$. Hence, $A = B$.

(vii) $A - B = A$ implies $A \cap \bar{B} = A$, i.e. $A \subseteq \bar{B}$. Hence, $A \cap B = \phi$. Conversely $A \cap B = \phi$ implies $A \subseteq \bar{B}$, which in turn means that $A \cap \bar{B} = A$, i.e. $A - B = A$.

(viii) If $A - B = \phi$, it implies that $A \cap \bar{B} = \phi$, i.e. $A \subseteq B$. Converse is proved by reversing the steps.

2.4.6 Symmetric Difference

The symmetric difference of two sets A and B, denoted by $A \oplus B$, is defined as
$$A \oplus B = \{x \mid x \in A - B \text{ or } x \in B - A\}$$
In other words, $A \oplus B = (A - B) \cup (B - A)$.

Examples:

(i) If $A = \{a, b, e, g\}$
$B = \{d, e, f, g\}$
then $A \oplus B = \{a, b, d, f\}$.

(ii) If $A = \{2, 4, 5, 9\}$
$B = \{x \in Z^+ \mid x^2 \leq 16\}$
then $A \oplus B = \{0, 1, 3, 5, 9\}$

(iii) If $A = \{\phi\}$,
$B = \{a, \phi, \{\phi\}\}$,
then $A \oplus B = \{a, \{\phi\}\}$.

2.4.7 Properties of Symmetric Difference

(i) $A \oplus A = \phi$

(ii) $A \oplus \phi = A$

(iii) $A \oplus U = \overline{A}$

(iv) $A \oplus \overline{A} = U$

(v) $A \oplus B = A \cup B - A \cap B$.

The properties (i) to (iv) are immediate consequences of the definition.

We shall prove the last property. Let $x \in A \cup B - A \cap B$. Then, $x \in A \cup B$ but $x \notin A \cap B$. This means that if $x \in A$, $x \notin B$. Similarly, if $x \in B$, then $x \notin A$. Hence, $x \in A - B$ or $x \in B - A$, which means that $x \in (A - B) \cup (B - A) = A \oplus B$. Conversely, let $x \in A \oplus B$. Then, $x \in A - B$ or $x \in B - A$. This means that $x \in A \cup B$ but $x \notin A \cap B$, i.e. $x \in (A \cup B) - (A \cap B)$. Hence, the two sets are equal.

2.4.8 Representation of Set Operations on Venn Diagrams

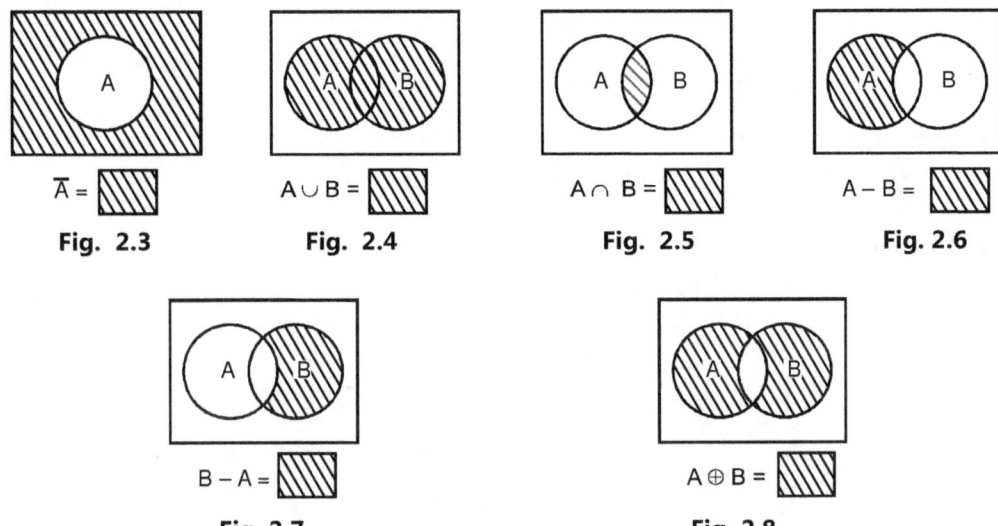

Fig. 2.3   Fig. 2.4   Fig. 2.5   Fig. 2.6

Fig. 2.7   Fig. 2.8

2.5 Algebra of Set Operations

The set operations obey the same rules as those of numbers, such as associativity, commutativity and distributivity. However, the cancellation rule which is true for numbers, is not true for sets in general. In addition, there are rules such as Idempotent laws, Absorption laws, De Morgan's laws, which are true only for sets.

Theorem: The set operations satisfy the following properties, for any sets A, B, C.

1. **Commutativity:**
   (i) $A \cup B = B \cup A$
   (ii) $A \cap B = B \cap A$

2. **Associativity:**
   (i) $A \cup (B \cup C) = (A \cup B) \cup C$, hence written as $A \cup B \cup C$
   (ii) $A \cap (B \cap C) = (A \cap B) \cap C$, hence written as $A \cap B \cap C$

3. **Distributivity:**
   (i) $A \cup (B \cap C) = (A \cup B) \cap (A \cup C)$
   (ii) $A \cap (B \cup C) = (A \cap B) \cup (A \cap C)$

4. **Idempotent Laws:**
   (i) $A \cup A = A$
   (ii) $A \cap A = A$

5. **Absorption Laws:**
   (i) $A \cup (A \cap B) = A$
   (ii) $A \cap (A \cup B) = A$

6. **De Morgan's Laws:**
   (i) $\overline{A \cup B} = \overline{A} \cap \overline{B}$
   (ii) $\overline{A \cap B} = \overline{A} \cup \overline{B}$

7. **Double Complement:** $\overline{\overline{A}} = A$

   Proof: We shall prove properties 3, 6 and 7. The remaining are easy exercises for the reader.

8. **Distributive Laws:**
   (i) $A \cup (B \cap C) = (A \cup B) \cap (A \cup C)$.
   Let $x \in A \cup (B \cap C)$. Then, $x \in A$ or $x \in B \cap C$. This further implies that $x \in A$ or ($x \in B$ and $x \in C$).
   i.e.   ($x \in A$ or $x \in B$) and ($x \in A$ or $x \in C$)
   i.e. $x \in A \cup B$ and $x \in A \cup C$
   i.e. $x \in (A \cup B) \cap (A \cup C)$
   Hence, $A \cup (B \cap C) \subseteq (A \cup B) \cap (A \cup C)$
   Similarly one can prove $(A \cup B) \cap (A \cup C) \subseteq A \cup (B \cap C)$.
   (ii) $A \cap (B \cup C) = (A \cap B) \cup (A \cap C)$ can be proved on similar lines.
   Refer to the figures below:

9. **De Morgan's Laws:**
   (i) $\overline{A \cup B} = \overline{A} \cap \overline{B}$

$$\overline{A \cup B} = \{x \mid x \notin A \cup B\}$$
$$= \{x \mid x \notin A \text{ and } x \notin B\}$$
$$= \{x \mid x \in \overline{A} \text{ and } x \in \overline{B}\}$$
$$= \overline{A} \cap \overline{B}$$

(ii) $\overline{A \cap B} = \overline{A} \cup \overline{B}$ can be proved in the same way, as above.

10. Double Complement:

$$\overline{\overline{A}} = A$$
$$\overline{\overline{A}} = \{x \mid x \notin \overline{A}\}$$
$$= \{x \mid x \in A\} = A.$$

The above properties can also be demonstrated by drawing suitable Venn diagrams, as shown below.

For Distributive Laws:

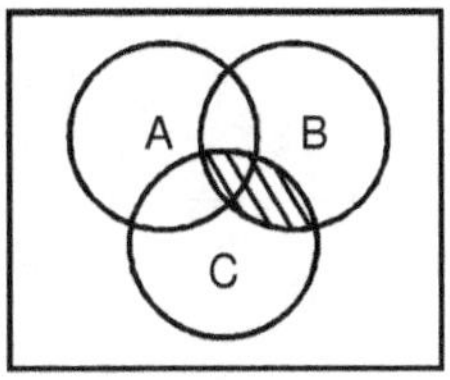

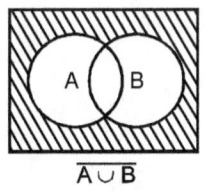

Fig. 2.9 $B \cap C$
Fig. 2.10 $A \cup (B \cap C)$
Fig. 2.11 $A \cup B$
Fig. 2.12 $A \cup C$
Fig. 2.13 $(A \cup B) \cap (A \cup C)$

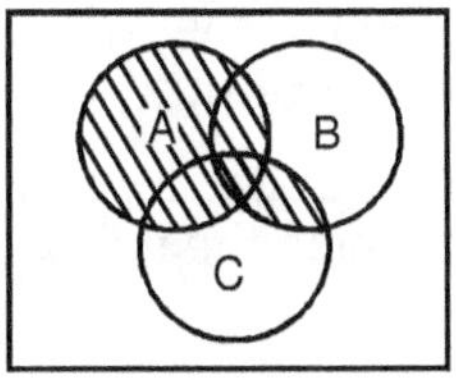

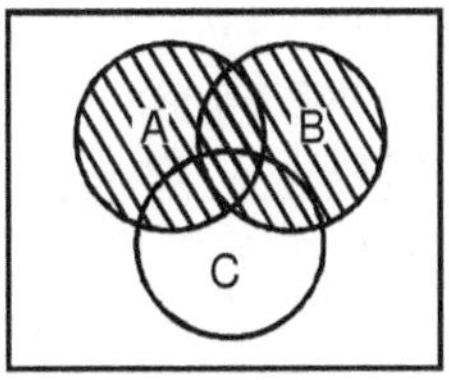

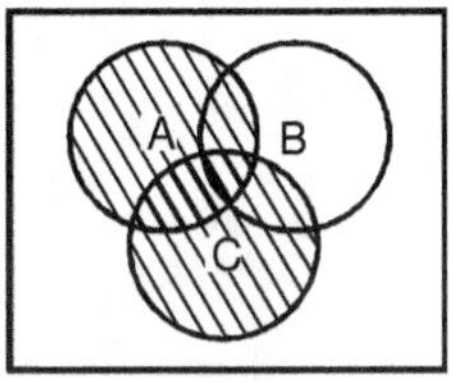

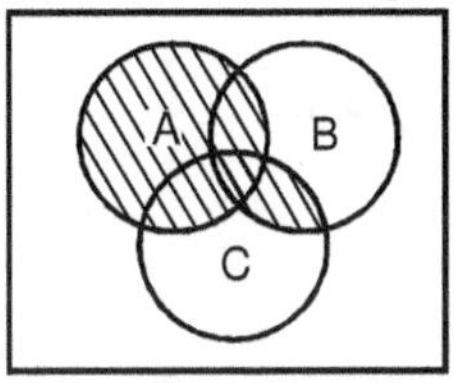

De Morgan's Laws:

Fig. 2.14 $\overline{A \cup B}$
Fig. 2.15 $\overline{A}$

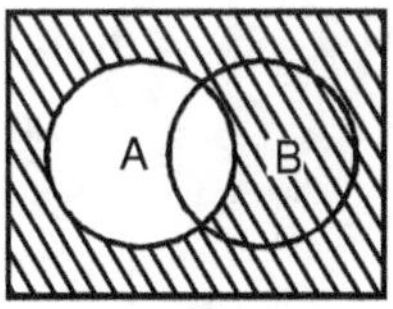

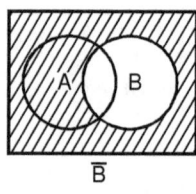

Fig. 2.16   Fig. 2.17

SOLVED EXAMPLES

Example 1: Determine whether the following statements are true or false. Justify your answers.

(i) $\{a, \phi\} \in \{a, \{a, \phi\}\}$.
(ii) $\{a, b\} \subseteq \{a, b, \{a, b\}\}$.
(iii) $\{a, b\} \in \{a, b, \{a, b\}\}$.
(iv) $\{a, c\} \in \{a, b, c, \{a, b, c\}\}$.

Solution: (i) True, since $\{a, \phi\}$ is an element of $\{a, \{a, \phi\}\}$.

(ii) True, since $\{a, b\}$ is a subset of $\{a, b, \{a, b\}\}$ containing the elements a, b.

(iii) True, since $\{a, b\}$ is an element in $\{a, b, \{a, b\}\}$.

(iv) False, since $\{a, c\}$ is not an element but a subset of $\{a, b, c, \{a, b, c\}\}$ containing the elements a, c.

Example 2 : If $A = \{a, b, \{a, c\}, \phi\}$, determine the following sets

(i) $A - \{a, c\}$
(ii) $\{\{a, c\}\} - A$
(iii) $A - \{\{a, b\}\}$
(iv) $\{a, c\} - A$.

Solution : (i) $A - \{a, c\} = \{b, \{a, c\}, \phi\}$

(ii) $\{\{a, c\}\} - A = \phi$
(iii) $A - \{\{a, b\}\} = A$
(iv) $\{a, c\} - A = \{c\}$.

Example 3: If
$U = \{n \mid n \in N, n \leq 15\}$,
$A = \{n \mid n \in N, 4 < n < 12\}$,
$B = \{n \mid n \in N, 8 < n < 15\}$,
$C = \{n \mid n \in N, 5 < n < 10\}$,

find $\overline{A} - \overline{B}$ and $\overline{C} - \overline{A}$.

Solution:
$\overline{A} = \{1, 2, 3, 4, 12, 13, 14, 15\}$
$\overline{B} = \{1, 2, 3, 4, 5, 6, 7, 8, 15\}$

$$\overline{C} = \{1, 2, 3, 4, 5, 10, 11, 12, 13, 14, 15\}$$

∴
$$\overline{A} - \overline{B} = \{12, 13, 14\}$$
$$\overline{C} - \overline{A} = \{5, 10, 11\}.$$

Example 4: Let A, B, C be subsets of the universal set U. Given that $A \cap B = A \cap C$ and $\overline{A} \cap B = \overline{A} \cap C$, is it necessary that $B = C$? Justify your answer.

Solution: Yes, $B = C$.
We can express B as

$$\begin{aligned}
B &= B \cap U = B \cap (A \cup \overline{A}) \\
&= (B \cap A) \cup (B \cap \overline{A}) && \text{(Distributive law)} \\
&= (A \cap B) \cup (\overline{A} \cap B) && \text{(Commutative law)} \\
&= (A \cap C) \cup (\overline{A} \cap C) && \text{(Given condition)} \\
&= (A \cup \overline{A}) \cap C && \text{(Distributive law)} \\
&= U \cap C \\
&= C.
\end{aligned}$$

Example 5: (i) Given that $A \cup B = A \cup C$, is it necessary that $B = C$?
(ii) Given that $A \cap B = A \cap C$, is it necessary that $B = C$?

Solution: (i) No. Let
$$A = \{1, 2, 3\}$$
$$B = \{1\}$$
$$C = \{3\}$$
$$A \cup B = \{1, 2, 3\} = A \cup C.$$
but $B \neq C$.

(ii) No. Let
$$A = \{1, 2\}$$
$$B = \{2, 3, 4, 5\}$$
$$C = \{2, 6, 7\}$$
then $A \cap B = \{2\} = A \cap C.$
but $B \neq C$

Example 6: If $A \oplus B = A \oplus C$, is $B = C$?

Solution: Yes. Consider any element $x \in B$. This element is then in A or not in A. Suppose $x \in A$. Then, $x \in A \cap B$ which implies that $x \notin A \oplus B$ and hence $\notin A \oplus C$. Now $A \oplus C = A \cup C - A \cap C$. Therefore, it follows that $x \in A \cap C$ which means that $x \in C$. Hence, if $x \in A$, then $B \subseteq C$.

Suppose we have the other possibility that x ∉ A. Then x ∉ A ∩ B so that x ∈ A ⊕ B which in turn implies that x ∈ A ⊕ C. This means that x ∈ A ∪ C. Therefore, x ∈ C. Hence, in this case also B ⊆ C.

Similarly we can show that C ⊆ B. Hence, B = C.

Problems involving Venn Diagrams:

Example 7: Show that $A \cup (\bar{B} \cap C) = (A \cup \bar{B}) \cap (A \cup C)$, using Venn diagram.

Solution:

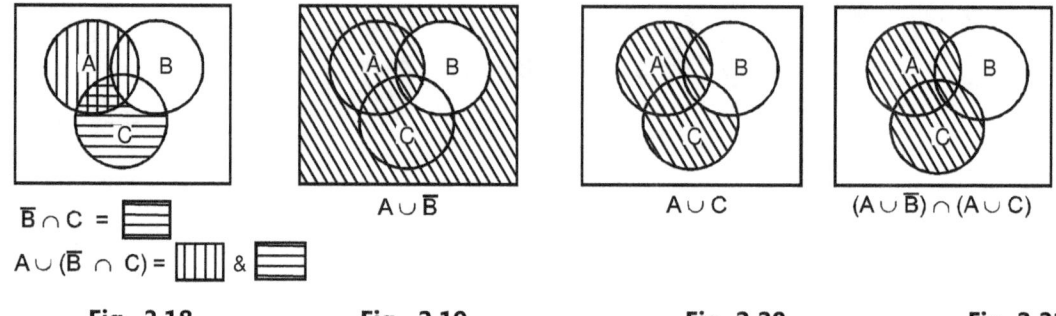

Fig. 2.18   Fig. 2.19   Fig. 2.20   Fig. 2.21

Example 8: Show that $(A - B) - C = A - (B \cup C)$ using Venn diagram.

Solution:

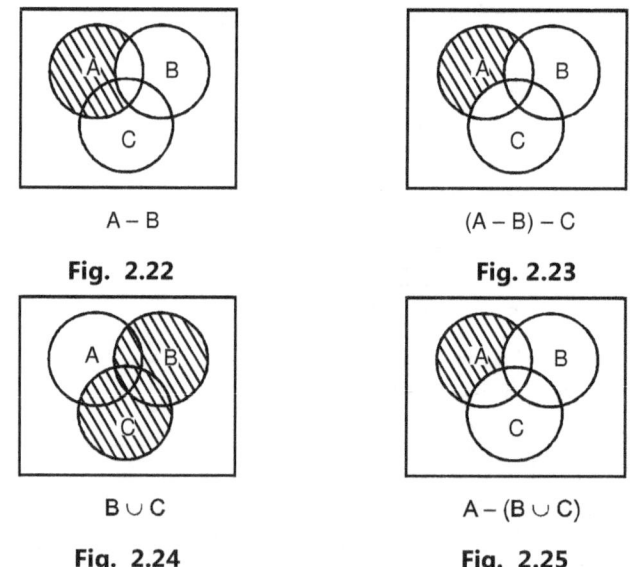

Example 9: Drawing Venn diagram, prove that A − (B − C) = (A − B) ∪ (A ∩ B ∩ C).
Solution:

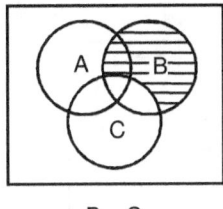

B − C

Fig. 2.26

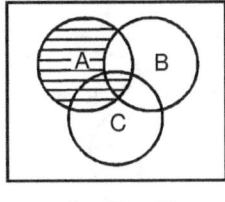

A − (B − C)

Fig. 2.27

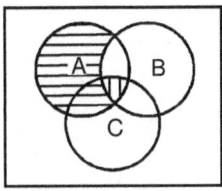

A − B = ▤
A ∩ B ∩ C = ▦

Fig. 2.28

Example 10: Using Venn diagram, prove or disprove
  (i)   A ⊕ (B ⊕ C) = (A ⊕ B) ⊕ C
  (ii)   A ∩ B ∩ C = A − [(A − B) ∪ (A − C)]

Solution:
(i)

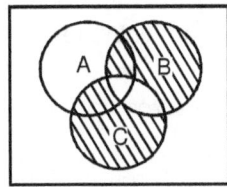

B ⊕ C

Fig. 2.29

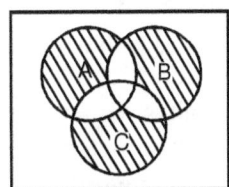

A ⊕ (B ⊕ C)

Fig. 2.30

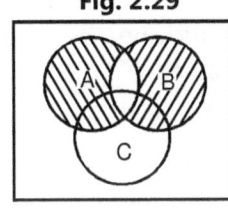

A ⊕ B

Fig. 2.31

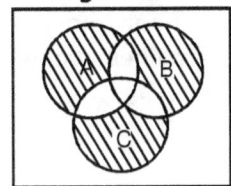

(A ⊕ B) ⊕ C

Fig. 2.32

(ii)

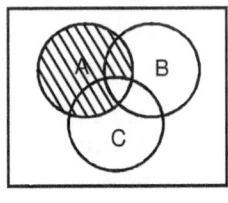

(A − B) ∪ (A − C)

Fig. 2.33

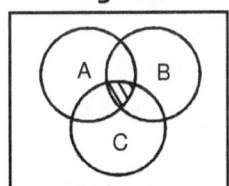

A − [(A − B) ∪ (A − C)]
= A ∩ B ∩ C

Fig. 2.34

Example 11: Using Venn diagram, prove or disprove

$$A \cap (B \oplus C) = (A \cap B) \oplus (A \cap C)$$

Solution:

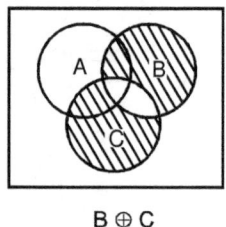
B ⊕ C
Fig. 2.35

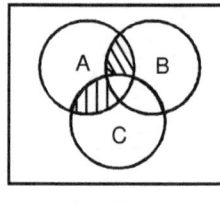
A ∩ (B ⊕ C)
Fig. 2.36

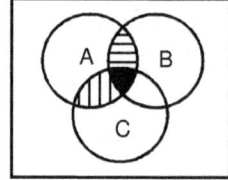
(A ∩ B) ⊕ (A ∩ C) = ▭ + ▭
Fig. 2.37

Hence, the equation is true.

Example 12: Let A denote the set of students who study Data Structures, B denote the set of students who study Discrete Mathematics, C denote the set of students who study Assembly Language Programming, D denote the set of students studying Theory of Computer Science. Let E denote the set of students who are staying in the Hostel and F denote the set of students who went to watch a cricket match last Monday. Express the following statements in set theoretic notation.

(i) All hostelites who study neither Data Structures nor Discrete Mathematics went to watch cricket match last Monday.

(ii) The students who went to see cricket match are only those who study Assembly Language Programming or Data Structures.

(iii) No student who is studying Data Structures went to see cricket match.

(iv) Those and only those students who are studying Theory of Computer Science and Discrete Mathematics went for a cricket match.

(v) All went to see cricket match.

Solution:

(i) $E \cap \bar{A} \cap \bar{B} \subseteq F$ or $(E - A) - B \subseteq F$

(ii) $F \subseteq C \cup A$

(iii) $A \cap F = \phi$

(iv) $F \subseteq D \cap B$

(v) If the universal set is $A \cup B \cup C \cup D \cup E$, then $A \cup B \cup C \cup D \cup E = F$. Otherwise $A \cup B \cup C \cup D \cup E \subseteq F$.

Example 13: Let A denote the set of all automobiles that are manufactured domestically. Let B denote the set of all imported automobiles. Let C denote the set of all automobiles manufactured before 1977. Let D denote the set of all automobiles with a current market value of less than 2000 $. Let E denote the set of all automobiles owned by students at the University.

Express the following in set theoretic notation.
(i) The automobiles owned by the students at the University are either domestically manufactured or imported.
(ii) All domestic automobiles manufactured before 1977 have a market value of less than 2000 $.
(iii) All imported automobiles manufactured after 1977 have a market value of more than 200 $.

Solution:
(i) $E \subseteq A \cup B$.
(ii) $A \cap C \subseteq D$.
(iii) $B \cap \bar{C} \subseteq \bar{D}$.
where the universal set U = set of all automobiles = $A \cup B$.
i.e. $B \cap ((A \cup B) - C) \subseteq (A \cup B) - D$.

Example 14: Tony, Mike and John belong to the Alpine Club. Every Club member is either a skier or mountain climber or both. No mountain climber likes rain and all skiers like snow. Mike dislikes whatever Tony likes and likes whatever Tony dislikes. Tony likes rain and snow. Is there a member of the Alpine Club who is a mountain climber but not skier?

Solution: Let A denote the set of all members of the Alpine Club. Let S denote the set of skiers and M the set of all mountain climbers. Then $A \subset M \cup S$. If $x \in M$, x does not like rain and if $y \in S$, y likes snow. Since, Tony likes both rain and snow, Tony $\in$ S−M. Since, Mike dislikes whatever Tony likes and likes what Tony dislikes, it follows that Mike $\in$ M−S. Hence, there is a member (that is Mike), of the Alpine Club, who is a mountain climber but not skier.

Example 15: Consider the following assumptions.
S_1 : Poets are happy people.
S_2 : Every doctor is wealthy.
S_3 : No one who is happy is also wealthy.

Determine the validity of the following arguments, using Venn diagram.
(1) No poet is wealthy.
(2) Doctors are happy people.
(3) No one can be both a poet and a doctor.

Solution: Let H be the set of happy people, P set of poets, W set of wealthy people and D, set of doctors. By S_1, $P \subseteq H$, S_2 implies $D \subseteq W$, S_3 implies $H \cap W = \phi$. We have the Venn diagram.

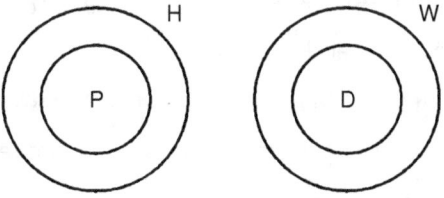

Fig. 2.38

From the Venn diagram, we observe that $P \cap W = \phi$, i.e. no poet is wealthy. Hence argument (1) is valid $D \cap H = \phi$, here doctors are not happy people so that (2) is invalid. $P \cap D = \phi$, hence no-one can be both a poet and doctor. Hence, (3) is valid.

2.6 Cardinality of Finite Set

A very important problem in Discrete Structures is that of determining the number of objects in a finite set. In the analysis of computer algorithms, one is often required to count the number of operations executed by various algorithms. This is necessary to estimate the cost effectiveness of a particular algorithm. In the study of data structures of files, determining the average and maximum lengths of searches for items stored in a data structure, also involve counting. Hence, in this section, we shall introduce the concept of **cardinality** of a finite set, and study its properties.

2.6.1 Definition

> Let A be a finite set. The cardinality of A, denoted by $|A|$ is the number of elements in the set.
>
> If $A = \phi$, then $|A| = 0$.
>
> If $A \subseteq B$, where B is a finite set, then $|A| \leq |B|$.

The following theorem enables us to find the cardinality of disjoint union of two sets.

2.6.2 Theorem (The Addition Principle)

> **Theorem (The Addition Principle):** Let A and B be finite sets which are disjoint. Then $|A \cup B| = |A| + |B|$.
>
> **Proof:**
>
> If A or B is the empty set, the proof is trivial.
> Hence, let us assume that $A \neq \phi$, $B \neq \phi$.
> Since, A and B are finite disjoint sets, let $A = \{a_1, a_2, \ldots a_m\}$ and $B = \{b_1, b_2, \ldots, b_n\}$, where $a_i \neq b_j$ for $1 \leq i \leq m$, $1 \leq j \leq n$. $|A| = m$ and $|B| = n$.
> Then $A \cup B = \{a_1, a_2, \ldots a_m, b_1, b_2, \ldots b_n\}$, i.e. $A \cup B$ contains exactly $m + n$ elements.
> Hence, $|A \cup B| = m + n = |A| + |B|$. Thus, the theorem is proved.

The above theorem can be extended to a finite collection of finite mutually disjoint sets.

2.6.3 Corollary

Let $A_1, A_2, \ldots A_n$ be a finite collection of mutually disjoint finite sets.
Then $|A_1 \cup A_2 \cup \ldots \cup A_n| = |A_1| + |A_2| + \ldots + |A_n|$.

Proof is left as an exercise.

2.6.4 Theorem

Let A be a finite set and let B be any set (not necessarily finite).
Then $|A - B| = |A| - |A \cap B|$.

Proof:

Consider the Venn diagram.

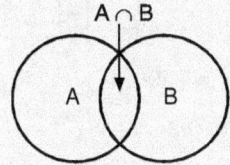

Fig. 2.39

From the Venn diagram, it is clear that $A = (A - B) \cup (A \cap B)$ (Disjoint union of two sets)
Hence, by the addition principle,

$$|A| = |A - B| + |A \cap B|,$$

so that $\quad |A - B| = |A| - |A \cap B|$.

2.6.5 Theorem (Principle of Inclusion–Exclusion)

Theorem: Let A and B be finite sets. Then $|A \cup B| = |A| + |B| - |A \cap B|$

Proof:

Consider the Venn diagram.

A – B is the shaded portion.

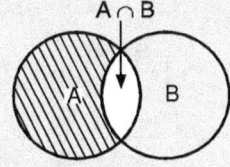

Fig. 2.40

We may express $A \cup B$ as disjoint union of two sets, by writing
$A \cup B = (A - B) \cup B$.

Hence, by the addition principle,

$$|A \cup B| = |A - B| + |B|$$
$$= |A| - |A \cap B| + |B| \text{ (by the previous theorem)}$$

Hence, $|A \cup B| = |A| + |B| - |A \cap B|$.

SOLVED EXAMPLES

Example 1: In a survey, 2000 people were asked whether they read India Today or Business Times. It was found that 1200 read India Today, 900 read Business Times and 400 read both. Find how many read at least one magazine and how many read none.

Solution: Let A denote the set of people who read India Today, B denote the set of people who read Business Times.

Now $|A| = 1200$, $|B| = 900$

and $|A \cap B| = 400$.

By the mutual inclusion-exclusion principle,

$$|A \cup B| = |A| + |B| - |A \cap B|$$
$$= 1200 + 900 - 400 = 1700$$

and $|U - (A \cup B)| = |U| - |A \cup B|$
$$= 2000 - 1700 = 300.$$

Hence, 1700 read at least one magazine and 300 read neither.

Example 2: Among the integers 1 to 300, find how many are not divisible by 3, nor by 5. Find also, how many are divisible by 3, but not by 7.

Solution: Let A denote the set of integers 1 – 300, divisible by 3; B, the set of integers divisible by 5; C, the set of integers divisible by 7. We have to find $|\overline{A} \cap \overline{B}|$ and $|A - C|$.

By De Morgan's laws, $\overline{A} \cap \overline{B} = \overline{A \cup B}$.

Hence,

$$|\overline{A \cup B}| = |U| - |A \cup B|$$
$$|A \cup B| = |A| + |B| - |A \cap B|$$
$$|A| = \left[\frac{300}{3}\right] = 100.$$
$$|B| = \left[\frac{300}{5}\right] = 60.$$

$$\therefore \quad |A \cap B| = \left\lceil \frac{300}{15} \right\rceil = 20.$$

$$\therefore \quad |A \cup B| = 100 + 60 - 20 = 140.$$

$$\therefore \quad |\overline{A \cup B}| = 300 - 140 = 160.$$

Hence, 160 integers between 1 to 300 are not divisible by 3, nor by 5.

Now
$$|A - C| = |A| - |A \cap C|$$
$$|A \cap C| = \left\lceil \frac{300}{21} \right\rceil = 14.$$

Hence, $\quad |A - C| = 100 - 14 = 86.$

Hence, 86 integers between 1 – 300 are divisible by 3, but not by 7.

2.6.6 Theorem (Mutual Inclusion – Exclusion Principle for Three Sets)

Theorem: Let A, B, C be finite sets.

Then $|A \cup B \cup C| = |A| + |B| + |C| - |A \cap B| - |B \cap C| - |A \cap C| + |A \cap B \cap C|$.

Proof:

Let D denote the union set $B \cup C$. Then $A \cup B \cup C = A \cup D$.

$|A \cup D| = |A| + |D| - |A \cap D|$ (by the previous theorem) ... (1)

$|D| = |B \cup C| = |B| + |C| - |B \cap C|$ ... (2)

$|A \cap D| = |A \cap (B \cup C)| = |(A \cap B) \cup (A \cap C)|$

$\quad = |A \cap B| + |A \cap C| - |A \cap B \cap C|$ ... (3)

Substituting equations (2) and (3) in (1), we have

$|A \cup B \cup C| = |A| + |B| + |C| - |A \cap B| - |B \cap C| - |A \cap C| + |A \cap B \cap C|$

Thus, the principle is proved for three sets. We now have the general theorem for a finite collection of finite sets.

Theorem: Let $\{A_1, A_2, ..., A_n\}$ be a finite collection of sets.

Then $|A_1 \cup A_2 \cup ...... \cup A_n| = \sum_{i=1}^{n} |A_i| - \sum_{1 \le i < j \le n} |A_i \cap A_j|$

$\quad + \sum_{1 \le i < j < k \le n} |A_i \cap A_j \cap A_k| + ... + (-1)^{n-1} |A_1 \cap A_2 \cap ... \cap A_n|$

Proof:
Proof is by induction on n.
We have already proved the theorem for n = 2, 3.
Hence, let us assume the theorem for (n − 1) numbers of sets and prove it for n sets.
Regarding $A_1 \cup A_2 \cup \ldots \cup A_n$ as $(A_1 \cup A_2 \cup \ldots \cup A_{n-1}) \cup A_n$, we have

$$|A_1 \cup A_2 \ldots \cup A_n| = |(A_1 \cup A_2 \cup \ldots \cup A_{n-1}) \cup A_n|$$

$$= |A_1 \cup A_2 \cup \ldots \cup A_{n-1}| + |A_n| - |(A_1 \cup A_2 \cup \ldots \cup A_{n-1}) \cap A_n| \quad \ldots (1)$$

By induction hypothesis,

$$|A_1 \cup A_2 \cup \ldots \cup A_{n-1}| = \sum_{i=1}^{n-1} |A_i| - \sum_{1 \leq i < j \leq n-1} |A_i \cap A_j|$$
$$+ \sum_{1 \leq i < j < k \leq n-1} |A_i \cap A_j \cap A_k| - \ldots + (-1)^{n-2} |A_1 \cap A_2 \cap \ldots \cap A_{n-1}| \quad \ldots (2)$$

Now $|(A_1 \cup A_2 \cup \ldots \cup A_{n-1}) \cap A_n| = |(A_1 \cap A_n) \cup (A_2 \cap A_n) \cup \ldots \cup (A_{n-1} \cap A_n)|$

$$= \sum_{i=1}^{n-1} |A_i \cap A_n| - \sum_{1 \leq i < j \leq n-1} |A_i \cap A_j \cap A_n| + \sum_{1 \leq i < j < k \leq n-1} |A_i \cap A_j \cap A_k \cap A_n| -$$
$$\ldots + (-1)^{n-2} |A_1 \cap A_2 \cap \ldots \cap A_{n-1} \cap A_n| \quad \ldots (3)$$

Substituting equations (2) and (3) in (1) we obtain the equation

$$|A_1 \cup A_2 \cup \ldots \cup A_n| = \sum_{i=1}^{n} |A_i| - \sum_{1 \leq i < j \leq n} |A_i \cap A_j|$$
$$+ \sum_{1 \leq i < j < k \leq n} |A_i \cap A_j \cap A_k| - \ldots + (-1)^{n-1} |A_1 \cap A_2 \cap \ldots \cap A_n|$$

SOLVED EXAMPLES

Example 1: In a computer laboratory out of 6 computers:
  (i) 2 have floating point arithmetic unit.
  (ii) 5 have magnetic disk memory.
  (iii) 3 have graphics display.
  (iv) 2 have both floating point arithmetic unit and magnetic disk memory.
  (v) 3 have both magnetic disk memory and graphics display.
  (vi) 1 has both floating point arithmetic unit and graphics display.

(vii) 1 has floating point arithmetic, magnetic disk memory and graphics display.

How many have at least one specification?

Solution: Let A be the set of computers having floating point arithmetic unit, B having magnetic disk memory and C having graphics display.

Then
$$|A| = 2, \quad |B| = 5, \quad |C| = 3,$$
$$|A \cap B| = 2, \quad |B \cap C| = 3,$$
$$|A \cap C| = 1, \quad |A \cap B \cap C| = 1$$

We have to determine $|A \cup B \cup C|$

$$|A \cup B \cup C| = |A| + |B| + |C| - |A \cap B|$$
$$- |B \cap C| - |A \cap C| + |A \cap B \cap C|$$
$$= 2 + 5 + 3 - 2 - 3 - 1 + 1 = 5.$$

Hence, 5 computers out of 6, have at least one specification.

Example 2: Among the integers 1 to 1000:

(i) How many of them are not divisible by 3, nor by 5, nor by 7?

(ii) How many are not divisible by 5 and 7 but divisible by 3?

Solution: (i) Let A, B, C denote respectively the set of integers from 1 to 1000 divisible by 3, by 5 and by 7. Then $\bar{A} \cap \bar{B} \cap \bar{C}$ denote the set of integers not divisible by 3, nor by 5, nor by 7.

By De Morgan's laws, $\bar{A} \cap \bar{B} \cap \bar{C} = \overline{(A \cup B \cup C)}$

Hence, $|\bar{A} \cap \bar{B} \cap \bar{C}| = 1000 - |A \cup B \cup C|$

$$|A| = \left[\frac{1000}{3}\right] = 333, |B| = \left[\frac{1000}{5}\right] = 200, |C| = \left[\frac{1000}{7}\right] = 142,$$

$$|A \cap B| = \left[\frac{1000}{15}\right] = 66$$

$$|B \cap C| = \left[\frac{1000}{35}\right] = 28$$

$$|A \cap C| = \left[\frac{1000}{21}\right] = 47$$

$$|A \cap B \cap C| = \left[\frac{1000}{105}\right] = 9.$$

Hence, $|A \cup B \cup C| = |A| + |B| + |C|$
$= |A \cap B| - |B \cap C| - |A \cap C| + |A \cap B \cap C|$
$= 333 + 200 + 142 - 66 - 28 - 47 + 9$
$= 543.$

Hence $|\bar{A} \cap \bar{B} \cap \bar{C}| = 1000 - 543 = 457.$

(ii) Consider the Venn diagram

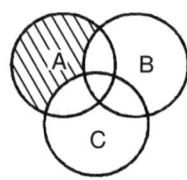

Fig. 2.41

The set of integers not divisible by 5 and 7 but divisible by 3 is the set $A \cap \bar{B} \cap \bar{C}$.

$A \cap \bar{B} \cap \bar{C} = A \cap \overline{(B \cup C)} = A - (B \cup C)$, the shaded portion shown in the Venn diagram. It is clear from the diagram that

$|A - (B \cup C)| = |A| - |(A \cap B) \cup (A \cap C)|$

Now $|(A \cap B) \cup (A \cap C)| = |A \cap B| + |A \cap C| - |A \cap B \cap C|$
$= 66 + 47 - 9 = 104$

$\therefore |A - (B \cup C)| = 333 - 104 = 229.$

Hence, 229 integers from 1 to 1000 are not divisible by 5 and 7 but divisible by 3.

Example 3: How many integers between 1 – 1000 are divisible by 2, 3, 5 or 7?

Solution: Let A, B, C, D denote respectively the set of integers from 1 to 1000 divisible by 2, 3, 5 or 7.

$\therefore |A| = \left\lceil \dfrac{1000}{2} \right\rceil = 500$

$|B| = \left\lceil \dfrac{1000}{3} \right\rceil = 333$

$|C| = \left\lceil \dfrac{1000}{5} \right\rceil = 200$

$|D| = \left\lceil \dfrac{1000}{7} \right\rceil = 142$

$|A \cap B| = \left\lceil \dfrac{1000}{6} \right\rceil = 166$

$$|A \cap C| = \left[\frac{1000}{10}\right] = 100$$

$$|A \cap D| = \left[\frac{1000}{14}\right] = 71$$

$$|B \cap C| = \left[\frac{1000}{15}\right] = 66$$

$$|B \cap D| = \left[\frac{1000}{21}\right] = 47$$

$$|C \cap D| = \left[\frac{1000}{35}\right] = 28$$

$$|A \cap B \cap C| = \left[\frac{1000}{30}\right] = 33$$

$$|B \cap C \cap D| = \left[\frac{1000}{105}\right] = 9$$

$$|A \cap C \cap D| = \left[\frac{1000}{70}\right] = 14$$

$$|A \cap B \cap D| = \left[\frac{1000}{42}\right] = 23$$

$$|A \cap B \cap C \cap D| = \left[\frac{1000}{210}\right] = 4$$

$\therefore$ $|A \cup B \cup C \cup D| = |A| + |B| + |C| + |D| - |A \cap B| - |A \cap C| - |A \cap D| - |B \cap C|$
$- |B \cap D| - |C \cap D| |A \cap B \cap C| + |A \cap B \cap D| + |A \cap C \cap D| - |A \cap B \cap C \cap D|$
$= 772$

Example 4: An investigator interviewed 100 students to determine their preferences for the three drinks – Milk (M), Coffee (C) and Tea (T). He reported the following:

10 students had all the three drinks, 20 had 'M' and 'C', 30 had 'C' and 'T', 25 had 'M' and 'T', 12 had 'M' only, 5 had 'C' only and 8 had 'T' only.

(i) How many did not take any of the three drinks?

(ii) How many take milk but not coffee?

(iii) How many take tea and coffee but not milk?

Solution: Consider the Venn diagram, incorporating the given data.

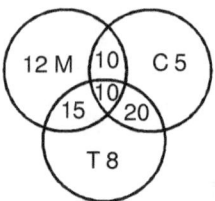

Fig. 2.42

(i) Taking the cardinalities of the disjoint sets into account,

$$|\overline{M} \cap \overline{C} \cap \overline{T}| = 100 - |M \cup C \cup T|$$
$$= 100 - [12 + 10 + 10 + 15 + 20 + 8 + 5]$$
$$= 100 - 80 = 20.$$

Hence, 20 students did not take any drink.

(ii) The set of students taking milk but not coffee is M − C.

$$|M - C| = 12 + 15 = 27$$

(iii) The set of students taking tea and coffee, but not milk is (T ∩ C) − M.

$$|(T \cap C) - M| = |T \cap C| - |T \cap C \cap M|$$
$$= 30 - 10 = 20.$$

Example 5: (i) Among 50 students in a class, 26 got an A in the first examination and 21 got an A in the second examination. If 17 students did not get an A in either examination, how many students got an A in both examinations?

(ii) If the number of students who got an A in the first examination is equal to that in the second examination, if the total number of students who got an A in exactly one examination is 40 and if 4 students did not get an A in either examination, then determine the number of students who got an A in the first examination only, who got an A in the second examination only, and who got an A in both the examinations.

Solution: (i) Let F denote the set of students who got an A in the first examination, S that of students who got an A in the second examination.

The set of students who did not get an A in either is $\overline{F \cup S}$.

$$|\overline{F \cup S}| = 50 - |F \cup S| = 17$$

∴ $$|F \cup S| = 50 - 17 = 33.$$

∴ $$|F \cap S| = |F| + |S| - |F \cup S|$$
$$= 26 + 21 - 33 = 14.$$

(ii) $|F| = |S|$, by given condition.

The set of students who got an A in exactly one examination is $(F - S) \cup (S - F) = F \oplus S$.

$|F \oplus S| = 40$, $|\overline{F \cup S}| = 4$ (given)

$\therefore \quad |F \cup S| = 50 - 4 = 46$

$|F \oplus S| = |F \cup S| - |F \cap S|$

$\Rightarrow \quad 40 = 46 - |F \cap S|$

$\therefore \quad |F \cap S| = 46 - 40 = 6.$

$|F \cup S| = |F| + |S| - |F \cap S|$

$= 2|F| - |F \cap S|$

i.e. $\quad 46 = 2|F| - 6$

$\therefore \quad |F| = \dfrac{52}{2} = 26 = |S|.$

The set of students who got an A in the first examination only is $F - S$.

$\therefore \quad |F - S| = |F| - |F \cap S| = 26 - 6 = 20.$

Similarly, the number of students who got an A in the second examination only is $|S - F| = |S| - |S \cap F| = 20.$

Example 6: In a survey, it is reported that of 1000 programmers, 650 habitually flowchart their programs, 788 are skilled COBOL programmers, 675 are men, 278 of the women are skilled COBOL programmers, 440 programmers both habitually flowchart and are skilled in COBOL, 210 women habitually flowchart and 166 women are both skilled in COBOL and habitually flowchart. Would you accept these data as being accurately reported? Justify your answer.

Solution: Let F denote the set of programs (both men and women) who habitually flow-chart their programs, and let C denote the set of all skilled COBOL programmers. Let M and W denote the set of men and women programmers respectively.

$|M| = 675$, $\therefore |W| = 1000 - 675 = 325.$

$|F| = 650$, $|C| = 788$

$|W \cap C| = 278$, $|W \cap F| = 210$, $|F \cap C| = 440$

$|W \cap F \cap C| = 166.$

$\therefore \quad |M \cap C| = |C| - |W \cap C| = 788 - 278 = 510.$

$$|M \cap F| = |F| - |W \cap F| = 650 - 210 = 440.$$
$$|M \cap F \cap C| = |F \cap C| -$$
$$= 440 - 166 = 274.$$

The set of M ∩ (F ∪ C) is the set of male programmers who habitually flowchart their programs or are skilled COBOL programmers.

∴ $$|M \cap (F \cup C)| = |M \cap F| + |M \cap C| - |M \cap F \cap C|$$
$$= 510 + 440 - 274$$
$$= 676.$$

Hence, there should be at least 676 men programmers. But this contradicts the given data that there are in all only 675 men programmers.

Hence, the data is inaccurately reported.

Example 7: 75 children went to an amusement park, where they can ride on the merry-go-round, roller coaster, and the Ferris wheel. It is known that 20 of them have taken all three rides, and 55 of them have taken at least 2. Each ride costs 5 rupees and the total collection of the park was 700 rupees. Determine the number of children who did not try any of the rides.

Solution: The total number of rides $= \frac{700}{5} = 140$.

The number of children who have taken exactly 2 rides = 55 – 20 = 35.
The number of children who have taken only one ride = 140 – 2 × 35 – 3 × 20
$$= 140 - 70 - 60 = 10$$
Hence, the number of children who have not taken any ride
$$= 75 - (35 + 20 + 10) = 75 - 65 = 10.$$

Example 8: It was found that in first year of computer science of 80 students 50 know Cobol, 55 know 'C', 46 know Pascal. It was also known that 37 know 'C' and Cobol, 28 know 'C' and Pascal, 25 know Pascal and Cobol. 7 students, however, know none of the languages. Find:

(i) How many know all the three languages?
(ii) How many know exactly two languages?
(iii) How many know exactly one language?

Solution: Let B, C and P denote the set of students who know Cobol, 'C' and Pascal respectively.

Then $$|B \cup C \cup P| = 80 - 7 = 73$$
is the number of students who know at least one of the languages.

(i) $$|B \cup C \cup P| = |B| + |C| + |P| - |B \cap C| - |B \cap P| - |C \cap P| + |B \cap C \cap P|$$
Hence, the number of students who know all the three languages is
$$|B \cap C \cap P| = 73 - 50 - 55 - 46 + 37 + 28 + 25 = 12$$

(ii) The number of students who know Cobol and 'C' but not Pascal is

$$|B \cap C \cap \bar{P}| = |B \cap C| - |B \cap C \cap P|$$
$$= 37 - 12 = 25$$

Similarly, the number of students who know Cobol and Pascal but not 'C' is

$$|B \cap P \cap \bar{C}| = 25 - 12 = 13$$

and the number of students who know Pascal and 'C' but not Cobol is

$$|\bar{B} \cap P \cap C| = 28 - 12 = 16$$

Hence, the number of students who known exactly two languages is
$$25 + 13 + 16 = 54$$

(iii) The number of students who know only Cobol (i.e. neither 'C' nor Pascal) is

$$|B| - |B \cap C| - |B \cap P| + |B \cap P \cap C| = 50 - 37 - 25 + 12 = 0$$

Similarly the number of students who know only 'C' is $55 - 37 - 28 + 12 = 2$ and the number of students knowing only Pascal is $46 - 28 - 25 + 12 = 5$.

Hence, the number of students who know exactly one language is $0 + 2 + 5 = 7$

Example 9: How many elements are in the union of five sets if the sets contain 10,000 elements each, each pair of sets has 1000 common elements, each triple of sets has 100 common elements, every four of the sets has 10 common elements, and there is 1 element common in all five sets?

Solution: Let A_1, A_2, A_3, A_4, A_5 denote the five sets.

Then $|A_1 \cup A_2 \cup A_3 \cup A_4 \cup A_5|$

$$= \sum_{1 \leq i \leq 5} |A_i| - \sum_{i<j} |A_i \cap A_j| + \sum_{i<j<k} |A_i \cap A_j \cap A_k|$$
$$- \sum_{i<j<k<l} |A_i \cap A_j \cap A_k \cap A_l| + |A_1 \cap A_2 \cap A_3 \cap A_4 \cap A_5|$$

Taking two sets at a time there are $5C_2 = 10$ such sets; taking three sets at a time, there are $5C_3 = 10$ such sets. Taking 4 sets at a time, there are $5C_4 = 5$ such sets.

$\therefore |A_1 \cup A_2 \cup A_3 \cup A_4 \cup A_5| = 5 \times 10,000 - 10 \times 1000 + 10 \times 100 - 5 \times 10 + 1 = 40,951$

Example 10: Find the number of positive integers not exceeding 100 that are either odd or the square of an integer.

Solution: Let A be the set of odd integers between 1 and 100, B the set of integers between 1 and 100, that are squares of an integer.

$$B = \{1, 4, 9, 16, 25, 36, 49, 64, 81, 100\}$$
$$|A \cup B| = |A| + |B| - |A \cap B|$$
$$= 50 + 10 - 5 = 55$$

Example 11: A college record gives the following information: 119 students enrolled in Introductory Computer Science; of these 96 took Data Structures, 53 took Foundations, 39 took Assembly Language, 31 took both Foundations and Assembly Language, 32 took both

Data Structures and Assembly Language, 38 took Data Structures and Foundations and 22 took all the three courses.

Is the information correct? Why?

Solution: Let D, F and A denote the set of students who took Data Structure, Foundations and Assembly Language respectively.

Given: $|D| = 96$, $|F| = 53$, $|A| = 39$, $|F \cap A| = 31$, $|D \cap A| = 32$, $|D \cap F| = 38$ and $|F \cap D \cap A| = 22$.

$$\therefore \quad |F \cup D \cup A| = |F| + |D| + |A| - |F \cap A| - |D \cap A| - |D \cap F| + |F \cap D \cap A|$$
$$= 53 + 96 + 39 - 31 - 32 - 38 + 22$$
$$= 109 \text{ which is less than } 119.$$

Since, there were 119 students enrolled for the course, assuming that all these students had taken at least one course, the given information is not correct.

Example 12: A software company writes a new package which integrates a word processing program with a spread sheet program and they wish it to run on a 64 K machine. The word processor requires 40 K for program and data and the spread sheet requires 32 K for the same. If 16 K must be reserved for the code integrator, what is the minimum amount of overlapping space that will be necessary?

Solution: Let A denote the memory space reserved for word processor and B that for spread sheet.

$|A| = 40$, $|B| = 32$.

Available memory is $64 - 16 = 48$

$$|A \cup B| = |A| + |B| - |A \cap B|$$
$\because \quad |A \cup B| \leq 48$
$\therefore \quad |A| + |B| - |A \cap B| \leq 48$
i.e. $\quad |A \cap B| \geq |A| + |B| - 48$
$$= 40 + 32 - 48 = 24$$

Hence, the minimum amount of overlapping space that will be necessary is 24 K.

Example 13: Among 130 students, 60 study Mathematics, 51 study Physics and 30 study both Mathematics and Physics. Out of 54 students studying Chemistry, 26 study Mathematics, 21 study Physics and 12 study both Mathematics and Physics. All the students studying neither Mathematics nor Physics are studying Biology.

Find:
1. How many are studying Biology?
2. How many not studying Chemistry are studying Mathematics but not Physics?
3. How many students are studying neither Mathematics nor Physics nor Chemistry?

Solution: 1. $\quad |M \cup P| = |M| + |P| - |M \cap P|$
$$= 60 + 51 - 30 = 81$$

∴ Number of students studying neither Mathematics nor Physics
$$= 130 - |M \cup P|$$
$$= 130 - 81 = 49$$

Hence, the number of students studying Biology is 49.

2. The set of students studying Mathematics but neither Chemistry nor Physics is $M - M \cap (C \cup P)$.

∴ $|M - [M \cap (C \cup P)]| = |M| - |M \cap C| - |M \cap P| + |M \cap C \cap P|$
$$= 60 - 26 - 30 + 12 = 16$$

3. Set of students studying neither Mathematics nor Physics nor Chemistry is the complement of the set $M \cup P \cup C$, i.e. $\overline{M \cup P \cup C}$.

∴ $|\overline{M \cup P \cup C}| = 130 - |M \cup P \cup C|$
$$= 130 - |M| - |P| - |C| + |M \cap P| + |M \cap C|$$
$$+ |P \cap C| - |M \cap P \cap C|$$
$$= 130 - 60 - 51 - 54 + 30 + 26 + 21 - 12$$
$$= 30$$

2.6.7 Infinite Sets

We have seen that if a set is finite; its elements can be counted or listed and this counting ceases in finite time. On the other hand if the counting is interminable or impossible, then such a set is said to be infinite. Familiar examples of infinite sets are:

(i) $N = \{1, 2, 3, ...\}$ the set of natural numbers.
(ii) The set of prime positive integers $\{2, 3, 5, 7, ...\}$.
(iii) The set of all points in the first quadrant of the plane, whose x and y co-ordinates are integers.
(iv) The set of all binary strings of odd length.

The above examples are of infinite sets, whose elements are although infinitely many in number can be listed or 'counted', in other words these elements are put into one-to-one correspondence with the set of natural numbers. The cardinality of such a set is denoted by N_0 (pronounced as aleph nought).

If a set is not countable, then it is called "uncountable" set. The set of real numbers, denoted by IR, is uncountable. The open interval (0, 1), as a set is uncountable. Another important example of an uncountably infinite set is the power set of N, the set of natural numbers. The cardinality of this set is 2^{N_0} denoted by C and is called the 'continuum'.

We shall discuss countably infinite and uncountably infinite sets, more in detail, in the chapter on functions.

2.7 Mathematical Induction

Mathematical Induction is a powerful technique in Mathematics; especially in Number Theory, where many properties of natural numbers are established by this method.

In Mathematics, we are often required to generalise a particular solution. In order to do this, we look for a pattern in the particular solution. Mathematical induction generalises this pattern of solutions by proving that it is always possible to extend the solution to a group that is one larger than the previous. The generalisation is achieved by using a statement involving a variable natural number.

The logic underlying the principle of mathematical induction, makes it an extremely suitable method to solve problems related to real life. A few examples of this type will be discussed in this section.

To the software engineer, mathematical induction is an important tool in algorithm verification, to check whether a program statement is loop invariant, that is, whether it is true before and after every pass through a programming loop.

2.7.1 Statement of the Principle of Mathematical Induction

Let $P(n)$ be a statement involving a natural number n.

1. If $P(n)$ is true for $n = n_0$, and
2. Assuming $P(k)$ is true, $(k \geq n_0)$ we prove $P(k + 1)$ is also true,

   then $P(n)$ is true for all natural numbers $n \geq n_0$.

Step (1) is called as the **basis of induction**. Step (2) is called as the **induction step**. The assumption that $P(n)$ is true for $n = k$ is called as the **induction hypothesis**.

$$\boxed{\text{SOLVED EXAMPLES}}$$

Example 1 : Prove that

$$\frac{1}{1.4} + \frac{1}{4.7} + \frac{1}{7.10} + \ldots + \frac{1}{(3n-2)(3n+1)} = \frac{n}{3n+1}$$

Solution: Let $P(n)$ be the statement:

$$\frac{1}{1.4} + \frac{1}{4.7} + \frac{1}{7.10} + \ldots + \frac{1}{(3n-2)(3n+1)} = \frac{n}{3n+1}.$$

For $n = 1$, $P(1) : \dfrac{1}{1.4} = \dfrac{1}{4}$

Hence, $P(1)$ is true.

Assume P(k) is true, and prove P(k + 1) is also true.

$$P(k+1) : \frac{1}{1 \cdot 4} + \frac{1}{4 \cdot 7} + \ldots + \frac{1}{(3k-2)(3k+1)} + \frac{1}{(3(k+1)-2)(3(k+1)+1)}$$

$$= \frac{k}{3k+1} + \frac{1}{(3k+1)(3k+4)}$$

$$= \frac{k(3k+4)+1}{(3k+1)(3k+4)} = \frac{3k^2+4k+1}{(3k+1)(3k+4)} = \frac{(3k+1)(k+1)}{(3k+1)(3k+4)}$$

$$= \frac{k+1}{3k+4} = \frac{k+1}{3(k+1)+1}$$

Hence, assuming P(k) is true, P(k + 1) is also true. Therefore, P(n) is true for all n ≥ 1.

Example 2: Prove that $5^n - 1$ is divisible by 4 for n ≥ 1.

Solution: (i) Basis of induction: For n = 1, $5^1 - 1 = 4$, divisible by 4.

(ii) Induction step: Assume that $5^k - 1$ is divisible by 4.

We have $5^{k+1} - 1 = (5^k \cdot 5 - 5) + 4$

$= 5(5^k - 1) + 4.$

By induction hypothesis, $5^k - 1$ is divisible by 4.

∴ Each term on the RHS is divisible by 4.

∴ $5^{k+1} - 1$ is divisible by 4.

Hence, $5^n - 1$ is divisible by 4 for n ≥ 1.

Example 3: Show that $n^3 + 2n$ is divisible by 3 for all n ≥ 1.

Solution: (i) Basis of induction:

$$n^3 + 2n = 1 + 2 = 3 \text{ divisible by 3.}$$

(ii) Induction step: Assume that for n = k, $k^3 + 2k$ is divisible by 3.

For n = k + 1,

$$(k+1)^3 + 2(k+1) = k^3 + 3k^2 + 3k + 1 + 2k + 2 = (k^3 + 2k) + 3(k^2 + k + 1)$$

Since, each term in the above is divisible by 3, it follows that the result is true for n = k + 1.

Hence, $n^3 + 2n$ is divisible by 3 for all n ≥ 1.

Example 4: Show that for any positive integer n > 1,

$$\frac{1}{\sqrt{1}} + \frac{1}{\sqrt{2}} + \ldots + \frac{1}{\sqrt{n}} > \sqrt{n}.$$

Solution: (i) Basis of induction:

For n = 2, $\quad \frac{1}{\sqrt{1}} + \frac{1}{\sqrt{2}} = 1 + 0.7071 = 1.7071$

$\sqrt{2} = 1.4142$

$\therefore \quad \frac{1}{\sqrt{1}} + \frac{1}{\sqrt{2}} > \sqrt{2}.$

(ii) Induction step: Assume that for n = k,

$$\frac{1}{\sqrt{1}} + \frac{1}{\sqrt{2}} + \ldots + \frac{1}{\sqrt{k}} > \sqrt{k}.$$

Now for n = k + 1

$$\frac{1}{\sqrt{1}} + \frac{1}{\sqrt{2}} + \ldots + \frac{1}{\sqrt{k}} + \frac{1}{\sqrt{k+1}} > \sqrt{k} + \frac{1}{\sqrt{k+1}}$$

To show that $\sqrt{k} + \frac{1}{\sqrt{k+1}} > \sqrt{k+1}$

We have to show $\sqrt{k} > \sqrt{k+1} - \frac{1}{\sqrt{k+1}}$

i.e. $\sqrt{k}\sqrt{k+1} > k + 1 - 1 = k.$

i.e. $k(k+1) > k^2$ which is true for $k \geq 1$.

Hence, the result is true for all $n \geq 1$.

Example 5: Show that $2^n > n^3$ for $n \geq 10$.

Solution: (i) Basis of induction: For n = 10, $2^{10} = 1024 > 10^3$

(ii) Induction step: Assume that $2^k > k^3$.

Then $\quad 2^{k+1} = 2^k \cdot 2 = 2^k(1+1)$

$> 2^k \left(1 + \frac{1}{10}\right)^3 \geq 2^k \left(1 + \frac{1}{k}\right)^3 \quad$ (Note this step)

$> k^3 \left(1 + \frac{1}{k}\right)^3 = k^3 \frac{(k+1)^3}{k^3} = (k+1)^3.$

Therefore, $2^n > n^3$ for $n \geq 10$.

Example 6: Show that for any positive integer n,
$(11)^{n+2} + (12)^{2n+1}$ is divisible by 133.

Solution: **(i) Basis of induction:** For n = 0, $(11)^{n+2} + (12)^{2n+1} = 121 + 12 = 133$, which is obviously divisible by 133.

For n = 1, $(11)^{n+2} + (12)^{2n+1} = 3059$ divisible by 133, since $133 \times 23 = 3059$.

(ii) Induction step: Assume the result for n = k.

Consider $(11)^{k+1+2} + (12)^{2(k+1)+1}$

$$= 11 \cdot (11)^{k+2} + (12)^{2k+1} \cdot 144$$
$$= 11 \cdot (11)^{k+2} + (133 + 11) \cdot (12)^{2k+1}$$
$$= 11 \cdot (11)^{k+2} + (12)^{2k+1}) + 133 \cdot (12)^{2k+1}$$

Since, both these terms are divisible by 133, the result follows.

Example 7: Formulate and prove by induction, a general formula stemming from the observations

$$1^3 = 1$$
$$2^3 = 3 + 5$$
$$3^3 = 7 + 9 + 11$$
$$4^3 = 13 + 15 + 17 + 19.$$

Solution: Note that the first term on the R.H.S., starting with the second equality can be written as

$$3 = 2.1 + 1$$
$$7 = 3.2 + 1$$
$$13 = 4.3 + 1$$

Hence, the first term for the nth equality can be written as

$$n(n-1) + 1.$$

Also note that in each equation, the number of terms of R.H.S. is equal to the value of n on L.H.S. Hence, the nth equation can be written as

$$n^3 = [n(n-1) + 1] + [n(n-1) + 3] + \ldots + [n(n-1) + (2n-1)]$$

Hence,
$$n^3 = \sum_{i=1}^{n} [n(n-1) + 2i - 1]$$

Let us verify the formula.

For n = 1, $\quad 1^3 = 1(1-1) + 2 - 1 = 1$

For n = 2, $\quad 2^3 = [2(2-1) + 1] + [2(2-1) + 3]$
$$= 3 + 5$$

For n = 3, $\quad 3^3 = [3(3-1) + 1] + [3(3-1) + 3] + [3(3-1) + 5]$
$$= 7 + 9 + 11$$

Now assume the result for n = k and prove it for n = k + 1

∴ $$k^3 = \sum_{i=1}^{k} [k(k-1) + 2i - 1] \qquad \ldots (1)$$

Now $(k+1)^3 = k^3 + 3k^2 + 3k + 1$

Consider for n = k + 1, the term on R.H.S., i.e.

$$\sum_{i=1}^{k+1} [(k+1)k + 2i - 1] = \sum_{i=1}^{k} [(k+1)k + 2i - 1] + [(k+1)k + 2(k+1) - 1]$$

$$= \sum_{i=1}^{k} [k(k-1) + 2i - 1] + \sum_{i=1}^{k} 2k + [(k+1)k + 2k + 1]$$

(Note this step)

$$= k^3 + 2k^2 + k^2 + 3k + 1 \qquad \text{by (1)}$$

$$= k^3 + 3k^2 + 3k + 1 = (k+1)^3.$$

Example 8 : Show that any integer composed of 3^n identical digits is divisible by 3^n.

Solution: (i) Basis of induction: For n = 1, the result is true, since an integer is divisible by 3 if the sum of the digits is divisible by 3. For example 111, 444, 555 etc. are divisible by 3.

(ii) Induction step: Let x be an integer composed of 3^{k+1} identical digits. Then we may express x as x = yz, where y is an integer composed of 3^k identical digits and

$$z = 10^{2 \cdot 3^k} + 10^{3^k} + 1$$

For example,

$$777777777 = 777(10^6 + 10^3 + 1), \text{ putting } k = 1.$$

In this case y = 777 and z = 1001001.

Now both y and z are divisible by 3 so that 777777777 is divisible by $3^2 = 9$.

In the general case y is divisible by 3^k, by induction hypothesis.

and   z = 10000 ... 01000 ... 01

$\phantom{\text{and}\ \ \ z = 10000}\ 3^k - 1\ \text{0's}\ \ \ \ 3^k - 1\ \text{0's}$

Clearly z is divisible by 3. Hence, x = yz is divisible by $3^k \cdot 3 = 3^{k+1}$.

Thus, the result is proved for any value of n.

Example 9: Prove by induction that the sum of the cubes of three consecutive integers is divisible by 9.

Solution: We have to show that $(n-1)^3 + n^3 + (n+1)^3$ is divisible by 9.

(i) **Basis of induction:** For n = 1, we have $0 + 1 + 2^3 = 9$, divisible by 9.

(ii) **Induction step:** Assume the result for n = k

∴ $(k-1)^3 + k^3 + (k+1)^3 = 3k^3 + 6k$ is divisible by 9.

For n = k + 1, we have
$$k^3 + (k + 1)^3 + (k + 2)^3 = 3k^3 + 9k^2 + 15k + 9$$
$$= 3k^3 + 6k + 9(k^2 + k + 1)$$
which is divisible by 9.
Hence, the result is proved.

Example 10: Show that $1 + 2 + 2^2 + 2^3 + \ldots + 2^n = 2^{n+1} - 1$.
Solution: (i) Basis of induction: For n = 1, we have
$$1 + 2 = 3 = 2^2 - 1$$
(ii) Induction step: Assume the result for n = k.
For n = k + 1, we have
$$1 + 2 + 2^2 + \ldots + 2^k + 2^{k+1} = (2^{k+1} - 1) + 2^{k+1} = 2 \cdot 2^{k+1} - 1 = 2^{k+2} - 1$$
Hence, the result is proved.

Example 11: Prove that $8^n - 3^n$ is a multiple of 5 by mathematical induction for $n \geq 1$.
Solution: (i) Basis of induction: For n = 1, we have $8 - 3 = 5$, obviously a multiple of 5.
(ii) Induction step: Assume the result for n = k, i.e. $8^k - 3^k = 5m$ for some integer m.
For n = k + 1, we have
$$8^{k+1} - 3^{k+1} = 8^k \cdot 8 - 3^k \cdot 3$$
$$= 8^k(5 + 3) - 3^k \cdot 3 = 5 \cdot 8^k + 3(8^k - 3^k)$$
$$= 5 \cdot 8^k + 3 \cdot 5m, \text{ clearly a multiple of 5.}$$
Hence, the result is proved.

Example 12: Prove that $n^3 - n$ is divisible by 3, for a positive integer n.
Solution: (i) Basis of induction: For n = 1, $1^3 - 1 = 0$ is divisible by 3.
(ii) Induction step: Assume for n = k, $n^3 - n$ is divisible by 3.
For n = k + 1, we have
$$(k + 1)^3 - (k + 1) = k^3 + 3k^2 + 3k + 1 - k - 1$$
$$= (k^3 - k) + 3(k^2 + k)$$
Since, $k^3 - k$ is divisible by 3, by induction hypothesis, the result follows.

Example 13: Prove that $1.1! + 2.2! + 3.3! + \ldots n.n! = (n + 1)! - 1$, where n is a positive integer.
Solution: (i) Basis of induction: For n = 1, $1.1! = 1$ and $(1 + 1)! - 1 = 2! - 1 = 1$.
(ii) Induction step: Assume for n = k, $1.1! + 2.2! + \ldots + k.k! = (k + 1)! - 1$.
For n = k + 1, $1.1! + 2.2! + \ldots + k.k! + (k + 1) \cdot (k + 1)!$
$$= (k + 1)! - 1 + (k + 1) \cdot (k + 1)!, \text{ (by induction hypothesis)}$$
$$= (k + 1)! + (k + 1) \cdot (k + 1)! - 1$$
$$= (k + 1)!(1 + k + 1) - 1 = (k + 1)!(k + 2) - 1$$
$$= (k + 2)! - 1.$$
Hence, the result is proved.

Example 14: For a positive integer $n > 1$, prove that $1 + \frac{1}{4} + \frac{1}{9} + \ldots + \frac{1}{n^2} < 2 - \frac{1}{n}$.

Solution: (i) Basis of induction:

For $n = 2$, $1 + \frac{1}{2^2} = 1 + \frac{1}{4} < 2 - \frac{1}{2}$ as $1 + \frac{1}{4} = \frac{5}{4} < \frac{3}{2}$.

(ii) Assume for $n = k$, i.e.

$$1 + \frac{1}{4} + \frac{1}{9} + \ldots + \frac{1}{k^2} < 2 - \frac{1}{k}.$$

For $n = k + 1$,

$$1 + \frac{1}{4} + \frac{1}{9} + \ldots + \frac{1}{k^2} + \frac{1}{(k+1)^2} < 2 - \frac{1}{k} + \frac{1}{(k+1)^2} \quad \text{(by induction hypothesis)}$$

$$= 2 - \frac{1}{k} + \frac{1}{(k+1)^2} = 2 - \frac{(k+1)^2 - k}{k(k+1)^2}$$

$$= 2 - \frac{k^2 + k + 1}{k(k+1)^2} = 2 - \left(\frac{k(k+1) + 1}{k(k+1)^2}\right)$$

$$= 2 - \left(\frac{1}{k+1} + \frac{1}{k(k+1)^2}\right)$$

$$= \left(2 - \frac{1}{k+1}\right) - \frac{1}{k(k+1)^2}$$

$$< 2 - \frac{1}{k+1}$$

Hence, the result.

Example 15: Show that $1^3 + 2^3 + \ldots + n^3 = (1 + 2 + \ldots + n)^2$.

Solution: Proof: (i) Basis of induction: For $n = 1$, $1^3 = 1^2$.

(ii) Induction step: Assume for $n = k$; hence $1^3 + 2^3 + \ldots + k^3 = (1 + 2 + \ldots + k)^2$

For $n = k + 1$, $1^3 + 2^3 + \ldots + k^3 + (k+1)^3$

$$= (1 + 2 + \ldots + k)^2 + (k+1)^3$$

$$= \frac{k^2(k+1)^2}{4} + (k+1)^3$$

$$= (k+1)^2 \left[\frac{k^2 + 4(k+1)}{4}\right]$$

$$= \frac{(k+1)^2(k+2)^2}{4}$$

$$= (1 + 2 + \ldots + k + 1)^2$$

Hence, the result is proved.

Following examples deal with real-life situations, where the principle of induction can be applied.

Example 16: Using mathematical induction, prove that

$$1^2 - 2^2 + 3^2 - 4^2 + \ldots + (-1)^{n-1} n^2 = (-1)^{n-1} \frac{n(n+1)}{2}$$

Solution: For $n = 1$, L.H.S. $= 1^2 = 1$

R.H.S. $= \frac{(-1) \, 1(2)}{2} = 1$

∴ Result is true for $n = 1$.

Assume result is true for $n = k$,

i.e. $1^2 - 2^2 + 3^2 - 4^2 + \ldots + (-1)^{k-1} k^2 = (-1)^{k-1} \frac{k(k+1)}{2}$

Consider $1^2 - 2^2 + 3^2 - 4^2 + \ldots + (-1)^{k-1} k^2 + (-1)^k (k+1)^2$

$$= (-1)^{k-1} \frac{k(k+1)}{2} + (-1)^k (k+1)^2$$

$$= (-1)^{k-1} \left\{ \frac{k(k+1) - 2(k+1)^2}{2} \right\} = (-1)^{k-1} \left\{ \frac{-k^2 - 3k - 2}{2} \right\}$$

$$= \frac{(-1)^k (k+1)(k+2)}{2}$$

Hence, result is true for $n = k + 1$.
Hence, result is true for all n.

Example 17: Prove by mathematical induction $0 \cdot 2^0 + 1 \cdot 2^1 + 2 \cdot 2^2 + 3 \cdot 2^3 + \ldots + n \, 2^n$
$= (n - 1) \, 2^{n+1} + 2;$ for $n \geq 0$.

Solution: Basis for induction : $n = 0$.
L.H.S. $= 0$, R.H.S. $= (0 - 1) \, 2^1 + 2 = 0$

Induction hypothesis: Assume the result is true for $n = k$.
For $n = k + 1 \, (0 \cdot 2^0 + 1 \cdot 2^1 + 2 \cdot 2^2 + \ldots + k \, 2^k) + (k+1) \, 2^{k+1}$.

$$= (k - 1) \, 2^{k+1} + 2 + (k+1) \, 2^{k+1}$$

$$= 2^{k+1} [k - 1 + k + 1] + 2$$

$$= 2^{k+1} \cdot 2k + 2 = k \, 2^{k+2} + 2$$

Hence, the equation is true for $n = k + 1$; hence it is true $\forall \, n$.

Example 18: Prove that $\frac{1}{2} + \frac{2}{2^2} + \frac{3}{2^3} + \ldots + \frac{n}{2^n} = 2 - \frac{n+2}{2^n}$, for $n \geq 1$

Solution: Basis of induction : $n = 1$.

L.H.S. $= \frac{1}{2}$

R.H.S. $= 2 - \frac{1+2}{2} = 2 - \frac{3}{2} = \frac{1}{2}$

Assume the equation for $n = k$. For $n = k + 1$

$$\left(\frac{1}{2} + \frac{2}{2^2} + \frac{3}{2^3} + \ldots + \frac{k}{2^k}\right) + \frac{k+1}{2^{k+1}}$$

$$= 2 - \frac{k+2}{2^k} + \frac{k+1}{2^{k+1}}$$

$$= 2 - \left[\frac{k+2}{2^k} - \frac{k+1}{2^{k+1}}\right]$$

$$= 2 - \left(\frac{2k+4-k-1}{2^{k+1}}\right)$$

$$= 2 - \frac{(k+1)+2}{2^{k+1}}$$

Thus, the result is true for $\forall \, n$.

Example 19: Let n be a positive integer. Show that any $2^n \times 2^n$ chessboard with one square removed can be covered using L-shaped pieces, where each piece covers three squares at a time.

Solution: Let P(n) be the proposition that any $2^n \times 2^n$ chessboard with one square removed can be covered using L-shaped pieces.

Basis of induction: For n = 1, P(1) implies that any 2 × 2 chessboard with one square removed can be covered using L-shaped pieces. P(1) is true, as seen in the following figure below.

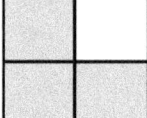 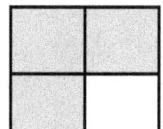 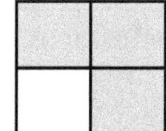 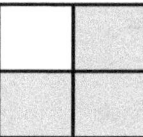

Fig. 2.43

Induction step: Assume P (n) is true and prove that P (n + 1) is true.

For this consider a $2^{n+1} \times 2^{n+1}$ chessboard with one square removed. Divide the chessboard into four equal halves of size $2^n \times 2^n$; as shown in the Fig. 2.44.

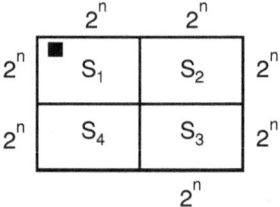

Fig. 2.44

Then the square which has been removed, would have been removed from one of the four chessboards, say S_1. Then by induction hypothesis, S_1 can be covered using L-shaped pieces. Now from each of the three remaining chessboards, remove that particular square lying at the centre of the larger chessboard. This is illustrated in the Fig. 2.45.

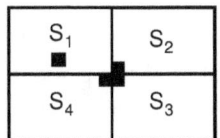

Fig. 2.45

Then by induction hypothesis, each of these $2^n \times 2^n$ chessboards with a square removed can be covered by the L-shaped pieces. Moreover, the three squares that have been temporarily removed can be covered by one L-shaped piece. Hence, the entire $2^{n+1} \times 2^{n+1}$ chessboard can be covered by L-shaped pieces. This completes the proof.

Example 20: Coin problem: Suppose we have coins of two different denominations, 2 rupees and 5 rupees. It is possible to make up exactly any denomination of 7 rupees or more, using only these two denominations, assuming of course that we have an unlimited supply of these.

Solution: For k = 7, we have one 5 rupee coin and one 2 rupee coin. For k = 8, we have four 2 rupee coins. Hence, let us assume that we can make up a denomination of k rupees (k ≥ 7). We discuss two cases. Suppose there is a 5 rupee coin in the k-denomination, we have made up. Replacing the 5 rupee coin by three 2 rupee coins, we can make up a denomination of k + 1 rupees. On the other hand, suppose that the k-denomination coins, we have made up, consist of only 2 rupee coins, then replacing two 2 rupee coins by one 5 rupee coin, we can still make up a denomination of k + 1 rupees. Thus, the process can be continued till the supply runs out.

Example 21: Solitaire game problem: For every integer i, there is an unlimited supply of balls marked with the number i. Initially, a tray of balls is given and the balls are thrown away one at a time. If a ball marked i is thrown away, it is replaced by any finite number of balls marked 1, 2, ..., i − 1. There is no replacement for a ball marked 1. The game ends when the tray is empty. Show that the game always terminates for any tray of balls given initially.

Solution:

(i) Basis of induction: For n = 1, there is a finite number of balls marked 1. Since, according to the rules of the game, there is no replacement if the balls are thrown away, the game terminates after a finite number of moves.

(ii) Induction step: Let us assume that the game terminates if the largest number that appears on the balls is k. Suppose k + 1 is the largest number appearing on the balls. If all these balls are thrown away, they are replaced by balls marked 1, 2, ..., k. Then the largest number appearing on the balls is k. Hence, by induction hypothesis, the game has to terminate after a finite number of steps.

2.7.2 Principle of Strong Mathematical Induction

We shall now state a more powerful form of the principle of mathematical induction.

Statement: Let P(n) be a statement involving a natural number n. If
(i) P(n) is true for $n = n_0$, and
(ii) P(n) is true for $n = k + 1$, **assuming that the statement is true for $n_0 \leq n \leq k$,** then the statement is true for all $n \geq n_0$.

Note that in the second principle of induction, we make a stronger assumption, that the statement is true for $n_0 \leq n \leq k$ (not merely for $n = k$).

SOLVED EXAMPLES

Example 1: Show that any positive integer n greater than or equal to 2 is either a prime or a product of primes.

Solution:

(i) Basis of induction: For $n = 2$, the statement is obviously true.

(ii) Induction step: Assume the result for $2 \leq n \leq k$. Consider $k + 1$. If $k + 1$ is a prime, the statement is true. If $k + 1$ is not a prime, then $k + 1 = pq$, where $p \leq k$, $q \leq k$. Hence, by induction hypothesis, p is either a prime or product of primes. Similarly, q is either a prime or a product of primes. Hence, $k + 1 = pq$ is a product of primes.

Example 2: Jigsaw Puzzle Problem: Show that for a jigsaw puzzle with n pieces, it will always take $n - 1$ moves to solve the problem.

Solution:

(i) Basis of induction: For $n = 1$, no moves are needed to solve the puzzle.

(ii) Induction step: Assume that for any jigsaw puzzle with m pieces, $1 \leq m \leq k$, it takes $m - 1$ moves to solve the puzzle.

Consider a jigsaw puzzle with $k + 1$ pieces. For the last move that produces the solution of the puzzle two blocks with m_1 pieces and m_2 pieces respectively, where $m_1 + m_2 = k + 1$, are put together to form a single block. Since, $1 \leq m_1 \leq k$, $1 \leq m_2 \leq k$, by induction hypothesis it takes $m_1 - 1$ moves to form one block and $m_2 - 1$ moves to form the other block.

Hence, the total number of moves to solve the puzzle
$$= (m_1 - 1) + (m_2 - 1) + 1 = m_1 + m_2 - 1$$
$$= k + 1 - 1 = k \text{ moves.}$$

2.8 Power Set

2.8.1 Definition

Let A be any set. The power set of A, denoted by P(A) is the set of all subsets of A.

Examples:
(i) If $A = \{a\}$, then $P(A) = \{A, \phi\}$.
(ii) If $A = \{a, b\}$, then $P(A)$
$= \{\phi, \{a\}, \{b\}, A\}$.

(iii) If $A = \{a, \{a\}\}$, then
$P(A) = \{\{a\}, \{\{a\}\}, A, \phi\}$.

The following theorem determines the size of the power set.

2.8.2 Theorem (Cardinality of a Power Set)

Let A be a finite set containing n elements. Then the power set of A has exactly 2^n elements.

Proof:
We prove the theorem by mathematical induction.
For $n = 1$, $A = \{a\}$, so that $P(A) = \{A, \phi\}$.
Hence, $|P(A)| = 2^1$ elements.
Assume that if $|A| = k$, $|P(A)| = 2^k$.
Let $|A| = k + 1$. For an element $a \in A$, consider the subset $B = A - \{a\}$. Since, $|B| = k$, by induction hypothesis $|P(B)| = 2^k$, i.e. there are exactly 2^k subsets of B.
Since, every subset of B is also a subset of A, it follows that A contains at least 2^k subsets.
In addition, for each subset of B, say C, we have another subset $C \cup \{a\}$ of A.
Hence, the total number of subsets of A is $2^k + 2^k = 2.2^k = 2^{k+1}$ subsets.
Hence, by induction, it follows that if $|A| = n$, $|P(A)| = 2^n$.

SOLVED EXAMPLES

Example 1: If $A = \{\phi, a\}$, then construct the sets $A \cup P(A)$, $A \cap P(A)$.
Solution : $P(A) = \{\phi, \{\phi\}, \{a\}, A\}$
∴ $A \cup P(A) = \{\phi, a, \{\phi\}, \{a\}, A\}$.
$A \cap P(A) = \{\phi\}$.

Example 2: Let $A = \{\phi\}$. Let $B = P(P(A))$.
(i) Is $\phi \in B$? $\phi \subseteq B$?
(ii) Is $\{\phi\} \in B$? $\{\phi\} \subseteq B$?
(iii) Is $\{\{\phi\}\} \in B$? $\{\{\phi\}\} \subseteq B$?

Solution: $P(A) = \{\phi, \{\phi\}\}$
$B = P(P(A)) = \{\phi, \{\phi\}, \{\{\phi\}\}, P(A)\}$.

(i) The element $\phi \in B$. The empty set ϕ is always a subset of B.
(ii) Both are true, one as element and the other as subset containing the single element ϕ.
(iii) Both are true, the first as element and the second as a single to n subset containing the element $\{\phi\}$.

Example 3: If $A \subseteq B$, then $P(A) \subseteq P(B)$.
Solution: Let $C \in P(A)$. Then $C \subseteq A$ which implies that $C \subseteq B$.
Hence, $C \in P(B)$. $\therefore$ $P(A) \subseteq P(B)$.

Example 4: Let A and B be two arbitrary sets.
(i) Show that $P(A \cap B) = P(A) \cap P(B)$ or give a counter example.
(ii) Show that $P(A \cup B) = P(A) \cup P(B)$ or give a counter example.

Solution: (i) Let $C \in P(A \cap B)$. Then $C \subseteq A \cap B$
$\Rightarrow \quad C \subseteq A$ and $C \subseteq B \Rightarrow C \in P(A)$ and $C \in P(B) \Rightarrow C \in P(A) \cap P(B)$
$\therefore \quad P(A \cap B) \subseteq P(A) \cap P(B)$.
Conversely, let $C \in P(A) \cap P(B)$.
This implies $C \in P(A)$ and $C \in P(B)$
$\Rightarrow \quad C \subseteq A$ and $C \subseteq B$
$\Rightarrow \quad C \subseteq A \cap B$, i.e. $C \in P(A \cap B)$.
Hence, $P(A) \cap P(B) \subseteq P(A \cap B)$
Hence, $P(A \cap B) = P(A) \cap P(B)$.

(ii) Equality is not true.
Consider $A = \{1\}$, $B = \{2\}$.
$A \cup B = \{1, 2\}$
$\therefore \quad P(A \cup B) = \{\phi, \{1\}, \{2\}, \{1, 2\}\}$
$P(A) = \{\phi, \{1\}\}$
$P(B) = \{\phi, \{2\}\}$
$\therefore \quad P(A) \cup P(B) = \{\phi, \{1\}, \{2\}\}$
$\neq P(A \cup B)$.

Example 5: Let $A = \{\phi, b\}$; construct the following sets:
(i) $A - \phi$
(ii) $\{\phi\} - A$
(iii) $A \cup P(A)$
(iv) $A \cap P(A)$
where P(A) is power set of A.

Solution: (i) $\quad A - \phi = A$
(ii) $\quad \{\phi\} - A = \phi$
(iii) $\quad A \cup P(A) = \{\phi, b, \{\phi\}, \{b\}, A\}$
(iv) $\quad A \cap P(A) = \{\phi\}$

EXERCISE - 2.1

1. If $A = \{\phi, \{\phi\}, \{\phi, \{\phi\}\}\}$, determine whether the following statements are true or false. Justify your answer.
   (i) $\phi \in A$
   (ii) $\{\phi\} \subseteq A$

(iii) $\{\phi\} \in A$
(iv) $\{\phi, \{\phi\}\} \subseteq A$
(v) $\{\{\phi\}\} \in A$

2. If $u = \{n \in N \mid 1 \leq n \leq 9\}$,
   $A = \{1, 2, 4, 6, 8\}$, $B = \{2, 4, 5, 9\}$, $C = \{x \in Z^+ \mid x^2 \leq 16\}$ and $D = \{7, 8\}$,
   find (i) $A \oplus B$, $B \oplus C$, $C \oplus D$
   (ii) $A - B$, $B - A$, $C - D$
   (iii) $\overline{A \cup B}$, $\overline{A \cap B}$
   (iv) $\overline{A} \cap (C \cup D)$

3. For $A = \{a, b, \{b, c\}, \phi\}$ determine the following sets:
   (i) $A - \{a\}$, (ii) $A - \{b, c\}$, (iii) $\{\{b, c\}\} - A$, (iv) $A - \{c, \phi\}$, (v) $\{a\} - \{A\}$.

4. Give an example of sets A, B, C such that $A \in B$, $B \in C$ and $A \notin C$.

5. Draw Venn diagrams for the following situations.
   (i) A, B, C are sets such that $A \subseteq B$, $A \subseteq C$, $(B \cap C) \subseteq A$ and $A \subseteq (B \cap C)$.
   (ii) $(A \cap B \cap C) = \phi$, $A \cap B \neq \phi$, $B \cap C \neq \phi$, $A \cap C \neq \phi$.

6. Using Venn diagrams, prove or disprove the following:
   (i) $(A - B) - C = (A - C) - B$
   (ii) $(A - B) - C = (A - C) - (B - C)$
   (iii) $(A - B) \cap (A - C) = A - (B \cup C)$
   (iv) $(A - C) \cup (B - C) = (A \cup B) - C$
   (v) $A - (B - C) = (A - B) \cup (A \cap C)$
   (vi) $A \cap (B - C) = (A \cap B) - (A \cap C)$
   (vii) $(A \cap B) - C = (A - C) \cap (B - C)$
   (viii) $(A \oplus B) \cap C = (A \cap C) \oplus (B \cap C)$
   (ix) $A \cup (\overline{B} \cap C) = (A \cup \overline{B}) \cap (A \cup C)$.

7. Using the rules of set operations, simplify the following:
   (i) $\overline{(A \cup B)} \cup (\overline{A} \cap B)$
   (ii) $[(A \cap B) \cup (A \cap \overline{B}) \cup (\overline{A} \cap B)] \cap B$
   (iii) $((A \cup B) \cap \overline{A}) \cup (\overline{B \cap A})$
   (iv) $[(A \cap B) \cup C] \cap \overline{B}$.

8. What can you say about sets A and B, if
   (i) $A - B = B$?
   (ii) $A - B = B - A$?
   (iii) $A \oplus B = A$?

9. It is known that at the University, 60 percent of the professors play tennis, 50 percent of them play bridge, 70 percent jog, 20 percent play tennis and bridge, 30 percent play tennis and jog and 40 percent play bridge and jog. If someone claimed that 20 percent of the professors jog and play bridge and tennis, would you believe this claim? Why?

10. A survey was conducted among 1000 people. Of these 595 are graduates, 595 wear glasses and 550 like ice cream, 395 of them are graduates who wear glasses, 350 of them are graduates who like ice cream and 400 of them wear glasses and like ice cream; 250 of them are graduates who wear glasses and like ice cream. How many of them who are not graduates do not wear glasses and do not like ice cream? How many of them are graduates who do not wear glasses and do not like ice cream?

11. Consider a set of integers from 1 to 250. Find how many of these numbers are divisible by 3 or 5 or 7? Also indicate how many are divisible by 3 or 7 but not by 5.

12. How many integers between 1 and 2000 are divisible by 2, 3, 5 or 7?

13. A college record gives the following information: 119 students enrolled in Introductory Computer Science; of these, 96 took Data Structures, 53 took Foundations, 39 took Assembly Language. Also 38 took both Data Structures and Foundations, 31 took both Foundations and Assembly Language, 32 took both Data Structures and Assembly language and 22 took all the three courses. Is the information correct? Why?

14. A survey of 100 students of the Management Programme shows that 70 read India Today, 31 read Fortune and 54 read Business India. Also the people who read Business India do not read Fortune. Draw a Venn diagram to represent the situation.

15. A software company writes a new package which integrates a word processing program with a spreadsheet program, and they wish it to run on a 64 K machine. The word processor requires 40 K for program and data and the spreadsheet requires 32 K for the same. If 16 K must be reserved for the code integrator, what is the minimum amount of overlapping space that will be necessary?

16. Consider a set of integers 1 to 500. Find how many of these numbers are divisible by 3 or by 5 or by 11?
    (i) Also indicate how many are divisible by 3 or by 11 but not by all 3, 5 and 11.
    (ii) How many are divisible by 3 or 11 but not by 5?

17. It was found that in first year of computer engineering out of 80 students, 50 know 'C' language, 55 know 'basic' and 25 know 'C++', while 8 did not know any language. Find,
    (i) How many know all the three languages?
    (ii) How many know exactly two languages?

18. In the survey of 60 people, it was found that 25 read Newsweek Magazine, 26 read time, 26 read fortune. Also 9 read both Newsweek and Fortune, 11 read both Newsweek and Time, 8 read both Time and Fortune and 8 read no magazine at all.

(i)   Find out the number of people who read all the three magazines.
   (ii) Fill in the correct numbers in all the regions of the Venn diagram.
   (iii) Determine number of people who reads exactly one magazine.
19. Among 130 students, 60 study Mathematics, 51 Physics and 30 both Mathematics and Physics. Of the 54 students studying Chemistry, 26 study Mathematics, 21 Physics and 12 both Mathematics and Physics. All the students studying neither Mathematics nor Physics are studying Biology.
   (i)   How many students are studying Biology?
   (ii) How many students not studying Chemistry are studying Mathematics but not Physics?
   (iii) How many students are studying neither Mathematics nor Physics nor Chemistry.
20. It was found that in first year of computer science of 80 students, 50 know COBOL, 55 know C language and 46 know Pascal. It was also known that 37 know C and COBOL, 28 know C and Pascal, and 25 know Pascal and COBOL. 7 students however know none of the language. Find:
   (i)   How many know all the three languages?
   (ii) How many know exactly two languages?
   (iii) How many know exactly one language?
21. A survey has been taken on methods of computer travels. Each respondent was asked to check BUS, TRAIN or AUTOMOBILE as a major method of traveling to work. More than one answer was permitted. The results reported were as follows: BUS – 30 people, TRAIN – 35 people, AUTOMOBILE – 15 people, TRAIN and AUTOMOBILE – 20 people and all three methods-5 people. How many people completed the survey form?
22. A survey of 500 television watchers produced the following information. 285 watch football, 195 watch hockey, 115 watch basket ball. 45 watch football and basket ball, 70 watch football and hockey, 50 watch hockey and basketball and 50 do not watch any of the three games.
   (i)   How many people in the survey watch all the three games?
   (ii) How many people watch exactly one game?
23. 100 of the 120 engineering students in a college take part in at least one of the activities: group discussion, debate and quiz. Also 65 participate in group discussion 45 participate in debate, 42 participate in quiz, 20 participate in group discussion and debate, 25 participate in group discussion and quiz, 15 participate in debate and quiz. Find the number of students:
   (i)   Who participate in all the three activities
   (ii) Who participate in exactly one of the activities.

24. In a class of 55 students, the number of students studying different subjects are as follows: Maths 23, Physics – 24, Chemistry 19, Maths + Physics – 12, Maths + Chemistry – 9, Physics + Chemistry – 7, all three subjects - 4. Find the numbers of students who have taken: (i) At least one subject, (ii) Exactly one subject, (iii) Exactly two subjects.
25. In a survey of 100 new cars, it is found that 60 had Air Conditioner (AC), 48 had Power-Steering (PS), 44 had Power Windows (PW), 36 had AC + PW, 20 had AC + PS, 16 had PW + PS, 12 had all three. Find the number of cars that had: (i) Only PW, (ii) PS and PW but not AC, (iii) AC and PS but not PW.

Exercise on Mathematical Induction
26. Show that $n^3 + 2n$ is divisible by 3 for all $n \geq 1$.
27. Show that $n^4 - 4n^2$ is divisible by 3 for all $n \geq 2$.
28. Show that $2^n \times 2^n - 1$ is divisible by 3 for all $n \geq 1$.
29. Show that $5^n - 4n - 1$ is divisible by 16 for all $n \geq 1$.
30. Prove that $1^3 + 2^3 + \ldots + n^3 = (1 + 2 + \ldots + n)^2$
31. Prove mathematical induction for $n \geq 1$
$$1 \cdot 2 + 2 \cdot 3 + \ldots + n(n + 1) = \frac{n(n + 1)(n + 2)}{3}.$$
32. Prove by mathematical induction, the given proposition
$$\frac{1}{1(3)} + \frac{1}{3(5)} + \frac{1}{5(7)} + \ldots + \frac{1}{(2n - 1)(2n + 1)} = \frac{n}{2n + 1}.$$
33. State the principle of mathematical induction and prove the following proposition
$$P(n) = 1 + 4 + 7 + \ldots + (3n - 2) = \frac{n(3n - 1)}{2}.$$
34. Prove that for any positive integer n, the number $n^5 - n$ is divisible by 5.
35. Prove De Morgan's laws for a finite collection of sets $A_1, A_2, \ldots, A_n$ using induction.
36. When n couples arrived at a party, they were greeted by the host and hostess at the door. After rounds of handshaking, the host asked the guests as well as his wife (the hostess) to indicate the number of hands each of them had shaken. He got 2n + 1 different answers. Given that no one shook hands with his or her spouse, how many hands had the hostess shaken? Prove your answer by induction.
37. We present a proof of the statement "Any n billiard balls are of the same colour", by induction.
    Basis of induction: For n = 1, the statement is trivially true.
    Induction step: Suppose we are given k + 1 billiard balls which we number 1, 2, ... (k + 1). According to the induction hypothesis, balls 1, 2, ..., k are of the same colour. Also balls 2, 3, ..., (k + 1) are of the same colour. Consequently, balls 1, 2, ..., k, (k + 1) are all of the same colour.
    What is wrong with the proof?

Problems on Power Sets:

38. Let A = {a, {a}}. Determine which of the following statements are true or false.
    (i) $\phi \in P(A)$
    (ii) $\phi \subseteq P(A)$
    (iii) $\{a\} \in P(A)$
    (iv) $\{a, \{a\}\} \in P(A)$
    (v) $\{\{\{a\}\}\} \subseteq P(A)$

39. Determine whether the following statements are true or false. Justify your answer.
    (i) $A \cup P(A) = P(A)$
    (ii) $\{A\} \cup P(A) = P(A)$
    (iii) $A - P(A) = A$
    (iv) $P(A) - \{A\} = P(A)$
    (v) $\{A\} \cap P(A) = A$.

40. For multisets, define in brief:
    (i) Multisets.
    (ii) Multiplicity of an element in a multiset.
    (iii) Cardinality of mulstiset.
    (iv) Union of multiset.
    (v) Intersection of multiset.
    (vi) Difference of multiset.

41. A survey has been taken on methods of computer travel. Each respondent was asked to check bus, train or automobile as a major method of travelling to work. More than one answer was permitted. The results reported were as follows:
    Bus - 30 people, train - 35 people, automobile - 100 people, bus and train - 15 people, bus and automobile - 15 people, train and automobile - 20 people and all three methods - 5 people. How many people completed a survey form?

42. In a survey of 260 college students, the following data were obtained: 64 had taken a Mathematical course, 94 has taken a Computer Science course, 58 had taken a Business course, 28 had taken both Mathematic and Business courses, 26 had taken both Mathematical and Computer Science course, 22 had taken both Computer Science and Business course and 14 had taken all 3 types of courses.
    (1) How many students were surveyed who had taken none of the three types of courses?
    (2) Of the students surveyed, how many had taken only Computer Science course?

ANSWERS - 2.1

1. (i) True, (ii) True, (iii) True, (iv) True, (v) False.
2. (i) $A \oplus B = \{1, 5, 6, 8, 9\}$
   (ii) $A - B = \{1, 6, 8\}$
   (iii) $\overline{A \cup B} = \{3, 7\}$.

3. (i) A – {a} = {b, {b, c}, φ} (v) {a} – {A} = {a}.
7. (i) $\bar{A}$, (iii) $\bar{A} \cup \bar{B}$.
9. Claim is false.
10. 155, 100
11. 86 numbers between 1 to 250 are divisible by 3 or 7 but not by 5.
12. 1499
19. (i) 49, (ii) 16, (iii) 30.
20. (i) 12, (ii) 66, (iii) 7.
22. (i) 20

Points to Remember

- A set is a **collection of** objects.
- An object in the collection is called an **element** or member of the set.
- The term **class** is also used to denote a set.
- A set may contain **finite** number of elements or **infinite** number of elements.
- A set is called an **empty set** or a **null set** if it contains no element. An empty set is denoted by the letter φ.
- If every element of a set A is also an element of a set B, then we say A is a **subset** of B, or A is **contained** in B. This is denoted by 'A ⊆ B'. This can be also denoted by 'B ⊇ A'. If A is not a subset of B, this is indicated by 'A ⊄ B'.
- If all sets, considered during a **specific discussion** are subsets of a given set, then this set is called as the **Universal Set**, and is denoted by 'U'.
- A Venn diagram (named after the British logician John Venn) is a pictorial depiction of a set.
- Let A be a given set. **Complement** of A, denoted by $\bar{A}$ is defined as

$$\bar{A} = \{x \mid x \notin A\}$$

- The union of two sets A and B is the set consisting of all elements which are in A, or in B, or in both sets A and B. It is denoted by A ∪ B.
- The intersection of two sets A and B, denoted by A ∩ B is the set consisting of elements which are in A **as well as** in B.
- If the counting of the elements of a set is interminable or impossible, then such a set is said to be infinite.

Chapter 3: PERMUTATIONS, COMBINATIONS AND DISCRETE POROBABILITY

SYLLABUS
- Permutations and Combinations, Rule of sum and products, Permutations, Combinations, Algorithms for generation of permutations and combinations.
- Discrete Probability, Conditional probability, Baye's Theorem.

OBJECTIVES:
- To study different types of counting problems and related probability.
- To learn various properties of binomial identities.

UTILITY:
- In solving combinatorial problems.
- In applying the counting procedures to problems on probability for discrete sample space.

KEY CONCEPTS:
- Permutation
- Combination
- Sample space
- Discrete probability

3.0 Introduction

This chapter is divided into two sections. In the first section, we shall study various counting techniques involving finite sets. Counting the objects in a finite set is a basic necessity in order to compare, evaluate and predict things. To compare the cost of applying two algorithms, one needs to estimate how many operations each of them executes to solve the same problem. Again to evaluate the cost efficiency of using a particular data structure for a file, one needs to determine the average and maximum lengths of searches for items stored in that particular data structure. Hence problems of this nature, ultimately involve counting the elements of a set.

The methods developed in this section are applied to solve problems on probability, related to discrete sample spaces, which are discussed in the second section.

3.1 Permutations and Combinations

Problems involving counting are generally of the type where we have to find the number of ways to arrange some or all elements of a set; or to select some elements or their combinations from a given set. Problems such as these are called as **combinatorial** problems. Some of these problems can be quite tricky as is evident from the following examples.

1. How many non-negative integer solutions are there of the equation
   $x + y + z + u + v = 10,000$?
2. In how many ways can the four walls of a room be painted with three colours so that no two adjacent walls have the same colour?

Problems such as those stated above are interpreted as "experiments" or "tasks" and solutions of the problems as "outcomes" of the experiments.

Suppose we have to consider several experiments and their outcomes, simultaneously. We observe the following self-evident rules of operations:

> **(i) Rule of Product:** If one experiment E_1 has n_1 possible outcomes and another experiment E_2 has n_2 possible outcomes, then there are $n_1 n_2$ possible outcomes when both the experiments ($E_1 \cap E_2$ or $E_1 E_2$) take place.
>
> This rule can be extended to a finite number of experiments $E_1, E_2, E_3, ..., E_k$, with outcomes $n_1, n_2, n_3, ..., n_k$ respectively.

> **(ii) Rule of Sum:** If one experiment E_1 has n_1 possible outcomes and another experiment E_2 has n_2 possible outcomes, then there are $n_1 + n_2$ possible outcomes when exactly one of these experiments take place i.e. $(E_1 \cup E_2) - E_1 \cap E_2$.

Example: Suppose there are 65 ways to select a class representative for FE-I and 75 ways to select a class representative for SE-(COM), then to select a representative for the combined FE and SE classes, there will be $65 \times 75 = 4875$ ways, by the rule of product. On the other hand, there will be $65 + 75 = 140$ ways to select a representative for either the FE class or the SE class.

The problems discussed in this section will deal with two basic ideas of counting, that of permutations and combinations.

3.1.1 Permutations

An arrangement in sequence of elements of a set is called a permutation of the elements. Essentially, there are three types of arrangement of elements to be considered.

> I. Let $0 \leq r \leq n$. The number of ways to have an ordered sequence of n distinct elements, taken r at a time is called as an r-permutation of n-elements and is denoted by P(n, r) or (^nP_r).

The first place in the sequence can be filled up in n ways, then the second in (n – 1) ways and proceeding in this manner the rth place can be filled up in (n – r + 1) ways.

Hence the number of permutations of n-distinct elements taken r at a time is given by the formula

$$P(n, r) = n(n-1)(n-2)\ldots(n-r+1)$$
$$= \frac{n!}{(n-r)!}, \quad \text{where } 0 \leq r \leq n$$

SOLVED EXAMPLES

Example 1: (a) Find the permutations of the set A = {1, 2, 3, 4}, taking the elements two at a time.

Solution: The permutations are the sequences

12, 13, 14, 21, 23, 24, 31, 32, 34, 41, 42, 43.

Note that the order in which the elements appear is important, 12 and 21 are **different** arrangements of the same elements.

(b) Find the permutations of the set A = {1, 2, 3}.

In this case, we permute all the three elements. Hence the permutations are the sequences: 123, 132, 231, 213, 312, 321.

Example 2: Four persons enter a bus in which there are six vacant seats. In how many ways can they take their places?

Solution: The first person may seat himself in 6 ways, then the second person can seat himself in 5 ways. Proceeding in this manner, the total number of ways in which the 4 persons can seat themselves is P(6, 4) = 6 × 5 × 4 × 3 = 360.

Example 3: A menu card in a restaurant displays four soups, five main courses, three desserts and 5 beverages. How many different menus can a customer select if
  (i) He selects one item from each group without omission?
  (ii) He chooses to omit the beverages, but selects one each from the other groups?
  (iii) He chooses to omit the desserts but decides to take a beverage and one item each from the remaining groups?

Solution: (i) The customer can select the soup in 4 ways, the main course in 5 ways, the dessert in 3 ways and beverage in 5 ways. Hence by the product rule, the number of ways in which he can select one item each, without omission, is 4 × 5 × 3 × 5 = 300.
  (ii) The number of ways in which the selection is made is 4 × 5 × 3 = 60.
  (iii) The number of ways to make the required selection is 4 × 5 × 5 = 100.

Example 4: In how many ways can one select a President, a General Secretary and a Treasurer from the members of a committee consisting of 9 men and 11 women, if the Treasurer must be a woman, and the General Secretary a man?

Solution: If the President is a man, he can be selected in 9 ways, in which case the General Secretary will be selected in 8 ways. If the President is a woman, she can be selected in 11 ways and then the Treasurer in 10 ways. Hence by the rules of sum and product, the total number of ways to make the selection is $9 \times 8 \times 11 + 11 \times 10 \times 9 = 1782$.

Example 5: Find how many words (meaningful or otherwise) of length 3 can be formed from the word COMPUTER, the beginning letter being C, and allowing no repetition of the letters.

Solution: The given word contains 8 distinct letters. Since the first letter of the word is already fixed, the remaining two letters can be selected in $7 \times 6 = 42$ ways.

Hence the number of words that can thus be formed is 42.

Example 6: Find how many symbol codes can be formed if the first two symbols are letters and the next 3 are digits, but no symbol is repeated.

Solution: The first two symbols can be chosen in P (26, 2) ways and the next three symbols can be chosen in P (10, 3) ways. Hence by the product rule, the number of symbol codes that can be formed is $\dfrac{26!}{24!} \cdot \dfrac{10!}{7!} = 26 \times 25 \times 10 \times 9 \times 8 = 468000$.

Example 7: (i) Suppose that repetitions are not permitted, then how many 4 digit numbers can be formed from the six digits 1, 2, 3, 5, 7, 8?
  (ii)   How many such numbers are less than 4000?
  (iii) How many of the numbers in (i) are even?
  (iv)   How many of the numbers in (ii) are odd?
  (v)   How many of the numbers in (i) contain both the digits 3 and 5?

Solution: (i) The number of 4 digit numbers is given by P (6, 4) = $\dfrac{6!}{2!}$ = 360.

  (ii) The numbers beginning with 1, 2, 3, will be the numbers which are less than 4000. The number of integers beginning with 1 is $5 \times 4 \times 3 = 60$.

The number of integers beginning with 2 is again $5 \times 4 \times 3 = 60$.

Thus the total number of integers less than 4000 is $3 \times 60 = 180$.

  (iii) Those numbers ending in 2 or 8 are even. Numbers ending in 2 are $5 \times 4 \times 3 = 60$. Similarly, the numbers ending in 8 are $5 \times 4 \times 3 = 60$. Hence the numbers ending in 2 or 8 are 120 numbers.

  (iv) The numbers ending in 1, 3, 5, 7 are odd. The 4 digit numbers ending in 1 and less than 4000 should begin with either 2 or 3. Then there are $2 \times 4 \times 3 = 24$ such numbers. Similarly, the numbers ending in 3 are 24. However, the numbers ending in 5 or 7 are $3 \times 4 \times 3 = 36$ for each. Hence there are in all $2 \times 24 + 2 \times 36 = 120$ such numbers.

(v) The digit 3 can occupy any of the 4 positions and the remaining 3 will be occupied by the digit 5. Hence the number of ways in which the digits 3 and 5 can appear is $4 \times 3 = 12$. Hence the number of integers containing both the digits 3 and 5 is $12 \times 4 \times 3 = 144$.

Example 8: Suppose repetitions are not possible.
1. How many three digit numbers can be formed from six digits 2, 3, 4, 5, 7 and 9?
2. How many of these numbers are less than 400?
3. How many are even?
4. How many are multiples of 5?

Solution:
1. Since repetition is not allowed, the first digit can be chosen in 6 ways, the second in 5 and the third in 4 ways.
Hence the total number of such 3 digit numbers is $6 \times 5 \times 4 = 120$.
2. Since the number is less than 400, the first digit has to be 2 or 3 only. Hence the first digit can be chosen in 2 ways, then the second in 5 and the last in 4 ways only.
Hence the total number of such numbers is $2 \times 5 \times 4 = 40$.
3. For the number to be even, the last digit has to be 2 or 4, then the middle digit can be chosen in 5 and the first in 4 ways.
Hence the total number of such numbers is $2 \times 5 \times 4 = 40$.
4. Since the last digit is 5, it can be filled up in only one way. Hence, the total number of such numbers is $1 \times 5 \times 4 = 20$.

Example 9: Six different Mathematics books, four different Discrete Structures books and three different Computer Science books are to be arranged on a shelf. How many different arrangements are possible if
(i) The books in each subject must all be together?
(ii) Only the Discrete Structures books must be together?

Solution: (i) The Mathematics books can be arranged among themselves in 6 ! ways, the Discrete Structures books in 4 ! ways and the Computer Science books in 3 ! ways.

Hence the total number of arrangements is 3 ! 3 ! 4 ! 6 ! = 103680 ways.

(ii) Consider the four Discrete Structures books as a single entity. Then we have 10 books which can be arranged in 10 ! ways. In each of these arrangements, the Discrete Structures books can be arranged among themselves in 4 ! ways. Hence, the number of arrangements is 4 ! 10 ! = 87091200 ways.

Example 10: In how many ways can 9 people be seated at a round table if
(i) they can sit anywhere?
(ii) 2 particular persons must not sit next to each other?

Solution:
(i) Since the people are seated in a circle, the total number of ways in seating them is $(9 - 1) ! = 8! = 40320$ ways.

(ii) Consider the two persons as a single entity. Then there are 8 people altogether and they can be seated in $(8 - 1)! = 7!$ ways. But the two particular persons can be arranged among themselves in $2!$ ways. Thus the number of ways of arranging 9 people at a round table with the two persons sitting together is $2! \, 7! = 10080$ ways.

Then from (i), the total number of ways in which 9 people can be seated at a round table so that 2 particular persons do not sit together $= 40320 - 10080 = 30240$ ways.

Example 11: How many different ways are there to arrange the letters in the word "PROBLEM" if
  (i) the letter P must come first?
  (ii) The letter P must come first and the letter M last?

Solution: (i) Since the letter P must come first, its position is fixed. Hence the remaining 6 letters can be arranged in $6!$ ways. Hence the required answer is $6!$.

(ii) Since the letter P must come first and the letter M last, the remaining 5 letters can be arranged in $5!$ ways.

Hence the required answer is $5!$ ways.

Example 12: The number of injective functions from a set with r elements to a set with n elements is $P(n, r)$, $r \leq n$.

Solution: Let A and B be sets with cardinalities r, n respectively. Let $A = \{a_1, a_2, \ldots a_r\}$ and $B = \{b_1, b_2, \ldots, b_n\}$. Let f be an injective function from A to B. $f(a_1)$ has n choices from elements of B. Since f is injective, $f(a_1) \neq f(a_2)$. Hence $f(a_2)$ has $(n-1)$ choices, $f(a_3)$ has $(n-2)$ choices and so on till $f(a_r)$ which has $(n - r + 1)$ choices. Hence by the product rule, the number of injective functions from A to B is $n(n-1)(n-2)\ldots(n-r+1) = P(n, r)$. We now deal with permutation problems of another type, which can be stated as follows:

> II. The number of ways in which of the n elements can be arranged, where r_1 elements are of one kind, r_2 are of another kind and so on till r_k elements are of another kind, is given by the formula $\dfrac{P(n, r)}{r_1! \, r_2! \ldots r_k!}$, where $r = r_1 + r_2 + \ldots + r_k$.

SOLVED EXAMPLES

Example 1: In how many ways can the letters in the word MISSISSIPPI be arranged?

Solution: The letter I occurs 4 times, hence there are $4!$ ways in which these I's can be re-arranged among themselves. But then as this does not change the word as such, we have to divide by $4!$ to count the word MISSISSIPPI once. Hence the I's are objects of one kind, similarly the 4 S's are objects of second kind and the two P's are objects of third kind. Hence the number of ways the letters of the word MISSISSIPPI can be rearranged is $\dfrac{11!}{4! \, 4! \, 2!}$.

Example 2: How many numbers can be formed with the digits 1, 2, 3, 4, 3, 2, 1, so that the odd digits always occupy the odd places?

Solution: The odd digits 1, 3, 3, 1 can be arranged in their four places in $\frac{4!}{2!2!}$ ways.

The even digits 2, 4, 2 can be arranged in their three places in $\frac{3!}{2!}$ ways.

Hence the required number of ways is $\frac{4!}{2!2!} \cdot \frac{3!}{2!} = 6 \times 3 = 18$.

Example 3: Fifteen new students are to be evenly distributed among three classes. Suppose there are three brilliant scholars among them. In how many ways can the distribution done, so that each class gets one? One class gets them all?

Solution: Since each class must get one scholar, we shall first assign these 3 students which is done in 3! ways. The other 12 students can be equally distributed in the 3 classes. Hence in this case, the number of ways in which the distribution can be done is $3! \frac{12!}{4!4!4!}$.

Next, if one class gets them all, then there are 3 possibilities according to which class it is. Hence the number of ways in which distribution can be done is $3 \cdot \frac{12!}{5!5!2!}$.

Example 4: In how many ways can the letters in the word "PIONEER" be arranged so that the two E's are always together?

Solution: The other five letters can be rearranged in 5! ways and for each such arrangement, the two E's can occupy any of the six remaining places. Hence the number of ways in which the letters of the word can be arranged, so that the two E's are always together, is $6 \cdot 5 = 6!$.

Example 5: Find the number of ways in which letters in the word "MALYALAM" be arranged so that the two M's are always together.

Solution: The remaining 6 letters in the word can be arranged in 6! ways and for each such arrangement the two M's can occupy any of the 7 remaining places; for instance one such arrangement is YMMALALA. For each such arrangement, since there are 3A's, 2L's (objects of the same kind), the total number of arrangements is $\frac{7 \cdot 6!}{3!\, 2!} = \frac{7!}{3!\, 2!} = 420$.

Example 6: In how many ways can 8 different books be divided among Sameer, Ajay and Leela if Sameer gets 4 books, Ajay and Leela get 2 each?

Solution: One of the arrangements can be SALSSLSA. Each such ordering determines a distribution of books.

Hence the total number of ways in distributing the 8 books, in the required manner is $\frac{8!}{4!2!2!} = 420$.

The third type of problems on permutation can be described as follows:

> III. The number of permutations of n elements, r at a time, when each element may be repeated once, twice, ... upto r times in any arrangement.

In this case, the first place may be filled up in n ways and when it has filled up in any one way, the second place may also be filled up in n ways since we are not precluded from using the same element. Proceeding in this manner, the number of ways in which the r places can be filled up is n^r.

SOLVED EXAMPLES

Example 1: A die is rolled three times, find the number of faces that can appear on top.

Solution: If the die is rolled once, the face appearing on the top can be any one of the six faces 1 to 6; when it is rolled the second time, then also there are 6 choices for the face appearing on top, and same is the situation when the die is rolled the third time. Hence the total number of ways of a face appearing on top is $6 \times 6 \times 6 = 6^3$.

Example 2: Find the number of ways in which three examinations can be scheduled within a five day period, with no restriction on the number of examinations scheduled each day.

Solution: The first examination can be held on any of the five days, hence it has 5 choices. There being no restriction, the second examination can also be held on any of the five days, and similar is the situation for the third examination.

Hence the number of ways in which the examinations can be held is $5 \times 5 \times 5 = 5^3$.

Example 3: (i) Find the number of binary sequences of length 5.

(ii) Find the number of four digit decimal numbers that contain one or more repeated digits.

Solution: (i) Each position in the sequence has 2 choices viz. 0 or 1. Hence the number of binary sequences of length 5 is $2 \times 2 \times 2 \times 2 \times 2 = 2^5$.

(ii) There are 9×10^3 four digit decimal numbers, including the non-repeated digits. Since we are required to find only those 4 digit numbers that contain one or more repeated digits, we have to omit those n numbers with non-repeated digits. There are $9 \times 9 \times 8 \times 7$ such numbers.

Hence the number of 4 digit decimal numbers, with one or more repeated digits, is $10^4 - 9 \times 9 \times 8 \times 7 = 5464$.

Example 4: How many auto license plates can be made if each is identified by 2 letters followed by 4 digits?

Solution: The first two positions in the sequence can be occupied in $26 \times 26 = 26^2$ ways. The next four positions can be occupied in $10 \times 10 \times 10 \times 10 = 10^4$ ways.

Hence the number of auto license plates that can be made is $26^2 \times 10^4$.

Example 5: In a Mathematics test, there are 10 multiple choice questions with 4 possible answers and 15 true-false questions. In how many ways can the 25 questions be answered?

Solution: If the student attempts to answer all the questions, he can answer the 10 multiple choice questions in 4^{10} ways and the 15 true-false questions in 2^{15} ways. Hence the required answer is $4^{10} \times 2^{15} = 2^{35} = 3436 \times 10^{10}$ ways.

Sometimes it is necessary to find the total number of ways in which it is possible to make a selection by taking **some or all** of the n elements. In this case, each element may be dealt within 2 ways, either taken or rejected. Hence the number of ways of dealing with them is $2 \times 2 \times ... \times 2$ (n times) i.e. 2^n. But since this includes the case when all the elements are rejected, omitting this case, the total number of ways is $2^n - 1$.

The following examples demonstrate this case.

Example 6: A man has 10 friends. In how many ways can he go to dinner with 1 or more of them?

Solution: Since he has to select some or all of his 10 friends, the number of ways is $2^{10} - 1$.

Example 7: There are 15 true or false questions in an exam. In how many ways can a student answer the exam if he or she can also choose not to answer some of them?

Solution: If the student attempts all the 15 questions, then he or she can do so in 2^{15} ways. But since he or she can choose not to answer some of them, the correct solution is $2^{15} - 1$.

Example 8: A bit is either 0 or 1. A byte is a sequence of 8 bits. Find:
  (i)   Number of bytes.
  (ii) Number of bytes that begin with 11 and end with 11.

Solution: (i) Total number of bytes is $2 \times 2 \times 2$ (8 times) $= 2^8 = 256$.

  (ii) Since the first two and last two bits are fixed, i.e. 11, the remaining bits in the sequence are either 0 or 1.

Hence, total number of bytes $= 2 \times 2 \times 2 \times 2 = 2^4 = 16$.

Example 9: In how many ways the letters in the word 'ORGANISE' can be arranged in such a way that all vowels come together and all consonants always come together.

Solution: The vowels are A, E, I, O, and consonants are R, G, N, S.

The vowels, being considered as a single block can be rearranged in 4 ! ways. Similarly, the consonants can be rearranged in 4 ! ways. The two blocks can be further arranged in 2 ! ways. Hence, required number of permutations is 2 ! 4 ! 4 ! = 1152.

3.1.2 Combinations

The counting methods that we have seen for permutations all apply to situations where order matters. In this section, we consider some problems where order does not matter.

Definition:

Let $0 \leq r \leq n$. A selection of a set of r elements from a set of n distinct elements is called a **combination**.

It is clear from the definition that in order to find the total number of r combinations of n elements, all that we have to do is to find all subsets of cardinality r, of a set whose cardinality is n. This can be done as follows.

Let B be a subset of A containing r elements. Let C (n, r) denote the number of ways to choose B. Now since a permutation of n-elements taken r at a time involves a subset B of r elements and a particular permutation of these r elements, it follows that

$$C(n, r) \cdot r! = P(n, r)$$

Hence $\quad C(n, r) = \dfrac{P(n, r)}{r!} = \dfrac{n!}{r!(n-r)!}$

The notation ^nC_r is also commonly used to denote C (n, r).

SOLVED EXAMPLES

Example 1: In how many ways can 25 late admitted students be assigned to three practical batches if the first batch can accommodate 10 students, the second 8 and third only 7?

Solution: The first batch can be assigned 10 students in C (25, 10) ways, then the second batch can be assigned 8 students in C(15, 8) ways, and the third batch can be assigned C (7, 7) = 1 way. Therefore, by the product rule (similar to that of permutations), the total number of ways of assigning the students is C (25, 10). C (15, 8) = $\dfrac{25!}{15!\,10!} \cdot \dfrac{15!}{7!\,8!}$.

Example 2: A and B are members of a club with a membership of 30. In how many ways can a committee of 10 be formed if

   (i)   A must be included in the committee?

   (ii)   A or B should be included but not both?

Solution: (i) Since A's choice is fixed, the remaining 9 members can be chosen in C (29, 9) ways.

   (ii) Since A's choice precludes the selection of B, the remaining 9 members can be chosen in C (28, 9) ways. Similarly if B is included, A should be excluded, again the number of ways to choose the remaining 9 members is C (28, 9). Hence by the rule of sum (similar to that of permutations), the number of ways to select a committee of 10 that includes A or B but not both is 2 C (28, 9).

Note that the rule of sum is based on the inclusion-exclusion principle of sets.

Example 3: A die is rolled 6 times and the sequence of faces is noted. In how many sequences does the face "5" appear an even number of times? Also find the number of sequences in which "5" appears exactly twice or the face "3" appears exactly 4 times.

Solution: There are 6 choices for each face and since the die is rolled 6 times, there are 6^6 possible sequences, each of length 6. For the face "5" to appear an even number of times, we have to find the number of times 5 does not appear, appears twice, four times or 6 times. The number of sequences in which 5 does not appear is $C(6, 0) \, 5^6$ since all the six positions in the sequence can be occupied by the remaining 5 numbers, in $5 \times 5 \times 5 \times 5 \times 5 \times 5 = 5^6$ ways. Similarly, if it has appear twice it can occupy any of the 6 positions in $C(6, 2)$ ways and the remaining 4 slots can be filled by any of the remaining numbers in $5 \times 5 \times 5 \times 5 = 5^4$ ways. Thus the number of sequences in which the face "5" appears an even number of times is $C(6, 0) \, 5^6 + C(6, 2) \, 5^4 + C(6, 4) \, 5^2 + C(6, 6) \, 5^0$.

The number of sequences in which "5" appears exactly twice is $C(6, 2) \, 5^4$. The number of sequences in which the "3" appears exactly 4 times is $C(6, 4) \, 5^2$. The common case to both the experiments, when "5" appears twice and "3" appears 4 times is $C(6, 2)$ ways. Hence by the mutual inclusion – exclusion principle for cardinalities of two sets, we have

$C(6, 2) \, 5^4 + C(6, 4) \, 5^2 - C(6, 2)$ sequences in which "5" appears exactly twice or "3" appears exactly 4 times.

Example 4: A fair coin is tossed 5 times. Find the number of sequences in which the head 'H' appears at the most 3 times.

Solution: Since the coin is tossed 5 times, we have a sequence of 5 slots to be filled either by 'H' or 'T' (eg. HTTTT or HHHHH). The number of sequences in which no head appears is $C(5, 0) = 1$. The number of sequences in which 1 head appears is $C(5, 1)$, 2 heads appear is $C(5, 2)$ and 3 heads appear is $C(5, 3)$. Since these are mutually exclusive cases, the total number of sequences in which H appears at the most 3 times is $C(5, 0) + C(5, 1) + C(5, 2) + C(5, 3) = 26$.

Example 5: Mathematics students have to attempt six out of ten questions in an examination in any order. How many choices have they? How many choices do they have if they must answer at least three out of the first five?

Solution: Since out of 10 distinct objects, we have to choose any six, the total number of selections is $C(10, 6) = 210$. For the second part we have three possibilities; one can answer three out of the first five and three out of the second five, or four out of the first five and two out of the second five, or five out of the first five and one out of the second five. Hence the total number of selections is: $C(5, 3) \, C(5, 3) + C(5, 4) \, C(5, 2) + C(5, 5) \, C(5, 1) = 100 + 50 + 5 = 155$.

Example 6: There are 10 points in a plane of which 4 are collinear. Find the number of triangles that can be formed with vertices at these points.

Solution: Since 4 points are collinear, it means that the remaining 6 points are non-collinear. These 6 points among themselves can form $C(6, 3) = 20$ triangles. Taking any two collinear points and one non-collinear point, we can form one triangle. Similarly, taking any two non-collinear points and any one of the collinear points, we can form another triangle. Hence taking the combination of collinear and non-collinear points, we can form

C (4, 2) · C (6, 1) + C (4, 1) C (6, 2) = 36 + 60 = 96 triangles. Hence the total number of triangles thus formed is 20 + 96 = 116 triangles.

Example 7: If no three diagonals of a convex decagon meet at the same point inside the decagon, into how many line segments are the diagonals divided by their intersections?

Solution: A decagon is a polygon with 10 sides. Since any two vertices of a decagon are joined either by a side or a diagonal, the total number of diagonals = C(10, 2) – 10 = 35. Since for every four vertices, there corresponds exactly one intersection of the diagonals, there are a total of C(10, 4) = 210 intersections between the diagonals. These intersections will give rise to 2 × 210 line segments. A diagonal itself can be considered as a line segment divided by its own intersection. Hence the total number of required line segments is 35 + 2 × 210 = 455.

Quite often we deal with problems on counting, where one has to make r-selections from n-types of objects with **repetitions** freely allowed. This problem can also be described in the following way, using the analogy of identical objects and distinct boxes.

In how many ways is it possible to distribute r identical objects in n distinct boxes, with no restriction put on the number of objects, a box may contain?

Problems of this nature are quite common place. Consider a few examples:

1. In how many ways is it possible to distribute 10 apples among 4 children?
2. In how many ways can 5 balls be selected from 8 identical red balls and 8 identical white balls?

In such problems what we are interested in, is the number of items to be selected and not which ones of them are selected.

To derive a formula for this type of distribution, we adopt the following approach, although there are other ways to solve the problem. Let us represent the r items by r circles and the distribution of r items into n distinct boxes by a sequence of r circles and n – 1 slashes. The slashes indicate the distribution of the items. For example, for n = 4, r = 8, consider the distribution represented by

$$00 / 00 / 0 / 000$$

This figure indicates that the first box receives two items, the second also two, the third one item and the last three items.

Next, consider the figure

$$000 / / 0000 / 0$$

This indicates that the first box receives three items, the second none, the third four and the last one.

In this manner, we can obtain any distribution by moving the three slashes to occupy any of the 8 + 4 – 1 = 11 positions.

Hence in the general case, the n – 1 slashes should occupy any of the r + n – 1 = n + r – 1 positions.

Hence the total number of ways to do this is C (n + r – 1, n – 1).

Example 8: In how many ways can one distribute 10 apples among 4 children?

Solution: Consider the apples as identical objects and let the children correspond to distinct boxes. The problem can then be considered as finding the number of ways to distribute 10 identical objects in 4 distinct boxes. This can be done in C (13, 3) = 286.

Example 9: In how many ways can 5 balls be selected from 8 identical red balls and 8 identical white balls?

Solution: The problem is that of distributing 5 identical objects in two distinct boxes, corresponding to their colours. Since we are required to select 5 objects from two types of objects, one must assume that there are at least 5 objects of each type, which is the case in this problem. Taking n = 2, r = 5, the number of ways to make the required selection is C (6, 1) = 6.

Example 10: Ten balls are picked from a pile of red, blue and white balls. Find how many such selections contain less than 5 red balls.

Solution: The number of ways to select 10 balls from a pile of red, blue and white balls is equivalent to distributing 10 identical objects into 3 distinct boxes. Hence there are

C (10 + 3 – 1, 3 – 1) = C (12, 2) = 66 ways of selection.

The number of ways to select 5 red balls is C (5 + 3 – 1, 2) = 21. Hence the number of ways to select 10 balls from a pile of red, blue and white balls, so that each selection contains less than 5 red balls is 66 – 21 = 45.

Example 11: How many non-negative integer solutions are there in the equation

x + y + z + u + v = 10,000?

Solution: The problem is that of distributing 10,000 identical objects in 5 distinct boxes, where there is no restriction on the number of objects, the box may contain.

Hence putting n = 5, r = 10,000 in the formula, C (n + r – 1, n – 1), we have C (10004, 4) = 417.0834792 × 10^{12} solutions.

Example 12: Find the number of ways a person can distribute Rs. 601 as pocket money to his three sons, so that no son should receive more than the combined total of the other two. (Assume no fraction of a rupee is allowed).

Solution: First without applying the restriction, the number of ways to distribute Rs. 601 among his three sons is C (601 + 3 – 1, 2) = C (603, 2).

Let the sons receive x, y, z rupees respectively. Suppose the first son receives more than the combined total of the other two it will follow that x + y + z = 601 means 2 (y + z) < 601 which means that y + z = 300, in which case x must be 301 at least. Hence the total number of ways in which the first son will receive more money than the combined total of the other two is C (300 + 3 – 1, 2) = C (302, 2).

The same result is applicable when the second son receives more than the combined total of the first and third sons or when the third son receives more than the combined total of the first and second.

Hence the number of ways so that no son receives more than the combined total of the other two is C (603, 2) – 3 C (302, 2)

$$= \frac{603 \times 602}{2} - 3\left(\frac{302 \times 301}{2}\right)$$

$$= 181503 - 136353$$

$$= 45150$$

Example 13: In how many ways can 15 different books be distributed among three students A, B, C so that A and B together receive twice as many books as C?

Solution: Let x, y, z denote the number of books that A, B, C receive such that

$$x + y + z = 15 \quad \text{and} \quad x + y = 2z$$

Hence z = 5 which means that C receives 5 books.

Hence C can receive the number of books in one way only. Now since z = 5, we have x + y = 10. We have to find all non-negative integer solutions to this equation. The number of ways in which the solutions are possible is

C (n + r – 1, n – 1) = C (2 + 10 – 1, 2 – 1) = C (11, 1) = 11.

Hence there are 11 ways in which the distribution can be done.

Example 14: Determine the number of ways to place 2t + 1 indistinguishable balls in three distinct boxes to that any two boxes together will contain more balls than the other one.

Solution: We shall first determine the number of ways in which the first box will contain more balls than the second and third considered together. For this, since 2t + 1 = t + 1 + t, place t + 1 balls in the first box and then the remaining t balls in the three boxes arbitrarily.

The total number of ways in which this can be done is C (3 + t – 1, t) = C (2 + t, t) (use the formula C (n + r – 1, r), where n = 3, r = t).

The same applies to the case when the second box contains more balls than the first and third, or when the third box contains more balls than the first and second. The total number of ways to place 2t + 1 balls in 3 boxes without any constraint is

C (3 + 2t + 1 – 1, 2t + 1) = C (2t + 3, 2t + 1)

Hence the total number of ways to place 2t + 1 balls in 3 boxes so that any two boxes together will contain more balls than the third is

$$C(2t+3, 2t+1) - 3C(t+2, t) = \frac{(2t+3)!}{2!(2t+1)!} - 3\frac{(t+2)!}{2!\, t!}$$

$$= \frac{(2t+3)(2t+2)}{2} - \frac{3(t+2)(t+1)}{2}$$

$$= \frac{(t+1)}{2}\, 4t + 6 - 3t - 6 = \frac{t(t+1)}{2}$$

3.1.3 Generation of Permutations and Combinations

Procedure to generate n ! permutations: An important but interesting problem in combinatorics is to find a systematic procedure for generating all the n! permutations of a set of n distinct elements, with no omissions or repetitions. In order to ensure that all the n ! permutations are indeed generated or that there is no repetition, some kind of hierarchy or ordering needs to be introduced on the permutations. One natural way to do so is to adopt the lexicographic order, which we shall now discuss.

Let $\{a_1, a_2, ..., a_n\}$ be a set of n distinct positive integers to be permuted. For two permutations $<a_1, a_2, ..., a_n>$ and $<b_1, b_2, ..., b_n>$ we shall say $<a_1, a_2, ... a_n>$ comes before $<b_1, b_2, ... b_n>$ in the lexicographic order if

(i) for some m, $1 \le m < n$.
$a_1 = b_1, a_2 = b_2, ..., a_{m-1} = b_{m-1}$,

(ii) $a_m < b_m$.

For example, $<1\ 3\ 4\ 2\ 5>$ comes before $<1\ 3\ 5\ 4\ 2>$, where m = 3. On the other hand, the permutation $<2\ 3\ 6\ 4\ 5>$ comes after $<2\ 3\ 5\ 4\ 6>$. Under this ordering a permutation $<b_1, b_2, ..., b_n>$ will immediately succeed $< a_1, a_2, ... a_n >$ if

(i) $a_i = b_i$ for $1 \le i \le m - 1$ and $a_m < b_m$ for the **largest possible m**
(ii) b_m is the smallest element from $\{a_{m+1}, a_{m+2}, ..., a_n\}$ that is larger than a_m.
(iii) $b_{m+1} < b_{m+2} < ... < b_m$.

Consider for example, the permutation $<1\ 2\ 3\ 4\ 5>$. By conditions (i) and (ii), m is the largest possible value for which $a_m < a_{m+1}$. In this case, obviously, m = 4, so that the permutation immediately following $<1\ 2\ 3\ 4\ 5>$ is $<1\ 2\ 3\ 5\ 4>$. Next for the permutation $<1\ 2\ 3\ 5\ 4>$, m = 3. Hence by condition (ii), $b_3 = 4$ and by condition (iii), $b_4 = 3$ and $b_5 = 5$. Hence $<1\ 2\ 4\ 3\ 5 >$ is the permutation, which comes immediately after $<1\ 2\ 3\ 5\ 4>$.

In this manner, all the 5 ! permutations of $< 1\ 2\ 3\ 4\ 5 >$ will be generated and order in which they appear, will be as follows:

$<1\ 2\ 4\ 3\ 5> \to <1\ 2\ 3\ 5\ 4> \to <1\ 2\ 4\ 3\ 5> \to <1\ 2\ 4\ 5\ 3> \to$
$<1\ 2\ 5\ 3\ 4> \to <1\ 2\ 5\ 4\ 3> \to <1\ 3\ 2\ 4\ 5> \to <1\ 3\ 2\ 5\ 4> \to ... \to$.

The procedure followed above can be succinctly stated in the following steps:

1. Examine the permutation $<a_1\ a_2\ ...\ a_n>$ element by element from right to left and let a_m be the right most element such that $a_m < a_{m+1}$ (this determines the value of m).
2. Next examine the permutation again, for the right most element such that $a_m < a_k$.
3. Interchange a_m and a_k.
4. Interchange a_{m+1} and a_n, a_{m+2} and a_{n-1}, a_{m+3} and a_{n-2}, and so on.

For example, consider $<1\ 2\ 5\ 4\ 3>$. Here m = 2 and k = 5. Hence interchange a_2 and a_5, i.e. 2 and 5. Hence $<1\ 2\ 5\ 4\ 3>$ becomes $<1\ 3\ 5\ 4\ 2>$. Next interchange a_3 and a_5. Hence we obtain $<1\ 3\ 2\ 4\ 5>$, which is the immediate successor to $<1\ 2\ 5\ 4\ 3>$.

Alternative Method:

In this method, we generate all the n! permutations of {1, 2, ..., n} by successively generating all the permutations of {1}, {1, 2}, {1, 2, 3}, ... and so on up to {1, 2, ... n – 1}. Let us see, how this is done. Beginning with <1>, we obtain the permutations <1 2> and <2 1> placing 2 on either side of 1. Next, in the permutation <1 2>, we place 3 at the extreme ends and between 1 and 2 to obtain the permutations <1 2 3>, <1 3 2> and <3 2 1>. Similarly from <2 1> we obtain <2 1 3>, <2 3 1>, <3 2 1>. Proceeding in this manner, we obtain all permutations of <1, 2, 3, ... n – 1> and then inserting n at both the ends and in then n – 2 gaps in between. We obtain all the n! permutations of {1, 2, 3, ... n}.

For example, suppose we wish to generate all the 24 permutations of {1, 2, 3, 4}. Then the sequential process, by which the permutations are generated is shown below:

<1> ;
<1 2>, <2 1> ;
<1 2 3>, <1 3 2>, <3 1 2>, <2 1 3>, <2 3 1>, <3 2 1> ;
<1 2 3 4>, <1 2 4 3>, <1 4 2 3>, <4 1 2 3> ;
<1 3 2 4>, <1 3 4 2>, <1 4 3 2>, <4 1 3 2> ;
<3 1 2 4 >, <3 1 4 2>, <3 4 1 2>, <4 3 1 2> ;
<2 1 3 4>, <2 1 4 3>, <2 4 1 3>, <4 2 1 3> ;
<2 3 1 4>, <2 3 4 1>, <2 4 3 1>, <4 2 3 1> ;
<3 2 1 4>, <3 2 4 1>, <3 4 2 1>, <4 3 2 1>.

Procedure to Generate Subsets of {1, 2, 3, ... n}.

Let $\{a_1, a_2, ..., a_k\}$ be a subset of size k of {1, 2, ..., n}, with $a_1 < a_2 < ... < a_k$.

Then the maximum possible value of a_{k-1} is n – 1 and so on. In general, the maximum possible value of a_i is n – k + i.

Consider the subset {1, 2, ..., k–1, k}. If k ≠ n, its maximum possible value, increase k by 1, so that the next subset {1, 2, ..., k – 1, k + 1} is generated. We continue this till the subset {1, 2, ..., k – 1, n} is reached.

Next repeat the procedure for k – 1. If k – 1 is not equal to its maximum value n – 1, increase it by 1 and let k take all large values. Continue this procedure with k – 1, till n – 1 is reached.

Then move to k – 2 and repeat the steps. In this manner, moving from right to left, we finally reach the a_n element a_j such that a_j can be increased to a_j + 1, but no a_i with i > j can be increased, which means that at some stage, a_i is equal to its maximum value n – k + i.

The procedure terminates when a_1 reaches its maximum value.

Let us apply this procedure to the following example.

Example: Generate all the subsets of size 4 of {1, 2, 3, 4, 5, 6}.

Solution: Begin with the subset {1, 2, 3, 4}. Now for any subset $\{a_1, a_2, a_3, a_4\}$ with $a_1 < a_2 < a_3 < a_4$, maximum possible value of a_4 is 6, of a_3 is 5, of a_2 is 4 and of a_1 is 3.

Hence increasing 4 by 1, we obtain the subset {1, 2, 3, 5}. Since a_4 has not still reached its maximum value, increasing 5 by 1, we obtain {1, 2, 3, 6}. We next move to the element 3 and repeat the procedure for 3 till 3 as a_3 reaches its maximum value 5, with the last element taking large values till it also reaches its maximum value. This gives us the subsets {1, 2, 4, 5}, {1, 2, 4, 6} and {1, 2, 5, 6}.

In this manner, we obtain the following 15 subsets:
{1, 2, 3, 4}, {1, 2, 3, 5}, {1, 2, 3, 6}, {1, 2, 4, 5}, {1, 2, 4, 6}, {1, 2, 5, 6}, {1, 3, 4, 5}, {1, 3, 4, 6}, {1, 3, 5, 6}, {1, 4, 5, 6}, {2, 3, 4, 5}, {2, 3, 4, 6}, {2, 3, 5, 6}, {2, 4, 5, 6}, {3, 4, 5, 6}.

SOLVED EXAMPLES

Example 1: How may four-digit numbers are there formed from the digits 1, 2, 3, 4, 5 (with possible repetition) that are divisible by 4?

Solution: A number is divisible by 4 if and only if the number formed by its two right most digits is divisible by 4. These numbers are 12, 32, 52, 24, 44. Numbers whose two right most digits are 12 are 5×5 numbers. Similarly in the other cases too, we have 5^2 numbers, whose last two digits are 32, 52, 24 or 44 respectively. Hence, in all there are $5^2 + 5^2 + 5^2 + 5^2 + 5^2 = 5^3$ numbers which are divisible by 4.

Example 2: How many sequences of length 5 can be formed using the digits 0, 1, 2, ..., 9 with the property that exactly two of the digits appear, (e.g. 03330)?

Solution: First we can select two digits from the ten digits in $^{10}C_2$ ways. Using these digits, we can form sequences of length 5 in $2 \times 2 \times 2 \times 2 \times 2$ ways. However, since the condition is that both the digits should appear, we should omit the two sequences in which exactly one digit appears. For example, if we choose 0 and 1, we should omit the sequences 00000 and 11111. Hence, such sequences are $2^5 - 2$ for each pair of digits chosen.

Hence, in all there are

$$^{10}C_2 (2^5 - 2) = \frac{10 \times 9 \times 30}{2} = 1350 \text{ sequences.}$$

Example 3: How many ways are there to pick 2 different cards from a standard 52-card deck such that

(i) the first is an ace and the second card is not a queen?

(ii) the first card is a space and the second card is not a queen?

Assume that the cards are not replaced.

Solution: (i) The first card, being an ace, can be chosen in 4 ways. Since we are not replacing the card and no queen should be chosen, we have only $52 - 1 - 4 = 47$ ways to choose the second card. Hence there are $3 \times 47 = 188$ ways to choose the pair.

(ii) The first card being a spade, there are 13 possibilities. If the first card happens to be a queen of spaces, for the second card there are 48 choices. If the first card is not a queen of spades, then for the second card there are 48 choices. If the first card is not a queen of spades, then for the second card there are $52 - 4 - 1 = 47$ choices; in this case the first card already having been chosen in 12 ways. Hence the total number of choices = $(1 \times 48) + (12 \times 47) = 612$.

Example 4: There are 10 different people at a party. How many ways are there to pair them of into a collection of 5 pairings?

Solution: Let A be an arbitrary person in the party; then he can be paired with the remaining 9 persons in 9 ways. Let {A, B} be one such pair. Then the third person C has 7 choices. In this manner we have $9 \times 7 \times 5 \times 3 \times 1 = 945$ ways of pairing.

Example 5: How many arrangements of the word INSTRUCTOR are there in which there are exactly two consonants between successive pairs of vowels?

Solution: There are 3 vowels I, O, U and 7 consonants in the word. The 3 vowels can rearrange themselves in 3! ways. Let I xx O xx U be one such arrangement in which 2 consonants are between the successive pairs of vowels. These pairs of consonants can be selected in $^7C_2 \times {^5C_2}$ ways, and then be arranged between I, O and O, U in 2 ways. The remaining 3 consonants can be regrouped in 3! ways and have 2 positions to occupy, either before I or after U. Hence, in all, there are

$3! \times {^7C_2} \times {^5C_2} \times 2 \times 3! \times 2 = 30,240$ ways of arrangement.

Example 6: A box contains 6 white balls and 5 black balls. Find the number of ways, 4 balls can be drawn from the box if

(i) two must be white

(ii) all of them must have the same colour.

Solution: (i) The two white balls can be selected in C (6, 2) ways. The remaining 2 balls can be selected in C (9, 2) ways. Hence the number of ways to make the necessary selection is
C (6, 2) · C (9, 2) = 540 ways.

(ii) All of them must have the same colour implies that the balls must be all white or all black. The number of ways in which exactly one of these combinations can be done is
C (6, 4) + C (5, 4) = 15 + 5 = 20.

Example 7: Suppose a valid computer password consists of 4 characters, the first of which is a letter chosen from the set {A, B, C, ... Z} and remaining 3 are chosen from English alphabets or digits from 0 to 9. How many passwords are there?

Solution: The first character has 26 choices. Each of the remaining characters have 26 + 10 = 36 choices. Hence the total number of passwords that are possible is 26×36^3.

Example 8: Consider all positive integers with three different digits.

(i) How many numbers are greater than 700?

(ii) How many numbers are even?

(iii) How many numbers are odd?

(iv) How many numbers are divisible by five?

Solution: (i) The first digit of a number greater than 700 is either 7, 8 or 9, hence can be chosen in three ways. The second digit of such a number will be any number from 0 to 9 but excluding the one which occurs as the first digit, hence can be chosen in 9 ways. Similarly the third digit will have 8 choices. Hence, the total number of numbers with three different digits and greater than 700 is $3 \times 9 \times 8 = 216$.

(ii) The last digit of an even number is either 0, 2, 4, 6 or 8. If the last digit is 0, number of such even numbers is $9 \times 8 = 72$. If the last digit is 2, 4, 6, or 8, the number of even numbers is $8 \times 8 \times 4 = 256$. Hence, there will be in all $72 + 256 = 328$ even numbers.

(iii) The last digit on an odd number is 1, 3, 5 or 9. For each such choice, the first digit can be chosen in 8 ways, as 0 has to be excluded, the second digit also in 8 ways, as 0 can be included. Hence, there will be $8 \times 8 \times 5 = 320$ odd numbers.

(iv) For a number to be divisible by 5, the last digit is 0 or 5 (with non-repeated digits). Total number of numbers (with non-repeated digits) with last digit 0 is $8 \times 9 = 72$. If the last digit is 5, total number of such numbers is $8 \times 8 = 64$. Hence, total number of numbers, which are divisible by 5 is $72 + 64 = 136$.

Example 9: Find the number of ways to paint 12 offices so that 3 of them will be green, 2 of them will be pink, 2 of them will be yellow and the remaining white. Also give the generalised formula.

Solution: The 12 offices can be painted in 12 ! ways, in general. However, since 3 of them should be green, 2 of them pink, 2 of them yellow and 5 white, the number of ways is

$$\frac{12!}{3!2!2!5!}$$

Generalised formula: $\dfrac{P(n, r)}{r_1! \, r_2! \, \ldots \, r_k!}$

where, $r = r_1 + r_2 + \ldots + r_k$

Example 10: From 12 mathematicians and 9 physicists, a committee of 8 is to be formed including two physicists. In how many ways can the committee be chosen so as to give majority of mathematicians?

(i) 2 physicists and 6 mathematicians.
(ii) 3 physicists and 5 mathematicians.

Solution : (i) The two physicists can be chosen in $^9C_2$ ways and 6 mathematicians in $^{12}C_6$ ways.

Hence the number of ways of forming the committee is $^9C_2 \cdot {}^{12}C_6 = 33264$ ways.

(ii) A committee of 3 physicists and 5 mathematicians can be chosen in

$^9C_3 \cdot {}^{12}C_5 = 66528$ ways.

Hence, the number of ways in which the committee can be chosen so as to give majority of mathematicians is $^9C_2 \cdot {}^{12}C_6 + {}^9C_3 \cdot {}^{12}C_5$ ways.

Example 11: There are 50 students in each of the junior and the senior classes. Each class has 25 male and 25 female students. In how many ways can eight representatives be selected so that there are four females and three juniors?

Solution: From the phrasing of the problem it is to be assumed that the four females belong to the senior class and so is the other 8th representative, obviously a male. The number of ways to select the four females from the senior class is C (25, 4). The number of ways to select the single male representative from the senior class is C (25, 1). Since the number of female students is specified in the group, it follows that the juniors are the male students from the junior class. Hence the number of ways in which the necessary selection can be made is C (25, 4) · C (25, 1) · C (25, 3).

Example 12: In how many ways can the letters in the English alphabet be arranged so that there are exactly seven letters between the letters a and b?

Solution: We have to permute the remaining 24 letters to obtain the desired result. Out of these 24 letters, 7 letters can be filled between a and b in P (24, 7) ways; also allowing for interchange between a and b, there are 2.P (24, 7) strings of 9 letters, each beginning with a and ending with b or vice-versa. The remaining 26 – 9 = 17 letters, together with the string form a group of 18 elements and hence be permuted in 18! ways. Hence, there are in all 2·P (24, 7) · 18 ! arrangements of the letters of the desired type.

Example 13: There are ten political leaders gathered at a party and two are known to be staunch opponents. In how many ways can they be seated in a row so that these two persons do not sit next to each other?

Solution: Let us name the two quarrelling leaders as A and B. The total number of ways to seat 10 persons is 10 !. Let us count the number of ways in which A and B can be seated together. We have to consider two types of arrangements where the order is AB (i.e. B is seated immediately after A) and BA (where B is seated before A). The number of ways for each such arrangement will however be the same. Treating AB as a single entity, the number of ways to seat the ten guests is (10 – 1) ! = 9 !. The other arrangement, involving BA, also has 9 ! ways. Hence A and B can be seated together in 2 × 9 ! ways. Hence the number of ways in which they are not seated next to each other is 10 ! – (2 × 9 !).

Example 14: In how many ways can 5 girls and 7 boys are seated in a row so that no two girls are seated next to each other?

Solution: First let the boys be seated, which can be done in 7 ! ways. Now, for any such arrangement there will be (7 – 1) = 6 gaps between adjacent pairs and two vacant spaces at the extreme ends. Hence, there are 6 + 2 = 8 vacant slots, which can be filled by the 5 girls. Since no gap should be assigned to more than one girl, this can be done in P(8, 5) ways. Hence, the total number of ways in which no two girls are seated next to each other is $7! \times \frac{8!}{3!}$ = 338688 × 10².

Example 15: Suppose we print all five digit numbers on slips of paper with one number on each slip. Find how many minimum distinct slips one has to make up for all the five digit numbers.

Solution: Note that there are 10^5 distinct five digit numbers (including the five digit number beginning with 0). Also note that the digits 0, 1, 6, 8 and 9 become 0, 1, 9, 8 and 6 when they are read upside down. Hence for numbers involving these digits, we can have common slip. For example, 1689 and 1986 can share the same slip, if the slips are read right side up or upside down. There are in all $5 \times 5 \times 5 \times 5 \times 5 = 5^5$ such numbers. There are some numbers among these which read the same whether inverted or not. For example, 16891, 86198, 18081 are such numbers. In all these numbers, the centre digit is either 0, 1 or 8. Hence numbers of this type are $3(5^2)$ numbers. Consequently there are $5^5 - 3(5^2)$ numbers that can be read right side up or upside down, but read differently. Hence these numbers can be divided into pairs that can share the same slip. Hence the total number of slips required is $\left[10^5 - \dfrac{5^5 - 3(5^2)}{2} \right]$.

Example 16: Five boys and five girls are to be seated in a row. In how many ways can they be seated if
   (i)   all boys must be seated in the five left-most seats?
   (ii)   no two boys can be seated together?
   (iii)   John and Mary must be seated together?

Solution: (i) Since the boys must be seated in the five left most seats, the girls must be seated in the right most seats. The boys can be seated in 5 ! ways and so are the girls. Hence the total number of ways in which they can be seated in this manner is 5 ! 5 !.

(ii) First let the girls be seated. This arrangement can be done in 5 ! ways. Now for each such seating arrangement there will be 5 – 1 = 4 gaps between any adjacent pair of girls, in addition to the 2 gaps at the extreme ends. Hence the seating arrangement of the boys should be such that these 6 gaps have to be filled in 5 ways so that no gap should be assigned to more than one boy. This will be done in P (6, 5) ways. Hence the number of ways of seating the boys, so that no two are seated adjacent is 5 ! P (6, 5) ways = 5 ! 6 ! ways.

(iii) The number of ways in which John and Mary are seated together is $2 \times 9 = 18$ ways. The remaining 8 people can be seated in 8 ! ways. Hence the number of ways in which the boys and girls are seated so that John and Mary are seated together is $8 ! \cdot 18$.

Example 17: In a class of 100 students 40 are boys.
   (i)   In how many ways can a 10 person committee be formed?
   (ii)   Repeat (i) if there must be an equal number of boys and girls in the committee.
   (iii)   Repeat (i) if the committee must consist of either 6 boys and 4 girls or 4 boys and 6 girls.

Solution: (i) A 10 person committee can be formed in C (100, 10) ways.
   (ii)   There should be 5 boys and 5 girls in the committee. This can be done in $C(40, 5) \cdot C(60, 5)$ ways.
   (iii)   The number of ways in which the committee consists of six boys and four girls is $C(40, 6) \cdot C(60, 4)$.

The number of ways in which the committee consists of four boys and six girls is $C(40, 4) \cdot C(60, 6)$.

Hence the number of ways in which the committee consists of either combination is $C(40, 6) \cdot C(60, 4) + C(40, 4) \cdot C(60, 6)$.

Example 18: A student has to answer 10 out of 13 questions in an examination.
  (i)   How many choices he has?
  (ii) How many choices he has if he has to answer the first two questions?
  (iii) How many choices he has if he must answer the first or second but not both?
  (iv) How many choices he has if he must answer exactly three out of first five?
  (v)   How many choices he has if he must answer at least three of the first five?

Solution: (i) C (13, 10) = 286
  (ii) C (11, 8) = 165
  (iii) [C (11, 9) + C (11, 9)] = 2 × 55 = 110
  (iv) C (5, 3) · C (8, 7) = 80
  (v)   C (5, 3) · C (8, 7) + C (5, 4) · C (8, 6) + C (5, 5) · C (8, 5) = 80 + 140 + 56 = 276.

Example 19: Three thieves have stolen a cash of Rs. 10,000, all of which is in the notes of denomination 10. How many ways can they distribute the money amongst themselves?

Solution: The number of notes of 10 are 1000, which can be treated as identical objects to be distributed amongst the three thieves. Hence the problem is equivalent to that of distributing 1000 identical objects in 3 distinct boxes, with no restriction on the number of objects a box may contain. Hence the number of ways is C (n + r − 1, n − 1) where n = 3, r = 1000, i.e. C (1002, 2).

(PROBLEMS ON DERANGEMENT)

Example 20: Five gentlemen attend a party, where before joining the party they leave their overcoats in a checkroom. After the party, the overcoats get mixed up are returned to the gentlemen in a random manner. Find the number of ways in which none receives his own overcoat.

Solution: Let us name the gentlemen as a, b, c, d, e. Let A denote the event a gets back his overcoat, B the event that b gets back his overcoat and similarly C, D, E are defined. Then |A| = |B| = |C| = |D| = |E| = 4 ! = 24. A ∩ B denotes the event that both A and B get their overcoats. Hence |A ∩ B| = 3 ! = 6.

  Similarly, |A ∩ C| = |A ∩ D| = |A ∩ E| = |B ∩ C|
                         = |B ∩ D| = |B ∩ E| = |C ∩ D| = |C ∩ E|
                         = |D ∩ E| = 3 ! = 6.

Similarly taking any three events, say A, B, C |A ∩ B ∩ C| = 2 ! = 2 and there are 10 such sets.

Taking 4 sets at a time, there are 5 such sets whose cardinalities are 1 each.
Finally |A ∩ B ∩ C ∩ D ∩ E| = 1.
Hence by the principle of mutual inclusion-exclusion,

|A ∪ B ∪ C ∪ D ∪ E| = ∑|A| − ∑|A ∩ B| + ∑|A ∩ B ∩ C| − ∑|A ∩ B ∩ C ∩ D| + |A ∩ B ∩ C ∩ D ∩ E|

= (5 × 24) − (10 × 6) + (10 × 2) − 5 + 1
= 120 − 60 + 20 − 4 = 76

Hence the number of ways in which any of the five gentlemen can get back his overcoat is 76. Therefore the number of ways in which no gentlemen gets back his overcoat is
$$5! - 76 = 120 - 76 = 44.$$

Example 21: In how many ways can the 4 walls of a room be painted with 3 colours so that no two adjacent walls have the same colour?

Solution: The number of ways in which 4 walls can be painted with 3 colours is $3^4 = 81$ ways. Label the walls as a, b, c, d in the clockwise manner (or anticlockwise manner). Let A denote the event that walls a and b have the same colour, B the event that walls b and c have the same colour. Similarly C and D are defined. Then $|A| = |B| = |D| = 3^3$. This is explained as follows. For the event A since walls a and b have the same colour, together they have 3 choices. The remaining two walls will have $3 \times 3 = 3^2$ choices.
Similarly $|A \cap B| = |A \cap C| = |A \cap D| = |B \cap C| = |B \cap D| = |C \cap D| = 3^2$
and $|A \cap B \cap C \cap D| = 3$.

Hence the number of ways in which any two adjacent walls will have the same colour is
$|A \cup B \cup C \cup D| = |A| + |B| + |C| - |A \cap B| - |A \cap C| - |A \cap D| - |B \cap C| - |B \cap D| - |C \cap D|$
$+ |A \cap B \cap C| + |A \cap B \cap D| + |A \cap C \cap D| + |B \cap C \cap D| - |A \cap B \cap C \cap D|$
$= 4 \times 3^3 - 6 \times 3^2 + 4 \times 3 - 3$
$= 108 - 54 + 12 - 3 = 63$

Hence the number of ways of painting 4 walls with 3 colours, so that no two adjacent walls have the same colour is $81 - 63 = 18$.

Example 22: A man has 7 relatives, 4 of them are ladies and 3 are gentlemen. His wife has 7 relatives, 3 of them are ladies and 4 are gentlemen. In how many ways can they invite a dinner party of 3 ladies and 3 gentlemen, so that there are 3 of man's relatives and 3 of wife's relatives?

Solution: Let us prepare the box as follows:

M		W	
4L	3G	3L	4G

Since there must be 3 relatives of M and 3 relatives of W, we can form the following combinations.

M	W
3L	3G
2L, 1G	1L, 2G
1L, 2G	2L, 1G
3G	3L

Hence, the total number of ways to invite the guests is
$4C_3 \cdot 4C_3 + 4C_2 \cdot 3C_1 \cdot 3C_1 \, 4C_2 + 4C_1 \, 3C_2 \cdot 3C_2 \cdot 4C_1 + 3C_3 \cdot 3C_3$
$= 16 + 324 + 144 + 1 = 485$

Example 23: (i) In how many ways can 6 men and 5 women be seated in a line so that no two women sit together.

(ii) In how many ways can 6 men and 5 women sit in a line so that women occupy the even places.

Solution: (i) Let the men be first seated which can be done in 6! ways. For each such arrangement, there will be 6 – 1 = 5 gaps between adjacent pairs and two vacant spaces at the extreme ends. These 5 + 2 = 7 slots can be filled by the girls in P (7, 5) ways, as no gap can be filled by more than one girl. Hence the total number of ways is $\frac{6! \, 7!}{2!}$.

(ii) Let the places be numbered 1 to 11, so that the women should occupy the places numbered as 2, 4, 6, 8, 10. This leaves the places numbered as 1, 3, 5, 7, 9 and 11 to be occupied by the men. Hence, the total number of ways to do so is 5! × 6!.

Example 24: A man, a woman, a boy, a girl, a dog and a cat are walking along a long and winding road, one after the other.

(i) In how many ways can this happen?
(ii) In how many ways can this happen if the dog comes first.
(iii) In how many ways can this happen if the dog immediately follows the boy?
(iv) In how many ways can this happen if only dog is in between the man and boy.

Solution: Let M, W, B, G, D, C denote respectively man, woman, boy, girl, dog and cat.

(i) We have 6! permutations of the 6 letters. Hence the number of ways in which they walk in sequence is 6! ways.

(ii) ∴ D must come first, the remaining 5 letters can be permuted in 5! ways. Hence, if dog the dog leads the sequence, the total number of ways is 5!.

(iii) We must have the combination BD in any arrangement of the 6 letters. Hence, this can be done in 5 × 4! = 5! ways, since the block BD can occupy any of the 5 places as follows:

… M … W … G … C … for one arrangement of the remaining letters.

(iv) If only D is between the man and boy, we must have MDB or BDM in any arrangement. The remaining 3 letters have in all 3! permutations.

Hence, the required number of ways is 2 × 4 × 3! = 2 × 4! ways.

Example 25: A family of 4 brothers and 3 sisters is to be arranged in a row of a photograph. In how many ways can they be seated if all sisters are together.

Solution: Consider all the sisters as one single object and the brothers as 4 distinct objects. Then the 5 objects can be permuted in 5! ways. The three sisters among themselves, can be seated in 3! ways.

Hence, the total number of ways, all can be seated is 3! 5! ways.

Example 26: In how many ways can 10 examination papers be arranged so that the best and worst are never together.

Solution: Total number of ways of arranging the 10 papers is 10!.

The number of ways in which the best worst papers are consecutive is 2! 9! ways.

Hence, total number of ways in which the ten papers can be arranged so that the best and worst papers are never together is 10! − 2! 9! = 8.9! ways.

Example 27: A menu card in a restaurant displays four soups, five main courses, three desserts and five beverages. How many different menus can a customer select if:

(i) He selects one item from each group without omission.

(ii) He chooses to omit the beverages, but selects one each from the other groups.

(iii) He chooses to omit he desserts, but decides to take a beverage and one item each from the remaining groups.

Solution: (i) Selecting one item from each group without omission can be done in $^4C_1$, $^5C_1$ $^3C_1$ $^5C_1$ ways.

(ii) Omitting beverages, selection can be done in $^4C_1$ $^5C_1$ $^3C_1$ ways.

(iii) Omitting the desserts, selection can be made in $^4C_1$ $^5C_1$ $^5C_1$ ways.

Example 28: How many automobile license plates can be made if each plate consists of different letters followed by three different digits. Solve the problem if first digit cannot be 0.

Solution: It is not mentioned in the problem how many different letters, the license plate must contain, whether 2 letters followed by 3 digits or 3 letters followed by 3 digits. Suppose we assume that the plate contains 2 alphabets followed by 3 digits, then the number of ways $26 \times 25 \times 9 \times 9 \times 8$.

On the other hand if the plate contains 3 alphabets followed by 3 digits, the number of ways is $26 \times 25 \times 24 \times 9 \times 9 \times 8$.

EXERCISE 3.1

1. How many permutations are there of the 26 letters of the alphabet in which the 5 vowels are in consecutive places?   **(Ans.** $5! \times 22!$ **)**

2. How many different necklaces can be designed from 6 different colours, using one bead of each colour?   **(Ans.** 60**)**

3. A car registration number is to consist of 2 letters followed by a 4 digit number. How many car numbers are possible?   **(Ans.** $26^2 \cdot (10^4 - 1)$**)**

4. How many numbers between 1000 and 3000 can be formed from the digits 1, 2, 3, 4, 5 if repetition of digits is (i) allowed (ii) not allowed?   **(Ans.** (i) 2×5^3, (ii) $2 \times 4!$ **)**

5. In how many ways can a 5-letter word be formed from an alphabet of 26 letters if repetitions are (i) allowed, (ii) not allowed?   **(Ans.** (i) 26^5, (ii) $\dfrac{26!}{21!}$ **)**

6. How many different arrangements of the letters in the word MONDAY can be formed if the vowels must be kept next to each other?   **(Ans.** 240**)**

7. In how many ways can the letters in the word COMMITTEE be rearranged?   **(Ans.** 45360**)**

8. The names of the 12 months of the year are listed in random order. Given that May and June are not next to each other, how many possible lists are there?

(**Ans.** $10 \times 11!$)

9. An eight member committee is to be formed from a group of 10 men and 15 women. In how many ways can the committee be chosen if –
   (i) the committee must contain 4 men and 4 women?
   (ii) there must be more men than women?
   (iii) there must be at least two men? (**Ans.** (i) $C(10, 4) \cdot C(15, 4)$,
   (ii) $C(10, 5) \cdot C(15, 3) + C(1, 6) \cdot C(15, 2) + C(10, 7) \cdot C(15, 1) + C(10, 8)$
   (iii) $C(25, 8) - C(15, 8) - 10C(15, 7)$)

10. A team of 11 players is to be chosen from a pool of 15. How many team selections are possible? How many if one of the 15 has already been appointed captain and must play?

(**Ans.** $C(15, 11), C(14, 10)$)

11. A man plans to visit one friend on each evening of a given week. There are 12 friends whom he would like to visit. In how many ways can he plan his week if
    (i) he can visit a friend more than once?
    (ii) he will not visit a friend more than once? (**Ans.** (i) 12^7, (ii) $\dfrac{12!}{5!}$)

12. 6 men are to be seated round a circular table. How many ways are there of achieving this? How many if A refuses to sit beside B? (**Ans.** (i) 120, (ii) 72)

13. 16 students, 4 each from FE, SE, TE and BE have to select 6 of their number to form a subcommittee. How many selections can be made if
    (i) each class is represented?
    (ii) no class can have more than two representatives?

(**Ans.** (i) $4^5 + 6^3 \cdot 4^2$ (ii) $4^2 6^3 + 4 \cdot 6^3$)

14. There are 10 different books and 2 copies of each. Find the number of ways in which a selection can be made from them. (**Ans.** $3^{10} - 1$)

15. A palindrome is a word that reads the same forward and backward. How many seven letter palindromes can be made out of the English alphabet? How many 6 letters palindromes? (**Ans.** (i) 26^4, (ii) 26^3)

16. 6 boys and 6 girls are to be seated in a row such that
    (i) All boys sit together and girls sit together.
    (ii) No two girls sit together.
    (iii) Boys and girls sit alternately.
    (iv) The extreme positions are occupied by boys.
    Find the number of ways in each case.

(**Ans.** (i) $2 \times (6!)^2$, (ii) $7!$ (iii) $2(6!)^2$ (iv) $P(6, 2) \times 10!$)

17. From a class of 11 students, what is the number of ways to select a committee of 5 students? Also find the number of ways if
    (i) Class representative should always be included.
    (ii) Last ranker should always be excluded. **(Ans.** $^{11}C_5$, (i) $^{10}C_4$, (ii) $^{10}C_5$)
18. A certain stationary shop has 6 types of ball pens available in 6 different colours. If a student wants to buy one, how many choices does he have? **(Ans. 36)**
19. In how many ways can 7 books be arranged on a shelf so that
    (i) two particular books are together?
    (ii) these two books are not together? **(Ans.** (i) 1440, (ii) 4320)
20. In how many ways can 6 letters be placed in 6 envelopes, if 2 of the letters are too large for one of the envelopes? **(Ans. 480)**
21. If 10 parallel straight lines are intersected by 8 other parallel straight lines, then find the number of different parallelograms so formed. **(Ans. 1260)**
22. 7 people enter the lift. The lift stops only at three floors. At each of the floor, none enters the lift, but at least 1 person leaves the lift. After the three floor stops, the lift is empty. In how many ways can this happen? **(Ans.** $3^7 - 3(2^7 - 1)$)
23. A student wishes to prepare for four subjects during a seven-day period; so that she may be able to devote at least one day for each subject. Find the number of ways in which she can plan her time table. **(Ans.** $4^7 - 4.3^7 + 6.2^7 - 4$)
24. In how many ways can 21 white balls be distributed in three distinct boxes so that any two boxes together contain more balls than the other one? **(Ans. 55)**
25. How many non-negative integer solutions are to the equation?
    (i) $x + y + z = 8$
    (ii) $x + y + z + t = 29$. **(Ans.** (i) 45, (ii) 4960)
26. There are 10 copies of one book and 1 copy each of 10 other books. In how many ways can we select 10 books? **(Ans.** 2^{10})
27. A fair coin is tossed 5 times. Determine how many heads occur exactly 3 times. Determine how many sequences have atmost 4 heads? **(Ans. 10, 31)**
28. Eight students are standing in line for an interview. Find the probability that there are exactly two freshman, two sophomores, two juniors and two seniors in the line.
29. A dice is rolled 6 times and sequence of faces is noted. In how many sequences does the face "5" appear an even number of times. Find the number of sequences in which "5" appears exactly twice or the face "3" appears exactly 4 times.
30. A box contains 6 white balls and 5 black balls. Find the number of ways in which 4 balls can be drawn from the box if:
    (i) Two must be white.
    (ii) All of them must have the same colour.

31. Five boys and five girls are to be seated in a row. In how many ways can they be seated if:
    (i) No two boys can be seated together.
    (ii) John and Mary must be seated together.
32. Find the number of ways that a party of seven persons can arrange themselves in:
    (i) a row of seven chairs.
    (ii) a round a circular table.
33. A women has 11 close friends:
    (i) In how many ways, can she invite five of them to dinner?
    (ii) In how many ways if two of the friends are married and will not attend separately?
    (iii) In how many ways if two of them are not on speaking terms and will not attend together?
34. A pair of fair dice is thrown. Find the probability p that sum is 10 or greater if:
    (i) 5 appears on the first die.
    (ii) 5 appears on at least one die.
35. In how many ways, five boys and five girls are to be seated in a row if:
    (i) All the boys must be seated in five leftmost seat?
    (ii) No two boys can be seated together?
    (iii) John and Mary may be seated together?
36. (i) Find the number m_1 of permutations that can be formed from all the letters of MISSISSIPPI.
    (ii) Find the number m_2 for the above case if words are to begin with an I.
    (iii) Find the number m_3 for the word in (i) if the two P's are to be next to each other.
    (iv) Find the number m_4 for the word in (i) if the four S's are to be next to each other.
37. Suppose repetitions are not permitted, how many four digit numbers can be formed from six digits 1, 2, 3, 5, 7, 8?
    (i) How many of such numbers are less than 4000?
    (ii) How many in (1) are even?
    (iii) How many in (1) are odd?
    (iv) How many in (1) contain both 3 and 5?
    (v) How many in (1) are divisible by 10?
38. A student has to answer 10 out of 13 questions in an examination.
    (i) How many choices he has?
    (ii) How many choices he has if he has to answer the first two questions?
    (iii) How many choices he has if he must answer exactly three out of first five?
    (iv) How many choices he has if he must answer at least three out of first five?

39. (i) Find the number m of permutations that can be formed from all the letters of ELEVEN.
    (ii) Find the number of permutations if word in (1) begins with L.
    (iii) Find the number of permutations if the words are to begin and end with E.
    (iv) Find the number of permutations if the words are to begin with E and end with N.
40. (i) How many distinguishable permutations of the letters in the word "BANANA' are there?
    (ii) Compute number of permutations of the set given: {1, 2, 3, 4, 5}.
    (iii) Find the number of permutations of A taken r at a time:
    A = {a, b, c, d, e, f}, r = 2.
    (iv) In how many ways can six men and six women be seated in a row if any person may sit next to any other.
41. A bit is either 0 or 1: a byte is a sequence of 8 bits. Find:
    (i) The number of bytes that can be formed from 8 bits.
    (ii) The number of bytes than begin with 11 and end with 11.
    (iii) The number of bytes that begin with 11 and do not end with 11.
    (iv) The number of bytes that begin with 11 or end with 11.
42. Five fair coins are tossed and the results are recorded:
    (i) How many different sequences of heads and tails are possible?
    (ii) How many of the sequence in part (i) have exactly one head recorded?
    (iii) How many of the sequences in part (i) have exactly three heads recorded?
43. Find the number of unordered samples of size five (repetition allowed) from the set {a, b, c, d, e, f}
    (i) No further restriction.
    (ii) 'a' occurs at least once.
    (iii) 'a' occurs exactly twice.
44. A computer password consists of a letter of the alphabet followed by 3 or 4 digits. Find:
    (i) The total number of passwords that can be formed.
    (ii) Number of passwords in which no digits repeat.
45. Find the number of permutation of letters a, b, c, d, e, f, g so that neither the pattern 'beg' nor 'cad' appears.
46. Given 6 flags of different colours, how many different signals can be generated, if signal requires the use of two flags, one below the other?
47. In how many ways can three prizes be distributed among 4 boys when:
    (i) No one gets more than one prize.
    (ii) A body can get number of prizes.

48. Find the number of arrangements that can be made out of the letters.
    (i)   ASSASSINATION (ii) GANESHOPURI
49. How many words with or without meanings can be formed using all the letters of the word 'EQUATION', using each letter exactly once.
50. Find the number of ways of arranging the letters of the word. TENNESSEE all at a time (i) if there is no restriction (ii) if the first two letters must be 'E'.
51. Suppose repetitions are permitted:
    (i)   How many ways three digit number can be formed from six digits 2, 3, 4, 5, 7 and 9?
    (ii)   How many of these numbers are less than 400?
    (iii) How many are even?
    (iv)   How many are odd?
    (v)   How many are multiples of 5?
    (vi)   How many are multiples of 10?
52. Out of 4 officers and 10 clerks, a committee of 2 officers and 3 clerks is to be formed. In how many ways can committee be formed if:
    (i)   any officer and any clerk can be included.
    (ii)   a particular clerk must be in the committee,
    (iii) a particular officer cannot be in the committee?
53. 12 persons are made to sit around a table. Find the number of ways they can sit such that 2 specific persons are not together.

3.2 Discrete Probability

In the previous section, we discussed various counting techniques to determine the number of ways in which an event can take place. In this section, we deal with the probability that a particular event shall occur. In daily life, we often come across such questions as "What is the chance of India winning the World Cup?" "What is the chance of the results being declared this week?" In all such problems, we are interested in obtaining a numerical measure of the possibility that a certain event (mostly desirable !) will take place. In other words, the question of finding probability often arises in situations referred to as "random experiments" or "trials". Some familiar examples of random experiments are: tossing one or more coins, rolling a pair of dice, drawing a card from a pack of cards etc. Hence in all problems dealing with probability, we must have a random experiment.

We first define various terms connected with probability theory.

3.2.1 Sample Space

A **sample space** of a random experiment is the set of all possible outcomes of the experiment. A sample space is generally denoted by S. An outcome is then an element of S and is denoted by x. An outcome is also called as a **Sample Point.**

A sample space that has a finite number or a countably infinite number of sample points is called a **Discrete Sample Space.**

We shall restrict our discussion to discrete sample space.

Examples:
(i) Suppose we toss a pair of coins. Let us denote appearance of head by H and tail by T. Then
$$S = \{(T, T), (T, H), (H, T), (H, H)\}$$
The element (T, T) is a sample point of S, and the cardinality of S = 2^2 = 4.

(ii) Suppose a pair of dice is rolled. Then the sample space is the set
$$S = \{(1, 1), (1, 2), ... (1, 6), (2, 1), (2, 2), ... (2, 6), (3, 1), (3, 2), ... (3, 6),$$
$$(4, 1), (4, 2), ... (4, 6), (5, 1), (5, 2), ... (5, 6), (6, 1), (6, 2), ... (6, 6)\}$$
The cardinality of the set S is the sample size which is 6×6 = 36.
An element (outcome) say (3, 4) of S is called as a sample point.

3.2.2 Event

A set of possible outcomes is called as an **event.** An event is a subset of the sample space.

Examples:
(i) Consider the experiment of tossing a pair of coins. The set
$$A = \{(T, H), (H, H), (H, T)\}$$ is an event. This event can also be described by the statement "At least one face is a head."

(ii) Consider the experiment of rolling a pair of dice. Suppose we describe an event by the statement "The sum of numbers recorded is less than 5". Then the event
$$A = \{(1, 1), (1, 2), (1, 3), (2, 1), (2, 2), (3, 1)\}$$

We can therefore describe an event by a set as well as by a statement. The sample space S itself is an event, called as the **certain event.** The empty subset of S is called the **impossible event.**

Since events are sets, we can combine them by applying the set operations of union, intersection and complementation, to form new events. These events are described as follows:

3.2.3 Complement of an Event

If A is an event, its set complement $\bar{A}$ = S – A is the complement event. If event A occurs, the event $\bar{A}$ will not occur and vice versa.

Example: In the experiment on tossing a pair of coins if we describe the event A as "at least one face is a head" the complement event $\bar{A}$ is "none of the faces is a head".

Hence, $\bar{A}$ = {(T, T)}.

3.2.4 Compound Event

> If A and B are two events, then the compound event is A ∪ B which is described as at least one of the events A or B occur.

Example: Consider the experiment of rolling a pair of dice. If two describe the event A as "The sum of numbers recorded is less than or equal to 3" and B as the event "The sum of numbers recorded is 4", the compound event A ∪ B will be described as "The sum of numbers recorded is less than or equal to 4".

Hence, A ∪ B = {(1, 1), (1, 2), (1, 3), (2, 1), (2, 2), (3, 1)}

3.2.5 Product Event

> If A and B are events, the product event is A ∩ B and is described as both events A and B occur.

Example: Consider the experiment of rolling a pair of dice. Suppose A is the event "sum of numbers is even" and B is the event "sum of numbers is a perfect square", then A ∩ B is the event" the sum of numbers is even and a perfect square".

Hence, A ∩ B = {(1, 3), (2, 2), (3, 1)}

3.2.6 Mutually Exclusive Events

> Events A and B are said to be **mutually exclusive** if the occurrence or non-occurrence of A precludes the occurrence or non-occurrence of B. In other words, if A occurs then B does not occur and vice versa. This is equivalent to saying that A ∩ B = ϕ.

Example: Consider the experiment of tossing a coin. Let A be the event "head appears" and B be the event "tail appears". Then A and B are mutually exclusive events.

3.2.7 Independent Events

> Events A and B are said to be **independent** if the occurrence or non-occurrence of one does not affect the occurrence or non-occurrence of the other.

Example: Consider the experiment of tossing a coin twice. In the first toss head or tail may appear, in the second toss also head or tail may appear. The result of the first toss does not affect the result of the second toss. Hence these two events are independent.

The above definitions can be briefly summarized as follows.

Statement corresponding to event	Set notations of event
Event A does not occur	$\bar{A}$
At least one of A or B occur	$A \cup B$
Both events A and B occur	$A \cap B$
Neither events A or B occur	$\overline{A} \cap \overline{B} = \overline{A \cup B}$
Event A occurs or B occurs but not both	$(A \cap \bar{B}) \cup (\bar{A} \cap B) = A \, H \, B$
Events A and B are mutually exclusive	$A \cap B = \phi$
Not more than one event occurs	$\overline{A \cap B} = \bar{A} \cup \bar{B}$

3.2.8 Probability of a Sample Point

Associated with each sample point in a sample space is a real number called as the probability of that sample point. For the sample point x_i, we use the notation $P(x_i)$ to denote its probability. The probabilities associated with the samples must satisfy the following conditions:

The probabilities associated with the samples must satisfy the following conditions:

(i) For each $x_i \in S$, $0 \leq P(x_i) \leq 1$.

(ii) $\sum_{x_i} P(x_i) = 1$.

The probability of a sample is a measure of the likelihood of occurrence of that sample. If two samples are equally likely, their probabilities will be the same. The probability of a sample point is also called as **elementary probability.**

The following examples illustrate some important elementary probabilities.

Examples:

1. Consider the experiment of tossing a coin. Then the sample space S = {H, T}. Since both the sample points are equally likely,

$$P(H) = P(T) = \frac{1}{2}$$

2. Consider the experiment of rolling a die. Then the sample space
$$S = \{1, 2, 3, 4, 5, 6\}.$$
Since all the sample points (outcomes) are equally likely for an unbiased die, for each $x_i \in S$, $P(x_i) = \frac{1}{6}$.

3. Consider the experiment of tossing a coin a couple of times. For convenience, we shall denote any outcome, say (H,T) by HT. The sample space S = {HH, TH, HT, TT}. Since all the outcomes are equally likely it follows that
P(HH) = P(TH) = P(HT) = P(TT) = 1/4.

3.2.9 Probability of an Event

Let A be an event which is finite or countably infinite, i.e. $A = \{x_1, x_2, \ldots x_n\}$ or
$$A = \{x_1, x_2, \ldots x_n, \ldots\}$$
Then probability of A is defined as
$$P(A) = \sum_{x_i \in A} P(x_i),$$
i.e. finite sum or countably infinite sum of elementary probabilities.

SOLVED EXAMPLES

Example 1: Consider the experiment of tossing a coin three times. What is the probability of getting exactly one head?

Solution: Let A denote the event of getting exactly one head.

Then A = {HTT, THT, TTH}

Hence P(A) = P(HTT) + P(THT) + P(TTH)

$$= \frac{1}{2^3} + \frac{1}{2^3} + \frac{1}{2^3} = \frac{3}{8}$$

Example 2: Consider the experiment of tossing a coin indefinitely until a head appears. Describe the sample space. What is the probability that the experiment ends before the 6th toss?

Solution: The sample space
$$S = \{H, TH, TTH, TTTH, \ldots\}.$$

Let A denote the event that the experiment ends before the 6th toss.

Then A = {H, TH, TTH, TTTH, TTTTH}.

Hence $P(A) = \frac{1}{2} + \frac{1}{4} + \frac{1}{8} + \frac{1}{16} + \frac{1}{32}$

$$= \frac{1}{2} \left[\frac{1 - \left(\frac{1}{2}\right)^5}{1 - \frac{1}{2}} \right] = 1 - \frac{1}{32} = \frac{31}{32}$$

Example 3: When a certain defective die is tossed, the numbers from 1 to 6 will appear with the following probabilities:

$$P(1) = \frac{2}{18}, \quad P(2) = \frac{3}{18}, \quad P(3) = \frac{4}{18},$$

$$P(4) = \frac{3}{18}, \quad P(5) = \frac{4}{18}, \quad P(6) = \frac{2}{18}.$$

Find the probability that
(i) an odd number is on top.
(ii) a prime number is on top.
(iii) a number less than 5 is on top.
(iv) a number greater than 3 is on top.

Solution: (i) $\quad A = \{1, 3, 5\}$

$$\therefore \quad P(A) = P(1) + P(3) + P(5) = \frac{2}{18} + \frac{4}{18} + \frac{4}{18} = \frac{10}{18} = \frac{5}{9}$$

(ii) $\quad A = \{2, 3, 5\}$

$$\therefore \quad P(A) = P(2) + P(3) + P(5) = \frac{3}{18} + \frac{4}{18} + \frac{4}{18} = \frac{11}{18}$$

(iii) $\quad A = \{1, 2, 3, 4\}$

$$\therefore \quad P(A) = \frac{2}{18} + \frac{3}{18} + \frac{4}{18} + \frac{3}{18} = \frac{12}{18} = \frac{2}{3}$$

(iv) $\quad A = \{4, 5, 6\}$

$$\therefore \quad P(A) = \frac{3}{18} + \frac{4}{18} + \frac{2}{18} = \frac{9}{18} = \frac{1}{2}$$

Let the sample space be a finite set with cardinality n. Let A be an event in S, with cardinality R.

Then $\quad A = \{x_1, x_2, ..., x_k\}$.

$$\therefore \quad P(A) = P(x_1) + P(x_2) + ... + P(x_k)$$

$$= \frac{1}{n} + \frac{1}{n} + ... + \frac{1}{n} \text{ (k times)}$$

$$= \frac{k}{n}, \text{ as all the outcomes are equally likely with probability } \frac{1}{n}, \text{ for}$$

a finite space S, in which all the outcomes are equally likely.

Hence $\quad P(A) = \frac{|A|}{|S|}$

By using the above formula, the computation of probability is reduced to finding the cardinalities of sets. For this reason, the methods of counting discussed in the previous section are quite useful.

However, this method can be applied when all the outcomes are equally likely. If the outcomes of the event have varying probabilities, then one should take the sum of the individual (elementary) probabilities to find the probability of that event.

SOLVED EXAMPLES

Example 1: If two cards are drawn without replacement from a pack, what is the probability that one of them is the ace of hearts?

Solution: Let A be the event that one of the cards drawn is an ace of hearts. Since the cards are drawn without replacement, the first card can be drawn in 52 ways and then the second card can be drawn in 51 ways. Hence the cardinality of the sample space S is 52.51. For the event A, since either the first card is the ace of hearts or the second card is the ace of hearts, its cardinality is $51 + 51 = 2.51$. Hence $P(A) = \dfrac{2.51}{52.51} = \dfrac{1}{26}$.

Example 2: If one card is drawn at random from each of two decks, what is the probability that at least one is the ace of hearts?

Solution: The sample space S consists of all such pairs (a, b) where a is a card from the first deck, and b from the second. Hence $|S| = 52.52 = 52^2$. Let A be the event under consideration.

Then A = {(a, b) | a or b is an ace of hearts}.

There will be $52 + 52 - 1 = 52 + 51$ such elements in A.

Hence $P(A) = \dfrac{|A|}{|S|} = \dfrac{52 + 51}{52^2} = \dfrac{103}{2704}$

Example 3: Cards are drawn one by one without replacement from a pack of 52 cards. What is the probability that the first ace will be drawn in the 10th draw?

Solution: Two cards can be drawn from a pack of 52 cards in $^{52}P_{10}$ ways. Hence the size of the sample space S is $^{52}C_{10}$. Let A be the event that the first ace is drawn in the 10th draw. The cardinality of A is $(48 \cdot 47 \cdot \ldots \cdot 40 \cdot 4)$ ways.

$$\therefore P(A) = \dfrac{|A|}{|S|}$$
$$= \dfrac{(48 \cdot 47 \ldots 40 \cdot 4)}{(52 \cdot 51 \ldots \cdot 43)} = \dfrac{328}{7735}$$

The following theorems on probability are important as they enable us to find the probabilities of new events formed from the given events.

Example 4: A students' committee consists of eight students. Find the probability that there will be exactly two FE, two SE, two TE and two BE students in the committee.

Solution: The sample space S will consist of 4.4 ... 4 (8 times) = 4^8 elements, since each of the 8 students can be selected in 4 different ways (corresponding to the class). Let A be the event that there will exactly 2 FE, 2 SE, 2 TE and 2 BE students. Then the number of elements in A is

$$\dfrac{8!}{2!2!2!2!}$$

Hence, $P(A) = \dfrac{|A|}{|S|} = \dfrac{8!}{(2!)^4 \, 4^8}$

3.2.10 Theorem (Addition law)

Let A and B be two events in a finite (or countably infinite) sample space. Then
$$P(A \cup B) = P(A) + P(B) - P(A \cap B)$$

Proof:

We shall prove the theorem only for finite events A and B, as it can be easily extended to the general case.

First let us assume that A and B are mutually exclusive events.

Let $A = \{a_1, a_2, ..., a_m\}$ and $B = \{b_1, b_2, ... b_m\}$,

where a_i and b_j are the outcomes in A and B respectively.

Then $A \cup B = \{a_1, a_2, ..., a_m, b_1, b_2, ... b_m\}$

Hence $P(A \cup B) = \sum_{\substack{1 \le i < m \\ 1 \le j \le n}} \{P(a_i) + P(b_j)\} = P(A) + P(B)$.

This result can obviously be extended to a finite number of mutually disjoint events, i.e.
$$P(A_1 \cup A_2 \cup ... \cup A_k) = P(A_1) + P(A_2) + ... + P(A_k)$$

Next, let us examine the case when A and B are not mutually exclusive.

From set theory we know that any set can be expressed as the disjoint union of two sets, i.e.
$$A = (A - B) \cup (A \cap B),$$
and
$$B = (B - A) \cup (A \cap B)$$

Similarly, $A \cup B$ can be expressed as the disjoint union of three sets, i.e.
$$A \cup B = (A - B) \cup (B - A) \cup (A \cap B)$$

Therefore, applying the mutually exclusive case to each of the above events, we obtain

$$P(A) = P(A - B) + P(A \cap B) \qquad ... (1)$$
$$P(B) = P(B - A) + P(A \cap B) \qquad ... (2)$$
$$P(A \cup B) = P(A - B) + P(B - A) + P(A \cap B) \qquad ... (3)$$

From the above equations it immediately follows that
$$P(A \cup B) = P(A) + P(B) - P(A \cap B)$$

The above theorem can be extended to a finite union of events, i.e.

$$P(A_1 \cup A_2 \cup ...... \cup A_n) = \sum_{i=1}^{n} P(A_i) - \sum_{1 \le i \le j \le n} P(A_i \cap A_j)$$
$$+ \sum_{1 \le i < j < k \le n} P(A_i \cap A_j \cap A_k) - ...... + (-1)^{n-1} P(A_1 \cap A_2 \cap ... \cap A_n)$$

3.2.11 Theorem

Let A be an event and let $\bar{A}$ denote its complementary event. Then $P(\bar{A}) = 1 - P(A)$.

Proof:

The sample space $S = A \cup \bar{A}$ is the disjoint union of two sets as A and $\bar{A}$ are mutually exclusive. $P(S) = 1$ as S is the universal set of all outcomes.
Hence by the above theorem,

$$P(S) = P(A) + P(\bar{A}) \Rightarrow P(\bar{A}) = 1 - P(A).$$

3.2.12 Definition of Independent Events (in terms of Probability)

Two events are said to be independent if $P(A \cap B) = P(A) \cdot P(B)$.
This rule is called as the multiplicative law of probability.

SOLVED EXAMPLES

Example 1: Two dice are rolled together. Event A denotes that the sum of the numbers on the top faces is even and event B denotes that there is a 4 on at least one of the top faces. Find $P(A \cup B)$ and $P(A \cap B)$.

Solution: Total number of points in the sample space S is 36.

$A = \{(1, 1), (1, 3), (1, 5), (2, 2), (2, 4), (2, 6), (3, 1), (3, 3), (3, 5),$
$\quad (4, 2), (4, 4), (4, 6), (5, 1), (5, 3), (5, 5), (6, 2), (6, 4), (6, 6)\}$

$|A| = 18$

Hence $P(A) = \dfrac{18}{36} = \dfrac{1}{2}$

$B = \{(1, 4), (2, 4), (3, 4), (4, 1), (4, 2), (4, 3), (4, 4), (4, 5),$
$\quad (4, 6), (5, 4), (6, 4)\}$

$\therefore P(B) = \dfrac{11}{36}$

$A \cap B = \{(2, 4), (4, 2), (4, 4), (4, 6), (6, 4)\}$

$P(A \cap B) = \dfrac{5}{36}$

$P(A \cup B) = P(A) + P(B) - P(A \cap B) = \dfrac{18 + 11 - 5}{36} = \dfrac{24}{36} = \dfrac{2}{3}.$

Example 2: A certain company encourages its employees to participate in cricket and hockey. A survey indicates that 40% play cricket, 50% play hockey and 25% play cricket and hockey both. Find the probability of the events that
    (i)   an employee plays only hockey.
    (ii)   an employee plays only cricket.
    (iii) an employee takes part in at least one of the games, cricket and hockey.

Solution: Let C denote the event that an employee plays cricket, and let H denote the event that an employee plays hockey.

$$P(H) = \frac{50}{100} = \frac{1}{2}, \quad P(C) = \frac{40}{100} = \frac{2}{5} \text{ and}$$

$$P(C \cap H) = \frac{25}{100} = \frac{1}{4}.$$

(i) An employee plays only hockey denotes the event H − C which is the same as H − C ∩ H.

(ii) Hence $P(H - C) = P(H) - P(C \cap H) = \frac{1}{2} - \frac{1}{4} = \frac{1}{4}$.

Hence $P(C - H) = P(C) - P(C \cap H) = \frac{2}{5} - \frac{1}{4} = \frac{3}{20}$.

(iii) $P(C \cup H) = P(C) + P(H) - P(C \cap H) = \frac{2}{5} + \frac{1}{2} - \frac{1}{9} = \frac{13}{20}$.

Example 3 : A problem on probability is given to four students A, B, C, D whose probabilities of solving the problem are 1/2, 3/4, 1/4, 2/5 respectively. What is the probability that (i) the problem will be solved? (ii) exactly one of them will solve the problem?

Solution: (i) It is easier to find the probability that the problem will not be solved. This is given by

$$P(\bar{A} \cap \bar{B} \cap \bar{C} \cap \bar{D}) = P(\bar{A}) P(\bar{B}) P(\bar{C}) P(\bar{D})$$

$$= (1 - P(A))(1 - P(B))(1 - P(C))(1 - P(D))$$

$$= \left(1 - \frac{1}{2}\right)\left(1 - \frac{3}{4}\right)\left(1 - \frac{1}{4}\right)\left(1 - \frac{2}{5}\right)$$

$$= \frac{1}{2} \cdot \frac{1}{4} \cdot \frac{3}{4} \cdot \frac{3}{5} = \frac{9}{160}$$

Hence the probability that the problem will be solved is

$$P(A \cup B \cup C \cup D) = 1 - P(\bar{A} \cap \bar{B} \cap \bar{C} \cap \bar{D})$$

$$= 1 - \frac{9}{160} = \frac{151}{160}$$

(ii) The probability that exactly one of them will solve the problem is

$$P(A \cap \bar{B} \cap \bar{C} \cap \bar{D}) + P(\bar{A} \cap B \cap \bar{C} \cap \bar{D}) + P(\bar{A} \cap \bar{B} \cap C \cap \bar{D}) + P(\bar{A} \cap \bar{B} \cap \bar{C} \cap D)$$

$$= \frac{1}{2} \cdot \frac{1}{4} \cdot \frac{3}{4} \cdot \frac{3}{5} + \frac{1}{2} \cdot \frac{3}{4} \cdot \frac{3}{4} \cdot \frac{3}{5} + \frac{1}{2} \cdot \frac{1}{4} \cdot \frac{1}{4} \cdot \frac{3}{5} + \frac{1}{2} \cdot \frac{1}{4} \cdot \frac{3}{4} \cdot \frac{2}{5} = \frac{9}{32}$$

Example 4: An urn contains 2 white and 4 black balls. Another urn B contains 5 white and 7 black balls. A ball is transferred from the urn A to urn B and then a ball is drawn from urn B. Find the probability that it is white.

Solution: We have to consider the following two cases:

Case I: The ball transferred from urn A to urn B is a white ball.

Let C denote the event of transferring a white ball from urn A to urn B and then drawing a white ball.

Then $\quad P(C) = \dfrac{2}{6} \cdot \dfrac{6}{13} = \dfrac{2}{13}$

Case II: Let D denote the event of transferring a black ball from A to B then drawing a white ball from B.

Then $\quad P(D) = \dfrac{4}{6} \cdot \dfrac{5}{13} = \dfrac{10}{39}$

C and D are mutually exclusive cases. The required probability is $P(C \cup D)$.

$$P(C \cup D) = P(C) + P(D) = \dfrac{2}{13} + \dfrac{10}{39} = \dfrac{16}{39}$$

Example 5: Four persons are chosen at random from a group containing 3 men, 2 women and 4 children. Find the chance that exactly two of them will be children.

Solution: We have to consider the following mutually exclusive cases:

(i) 2 men and 2 children, denoted by event A.
(ii) 2 women and 2 children, denoted by event B.
(iii) 1 man, 1 woman and 2 children, denoted by event C.

$$P(A \cup B \cup C) = P(A) + P(B) + P(C)$$

Number of ways of selecting 2 men and 2 children from the group is $C(3, 2) \cdot C(4, 2) = 18$. Total number of ways of selecting 4 persons from a group of 9 persons is

$$C(9, 4) = 126 \text{ ways}$$

$\therefore \quad P(A) = \dfrac{18}{126} = \dfrac{1}{7}$

Number of ways of selecting 2 women and 2 children is $^2C_2 \cdot {}^4C_2 = 6$

$\therefore \quad P(B) = \dfrac{6}{126} = \dfrac{1}{21}$

Number of ways of selecting 1 man, 1 woman and 2 children is

$C(3, 1) \cdot C(2, 1) \cdot C(4, 2) = 36$

$\therefore \quad P(C) = \dfrac{36}{126} = \dfrac{2}{7}$

$\therefore \quad P(A \cup B \cup C) = P(A) + P(B) + P(C)$

$= \dfrac{1}{7} + \dfrac{1}{21} + \dfrac{2}{7} = \dfrac{3 + 1 + 6}{21} = \dfrac{10}{21}$

DISCRETE STRUCTURE AND GRAPH THEORY (NMU) PERMUTATIONS, COMBINATIONS ......

3.2.13 Conditional Probability

Quite often, the probability of occurrence of one event depends on the occurrence or non-occurrence of another event. For example, consider the following statements,

"If it continues to rain, the match scheduled for tomorrow shall be cancelled".

"If the professor is in town, he will inaugurate the conference". Such events are called as conditional events, which we shall now define.

Definition:

Let A be an event that has already occurred. Then the **conditional probability** of an event B with respect to that of A is given by

$$P(B/A) = \frac{P(A \cap B)}{P(A)}$$

Note that if A and B are independent events, then P(B/A) = P(B), since for independent events A and B, $P(A \cap B) = P(A) \cdot P(B)$.

SOLVED EXAMPLES

Example 1: Two dice are rolled. What is the probability that the sum of the faces will not exceed 7? Given that at least one face shows a 4.

Solution: Let   A = {(a, b) | a + b ≤ 7}

∴   A = {(1, 1), (1, 2), (1, 3), (1, 4), (1, 5), (1, 6),
           (2, 1), (2, 2), (2, 3), (2, 4), (2, 5)
           (3, 1), (3, 2), (3, 3), (3, 4), (4, 1)
           (4, 2), (4, 3), (5, 1), (5, 2), (6, 1)}.

Let   B = {(a, b) | a = 4 or b = 4}

∴   B = {(1, 4), (4, 1), (2, 4), (4, 2), (3, 4), (4, 3),
           (4, 4), (4, 5), (5, 4), (4, 6), (6, 4)}

A ∩ B = {(1, 4), (2, 4), (3, 4), (4, 1), (4, 2), (4, 3)}

∴ $P(A/B) = \frac{P(A \cap B)}{P(B)} = \frac{6/36}{11/36} = \frac{6}{11}$

Example 2: In an university, 60% of the professors are men and 40% are women. It is also found that 50% of the male professors and 60% of the female professors know computer programming. Find the probability that a professor knowing programming is a women.

Solution: Let M denote the event that a person selected is a male and let F denote the event that the person selected is a female. Let C denote the event that the person selected knows programming.

P(M) = 0.6, P(F) = 0.4
P(C/M) = 0.5, P(C/F) = 0.6.

Chp 3 | 3.41

We have to find the probability P(F/C).

$$P(F|C) = \frac{P(C \cap F)}{P(C)}$$

Since $P(C|F) = 0.6$

we have, $\frac{P(C \cap F)}{P(F)} = 0.6$, $P(C \cap F) = 0.6 \times 0.4 = 0.24$

Similarly $P(C \cap M) = 0.5 \times 0.6 = 0.30$

Now $P(C) = P(C \cap F) + P(C \cap M)$
$= 0.24 + 0.30 = 0.54$

$\therefore P(F|C) = \frac{P(C \cap F)}{P(C)} = \frac{.24}{0.54} = \frac{4}{9} = 0.44$

Example 3: The probability that a manufacturing process will be completed on time is 0.8, and the probability that all the machines are in working condition is 0.7. The probability that the process will be completed, given that all the machines are in working condition is 0.9.
   (i)   What is the probability that the process will be finished on time and all the machines are in working condition?
   (ii)   What is the probability that all the machines were working, given that the process was completed on time?

Solution: Let A denote the event that the manufacturing process is complete and B, the event that the machines are working.
Given: P(A) = 0.8, P(B) = 0.7, P(A/B) = 0.9.

(i) $P(A/B) = \frac{P(A \cap B)}{P(B)}$

$\therefore P(A \cap B) = P(A/B) \cdot P(B) = (0.9)(0.7) = 0.63$

(ii) $P(B|A) = \frac{P(A \cap B)}{P(A)} = \frac{0.63}{0.80} = 0.79$

Example 4: Given that a student had prepared, the probability of passing a certain entrance exam is 0.99. Given that a student did not prepare, the probability of passing the entrance exam is 0.05. Assume that the probability of preparing is 0.7. The student fails in the exam. What is the probability that he or she did not prepare?

Solution: Let A denote the event that the student having prepared for the exam, and B denote the event that the student passing in the entrance exam.

Given: $P(B|A) = 0.99$, $P(B|\bar{A}) = 0.05$
$P(A) = 0.7$

We have to find $P(\bar{A}|\bar{B})$.

$$P(\bar{A}|\bar{B}) = \frac{P(\bar{A} \cap \bar{B})}{P(\bar{B})}$$

Now $\quad$ $P(A \cap B) = P(B/A) \cdot P(A)$
$\qquad\qquad\qquad\quad = (0.99)(0.7) = 0.693$

Also $\quad$ $P(\bar{A} \cap B) = P(B/\bar{A}) \cdot P(\bar{A})$
$\qquad\qquad\qquad\quad = (0.05)(0.3) = 0.015$

$\qquad\qquad P(B) = P(A \cap B) + P(\bar{A} \cap B) = 0.693 + 0.015 = 0.708$

Hence $\quad P(\bar{B}) = 1 - 0.708 = 0.292$

Now $\quad P(\bar{A} \cap \bar{B}) = P(\overline{A \cup B})$
$\qquad\qquad\qquad\quad = 1 - P(A \cup B) = 1 - [P(A) + P(B) - P(A \cap B)]$
$\qquad\qquad\qquad\quad = 1 - 0.7 - 0.708 + 0.693 = 0.285$

Hence $\quad P(\bar{A} \mid \bar{B}) = \dfrac{0.285}{0.292} = 0.976$

Let us summarize the various results on probabilities, we have obtained so far.

(i) $\qquad\qquad P(S) = 1$
(ii) $\qquad\qquad P(\phi) = 0$
(iii) $\qquad\qquad P(\bar{A}) = 1 - P(A)$
(iv) $\qquad\qquad P(A \cup B) = P(A) + P(B) - P(A \cap B)$
(v) $\qquad\qquad P(A \cup B \cup C) = P(A) + P(B) + P(C) - P(A \cap B)$
$\qquad\qquad\qquad\qquad\quad - P(B \cap C) - P(C \cap A) + P(A \cap B \cap C)$
(vi) $\qquad\qquad P(A \cup B) = P(A) + P(B)$ for mutually exclusive events.
(vii) $\qquad\qquad P(A \cap B) = P(A) \cdot P(B)$ for independent events
(viii) $\qquad\qquad P(\overline{A \cup B}) = P(\bar{A} \cap \bar{B}) = (1 - P(A))(1 - P(B))$
$\qquad\qquad\qquad\qquad$ for independent events A and B

3.2.14 Binomial Probability

Suppose an experiment is performed repeatedly, say n number of times. Let A be an event with its probability of occurrence being p. If the event A occurs among the n-trials, we say that the trial has a success, otherwise it has a failure. Hence if the event A occurs r times (for $0 \leq r \leq n$), the trial is said to have r 'successes'. The probability that the trial has r successes is given by the formula

$$P(r) = {}^nC_r \, p^r \, q^{n-r}, \text{ where } q = 1 - p. \qquad ({}^nC_r \text{ denotes } C(n, r))$$

Since the binomial coefficients appear in the formula, the probability is called as binomial probability.

SOLVED EXAMPLES

Example 1: An examination containing multiple choice questions is designed so that the probability of a correct choice by mere guessing is 0.2. What is the probability that a student will not get more than 2 questions right out of 10, by guessing alone?

Solution: The ten questions are the 10 trials. Getting a right answer by guessing is a success, getting a wrong answer is a failure.

Hence $n = 10$, $p = 0.2$, $q = 0.8$, $0 \le r \le 2$.

$\therefore \quad P(0 \le r \le 2) = P(0) + P(1) + P(2)$

$= {}^{10}C_0 (0.2)^0 (0.8)^{10} + {}^{10}C_1 (0.2)(0.8)^9 + {}^{10}C_2 (0.2)^2 (0.8)^8$

$= 0.1073 + 0.2684 + 0.30198$

$= 0.68$

Example 2: If on an average one candidate out of ten fails in a certain examination, then find the probability that out of 5 candidates that have appeared for the examination, at least 4 will be successful.

Solution: Let A denote the event that a candidate is successful in the examination.

p = Probability of success in the examination
$= 1 - 0.1 = 0.9$

$q = 0.1$

$n = 5$, $r \ge 4$

$\therefore \quad P(r \ge 4) = P(4) + P(5) = {}^5C_4 (0.9)^4 (0.1) + {}^5C_5 (0.9)^5$

$= 0.32805 + 0.59049 = 0.91854 = 0.92$

Example 3: There is a 30% chance that it rains on any particular day. What is the probability that there is at least one rainy day during a 7-day period? Given that there is at least one rainy day. What is the probability that there are at least two rainy days.

Solution: Let A be the event of a day being a rainy days.

Then $p = \dfrac{30}{100} = 0.3$, $\therefore q = 0.7$, and $n = 7$.

$= 1 - P(r < 1)$

$\therefore \quad P(r \ge 1) = 1 - P(0) = 1 - {}^7C_0 (0.7)^7$

$= 1 - 0.082 = 0.9176$

Probability that there are at least 2 rainy days

$= P(r \ge 2)$

$= 1 - P(r < 2) = 1 - P(0) - P(1)$

$= 1 - [{}^7C_0 (0.7)^7 + {}^7C_1 (0.3)(0.7)^6]$

$= 1 - (0.082 + 0.2470)$

$= 0.6709$

Let B denote the event that there is at least one rainy day, and C the event that there are at least two rainy days. Then we have to find P(C/B).

$$P(C/B) = \frac{P(C \cap B)}{P(B)} = \frac{P(C)}{P(B)} = \frac{0.6709}{0.9176} = 0.731$$

Example 4: The probability that a man, aged 60 will live upto 70 is 0.65. What is the probability that out of 10 men, now 60, at least 8 would live upto 70?

Solution: Let A be the event that a man, aged 60 lives upto 70.

Then $p = 0.65$, $\therefore q = 0.35$
$n = 10$, $r \geq 8$

$\therefore \quad P(r \geq 8) = P(8) + P(9) + P(10)$
$= {}^{10}C_8 (0.65)^8 (0.35)^2 + {}^{10}C_9 (0.65)^9 (0.35) + {}^{10}C_{10} (0.65)^{10}$
$= 0.1756 + 0.0725 + 0.01346 = 0.2616$

Example 5: A typist makes one error on the average in every fifth typed page. If 9 pages are typed in 1 day, what is the probability that

(i) exactly three of them have errors?

(ii) none of them has an error?

(iii) not more than 7 pages have errors?

Solution: $n = 9$, $p = \frac{1}{5} = 0.2$, $q = 0.8$.

(i) $P(r = 3) = {}^9C_3 (0.2)^3 (0.8)^6 = 0.1762$

(ii) $P(r = 0) = {}^9C_0 (0.2)^0 (0.8)^9 = 0.1342$

(iii) $P(r \geq 7) = 1 - P(r \geq 8) = 1 - \{{}^9C_8 (0.2)^8 (0.8) + {}^9C_9 (0.2)^9\} = 0.99998$

Example 6: There are 50 cards numbered from 1 to 50. Two different cards are chosen at random. What is the probability that one number is twice the other number?

Solution: There are 25 pairs (a, b) where b = 2a and also 25 pairs (a, b) where a = 2b, for example we have (1, 2) and (2, 1). Hence the number of ways of selecting two cards such that one number is twice the other is 25 + 25 = 2 × 25 ways. The number of ways of selecting any two cards is 50 × 49.

Hence the required probability is $\frac{2 \times 25}{50 \times 49} = \frac{1}{49}$.

Example 7: Suppose a subset of 60 different days of the year is selected at random. What is the probability that there are 5 days from each month in the subset? (Assume for simplicity that a year has 12 months with 30 days each.

Solution: The number of days of selecting 5 days from each month is

$${}^{30}C_5 \times {}^{30}C_5 \times ... \times {}^{30}C_5 \text{ (12 times)}.$$

The total number of ways of selecting 60 days in a year (12 × 30 = 360) is $^{360}C_{60}$. Hence the required probability is $\dfrac{^{30}C_5}{^{360}C_{60}}$.

Example 8: What is the probability that 2 (or more) people in a random group of 25 people have a common birthday?

Solution : First we shall find the probability that no one has a common birthday. All possibilities of birthdays for the 25 people are 365 × 365 × ... × 365 (25 times) = 365^{25}. The number of possibilities that everyone has a different birthday is P (365, 25). Hence the required probability is $1 - P(365, 25)/365^{25}$.

Example 9: A four digit number is formed from 1, 2, 3, 5 with no repetition. Find the probability that the number is (i) divisible by 5, (ii) odd.

Solution: Total number of ways of forming a 4 digit number with no repetition is 4 ! ways.

(i) The number is divisible by 5, if the last digit is 5. This number can be chosen in 3 ! ways. Hence probability of getting a number that is divisible by 5 is $\dfrac{3!}{4!} = \dfrac{1}{4}$.

(ii) The number is odd if the last number is 1, 3 or 5.

The number of ways of finding an odd number with the digits not repeating is 3.3 ! ways. Hence the required probability is $\dfrac{3.3!}{4!} = \dfrac{18}{24} = \dfrac{3}{4}$.

Example 10: All picture cards are removed from a deck of 52 cards and then 4 cards are drawn. Find the probability that (i) they belong to different suits, (ii) they belong to different suits and are of different denominations.

Solution: The number of cards remaining after removing the picture cards is

52 − 3 × 4 = 40 cards.

(i) The number of ways of choosing 4 cards from 40 cards is $^{40}C_4$ ways. The number of ways of choosing the cards so that they all belong to different suits is

$^{10}C_1 \cdot {}^{10}C_1 \cdot {}^{10}C_1 \cdot {}^{10}C_1 = 10^4$ ways.

$$= \dfrac{10{,}000 \times 24}{40 \times 39 \times 38 \times 37} = \dfrac{1000}{9139}$$

(ii) The number of ways of choosing the cards so that they belong to different suits and are of different denomination is 10 × 9 × 8 × 7 ways.

Hence the required probability is $\dfrac{10 \times 9 \times 8 \times 7 \times 24}{40 \times 39 \times 38 \times 37} = \dfrac{504}{9139}$ ways.

Example 11: An urn contains 6 red balls and 4 green balls. 4 balls are selected at random from the box. What is the probability that 2 of the selected balls will be red and 2 will be green?

Solution: The total number of ways of choosing 4 balls from a total of 10 balls is $^{10}C_4$ ways. The number of ways of selecting 2 red balls is $^6C_2$ and the number of ways of selecting 2 green balls is $^4C_2$ ways.

Hence the required probability is $\dfrac{^6C_2 \cdot {}^4C_2}{^{10}C_4} = \dfrac{15 \times 6}{210} = \dfrac{3}{7}$.

Example 12: 2 cards are drawn from a deck of 54 cards (52 + 2 Jokers). What is the probability that
  (i) both of them are spades?
  (ii) both are kings?
  (iii) at least one joker is drawn?
  (iv) both are black queens?

Solution: Any 2 cards can be chosen in $^{54}C_2$ ways.

(i) Required probability is $\dfrac{^{13}C_2}{^{54}C_2}$, as 2 spades can be chosen from 13 spades in $^{13}C_2$ ways.

(ii) Required probability is $^4C_2 / {}^{54}C_2$ as there are 4 kings out of which 2 can be chosen in $^4C_2$ ways.

(iii) When 1 joker is drawn, the remaining one card is to be chosen from the remaining 53 cards. The joker can be drawn in $^2C_1$ ways. Hence the required probability is $(^2C_1 \cdot {}^{53}C_1) / {}^{54}C_2$.

(iv) The number of ways of choosing 2 black queens is $^2C_2 = 1$ way only. Hence the required probability is $\dfrac{1}{^{54}C_2}$.

Example 13: A husband and wife appear in an interview for two vacancies in the same post. The probability of husband's selection is $\dfrac{1}{3}$ and that of wife's selection is $\dfrac{1}{2}$. What is the probability that
  (i) both of them will be selected?
  (ii) only one of them will be selected?
  (iii) none of them will be selected?

Solution: Let A be the event that the husband is selected and B. The event that the wife is selected. Then $P(A) = \dfrac{1}{3}$, $P(B) = \dfrac{1}{2}$.

(i) Both of them will be selected corresponds to the event $A \cap B$.
∴ $P(A \cap B) = P(A) \cdot P(B)$ as both are independent events.
∴ $P(A \cap B) = \dfrac{1}{3} \cdot \dfrac{1}{2} = \dfrac{1}{6}$.

(ii) Only one of them is selected corresponds to the event $(A \cap \bar{B}) \cup (\bar{A} \cap B)$

$\therefore \quad P((A \cap \bar{B}) \cup (\bar{A} \cap B)) = P(A \cap \bar{B}) + P(\bar{A} \cap B)$
$= P(A)(1 - P(B)) + (1 - P(A)) P(B)$
$= \left(\dfrac{1}{3}\right)\left(\dfrac{1}{2}\right) + \left(\dfrac{2}{3}\right)\left(\dfrac{1}{2}\right) = \dfrac{1}{6} + \dfrac{1}{3} = \dfrac{3}{6} = \dfrac{1}{2}$

(iii) None of them is selected corresponds to the event $\bar{A} \cap \bar{B}$.

$P(\bar{A} \cap \bar{B}) = P(\bar{A}) \cdot P(\bar{B}) = (1 - P(A))(1 - P(B))$
$= \left(1 - \dfrac{1}{3}\right)\left(1 - \dfrac{1}{2}\right) = \dfrac{2}{3} \cdot \dfrac{1}{2} = \dfrac{1}{3}$

Example 14: A company purchased 10,000 transistors, 5,000 from supplier A; 3,000 from supplier B and 2,000 from supplier C. It is known that 2% of supplier A are defective, 4% of supplier B are defective and 5% of supplier C are defective.

(i) If transistor from 10,000 is selected at random, what is the probability that it is defective?

(ii) If transistor selected at random is defective, what is the probability that it is from supplier A?

(iii) Given that transistor selected at random is not from supplier A, what is the probability that it is defective?

Solution: Let A, B, C denote the events that a transistor is from supplier A, B, C respectively. Let D denote the event that the transistor is defective.

(i) The defective transistor may be from A, B or C.

$P(D) = P(A \cap D) + P(B \cap D) + P(C \cap D)$ as there are mutually exclusive cases.

Hence $P(D) = \dfrac{2}{100} \times \dfrac{5000}{10{,}000} + \dfrac{3}{100} \times \dfrac{3000}{10000} + \dfrac{5}{100} \times \dfrac{2000}{10000}$

$= 0.01 + 0.009 + 0.01 = 0.029$

(ii) We have to find the conditional probability $P(A|D)$

$P(A|D) = \dfrac{P(A \cap D)}{P(D)} = \dfrac{0.01}{0.029} = 0.345$

(iii) We have to find the conditional probability $P(D | \bar{A})$

$P(D | \bar{A}) = \dfrac{P(\bar{A} \cap D)}{P(\bar{A})}$

$= \dfrac{P(B \cap D) + P(C \cap D)}{1 - P(A)} = \dfrac{0.009 + 0.01}{1 - 0.5} = 0.038$

Example 15: In a certain college, 25% of male students and 10% of female students are studying Mathematics. Women constitute 60% of the student body. A student is chosen at random.

(i) Find the probability that the student is studying Mathematics.

(ii) If the student is studying Mathematics, find the probability that the student is female.

Solution: Let A denote the event that the student is a male and B denote the event that the student is female. Let C denote the event that the student is studying Mathematics.

Then $P(A) = \frac{2}{5}$, $P(B) = \frac{3}{5}$

$$P(A \cap C) = \frac{25}{100} \times \frac{2}{5} = \frac{1}{10}$$

$$P(B \cap C) = \frac{10}{100} \times \frac{3}{5} = \frac{3}{50}$$

(i) $P(C) = P(A \cap C) + P(B \cap C) = \frac{1}{10} + \frac{3}{50} = \frac{8}{50} = 0.16$

(ii) $P(B|C) = \frac{P(B \cap C)}{P(C)} = \frac{3/50}{8/50} = \frac{3}{8} = 0.375$

Example 16: In a certain college, 25% of students failed in Maths, 15% failed in Chemistry, and 10% failed in both Maths and Chemistry. A student is selected at random.

(i) If he has failed in Chemistry, what is the probability that he fails in Maths?

(ii) What is the probability that he fails in Maths or Chemistry?

Solution: Let A denote the event that the student fails in Maths, and B denote the event that he fails in Chemistry.

$$P(A) = \frac{1}{4}, \quad P(B) = \frac{3}{20}$$

$$P(A \cap B) = \frac{1}{10}$$

(i) $P(A|B) = \frac{P(A \cap B)}{P(B)} = \frac{1/10}{3/20} = \frac{2}{3}$

(ii) $P(A \cup B) = P(A) + P(B) - P(A \cap B) = \frac{1}{4} + \frac{3}{20} - \frac{1}{10} = \frac{3}{10} = 0.3$

Example 17: A shelf has 8 Mathematics books and 4 Physics books. Find the probability that 3 particular Mathematics books will be together.

Solution: The total number of ways for arranging the 8 + 4 = 12 books = 12 ! ways.

Treating the 3 books as 1 single entity, the total number of ways to arrange the books is 10 ! × 3 ! ways, as the three Mathematics books can be rearranged among themselves in 3 ! ways. Hence the required probability is $\frac{10!\,3!}{12!} = \frac{1}{22}$.

Example 18: Find the probability of getting a total 7 at least once in three tosses of a pair of fair dice.

Solution: For a single toss of a pair of fair dice, the event
$$A = \{(1, 6), (2, 5), (3, 4), (4, 3), (5, 2), (6, 1)\}$$
$$P(A) = \frac{6}{36} = \frac{1}{6}$$

We have to use binomial probability $^nC_r\, p^q\, q^r$, where $n = 3$, $r \geq 1$, $p = \frac{1}{6}$, $q = \frac{5}{6}$.

Required probability is $P(r \geq 1)$
$$= 1 - P(0)$$
$$= 1 - {}^3C_0 \left(\frac{5}{6}\right)^3 = 1 - 0.5787 = 0.42$$

Example 19: If 3 dice are rolled, then find out the probability that exactly 1 face shows a number less than or equal to 4.

Solution: The experiment of rolling 3 dice is equivalent to that of rolling 1 die 3 times. Let A be the event that the face appearing on top is less than or equal to 4. Then $A = \{1, 2, 3, 4\}$. Then $P(A) = \frac{4}{6} = \frac{2}{3}$. We have to use binomial probability where $n = 3$, $r = 1$, $p = \frac{2}{3}$, $q = \frac{1}{3}$.

$$\therefore \quad P(r = 1) = {}^3C_1 \left(\frac{2}{3}\right)\left(\frac{1}{3}\right)^2$$
$$= 3 \cdot \frac{2}{3} \cdot \frac{1}{9} = \frac{2}{9}$$

Example 20: There are 10 adjacent parking spaces in a parking lot. When you arrive in your Maruti car, there are already 7 cars in the lot. What is the probability that you can find 2 adjacent unoccupied spaces for your car?

Solution: The 7 cars occupy the lot in $^{10}C_7$ ways. Hence the three unoccupied parking spaces can be chosen in $^{10}C_3$ ways. Treating the two adjacent unoccupied spaces as one single unit, it can occupy any of the 9 spaces. Since there are 3 empty lots, the two adjacent ones can be chosen in $^3C_2$ ways. Hence required probability is $\dfrac{{}^3C_2 \cdot 9}{{}^{10}C_3} = \dfrac{9}{40}$.

Example 21: A number is chosen at random from the 30 numbers
$$\{10, 11, \ldots, 19, 20, 21, 30, 31, \ldots 39\}.$$

It is known that numbers with the first digit have an equal chance of being chosen. Also a number with 2 as the first digit is twice as likely to be chosen as one with 1 as the first digit and a number with 3 as the first digit is three times as likely to be chosen as one with 1 as the first digit. What is the probability that

(i) a number with 1 as its first digit is chosen?

(ii) a number between 25 and 30 (both inclusive) is chosen?
(iii) a two digit number, the sum of whose digits is 9 is chosen?

Solution: Let p be the probability of a number being chosen whose first digit is 1, hence 2p will be the probability of a number being chosen whose first digit is 2 and 3p that of a number whose first digit is 3.

Then $10p + 20p + 30p = 1$. $\therefore p = \frac{1}{60}$.

(i) The probability that a number with 1 as its first digit being chosen is $\frac{1}{60}$.

(ii) Let A denote the event that a number between 25 and 30 being chosen.
Then $A = \{25, 26, 27, 28, 29, 30\}$
$\therefore P(A) = 10p + 3p = 13p = \frac{13}{60}$.

(iii) Let B be the event that a 2 digit number is chosen ; sum of whose digits is 9.
$\therefore B = \{18, 27, 36\}$
$\therefore P(B) = p + 2p + 3p = 6p = \frac{6}{60} = \frac{1}{10}$

Example 22: Consider the experiment of tossing a fair coin, until two heads or tails appear in succession.

(i) Describe the sample space.
(ii) What is the probability that the experiment ends before the sixth toss?
(iii) What is the probability that the experiment ends after an even number of tosses?
(iv) Given that the experiment ends with two heads, what is the probability that the experiment ends before the sixth toss?
(v) Given that the experiment does not end before the third toss, what is the probability that the experiment does not end after the sixth toss?

Solution: Let h denote head and t denote tail.
(i) $S = \{hh, tt, htt, thh, hthh, thtt, hthtt, thhh, ...\}$
(ii) The experiment may end at the second, third or fourth or fifth toss.
$\therefore A = \{hh, tt, htt, thh, hthh, thtt, hthtt, ththh\}$
$P(A) = 2\left[\frac{1}{4} + \frac{1}{8} + \frac{1}{16} + \frac{1}{32}\right] = 2 \times \frac{15}{32} = \frac{15}{16}$

(iii) $A = \{hh, tt, hthh, thtt, ...\}$
$P(A) = 2\left[\frac{1}{4} + \frac{1}{16} + \frac{1}{64} + ...\right]$
$= \frac{1}{2} + \frac{1}{2^3} + \frac{1}{2^5} + ... = \frac{1}{2}\left[1 + \frac{1}{4} + \frac{1}{16} + ...\right]$

$$= \frac{1}{2}\left[\frac{1}{1-\frac{1}{4}}\right] = \frac{1}{2} \times \frac{4}{3} = \frac{2}{3}$$

(iv) Let A be the event that the experiment ends two heads

∴ A = {hh, thh, hthh, ththh, hththh, ...}

$$P(A) = \frac{1}{4} + \frac{1}{8} + \frac{1}{16} + \frac{1}{32} + \frac{1}{64} + \ldots$$

$$= \frac{1}{4}\left[1 + \frac{1}{2} + \frac{1}{2^2} + \frac{1}{2^3} + \ldots\right]$$

$$= \frac{1}{4} \cdot \frac{1}{1-\frac{1}{2}} = \frac{1}{4} \cdot 2 = \frac{1}{2}$$

Let B be the event that the experiment ends before the sixth toss.
We have to find P(B|A)

$$P(B|A) = \frac{P(A \cap B)}{P(A)}$$

$A \cap B$ = {hh, thh, hthh, ththh}

$$P(A \cap B) = \frac{1}{2^2} + \frac{1}{2^3} + \frac{1}{2^4} + \frac{1}{2^5} = \frac{15}{32}$$

Hence $P(B|A) = \dfrac{15/32}{1/2} = \dfrac{30}{32} = \dfrac{15}{16}$

Example 23: Seven (distinct) car accidents occurred in a week. What is the probability that they all occurred on the same day?

Solution: The number of ways in which the seven accidents can occur in a week is $^{13}C_7$ ways. The number of ways in which all the accidents can occur on the same day is 7 ways.

Hence required probability is $\dfrac{7}{^{13}C_7} = \dfrac{7}{1716}$.

Example 24: Ten passengers got into an elevator on the ground floor of a 20 storey building. What is the probability that they will all get off at different floors?

Solution: The number of ways in which 10 people can get off at the 20 floors is 20^{10} ways.

The number of ways in which the passengers can get off at different floors is $20 \times 19 \times \ldots \times 11$ ways. Hence required probability is $\dfrac{^{20}P_{10}}{20^{10}}$.

Example 25: A, B, C throw a fair coin in that order one who throws a head first wins. Find the probabilities of their winning.

Solution: Let A, B, C denote the corresponding events, that A wins or B wins or C wins. Then event

$$A = \{h, tth, tttttth, \ldots\}$$
$$B = \{th, ttth, tttttth, \ldots\}$$
$$C = \{tth, tttttth, tttttttth, \ldots\}$$

$$\therefore P(A) = \frac{1}{2} + \frac{1}{2^3} + \frac{1}{2^6} + \ldots = \frac{1}{2}\left(\frac{1}{1-\frac{1}{8}}\right) = \frac{1}{2} \cdot \frac{8}{7} = \frac{4}{7}$$

$$P(B) = \frac{1}{2^2} + \frac{1}{2^5} + \frac{1}{2^8} + \ldots$$
$$= \frac{1}{4}\left(\frac{1}{1-\frac{1}{8}}\right) = \frac{1}{4} \cdot \frac{8}{7} = \frac{2}{7}$$

$$P(C) = \frac{1}{2^3} + \frac{1}{2^6} + \frac{1}{2^9} + \ldots$$
$$= \frac{1}{2^3}\left[\frac{1}{1-\frac{1}{8}}\right] = \frac{1}{8} \cdot \frac{8}{7} = \frac{1}{7}$$

Example 26: 10 letters each of which corresponds to an envelope are placed in the envelopes at random. What is the probability that no letter is placed in the right envelope?

Solution: Let A_i ($1 \le i \le 10$) denote the event that the i-th letter is placed in the right envelope. We have to find the probability $P(\bar{A}_1 \cap \bar{A}_2 \cap \ldots \cap \bar{A}_{10})$

$$P(\bar{A}_1 \cap \bar{A}_2 \cap \ldots \cap \bar{A}_{10}) = 1 - P(A_1 \cup A_2 \cup \ldots \cup A_{10})$$
$$= 1 - \sum_{i=1}^{10} P(A_i) + \sum_{i<j} P(A_i \cap A_j) - \ldots + \ldots + (-1)^n P(A_1 \cap \ldots \cap A_{10}) \ldots (1)$$

$$P(A_i) = \frac{1}{10}; \quad 1 \le i \le 10 \qquad \ldots (2)$$

$$P(A_i \cap A_j) = P(A_i) P(A_j | A_i) = \frac{1}{10} \cdot \frac{1}{9}, \quad i \le j$$

$$P(A_i \cap A_j \cap A_k) = P(A_i) P(A_j | A_i) P(A_k | A_i \cap A_j)$$
$$= \frac{1}{10} \cdot \frac{1}{9} \cdot \frac{1}{8}; \quad i < j < k \qquad \ldots (3)$$

Continuing in this manner, the last term is

$$P(A_1 \cap A_2 \cap \ldots A_{10}) = \frac{1}{10} \cdot \frac{1}{9} \cdot \frac{1}{8} \ldots \frac{1}{2} \cdot 1 \ldots (n+1)$$

Hence the required probability is obtained by substituting (2), (3), ... (n + 1) equations in (1).

Hence,

$$P(\bar{A}_1 \cap \bar{A}_2 \cap ... \cap \bar{A}_{10}) = 1 - {}^{10}C_1 \cdot \frac{1}{10} + {}^{10}C_2 \cdot \frac{1}{10 \cdot 9} + {}^{10}C_3 \cdot \frac{1}{10 \cdot 9 \cdot 8} + ... + \frac{1}{10!}$$

$$= \frac{1}{2!} - \frac{1}{3!} + \frac{1}{4!} - ... + \frac{1}{10!}$$

Example 27: Consider the experiment of tossing a fair coin until two heads or tails appear in succession.

(i) Describe the sample space.

(ii) What is the probability that the experiment ends after even number of tosses?

Solution: (i) S = {HH, TT, THH, HTT, THTT, HTHH, THTHH, HTHTT, THTHTT, HTHTHH ...}

(ii) $P(T) = P(H) = \frac{1}{2}$

A : Experiment ends after even number of tosses

$$P(A) = \frac{1}{2^2} + \frac{1}{2^2} + \frac{1}{2^4} + \frac{1}{2^4} + \frac{1}{2^6} + \frac{1}{2^6} + ...$$

$$= 2\left\{\frac{1}{2^2} + \frac{1}{2^4} + \frac{1}{2^6} + ...\right\}$$

$$= 2\left\{\frac{1}{2^2}\left\{1 + \frac{1}{2^2} + \frac{1}{2^4} + ...\right\}\right\}$$

$$= \frac{1}{2}\left\{\frac{1}{1 - \frac{1}{4}}\right\} = \frac{1}{2} \times \frac{4}{3} = \frac{4}{6} = \frac{2}{3}$$

Example 28: Give the sample space for the following:

(i) Tossing the two coins at a time.

(ii) Waiting for the arrival of bus at bus stop after 30 minutes.

(iii) Shooting a target until there is a hit.

Solution: (i) S = {TH, HT, TT, HH}

(ii) The elements in the sample space are the number of minutes one is waiting for the arrival of the bus.

∴ S = {0, 1, 2, ..., 30}

(iii) S = {H, MH, MMH, MMMH, ..., MMM ... MH, ...}

where, M stands for missing the target and
H stands for hitting the target.

Example 29: Three dice were rolled. Given no two faces were the same. What is the probability that there was an ace?

Solution: Let A be the event that there was an ace and B be the event that no two faces are same.

$$\therefore P(A|B) = \frac{P(A \cap B)}{P(B)}$$

$$P(A \cap B) = \frac{3 P(5, 2)}{6^3}$$

$$P(B) = \frac{P(6, 3)}{6^3}$$

$$\therefore P(A|B) = \frac{3 P(5, 2)}{P(6, 3)} = \frac{1}{2}.$$

Example 30: A bag contains 4 white and 6 black balls and two draws of 3 balls are made from it successively. Find the probability of drawing first 3 white and then 3 black balls when
(i) balls are replaced, (ii) balls are not replaced.

Solution: (i) The number of ways in which two draws of 3 balls of any colour can be made successively if the balls are replaced is $^{10}C_3 \cdot {}^{10}C_3$. The number of ways whereby first 3 white balls are drawn and then replacing them back 3 black balls are drawn is $^4C_3 \cdot {}^6C_3$. Hence the required probability is $\frac{{}^4C_3 \cdot {}^6C_3}{{}^{10}C_3 \cdot {}^{10}C_3} = \frac{1}{180}$.

(ii) If the balls are not replaced, then the number of ways in which two draws of 3 balls, of any colour, can be made is $^{10}C_3 \cdot {}^7C_3$. In this case, the required probability is $\frac{{}^4C_3 \cdot {}^6C_3}{{}^{10}C_3 \cdot {}^7C_3}$

$$= \frac{2}{105}.$$

Example 31: A box contains 100 slips of paper numbered from 1 to 100. If 3 slips are drawn in succession with replacement, what is the probability that at least 2 of them have the same number?

Solution: The total number of ways in which the 3 slips are drawn in succession with replacement from 100 slips of paper are $100 \times 100 \times 100 = 10^6$. The number of ways in which 2 of them have the same number is $100 \times 99 + 100 \times 99 + 100 \times 99 = 3 \times 10^2 \times 99$.

Hence the required probability is $\frac{3 \times 10^2 \times 99}{10^6} = \frac{297}{10^4} = 0.0297$.

Example 32: A room contains 10 married couples. Two people are chosen randomly from the room. What is the probability that they are husband and wife?

Solution: Total number of ways to select 2 people from the 10 pairs is $^{20}C_2 = \frac{20 \times 19}{2} = 190$. Number of ways of selecting a husband-wife pair is $^{10}C_1 = 10$.

Hence, the required probability is $\dfrac{10}{190} = \dfrac{1}{19} = 0.0526$.

Example 33: Four boys are chosen at random. What is the probability that
  (i) all are born on the same day of the week?
  (ii) all are born on different days of the week?

Solution: (i) Number of ways the boys could have been born in the week $= 7 \times 7 \times 7 \times 7 = 7^4$.

Number of ways all the boys are born on the same day in the week = 7. Hence the required probability is $\dfrac{7}{7^4} = \dfrac{1}{343} = 0.0029$.

  (ii) Probability that all are born on different days of the week

$$= \dfrac{7 \times 6 \times 5 \times 4}{7^4} = \dfrac{120}{343} = 0.3498.$$

Example 34: A box contains 6 red and 4 white balls. Find out the probability of drawing out the balls in the order: red–white–red–white etc., until only red balls (two of them) are left in the box.

Solution: The sequence in which the balls are drawn is RWRWRWRW.

Hence the required probability is $\dfrac{6}{10} \cdot \dfrac{4}{9} \cdot \dfrac{5}{8} \cdot \dfrac{3}{7} \cdot \dfrac{4}{6} \cdot \dfrac{2}{5} \cdot \dfrac{3}{4} \cdot \dfrac{1}{3} = \dfrac{1}{120} = 0.0083$.

Example 35: A and B throw alternatively with a pair of dice. A wins if he throws 6 before B throws 7 and B wins if he throws 7 before A throws 6. If A begins, show that the chance of A winning is $\dfrac{30}{61}$.

Solution: The event corresponding to A throwing 6 is {(1, 5), (5, 1), (2, 4), (4, 2), (3, 3)}.

The probability of A throwing a 6 with a pair of dice is $\dfrac{5}{36}$.

Similarly, event corresponding to B throwing 7 is {(1, 6), (6, 1), (2, 5), (5, 2), (3, 4), (4, 3)}.

Hence, the probability of B throwing a 7 is $\dfrac{6}{36}$.

$\therefore \quad P(\bar{A}) = 1 - \dfrac{5}{36} = \dfrac{31}{36}$ and $P(\bar{B}) = 1 - \dfrac{6}{36} = \dfrac{30}{36}$

Hence, the probability of A winning is

$$\dfrac{5}{36} + \dfrac{31}{36} \cdot \dfrac{30}{36} \cdot \dfrac{5}{36} + \left(\dfrac{31 \cdot 30}{36 \cdot 36}\right)^2 \dfrac{5}{36} + \ldots = \dfrac{5}{36}\left[\dfrac{1}{1 - \left(\dfrac{31 \times 30}{36 \times 36}\right)}\right] = \dfrac{5 \times 36}{6 \times 61} = \dfrac{30}{61}$$

Example 36: A committee of 12 students consists of 3 representatives from first year, 4 from second year and 5 from third year. Out of these 12 students, 3 are to be excluded from the committee by drawing lots. What is the chance that:
(i) 3 students belong to 3 different classes?
(ii) 2 belong to one class and 1 belongs to another class?
(iii) 3 belong to the same class?

Solution: Number of ways of selecting 3 students from 12 is $^{12}C_3 = 220$.

(i) Number of ways of selecting 3 belonging to three different groups is $^3C_1 \cdot {}^4C_1 \cdot {}^5C_1 = 60$.

∴ Required probability $= \dfrac{60}{220} = \dfrac{3}{11}$.

(ii) Number of ways of selecting 2 from one class and 1 from another class is
$^3C_2 \cdot {}^4C_1 + {}^3C_2 \cdot {}^5C_1 + {}^4C_2 \cdot {}^3C_1 + {}^4C_2 \cdot {}^5C_1 + {}^5C_2 \cdot {}^3C_1 + {}^5C_2 \cdot {}^4C_1 = 145$.

∴ Required probability $= \dfrac{145}{220} = \dfrac{29}{44}$.

(iii) Number of ways of selecting 3 from the same class is $^3C_3 + {}^4C_3 + {}^5C_3 = 15$.

∴ Required probability $= \dfrac{15}{220} = \dfrac{3}{44}$.

Example 37: In a test an examinee either guesses or copies or knows the answer to multiple choice questions with 4 choices, only one answer being correct. The probability that he makes a guess is $\dfrac{1}{3}$, the probability that he copies the answer is 1/6. The probability that his answer is correct, given that he copies it is 1/8. Find the probability that he knew the answer to that question, given that he correctly answers it.

Solution: Let A: event that the examinee knows the answer.
B: event that he guesses the answer.
C: event that he copies the answer.
D: event of obtaining the correct answer.

It is given that $P(B) = \dfrac{1}{3}$, $P(C) = \dfrac{1}{6}$.

∴ $1 = P(A) + P(B) + P(C)$

$P(A) = 1 - \dfrac{1}{3} - \dfrac{1}{6} = \dfrac{1}{2}$.

Probability that an answer is correct is 1/4.

Also it is given that $P(D|C) = \dfrac{1}{8}$.

∴ $P(D \cap C) = \dfrac{1}{8} \cdot \dfrac{1}{6} = \dfrac{1}{48}$

$$P(D \cap B) = \frac{1}{4} \cdot \frac{1}{3} = \frac{1}{12}$$

$$\therefore \quad P(D) = P(A \cap D) + P(B \cap D) + P(C \cap D)$$

$$= \frac{1}{2} + \frac{1}{12} + \frac{1}{48} = \frac{29}{48}$$

$$\therefore \quad \text{Required probability} = P\left(\frac{A}{D}\right)$$

$$= \frac{P(A \cap D)}{P(D)} = \frac{\frac{1}{2}}{\frac{29}{48}} = \frac{24}{29}$$

Example 38: Suppose that the probability of a person having a headache is 0.01; person having fever, given that he has a headache is 0.4 and the probability of a person having fever is 0.02. Find the probability that a person has a headache, given that he has fever.

Solution: Let H denote the event of person having headache, F the event of person having fewer. $P(H) = 0.01$, $P(F|H) = 0.$, $P(F) = 0.02$.

$$P(F|H) = \frac{P(F \cap H)}{P(H)}$$

$$\Rightarrow \quad 0.4 = \frac{P(F \cap H)}{0.01}$$

$$\therefore \quad P(F \cap H) = 0.004$$

$$\therefore \quad P(H|F) = \frac{P(H \cap F)}{P(F)} = \frac{0.004}{0.02} = 0.2$$

Example 39: Two unbiased dice are thrown. Find the probability that:
  (i) Getting a sum 6.
  (ii) Numbers shown are equal.
  (iii) Difference is 1.
  (iv) Sum is greater than 8.
  (v) First die shows 6.
  (vi) Difference is 3.

Solution: Sample space $S = \{(1, 1), (1, 2) \ldots (6,1) \ldots (6, 6)\}$

$$|S| = 36$$

(i) $A = \{(1, 5), (5, 1), (2, 4), (4, 2), (3, 3)\}$

$$\therefore \quad P(A) = \frac{5}{36}$$

(ii) $B = \{(1, 1), (2, 2), (3, 3), (4, 4), (5, 5), (6, 6)\}$

(iii) C = {(1, 2), (2, 1), (3, 2), (2, 3), (3, 4), (4, 3), (4, 5), (5, 4), (5, 6), (6, 5)}

$P(B) = \dfrac{6}{36} = \dfrac{1}{6}$

$P(C) = \dfrac{10}{36} = \dfrac{5}{18}$

(iv) D = {(3, 6), (6, 3), (4, 5), (5, 4), (4, 6), (6, 4), (5, 5), (5, 6), (6, 5), (6, 6)}

$P(D) = \dfrac{10}{36} = \dfrac{5}{16}$

(v) E = {(6, 1), (6, 2), (6, 3), (6, 4), (6, 5), (6, 6)}

$P(E) = \dfrac{6}{36} = \dfrac{1}{6}$

(vi) F = {(1, 4), (4, 1), (2, 5), (5, 2), (3, 6), (6, 3)}

$P(F) = \dfrac{6}{36} = \dfrac{1}{6}$

Example 40: Three fair coins, a penny, a nickel and a dime are tossed. Find the probability that they are all heads if (i) the penny is heads, (ii) at least one of the coins is heads.

Solution: Sample space S = {HHH, HTH, HHT, THH, THT, TTH, HTT, TTT}

(i) Let A be the event that the penny is heads. Then A = {HHH, HHT, HTH, HTT}, i.e. penny is heads, whereas the other two coins may be heads or tails. Then required probability is 1/4.

(ii) The event corresponding to at least one of the coins is heads is

B = {HHH, HTH, HHT, THH, HTT, THT, TTH}

Then required probability is 1/7.

EXERCISE - 3.2

1. Find the probability that three cards drawn at random without replacement, from a well shuffled pack of 52 playing cards, all are face cards. **(Ans. 11/1105)**

2. While shuffling a pack of cards, four cards are accidently dropped. Find the chance that the missing cards would be
   (i) one from each suit
   (ii) all from the same suit. **(Ans. (i) 0.1055, (ii) 0.0106)**

3. Two fair dice are rolled simultaneously. Find the probabilities of the following events:
   (i) A: the sum of two numbers is odd.
   (ii) B: the sum of two numbers is greater than 8.
   (iii) C: the sum of two numbers is odd or less than 7. **(Ans. (i) 1/2, (ii) 5/18, (iii) 3/4)**

4. A two digit number ending in 6 is chosen from integers 1 to 100. What is the probability that it is divisible by 3? **(Ans. 1/11)**

5. Two brothers A and B appear for the same examination. Probability that at least one of them will pass is 5/6 and probability that both of them will pass is 1/3 and the probability that A will not pass is 1/2. Find the probability of (i) A passing, (ii) B passing the exam. **(Ans. P(A) = 1/2, P(B) = 2/3)**

6. Three urns identical in appearances contain respectively 2 red and 2 green balls, 1 red and 3 green balls, 2 red and 3 green balls. One ball is drawn at random from each urn. Find the probability of getting 1 green and 2 red balls. **(Ans. 11/40)**

7. In the World Cup Soccer tournament, the probability that Brazil will enter the semi-final is 0.6, and the probability that it will win the final is 0.7. The probability that Brazil will win given that it has entered the semi-final is 0.9. Find the probability that at least one of these events will happen. **(Ans. 0.76)**

8. If the probability that a new born child is a female is 0.6, then find the probability that in a family of 3 children, there will be exactly 2 girls. **(Ans. 0.432)**

9. Two brothers appear in an interview for ME admission for the first type of vacancy. The probability of one brother's admission is 1/3 and that of another brother's admission is 1/2. What is the probability that
   (i)   both of them will get admission?   (ii) only one of them will get it?
   (iii) none of them will get it? **(Ans. (i) $\frac{1}{6}$, (ii) $\frac{1}{2}$, (iii) $\frac{1}{3}$)**

10. A boy is throwing stones to get a mango from a tree 12 times. In each trial the probability of getting the mango is $\frac{1}{2}$. Find the probability of getting
    (i)   exactly 10 mangoes.
    (ii) not more than 10 mangoes.
    (iii) at least 4 mangoes. **(Ans. (i) $^{12}C_{10}\left(\frac{1}{2}\right)^{10}\left(\frac{1}{2}\right)^2$, (ii) $1 - {}^{12}C_{11}\left(\frac{1}{2}\right)^{11}\left(\frac{1}{2}\right)$**
    (iii) $1 - \sum_{r=0}^{3} \left(\frac{1}{2}\right)^r \left(\frac{1}{2}\right)^{10-r}$)

11. A fair coin is thrown 10 times. Find the probability of getting exactly 6 heads and at least 6 heads.

    (Ans. $^{10}C_6\left(\frac{1}{2}\right)^{10}$, $\sum_{r=6}^{10} {}^{10}C_r \left(\frac{1}{2}\right)^r \left(\frac{1}{2}\right)^{10-r}$)

12. Bag I contains 6 blue and 4 red balls, bag II contains 2 blue and 6 red balls and bag III contains 1 blue and 8 red balls.
    (i) A bag is chosen at random and a ball is drawn randomly from this bag. It turns out to be blue. Find the probability that bag I was chosen.
    (ii) A bag is chosen at random, two balls are drawn without replacement from this bag. Both the balls were blue. Find the probability that bag II was chosen.
    (Ans. (i) 0·6243, (ii) 0·0968)

13. A coin is tossed until a head appears or until it has been tossed three times. Given that the head does not occur on the first toss, what is the probability, that the coin is tossed three times? **(Ans. 1/2)**
14. What is the probability that the 4 'S' appearing in the word 'MISSISSIPPI' be together if the letters are rearranged? **(Ans. 4/165)**
15. In a bag there are 4 white and 3 black balls. If four balls are drawn one by one at random, what is the probability that the balls so drawn are alternately of different colour? **(Ans. 6/35)**
16. There are 3 events A, B, C, one of which must and only one can happen; the odds are 7 to 3 against A and 6 to 4 against B. Find the odds against C.
17. A committee of 12 students consists of 3 representatives from first year, 4 from second year and 5 from third year classes. Out of these 12 students, three are to be excluded from the committee by drawing lots. What is the chance that (i) the three students belong to different classes? (ii) two belong to one class and the third to a different class? (iii) the three belong to the same class?
(Ans. (i) 3/11, (ii) 29/44, (iii) 3/44)
18. A student takes his examination in 4 subjects A, B, C and D. He estimates his chance of passing in A as 4/5, in B as 3/4, in C as 5/6 and in D as 2/3. To qualify he must pass in A and at least two other subjects. What is the probability that he will qualify?
(Ans. 61/90)
19. An integer between 1 and 100 (both inclusive) is selected at random. Find the probability of selecting a perfect square if (i) all integers are equally likely (ii) an integer between 1 and 50 is twice as likely to occur than an integer between 51 and 100. **(Ans. (i) 0.10, (ii) 0.113)**
20. The chances that a doctor will diagnose a disease correctly is 60%. The chances that a patient will die by his treatment after correct diagnosis is 40% and the chances of death by wrong diagnosis is 70%. A patient of the doctor, who had the disease, died. What is the chance that his disease was diagnosed correctly? **(Ans. 6/13)**
21. The probability that a man, aged 60 will live to be 70 is 0.65. What is the probability that out of 10 men, now 60, at least 7 will live to be 70? **(Ans. 0.5137)**
22. In how many ways can 4 Maths books, three History books, three Chemistry books and two Sociology books be arranged on a shelf so that all the books of the same subject are together? **(Ans. 41472)**
23. There are 3 different pairs of socks in a box. If two socks are chosen at random, what is the probability that they form an exact pair? **(Ans. 1/5 = 0.2)**
24. A can hit a target 3 times in 5 shots, B, 2 times in 5 shots, 3 times in 4 shots. They fire a volley. What is the probability that 2 shots hit the target? **(Ans. 9/20)**
25. A computer consists of 5 subsystems and the computer crashes if at least one of the subsystem crashes. The probabilities of subsystems 1, 2, 3, 4 and 5 crashing are 0.2,

0.5, 0.7, 0.1 and 0.3 respectively. Suppose the computer has crashed, what is the probability that

(i) only subsystem number 1 has crashed?

(ii) subsystem number 1 has crashed?

(iii) all the subsystems have crashed?

(**Ans.** (i) 0.0189, (ii) 0.2, (iii) 0.0021, (iv) 8.897)

26. An educational institute encourages its students to participate in group discussions and debates. A survey indicates that 40% participate in group discussions, 50% participate in debates and 25% participate in both. Find the probability of the events:

    (i) A student participates only in debates.

    (ii) A student participates only in group discussions.

    (iii) A student participates in at least one of the activity.

27. Suppose that 3 balls are selected at random from a user containing 7 red balls and 5 black balls. Compute the probability that:

    (i) All three balls are red.

    (ii) At least two balls are black.

    (iii) At most two balls are black.

    (iv) At least one ball is red.

28. A pair of fair deice is thrown. If the two numbers appearing are different, find the probability that (a) the sum is 6, (b) an ace appears, (c) the sum is 4 or less.

29. Suppose that three balls are selected at random from an urn containing seven red balls and five black balls. Compute probability that:

    (i) All three balls are red.

    (ii) At least two balls are black.

    (iii) At most two balls are black.

    (iv) At least one ball is red.

3.4 Binomial Coefficients and Combinatorial Identities

The numbers C (n, r) described in article 8.1.2, occur as coefficients in the binomial expansion $(a + b)^n$, and hence are called as binomial coefficients. The binomial coefficients surprisingly satisfy quite a large number of identities, which are well adapted to algebraic manipulation. Hence these identities find important applications in problems involving counting. (This branch of study is called as Combinatorics.)

In this section we will deal with some of the basic identities and their properties.
Let us first, take a review of the Binomial Theorem.
The Binomial Theorem gives the expansion of $(a + b)^n$ (n positive integer) as

$$(a + b)^n = C(n, 0) a^n b^0 + C(n, 1) a^{n-1} b^1 + C(n, 2) a^{n-2} b^2 + \ldots + C(n, n-1) a^1 b^{n-1} + C(n, n) a^0 b^n$$

Although the Binomial Theorem is normally proved, using induction on n, a combinatorial approach will be more appropriate here.

For n = 3, consider

$$(a + b)^3 = (a + b)(a + b)(a + b)$$
$$= aaa + aab + aba + abb + baa + bab + bba + bbb$$

The first term aaa occurs, when we select a from each factor $(a + b)$ and there is only one such term, i.e. a^3 in the final expansion. There are 3 terms viz. aab, aba, baa in which a appears twice and b only once. The same is the case with b twice and a only once. The last term bbb occurs only once, like aaa.

Putting the above observations differently, we note:

(i) There are two choices a or b for each term in the product and so there are $2 \times 2 \times 2 = 8$ formal products.

(ii) In the 8 formal products, there are 3 in which a appears twice and same is the case for b.

(iii) There is only a single product in which a (as well as b) has all the three choices.

Using the above combinational argument we conclude that

$$(a + b)^3 = a^3 + 3a^2 b + 3ab^2 + b^3$$

For the general case $(a + b)^n$, we can argue similarly. Each product in the expansion contains n factors. Suppose we want to find how many times the product $a^k b^{n-k}$ appears in the expansion. Since a must have k choices, these can be found in $C(n, k)$ ways. The number of choices is exactly the same for b to have $n - k$ choices. Hence it follows that

$$C(n, k) = C(n, n - k)$$

The binomial coefficient $C(n, k)$ can also be interpreted differently using set theory, and this interpretation is found very often useful.

Let us suppose that we have a set of n people, from which we want to form a committee of k persons. This is equivalent to finding k-element subsets of a set containing n objects and this number is $C(n, k)$.

Let us now consider some basic properties of the binomial coefficients, which are considered as **Combinational Identities.**

Theorem 1: $C(n + 1, k) = C(n, k - 1) + C(n, k)$, for $1 \leq k \leq n$
Proof:
The theorem can easily be verified by algebraic method. However, a combinational proof will be more in place here. Let A be a set containing n elements. Choose $b \notin A$, and form the set $B = A \cup \{b\}$.

Then $C(n+1, k)$ is the number of k-element subsets of B.
These can be divided into two disjoint classes.
Subsets of B not containing b.
Subsets of B containing b.
The subsets of class 1 are just k-element subsets of A, and those of class 2 consist of a $k-1$ element subset of A together with b.
Number of subsets of the first type is $C(n, k)$ and that of the second type is $C(n, k-1)$.
Hence $C(n+1, k) = C(n, k-1) + C(n, k)$

Theorem 2: $C(n, k) \cdot C(k, m) = C(n, m) \cdot C(n-m, k-m)$; $1 \leq m \leq k \leq n$

Proof:
L.H.S. gives the number of ways to select k-element subsets of a set of n elements and then to select m-element subsets from each of these k-subsets.
This can be equivalently substituted by selecting m-element subsets from the set of n elements and the remaining $k-m$ element subsets from remaining $n-m$ elements.

Theorem 3: $C(n, 0) + C(n, 1) + C(n, 2) + \ldots + C(n, n) = 2^n$

Proof:
Let A be a set containing n elements.
Then the number of subsets of $A = 2^n$ = R.H.S. On the L.H.S., $C(n, 0), C(n, 1), \ldots, C(n, n)$ gives the count of all the subsets of A, containing 0 elements, 1 element, 2 elements, and so on.
Hence the total number of subsets by L.H.S. count is the same as the total number of subsets of A which is equal to 2^n.

Theorem 4: $C(k, k) + C(k+1, k) + C(k+2, k) + \ldots + C(n, k) = C(n+1, k+1)$.

Proof:
We know that
$$C(i+1, k) = C(i, k-1) + C(i, k) \quad ; \quad \forall\ 1 \leq k \leq i \leq n$$
Hence we can deduce from the above that
$$C(i, k) = C(i+1, k+1) - C(i, k+1)$$
(replacing k by $k+1$ in the above identity)
Now in L.H.S., $C(k, k) = 1$
$C(k+1, k) = C(k+2, k+1) - C(k+1, k+1)$ (putting $i = k+1$)
Similarly $C(k+2, k) = C(k+3, k+1) - C(k+2, k+1)$
and so on.
Hence, L.H.S. = $1 + C(k+2, k+1) - C(k+1, k+1) + C(k+3, k+1)$
$C(k+2, k+1) + \ldots + C(n+1, k+1) - C(n, k+1)$
$= C(n+1, k+1)$
as all other terms mutually cancel.

The following examples illustrate how the binomial identities can be applied to evaluate sum of a series, whose coefficients are closely related to binomial coefficients.

SOLVED EXAMPLES

Example 1: Find the sum of $1 + 2 + \ldots + n$

Solution:
$$1 + 2 + \ldots + n = C(1, 1) + C(2, 1) + \ldots + C(n, 1)$$
$$= C(n + 1, 2) \quad \text{(by theorem)}$$
$$= \frac{(n + 1)!}{2!(n - 1)!} = \frac{n(n + 1)}{2}$$

Example 2: Find the sum $1^2 + 2^2 + 3^2 + \ldots + n^2$

Solution: The general term k^2, we can express as
$$k^2 = k(k - 1) + k$$
By this strategy we can relate $k(k - 1)$ to $C(k, 2)$.
Hence the given sum can be rewritten as
$$(1 \times 0 + 1) + [(2 \times 1) + 2] + [(3 \times 2) + 3] + \ldots + [n(n - 1) + n]$$
$$= [2 \times 1 + 3 \times 2 + \ldots + n(n - 1)] + (1 + 2 + 3 + \ldots + n)$$
$$= [2\,C(2, 2) + 2\,C(3, 2) + \ldots + 2\,C(n, 2)] + C(n + 1, 2)$$
$$= 2\,C(n + 1, 3) + C(n + 1, 2)$$
$$= 2 \cdot \frac{(n + 1)!}{3!(n - 2)!} + \frac{n(n + 1)}{2} = \frac{(n + 1)\,n(n - 1)}{3} + \frac{n(n + 1)}{2}$$
$$= \frac{n(n + 1)(2n + 1)}{6}$$

Example 3: Evaluate the sum
$$C(n, 0) + 2\,C(n, 1) + 2^2\,C(n, 2) + \ldots + 2^k\,C(n, k) + \ldots + 2^n\,C(n, n)$$

Solution: By binomial theorem,
$$(1 + x)^n = C(n, 0) + C(n, 1)\,x + C(n, 2)\,x^2 + \ldots + C(n, n)\,x^n$$
Hence putting $x = 2$,
$$\text{R.H.S.} = C(n, 0) + 2\,C(n, 1) + \ldots + 2^n\,C(n, n)$$
$$= (1 + 2)^n = 3^n$$

Example 4: Evaluate the sum $1 \times 2 \times 3 + 2 \times 3 \times 4 + \ldots + (n - 2)(n - 1)n$

Solution: The general term is $k(k - 1)(k - 2) = 3!\,C(k, 3)$
Hence the given sum can be rewritten as
$$3!\,C(3, 3) + 3!\,C(4, 3) + \ldots + 3!\,C(n, 3)$$
$$= 3!\,[C(3, 3) + C(4, 3) + \ldots + C(n, 3)]$$
$$= 3!\,C(n + 1, 4)$$
$$= \frac{3!\,(n + 1)!}{4!\,(n - 3)!}$$
$$= \frac{1}{4}(n + 1)\,n(n - 1)(n - 2)$$

Example 5: Prove that: $C(n, 0)^2 + C(n, 1)^2 + \ldots + C(n, n)^2 = C(2n, n)$

Solution: We use the equality

$$(1 + x)^n + (1 + x)^n = (1 + x)^{2n} \qquad \ldots (1)$$

$$(1 + x)^n = \sum_{r=0}^{n} C(n, r) x^r$$

$$(1 + x)^{2n} = \sum_{k=0}^{2n} C(2n, k) x^k$$

Hence equation (1) can be expressed as

$$\left[\sum_{r=0}^{n} C(n, r) x^r\right]\left[\sum_{m=0}^{n} C(n, m) x^m\right] = \sum_{k=0}^{2n} C(2n, k) x^k$$

The coefficient of x^n should be equal on both the sides. Hence,

$C(n, 0) C(n, n) + C(n, 1) C(n, n-1) + C(n, 2) C(n, n-2) + \ldots + C(n, n) C(n, 0) = C(2n, n)$

But $\quad C(n, 0) = C(n, n), \quad C(n, 1) = C(n, n-1)$ and so on.

Hence, $\quad C(n, 0)^2 + C(n, 1)^2 + \ldots + C(n, n)^2 = C(2n, n)$

Example 6: Show that $C(n, 1) + 2C(n, 2) + 3C(n, 3) + \ldots + nC(n, n) = n \cdot 2^{n-1}$

Solution: We use the identity

$$C(n, n-k) = C(n, k)$$

Let, $\quad S_n = C(n, 1) + 2C(n, 2) + 3C(n, 3) + \ldots + nC(n, n) \qquad \ldots (1)$

Then using the above identity, we see that

$$S_n = C(n, n-1) + 2C(n, n-2) + 3C(n, n-3) + \ldots + nC(n, 0) \ldots (2)$$

We reverse the order of the equation (2) and rewrite

$$S_n = nC(n, 0) + (n-1) C(n, 1) + (n-2) C(n, 2) + \ldots + C(n, n-1)$$
$$\ldots (3)$$

Adding equations (1) and (3) we obtain

$$2S_n = n[C(n, 0) + C(n, 1) + C(n, 2) + \ldots + C(n, n)] = n \cdot 2^n$$

$\therefore \qquad S_n = \dfrac{n \cdot 2^n}{2} = n \cdot 2^{n-1}$

Example 7: Simplify the expression: $C(3, 3) + C(4, 3) + C(5, 3) + \ldots + C(27, 3)$

Solution: Note that there are 25 terms in the series. We use the identity

$$C(n, k) + C(n, k-1) = C(n+1, k)$$

Also we can replace $C(3, 3)$ by $C(4, 4)$.

Hence the given sum is

$[C(4, 4) + C(4, 3)] + C(5, 3) + C(6, 3) + \ldots + C(27, 3)$

$= C(5, 4) + C(5, 3) + C(6, 3) + \ldots + C(27, 3)$

$$= C(6, 4) + C(6, 3) + \ldots + C(27, 3)$$
$$= C(7, 4) + \ldots + C(27, 3)$$

Continuing in this way, the last two terms
$$= C(27, 4) + C(27, 3) = C(28, 4)$$

EXERCISE - 3.3

1. Show that: $C(2n, n) + C(2n, n-1) = C(2n+2, n+1)$
2. If $C(n, 3) + C(n+2, 3) = P(n, 3)$, find n. **(Ans.: n = 4)**
3. Prove that: $C(2n, 2) = 2 C(n, 2) + n^2$
4. Show that: $C(n, 1) + 6C(n, 2) + 6C(n, 3) = n^3$
5. Evaluate: $1^3 + 2^3 + 3^3 + \ldots + n^3$ **(Ans.:** $C(n+1, 2) + 6C(n+1, 3) + 6C(n+1, 4)$**)**
6. Evaluate the sum: $1 + 2C(n, 1) + \ldots + (k+1) C(n, k) + \ldots + (n+1) C(n, n)$

    (Ans.: $2^n + n2^{n-1}$**)**
7. Find the sum: $C(n, 0) - 2C(n, 1) + 3C(n, 2) + \ldots + (-1)^n (n+1) C(n, n)$ **(Ans.: 0)**
8. Evaluate: $C(n, 0) + 2C(n, 1) + C(n, 2) + 2C(n, 3) + \ldots$ **(Ans.:** $3 \cdot 2^{n-1}$**)**

POINTS TO REMEMBER

- Let $0 \le r \le n$. The number of ways to have an ordered sequence of n distinct elements, taken r at a time is called as an r-permutation of n-elements and is denoted by P(n, r) or (^nP_r).
- The number of ways in which of the n elements can be arranged, where r_1 elements are of one kind, r_2 are of another kind and so on till r_k elements are of another kind, is given by the formula $\dfrac{P(n, r)}{r_1! \, r_2! \, \ldots \, r_k!}$, where $r = r_1 + r_2 + \ldots + r_k$.
- The number of permutations of n elements, r at a time, when each element may be repeated once, twice, ... upto r times in any arrangement.
- Let $0 \le r \le n$. A selection of a set of r elements from a set of n distinct elements is called a combination.
- A set of possible outcomes is called as an event. An event is a subset of the sample space.
- If A is an event, its set complement $\bar{A} = S - A$ is the complement event. If event A occurs, the event $\bar{A}$ will not occur and vice versa.
- If A and B are two events, then the compound event is $A \cup B$ which is described as at least one of the events A or B occur.
- If A and B are events, the product event is $A \cap B$ and is described as both events A and B occur.

- Events A and B are said to be mutually exclusive if the occurrence or non occurrence of A precludes the occurrence or non-occurrence of B. In other words, if A occurs then B does not occur and vice versa. This is equivalent to saying that $A \cap B = \phi$.
- Events A and B are said to be independent if the occurrence or non-occurrence of one does not affect the occurrence or non-occurrence of the other. Two events are said to be independent if $P(A \cap B) = P(A) \cdot P(B)$. This rule is called as the multiplicative law of probability.
- Let A be an event, with its probability of occurrence P(A). Then the information contained in a statement regarding the occurrence of A is given by the formula $I(A) = -\log P(A)$.

  Note that since $0 \leq P(A) \leq 1$, log P(A) is a non-positive number and hence $-\log P(A)$ is a non-negative number.

Unit 2

Chapter 4: RELATIONS

SYLLABUS:
- Relations: Definitions, Properties of Binary Relations, Equivalence Relations and Partitions, Partial ordering relations and Lattices, Chains and Antichains, Job Scheduling problem, Transitive closure and Warshall's algorithm.

OBJECTIVES:
- To study relations among objects of sets.
- To study function as input-output relation.

UTILITY:
- In preparing relational database.
- Recursive and generating functions are important tools in software development.

KEY CONCEPTS:
- Binary relation
- Equivalence relation
- Partial order
- Partition

4.0 Introduction

In the preceding chapter we dealt with sets, elements and general properties of sets. Now we progress further and study the various relationships that may exist between elements of a set. We study various properties of a relation, including its matrix and graphical representations.

The concept of relation is of primary importance in computer science, especially in the study of data structure such as linked list, array, relational models etc. Relations are also important in the analysis of algorithms, information system etc.

4.1 Relations

A common notion of relation is a type of association that exists between two or more objects. Consider the following examples:

(i) x is the father of y.
(ii) x was born in the city y in the year z.
(iii) The number x is greater than the number y.
(iv) Prof. x teaches the subject y to the class z in classroom u.

In general, one can have relation among n objects, (where n is a positive integer). In describing a relation, it is necessary not only to specify the objects, but also the order in which they appear. In the example "x is the father of y", the respective positions of x and y matter; x should precede y, and not vice-versa. Hence in the following definition, we introduce the concept which gives the necessary ordering of the objects.

4.1.1 Definition

> An **ordered n-tuple,** for n > 0, is a sequence of objects or elements, denoted by $(a_1, a_2,\ldots, a_n)$.
>
> If n = 2, the ordered n-tuple is called an **ordered pair.**
>
> If n = 3, the ordered n-tuple is called an ordered triple; and so on.

As pre-requisite to study relations, we consider sets whose elements are ordered n-tuples and study their properties.

4.2 Product Sets

Definition:

> Let A and B be non-empty sets. The **product set** or the **Cartesian product** $A \times B$ is defined as
>
> $$A \times B = \{ (a, b) \mid a \in A \text{ and } b \in B \}.$$
>
> If $A = \phi$ or $B = \phi$, then $A \times B = \phi$.

Examples:

(i) Let $A = \{a, b, c\}$, $B = \{1, 2\}$.
   Then $A \times B = \{(a, 1), (a, 2), (b, 1), (b, 2), (c, 1), (c, 2)\}$

(ii) Let A = set of students = {Shilpa, Ramesh, Aparna}
   and B = set of marks in DSGT = {65, 56, 72},

Then A × B = {(Shilpa, 65), (Shilpa, 56), (Shilpa, 72), (Ramesh, 65), (Ramesh, 56), (Ramesh, 72), (Aparna, 65), (Aparna, 56), (Aparna, 72)}.

(iii) If **R** denotes the set of all real numbers, then **R** × **R** denotes the set of all points in the co-ordinate plane.

(iv) We know that a complex number x + iy can be considered as an ordered pair (x, y). Hence if **C** denotes the set of all complex numbers, then C is the Cartesian product **R** × **R**.

From the above examples, it is clear that product of sets is non-commutative,

i.e. A × B ≠ B × A.

The following theorem establishes certain important properties of the product operation.

4.2.1 Theorem

(i) A × (B ∪ C) = (A × B) ∪ (A × C)
Proof:
We shall show that every element (x, y) of A × (B ∪ C) is an element of (A × B) ∪ (A × C) and vice-versa.
(x, y) ∈ A × (B ∪ C) × x ∈ A and y ∈ (B ∪ C) × x ∈ A and (y ∈ B or y ∈ C).
Since 'and' distributes over 'or', this implies (x ∈ A and y ∈ B) or (x ∈ A and y ∈ C)
(x, y) ∈ (A × B) or (x, y) ∈ (A × C)
x ∈ (A × B) ∪ (A × C).
Thus (i) is proved.

(ii) A × (B ∩ C) = (A × B) ∩ (A × C)
Proof:
(x, y) ∈ A × (B ∩ C) ↔ x ∈ A and y ∈ (B ∩ C) ↔ x ∈ A and (y ∈ B and y ∈ C)
↔ (x ∈ A and y ∈ B) and (x ∈ A and y ∈ C)
↔ (x, y) ∈ (A × B) and (x, y) ∈ (A × C)
↔ (x, y) ∈ (A × B) ∩ (A × C)

(iii) (A ∪ B) × C = (A × C) ∪ (B × C)
Proof:
(x, y) ∈ A × (B ∩ C) ↔ x ∈ A and y ∈ (B ∩ C) ↔ x ∈ A and (y ∈ B and y ∈ C)

$\leftrightarrow$ ($x \in A$ and $y \in B$) and ($x \in A$ and $y \in C$)
$\leftrightarrow$ $(x, y) \in (A \times B)$ and $(x, y) \in (A \times C)$
$\leftrightarrow$ $(x, y) \in (A \times B) \cap (A \times C)$

(iv) $(A \cap B) \times C = (A \times C) \cap (B \times C)$
$(x, y) \in (A \cap B) \times C \leftrightarrow x \in (A \cap B)$ and $y \in C \leftrightarrow (x \in A$ and $x \in B)$ and $y \in C$
$\leftrightarrow (x \in A$ and $y \in C)$ and $(x \in B$ and $y \in C)$
$\leftrightarrow (x, y) \in (A \times C)$ and $(x, y) \in (B \times C)$
$\leftrightarrow (x, y) \in (A \times C) \cap (B \times C)$.

The next theorem gives an important result pertaining to the cardinality of the product set.

4.2.2 Theorem

If A and B are finite sets with cardinalities m, n respectively then $|A \times B| = m \cdot n$.

Proof:

Since $|A| = m$,

Let $A = \{a_1, a_2, ..., a_m\}$.

Similarly, $B = \{b_1, b_2, ..., b_n\}$, as $|B| = n$.

Now $A \times B = \{(a_i, b_j) \mid 1 \leq i \leq m, 1 \leq j \leq n\}$

Since for each element a_i in A, there exists a corresponding element $b_j \in B$ in the ordered pair (a_i, b_j), the set $A \times B$ consists of exactly $m \cdot n$ elements.

Hence $|A \times B| = m \cdot n$.

Example: If $A = \{n \in N \mid 1 \leq n \leq 100\}$

and $B = \{n \in N \mid 1 \leq n \leq 50\}$

then $|A \times B| = 100 \times 50 = 5000$

The definition of product of two sets is generalised for a finite collection of sets $\{A_1, A_2, ..., A_n\}$ by defining $A_1 \times A_2 \times ...... \times A_n = \{(a_1, a_2, ..., a_n) \mid a_i \in A_i, 1 \leq i \leq n\}$.

If all $A_i = A$, then $A_1 \times A_2 \times ... \times A_n = A^n$.

If A, B, C are non-empty sets ;

then $A \times B \times C = \{(a, b, c) \mid a \in A, b \in B, c \in C\}$

This set is clearly different from

$$A \times (B \times C) = \{(a, (b, c)) \mid a \in A, (b, c) \in B \times C\}$$

and also different from the set

$$(A \times B) \times C = \{((a, b), c) \mid (a, b) \in A \times B, c \in C\}$$

Distinguishing the three types is quite a problem sometimes, though normally by product of sets A, B, C, we mean $A \times B \times C$.

SOLVED EXAMPLES

Example 1: If $A = \{1\}$, $B = \{a, b\}$, $C = \{2, 3\}$, find $A \times B \times C$, A^2, $B^2 \times A$, C^3.

Solution:
$A \times B \times C = \{(1, a, 2), (1, b, 2), (1, a, 3), (1, b, 3)\}$
$A^2 = \{(1, 1)\}$
$B^2 = \{(a, a), (a, b), (b, a), (b, b)\}$
$B^2 \times A = \{((a, a), 1), ((a, b), 1), ((b, a), 1), ((b, b), 1)\}$
$C^3 = C \times C \times C = \{(2, 2, 2), (2, 2, 3), (2, 3, 3), (2, 3, 2), (3, 2, 2), (3, 3, 2), (3, 2, 3), (3, 3, 3)\}$

Example 2: If $A \subseteq C$ and $B \subseteq D$, prove that $A \times B \subseteq C \times D$.

Solution: Let $(a, b) \in A \times B$.
This implies $a \in A$ and $b \in B$. Since $A \subseteq C$ and $B \subseteq D$, $a \in C$ and $b \in D$ so that $(a, b) \in C \times D$. Hence $A \times B \subseteq C \times D$.

Example 3: Show that $A \times B = B \times A \leftrightarrow A = \phi$ or $B = \phi$ or $A = B$.

Solution: Let $A \times B = B \times A$. Then $(a, b) \in A \times B \leftrightarrow (a, b) \in B \times A \leftrightarrow a \in A$ iff $a \in B$ and $b \in B$ iff $b \in A \leftrightarrow A = B$ iff $A \times B \neq \phi$. If $A \times B = \phi$, then $A = \phi$ or $B = \phi$. Hence the result.

Example 4: If $A = \{1, 2\}$, $B = \{1, 2, 3\}$, find $(A \times B) \cap (B \times A)$

Solution:
$A \times B = \{(1, 1), (1, 2), (1, 3), (2, 1), (2, 2), (2, 3)\}$
$B \times A = [(1, 1), (1, 2), (2, 1), (2, 2), (3, 1), (3, 2)\}$.
Hence $(A \times B) \cap (B \times A) = \{(1, 1), (1, 2), (2, 1), (2, 2)\}$.

EXERCISE 4.1

1. Let $A = \{a, b\}$ and $B = \{4, 5, 6\}$. List the elements in
   (a) $A \times B$, (b) $B \times A$, (c) $A \times A$, (d) $B \times B$,
   (e) $(A \times B) \times A$, (f) $A \times A \times B$, (g) $A \times (B \times A)$.

2. If A = {a, b, c}, B = {1, 2} and C = {#, *}, list all the elements in A × B × C.
3. If A = {1, 2} construct the set P(A) × A.
4. If A × B ⊆ C × D, does it necessarily follow that A ⊆ C and B ⊆ D?
5. Is it possible A ⊆ A × A, for some set A?
6. Prove or disprove
   (i)   (A ∪ B) × (C ∪ D) = (A × C) ∪ (B × D)
   (ii) (A − B) × (C − D) = (A × C) − (B × D)
   (iii) (A ⊕ B) × (C ⊕ D) = (A × C) ⊕ (B × D)
   (iv) (A ⊕ B) × C = (A × C) ⊕ (B × C)
7. Prove that A × B = B × A iff A = B.
8. Consider the ordered triple {1, 3, 5}.
   (a) Represent the ordered triple as an ordered pair.
   (b) Represent the ordered pair in (a) as a set.
9. Let $A = \{a \mid 1 \leq a \leq 2\}$ and
   $B = \{b \mid 0 \leq b \leq 1\}$.

   Find : (a) A × B
   (b) B × A
   (c) Represent A × B and B × A graphically.
10. Is (A × B) × C = A × (B × C)? Justify?

4.3 Basic Concepts Of Relation

4.3.1 Definition

Let $\{A_1, A_2, ..., A_n\}$ be a finite collection of sets. A subset R of $A_1 \times A_2 \times ... \times A_n$ is called an **n-ary relation** on $A_1, A_2, ..., A_n$.

If R = φ, then R is called **void** or empty relation.

If R = $A_1 \times A_2 \times ... \times A_n$, then R is called the **universal** relation.

If A_i = A for all i, then R is called an n-ary relation on A.

If n = 1, 2 or 3, then R is called a **unary, binary** or **ternary** relation respectively.

Examples:
(i) Let **Z** be the set of all integers. Then the property "x is an even integer", can be characterised as a relation which is unary. In this case, the relation
$R = \{x \in Z \mid x \text{ is even}\}$.

(ii) Let A = {1, 2, 5, 6} and let R be the relation characterised by the property "x is less than y". Then R = {(1, 2), (1,5), (1, 6), (2, 5), (2, 6), (5, 6)}, where R is binary.

(iii) Let A = {1, 2, 3} and let R be the relation characterised by the property "x + y is less than z". Then R = {1, 1, 3}, which is a ternary.

(iv) Let A = {2, 3, 4} and let R be the relation characterised by the property "x + y is divisible by z". Then R = {(2, 2, 2), (2, 2, 4), (2, 4, 2), (2, 4, 3), (3, 3, 2), (3, 3, 3), (4, 2, 2), (4, 2, 3), (4, 4, 2), (4, 4, 4)}, where R is a ternary relation.

Among the relations, binary relations are the most important, being widely used in various applications. Hence in what follows, we will discuss binary relations and their properties in detail.

4.3.2 Binary Relation

Let A and B be non-empty sets. Then a binary relation R from A to B is a subset of A × B, i.e. R ⊆ A × B. The **domain** of R, denoted by D(R), is the set of elements in A that are related to some element in B, i.e.

$$D(R) = \{a \in A \mid \text{for some } b \in B, (a, b) \in R\}$$

The range of R denoted by Rn (R) is the set of elements in B, that are related to some element in A, i.e.

$$Rn(R) = \{b \in B \mid \text{for some } a \in A, (a, b) \in R\}.$$

Clearly D(R) ⊆ A and Rn (R) ⊆ B.

Example 5: Let A = {2, 3, 4, 5} and let R be the relation on A defined as aRb iff a < b. Find D(R) and Rn(R).

Solution: R = {(2, 3), (2, 4), (2, 5), (3, 4), (3, 5), (4, 5)}
Then   D(R) = {2, 3, 4} and   Rn (R) = {3, 4, 5}

As R is basically a set, all the rules of set operations are applicable to R. Hence if A, B are sets with binary relations R and S, then

$$R \cup S = \{(a, b) \mid (a, b) \in R \vee (a, b) \in S\}$$

$$R \cap S = \{(a, b) \mid (a, b) \in R \wedge (a, b) \in S\}$$

The set A × B is the **universal** relation and the empty set φ is the **void** relation.

4.3.3 Complement of a Relation

> The complement of a relation R, denoted by $\overline{R}$ is defined as the set
> $$\overline{R} = \{(a, b) \mid (a, b) \in R\}, \text{ i.e. } a\overline{R}b \text{ iff } aRb.$$

Example 1:

Let $A = \{1, 2, 3, 4\}$ and $B = \{a, b, c\}$.
Let $R = \{(1, a), (1, b), (2, c), (3, a), (4, b)\}$
and $S = \{(1, b), (1, c), (2, a), (3, b), (4, b)\}$

Find (i) $\overline{R}$ and $\overline{S}$ (ii) Verify De Morgan's laws for R and S.

Solution:

(i) $A \times B = \{(1, a), (1, b), (1, c), (2, a), (2, b), (2, c), (3, a), (3, b), (3, c),$
$(4, a), (4, b), (4, c)\}$.

$\therefore \quad \overline{R} = \{(1, c), (2, a), (2, b), (3, b), (3, c), (4, a), (4, c)\}$

$\overline{S} = \{(1, a), (2, b), (2, c), (3, a), (3, c), (4, a), (4, c)\}$.

(ii) De Morgan's laws states that

$\overline{R \cup S} = \overline{R} \cap \overline{S}$ and $\overline{R \cap S} = \overline{R} \cup \overline{S}$

$R \cup S = \{(1, a), (1, b), (1, c), (2, a), (2, c), (3, a), (3, b), (4, b)\}$

$\overline{R \cup S} = \{(2, b), (3, c), (4, a), (4, c)\}$

$\overline{R} \cap \overline{S} = \{(2, b), (3, c), (4, a), (4, c)\}$

Hence $\overline{R \cup S} = \overline{R} \cap \overline{S}$

$R \cap S = \{(1, b), (4, b)\}$

$\therefore \quad \overline{R \cap S} = \{(1, a), (1, c), (2, a), (2, b), (2, c), (3, a), (3, b), (3, c), (4, a), (4, c)\}$

$\overline{R} \cup \overline{S} = \{(1, a), (1, c), (2, a), (2, b), (2, c), (3, a), (3, b), (3, c), (4, a), (4, c)\}$

Hence $\overline{R \cap S} = \overline{R} \cup \overline{S}$

Thus De Morgan's laws are verified for relations R and S.

DISCRETE STRUCTURE AND GRAPH THEORY (NMU) RELATIONS

4.3.4 Converse of a Relation

Given a relation from A to B, one may define a relation from B to A as follows.

> Let R be a relation from A to B. Then the **converse** of R, denoted by R^c is the relation from B to A, defined as
>
> $$R^c = \{(b, a) \mid (a, b) \in R\}$$
>
> Clearly $R^c \subseteq B \times A$

For example, if $A = N$ is the set of natural numbers and R is the relation <, then R^c is the relation >. The converse relation is also called as the **inverse** relation and is denoted by R^{-1}.

The following theorem gives important properties of the converse relation.

4.3.5 Theorem

Let R, S be the relations from A to B. Then

(i) $(R^c)^c = R$
Proof:
(i) is immediate, by the definition of the converse.

(ii) $(R \cup S)^c = R^c \cup S^c$
Proof:
$(R \cup S)^c = \{(b, a) \mid (a, b) \in R \text{ or } (a, b) \in S\}$
$= \{(b, a) \mid (b, a) \in R^c \vee (b, a) \in S^c\}$
$= R^c \cup S^c$

(iii) $(R \cap S)^c = R^c \cap S^c$
Proof:
$(R \cap S)^c = \{(b, a) \mid (a, b) \in R \wedge (a, b) \in S\}$
$= \{(b, a) \mid (b, a) \in R^c \wedge (b, a) \in S^c\}$

SOLVED EXAMPLES

Example 1: Let $A = \{1, 2, 3, 4\}$ and $B = \{a, b, c\}$
Let $R = \{(1, a), (3, a), (3, c)\}$.
Find (i) R^c, (ii) $D(R^c)$, (ii) $Rn(R^c)$.

Solution: (i) $R^c = \{(a, 1), (a, 3), (c, 3)\}$
(ii) $D(R^c) = \{a, c\} = Rn(R)$
(iii) $Rn(R^c) = \{1, 3\} = D(R)$

Example 2: Let $A = \{2, 3, 4, 6\}$. Let R and S be relations on A such that
$R = \{(a, b) \mid a = b + 1 \text{ or } b = 2a\}$

and $S = \{(a, b) \mid a \text{ divides } b\}$, find $(R \cap S)^c$.

Solution: $R = \{(3, 2), (4, 3), (2, 4), (3, 6)\}$
and $S = \{(2, 2), (2, 4), (2, 6), (3, 3), (3, 6), (4, 4), (6, 6)\}$
∴ $R \cap S = \{(2, 4), (3, 6)\}$
∴ $(R \cap S)^c = \{(4, 2), (6, 3)\}$.

4.3.6 Composition of Binary Relations

We shall now discuss relations that are formed from an existing **sequence** of relations. These are called as composite relations. Real life abounds with such relations. Consider for example, the relationship of grandfather who is father's (or mother's) father.

The concept of composite relations plays an important role in the execution of programs, where a sequence of data conversions takes place from decimal to binary and from binary to floating point. Let us now formally define composite relation.

Definition:

Let R_1 be a relation from A to B and R_2 a relation from B to C. The **composite relation** from A to C, denoted by $R_1 \cdot R_2$ (or $R_1 R_2$) is defined as

$$R_1 \cdot R_2 = \{(a, c) \mid a \in A \land c \in C \land \exists b [b \in B \land (a, b) \in R_1 \land (b, c) \in R_2]\}$$

Note that if R_1 is a relation from A to B and R_2 from C to D, $R_1 \cdot R_2$ is not defined unless B = C. In general, if $\{A_1, A_2, ..., A_{n+1}\}$ is a finite collection of sets where R_1 is a relation from A_1 to A_2, R_2 from A_2 to A_3, ... R_n from A_n to A_{n+1}, then $R_1 \cdot R_2 \cdot ... \cdot R_n$ is a relation from A_1 to A_{n+1}. We shall denote this relation simply as $R_1 R_2 R_3 ... R_n$.

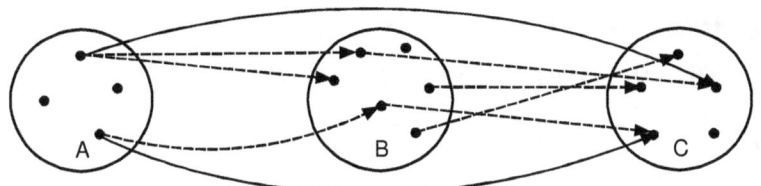

Fig. 4.1

In particular, if $A_1 = A_2 = \ldots = A_{n+1} = A$ and $R_1 = R_2 = \ldots = R_n = R$, then we denote $R_1 R_2 \ldots R_n$ by R^n which is a relation on A. Hence given R, one can compute R^2, R^3, and so on. The operation of composition is clearly not commutative; i.e. $R_1 R_2 \neq R_2 R_1$. In fact $R_2 R_1$ may not be defined, even though $R_1 R_2$ is. However, the operation is associative, as established in the following theorem.

4.3.7 Theorem

Let R_1, R_2 and R_3 be relations from A to B, B to C and C to D. Then $(R_1 R_2) R_3 = R_1 (R_2 R_3)$.
Proof:
Since we have to prove essentially the equality of two sets, we shall show that $(R_1 R_2) R_3 \subseteq R_1 (R_2 R_3)$ and conversely. Let $(a, d) \in (R_1 R_2) R_3$, where $a \in A$, $d \in D$. Note that $R_1 R_2$ is a relation from A to C. Then this means that there exists an element $c \in C$ such that $(a, c) \in R_1 R_2$ and $(c, d) \in R_3$. Now $(a, c) \in R_1 R_2$ implies there exists an element $b \in B$ such that $(a, b) \in R_1$ and $(b, c) \in R_2$. Since $(b, c) \in R_2$ and $(c, d) \in R_3$, if follows that $(b, d) \in R_2 R_3$. Again since $(a, b) \in R_1$ and $(b, d) \in R_2 R_3$, $(a, d) \in R_1 (R_2 R_3)$. Similarly, we can prove $R_1 (R_2 R_3) \subseteq (R_1 R_2) R_3$. This proves the associativity property of relations. The next result deals with the converse of the composition.

4.3.8 Theorem

Let R_1 be a relation from A to B and R_2 from B to C. Then $(R_1 R_2)^c = R_2^c R_1^c$.
Proof:
R_1^c is a relation from B to A and R_2^c from C to B. Hence anyway both $(R_1 R_2)^c$ and $R_2^c R_1^c$ are relations from C to A. We shall now prove that these relations are equal. Let $(c, a) \in (R_1 R_2)^c$. This implies that $(a, c) \in R_1 R_2$.

Hence there exists an element $b \in B$ such that $(a, b) \in R_1$ and $(b, c) \in R_2$.

It follows that $(b, a) \in R_1^c$ and $(c, b) \in R_2^c$, so that $(c, a) \in R_2^c R_1^c$.

Hence $(R_1 R_2)^c \subseteq R_2^c R_1^c$. Similarly, we can prove $R_2^c R_1^c \subseteq (R_1 R_2)^c$. Hence the equality is proved.

SOLVED EXAMPLES

Example 1: Let $A = \{a, b, c, d\}$ where

where $R_1 = \{(a, a), (a, b), (b, d)\}$

and $R_2 = \{(a, d), (b, c), (b, d), (c, b)\}$

Find $R_1 R_2$, $R_2 R_1$, R_2^2, R_2^3.

Solution:
$R_1 R_2 = \{(a, d), (a, c)\}$

$R_2 R_1 = \{(c, d)\}$.

$R_1^2 = \{(a, a), (a, b), (a, d)\}$

$R_2^2 = \{(b, b), (c, c), (c, d)\}$

$R_2^3 = R_2 R_2^2 = \{(b, c), (c, b), (b, d)\}$

Example 2: Let $A = \{2, 3, 4, 5, 6\}$ and let R_1, R_2 be relations on A such that

$R_1 = \{(a, b) \mid a - b = 2\}$

and $R_2 = \{(a, b) \mid a + 1 = b \text{ or } a = 2b\}$.

Find the composite relations

(i) $R_1 R_2$, (ii) $R_2 R_1$ (iii) $R_1 R_2 R_1$ (iv) R_1^2 (v) $R_1 R_2^2$.

Solution:
$R_1 = \{(4, 2), (5, 3), (6, 4)\}$

$R_2 = \{(2, 3), (3, 4), (4, 5), (5, 6), (4, 2), (6, 3)\}$

(i) $R_1 R_2 = \{(4, 3), (5, 4), (6, 2), (6, 5)\}$

(ii) $R_2 R_1 = \{(3, 2), (5, 4), (4, 3)\}$

(iii) $R_1 R_2 R_1 = R_1 (R_2 R_1)$

$= \{(5, 2), (6, 3)\}$

Example 3: Let $A = \{1, 2, 3, 4\}$,

Let R_1 be the relation on A defined as

$R_1 = \{(x, y) \mid x + y = 5\}$

and R_2 be the relation defined as
$$R_2 = \{(x, y) \mid y - x = 2\}.$$
Verify that $(R_1 R_2)^C = R_2^C R_1^C$.

Solution:
$$R_1 = \{(1, 4), (2, 3), (3, 2), (4, 1)\}$$
$$R_2 = \{(1, 3), (2, 4)\}$$
$$R_1 R_2 = \{(3, 4), (4, 3)\}$$
∴ $(R_1 R_2)^C = \{(4, 3), (3, 4)\}$
$$R_1^C = \{(4, 1), (3, 2), (2, 3), (1, 4)\}$$
$$R_2^C = \{(3, 1) (4, 2)\}$$
$$R_2^C R_1^C = \{(3, 4), (4, 3)\} = (R_1 R_2)^C$$

4.4 Matrix Representation of a Relation

Let $A = \{a_1, a_2, \ldots, a_n\}$
and $B = \{b_1, b_2, \ldots, b_n\}$

be finite sets containing respectively m and n elements.

Let R be a relation from A to B. By definition, $R \subseteq A \times B$. Hence we can represent R by a $m \times n$ matrix $M_R = [m_{ij}]$, which is defined as follows:

$$m_{ij} = 1 \quad ; \quad \text{if } (a_i, b_j) \in R$$
$$= 0 \quad ; \quad \text{if } (a_i, b_j) \notin R.$$

The matrix M_R is called as the matrix of R.

The matrix representation of R is useful in verifying certain properties of R.

SOLVED EXAMPLES

Example 1: Let $A = \{a, b, c, d\}$ and $B = \{1, 2, 3\}$.
Let $R = \{(a, 1), (a, 2), (b, 1), (c, 2), (d, 1)\}$
Find the relation matrix.

Solution: M_R will have 4 rows and 3 columns.

$$M_R = \begin{array}{c} \\ a \\ b \\ c \\ d \end{array} \begin{array}{ccc} 1 & 2 & 3 \end{array} \\ \left[\begin{array}{ccc} 1 & 1 & 0 \\ 1 & 0 & 0 \\ 0 & 1 & 0 \\ 1 & 0 & 0 \end{array} \right]$$

Example 2:

Let $A = \{1, 2, 3, 4, 8\}$, $B = \{1, 4, 6, 9\}$.

Let $a R b$ iff $a | b$ (a divides b).

Find the relation matrix.

Solution: $R = \{(1, 1), (1, 4), (1, 6), (1, 9), (2, 4), (2, 6), (3, 6), (3, 9), (4, 4)\}$

$$M_R = \begin{array}{c} \\ 1 \\ 2 \\ 3 \\ 4 \\ 8 \end{array} \begin{array}{cccc} 1 & 4 & 6 & 9 \\ \left[\begin{array}{cccc} 1 & 1 & 1 & 1 \\ 0 & 1 & 1 & 0 \\ 0 & 0 & 1 & 1 \\ 0 & 1 & 0 & 0 \\ 0 & 0 & 0 & 0 \end{array}\right] \end{array}$$

Example 3:

Let $A = \{1, 2, 3, 4, 8\} = B$; $a R b$ iff $a + b \leq 9$. Find its relation matrix.

Solution: $R = \{(1, 1), (1, 2), (1, 3), (1, 4), (1, 8), (2, 1), (2, 2), (2, 3), (2, 4), (3, 1),$
$(3, 2), (3, 3), (3, 4), (4, 1), (4, 2), (4, 3), (4, 4), (8, 1)\}$

$$M_R = \begin{bmatrix} 1 & 1 & 1 & 1 & 1 \\ 1 & 1 & 1 & 1 & 0 \\ 1 & 1 & 1 & 1 & 0 \\ 1 & 1 & 1 & 1 & 0 \\ 1 & 0 & 0 & 0 & 0 \end{bmatrix}$$

Example 4:

Let $A = \{a, b, c, d\}$ and let

and let $M_R = \begin{bmatrix} 1 & 1 & 0 & 0 \\ 0 & 0 & 1 & 1 \\ 0 & 0 & 1 & 1 \\ 1 & 0 & 1 & 0 \end{bmatrix}$.

Find R.

Solution: $R = \{(a, a), (a, b), (b, c), (b, d), (c, c), (c, d), (d, a), (d, c)\}$

4.4.1 Relation Matrix Operations

A relation matrix has entries which are either one or zero. Such a matrix is called a Boolean matrix. Let us see how to add or multiply two such matrices.

Let $A = [a_{ij}]$ and $B = [b_{ij}]$ be $m \times n$ Boolean matrix. We define
$A + B = [c_{ij}]$ where,
$c_{ij} = 1$; if $a_{ij} = 1$ or $b_{ij} = 1$
$\phantom{c_{ij}} = 0$; if a_{ij} and b_{ij} are both zero.

Similarly, if $A = [a_{ij}]$ is an $m \times n$ Boolean matrix and $B = [b_{ij}]$ is an $n \times r$ Boolean matrix, then $A \cdot B = [d_{ij}]$ is an $m \times r$ matrix.

where, $d_{ij} = 1$; if $a_{ij} = b_{ij} = 1$
$\phantom{d_{ij}} = 0$; if $a_{ij} = 0$ or $b_{ij} = 0$

Example: Let $A = \begin{bmatrix} 1 & 0 & 1 \\ 0 & 1 & 1 \\ 1 & 1 & 0 \end{bmatrix}$ and $B = \begin{bmatrix} 1 & 1 & 0 \\ 1 & 0 & 1 \\ 0 & 0 & 1 \end{bmatrix}$

then $A + B = \begin{bmatrix} 1 & 1 & 1 \\ 1 & 1 & 1 \\ 1 & 1 & 1 \end{bmatrix}$ and $A \cdot B = \begin{bmatrix} 1 & 1 & 1 \\ 1 & 0 & 1 \\ 1 & 1 & 1 \end{bmatrix}$

4.4.2 Properties of Relation Matrix

Let R_1 be a relation from A to B, R_2 from B to C. Then the relation matrices satisfy the following properties:

1. $M_{R_1 \cdot R_2} = M_{R_1} \cdot M_{R_2}$
2. M_{R^C} = transpose of M_R (for $R = R_1$ or $R = R_2$)
3. $M_{(R_1 \cdot R_2)^C} = M_{R_2^C R_1^C} = M_{R_2^C} \cdot M_{R_1^C}$

The proofs are left as exercises.

SOLVED EXAMPLES

Example 1: Let $A = \{1, 2, 3, 4\}$,
and let $R_1 = \{(1, 1), (1, 2), (2, 3), (2, 4), (3, 4), (4, 1), (4, 2)\}$
and $R_2 = \{(3, 1), (4, 4), (2, 3), (2, 4), (1, 1), (1,4)\}$

Verify (i) $M_{R_1 R_2} = M_{R_1} \cdot M_{R_2}$

(ii) $M_{R_1^c} = $ Transpose of M_{R_1}

(iii) $M_{(R_1 R_2)^c} = M_{R_2^c} \cdot M_{R_1^c}$

Solution: (i) $M_{R_1} = \begin{bmatrix} 1 & 1 & 0 & 0 \\ 0 & 0 & 1 & 1 \\ 0 & 0 & 0 & 1 \\ 1 & 1 & 0 & 0 \end{bmatrix}$, $M_{R_2} = \begin{bmatrix} 1 & 0 & 0 & 1 \\ 0 & 0 & 1 & 1 \\ 1 & 0 & 0 & 0 \\ 0 & 0 & 0 & 1 \end{bmatrix}$

$R_1 R_2 = \{(1, 1), (1, 4), (1, 3), (2, 1), (2, 4), (3, 4), (4, 4), (4, 1), (4, 3)\}$

$\therefore M_{R_1 R_2} = \begin{bmatrix} 1 & 0 & 1 & 1 \\ 1 & 0 & 0 & 1 \\ 0 & 0 & 0 & 1 \\ 1 & 0 & 1 & 1 \end{bmatrix}$

$M_{R_1} \cdot M_{R_2} = \begin{bmatrix} 1 & 1 & 0 & 0 \\ 0 & 0 & 1 & 1 \\ 0 & 0 & 0 & 1 \\ 1 & 1 & 0 & 0 \end{bmatrix} \begin{bmatrix} 1 & 0 & 0 & 1 \\ 0 & 0 & 1 & 1 \\ 1 & 0 & 0 & 0 \\ 0 & 0 & 0 & 1 \end{bmatrix} = \begin{bmatrix} 1 & 0 & 1 & 1 \\ 1 & 0 & 0 & 1 \\ 0 & 0 & 0 & 1 \\ 1 & 0 & 1 & 1 \end{bmatrix}$

(ii) $R_1^c = \{(1, 1), (2, 1), (3, 2), (4, 2), (4, 3), (1, 4), (2, 4)\}$

$M_{R_1^c} = \begin{bmatrix} 1 & 0 & 0 & 1 \\ 1 & 0 & 0 & 1 \\ 0 & 1 & 0 & 0 \\ 0 & 1 & 1 & 0 \end{bmatrix} = $ Transpose of M_{R_1}

(iii) $(R_1 R_2)^c = \{(1, 1), (4, 1), (3, 1), (1, 2), (4, 2), (4, 3), (4, 4), (1, 4), (3, 4)\}$

$\therefore M_{(R_1 R_2)^c} = \begin{bmatrix} 1 & 1 & 0 & 1 \\ 0 & 0 & 0 & 0 \\ 1 & 0 & 0 & 1 \\ 1 & 1 & 1 & 1 \end{bmatrix}$

Now $M_{R_2^c} \cdot M_{R_1^c} = \begin{bmatrix} 1 & 0 & 1 & 0 \\ 0 & 0 & 0 & 0 \\ 0 & 1 & 0 & 0 \\ 1 & 1 & 0 & 1 \end{bmatrix} \begin{bmatrix} 1 & 0 & 0 & 1 \\ 1 & 0 & 0 & 1 \\ 0 & 1 & 0 & 0 \\ 0 & 1 & 1 & 0 \end{bmatrix}$

$= \begin{bmatrix} 1 & 1 & 0 & 1 \\ 0 & 0 & 0 & 0 \\ 1 & 0 & 0 & 1 \\ 1 & 1 & 1 & 1 \end{bmatrix} = M_{R_2^c} \cdot M_{R_1^c}$

4.5 Graphical Representation of a Relation

If A is a finite set and R is a relation on A, it is possible to represent R pictorially by means of a graph. The elements of A are represented by points or circles, called as **nodes** or **vertices**. If aRb, this is indicated by drawing an arc from a to b with an arrowhead pointing in the direction a → b. If aRa, this is shown by drawing a loop around a. These arcs (or loops) are called as **edges** of the graph. The resulting graph is called a **directed graph** or **digraph** of R. The various types are illustrated in the following figures.

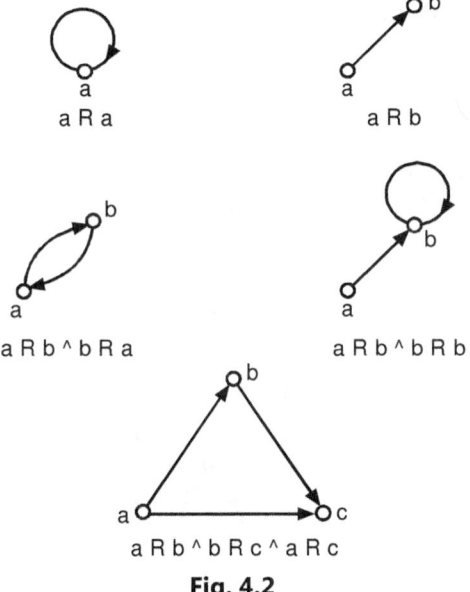

Fig. 4.2

SOLVED EXAMPLES

Example 1: Let A = {2, 3, 4, 5} and let
R = {(2, 3), (3, 2), (3, 4), (3, 5), (4, 3), (4, 4), (4, 5)}
Draw its digraph.

Solution:

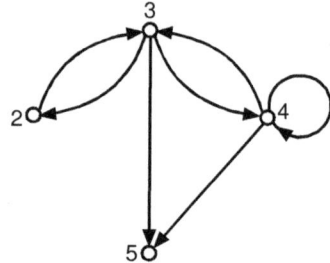

Fig. 4.3

Example 2: Let A = {a, b, c, d}

and $M_R = \begin{bmatrix} 1 & 1 & 0 & 1 \\ 0 & 1 & 1 & 0 \\ 0 & 0 & 1 & 1 \\ 1 & 0 & 0 & 0 \end{bmatrix}$

Draw the digraph of R.

Solution: R = {(a, a), (a, b), (a, d), (b, b), (b, c), (c, c), (c, d), (d, a)}

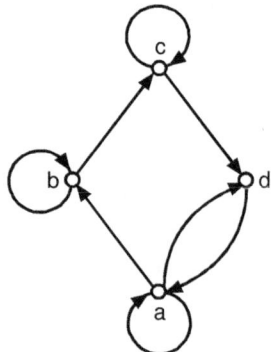

Fig. 4.4

Example 3: Find the relation determined by the digraph and give its matrix.

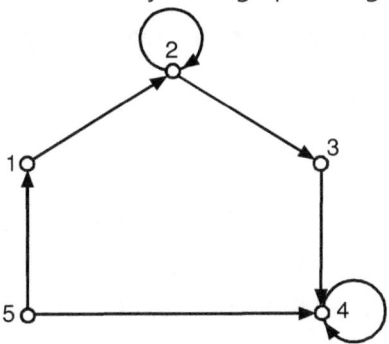

Fig. 4.5

Solution: A = {1, 2, 3, 4, 5}   R = {(1, 2), (2, 2), (2, 3), (3, 4), (4, 4), (5, 1), (5, 4)}

$$M_R = \begin{bmatrix} 0 & 1 & 0 & 0 & 0 \\ 0 & 1 & 1 & 0 & 0 \\ 0 & 0 & 0 & 1 & 0 \\ 0 & 0 & 0 & 1 & 0 \\ 1 & 0 & 0 & 1 & 0 \end{bmatrix}$$

EXERCISE - 4.2

1. Let A be the product set {1, 2, 3} × {a, b}. How many relations are there on A?
2. A = {1, 2, 3, 4}, B = {1, 4, 6, 8, 9}; aRb if and only if b = a². Find the domain, range of R. Also find also its relation matrix and draw its digraph.
3. Let A = **R**, set of real numbers. Consider the following relation on A ; (a, b) ∈ R iff 2a + 3b = 6. Find domain of R and also its range.
4. Let A = {1, 2, 3, 4, 5} and let R = {(1, 1,), (1, 2), (2, 1), (1, 3), (1, 4), (4, 5), (5, 1),   (1, 5), (4, 1)}. Draw the digraph of R.
5. For a set A = {1, 2, 3, 4, 5}, the relation matrix is

$$\begin{bmatrix} 1 & 1 & 1 & 1 & 1 \\ 0 & 0 & 1 & 0 & 0 \\ 0 & 0 & 0 & 0 & 0 \\ 1 & 0 & 0 & 0 & 1 \\ 1 & 0 & 0 & 0 & 0 \end{bmatrix}$$

Draw its digraph.

6. Let $A = \{1, 2, 3, 4\}$.

   If $R = \{(a, b) \mid (a - b)$ is an integral non-zero multiple of $2\}$

   and $S = \{(a, b) \mid (a - b)$ is an integral non-zero multiple of $3\}$

   Find $R \cup S$ and $R \cap S$.

7. For a set $A = \{1, 2, 3, 4, 5\}$ relations R_1 and R_2 are given by
   $R_1 = \{(1, 2), (3, 4), (2, 2)\}$ and $R_2 = \{(4, 2), (2, 5), (3, 1), (1, 3)\}$
   Find (a) $R_1 R_2$, (b) $R_2 R_1$, (c) $R_1 (R_2 R_1)$, (d) $(R_1 R) R_1$, (e) R_1^3, (f) R_2^2.

8. If $A = B = \{1, 2, 3\}$, $R_1 = \{(1, 1), (1, 2), (2, 3), (3, 1)\}$
   and $R_2 = \{(2, 1), (3, 1), (3, 2), (3, 3)\}$

   Compute
   (a) Complement of R_1,
   (b) Converse of R_2
   (c) $R_1 \oplus R_2$.

9. Let $A = B = \{1, 2, 3, 4\}$, $R = \{(1, 1), (1, 3), (2, 3), (3, 1), (4, 2), (4, 4)\}$ and
   $S = \{(1, 2), (2, 3), (3, 1), (3, 2), (4, 3)\}$
   Compute: (a) $M_{R \cap S}$ (b) $M_{R \cup S}$ (c) M_{R^c} (d) $M_{\overline{S}}$

10. Let A be set of workers and B be a set of jobs. Let R_1 be a binary relation from A to B such that (a, b) is in R_1 if worker a is assigned to job b. (We assume that a worker might be assigned to more than one job and more than one worker might be assigned to the same job.) Let R_2 be a binary relation on A such that (a_1, a_2) is in R_2 if a_1, a_2 can get along with each other if they are assigned to the same job. State a condition in terms of R_1, R_2 and (possibly) binary relations derived from R_1 and R_2 such that an assignment of the workers to the jobs according to R_1 will not put workers that cannot get along with one another on the same job.

4.6 Special Properties of Binary Relations

In many applications to computer science, we deal with relations on a set A, rather then relations from A to B. These relations have certain properties which are useful in storing data, more efficiently, on the computer. Let R be a relation on a set A.

(A) Reflexive relation: R is reflexive if for **every** element $a \in A$, $a R a$ i.e. $(a, a) \in R$.

R is not a reflexive relation if for **some** element $a \in A$, $a \not R a$, i.e. $(a, a) \notin R$.

Examples:

(i) Let A = {a, b} and let R = {(a, a), (a, b), (b, b)}.
Then R is reflexive.

(ii) Let A = {1, 2} and let R = {(1, 1), (1, 2)}.
R is not reflexive since (2, 2) ∉ R.

(B) Irreflexive relation R is said to be **irreflexive** if for every element a ∈ A, a R̸ a, i.e. (a, a) ∉ R.

Examples:

(i) Let A = {1, 2) and let R = {(1, 2), (2, 1)}. Then R is irreflexive since (1, 1), (2, 2) ∉ R.

(ii) Let A = {1, 2} and let R = {(1, 2), (2, 2). Then R is not irreflexive since (2, 2) ∈ R.

Note that R is not reflexive either; since (1, 1) ∉ R.

If R is reflexive, the corresponding relation matrix M_R will have its diagonal entries as one. If R is irreflexive, the diagonal elements will be zeros.

Digraph of a reflexive relation.

Fig. 4.6

(C) Symmetric relation: R is said to be **Symmetric** if whenever a R b, then b R a. It then follows that, R is not symmetric if for some a and b ∈ A, a R b but b R̸ a.

The relation matrix corresponding to a symmetric relation is a symmetric matrix. If its ij-th entry is 1, its jith entry is also 1. If its jith entry is 0, its ij-th entry is also 0 (for i ≠ j).

Examples:

(i) Let A be set of people. Let a R b if a is a friend of b. Then obviously b is related to a. Hence the relation of being "friend" is a symmetric relation.

(ii) Let A be set of lines in a plane. For lines l_1, l_2 ∈ A, let l_1 R l_2 if l_1 is parallel to l_2. Then l_2 R l_1 since the relation of being "parallel to" is a symmetric relation.

(iii) Let A be set of people and let a R b if a is brother of b. Then this is not a symmetric relation since b can be the sister of a. This relation will be symmetric only if A is the set of males.

(iv) Let A = {1, 2} and let R = {(1, 1), (2, 2)}. This is an example of a symmetric relation which is also reflexive.

Digraph of a Symmetric Relation:

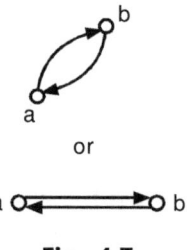

or

a ⚪⇄⚪ b

Fig. 4.7

(D) Asymmetric relation R is said to be **asymmetric** if whenever a R b, then b R̸ a. Hence R is not asymmetric if for some a and b ∈ A, we have both a R b and b R a.

Examples:

(i) Let A = **R** the set of real numbers and let R be the relation ' < '. Then a < b → b < a. Hence < is asymmetric.

(ii) Let A = {2, 4, 5} and let R be the relation "is a divisor of".
Then R = {(2, 2), (2, 4), (4, 4), (5, 5)}.
R is not asymmetric since (2, 2) (also (4, 4), (5, 5)) ∈ R.

(E) Antisymmetric relation R is antisymmetric if whenever a R b and b R a then a = b. It follows that R is not antisymmetric if we have elements a, b ∈ A such that a ≠ b but both a R b and b R a.
An equivalent definition of antisymmetric relation R is: If a ≠ b, then either a R̸ b or b R̸ a.

This definition is sometimes useful to verify whether a given relation is antisymmetric.

Examples:

(i) Let A = **R** and let R be the relation ' ≤ '. Then a ≤ b and b ≤ a → a = b. Hence ' ≤ ' is an antisymmetric relation.

(ii) Let A = {1, 2, 3} and let R = {(1, 2), (2, 1), (2, 3)}.
R is not antisymmetric since (1, 2) and (2, 1) ∈ R.
R is not symmetric either since (2, 3) ∈ R but (3, 2) ∉ R.
R is also not asymmetric since both (1, 2) and (2, 1) ∈ R.

(F) Transitive relation R is said to be **transitive** if whenever a R b and b R c, then a R c. It follows that a relation R is not transitive if there exist elements a, b, c ∈ A such that a R b and b R c, but a R̸ c. If such elements a, b, c do not exist, then R is transitive.

Examples:

(i) Let A = **R** and let R be the relation '≤'. Then R is clearly transitive.

(ii) Let A = set of triangles and let R be the relation of being congruent. Then for triangles a, b, c ∈ A, a R b and b R c → a R c. Hence R is transitive.

(iii) Let A be set of people and let R be the relation of being "brother of". Then a is brother of b and b is brother of c implies a is brother of c. Hence R is transitive.

(iv) Let A = N the set of natural numbers, and let

$$R = \{(a, b) \, a, b \in N \mid a + b \text{ is an odd number}\}$$

Then R is not transitive since (1, 2) and (2, 1) ∈ R, but (1, 1) ∉ R.

Digraphs of transitive relation.

(i)

(ii)

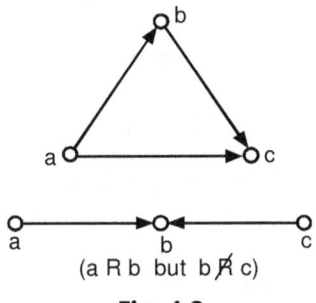

(a R b but b R̸ c)

Fig. 4.8

4.7 Equivalence Relation

A binary relation R on a set A is called as equivalence relation if it is reflexive, symmetric and transitive.

The following are some of the common but important examples of equivalence relations.

Examples:

(i) Let A = **R** and R be 'equality' of numbers.

(ii) Consider all subsets of a universal set and R be the relation, "equality" of sets.

(iii) A is the set of triangles and R is 'similarity' of triangles.

(iv) A is a set of students and R is the relation of being in "the same class or division."

(v) Let A be set of statement forms and R be the relation of "logical equivalence".

(vi) A is set of lines in a plane and R is the relation of lines being "parallel."

The digraph of an equivalence relation will have the following characteristics. Every vertex will have a loop; if there is an arc from a to b, there should be an arc from b to a; if there is an arc from a to b and one from b to c, there should be an arc from a to c. In short, the following is a typical digraph of an equivalence relation.

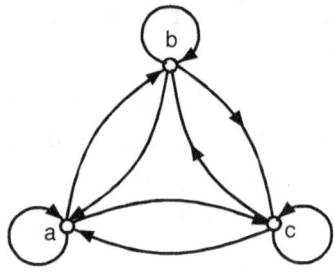

Fig. 4.9

Examples:
1. Let A = {a, b, c, d}, R = {(a, a), (b, a), (b, b), (c, c), (d, d), (d, c)}.
   Determine whether R is an equivalence relation.

Solution:
R is reflexive since (a, a), (b, b), (c, c) and (d, d) ∈ R.
But R is not symmetric since (b, a) ∈ R but (a, b) ∉ R. Hence R is not an equivalence relation.

---

2. Let A = {a, b, c} and let

$$M_R = \begin{bmatrix} 1 & 0 & 0 \\ 0 & 1 & 1 \\ 0 & 1 & 1 \end{bmatrix}$$. Determine whether R is an equivalence relation.

Solution: R = {(a, a), (b, b), (b, c), (c, b), (c, c)}.
R is reflexive since (a, a), (b, b), (c, c) ∈ R.
R is symmetric since (b, c) ∈ R → (c, b) ∈ R,
R is transitive since
  (b, b) and (b, c) ∈ R implies (b, c) ∈ R,
  (b, c) and (c, b) ∈ R implies (b, b) ∈ R,
  (c, c) and (c, b) ∈ R implies (c, b) ∈ R,
  (c, b) and (b, b) ∈ R implies (c, b) ∈ R
  (c, b) and (b, c) ∈ R implies (c, c) ∈ R
  (b, c) and (c, c) ∈ R implies (b, c) ∈ R.
Hence R is an equivalence relation.

3. Determine whether the relation R whose digraph is given below is an equivalence relation.

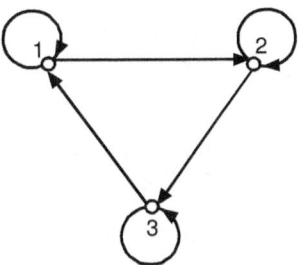

Fig. 4.10

Solution: R is reflexive since there is a loop around each vertex. But R is not symmetric, since (1, 2) ∈ R but (2, 1) ∉ R. Hence R is not an equivalence relation.

4. Determine whether the relation R whose digraph is given below is an equivalence relation.

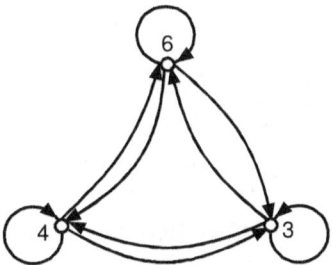

Fig. 4.11

Solution: R is reflexive since each vertex has a loop. R is also symmetric since every pair of distinct vertices is connected by a pair of double arcs, each pointing in the opposite direction.

In fact R = {(3, 3), (3, 4), (3, 6), (4, 3), (4, 4), (4, 6), (6, 3), (6, 4), (6, 6)}

Hence it is clear that R is also transitive. Therefore R is an equivalence relation.

4.7.1 Some Important Properties of Equivalence Relations

1. If R_1 and R_2 are equivalence relations on a set A, then $R_1 \cap R_2$ is an equivalence relation.
Proof:
For each a ∈ A, (a, a) ∈ R_1 and (a, a) ∈ R_2; hence (a, a) ∈ $R_1 \cap R_2$.
Therefore $R_1 \cap R_2$ is reflexive.
Let (a, b) ∈ $R_1 \cap R_2$; then (a, b) ∈ R_1 and (a, b) ∈ R_2.

Since R_1 and R_2 are both symmetric this implies $(b, a) \in R_1$ and $(b, a) \in R_2$, so that $(b, a) \in R_1 \cap R_2$.

Hence $R_1 \cap R_2$ is symmetric. Let (a, b), and $(b, c) \in R_1 \cap R_2$.

Then $(a, b), (b, c) \in R_1$ and $(a, b), (b, c) \in R_2$. But R_1 and R_2 are transitive; therefore $(a, c) \in R_1$ and $(a, c) \in R_2$, so that $(a, c) \in R_1 \cap R_2$.

Hence $R_1 \cap R_2$ is transitive. This proves that $R_1 \cap R_2$ is an equivalence relation.

2. If R_1 and R_2 are equivalence relations, it is not necessary that $R_1 \cup R_2$ is also an equivalence relation.

Proof:

Counter-example:

Let $A = \{a, b, c\}$

$R_1 = \{(a, a), (b, b), (c, c), (a, b), (b, a)\}$

and $R_2 = \{(a, a), (b, b), (c, c), (a, c), (c, a)\}$

Both R_1 and R_2 are equivalence relations.

$R_1 \cup R_2 = \{(a, a), (b, b), (c, c), (a, b), (b, a), (a, c), (c, a)\}$

is not an equivalence relation since it is not transitive (b, a) and $(a, c) \in R_1 \cup R_2$ but $(b, c) \notin R_1 \cup R_2$.

In general, if a relation R is not transitive, we can find a relation containing R which is transitive and is the smallest set with this property.

This set is called as the **transitive closure** of R. This notion is discussed in Art 4.11.

4.7.2 Equivalence Classes

Let R be an equivalence relation on a set A. For every $a \in A$, let $[a]_R$ denote the set $\left\{ x \in A \mid x\, R\, a \right\}$. Then $[a]_R$ is called as the **equivalence class of a with respect to R.**

$[a]_R \neq \phi$ since $a \in [a]_R$.

The **rank** of R is the number of distinct equivalence classes of R if the number of classes is finite; otherwise the rank is said to be infinite.

In what follows, we will drop the suffix R, and denote the equivalence class of a simply as $[a]$. The following theorem gives an important characterisation of the equivalence classes.

(i) For all a, b ∈ A, either [a] = [b] or [a] ∩ [b] = φ.

Proof:

If A = φ, there is nothing to prove.

Hence assume A ≠ φ. If A = {a}, singleton set, the result is trivially true.

Therefore consider elements a, b ∈ A.

Suppose [a] ≠ [b]. Then we have to show that [a] ∩ [b] = φ.

Suppose this is not true.

Let c ∈ [a] ∩ [b] then c R a and c R b.

Since R is symmetric it follows that a R c and c R b. But R is transitive as well.

Hence we have a R b, i.e. b ∈ [a] and a ∈ [b], which means that [a] = [b], a contradiction.

Hence [a] ∩ [b] = φ.

(ii) $A = \bigcup_{a \in A} [a]$

$a \in A$

Proof:

If A = φ, there is nothing to prove.

Hence assume A ≠ φ. If A = {a}, singleton set, the result is trivially true.

Therefore consider elements a, b ∈ A.

Suppose [a] ≠ [b]. Then we have to show that [a] ∩ [b] = φ.

Suppose this is not true.

Let c ∈ [a] ∩ [b] then c R a and c R b.

Since R is symmetric it follows that a R c and c R b.

But R is transitive as well.

Hence we have a R b, i.e. b ∈ [a] and a ∈ [b], which means that [a] = [b], a contradiction.

Hence [a] ∩ [b] = φ.

Examples:

1. Let A = {a, b, c} and let R = {(a, a), (b, b), (c, c), (a, b), (b, a)}
   where, R is clearly an equivalence relation.

The equivalence classes of the elements of A are:

$$[a] = \{a, b\}$$
$$[b] = \{b, a\} = [a]$$
$$[c] = \{c\}.$$

The rank of R is 2.

2. Let A = {1, 2, 3, 4} and let R = {(1, 1), (1, 2), (1, 3), (2, 1), (2, 2), (3, 1), (2, 3), (3, 2), (3, 3), (4, 4)}. Show that R is an equivalence relation and determine the equivalence classes, and hence find the rank of R.

Solution: R is reflexive since (1, 1), (2, 2), (3, 3), (4, 4) ∈ R.
R is symmetric since both (1, 2), (2, 1) ∈ R.
Similarly (2, 3), (3, 2), (1, 3), (3, 1) ∈ R.
R is transitive since (1, 2) and (2, 1) ∈ R implies (1, 1) ∈ R.
Similarly

(1, 3), (3, 1) ∈ R → (1, 1) ∈ R,
(2, 3), (3, 2) ∈ R → (2, 2) ∈ R
(3, 1), (1, 3) ∈ R → (3, 3) ∈ R
(3, 2), (2, 1) ∈ R → (3, 1) ∈ R.

Hence R is an equivalence relation. The equivalence classes of A are:

[1] = {1, 2, 3}
[2] = {1, 2, 3} = [1]
[3] = {3, 1, 2} = [1]
[4] = {4}.

Hence there two distinct equivalence classes. Hence rank of R is 2.
The following is an important example of an equivalence relation and equivalence classes.

---

3. (Residue classes modulo a positive integer)

Let Z denote the set of integers. Let n be a positive integer and define a relation R on Z by setting a R b iff $n \mid (a-b)$. Show that R is an equivalence relation and determine its equivalence classes.

Solution: R is reflexive since $n \mid (a-a)$ i.e. n divides zero.

R is symmetric, since a R b → $n \mid a-b$ which implies $n \mid (b-a)$, i.e. b R a. Let a R b and b R c. Then $n \mid (a-b)$ and $n \mid (b-c)$ which implies $n \mid [(a-b) + (b-c)] \to n \mid (a-c)$, i.e. a R c. Hence R is transitive. R is therefore an equivalence relation.

The equivalence classes are [0], [1], [2], ..., [n – 1]. This is because [n] = [0], [n + 1] = [1] and so on. Also note that for any integer m, [–m] = [m].
We denote the set of these equivalence classes by Z_n.

$$Z_1 = \{[0]\} = \{... -1, 0, 1, 2 ...\}$$

Chp 4 | 4.28

$$= Z$$
$$Z_2 = \{[0], [1]\}$$
$$Z_3 = \{[0], [1], [2]\}$$
$$Z_4 = \{[0], [1], [2], [3]\} \text{ and so on.}$$

The relation R is known as the congruence relation.

4.7.3 Partitions

We shall now discuss the concept of partition which is closely related to that of equivalence relation.

Definition:

> A partition of a non-empty set A is a collection of sets $\{A_1, A_2, ..., A_n\}$ such that
> (i) $A = \bigcup_{i=1}^{n} A_i$
> (ii) $A_i \cap A_j = \phi$, for $i \neq j$ (i.e. the sets A_i are mutually disjoint).

We denote a partition of A by the symbol π. An element of a partition is called a **block**. The **rank** of π is the number of blocks of π.

For a given non-empty set, its partition is not unique; we can have different partitions of the same set.

Examples :

1. Let $A = \{1, 2, 3\}$
   Then $\pi_1 = \{\{1, 2\}, \{3\}\}$ is a partition of A.
   Similarly, $\pi_2 = \{\{1, 3\}, \{2\}\}$ is another partition of A. A third partition is
   $\pi_3 = \{\{1\}, \{2\}, \{3\}\}$ and so on.

2. Let Z = set of all integers,
   E = set of all even integers,
   O = set of all odd integers.
   Then $\{E, O\}$ is a partition of Z.

3. The rooms (flats) in a building block form a partition.

4. The main memory of a multi-programmed computer system is partitioned and a separate program is stored in each block of the partition.
   The following diagram represents a partition of a set.

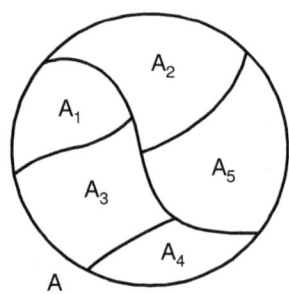

Fig. 4.12

The following theorem establishes the fact that equivalence relations and partitions are different descriptions of the same concept.

Theorem 1: Let A be a non-empty set and R an equivalence relation on A, then the set of equivalence classes $\{[a]_R \mid a \in A\}$ constitutes a partition of A.

Proof:

This theorem is actually a corollary to Theorem 1 of Art 4.9.2 in which we have shown that
(i) $A = \bigcup_{a \in A} [a]$
(ii) $[a] \cap [b] = \phi$ if $[a] \neq [b]$.

The above conditions are the same as that at required for a partition of A. Thus the theorem is proved.

In the above theorem, we have shown that an equivalence relation induces a partition on A. The converse is also true, as proved in the following theorem.

Theorem 2: Let A be a non-empty set, and let π be a partition of A. Then π induces an equivalence relation on A.

Proof:

Let π be a partition of the set A, and define the binary relation R on A as a R b iff there exists a set A_i in π such that a, b ∈ A_i. We shall show that R is an equivalence relation.

(i) R is reflexive since a R a. This is because π being a partition of A, a ∈ A_i for some i.
(ii) R is symmetric by definition of R.
(iii) R is transitive. Let a R b and b R c.

This implies that for some i, a, b ∈ A_i, and for some j, b, c ∈ A_j.
Therefore b ∈ $A_i \cap A_j$.
But since π is a partition, this is possible only if $A_i = A_j$.
Hence a, c ∈ A_i which means that a R c. This proves that R is transitive.

The above theorems, thus, establish a natural correspondence between partition of a set and equivalence relation on the set.

Examples:

1. Let A = {a, b, c, d}, π = {{a, b}, {c}, {d}}. Find the equivalence relation induced by π and construct is digraph.

   Solution: R = {(a, a), (a, b), (b, a), (b, b), (c, c), (d, d)}.

   The digraph of R is:

   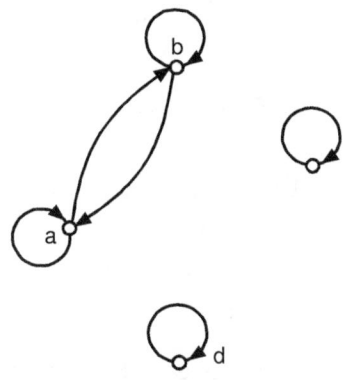

   Fig. 4.13

2. Let A = {1, 2, 3, 5} and π = {{1, 2}, {3}, {4, 5}}. Find the equivalence relation determined by π and draw its digraph.

   Solution: R = {(1, 1), (1 2), (2, 1), (2, 2), (3, 3), (4, 4), (4, 5), (5, 4), (5, 5)}.

   Digraph of R

   Fig. 4.14

Let R be an equivalence relation on A. We denote by A/R the partition induced by R. Hence a partition of A is called as a **quotient** set of A.

Examples:

1. Let   A = {1, 2, 3} and let R = {(1, 1), (2, 2), (1, 3), (3, 1), (3, 3)}. Find A/R.

   Solution: A/R is the partition of A induced by R.

   Hence A/R = {{1, 3}, {2}}.

2. Let Z be the set of integers. Define a relation R on Z as a R b iff $6 \mid (a-b)$, show that R is an equivalence relation and find Z/R.

Solution: Since $6 \mid (a-a)$, a R a. Hence R is reflexive.

If $6 \mid (a-b)$, then $6 \mid (b-a)$, which shows that R is symmetric.

If $6 \mid (a-b)$ and $6 \mid (b-c)$ then obviously $6 \mid ((a-b)+(b-c))$, i.e. $6 \mid (a-c)$. Hence R is also transitive. R is therefore an equivalence relation.

where
$$Z/R = \{[0], [1], [2], [3], [4], [5]\}$$
$$[0] = \{\ldots -12, -6, 0, 6, 12, 18 \ldots\}$$
$$[1] = \{, -11, -5, 1, 7, 13, \ldots\}$$
$$[2] = \{, \ldots -10, -4, 2, 8, 14, \ldots\}$$
$$[3] = \{\ldots, \ldots, -3, 3, 9, 15, \ldots\}$$
$$[4] = \{\ldots, \ldots, -2, 4, 10, 16, \ldots\}$$
$$[5] = \{\ldots, -7, -1, 5, 11, 17, \ldots\}$$

The quotient set Z/R is denoted by Z_6 and is called as the set of congruence classes modulo 6. R is also called as a congruence relation.

3. Let X = {a, b, c, d, e} and C = {{a, b}, {c}, {d, e}}. Show that the partition C defines an equivalence relation on X. **(Dec. 2002)**

Solution: C induces a relation R on X, as follows: For elements x, y∈ X, xRy if and only if x and y are members of the same subset element of C.

For example, aRb since both a, b∈ {a, b} in C. R is reflexive since aRa, bRb, cRc, dRd, eRe. Also R is symmetric since aRb and bRa. R is also transitive since aRb, bRa, aRa, bRb, dRe, eRd, dRd, eRe. Hence R is an equivalence relation.

4.7.4 Refinement of Partition

Definition:

Let π and π' be partitions of a non-empty set A. Then π' is called a refinement of π if every block (element) of π' is contained in a block of π.

Example: Let A = {a, b, c}.
Let π = {{a}, {b, c}} and π' = {{a}, {b}, {c}}.

Then π' is a refinement of π.

Let R and R' be the equivalence relations induced by π and π' respectively. Then the following theorem relates R' and R.

Theorem 1: Let π and π' be partitions of a non-empty set A and let R, R' be the equivalence relations induced by π and π' respectively. Then π' refines π if and only if $R' \subseteq R$.
Proof:
Let π' be a refinement of π. We have to prove that $R' \subseteq R$. Let a R' b. Then there is some block $A_i' \in \pi'$ such that a, b $\in A_i'$. Since π' refines π, $A_i' \subseteq A_i$ for some block $A_i \in \pi$. Hence a, b $\in A_i$ which implies a R b. Hence $R' \subseteq R$. Next, let $R' \subseteq R$. We have to prove π' is a refinement of π. Let $A_i' \in \pi'$ and let a $\in A_i'$. Then $A_i' = [a]_{R'}$. Let x $\in A_i'$. This implies x R' a and hence x R a since $R' \subseteq R$. This means that $[a]_{R'} \subseteq [a]_R$. Denote by A_i the block $[a]_R$. Then $A_i' \subseteq A_i$ which means that π' is a refinement of π

Remark on Product and Sum of Partitions:

The product $\pi_1 \cdot \pi_2$ consists of the set of intersections of every element of π_1 with every element of π_2, omitting the empty intersections.

For example, if $\quad$ S = {a, b, c, d, e, f}
$$\pi_1 = \{\{a, b\}, \{c, d, e\}, \{f\}\}, \quad \pi_2 = \{\{a, b, c\}, \{d\}, \{e, f\}\}$$
then $\quad \pi_1 \cdot \pi_2 = \{\{a, b\} \{c\}, \{d\}, \{e\}, \{f\}\}$

Let $\pi(S)$ denote the set of all partitions of S. Then a subset T of S is in the sum $\pi_1 + \pi_2$ if

(i) T is the union of one or more elements of π_1.

(ii) T is the union of one or more elements of π_2.

(iii) No subset of T satisfies (i) and (ii) except T itself.

For example, if $\quad \pi_1 = \{\{a, b\}, \{c\}, \{d, e, f\}\}$
$$\pi_2 = \{\{a, b, c\}, \{d\}, \{e, f\}\}$$
then $\quad \pi_1 + \pi_2 = \{\{a, b, c\}, \{d, e, f\}\}$

4.7.5 Sums and Products of Partitions

Definition:

Let π_1 and π_2 be partitions of a non-empty set A. The product of π_1 and π_2, denoted $\pi_1 \cdot \pi_2$ is a partition π of A such that
  (i) π refines both π_1 and π_2.
  (ii) If π' refines both π_1 and π_2, then π' refines π.

The following theorem tells us how to determine the product $\pi_1 \cdot \pi_2$.

Theorem 1: Let R_1, R_2 be the equivalence relations induced by partitions π_1 and π_2 respectively. Then the relation $R = R_1 \cap R_2$ induces the product partition $\pi_1 \cdot \pi_2$.

Proof:

By property 1 (article 4.9.1) we know that $R_1 \cap R_2$ is an equivalence relation.
Let π be the partition induced by $R_1 \cap R_2$.
Then by theorem 1 (4.9.4) π refines both π_1 and π_2.
Next suppose π' refines both, π_1 and π_2.
If π' induces R', then by theorem 1 (4.9.4) $R' \subseteq R_1$ and $R' \subseteq R_2$ which implies $R' \subseteq R_1 \cap R_2$.
Hence again by theorem 1 (4.9.4) π' refines π.

We now deal with sum of two partitions.

Definition:

Let π_1 and π_2 be partitions of a non-empty set. The sum of π_1 and π_2, denoted by $\pi_1 + \pi_2$, is a partition π such that
  (i) Both π_1 and π_2 refine π.
  (ii) If π' is a partition of A such that both π_1 and π_2 refine π', then π refines π'.

We have the following theorem.

Theorem 2: Let R_1 and R_2 be equivalence relations on a non-empty set A induced by the partitions π_1 and π_2. Let $R = (R_1 \cup R_2)^*$ the transitive closure of $R_1 \cup R_2$. Then R is an equivalence relation on A and induces the partition $\pi_1 + \pi_2$.

Proof:

$R_1 \cup R_2$ is reflexive and symmetric.
Hence $(R_1 \cup R_2)^*$ be also transitive is the smallest equivalence relation containing both R_1 and R_2.

Since $R_1 \subseteq R$ and $R_2 \subseteq R$ both π_1 and π_2 induce an equivalence relation which contains both R_1 and R_2.

Since $(R_1 \cup R_2)^*$ is the smallest such equivalence relation, it follows that π refines all such partitions.

Hence π is a sum of π_1 and π_2.

Note that the product and sum of two partitions always exists and is unique.

Example :

1. Let $A = \{a, b, c, d, e, f, g, h, i, j, k\}$
   $\pi_1 = \{\{a, b, c, d\}, \{e, f, g\}, \{h, i\}, \{j, k\}\}$
   and $\pi_2 = \{\{a, b, c, h\}, \{d, i\}, \{e, f, j, k\}, \{g\}\}$
   be two partitions of A. Find $\pi_1 \cdot \pi_2$ and $\pi_1 + \pi_2$.

   Solution: $\pi_1 \cdot \pi_2 = \{\{a, b, c\}, \{d\}, \{e, f\}, \{g\}, \{h\}, \{i\}, \{j, k\}\}$
   $\pi_1 + \pi_2 = \{\{a, b, c, d, h, i\}, \{e, f, g, j, k\}\}$

4.8 Compatible Relation

Definition:

A relation R on a set A is said to be compatible if it is reflexive and symmetric.

Examples:

(i) All equivalence relations are compatible relations.

(ii) The relation of 'being friend of' is a compatible relation.

(iii) Let $A = \{a, b, c\}$
   $B = \{b, c, d\}$
   $C = \{d, e, f\}$.

Define a relation R on these sets as: A set X is related to a set Y, i.e. X R Y iff $X \cap Y \neq \phi$.

In this example A R B, B R C, but A R C. R is therefore a compatible relation which is not an equivalence relation. The graph of a compatible relation is drawn by omitting the loop at each vertex and using a single edge with no arrow between them. If R is a compatible relation, its relation matrix is symmetric with the diagonal elements being 1.

Definition:

A **covering** of a set A is a collection of subsets $\{A_1, A_2, \ldots, A_k\}$ of A, such that $\bigcup_{i=1}^{k} A_i = A$.

We have seen that an equivalence relation induces a partition on A. We shall now show that a compatible relation induces a covering on A.

Definition:

> Let A be a non-empty set and let R be a compatible relation on A. A subset M of A is called a **maximal compatibility block** if every element of M is compatible with every other element of M and no element of A − M is compatible with all elements of M.

For example, consider the diagram given below for the compatible relation R on the set A = {1, 2, 3, 4, 5}.

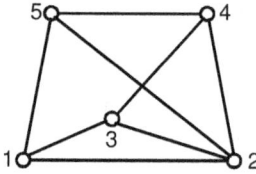

Fig. 4.15

The maximal compatibility blocks are

$$M_1 = \{1, 2, 3\}, \quad M_2 = \{2, 3, 4\}, \quad M_3 = \{1, 2, 5\}, \quad M_4 = \{2, 4, 5\}.$$

$A = M_1 \cup M_2 \cup M_3$. Hence $\{M_1, M_2, M_3\}$ forms a covering for A.

Similarly, $\{M_1, M_4\}$ forms a covering for A.

4.9 Transitive Closure

Definition:

> The transitive closure of a relation R is the smallest transitive relation containing R. We denote transitive closure of R by R^*.

The following theorem gives a method to find the transitive closure.

> **Theorem:** Let A be a set with $|A| = n$, and let R be a relation on A. Then
> $$R^* = R \cup R^2 \cup R^3 \cup \ldots \cup R^n.$$
>
> **Proof:**
>
> Let $(a, b) \in R^*$. Then since R^* is the transitive closure of R, there exists a sequence of elements $x_1, x_2, \ldots, x_R$ in A such that $a = x_1$, $b = x_R$ and $(x_i, x_{i+1}) \in R$ for $1 \leq i \leq R − 1$.
>
> This means that $(a, b) \in R^{k-1}$. Hence, $R^* \subseteq R \cup R^2 \cup R^3 \cup \ldots \cup R^n$.
>
> Conversely $R^i \subseteq R^*$ for $1 \leq i \leq n$. Hence $R^* = R \cup R^2 \cup R^3 \cup \ldots \cup R^n$.
>
> Now we have only to show that R^* is the smallest transitive relation, containing R.

Let S be a transitive relation containing R. Let $(a, c) \in R^2$.
This implies that there exists an element $b \in A$ such that $(a, b) \in R$ and $(b, c) \in R$.
Since $R \subseteq S$ and S is transitive it follows that $(a, c) \in S$.
Hence $R^2 \subseteq S$. Proceeding thus, we can show that $R^3, R^4, \ldots, R^n$ are all subsets of S.
Hence $R \cup R^2 \cup \ldots \cup R^n \subseteq S$, which proves the claim.

Examples:

1. Let $A = \{1, 2, 3, 4\}$ and $R = \{(1, 2), (2, 3), (3, 4)\}$ be a relation on A. Find R^* and draw its digraph.

Solution:
$R = \{(1, 2), (2, 3), (3, 4)\}$
$R^2 = \{(1, 3), (2, 4)\}$
$R^3 = \{(1, 4)\}$
$R^4 = \phi$

Hence $R^* = R \cup R^2 \cup R^3$
$= \{(1, 2), (2, 3), (3, 4), (1, 3), (2, 4), (1, 4)\}$

Digraph of R^*

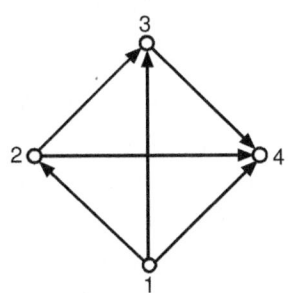

Fig. 4.16

2. Let $A = \{a, b, c, d\}$,
$R_1 = \{(a, a), (b, b), (c, c), (a, b)\}$ and
$R_2 = \{(a, a), (b, d), (d, c)\}$

Find $(R_1 \cup R_2)^*$ and draw its digraph.

Solution:
$R = R_1 \cup R_2 = \{(a, a), (b, b), (c, c), (a, b), (b, d), (d, c)\}$
$R^2 = \{(a, b), (b, d), (a, d), (b, c), (a, a), (b, b), (c, c) (d, c)\}$
$R^3 = \{(a, a), (a, b), (a, c), (a, d), (b, b), (b, c), (b, d), (d, c), (c, c)\}$
$R^4 = \{(a, a), (a, b), (a, c), (a, d), (b, b), (b, c), (b, d), (c, c), (d, c)\}$

$\therefore R^* = R \cup R^2 \cup R^3$
$= \{(a, a), (b, b), (c, c), (a, b), (b, d), (d, c), (a, d), (b, c), (a, c)\}$

Digraph of R*

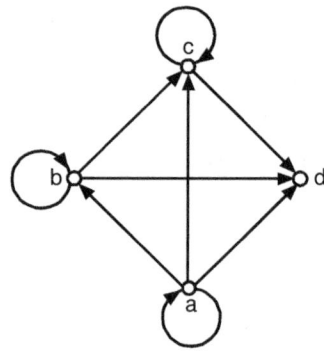

Fig. 4.17

4.9.1 Warshall's Algorithm

Finding the transitive closure of a relation, by computing various powers of R or products of the relation matrix M_R, is quite impractical for large sets and relations. Warshall's Algorithm offers an alternative but efficient method for computing the transitive closure.

Let R be a relation on a set $A = \{a_1, a_2, \ldots a_n\}$ and let R^* denote the transitive closure of R. A **path** of length m in R from a to b is a finite sequence $a, x_1, x_2, \ldots, x_{m-1}, b$, beginning with a and ending with b, such that $a\ R\ x_1, x_1\ R\ x_2, \ldots, x_{m-1}\ R\ b$. Note that a path of length m involves m + 1 elements of A, not necessarily distinct. All vertices in the path, except a and b are called as **interior vertices** of the path. For $1 \leq k \leq n$, define a Boolean matrix W_k as W_R has 1 in position i, j if and only if there is a path from a_i to a_j in R whose interior vertices, if any, come from the set $\{a_1, a_2, \ldots, a_k\}$.

Suppose we have a path as shown in the diagram below,

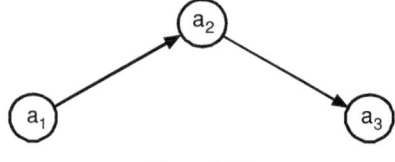

Fig. 4.18

then W_2 will have a 1 in the first row and third column.

Since any vertex must come from the set $\{a_1, a_2, \ldots a_n\}$, it follows that the matrix W_n has 1 in position i, j if and only if some path in R connects a_i and a_j. Hence $W_n = M_{R^*}$. Define $W_0 = M_R$. Then we will have a sequence $W_0, W_1, \ldots, W_n$ whose first term is M_R and last term is M_{R^*}. Suppose we have a path as shown in the diagram below,

Warshall's algorithm gives a procedure to compute each matrix W_R from the previous matrix W_{R-1}. Beginning with the matrix of R, we proceed one step at a time, until we reach the matrix of R^*, in n steps. The matrices W_R, being different from powers of the matrix M_R, results in a considerable saving of steps in the computation of the transitive closure of R.

Suppose $W_{k-1} = [u_{ij}]$ and $W_k = [v_{ij}]$. If $v_{ij} = 1$, there is a path from a_i to a_j whose interior vertices come from the set $\{a_1, a_2, ... a_k\}$. If a_k is not an interior vertex of this path, then all the interior vertices must come actually from $\{a_1, a_2, ..., a_{k-1}\}$, hence $u_{ij} = 1$. If a_k is an interior vertex of the path, then we have the situation as shown below.

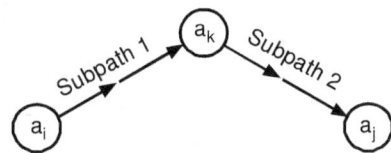

Fig. 4.19

Since there is a sub path from a_i to a_k whose interior vertices come from $\{a_1, a_2, ..., a_{k-1}\}$, we must have $u_{ik} = 1$. Similarly $u_{kj} = 1$.

Hence, $v_{ij} = 1$ if and only if

(1) $u_{ij} = 1$

(2) $u_{ik} = 1$ and $u_{kj} = 1$.

This is the basis for Warshall's algorithm. If W_{k-1} has 1 in position i, j then by (1) so will W_k. A new 1 can be added in position i, j of W_k if and only if column k of W_{k-1} has a 1 in position i, and row k of W_{k-1} has a 1 in position j.

Thus we have the following procedure for computing W_k from W_{k-1}.

Step 1: Transfer to W_k, all the 1's in W_{k-1}.

Step 2: List the locations $p_1, p_2, ...$ in column k of W_{k-1} where the entry is 1, and the locations $q_1, q_2, ...$ in row k of W_{k-1}, where the entry is 1.

Step 3: Put 1's in all the positions p_i, q_j of W_R (if they are not already there).

The above procedure is illustrated in the following problems.

SOLVED EXAMPLES

Examples 1: Let $A = \{1, 2, 3, 4\}$ and $R = \{(1, 2), (2, 4), (1, 3), (3, 2)\}$. Find the transitive closure of R by Warshall's algorithm.

Solution:
$$W_0 = M_R = \begin{bmatrix} 0 & 1 & 1 & 0 \\ 0 & 0 & 0 & 1 \\ 0 & 1 & 0 & 0 \\ 0 & 0 & 0 & 0 \end{bmatrix}$$

For W_1, $k = 1$, $a_k = 1$ is not an interior vertex for any path in R. Hence $W_1 = W_0$, without any addition to the entries.

For W_2, $k = 2$; $a_k = 2$ is an interior vertex for the path from 3 to 4. It is also an interior vertex for the path from 1 to 4. Hence W_2 has 1 in the position (3, 4) and also 1 in the position (1, 4).

Hence
$$W_2 = \begin{bmatrix} 0 & 1 & 1 & 1 \\ 0 & 0 & 0 & 1 \\ 0 & 1 & 0 & 1 \\ 0 & 0 & 0 & 0 \end{bmatrix}$$

For W_3, $k = 3$, $a_k = 3$. Although 3 is an interior vertex for the path from 1 to 2, since the entry 1 is already in the position (1, 2), there is no new addition to the entries in W_2. Hence $W_3 = W_2$.

For W_4, $k = 4$, $a_k = 4$ which is not an interior vertex of any path in R. Hence $W_4 = W_3 = W_2$.

But $M_{R^*} = W_4$

Hence
$$M_{R^*} = \begin{bmatrix} 0 & 1 & 1 & 1 \\ 0 & 0 & 0 & 1 \\ 0 & 1 & 0 & 1 \\ 0 & 0 & 0 & 0 \end{bmatrix}$$

Therefore, we obtain the transitive closure R^* as $\{(1, 2), (1, 3), (1, 4), (2, 4), (3, 2), (3, 4)\}$.

Example 2: Let $A = \{a_1, a_2, a_3, a_4, a_5\}$ and let R be a relation on A whose matrix is

$$M_R = \begin{bmatrix} 1 & 0 & 0 & 1 & 0 \\ 0 & 1 & 0 & 0 & 0 \\ 0 & 0 & 0 & 1 & 1 \\ 1 & 0 & 0 & 0 & 0 \\ 0 & 1 & 0 & 0 & 1 \end{bmatrix}$$

Find M_{R^*} by Warshall's algorithm.

Solution: $R = \{(a_1, a_1), (a_1, a_4), (a_2, a_2), (a_3, a_4), (a_3, a_5), (a_4, a_1), (a_5, a_2), (a_5, a_5)\}$

$W_0 = M_R$

For $k = 1$, a_1 is an interior vertex for the path a_4 to a_4. Hence W_1 has 1 in the position (4, 4).

$$W_1 = \begin{bmatrix} 1 & 0 & 0 & 1 & 0 \\ 0 & 1 & 0 & 0 & 0 \\ 0 & 0 & 0 & 1 & 1 \\ 1 & 0 & 0 & 1 & 0 \\ 0 & 1 & 0 & 0 & 1 \end{bmatrix}$$

$W_2 = W_1$ as there is already 1 in the position (5, 2). a_3 is not an interior vertex for any path in R. Hence $W_3 = W_2 = W_1$.

a_4 is an interior vertex for the path a_3 to a_1. Hence W_4 has 1 in the position (3, 1).

$$\therefore \quad W_4 = \begin{bmatrix} 1 & 0 & 0 & 1 & 0 \\ 0 & 1 & 0 & 0 & 0 \\ 1 & 0 & 0 & 1 & 1 \\ 1 & 0 & 0 & 1 & 0 \\ 0 & 1 & 0 & 0 & 1 \end{bmatrix}$$

a_5 is an interior vertex in the path from a_3 to a_2. Hence

$$W_5 = \begin{bmatrix} 1 & 0 & 0 & 1 & 0 \\ 0 & 1 & 0 & 0 & 0 \\ 1 & 1 & 0 & 1 & 1 \\ 1 & 0 & 0 & 1 & 0 \\ 0 & 1 & 0 & 0 & 1 \end{bmatrix}$$

$W_5 = M_{R^*}$

Hence $M_{R^*} = \begin{bmatrix} 1 & 0 & 0 & 1 & 0 \\ 0 & 1 & 0 & 0 & 0 \\ 1 & 1 & 0 & 1 & 1 \\ 1 & 0 & 0 & 1 & 0 \\ 0 & 1 & 0 & 0 & 1 \end{bmatrix}$

The algorithm for Warshall's method is given below:

Example 3: Find the transitive closure of R by Warshall's algorithm, where $A = \{1, 2, 3, 4, 5, 6\}$ and $R = \{(x, y) \mid |x - y| = 2\}$.

Solution: $R = \{(1, 3), (3, 1), (2, 4), (4, 2), (3, 5), (5, 3), (4, 6), (6, 4)\}$

$$M_R = W_0 = \begin{bmatrix} 0 & 0 & 1 & 0 & 1 & 0 \\ 0 & 0 & 0 & 1 & 0 & 0 \\ 1 & 0 & 0 & 0 & 1 & 0 \\ 0 & 1 & 0 & 0 & 0 & 1 \\ 0 & 0 & 1 & 0 & 0 & 0 \\ 0 & 0 & 0 & 1 & 0 & 0 \end{bmatrix}$$

For $k = 1$, 1 is in the 3rd row and 3rd and 5th columns.

Hence, put 1 in the positions (3, 3) and (3, 5).

$$\therefore W_1 = \begin{bmatrix} 0 & 0 & 1 & 0 & 1 & 0 \\ 0 & 0 & 0 & 1 & 0 & 0 \\ 1 & 0 & 1 & 0 & 1 & 0 \\ 0 & 1 & 0 & 0 & 0 & 1 \\ 0 & 0 & 1 & 0 & 0 & 0 \\ 0 & 0 & 0 & 1 & 0 & 0 \end{bmatrix}$$

For $k = 2$, 1 is in 4th row and 4th column.

Hence, put 1 in the position (4, 4).

Thus, $W_2 = \begin{bmatrix} 0 & 0 & 1 & 0 & 1 & 0 \\ 0 & 0 & 0 & 1 & 0 & 0 \\ 1 & 0 & 1 & 0 & 1 & 0 \\ 0 & 1 & 0 & 1 & 0 & 1 \\ 0 & 0 & 1 & 0 & 0 & 0 \\ 0 & 0 & 0 & 1 & 0 & 0 \end{bmatrix}$

Proceeding in this manner.

$W_3 = \begin{bmatrix} 1 & 0 & 1 & 0 & 1 & 0 \\ 0 & 0 & 0 & 1 & 0 & 0 \\ 1 & 0 & 1 & 0 & 1 & 0 \\ 0 & 1 & 0 & 1 & 0 & 1 \\ 1 & 0 & 1 & 0 & 1 & 0 \\ 0 & 0 & 0 & 1 & 0 & 0 \end{bmatrix}$

$W_4 = \begin{bmatrix} 1 & 0 & 1 & 0 & 1 & 0 \\ 0 & 1 & 0 & 1 & 0 & 1 \\ 1 & 0 & 1 & 0 & 1 & 0 \\ 0 & 1 & 0 & 1 & 0 & 1 \\ 1 & 0 & 1 & 0 & 1 & 0 \\ 0 & 1 & 0 & 1 & 0 & 1 \end{bmatrix}$

$W_5 = \begin{bmatrix} 1 & 0 & 1 & 0 & 1 & 0 \\ 0 & 1 & 0 & 1 & 0 & 1 \\ 1 & 0 & 1 & 0 & 1 & 0 \\ 0 & 1 & 0 & 1 & 0 & 1 \\ 1 & 0 & 1 & 0 & 1 & 0 \\ 0 & 1 & 0 & 1 & 0 & 1 \end{bmatrix}$

$M_R = W_6 = W_5$

Hence, $R^* = \{(1, 1), (1, 3), (1, 5), (2, 2), (2, 4), (2, 6), (3, 1), (3, 3), (3, 5), (4, 2), (4, 4),$ $(4, 6), (5, 1), (5, 3), (5, 5), (6, 2), (6, 4), (6, 6)\}$

Warshall Algorithm

```
FOR  i: = 1 TO n DO
   FOR j: = 1 TO n DO
      If  a [j, i] = 1  THEN
         FOR  k: = 1  TO  n DO
            If a [i, k] = 1  THEN
               a [j, k]: = 1 ;
                  END;
               END;
            END;
      END;
END;
```

4.10 Partial Ordering Relations

An **order relation** is a transitive relation on a set by means of which we can compare elements of set.

Definition:

A binary relation R on a non-empty set A is a **partial order** if R is reflexive, antisymmetric and transitive.

The ordered pair (A, R) is called a **partially ordered set** or **poset.**

Examples:
  (i)   The relation ' $\leq$ ' is a partial order relation on the set of real numbers.
  (ii) The relation of 'being a subset' is a partial order on any collection of subsets of a set A; i.e. the ordered pair (P(A), $\subseteq$) is a poset.
  (iii) The lexicographic ordering on the set of alphabets is a partial order.

We will use the symbol $\leq$ to denote an arbitrary partial order. This notation should not be confused with the ' $\leq$ ' of number systems. Thus a $\leq$ b will mean a R b for an arbitrary partial order relation R, and (A, $\leq$) will be the corresponding poset.

4.10.1 Hasse Diagrams

The posets can be depicted by digraphs. However a more economical way to describe a poset is by **Hasse diagrams**. A Hasse diagram is a simpler version of a digraph, incorporating the following rules:

(i) All arrow heads that appear on the edges are omitted.
(ii) Loops are omitted as reflexivity is implied, by definition of a partial order.
(iii) Similarly an arc (or edge) is not present in the diagram if it is implied by transitivity. There is an arc from a to b only if there is no element c such that a ≤ c and c ≤ b.
(iv) An arc pointing upward is drawn from a to b if a ≠ b and a ≤ b. Arrow heads are not used.

SOLVED EXAMPLES

Examples 1: Let A = {2, 3, 4, 6} and let a R b if a divides b. Show that R is a partial order and draw its Hasse diagram.

Solution: R = {(2, 2), (2, 4), (2, 6), (3, 3), (3, 6), (4, 4), (6, 6)}

R is reflexive since (2, 2), (3, 3), (4, 4), (6, 6) ∈ R. R is antisymmetric since if a | b b | a unless a = b. R is also transitive since a | b and b | c implies a | c. Hence R is a partial order.

Hasse diagram for R

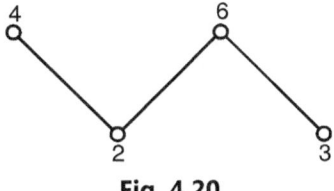

Fig. 4.20

Example 2: If A = {1, 2, 3, 4},
R = {(1, 1), (1, 2), (2, 2), (2, 4), (1, 3), (3, 3), (3, 4), (1, 4), (4, 4)}
then show that R is a partial order and draw its Hasse diagram.

Solution: R is reflexive since (1, 1), (2, 2), (3, 3), (4, 4) ∈ R.
R is antisymmetric since (1, 2) ∈ R but (2, 1) ∉ R, (2, 4) ∈ R but (4, 2) ∉ R. Similarly (1, 3), (1, 4), (3, 4) ∈ R but (3, 1), (4, 1), (4, 3) ∉ R. One can also similarly check that R is transitive.

Hasse diagram:

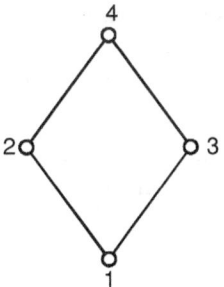

Fig. 4.21

Example 3: Let A = {a, b, c}. Show that (P(A), ⊆) is a poset and draw its Hasse diagram.

Solution: P(A) = {A, φ, {a, b}, {b, c}, {a, c}, {a}, {b}, {c}}

Set containment ⊆ is always a partial order since for any subset B of A, B ⊆ B, i.e. ⊆ is reflexive. If B ⊆ C and C ⊆ B, B = C antisymmetry. If B ⊆ C and C ⊆ D then B ⊆ D (transitivity).

Hasse diagram:

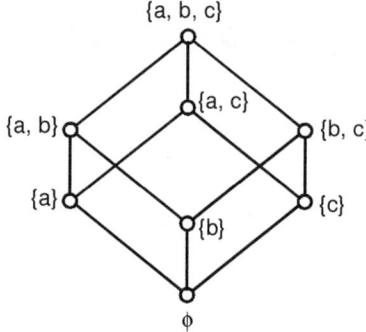

Fig. 4.22

4.11 Chains and Antichains

Definition:

Let (A, ≤) be a poset. A subset of A is called a **chain** if every pair of elements in the subset is related.

In any chain with a finite number of elements $\{a_1, a_2, ..., a_k\}$ there is an element a_{i_1} that is less than (i.e. related to) every element in the chain, and there is an element a_{i_2} that is less than every other element except a_{i_1}. Continuing in this manner, we shall have a sequence $a_{i_1} \leq a_{i_2} \leq a_{i_3} \leq ... \leq a_{i_k}$. The number of elements in the chain is called as the length of the chain.

If A itself is a chain, the poset (A, ≤) is called a totally ordered set or linearly ordered set.

Definition:

A subset of A is called an antichain if no two distinct elements in the subset are related.

Examples:

(i) Let A = {1, 2, 3} and let the partial order ≤ mean " less than or equal to ". Then (A, ≤) is a chain and its Hasse diagram is

Fig. 4.23

(ii) Let A = {a, b} and consider its poset {P(A), ⊆}

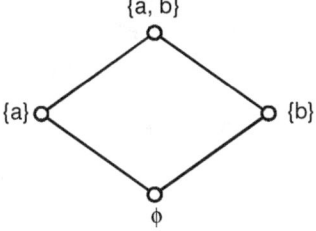

Fig. 4.24

Then the following subsets are chains

{ϕ, {a}, {a, b}}, {ϕ, {b}, {a, b}}, {ϕ, {a}}, {ϕ, {b}}, {{a}, {a, b}}, {{b}, {a, b}}.

The following subset is an antichains is {{a}, {b}}.

In the above example the length of the longest chain is 3 and the number of elements in the antichain is 2.

We state the following theorem (without proof) that shows a close relation between chains and antichains.

Theorem 1: Set (A, ≤) be a poset. Suppose the length of the longest chain in A is n. Then the elements is A can be partitioned into n disjoint antichains.

SOLVED EXAMPLES

Example 1: Let R_1 be a binary relation on A such that (a, b) is in R_1 if book a costs more and contains fewer pages than book b. Is R_1 reflexive? Symmetric? Antisymmetric? Transitive?

Solution: R_1 is obviously not reflexive and not symmetric. If a R b, then b R a. Similarly if b R a, then a R b. Hence both the conditions a R b and b R a cannot be fulfilled simultaneously. Hence by the law of contrapositive, R_1 is antisymmetric. Let a R b and b R c. This implies a costs more than b, b costs more than c, a contains fewer pages than b, b contains fewer pages than c. Hence combining all these statements a costs more than c and contains few pages than c. Hence R is a transitive relation.

Example 2: Let R be a binary relation on the set of all positive integers such that
$$R = \{(a, b) \mid a - b \text{ is an odd positive integer}\}.$$

Is R reflexive, symmetric, antisymmetric, transitive?
Is R an equivalence relation? a partial ordering relation.

Solution: R is not reflexive since (a, a) ∉ R as a − a = 0.
R is not symmetric since a − b is odd implies b − a is odd, but it is not positive. (3, 2), ∈ R but (2, 3) ∈ R. R is also not transitive, since although a − b is odd and b − c is odd, a − c = (a − b) + (b − c) which is even. Hence (a, c) ∉ R whenever (a, b) ∈ R and (b, c) ∈ R. R is antisymmetric since a R b → b R a. None of the conditions for an equivalence relation are satisfied. Hence R is not an equivalence relation. R is also not a partial order.

Example 3: Let R be a binary relation on the set of all strings of 0's and 1's such that
$$R = \{(a, b) \mid a \text{ and } b \text{ are strings that have the same number of 0's}\}$$

Is R reflexive? Symmetric? Antisymmetric? Transitive? An equivalence relation? A partial order?

Solution: R is reflexive since (a, a) ∈ R. R is symmetric since if a and b have the same number of 0's, then b and a will have the same number of 0's. R is transitive since if a and b have the same number of 0's, b and c have the same number of 0's, then obviously a and c have the same number of 0's. R is obviously not antisymmetric. R is an equivalence relation but not a partial order.

Example 4: Let S be the set of all points in a plane. Let R be the relation such that for any two points a and b, (a, b) ∈ R if b is within one inch from a. Examine if R will be an equivalence relation.

Solution: R is reflexive since a is **within** one inch (i.e. 0 inch) from itself.
R is symmetric since if b is within 1 inch from a, a is also within 1 inch from b.
But R is not transitive since b is within 1 inch from a, c is within 1 inch from b need not imply that c is within 1 inch from a. Hence R is not an equivalence relation.

Example 5: Let T be a set of triangles in a plane and define R as the set
$$R = \{(a, b) \mid a, b \in T, a \text{ is congruent to } b\}.$$

Show that R is an equivalence relation.

Solution: a triangle is congruent to itself. Hence R is reflexive. If a is congruent to b, then b is congruent to a. Hence R is symmetric. If a is congruent to b, b is congruent to c, then a is congruent to c. Hence R is transitive. The relation satisfies all the three properties of an equivalence relation.

Example 6: Consider subset as a relation on a given set. Check whether it is reflexive, symmetric, antisymmetric, equivalence or partial ordering relation.

Solution: Let A be the given set. Consider subsets B, C of A. Any set is its own subset. Hence the relation is reflexive. If $B \subseteq C$, then $C \subseteq B$ only if B = C. Hence the relation is not symmetric but antisymmetric. If $B \subseteq C$ and $C \subseteq D$ then $B \subseteq D$. Hence the subset relation is transitive. The relation is therefore not an equivalence relation but a partial ordering relation.

Example 7: From the following digraphs, write the relation a set of ordered pairs. Are the relations equivalence relations?

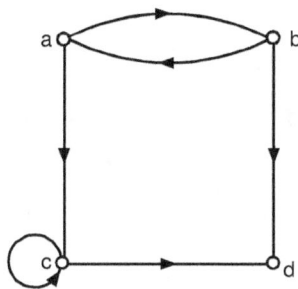
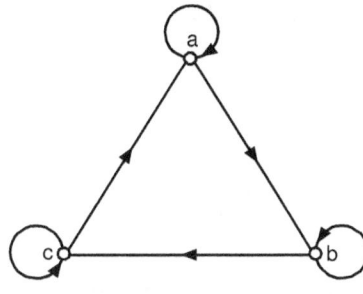

Fig. 4.25   Fig. 4.26

Solution: R_1 = {(a, b), (b, a), (a, c), (c, d), (b, d), (c, c)} and
R_2 = {(a, a), (b, b), (c, c), (c, a), (c, c), (a, b)}

R_1 is not an equivalence relation since R_1 is not reflexive. R_2 is also not an equivalence relation since R_2 is not symmetric, as (a, b) ∈ R but (b, a) ∉ R.

Example 8: Consider the following relation on {1, 2, 3, 4, 5, 6}, $R = \{(i, j) \mid |i - j| = 2\}$

Is R reflexive, symmetric, transitive? Draw a graph of R.

Solution: R is not reflexive. R is symmetric but not transitive.

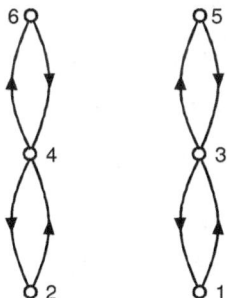

Fig. 4.27

DISCRETE STRUCTURE AND GRAPH THEORY (NMU) — RELATIONS

Example 9: Consider the relations defined by the digraphs. Determine whether the given relations are reflexive, symmetric, antisymmetric or transitive. Which graphs are equivalence relations and which are partial orders?

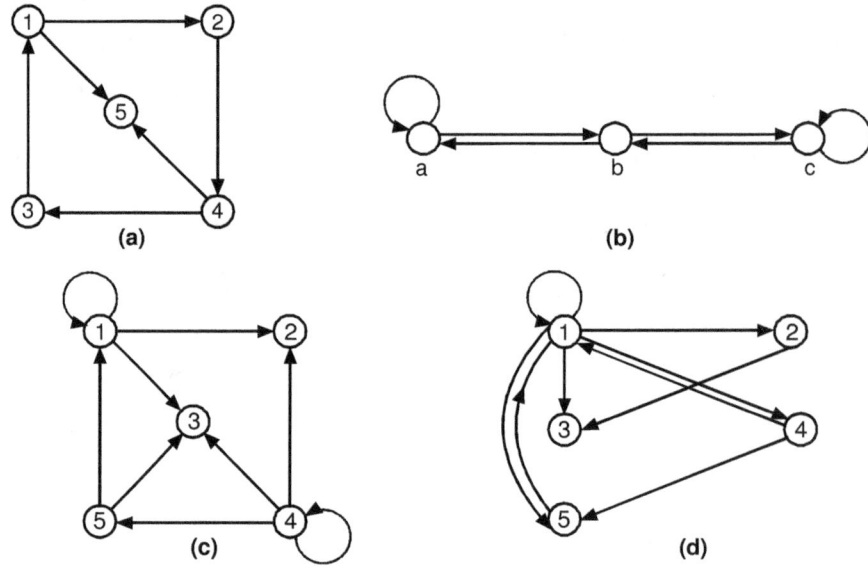

Fig. 4.28

Solution: $R_1 = \{(1, 2), (1, 5), (2, 4), (3, 1), (4, 3), (4, 5)\}$
$R_2 = \{(a, a), (a, b), (b, a), (b, c), (c, b), (c, c)\}$
$R_3 = \{(1, 1), (1, 2), (1, 3), (2, 4), (4, 3), (4, 4), (4, 5), (5, 1)\}$
$R_4 = \{(1, 1), (1, 2), (1, 3), (1, 4), (1, 5), (2, 3), (4, 1), (4, 5), (5, 1)\}$

R_1 is not reflexive, not symmetric and not transitive also.

R_1 is also antisymmetric since $a \neq b \rightarrow a\,R\,b \vee b\,R\,a$.

R_2 is not reflexive, not transitive but symmetric. R_2 is not antisymmetric.

R_3 is not reflexive, not symmetric, but is transitive and antisymmetric.

R_4 is not reflexive, not symmetric and not transitive since $(4, 1) \in R$ and $(1, 3) \in R$ but $(4, 3) \notin R$. R_4 is not antisymmetric.

None of the relations are equivalence relations or partial orders.

Example 11: The following relations R_1 and R_2 are defined over the set $A = \{1, 2, 3, 4, 5\}$. Show that they are partial order relations and draw their Hasse diagram.

R_1	1	2	3	4	5
1	✓				
2	✓	✓			
3	✓	✓	✓		
4	✓	✓		✓	✓
5	✓				✓

R_2	1	2	3	4	5
1	✓	✓	✓	✓	
2		✓	✓	✓	
3			✓	✓	
4				✓	
5			✓	✓	✓

Solution: R_1 is reflexive since (1, 1), (2, 2), (3, 3), (4, 4), (5, 5) ∈ R_1. R_1 is also antisymmetric since (1, 2) ∉ R_1, but (2, 1) ∈ R_1 (1, 3) ∉ R_1 but (3, 1) ∈ R_1. Likewise we can check for other elements. R_1 is transitive (4, 5) ∈ R_1, (5, 1) ∈ R_1, → (4, 1) ∈ R_1. Hence R_1 is a partial order relation.

R_2 is reflexive since ✓ appears along the diagonal of the square. R_2 is antisymmetric since whenever (a, b) ∈ R_2, (b, a) ∉ R_2, unless a = b. R_2 is also transitive.

(1, 3) and (3, 4) ∈ R_2 → (1, 4) ∈ R_2. (5, 3) and (3, 4) ∈ R_2 → (5, 4) ∈ R_2. Likewise we can check transitivity for all possible combinations. Hence R_2 is also a partial order.

Hasse diagrams:

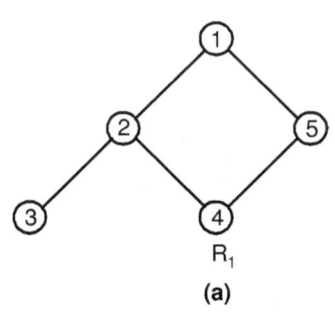
R_1
(a)

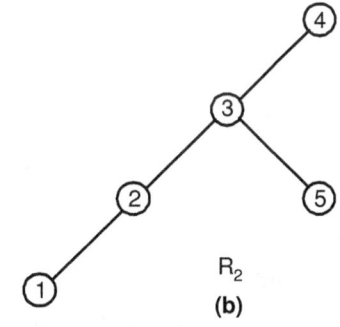
R_2
(b)

Fig. 4.29

Example 11: Let R be a symmetric and transitive relation on a set A. Show that if for every a in A there exists b in A such that (a, b) is in R, then R is an equivalence relation.

Solution: We have only to show that R is reflexive. Let a ∈ A, then there exists b ∈ A, such that (a, b) ∈ R. Since R is symmetric, this implies (b, a) ∈ R. Now (a, b) and (b, a) ∈ R. Hence by transitivity (a, a) ∈ R, i.e. R is reflexive.

Example 12: Show that the transitive closure of a symmetric relation is symmetric.

Solution: Let R^* denote the transitive closure of R. $R^* = R \cup R^2 \cup$. Let (a, b) ∈ R^*. Then (a, b) ∈ R^k for some positive integer k. Then there exists a sequence of elements a, $x_1, x_2, \ldots x_{k-1}$, b, such that (a, x_1) ∈ R, (x_1, x_2) ∈ R, ..., (x_{k-1}) ∈ R.

Since R is symmetric this implies (b, x_{k-1}), (x_{k-1}, x_{k-2}), ... , (x_2, x_1), (x_1, a) ∈ R. Since R^* is transitive this implies that (b, a) ∈ R^*. Hence R^* is transitive.

Example 13: Let X = {1, 2, 3, 4} and R = {(x, y) | x > y}. Draw the graph of R and also give its matrix.

$$R = \{(2, 1), (3, 1), (3, 2), (4, 1), (4, 2), (4, 3)\}$$

Graph of R:

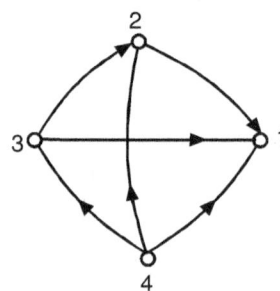

Fig. 4.30

$$M_R = \begin{bmatrix} 0 & 0 & 0 & 0 \\ 1 & 0 & 0 & 0 \\ 1 & 1 & 0 & 0 \\ 1 & 1 & 1 & 0 \end{bmatrix}$$

Example 14: Let X = {1, 2, ... 7} and R = {(x, y) | x − y is divisible by 3}. Show that R is an equivalence relation. Draw the graph of R.

Solution: R is reflexive since ∀ x ∈ X, x − x = 0 is divisible by 3. Hence for ∀ x ∈ X, (x, x) ∈ R. R is symmetric since for every (x, y) ∈ R, (y, x) ∈ R, as y − x = − (x − y) is divisible by 3. Let (x, y) and (y, z) ∈ R. Then ± x − z = (x − y) + (y − z) is clearly divisible by 3. Hence R is an equivalence relation.

Graph of R: R = {(1, 1), (1, 4), (1, 7), (2, 2), (2, 5), (3, 3), (3, 6), (4, 1), (4, 4), (4, 7), (5, 2), (5, 5), (6, 3), (6, 6), (7, 1), (7, 4), (7, 7)}

  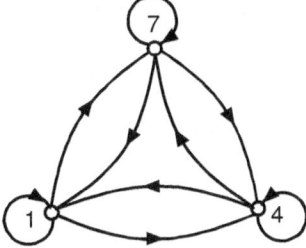

Fig. 4.31

Example 15: Draw the Hasse diagram.

Let A be the set of factors of a particular positive integer m and let ≤ be a relation divides, i.e.
$$\leq \ = \ \{(x, y) \mid x \in A \wedge y \in A \wedge (x \text{ divides } y)\}.$$

(i) m = 2,   (ii) m = 6,   (iii) m = 12,   (iv) m = 45.

Solution: (i) m = 2,   A = {1, 2},   R = {(1, 1), (1, 2), (2, 2)}

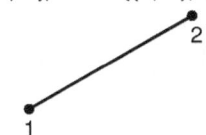

(ii) m = 6,   A = {1, 2, 3, 6}
R = {(1, 1), (1, 2), (1, 3), (1, 6), (2, 2), (2, 6), (3, 3), (3, 6), (6, 6)}

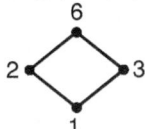

(iii) m = 12,   A = {1, 2, 3, 4, 5, 6, 12}

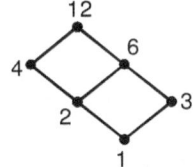

(iv) m = 45,   A = {1, 3, 9, 15, 45}

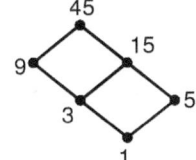

Example 16: Let R be the relation on the set A = {5, 6, 8, 10, 28, 36, 48}. Let R = {(a, b) | a is a divisor of b}. Draw the Hasse diagram and compare it with digraph. Determine whether R is reflexive, transitive and symmetric.

Solution: R = {(5, 5), (5, 10), (6, 6), (6, 36), (6, 48), (8, 8), (8, 48), (10, 10), (28, 28), (36, 36), (48, 48)}.

Hasse diagram:

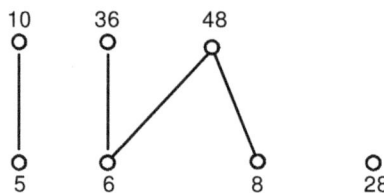

Digraph:

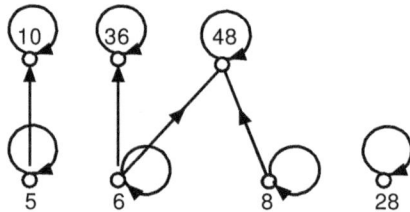

R is reflexive, but not symmetric or transitive.

Example 17: Find the transitive closure of R by Warshall Algorithm where A = {1, 2, 3, 4, 5, 6} and R = {(x, y) | |x − y| = 2}.

Solution: R = {(1, 3), (3, 1), (2, 4), (4, 2), (3, 5), (5, 3), (4, 6), (6, 4)}

$$W_R = M_R = \begin{bmatrix} 0 & 0 & 1 & 0 & 0 & 0 \\ 0 & 0 & 0 & 1 & 0 & 0 \\ 1 & 0 & 0 & 0 & 1 & 0 \\ 0 & 1 & 0 & 0 & 0 & 1 \\ 0 & 0 & 1 & 0 & 0 & 0 \\ 0 & 0 & 0 & 1 & 0 & 0 \end{bmatrix}$$

By notation, let $a_1 = 1$, $a_2 = 2$, $a_3 = 3$, $a_4 = 4$, $a_5 = 5$, $a_6 = 6$. For k = 1, $W_k = W_1$, $a_k = 1$ is an interior vertex for the path from 3 to 1 and 1 to 3. Hence W_1 has 1 in the position (3, 3).

$$\therefore \quad W_1 = \begin{bmatrix} 0 & 0 & 1 & 0 & 0 & 0 \\ 0 & 0 & 0 & 1 & 0 & 0 \\ 1 & 0 & 1 & 0 & 1 & 0 \\ 0 & 1 & 0 & 0 & 0 & 1 \\ 0 & 0 & 1 & 0 & 0 & 0 \\ 0 & 0 & 0 & 1 & 0 & 0 \end{bmatrix}$$

Similarly for $k = 2$, $a_2 = 2$ is an interior vertex for the path (4, 2) and (2, 4). $k = 3$, $a_3 = 3$ is an interior vertex for the path (1, 3) and (3, 1). $k = 4$, $a_4 = 4$ is an interior vertex for the path (2, 4) and (4, 2). $k = 5$, $a_5 = 5$ is an interior vertex for the path (3, 5) and (5, 3). $k = 6$, $a_k = 6$ is an interior vertex for the path (4, 6) and (6, 4).

Hence the final matrix becomes

$$W_6 = \begin{bmatrix} 1 & 0 & 1 & 0 & 1 & 0 \\ 0 & 1 & 0 & 1 & 0 & 1 \\ 1 & 0 & 1 & 0 & 1 & 0 \\ 0 & 1 & 0 & 1 & 0 & 1 \\ 1 & 0 & 1 & 0 & 1 & 0 \\ 0 & 1 & 0 & 1 & 0 & 1 \end{bmatrix}$$

Hence transitive closure of R is

$R^* = \{(1, 1), (1, 3), (1, 5), (2, 2), (2, 4), (2, 6), (3, 1), (3, 3), (3, 5), (4, 2),$
$(4, 4), (4, 6), (5, 1), (5, 3), (5, 5), (6, 2), (6, 4), (6, 6)\}$

Example 18: Use Warshall's Algorithm to find the transitive closure of R, where

$$M_R = \begin{bmatrix} 1 & 0 & 1 \\ 0 & 1 & 0 \\ 1 & 1 & 0 \end{bmatrix} \quad \text{and } A = \{1, 2, 3\}.$$

Solution: $R = \{(1, 1), (1, 3), (2, 2), (3, 1), (3, 2)\}$

$W_0 = W_R$

For $k = 1$, $a_k = 1$ is an interior vertex for the path (3, 1) and (1, 3). Hence W_1 will have 1 as its (3, 3) entry.

For $k = 2$, $a_k = 2$ is an interior vertex for the path (3, 2) and (2, 2), but already there is 1 at (3, 2) position.

For $k = 3$, $a_k = 3$ is an interior vertex for the paths (1, 3), (3, 2) and (1, 3), (3, 1). Hence we have to include 1 at the (1, 2) position, whereas there is already 1 at the (1, 1) position.

$$W_3 = \begin{bmatrix} 1 & 0 & 1 \\ 1 & 1 & 0 \\ 1 & 1 & 1 \end{bmatrix}$$

Hence transitive closure of R

$$R^* = \{(1, 1), (1, 3), (2, 1), (2, 2), (3, 1), (3, 2), (3, 3)\}$$

Example 19: Let $R = \{(1, 4), (2, 1), (2, 5), (2, 4), (4, 3), (5, 3), (3, 2)\}$

Use Warshall's algorithm to find the matrix of transitive closure.

Solution:
$$W_0 = M_R = \begin{bmatrix} 0 & 0 & 0 & 1 & 0 \\ 1 & 0 & 0 & 1 & 1 \\ 0 & 1 & 0 & 0 & 0 \\ 0 & 0 & 1 & 0 & 0 \\ 0 & 0 & 1 & 0 & 0 \end{bmatrix}$$

For k = 1, place 1 is already in the position (2, 4). Hence, $W_0 = W_1$.

For k = 2, place 1 in the positions (3, 1), (3, 4) and (3, 5).

$$\therefore W_2 = \begin{bmatrix} 0 & 0 & 0 & 1 & 0 \\ 1 & 0 & 0 & 1 & 1 \\ 1 & 1 & 0 & 1 & 1 \\ 0 & 0 & 1 & 0 & 0 \\ 0 & 0 & 1 & 0 & 0 \end{bmatrix}$$

Similarly,
$$W_3 = \begin{bmatrix} 1 & 1 & 1 & 1 & 1 \\ 1 & 0 & 0 & 1 & 1 \\ 1 & 1 & 0 & 1 & 1 \\ 1 & 1 & 1 & 1 & 1 \\ 1 & 1 & 1 & 1 & 1 \end{bmatrix}$$

Finally,
$$W_5 = \begin{bmatrix} 1 & 1 & 1 & 1 & 1 \\ 1 & 1 & 1 & 1 & 1 \\ 1 & 1 & 1 & 1 & 1 \\ 1 & 1 & 1 & 1 & 1 \\ 1 & 1 & 1 & 1 & 1 \end{bmatrix}$$

Example 20: Find the transitive closure of the relation R on A = {1, 2, 3, 4} defined by R = {(1, 2), (1, 3), (1, 4), (2, 1), (2, 3), (3, 4), (3, 2), (4, 2), (4, 3).

Solution:
$$W_0 = M_R = \begin{bmatrix} 0 & 1 & 1 & 1 \\ 1 & 0 & 1 & 0 \\ 0 & 1 & 0 & 1 \\ 0 & 1 & 1 & 0 \end{bmatrix}$$

For k = 1, place 1 in the positions (2, 2), (2, 3) and (2, 4).

$$\therefore W_1 = \begin{bmatrix} 0 & 1 & 1 & 1 \\ 1 & 1 & 1 & 1 \\ 0 & 1 & 0 & 1 \\ 0 & 1 & 1 & 1 \end{bmatrix}$$

For k = 2, we have 1 in (1, 2), (2, 2), (3, 2) and (3, 4) (in 2nd column) and (2, 1), (2, 2), (2, 3) and (2, 4) (in the 2nd row).

Hence, we place 1 in the new locations (1, 1), (3, 1), (3, 3), keeping infact the 1's, which are already there in other locations.

Hence,
$$W_2 = \begin{bmatrix} 1 & 1 & 1 & 1 \\ 1 & 1 & 1 & 1 \\ 1 & 1 & 1 & 1 \\ 0 & 1 & 1 & 1 \end{bmatrix}$$

For k = 3, as before we place 1 in the position (4, 4), considering the combination of (4, 3) and (3, 4) positions, where 1 is located.

$$\therefore W_3 = \begin{bmatrix} 1 & 1 & 1 & 1 \\ 1 & 1 & 1 & 1 \\ 1 & 1 & 1 & 1 \\ 1 & 1 & 1 & 1 \end{bmatrix} = M_R^*$$

∴ Transitive closure R* = {(1, 1), (1, 2), (1, 3), (1, 4), (2, 1), (2, 2), (2, 3), (2, 4), (3, 1), (3, 2), (3, 3), (3, 4), (4, 1), (4, 2), (4, 3), (4, 4)}

Example 21: Determine the properties of the relations given by the graphs below:

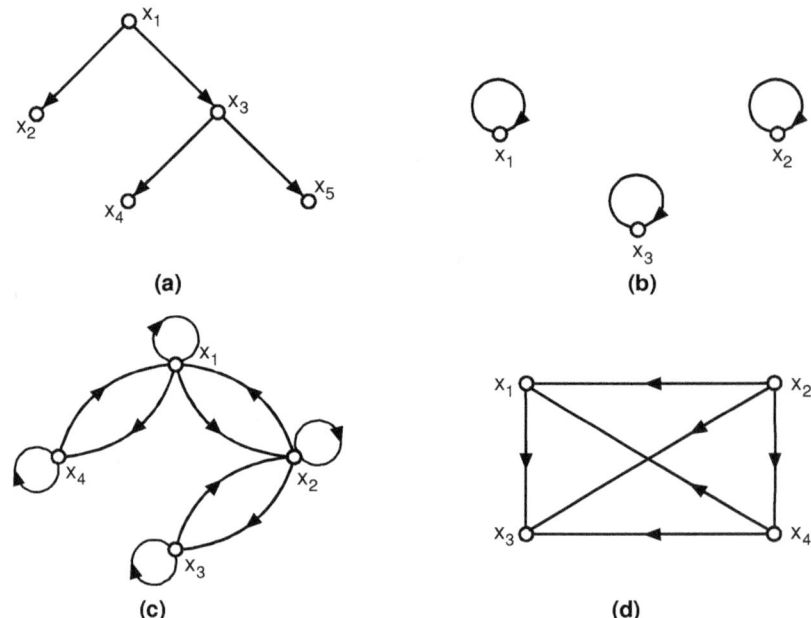

Fig. 4.32

Solution:

$$M_{R_1} = \begin{array}{c} \\ x_1 \\ x_2 \\ x_3 \\ x_4 \\ x_5 \end{array} \begin{array}{c} x_1 \ x_2 \ x_3 \ x_4 \ x_5 \\ \begin{bmatrix} 0 & 1 & 1 & 0 & 0 \\ 0 & 0 & 0 & 0 & 0 \\ 0 & 0 & 0 & 1 & 1 \\ 0 & 0 & 0 & 0 & 0 \\ 0 & 0 & 0 & 0 & 0 \end{bmatrix} \end{array}$$

∴ R_1 is not reflexive, not symmetric and not transitive. R_1 is reflexive and antisymmetric.

(b)
$$M_{R_2} = \begin{array}{c} \\ x_1 \\ x_2 \\ x_3 \end{array} \begin{array}{c} x_1 \ x_2 \ x_3 \\ \begin{bmatrix} 1 & 0 & 0 \\ 0 & 1 & 0 \\ 0 & 0 & 1 \end{bmatrix} \end{array}$$

R₂ is reflexive.

(c) $M_{R_3} = \begin{array}{c} \\ x_1 \\ x_2 \\ x_3 \\ x_4 \end{array} \begin{array}{cccc} x_1 & x_2 & x_3 & x_4 \\ \begin{bmatrix} 1 & 1 & 0 & 1 \\ 1 & 1 & 1 & 0 \\ 0 & 1 & 1 & 0 \\ 1 & 0 & 0 & 1 \end{bmatrix} \end{array}$

R₃ is reflexive, symmetric R₃ is not transitive and not antisymmetric.

(d) $M_{R_4} = \begin{array}{c} \\ x_1 \\ x_2 \\ x_3 \\ x_4 \end{array} \begin{array}{cccc} x_1 & x_2 & x_3 & x_4 \\ \begin{bmatrix} 0 & 0 & 0 & 1 \\ 1 & 0 & 1 & 1 \\ 1 & 0 & 0 & 1 \\ 0 & 0 & 0 & 0 \end{bmatrix} \end{array}$

R₄ is not reflexive, not symmetric and not antisymmetric. R₄ is reflexive and transitive.

Example 22: Let R, S and T be the relations on
$$A = \{1, 2, 3\} \text{ defined by}$$
$$R = \{(1, 1), (2, 2), (3, 3)\}$$
$$S = \{(1, 2), (2, 1), (3, 3)\}$$
$$T = \{(1, 2), (2, 3), (1, 3)\}$$
Determine which of the relations are reflexive, symmetric, transitive, antisymmetric.

Solution: R is reflexive, symmetric and transitive.
S is not reflexive and not transitive. But R is symmetric. T is irreflexive, not symmetric.
T is transitive and antisymmetric.

Example 23: Consider the set of words
$$W = \{Sheet, Last, Sky, Wash, Wind, Sit\}$$
Let R be the equivalence relation on W defined by
(i) "has the same number of letter as"
(ii) "begins with the same letter as".
Find the quotient W/R.

Solution: (i) Quotient set W/R is the set of equivalence clauses of R
∴   W/R = {{Sheet}, {Last, Wash, Wind}, {Sky, Sit}}
(ii)   W/R = {{Last}, {Sheet, Sky, Sit} {Wash, Wind}}

Example 24: For A = {1, 2, 3, 4, 5, 6, 7, 8, 9, 10}. Consider the poset (A, R) whose Hasse diagram is shown below.

Find:

(i) GLB {2, 3}, (ii) GLB = {2, 7}, (iii) GLB {5, 8}, (iv) LUB {3, 2}, (v) LUB {4, 8}, (vi) LUB {3, 5}.

Solution:

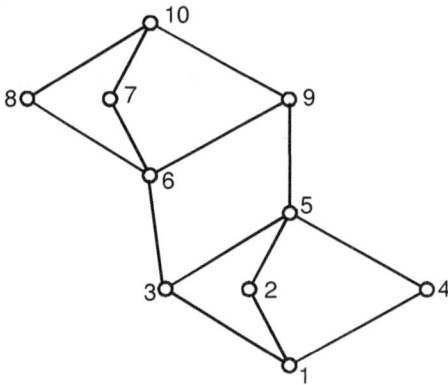

Fig. 4.33

(i) GLB {2, 3} = 1
(ii) GLB {2, 7} = 1
(iii) GLB {5, 8} = 3
(iv) LUB {3, 2} = 5
(v) LUB {4, 8} = 10
(vi) LUB {3, 5} = 5.

EXERCISE - 4.3

1. Let A = {1, 2, 3, 4}. Consider the following relations on A.
   R_1 = {(1, 3), (2, 3), (4, 1)}
   R_2 = {(1, 1), (2, 1)}
   R_3 = {(3, 4)}
   R_4 = {(1, 1), (2, 2), (3, 3)}
   R_5 = {(1, 3), (2, 4)}.

   Determine which relations are (i) reflexive, (ii) symmetric, (iii) transitive, (iv) equivalence, (v) partial ordering relation?

2. Let A = {a, b, c}. Determine whether the relation R whose matrix M_R is given is an equivalence relation.

(a) $M_R = \begin{bmatrix} 1 & 0 & 0 \\ 0 & 1 & 1 \\ 0 & 1 & 1 \end{bmatrix}$

(b) $M_R = \begin{bmatrix} 1 & 0 & 1 \\ 0 & 1 & 0 \\ 0 & 0 & 1 \end{bmatrix}$

3. Determine whether the relation R whose digraph is given is reflexive, irreflexive, symmetric, antisymmetric or transitive?

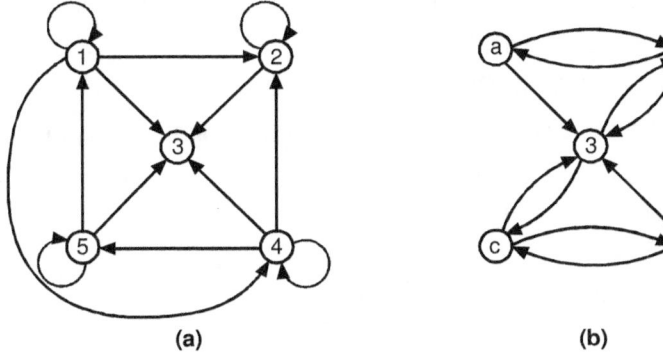

(a) (b)

Fig. 4.34

4. Let Z be the set of integers and let a R b iff b is a multiple of a. Determine which of the five properties are satisfied by R?
5. Let A be a set of lines in a plane. Define the following relation on A: l_1 A l_2 if and only if l_1 is perpendicular to l_2. Determine what properties of a relation are satisfied by R?
6. Let P be the set of all people. Let R be a binary relation on P such that a R b iff a is a brother of b. What properties of a relation are satisfied by R?
7. Let R_1 and R_2 be relations on a set A. Prove the following:

    (a) If R_1 is symmetric, then so are R_1^c and $\overline{R}_1$.
    (b) If R_1 and R_2 are symmetric, then so are $R_1 \cap R_2$ and $R_1 \cup R_2$.
    (c) If R_1 and R_2 are transitive, then so is $R_1 \cap R_2$. Is $R_1 \cup R_2$ transitive?

8. If R_1 and R_2 are relations on any set A, prove or disprove the following:

    (a) If R_1 and R_2 are reflexive then so is $R_1 R_2$.
    (b) If R_1 and R_2 are irreflexive, then so is $R_1 R_2$.
    (c) If R_1 and R_2 are symmetric, then so is $R_1 R_2$.
    (d) If R_1 and R_2 are antisymmetric, then so is $R_1 R_2$.
    (e) If R_1 and R_2 are transitive, then so is $R_1 R_2$.

9. If A = {1, 2, 3, 4, 5} and R = {(1, 2), (3, 4), (4, 5), (4, 1), (1, 1)}, find its transitive closure.
10. Let R be a transitive and reflexive relation on A. Let T be a relation on A such that (a, b) ∈ T iff both (a, b) and (b, a) are in R. Show that T is an equivalence relation.
11. Let R be a reflexive relation on a set A. Show that R is an equivalence relation iff (a, b) and (a, c) ∈ R implies that (b, c) ∈ R.
12. Let R be the relation defined on the integers by a R b iff a − b is even. Show that R is an equivalence relation and determine the equivalence classes.
13. Partition the set A = {1, 2, 3, 4, 5} by collection of sets {{1, 2}, {3}, {4, 5}}.
    Determine the equivalence relation induced by the partition.
14. Let, A = {1, 2, 3, 4} and
    R = {(1, 1), (1, 2), (1, 3), (2, 1), (2, 2), (3, 1), (2, 3), (3, 2), (3, 3), (4, 4)}
    Show that R is an equivalence relation and determine the equivalence classes.
15. Let, A = {1, 2, 3, 4, 5, 6, 7, 8, 9, 10}
    and let, A_1 = {1, 2, 3, 4}
    A_2 = {5, 6, 7}
    A_3 = {8, 9, 10}
    From a partition
    π_1 = {A_1, A_2, A_3} of A.
    Let, $_4$ = {4, 8, 10}, A_5 = {3, 7, 9}, A_6 = {1, 2, 5, 6} form another partition
    π_2 = {A_4, A_5, A_6} of A.
    Find the sum and product of the two partitions.
16. Let A be a set of people and R be a binary relation on A such that (a, b) is in R if a is a friend of b. Show that R is a compatible relation.
17. Let R_1 and R_2 be two compatible relations on A. Is $R_1 \cap R_2$ a compatible relation?
18. Let A be a set of English words and R be a binary relation on A such that two words in A are related if they have one or more letters in common. Show that R is a compatible relation.
19. Determine whether the relation R is a partial order on the set A.
    (i) A = Z, and a R b iff a = 2b
    (ii) A = Z, and a R b iff b^2 | a.
20. Let A = {1, 2, 3, 4} and R = {(1, 1), (1, 2), (2, 2), (2, 4), (1, 3), (3, 3), (3, 4), (1, 4), 4)}. Show that R is a partial order and draw its Hasse diagram. Determine the chains and antichains.

21. Consider the poset whose Hasse diagram is given below. Find the length of the longest chain. Find also the antichains.

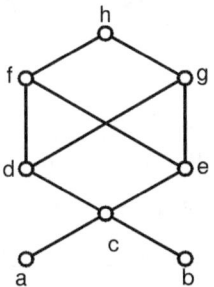

Fig. 4.35

22. Given S = {1, 2, 3, 4, 5} and relation R on S, where R = {(x, y) | x + y = 5}. What are the properties of R?

23. Let R be a relation on a set A,

$$A = \{2, 3, 4, 6, 8, 12, 38, 48\} \text{ defined by}$$
$$R = \{(a, b) \mid a \text{ is divisor of } b\}$$

Draw the diagraph and Hasse diagram.

24. Draw the Hasse diagram of the following sets under the partial ordering relation 'divides' and indicate those which are chains:
    (i) {2, 4, 12, 24}
    (ii) {1, 3, 5, 15, 30}

25. Draw the diagraph for the following relation and determine whether the relation is reflexive, symmetric, transitive and antisymmetric.
    A = {1, 2, 3, 4, 5, 6, 7, 8} and let xRy whenever y is divisible by x.

26. Let A = {1, 2, 3} and consider two reflexive relations R = {(1, 1), (1, 2), (1, 3), (2, 2), (3, 3)} and S = {(1, 1), (1, 2), (2, 2), (3, 2), (3, 3)}. Determine whether the following relations are reflexive or irreflexive.

    (i) R^{-1}, (ii) $\bar{R}$, (iii) $R \cap S$, (iv) $R \cup S$.

27. For the relation R whose matrix is given, find the matrix of transitive closure, using Warshall's Algorithm:

$$\begin{bmatrix} 1 & 0 & 0 & 1 \\ 1 & 1 & 0 & 0 \\ 0 & 0 & 1 & 0 \\ 0 & 0 & 0 & 1 \end{bmatrix}$$

4.12 Lattice

Let (A, ≤) be a poset with partial order ≤. We first define the following terms given in next section.

4.12.1 Maximal and Minimal Elements

> An element a ∈ A is called a **maximal element** if there is no element b ∈ A such that b ≠ a and a ≤ b. An element c ∈ A is called a minimal element if there is no element d ∈ A such that d ≠ c and d ≤ a.

Example: Consider the poset whose Hasse diagram is given below.

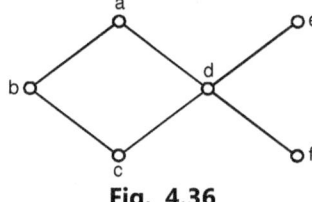

Fig. 4.36

Maximal elements are a, e. Minimal elements are c, f.

4.12.2 Upper Bound and Lower Bound

> Let a, b be elements in a poset (A, ≤). An element c is said to be an **upper bound** of a and b if a ≤ c and b ≤ c. An element c is said to be a **least upper bound** (lub) of a and b if c is an upper bound of a and b and if there is no other upper bound d of a and b such that d ≤ c.

> Similarly an element e is said to be a **lower bound** of a and b if e ≤ a and e ≤ b; and e is called a **greatest lower bound** (glb) of a and b if there is no other lower bound f of a, b such that e ≤ f.

Example: Consider the poset whose diagram is given below.

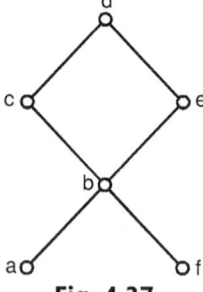

Fig. 4.37

Then
- (i) upper bounds for {c, e} is d

  lub {c, e} = d.

  lower bounds for {c, e} are the elements b, a and f

  glb {c, e} = b.
- (ii) upper bounds for {a, f} are the elements b, c, e, d.

  lub {a, f} = b.

  lower bounds for a, f do not exist.
- (iii) upper bounds for {b, d} is d.

  lub {b, d} = d.

  lower bounds for {b, d} are b, a and f.

  glb {b, d} = b.

In this manner, one can find the bounds for various pairs of elements.

4.12.3 Lattice – Definition

A lattice is a poset (L, ≤) in which every subset {a, b} of L, has a least upper bound and a greatest lower bound.

Examples:
1. For any set A, consider its power set P(A). Then (P(A), ⊆) is a poset. It is also a lattice since for any pair of subsets B, C of A, lub {B, C} = B ∪ C and glb {B, C} = B ∩ C.
2. Let N be the set of natural numbers. For a, b ∈ N, let a ≤ b if b is divisible by a. Then (N, ≤) is a lattice since for any pair of elements a, b ∈ N, lub {a, b} = lcm of a and b and glb {a, b} = gcd of a and b.
3. Consider the poset whose diagram is given below.

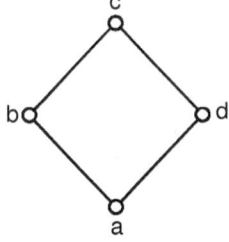

Fig. 4.38

If A = {a, b, c, d}, every pair of elements has a lub and glb. Hence (A, ≤) is a lattice.

4. Let A = {2, 3, 4, 6, 12} and define a ≤ b as a divides b.

Consider the diagram of the poset (A, ≤).

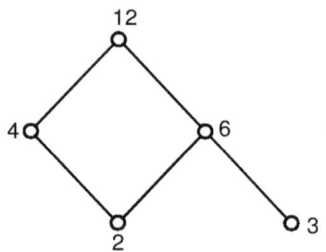

Fig. 4.39

The poset is not a lattice since the pair {2, 3} does not have a greatest lower bound. If the element 1 is included in A, then (A, ≤) will be a lattice.

4.12.4 Lattice Operators

Let $(L, \leq)$ be a lattice. For any pair of elements $a, b \in L$, denote lub $\{a, b\}$ by $a \vee b$ and glb $\{a, b\}$ by $a \wedge b$. $a \vee b$ is called as the **join** of a and b. $a \wedge b$ is called as the meet of a and b. The meet and join are therefore binary operators.

4.12.5 Basic Properties of Lattices

Theorem 1: For any element $a \in L$, $a \vee a = a$ and $a \wedge a = a$ (Idempotent property).

Proof:

Since $a \vee a$ is an upper bound for a, $a \leq a \vee a$

By reflexivity, $a \leq a$ ... (2)

Since $a \vee a =$ lub $\{a, a\}$, from (1) and (2) it follows that

$a \vee a \leq a$ ... (3)

But ≤ is antisymmetric.

Hence $a \vee a = a$

Similarly, we can prove $a \wedge a = a$

Theorem 2: For any $a, b \in L$

$a \vee (a \wedge b) = a$

$a \wedge (a \vee b) = a$ (Absorption property of join and meet)

Proof:

Since $a \vee (a \wedge b)$ is an upper bound for a and $a \wedge b$, it follows that

$a \leq a \vee (a \wedge b)$ ... (1)

> Now $a \wedge b$ is a lower bound for a and b, hence $a \wedge b \leq a$.
> Now $a \leq a$ and $a \wedge b \leq a$. Hence a is an upper bound for the pair $\{a, a \wedge b\}$.
> Since $a \vee (a \wedge b) = \text{lub } \{a, a \wedge b\}$, it follows that
> $a \vee (a \wedge b) \leq a$ ... (2)
> From (1) and (2) by antisymmetry of $\leq$, we have
> $a = a \vee (a \wedge b)$
> Similarly, we can prove $a \wedge (a \vee b) = a$.

Theorem 3: The meet and join operations are associative,

    i.e. $a \vee (a \vee c) = (a \vee b) \vee c$

    and $a \wedge (b \wedge c) = (a \wedge b) \wedge c$.

Proof: Proof is left as an exercise.

Theorem 4: The meet and join operations are commutative.

Proof: Left as an easy exercise.

In general, the distributive law is not satisfied for a lattice, as the following example demonstrates.

4.12.6 Example of a Non-distributive Lattice

1. Consider the Hasse diagram given below of a lattice.

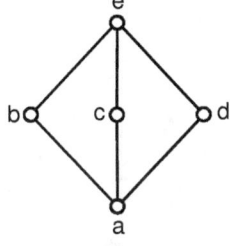

Fig. 4.40

We have $b \wedge (c \vee d) = b \wedge e = b$ ... (1)

On the other hand $(b \wedge c) \vee (b \wedge d) = a \vee a = a$.

Since $a \neq b$, the distributive law does not hold for this lattice.

4.12.7 Universal Bounds

An element in a lattice $(L, \leq)$ is called universal lower bound if for every $a \in L, l \leq a$. Similarly an element u in L is called universal upper bound if for every $a \in L, a \leq u$.

One can easily see that these universal bounds are unique. We denote the universal lower bound by 0 and the universal upper bound by 1. 0 and 1 are merely symbols and should not confuse with the numbers 0 and 1. All lattices do not have the universal bounds. The set of real numbers with the usual order (≤) has neither the universal lower bound nor the universal upper bound.

Theorem 1: Let (L, ≤) be a lattice with universal bounds 0 and 1. Then for every a ∈ L, a ∨ 1 = 1, a ∧ 1 = a, a ∨ 0 = a, a ∧ 0 = 0.

Proof: Easy exercise

4.12.8 Complement and Complemented Lattice

Definition:

> Let (L, ≤) be a lattice with universal bounds 0 and 1. For an element a ∈ L, b is said to be a complement of a if a ∨ b = 1 and a ∧ b = 0.

Note by the commutativity property of meet and join, if b is the complement of a, then a is the complement of b.

In a lattice an element can have more than one complement, as demonstrated in the following example.

Example: Let A = {1, 2, 3, 5, 30} and let a ≤ b iff a divides b. The Hasse diagram is

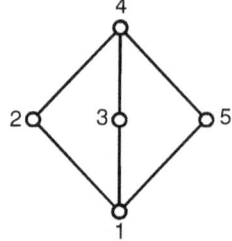

Fig. 4.41

Now $\quad$ 2 ∧ 3 = 1, $\quad$ 2 ∨ 3 = 30

$\quad\quad\quad\quad\quad$ 2 ∧ 5 = 1, $\quad$ 2 ∨ 5 = 30

Hence 2 has two complements 3 and 5.

Hence complement is not unique.

However, as the following theorem will prove, there is a special type of lattice, in which every element has a unique complement.

Theorem 1: Let $(L, \leq)$ be a complemented distributive lattice. Then every element in L has a unique complement.

Proof:
Let $a \in L$. Suppose there exist elements $a_1, a_2 \in L$.
Such that $\quad a \wedge a_1 = 0$ and $a \vee a_1 = 1$,
and $\qquad\quad a \wedge a_2 = 0$ and $a \vee a_2 = 1$,
then, we have to prove $a_1 = a_2$.

Consider $a_1 \quad = a_1 \wedge 1 = a_1 \wedge (a \vee a_2)$
$\qquad\qquad\quad = (a_1 \wedge a) \vee (a_1 \wedge a_2) \quad$ (by distributivity)
$\qquad\qquad\quad = 0 \vee (a_1 \wedge a_2) = a_1 \wedge a_2 \qquad$ ... (1) (Commutativity)

Similarly, $\quad a_2 = a_2 \wedge 1 = a_2 \wedge (a \vee a_1)$
$\qquad\qquad\quad = (a_2 \wedge a) \vee (a_2 \wedge a_1) = 0 \vee (a_2 \wedge a_1) = a_1 \wedge a_2 \quad$ ... (2)

From (1) and (2), a_1 and a_2 are both equal to $a_1 \wedge a_2$.
Hence $a_1 = a_2$, which proves the uniqueness of the complement.
We denote the complement of a by a'.

The following theorem proves De Morgan's laws for a complemented distributive lattice.

Theorem 2: Let $(L, \leq)$ be a complemented distributive lattice.
$\qquad\qquad$ Show that $(a \vee b)' = a' \wedge b'$ and $(a \wedge b)' = a' \vee b'$.

Proof:
We use the uniqueness of complement.
Consider $(a \vee b) \vee (a' \wedge b')$
$\qquad\qquad\qquad = (a \vee b \vee a') \wedge (a \vee b \vee b')$
$\qquad\qquad\qquad = ((a \vee a') \vee b) \wedge (a \vee 1)$
$\qquad\qquad\qquad\quad$ (By associativity, commutativity and distributivity)
$\qquad\qquad\qquad = (1 \vee b) \wedge (a \vee 1) = |\wedge| = 1$

Next consider $(a \vee b) \wedge (a' \wedge b')$
$\qquad\qquad\qquad = ((a \wedge a') \wedge b') \vee (b \wedge b' \wedge a')$
$\qquad\qquad\qquad\quad$ (Using distributivity, commutativity and associativity)
$\qquad\qquad\qquad = (0 \wedge b) \vee (0 \wedge a')$
$\qquad\qquad\qquad = 0 \vee 0 = 0$

Hence $a' \wedge b'$ satisfies the conditions for complement of $a \vee b$. By uniqueness of complement, it follows that
$\qquad\qquad (a \vee b') = a' \wedge b'$.
One can similarly prove that
$\qquad\qquad (a \wedge b)' = a' \vee b'$.

4.12.9 Principle of Duality

Any statement about lattices involving the join and meet operations and the relations $\leq = \geq$ remains true if $\wedge$ is replaced by $\vee$ and $\vee$ by $\wedge$, $\leq$ by $\geq$ and $\geq$ by $\leq$. (= remains as =).
Hence if "a $\vee$ a = a" is true, then so is "a $\wedge$ a = a".
If " a $\wedge$ b $\leq$ a " is true, then so is "a $\vee$ b' $\geq$ a" (or " a $\leq$ a $\vee$ b") is true.
If a lattice has universal bounds 0 and 1, then in the dual statement, 0 is replaced by 1 and 1 is replaced by 0.

This concept is known as the principle of duality. Use this principle in the following theorem.

Theorem 1: If the meet operation is distributive over the join operation in a lattice, then the join operation is also distributive over the meet operation. The converse is also true.

Proof:
It is given that a $\wedge$ (b $\vee$ c) = (a $\wedge$ b) $\vee$ (a $\wedge$ c)
We obtain (a $\vee$ b) $\wedge$ (a $\vee$ c) = [(a $\vee$ b) $\wedge$ a] $\vee$ [(a $\vee$ b) $\wedge$ c]
$$= a \vee [(a \vee b) \wedge c]$$
$$= a \vee [(a \wedge c) \vee (b \wedge c)]$$
$$= [a \vee (a \wedge c)] \vee (b \wedge c)$$
$$= a \vee (b \wedge c)$$
Hence we have proved that if the meet operation is distributive over the join operation, the join operation is also distributive over the meet operation.

The converse is obtained by the principle of duality.

SOLVED EXAMPLES

Example 1: Show that in a distributive lattice (A, $\leq$) if a $\wedge$ x = a $\wedge$ y and a $\vee$ x = a $\vee$ y for some a, then x = y.

Solution: By Absorption property

$$\begin{aligned}
x &= x \wedge (a \vee x) = (x \wedge a) \vee (x \wedge x) & \text{(Distributive law)} \\
&= (a \wedge x) \vee x & \text{(Commutativity and Idempotent)} \\
&= (a \wedge y) \vee x \\
&= (a \vee x) \wedge (y \vee x) \\
&= (a \vee y) \wedge (x \vee y) \\
&= (a \wedge x) \vee y = (a \wedge y) \vee y = y
\end{aligned}$$

Example 2: Let $(A, \leq)$ be a lattice with a universal upper and lower bounds 0 and 1. For any element $a \in A$, prove

$$a \vee 1 = a, \qquad a \wedge 1 = a$$
$$a \vee 0 = a, \qquad a \wedge 0 = 0$$

Solution: $a \vee 1 = \text{lub } \{a, 1\}$

Hence by definition $1 \leq a \vee 1$, but by definition glb, $a \vee 1 \leq 1$

Hence $\qquad a \vee 1 = 1$

$\qquad\qquad a \vee 0 = \text{lub } \{a, 0\}$

Hence $\qquad a \leq a \vee 0$

Now $\qquad 0 \leq a$ for any $a \in A$

and $\qquad a \leq a$.

Hence a is an upper bound for $\{a, 0\}$. But $a \vee 0$ is the least upper bound for $\{a, 0\}$.

Hence it follows that $a \vee 0 \leq a$.

By reflexivity of $\leq$, we obtain

$\qquad\qquad a \vee 0 = a$

$\qquad\qquad a \wedge 1 = a$ is the dual statement of

$\qquad\qquad a \vee 0 = a$, and

$\qquad\qquad a \wedge 0 = 0$ is the dual of

$\qquad\qquad a \vee 1 = 1$

Hence by the principle of duality, these statements are also true.

Example 3: Let $(A, \leq)$ be a lattice. For any $a, b \in A$, prove that $a \leq b$ iff $a \wedge b = a$ iff $a \vee b = b$.

Let $a \leq b$. Then a is a lower bound for $\{a, b\}$. But $a \wedge b = \text{glb } \{a, b\}$. Hence $a \leq a \wedge b$, By definition of $a \wedge b$, $a \wedge b \leq a$. Hence by reflexivity of $\leq$, $a \wedge b = a$.

Conversely let $a \wedge b = a$.

Hence $\qquad a = \text{glb } \{a, b\}$

Therefore $\qquad a \leq b$.

Similarly, we can prove that $a \leq b$ iff $a \vee b = b$.

Example 4: Prove that in a complemented distributive lattice, if $b \wedge \bar{c} = 0$, then $b \leq c$.

Solution: $\qquad b = b \wedge 1 = b \wedge (c \vee \bar{c})$

$\qquad\qquad\qquad = (b \wedge c) \vee (b \wedge \bar{c}) = (b \wedge c) \vee 0 = b \wedge c$

But $\qquad b \wedge c = \text{glb } \{b, c\}$

Hence $\qquad b \leq c$.

Example 5: Show that the set of all divisors of 70 forms a lattice.

Solution: Let A = {1, 2, 5, 7, 10, 14, 35, 70}, and let '≤' is "a divisor of ".

The join operation ∨ = lcm {a, b} and meet ∧ = gcd {a, b}.

The universal upper bound '1' is 70 and the lower bound '0' is 1.

The Hasse diagram is

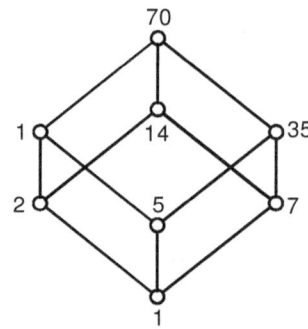

Fig. 4.42

Example 6: For the set X = {2, 3, 6, 12, 24, 36}, a relation ≤ is defined as x ≤ y if x divides y. Draw the Hasse diagram for (X, ≤). Answer the following:

   (i)   What are the maximal elements?

   (ii)   What are the minimal elements?

   (iii) Give one example of chain and one example of antichain.

   (iv) What is the maximum length of chain?

   (v)   Is the poset a lattice?

Solution:

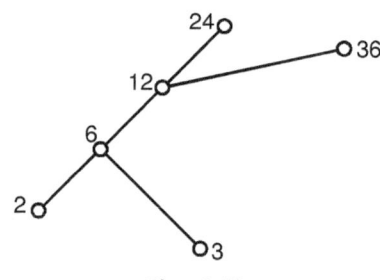

Fig. 4.43

   (i)   Maximal elements are 24, 36.

   (ii) Minimal elements are 2, 3.

   (iii) Chain: {2, 6, 12, 24}

        Antichain: {2, 3} or {24, 36}.

(iv) Maximum length of chain is 3.

(v) The poset is not a lattice since the set {2, 3} has no greatest lower bound.
The set {24, 36} has no least upper bound.

Example 7: Let A is set of factors of positive integer m and relation is divisibility on A.
i.e. R = {(x, y) | x, y ∈ A, x divides y}.
For m = 45, show that POSET (A, ≤) is a lattice. Draw Hasse diagram and give join and meet for the lattice.

Solution: A = {1, 3, 5, 9, 15, 45}
R = {(1, 1), (1, 3), (1, 5), (1, 9), (1, 15), (1, 45), (3, 3), (3, 9), (3, 15), (3, 45), (5, 5), (5, 15), (5, 45), (9, 9), (9, 45), (15, 15), (15, 45), (45, 45)}

For any pair of elements a, b ∈ A,

lub {a, b} = lcm of a and b
and   glb {a, b} = gcd of a and b
For e.g. lub {3, 5} = 15
and   gcd {3, 5} = 1

Tables of operations for ∧ and ∨ operations where ∧ = gcd and ∨ = lcm.

∧	1	3	5	9	15	45
1	1	1	1	1	1	1
3	1	3	1	3	3	3
5	1	1	5	1	5	5
9	1	3	1	9	3	9
15	1	3	5	3	15	15
45	1	3	5	9	15	45

∨	1	3	5	9	15	45
1	1	3	5	9	15	45
3	3	3	15	9	15	45
5	5	15	5	45	15	45
9	9	9	45	9	45	45
15	15	15	15	45	15	45
45	45	45	45	45	45	45

Hasse Diagram:

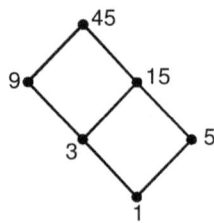

Fig. 4.44

Hence (A, ≤) is a lattice.

Example 8: For any a, b, c, d in a lattice (A, ≤), if (a ≤ b) and (c ≤ d) then prove
(i) a ∨ c ≤ b ∨ d, (ii) a ∧ c ≤ b ∧ d.

Solution: (i) a ≤ b and b ≤ b ∨ d.
Hence   a ≤ b ∨ d.   (by transitivity of ≤)
Similarly   c ≤ d and d ≤ b ∨ d
              c ≤ b ∨ d.
Hence b ∨ d is an upper bound for {a, c}. But by definition
              a ∨ c = lub {a, c}
Hence   a ∨ c ≤ b ∨ d.

(ii) is proved on similar lines.

Example 9: For set A = {a, b} and lattice (P(A), ⊆), construct the tables for ∨ and ∧.

P(A) = {A, ϕ {a}, {b}}

A + 1 and ϕ = 0

∨ + ∪ (union),   ∧ + ∩ (intersection)

We have the following tables for ∨ and ∧ operations.

∨	0	1	{a}	{b}
0	0	1	{a}	{b}
1	1	1	1	1
{a}	{a}	1	{a}	1
{b}	{b}	1	1	{b}

∧	0	1	{a}	{b}
0	0	0	0	0
1	0	1	{a}	{b}
{a}	0	{a}	{a}	0
{b}	0	{b}	0	{b}

EXERCISE - 4.4

1. Determine all the maximal and minimal elements of the poset.

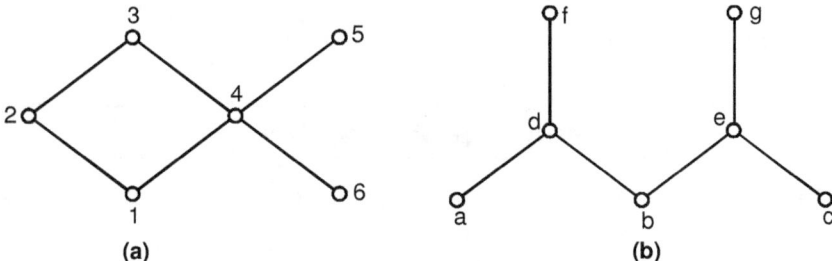

Fig. 4.45

2. In (1) above, determine, if any, least upper bound and greatest lower bound of the following sets:

   (a) {2, 4, 6}, {3, 5}, {1, 6}, {2, 3, 5}.

   (b) {d, e}, {f, g}, {a, d, e}, {d, g}.

3. On each of the following sets, let the partial order ≤ denote 'is a divisor of '. Draw the corresponding Hasse diagrams and determine which posets are lattices.

   (i)   A = {1, 2, 3, 5, 30}
   (ii) A = {1, 2, 3, 4, 6}
   (iii) A = {2, 3, 4, 16, 12, 24, 36}
   (iv) A = {1, 3, 5, 9, 15, 45}
   (v)   A = {2, 3, 5, 7, 10, 14, 21}

4. Is the Cartesian product of two lattices always a lattice? Prove your claim.
5. If a and b are elements in a lattice (A, ≤), then show that a ∧ b = b iff a ∨ b = a.
6. Prove the associative laws for a lattice.

   i.e. a ∨ (b ∨ c) = (a ∨ b) ∨ c and
         a ∧ (b ∧ c) = (a ∧ b) ∧ c

7. For elements a, b, c in a lattice (A, ≤), show that if a ≤ b then a ∨ (b ∧ c) ≤ b ∧ (a ∨ c).
8. Show that a lattice (A, ≤) is distributive iff for any element a, b, c in A,
   (a ∧ b) ∨ (b ∧ c) ∨ (c ∧ a) = (a ∨ b) ∧ (b ∨ c) ∧ (c ∨ a)

[**Hint:** To show that (A, ≤) is distributive, consider the elements a, b ∨ c and (a ∨ b) ∧ (a ∨ c)].

9. A lattice (A, ≤) is called a modular lattice if for any a, b, c in A where a ≤ c,
   a ∨ (b ∧ c) = (a ∨ b) ∧ c.
   Show that a lattice is modular iff a ∨ (b ∧ (a ∨ c)) = (a ∨ b) ∧ (a ∨ c).

10. Show that for any elements a, b, c in a modular lattice,
    (a ∨ b) ∧ c = b ∧ c implies
    (a ∨ b) ∧ a + b ∨ a.

Points to Remember

- A common notion of relation is a type of association that exists between two or more objects.
- An **ordered n-tuple,** for n > 0, is a sequence of objects or elements, denoted by $(a_1, a_2, ..., a_n)$.

  If n = 2, the ordered n-tuple is called an **ordered pair.**

  If n = 3, the ordered n-tuple is called an ordered triple; and so on.

- Let A and B be non-empty sets. The **product set** or the **Cartesian product** A × B is defined as

  A × B = { (a, b) | a ∈ A and b ∈ B }.

  If A = ϕ or B = ϕ, then A × B = ϕ.

- Let $\{A_1, A_2, ..., A_n\}$ be a finite collection of sets. A subset R of $A_1 \times A_2 \times ... \times A_n$ is called an **n-ary relation** on $A_1, A_2, ..., A_n$.

- Let A and B be non-empty sets. Then a binary relation R from A to B is a subset of A × B, i.e. R ⊆ A × B. The **domain** of R, denoted by D(R), is the set of elements in A that are related to some element in B, i.e.

  D(R) = { a ∈ A | for some b ∈ B, (a, b) ∈ R }

- Let R be a relation from A to B. Then the **converse** of R, denoted by R^C is the relation from B to A, defined as
$$R^C = \{(b, a) \mid (a, b) \in R\}$$

- Let R_1 be a relation from A to B and R_2 a relation from B to C. The **composite relation** from A to C, denoted by $R_1 \cdot R_2$ (or $R_1 R_2$) is defined as
$$R_1 \cdot R_2 = \{(a, c) \mid a \in A \wedge c \in C \wedge \exists b \, [b \in B \wedge (a, b) \in R_1 \wedge (b, c) \in R_2]\}$$

- A relation matrix has entries which are either one or zero. Such a matrix is called a Boolean matrix.

- **Properties of Relation Matrix are:**
    1. $M_{R_1 \cdot R_2} = M_{R_1} \cdot M_{R_2}$
    2. M_{R^C} = transpose of M_R (for $R = R_1$ or $R = R_2$)
    3. $M_{(R_1 \cdot R_2)^C} = M_{R_2^C R_1^C} = M_{R_2^C} \cdot M_{R_1^C}$

- Special properties of Binary Relations are
  (A) Reflexive relation
    (B) Irreflexive relation
  (C) Symmetric relation
    (D) Asymmetric relation
    (E) Antisymmetric relation
    (F) Transitive relation

- A binary relation R on a set A is said to be compatible if it is reflexive and symmetric.
- Let π and π' be partitions of a non-empty set A. Then π' is called a refinement of π if every block (element) of π' is contained in a block of π.
- Let π_1 and π_2 be partitions of a non-empty set A. The product of π_1 and π_2, denoted $\pi_1 \cdot \pi_2$ is a partition π of A such that
    (i) π refines both π_1 and π_2.
    (ii) If π' refines both π_1 and π_2, then π' refines π.
- Let π_1 and π_2 be partitions of a non-empty set. The sum of π_1 and π_2, denoted by $\pi_1 + \pi_2$, is a partition π such that

(i) Both π_1 and π_2 refine π.

(ii) If π' is a partition of A such that both π_1 and π_2 refine π', then π refines π'.

- A relation R on a set A is said to be compatible if it is reflexive and symmetric.
- A binary relation R on a non-empty set A is a **partial order** if R is reflexive, antisymmetric and transitive.
- The ordered pair (A, R) is called a **partially ordered set** or **poset.**
- The transitive closure of a relation R is the smallest transitive relation containing R. We denote transitive closure of R by R^*.
- A binary relation R on a non-empty set A is a **partial order** if R is reflexive, antisymmetric and transitive.
- Let (A, ≤) be a poset. A subset of A is called a **chain** if every pair of elements in the subset is related.
- A subset of A is called an antichain if no two distinct elements in the subset are related.
- An element a ∈ A is called a **maximal element** if there is no element b ∈ A such that b ≠ a and a ≤ b. An element c ∈ A is called a minimal element if there is no element d ∈ A such that d ≠ c and d ≤ a.
- A lattice is a poset (L, ≤) in which every subset {a, b} of L, has a least upper bound and a greatest lower bound.
- Let (L, ≤) be a lattice with universal bounds 0 and 1. For an element a ∈ L, b is said to be a complement of a if a ∨ b = 1 and a ∧ b = 0.

Chapter 5: FUNCTIONS

SYLLABUS:
- Functions : Functions, Definition, Composition of Functions, Types of functions, Recursive functions, Pigeonhole Principle.

OBJECTIVES:
- To study function as input output relation.

UTILITY:
- Used in discrete numeric functions, Generating functions and Recurrence relations.

KEY CONCEPTS:
- Bijective.
- Pigeonhole principle.

5.0 Introduction

Function is a special type of relation. It is basically an input–output relation. Many concepts in computer science can be conveniently stated in the language of functions. Recursive and generating functions are of special importance in software development.

In this chapter, we discuss infinite sets and their cardinalities, where the concept of bijective function is used. We will also briefly discuss an important principle called as the Pigeonhole Principle, and use it to solve some problems related to counting.

5.1 Functions

In this section, we deal with functions which form a special class of binary relations. We shall discuss the various properties of functions and focus our attention on some special types of functions.

5.1.1 Definitions

Let A and B be non-empty sets. A **function** f from A to B, denoted as f: A → B, is a relation from A to B such that for every a ∈ A, there exists a **unique** b ∈ B such that (a, b) ∈ f. Normally if (a, b) ∈ f, we write f(a) = b.

An important point to be re-emphasised is that f is a relation with the following special property:

If f(a) = b and f(a) = c then b = c.

This condition implies that to each element a ∈ A, a unique element b ∈ B should be assigned by the relation f.

Consider the following relation

$$f: R^+ \to R \text{ where}$$
$$f(x) = \sqrt{x}$$

f is obviously not a function since f(4) = + 2 as well as $-\sqrt{2}$.

Hence in general only a many-to-one relation or a one-to-one relation is a function. A one-to-many relation is not a function.

The set A is called as the **domain** of f, denoted **D(f)**. The set B is called as the **codomain**, and the set { f(a) | a ∈ A }, which is a subset of B, is called as the **range** of f, and denoted as **R(f)**.

The element a is called an **argument** of the function f and f(a) is called the **value** of the function for the argument a.

As t is a relation we may also express f as a set of ordered pairs, i.e.

$$f = \{(a, f(a))) \ a \in A, f(a) \in B\}.$$

Functions are also called as **mappings** or **transformations,** since they can be thought of as rules for assigning to each element a ∈ A, the unique element f(a) ∈ B. In this context, it is customary to refer to f(a) as **image** of a and a as the **pre-image** of b which is equal to f(a).

A typical way of representing a function graphically is given below.

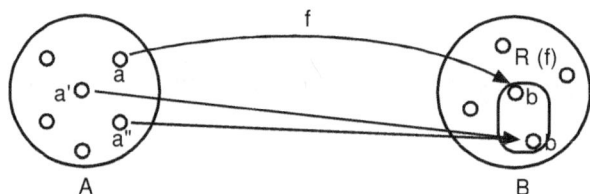

Fig. 5.1

R(f) ⊆ B, i.e. range of f is a proper subset of B or is equal to B.

To describe a function completely it is necessary to specify its domain, codomain and the value f(a), for each argument a.

Examples :

1. Let A be a non-empty set. Then we can always define a function f: A → A (i.e. B = A) as f(a) = a.
   f is called the **identity** function on A and is denoted by 1_A.

2. Let f: N → N be defined as f(x) = 2x.
   f is a function with R(f) being the set of even natural numbers.

3. Let f: **R** → **R** be defined as $f(x) = x^2$.
   f is a function. Geometrically, R(f) is the parabola $y = x^2$.

4. Let A = {1, 2, 3} and B = {a, b, c, d}
   Let f: A → B be defined as
   f(1) = a
   f(2) = c
   f(3) = a

   f is a function, which is graphically represented as

   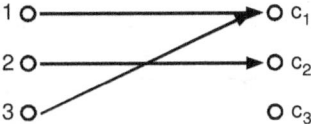

   Fig. 5.2

   R(f) = {a, c}.

5. Let A = {a, b, c} and B = {e, f}
   Let R = {(a, e), (b, e), (a, f), (c, e)}
   The graph of R is

   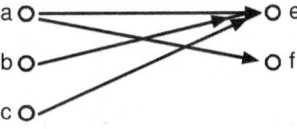

   Fig. 5.3

   The relation R is not a function since f(a) = e as well as f(a) = f, which violates the definition of a function.

   To the computer engineer, a function is a procedure which gives a unique output for any suitable input. The next example demonstrates this aspect.

6. Let P be a computer program that accepts an integer as input and produces an integer as output. Let A = B = Z. Then P determines a relation f_P as follows: (a, b) ∈ f_P implies

that b is the output produced by program P when the input is a. f_P is clearly a function, since any particular input corresponds to a unique output.

7. Let A be a finite set and let P(A) denote its power set. Define
$$f: P(A) \to Z^+ \text{ by}$$
$$f(S) = |S|, \text{ for any } S \in P(A), \text{ (i.e. } S \subseteq A),$$
|S| denotes the cardinality of S. f is clearly a function.

5.1.2 Partial Functions

In actual application of functions, it is often convenient to treat the domain of a function as a subset of another set known as the **source**. (In this case, the codomain is appropriately called as the **target** set). In other words, the function has the set A as its domain but is not defined for some arguments. This leads to the following definition.

Definition:

Let A and B be two sets. A partial function f with **domain A** and codomain B is any function from A' to B where A' $\subset$ A. For any element x $\in$ A − A', the value of f(x) is said to be undefined

A partial function

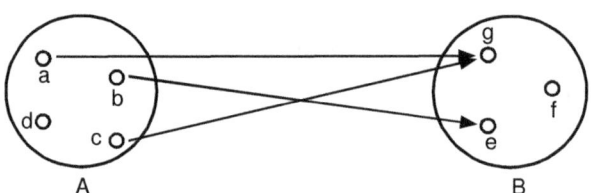

Fig. 5.4

To make the distinction more clear, the function which is not a partial function is sometimes called as a **total function**.

However, in what follows, we will use the unqualified term "function" to denote total function and the qualifier "partial" while referring to partial functions.

5.1.3 Examples

(i) The function f: **R** → **R** defined as f(x) = 1/x, is a partial function, as it is undefined for x = 0.

(ii) The function f: **R** → **R** defined as $f(x) = \sqrt{x}$ is a partial function, as $\sqrt{x}$ is not defined for x < 0, in **R**.

(iii) Computer programs represent partial functions. Let P be a program which has one natural number as its input, and which, for some input values will never terminate, or terminates abnormally (e.g. while attempting to divide by 0, an illegal operation). Then P is not defined for such arguments and hence can be regarded as a partial function from N to **R**. The following function plays an important role in computer applications.

(iv) Hashing functions:

A symbol table is constructed by a compiler.

The identifiers in a program are read and inserted into a table (say) with 1000 spaces, labelled 0 to 999.

A unique identifier is called a key.

To determine to which space (location) in the table a particular key is assigned we create a hashing function from the set of keys to the set of locations.

Hashing functions generally use a mod function.)

Let I = Set of all possible identifiers
and $N = \{0, 1, ..., 999\}$. We may define
$f: I \to N$ as
$f(i) = |i|^3 \pmod{1000}$

For example,
$f(23) = 23^3 \pmod{1000}$
$= 12167 \pmod{1000}$
$= 167$

Hence an identifier with length 23 characters is inserted in position 167.

5.1.4 Equivalent Functions

Definition:

> Let $f: A \to B$ and $g: C \to D$ be functions. Then f and g are said to be equivalent or **identical** only if $A = C$, $B = D$ and $f(a) = g(a)$ for all $a \in A$.
> The function $f: Z \to Z$ given by $f(x) = x$ and $g: Z \to Z^+$ given by $g(x) = x$ are not equivalent.

5.1.5 Composite Function

Let $f: A \to B$ and $g: B \to C$ be two functions. Then the composition of f and g denoted as **gof** is a relation from A to C, where $gof(a) = g(f(a))$. $gof: A \to C$ is also a function. This is because if there exists elements $c, d \in C$ such that $gof(a) = c$ and $gof(a) = d$, for some $a \in A$, this would imply that f(f(a)) = c and g (f(a)) = d. But f is a function, hence f(a) is unique. Then since g is also a function, it follows that c = d. Hence gof is a function from A to C. Note that gof is defined only when the range of f is a subset of the domain of g. The diagram given below depicts a composite function.

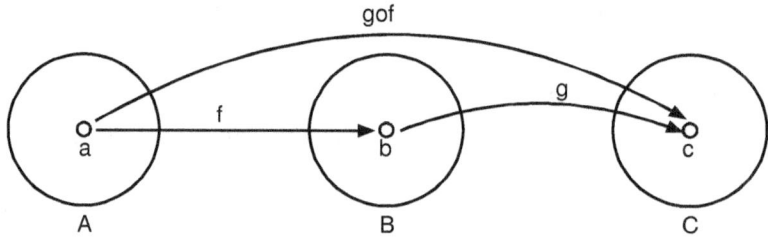

Fig. 5.5

The rule to compose two functions can be extended to a finite number of functions: $f_1: A_1 \to A_2, f_2: A_2 \to B_3, ..., f_n: A_n \to A_{n+1}$, where range of f_i = domain of f_{i+1}, for $1 \leq i \leq n$. Thus $f_n \circ f_{n-1} \circ ... \circ f_1$ (denoted usually as $f_n f_{n-1} ... f_1$) is a function from A_1 to A_{n+1}. In particular if $A_1 = A_2 = ... = A_{n+1} = A$ and $f_1 = f_2 = ... = f_n = f$ then f o f o ... o f (n times) denoted as f^n is the composite function from A to A.

Examples:

1. Let f: Z → Z be defined as
$f(x) = x^2 + 2x + 2$, and
g: Z → Z be defined as
$g(x) = x - 1$
Then gof: Z → Z is defined as
gof (x) $= x^2 + 2x + 2 - 1$
$= (x + 1)^2$

In this case, we also have the function fog: Z → Z which is defined
fog (x) $= (x - 1)^2 + 2 (x - 1) + 2$
$= x^2 + 1$
fof: Z → Z is defined as
fof (x) $= f (x^2 + 2x + 2)$
$= (x^2 + 2x + 2)^2 + 2 (x^2 + 2x + 2) + 2$
gog: Z → Z is defined as
gog (x) $= g (x - 1) = x - 1 - 1 = x - 2$.

2. Let $f: Z \to R$ be defined as $f(x) = \frac{(x+1)}{2}$, and

   $g: R \to R$ be defined as

   $g(x) = x^2$

   Then $gof: Z \to R$ is defined as $gof(x) = g(f(x))$

   $= g\left(\frac{x+1}{2}\right) = \frac{(x+1)^2}{4}$

3. Let A = Set of students (or their names)

   B = Set of their examination seat numbers,

   and C = Set of the students mark lists.

   $f: A \to B$ is defined as

   $f(s) = n$, where n is the seat number of the students

   $g: B \to C$ is defined as

   $g(x) = l$, where l is the mark list corresponding to the seat number n.

   Then $gof: A \to C$ is the function defined as $gof(s) = l$, l being the mark list of the students whose seat number is n.

4. Suppose a manufacturer has a list of all the parts which are supplied to him, together with the supplier's name. He has also a list of suppliers names, together with the suppliers addresses. To obtain the address from which to order a given part, he composes two functions $f: P \to S$ and $g: S \to A$ to obtain $gof: P \to A$, which gives the address a of the supplier of part p.

5. Let $f: A \to B$, $g: B \to C$ and $h: C \to D$ be defined as shown in the following graphs.

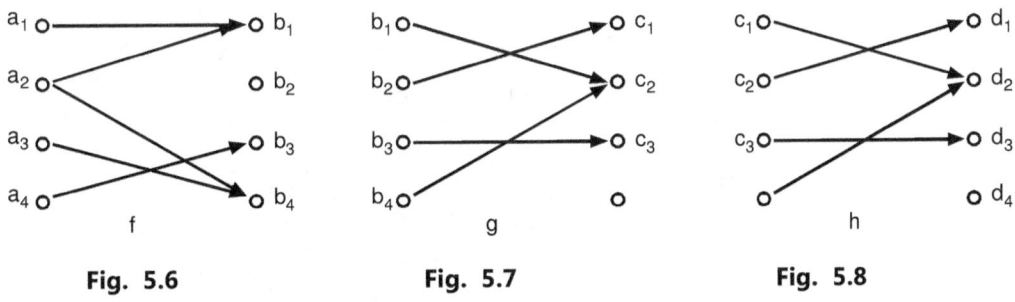

Fig. 5.6   Fig. 5.7   Fig. 5.8

Then we have the following composite functions

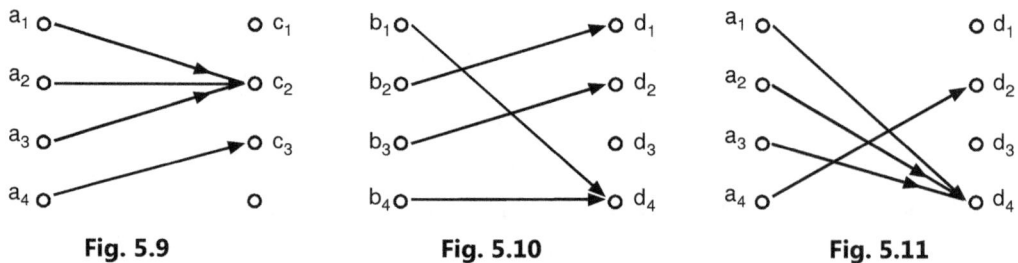

Fig. 5.9 Fig. 5.10 Fig. 5.11

Note that composition is associative. Hence ho (gof) = (hog) of. Hence dispersing with the brackets, we simply write hogof.

5.1.6 Special Types of Functions
Definitions:

Let f: A → B be a function.
  (i) f is called a **surjective** (onto) function if f(A) = B, i.e. range of f is equal to the codomain of f.
  (ii) f is called an **injective** (one-to-one) function if for elements a, a' ∈ A, a ≠ a' implies
      f(a) ≠ f(a'), or equivalently if f(a) = f(a'), then a = a'.
  (iii) f is called bijection (one-to-one and onto) function if f is both surjective and injective.

Functions with these properties are called **surjections, injections** and **bijections** respectively. The following diagrams represent these three types of functions.

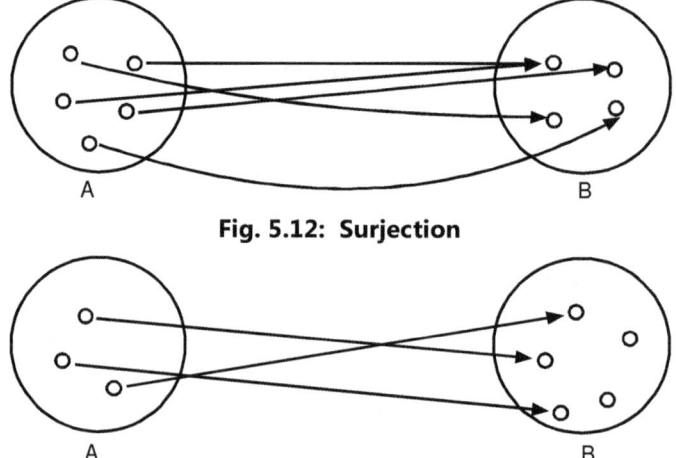

Fig. 5.12: Surjection

Fig. 5.13: Injection

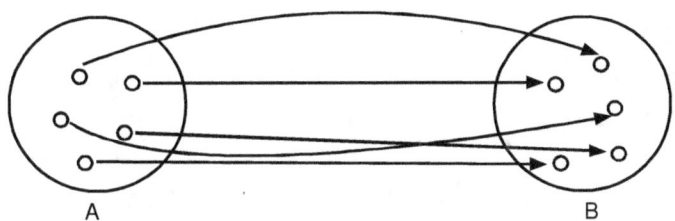

Fig. 5.14: Bijection

Examples:

(i) The identity function $1_A: A \to A$ is both surjective and injective, hence is a bijective function.

(ii) Let $f: \mathbf{R} \to \mathbf{R}$ be defined as $f(x) = x + 1$. Then f is an injective function. We know that geometrically, this function represents a straight line.

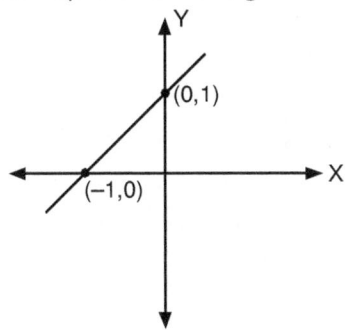

Fig. 5.15

In general, any function f defined as $f(x) = mx + c$ is an injective function.

(iii) Let $f: \mathbf{R} \to \mathbf{R}^+$ be defined as $f(x) = x^2$

This is a surjective function, since for any $y \in \mathbf{R}^+$, (i.e. $y > 0$) there exists $x \in \mathbf{R}$ such that $f(x) = y$, i.e. $x = \pm\sqrt{y}$.

Geometrically this function represents the parabola $y = x^2$, symmetric about the y-axis.

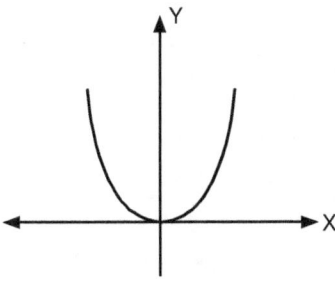

Fig. 5.16

Clearly the function is not injective.

(iv) The function in example (ii) is also a surjective function, since for any $y \in \mathbf{R}$ there exists $x \in \mathbf{R}$ such that f(x) = y, i.e. x + 1 = y which implies x = y – 1. This means that for every element y in the co-domain $\mathbf{R}$, there is a pre-image x in the domain $\mathbf{R}$, whose image is y. Hence the function f is surjective. f is therefore a bijective function.

(v) Let E be the set of even integer and define a function f: E → Z as f(x) = 2x. Then f is an injective function, which is not surjective.

(vi) Let A be the set of students in a class, and B be the set of their roll numbers. Assign to a student his or her roll number. The assignment is then a bijective function.

(vii) Let A be the set of students and B be the set of their ages (in years). Assign to a student his or her age. This assignment is then a many-one function (i.e. not injective) which is surjective.

(viii) Let A be the set of students and B be the set of integers {0, 1, 2, ... 100}. Assign to a student an integer which is his marks (out of 100) in a particular subject, assuming that all the students in the set, appeared for this subject. Then this assignment is a function which is not necessarily injective or surjective.

The following theorems, give some important properties of the injective, surjective and bijective functions, for composite functions.

Theorem 1:

Let f: A → B and g: B → C be functions. Then
(i) If f and g are surjective functions, then gof is surjective.
Proof:
gof: A → C. We have to show gof (A) = C. Let $c \in C$; then since g is surjective, there exists an element $b \in B$ such that g(b) = c. Since f is surjective as well, for the element $b \in B$, there exists an element $a \in A$ such that f(a) = b. Then gof (a) = g (f(a)) = g(b) = c. Hence $c \in$ gof (A), i.e. gof is surjective.

Let f: A → B and g: B → C be functions. Then
(ii) If f and g are injective, then gof is injective
Proof:
Let elements a, a' $\in$ A such that gof (a) = gof (a').

We have to prove a = a'.
Let f(a) = b and f(a') = b', where elements b, b' ∈ B.
Then gof (a) = gof (a') implies g(b) = g(b').
But g is injective; hence b = b'.
This implies f(a) = f(a').
Since f is injective, we have a = a'.
Hence gof is injective.

Let f: A → B and g: B → C be functions. Then
(iii) If f and g are bijective, then gof is bijective.

Proof:

(iii) Since (i) and (ii) are true, it follows that gof is bijective.

However, converse to the theorem is not true; as shown by the following examples:

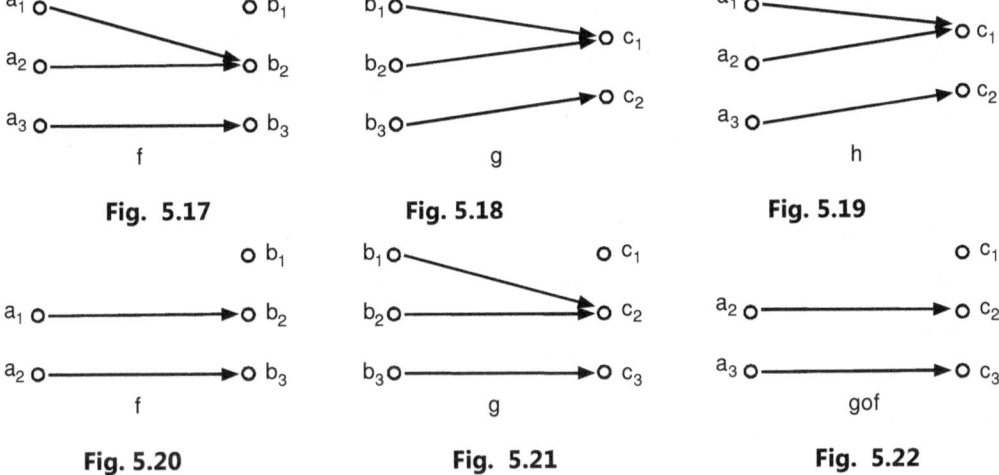

Fig. 5.17 **Fig. 5.18** **Fig. 5.19**

Fig. 5.20 **Fig. 5.21** **Fig. 5.22**

The following theorem, however gives a "partial converse" to the above theorem.

Theorem 2:

Let f: A → B and g: B → C be functions. Then
If gof is surjective, then g is surjective.

Proof:

We have to prove g(B) = C.
Let c ∈ C. Since gof is surjective, there exists an element a ∈ A such that gof (a) = c, i.e. g

$(f(a)) = c$.

Let $f(a) = b$.

Then $g(b) = c$ which implies that b is the pre-image of c in B.

Hence $g(B) = C$, i.e. g is surjective.

Let $f: A \to B$ and $g: B \to C$ be functions. Then

If gof is injective, then f is injective.

Proof:

Let for elements $a, a' \in A$, $f(a) = f(a')$.

We have to prove $a = a'$. Since $f(a) = f(a')$, if follows that $g(f(a)) = g(f(a'))$ i.e. gof (a) = gof (a').

Since gof is injective, it follows that $a = a'$.

Hence f is injective

Let $f: A \to B$ and $g: B \to C$ be functions. Then

If gof is bijective, then g is surjective and f is injective.

Proof:

This statement is true, as consequence of (i) and (ii).

5.1.7 Inverse Function

The concept of inverse of a function is analogous to that of the converse of a relation.

Definition:

Let $f: A \to B$ be a bijection from A to B. The inverse of f denoted by f^{-1} is the function $f^{-1}: B \to A$ such that

$$f^{-1} o f = 1_A \text{ and}$$
$$f o f^{-1} = 1_B$$

Example: Let $f: \{a_1, a_2, a_3\} \to \{b_1, b_2, b_3\}$ be defined as

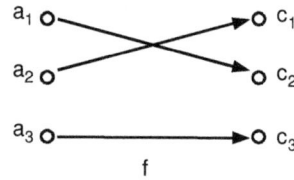

Fig. 5.23

Then f^{-1} is given by the graph

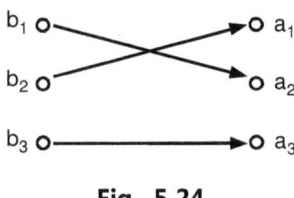

Fig. 5.24

Then $f^{-1} \circ f = 1_A$ and $f \circ f^{-1} = 1_B$.

1. Properties of the Inverse Function

(i) $(f^{-1})^{-1} = f$. (Proof left as an easy exercise)

(ii) If f and g are bijective functions from A to B, and B to C respectively, then $(g \circ f)^{-1} = f^{-1} \circ f^{-1}$.
Proof:
First observe that both $(g \circ f)^{-1}$ and $f^{-1} \circ ^{-1}$ are functions from C to A.
Hence domains of $(g \circ f)^{-1}$ and $f^{-1} \circ g^{-1}$ are equal; and so are their codomains.
We have only to prove $(g \circ f)^{-1}(c) = f^{-1} \circ g^{-1}(c)$ for all $c \in C$.
Let $(g \circ f)^{-1}(c) = a$, then $(g \circ f)(a) = c$ which means that $g(f(a)) = c$ since g^{-1} exists, we have $f(a) = g^{-1}(c)$.
Since f^{-1} also exists, $a = f^{-1}(g^{-1}(c)) = f^{-1} \circ g^{-1}(c)$.
Hence $(g \circ f)^{-1}(c) = f^{-1} \circ g^{-1}(c)$ for all $c \in C$.
Hence $(g \circ f)^{-1} = f^{-1} \circ g^{-1}$

2. One-sided Inverse Functions

We have seen that if $f: A \to B$ is a bijective function, then f^{-1} exists and $f^{-1} \circ f = 1_A$ and $f \circ f^{-1} = 1_B$.

We then say that f has a **left inverse** as well as a **right inverse**. Only bijections have a two sided inverse. However, there are some functions which possess one-sided inverses. The existence of these one-sided inverses is determined by whether the function is injective or surjective.

Definition:

Let $f: A \to B$ and $g: B \to A$ be functions. If $g \circ f = 1_A$ then g is a left inverse of f, while f is a right inverse of g.

We have the following theorem.

> Let f: A → B be a function (A ≠ φ, B ≠ φ) f has a left inverse if and only if f is injective.

Proof:

Assume first that f is injective.

We have to show that f has a left inverse, i.e. we must define a function g: B → A such that gof = 1_A.

Let b ∈ B.

Then either b ∈ f(A) or b ∈ B − f(A).

If b ∈ f(A), then b = f(a) for some a ∈ A.

In that case, define g(b) = a.

Otherwise, if b ∈ B − f(A), choose any arbitrary element a' ∈ A and define g(b) = a'.

The function g is well-defined since exactly one value is specified for each b ∈ B as f is injective.

Then gof (b) = g(b) = a. Hence gof = 1_A.

Conversely, let f have a left inverse.

We have to show that f is injective.

Let g: B → A such that gof = 1_A. Let f(a) = f(a').

We have to show a = a'.

Now g(f(a)) = g(f(a')) since g is well defined.

This implies 1_A (a) = 1_A (a') i.e. a = a'.

Hence f is injective.

> Let f: A → B be a function (A ≠ φ, B ≠ φ)
> f has a right inverse if and only if f is surjective.

Proof:

Let f be surjective.

We have to show that f has a right inverse, i.e. we must define a function g: B → A so that fog = 1_B.

Let b ∈ B.

Since f is surjective, there exists an element a ∈ A such that f(a) = b.

Define g(b) = a.

Then fog (b) = f(a) = b. Hence fog = 1_B.

Conversely, let f have a right inverse g: B → A such that fog = 1_B.

We have to show that f is surjective.

Let b ∈ B and let g(b) = a.

Then fog (b) = b which implies that f(a) = b.

Hence f is surjective, as there exists an element a ∈ A such that f(a) = b.

The next theorem deals with bijective function.

Theorem 2: If f: A → B is bijective, then the left and right inverses of f are equal.

Proof: Left as an exercise.

SOLVED PROBLEMS

Example 1: A function f: N → N, where N is the set of natural members including 0. Comment on the type of the following functions (one-one/onto etc.)

(i)   f (j) = $j^2 + 2$

(ii)   f (j) = 1   ;   if j is odd

               = 0   ;   if j is even.

Solution: (i) f is one-one function since if f(j) = f (k), then $j^2 + 2 = k^2 + 2$ which implies j = k. But f is not onto since there is no natural number j ∈ N, such that f (j) = 0, since $j^2 + 2 = 0 → j^2 = -2$. Hence 0 has no pre-image. Hence f is not onto.

(ii) f is not onto since R(f) = {0, 1}. f is also not one-one since all odd numbers (even numbers) have the same image.

Example 2: Functions f, g, h are defined on a set

               X = {1, 2, 3} as

               f = {(1, 2), (2, 3), (3, 1)}

               g = {(1, 2), (2, 1), (3, 3)}

               h = {(1, 1), (2, 2), (3, 1)}.

(i) Find fog, gof. Are they equal?

(ii) Find fogoh and fohog.

Solution: We may depict f, g, h graphically as

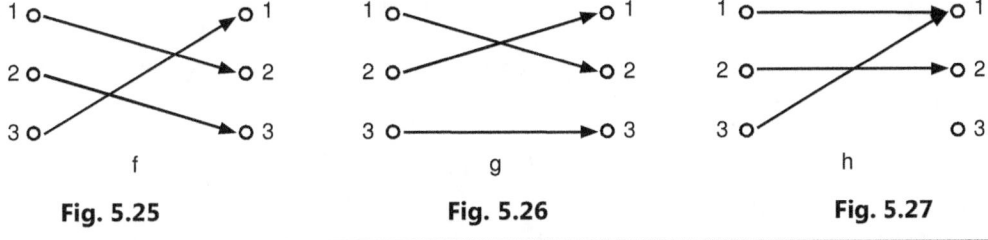

Fig. 5.25   Fig. 5.26   Fig. 5.27

(i) fog is depicted as

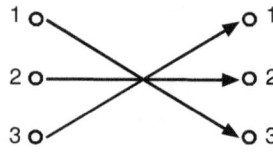

Fig. 5.28

Hence   fog = {(1, 3), (3, 1), (2, 2)}

gof is depicted as

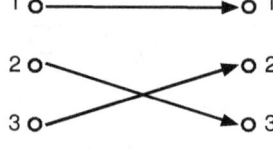

Fig. 5.29

∴   gof = {(1, 1), (2, 3), (3, 2)}
∴   fog ≠ gof

(ii)   fogoh = (fog) oh, which can be depicted as

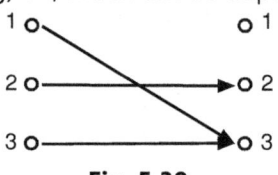

Fig. 5.30

∴   fogoh = {(1, 3), (2, 2), (3, 3)}

         fohog = fo (hog)

hog can be depicted as

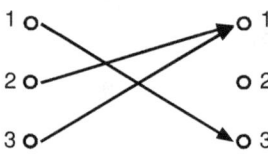

Fig. 5.31

∴ fo (hog) is

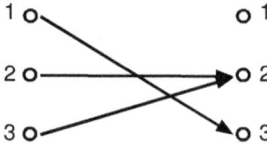

Fig. 5.32

∴   fohog = {(1, 3), (2, 2), (3, 2)}

Example 3: Let A = {a, b, c, d}, B = {s, t, u}, C = {l, m, n}.
Obtain the composition of the following functions f: A → B, g: B → C
where   f = {(a, s), (b, t), (c, u), (d, t)}
            g = {(s, m), (t, l), (u, n)}.

Solution:

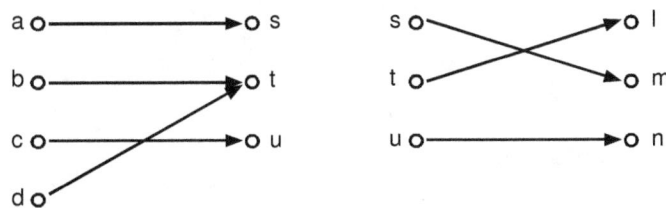

Fig. 5.33   Fig. 5.34

then gof is

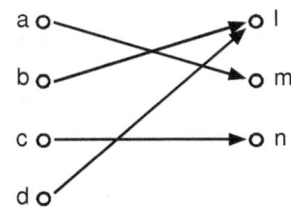

Fig. 5.35

∴   gof = {(a, m), (b, l), (c, n), (d, l)}.

Example 4: Let A = {1, 2, 3, 4, 5}, g: A → A is as shown in the figure.

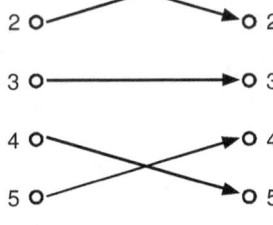

Fig. 5.36

Find the composition gog, go (gog). Determine whether each is one-to-one or onto function.

Solution: gog is

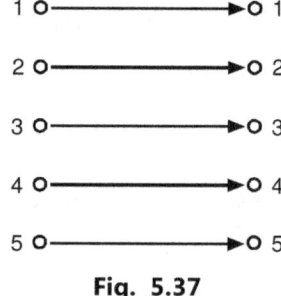

Fig. 5.37

gog is one-one and onto function.

go (gog) is

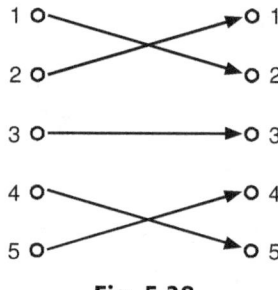

Fig. 5.38

go (gog) is also one-one and onto function.

Example 5: The functions f: A → B, g: B → C, h: C → D are defined in the following diagram. Determine the range of each function. State which functions are into and which are onto. Draw the diagram of the composite function hogof.

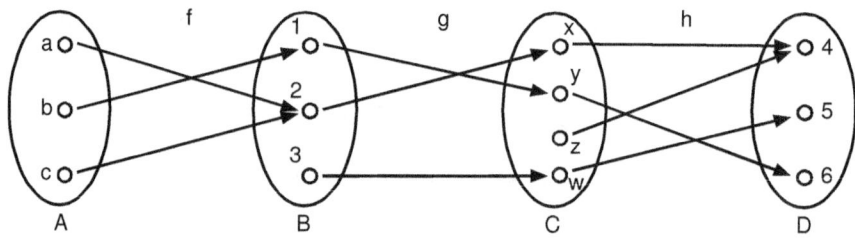

Fig. 5.39

Solution: R(f) = {1, 2},   f is onto
R(g) = {x, y, w},   g is into
R(h) = {4, 5, 6},   h is onto.

gof is

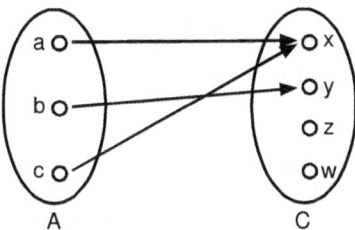

Fig. 5.40

h o (gof) is

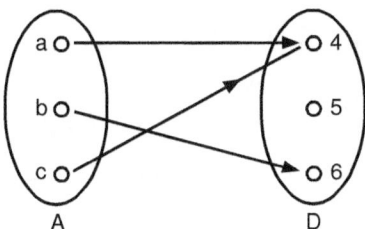

Fig. 5.41

Example 6: State whether the following functions are one-one
   (i) To each person on the earth assign the number which corresponds to his age.
   (ii) To each country assign the number of people living in the country.
   (iii) To each book written by only one author, assign the author.
   (iv) To each country having prime minister, assign the prime minister.

Solution:
   (i) Many than one person can have the same age. f is not one-one but many-one.
   (ii) More than one country may not have exactly the same population. Hence function is one-one.
   (iii) The same author may have written more than one book. Hence function is many-one and not one-one.
   (iv) function is one-one.

Example 7: Let $f(x) = x + 2$, $g(x) = x - 2$ and $h(x) = 3x$ for $x \in R$, where R = set of real numbers. Find gof, fog, fof, gog, foh, hog, hof, fohog.

Solution:
$$gof(x) = g(f(x)) = g(x+2)$$
$$= (x+2) - 2 = x$$

$$\begin{aligned}
\text{fog}(x) &= f(g(x)) = f(x-2) \\
&= (x-2) + 2 = x \\
\text{fof}(x) &= f(f(x)) = f(x+2) \\
&= (x+2) + 2 = x + 4 \\
\text{gog}(x) &= g(g(x)) = g(x-2) = (x-2) - 2 = x - 4 \\
\text{foh}(x) &= f(h(x)) = f(3x) = 3x + 2 \\
\text{hog}(x) &= h(g(x)) = h(x-2) \\
&= 3(x-2) = 3x - 6 \\
\text{hof}(x) &= h(f(x)) = h(x+2) \\
&= 3(x+2) = 3x + 6 \\
\text{fohog}(x) &= \text{foh}(g(x)) \\
&= \text{foh}(x-2) = f(h(x-2)) \\
&= f(3x-6) = (3x-6) + 2 \\
&= 3x - 4
\end{aligned}$$

Example 8: Let $f(x) = 2x + 3$, $g(x) = 3x + 4$, $h(x) = 4x$ for $x \in R$, where R = set of real numbers. Find gof, fog, foh, hof, goh.

Solution:
$$\begin{aligned}
\text{gof}(x) &= g(f(x)) \\
&= g(2x+3) = 3(2x+3) + 4 \\
&= 6x + 13 \\
\text{fog}(x) &= f(g(x)) = f(3x+4) = 2(3x+4) + 3 = 6x + 11 \\
\text{foh}(x) &= f(h(x)) = f(4x) \\
&= 2(4x) + 3 = 8x + 3 \\
\text{hof}(x) &= h(2x+3) = 4(2x+3) = 8x + 12 \\
\text{goh}(x) &= g(4x) = 3(4x) + 4 = 12x + 4.
\end{aligned}$$

Example 9: If $f(x) = x^2 + 1$ and $g(x) = x + 2$ are functions from R to R, where R is the set of real numbers, find fog and gof.

Solution:
$$\begin{aligned}
\text{fog}(x) &= f(g(x)) = f(x+2) \\
&= (x+2)^2 + 1 = x^2 + 4x + 5 \\
\text{gof}(x) &= g(f(x)) = g(x^2 + 1) \\
&= (x^2 + 1) + 2 = x^2 + 3.
\end{aligned}$$

Example 10: Let $f(x) = ax + b$ and $g(x) = cx + d$, where a, b, c, d are constants. Determine for which constants a, b, c, d it is true that fog = gof.

Solution:
$$fog(x) = f(g(x)) = f(cx+d)$$
$$= a(cx+d) + b = acx + ad + b$$
$$gof(x) = g(f(x)) = g(ax+b)$$
$$= c(ax+b) + d = acx + cb + d$$

∴ $\quad$ fog = gof $\Rightarrow$ acx + ad + b
$$= acx + cd + d$$

∴ $\quad$ ad + b = cb + d
$\Rightarrow \quad$ d(a − 1) = b(c − 1)

i.e. $\quad \dfrac{b}{d} = \dfrac{a-1}{c-1}$

is the relation between the constants if fog = gof.

Example 11: Let $A = B = C = R$ and let $f: A \rightarrow B$, $g: B \rightarrow C$ be defined by $f(a) = a - 1$ and $g(b) = b^2$. Find (i) fog (2), (ii) gof (2), (iii) gof (x), (iv) fog (x), (v) fof (y), (vi) gog (y).

Solution: (i) fog (2) $= f(4) = 4 - 1 = 3$
(ii) $\quad$ gof ((2) $= g(2-1) = 1$
(iii) $\quad$ gof (x) $= g(x-1) = (x-1)^2$
(iv) $\quad$ fof (x) $= f(x^2) = x^2 - 1$
(v) $\quad$ fof (y) $= f(y-1) = y - 2$
(vi) $\quad$ gog (y) $= g(y^2) = y^4$

5.2 Bijection and Cardinality of Finite Sets

Recall that cardinality of a finite set $\Big(\text{denoted as } |A|\Big)$ is the number of distinct elements in that set. The concept of bijection is a powerful tool to compare the cardinalities of two sets, especially for infinite sets, as we shall see later. For the present, we shall confine ourselves to finite sets. We have the following theorem.

5.2.1 Theorem 1

Let A and B be finite sets and suppose there is a bijection from A to B. Then $|A| = |B|$.
Proof:
Let $|A| = m$ and $|B| = n$. Then, $A = \{a_1, a_2, a_3, \ldots, a_m\}$ and $B = \{b_1, b_2, \ldots, b_n\}$. Let $f: A \to B$ be the bijection. Then since f is surjective for each $b_i \in B$ $(1 \leq i \leq n)$, there exists an element $a_i \in A$ such that $f(a_i) = b_i$. This means that $m \geq n$. But f is also injective ; hence for $a_i \neq a_j$, $f(a_i) \neq f(a_j)$, i.e. $b_i \neq b_j$, i.e. $m \leq n$. Hence $|A| = |B|$.

Conversely if A and B are finite sets of same cardinality, we have the following theorem.

5.2.2 Theorem 2

If A and B are finite sets of same cardinality, and $f: A \to B$ is a function then f is injective iff f is surjective.
Proof:
Let $f: A \to B$ be injective. Then $|\text{Range}(f)| = |A|$. As A and B have the same cardinality, and $\text{Range}(f) \subseteq B$, it follows that $\text{Range}(f) = B$. This proves that f is surjective. Conversely, let f be surjective. We have to prove f is injective. Let $f(a) = f(a')$ for elements $a, a' \in A$. Suppose $a \neq a'$. Then, assuming $|A| = m \left(= |B| \right)$, this would imply that the remaining $(m - 2)$ elements of B.
This is possible only if at least one element is mapped onto two different elements in B, which contradicts the fact that f is a function. Hence our supposition that $a \neq a'$ is false. Hence $a = a'$ which means that f is injective.

5.2.3 Pigeonhole Principle

In theorem 5.6.1 we have proved that if A and B are finite sets and a bijection exists from A to B, then their cardinalities are the same.

Hence if A and B are any two sets such that $|A| > |B|$, then no bijection can exist from A to B. This fact is stated as a principle, famously known as the 'Pigeon hole principle'.

This principle states that if there are n + 1 pigeons and only n pigeonholes, then two pigeons will share the same hole.

This pigeonhole principle though self-evident (and seemingly trivial) serves as a powerful tool in solving many intricate problems in counting.

SOLVED EXAMPLES

Example 1: Show that if seven numbers from 1 to 12 are chosen, then two of them will add upto 13.

Solution: We form the six different sets, each containing two numbers that add upto 13, $A_1 = \{1, 12\}$, $A_2 = \{2, 11\}$, $A_3 = \{3, 10\}$, $A_4 = \{4, 9\}$, $A_5 = \{5, 8\}$, $A_6 = \{6, 7\}$. Each of the seven numbers chosen must belong to one of these sets. Since there are only six sets, by pigeonhole principle, two of the chosen numbers must belong to the same set; hence their sum is 13.

Example 2: Let S be a square whose sides have length 2 units. Show that for any five points on or inside S, there must be two points whose distance apart is almost $\sqrt{2}$ units.

Solution: Divide the square into four equal squares, as shown in Fig. 5.42. If five points are chosen in the square, we can assign each of them to a square that contains it. If a point belongs to more than one square, we assign it to one of them arbitrarily. Then the five points are assigned to four square regions, so by the pigeonhole principle at least two points must belong to the same region. These two cannot be more than $\sqrt{2}$ units apart, as the side of each square being 1 unit, the length of the diagonal is $\sqrt{2}$ units, which is the maximum distance, that the two points can be apart.

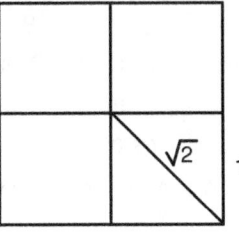

Fig. 5.42

Example 3: Show that if any 51 numbers are chosen from the set {1, 2, ..., 100}, then one of them will be a multiple of the other.

Solution: Every positive integer n can be written as $n = 2^k m$, where m is odd and $k \geq 0$. Since the set contains only 50 odd numbers and 51 numbers are chosen, it follows from pigeonhole principle that two of the numbers chosen will have the same odd factor. Let these numbers be n_1 and n_2. Then $n_1 = 2^{k_1} m$ and $n_2 = 2^{k_2} m$, for some $k_1, k_2 \geq 0$. Then if $k_1 \geq k_2$, n_1 is a multiple of n_2; otherwise n_2 is a multiple of n_1.

Example 4: Show that among n + 1 arbitrarily chosen positive integers, there are two whose difference is divisible by n.

Solution: We use Euclid's division algorithm. Given positive integers a and b, we can divide a by b and get a quotient q and remainder r, i.e.

$$a = bq + r.$$

Let $S = \{a_1, a_2, ..., a_{n+1}\}$ be the set of n + 1 arbitrarily chosen positive integers.

Define $f: S \rightarrow \{0, 1, 2, ..., n-1\}$

by $f(a_i) = r_i$, the remainder left after dividing by n.

Here $|S| = n + 1$ and cardinality of the co-domain is n. Hence by pigeonhole principle $f(a_i) = f(a_j)$ for $i \neq j$. This means that $r_i = r_j$. Hence $a_i - a_j = n(q_i - q_j)$. This means that there are two integers a_i and a_j in S whose difference is divisible by n.

Example 5: A sports tournament consisting of 45 events is spread over 30 days. There is at least one event per day. Prove that no matter how the events are arranged there will be a period of consecutive days during which exactly 14 events will take place.

Solution: Let a_i denote the total number of events that takes place upto and including the i-th day. Hence $a_1 \geq 1$ and $a_{30} = 45$, and we have a sequence $a_1, a_2, a_3, ..., a_{30} = 45$, which is strictly increasing since there is at least one event per day. Adding 14 to each term in the sequence, we obtain $a_1 + 14, a_2 + 14, ..., a_{30} + 14 = 59$. Now consider the sequence $a_1, a_2, ..., a_{30}, a_1 + 14, a_2 + 14, ..., a_{30} + 14$, which consists of 60 numbers ranging from 1 to 59. Hence by pigeonhole principle, two of these numbers must be the same. Since $a_i \neq a_j$ for $i \neq j$, it follows that $a_j = a_i + 14$ for some $j > i$. Hence $a_j - a_i = 14$, which means that there is a period of consecutive days from the i-th day, during which exactly 14 games take place.

Example 6: If a set of 16 numbers is selected from {2, ..., 50}, at least 2 numbers will be in the set with a common divisor greater than 1.

Solution: In the set {2, ..., 50}, there are 15 prime numbers viz. {2, 3, 5, 7, 11, 13, 17, 19, 23, 29, 31, 37, 41, 43, 47}.

Suppose in any set of 16 numbers from 2 to 50, no two have a common divisor greater than one. Consider the prime factors of these numbers. By our assumption no two numbers will have common prime factor. This would mean that there should be at least 16 different prime numbers. This contradicts the fact that there are only 15 prime numbers. Hence our assumption is wrong. Therefore, in any set of 16 numbers from 2 to 50, 2 numbers will have a common divisor greater than 1.

Example 7: Show that among any n + 1 positive integers not exceeding 2n, there must be an integer that divides one of the other integers.

Solution: Let us denote the n + 1 positive integers as $a_1, a_2, ..., a_{n+1}$. Then we can write each integer a_i as $a_i = 2^{k_j} b_j$, for j = 1, 2, ..., n + 1, where k_j is a non-negative integer and b_j is odd positive integer. For example, $1 = 2^0 \cdot 1$, $2 = 2^1 \cdot 1$, $4 = 2^2 \cdot 1$, $6 = 2^1 \cdot 3$, and so on. Now $b_1, b_2, ..., b_{n+1}$ are all odd positive integers less than 2n. Since there are only n odd positive integers which are less than 2n, it follows from pigeon-hole principle that $b_i = b_j$ for some i and j. Then $a_i = 2^{k_j} q$ and $a_j = 2^{k_j} q$, where $q = q_i = q_j$. If $k_i < k_j$, a_i divides a_j; otherwise a_j divides a_i. Hence the result.

5.2.4 The Extended Pigeonhole Principle

Let A and B be two non-empty finite sets. If cardinality of A is greater than B, the following theorem (without proof) is a stronger version of the pigeonhole principle.

> **Theorem 3:** Let f: A → B be a function and let |A| = m, |B| = n, m > n.
> Let $k = \left\lceil \frac{(m-1)}{n} \right\rceil + 1$.
> Then there exist k elements $a_1, a_2, ..., a_k \in A$ such that $f(a_1) = f(a_2) ... = f(a_k)$.

SOLVED EXAMPLES

Examples 1: Prove that among 100,000 people, there are two who are born at exactly the same time (hour, minute and second).

Solution: Let A be the set of people (pigeons) and B, the set of seconds (pigeonholes) of one day.

$$|A| = 100{,}000 = m, \quad |B| = 24 \times 3600 = 86400 = n.$$

Then $\quad k = \left\lceil \dfrac{100000 - 1}{86400} \right\rceil + 1 = 1 + 1 = 2.$

Hence there are at least two who are born on the same day.

Example 2: Show that there must be at least 90 ways to choose six numbers from 1 to 15 so that all the choices have the same sum.

Solution: $m = {}^{15}c_6 = 5005$

The lowest sum of 6 numbers chosen from 1 to 15
$$= 1 + 2 + 3 + 4 + 5 + 6 = 21$$
Highest sum $= 10 + 11 + 12 + 13 + 14 + 15 = 75$

Hence $\quad n = 75 - 21 + 1 = 55$

Hence by the pigeonhole principle
$$k = \left\lceil \dfrac{m-1}{n} \right\rceil + 1 = \left(\dfrac{5004}{55}\right) + 1 = 91$$

Hence in at least 90 ways, we can choose six numbers from 1 to 15 so that all the choices have the same sum.

Example 3: There are 3000 students in a college which offers 7 distinct courses of 4 year's duration. A student who has taken a course in Discrete Mathematics learns that the largest classroom can hold only 100 students. She at once realizes there is a problem. What is the problem?

Solution: Since there are 7 distinct classes of 4 year's duration, we have $7 \times 4 = 28$ different classes. Hence, by extended pigeon-hole principle, each classroom must hold at least $\left\lceil \dfrac{3000 - 1}{28} \right\rceil + 1 = 107 + 1 = 108$ students. But since the capacity of the largest classroom is only 100, this is obviously a problem.

Example 4: In a group of six people at a party, each pair of individuals consists of two mutual acquaintances or two strangers. Show that there are either three mutual acquaintances or three mutual strangers in the group.

Solution: Let A be one of the six people. Divide the remaining five into two sets, one consisting only of acquaintances of A, the other only of strangers to A. By Extended Pigeon-hole Principle, cardinality of one of the sets must be at least [5/2] = 3. Hence it follows that in the group there are either 3 or more who are acquaintances of A, or there are 3 or more who are strangers to A. Let us assume the former, i.e. say B, C, D are acquaintances of A. Since any pair of individuals are either acquaintances or strangers, if say B, C are acquaintances, then together with A, A, B, C form a group of 3 mutual acquaintances. On the other hand if B, C, D are mutual strangers, they form a group of three mutual strangers.

If we assume the latter, when B, C, D are strangers to A, the proof follows in similar manner.

Example 5: A man hiked for 10 hours and covered a total distance of 45 miles. It is known that he hiked 6 miles in the first hour and only 3 miles in the last hour. Show that he must have hiked at least 9 miles within a certain period of two consecutive hours.

Solution: Let a_i, $1 \le i \le 10$, denote the number of miles hiked by the man during the ith hour. Then $a_1 = 6$, $a_{10} = 3$. Hence $a_2 + a_3 + \ldots + a_9 = 45 - (6 + 3) = 36$ miles. Consider the set

$$A = \{(a_2, a_3), (a_4, a_5), (a_6, a_7), (a_8, a_9)\}$$

of pairs of consecutive hours.

Apply Pigeon-hole Principle to the sum $(a_2 + a_3) + (a_4 + a_5) + (a_6 + a_7) + (a_8 + a_9) = 36$.

Since sum of 4 numbers is 36, value of one number should be at least 9.

Hence the man must have hiked at least 9 miles within a certain period of two consecutive hours.

Example 6: Show that if 7 colours are used to paint 50 bicycles, at least 8 bicycles will be the same colour.

Solution: Let A be the set of bicycles and B be the set of colours. Let $f: A \to B$ be a function, assigning a bicycle in A, a colour in B. Let $|A| = m$ and $|B| = n$. Then $m = 50$ and $n = 7$.

Let $K = \left\lceil \dfrac{m-1}{n} \right\rceil + 1 = \left\lceil \dfrac{50-1}{7} \right\rceil + 1 = 8$. Then by Extended Pigeon Hole Principle, there exist 8 elements in A such that $f(a_1) = f(a_2) = f(a_8)$, i.e. there exist at least 8 bicycles in A, which have the same colour.

EXERCISES - 5.1

1. Let $A = \{a, b, c, d\}$, $B = \{s, t, v\}$, $C = \{1, 2\}$. Define $f: A \to B$, $g: B \to C$, $h: C \to D$ as shown in the figures.

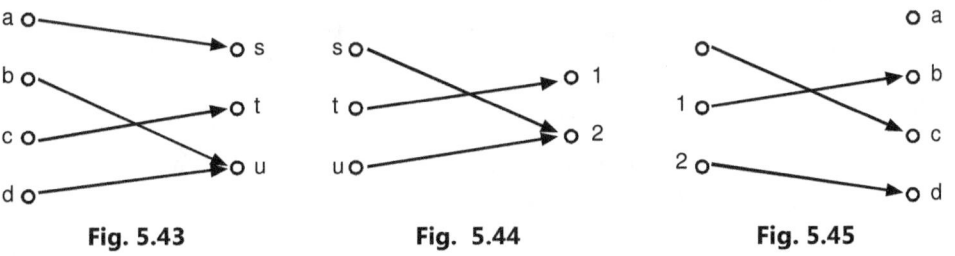

Fig. 5.43   Fig. 5.44   Fig. 5.45

Find the compositions.

(i) goh, (ii) foh, (iii) hog, (iv) gof.

Find in each case the domain and codomain.

2. The following diagrams define functions f_1 g_1 h which map the set {1, 2, 3, 4} into itself. Find (i) range of f, (ii) range of g, (iii) range of h, (iv) fog, (v) hof, (vi) gog.

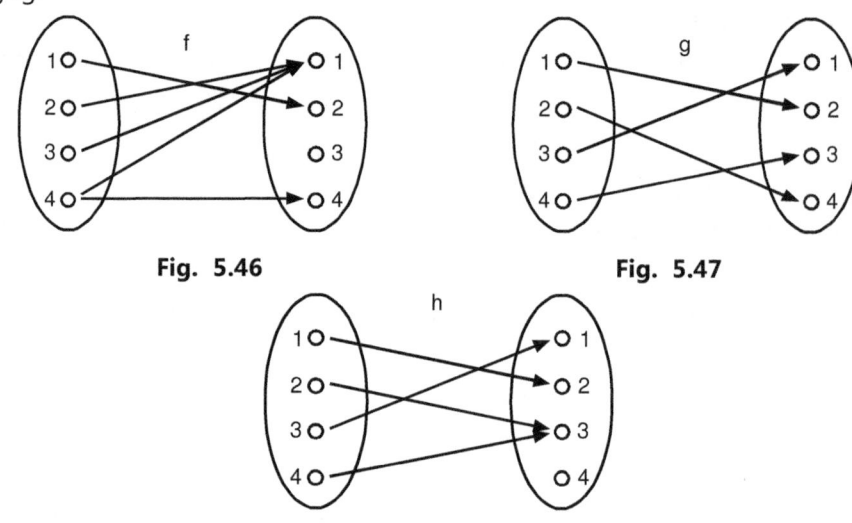

Fig. 5.46   Fig. 5.47

Fig. 5.48

3. Let f, g, h be defined by the following diagrams. Find which of them are injective, surjective or bijective.

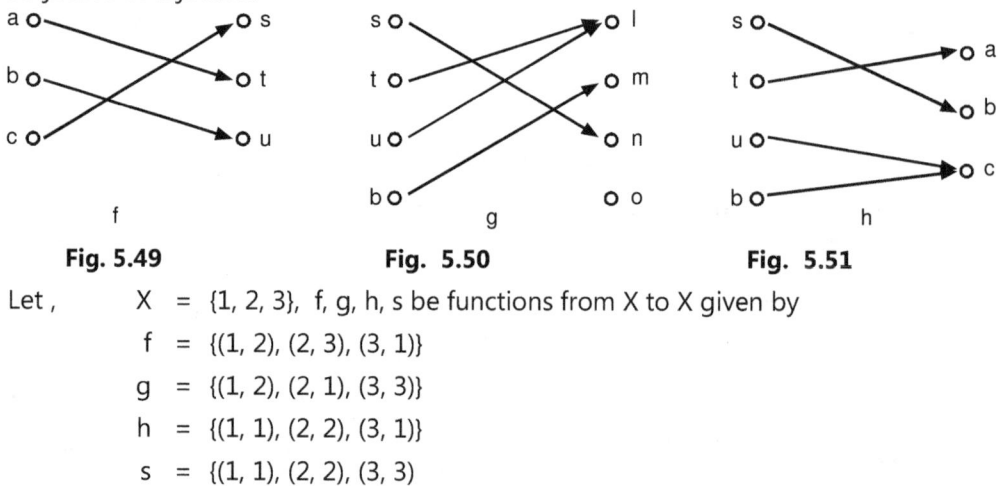

Fig. 5.49   Fig. 5.50   Fig. 5.51

Let, X = {1, 2, 3}, f, g, h, s be functions from X to X given by

f = {(1, 2), (2, 3), (3, 1)}

g = {(1, 2), (2, 1), (3, 3)}

h = {(1, 1), (2, 2), (3, 1)}

s = {(1, 1), (2, 2), (3, 3)

Find fohog, sog, fos.

5. Give example one each of the following functions:
   (i) A function which is injective but not surjective.
   (ii) A function which is surjective but not injective.
   (iii) A function which is neither surjective nor injective.
   (iv) A function which is bijective.
6. Construct an example to show that for two functions f and g from A to A, fog ≠ gof.
7. Let f, g, h be functions from N to N where N, is the set of natural numbers including 0, such that

$$f(n) = n + 1$$
$$g(n) = 2n$$
$$h(n) = \begin{cases} 0 & \text{if n is even} \\ 1 & \text{if n is odd.} \end{cases}$$

   Determine fof, fog, gof, goh, hog, (fog)oh.
8. Show that for any functions f: A → B, g: B → C and h: C → D,

   ho (gof) = (hog)of
9. Let A = {1, 2, 3, 4} and B = {a, b, c, d} and let f: A → B be given by

   f = {(1, a), (2, a), (3, c), (4, a)}.

   Determine whether f^{-1} exists. If so, find f^{-1}.
10. Let f: **R** → **R**, g: **R** → **R** be defined by f(a) = 2a + 1, g(b) = b/3. Verify $(gof)^{-1} = f^{-1}og^{-1}$.
11. Let A = {a, b, c, d} and B = {1, 2, 3}. Determine whether the following relations from A to B is a function. If it is a function, find its range.
    (i)   R = {(a, 1), (b, 2), (c, 1), (d, 2)}
    (ii) R = {(a, 1), (b, 2), (a, 2), (c, 1), (d, 2)}
    (iii) R = {(a, 3), (b, 2), (c, 1)}
    (iv) R = {(a, 1), (b, 1), (c, 1), (d, 1)}
12. Determine whether the following functions are one-one, onto (or both or neither).
    (i)   A = {1, 2, 3, 4} = B
          f = {(1, 1), (2, 3), (3, 4), (4, 2)}
    (ii) A = {1, 2, 3}, B = {a, b, c, d}
          f = {(1, a), (2, a), (3, c)}
    (iii) A = B = {1, 2, 3, 4, 5},
          f = {(1, 3), (2, 2), (3, 4), (4, 5), (5, 1)}
    (iv) A = {1, 2, 3, 4, 5}, B = {a, b, c, d}
          f = {(1, a), (2, c), (3, b), (4, d)}

13. Show that one of any m consecutive integers is divisible by m.
14. Suppose the figures from 1 to 12 on a clock dial are reshuffled among themselves. Prove that there exists a pair of adjacent figures which add up to at least 14.
15. Suppose that at a party, there are at least 6 persons. Prove that either there exist 3 persons, every two of whom know each other or else there exist 3 persons no two of whom know each other.
16. Suppose 18 students in a class appear at an entrance examination. Prove that there exist two among them whose seat numbers differ by a multiple of 17.
17. If 101 integers are selected from the set {1, 2, ..., 200}, prove that among the selected integers there exist two integers such that one of them is a multiple of the other.
18. Show that if seven points are chosen a region bounded by a regular hexagon of side 1 unit each, two of the points must be no further apart than 1 unit.
19. How many friends must you have to guarantee that at least five of them will have birthdays in the same month?

5.3 Infinite Sets

Although many problems in counting involve only finite sets, it is the infinite set which plays a more important and significant role in computability theory. It is the infinite set which provides an insight into the limitations of that which can be computed algorithmically. One can show, with the help of infinite sets that there are tasks which cannot be performed by any computer.

This section is therefore devoted to the study of some important infinite sets and their properties.

5.3.1 Infinite Sets

We have an intuitive idea of an 'infinite' set, it is a set with an infinite number of elements, an inexhaustible storehouse of elements which do not cease to appear; one will never reach the last element in the set. We are also familiar with some infinite sets; the set of natural numbers, set of integers etc. Let us now formally define an infinite set.

Definition:

A set A is infinite if there exists an injection $f: A \to A$ such that $f(A)$ is a proper subset of A. If no such injection exists, the set is finite.

Examples:
1. The set of natural numbers N is an infinite set.
   Consider f: N → N, where f(x) = 2x.
   f(N) is the set of all positive even integers which is a proper subset of N.
2. The set of real numbers **R** is an infinite set.
   Define f: **R** → **R** as
   $$f(x) = x + 1, \quad \text{if } x \geq 0$$
   $$= x, \quad \text{if } x < 0.$$
   Clearly f is an injective function. Note that if $y \in R$ such that $y = x + 1$, then $x = y - 1$. Hence $x \geq 0$ implies $y \geq 1$. Hence range (f) = $\{y \in R \mid y < 0 \wedge y \geq 1\}$, which is a proper subset of **R**.

5.3.2 Properties of Infinite Sets

1. Let B be a subset of A. Then if B is infinite, A is infinite.

Proof:
Since B is infinite, we have an injection f: B → B such that f(B) is a proper subset of B.
Define a function g: A → A as
$$g(a) = f(a), \quad \text{if } a \in B$$
$$g(a) = a \text{ if } a \in A - B.$$
g is injective and g(A) does not include the elements in B − g(B). Hence A is infinite.

2. If A is infinite, its power set P(A) is infinite.

Proof:
The mapping f: A → P(A), where f(a) = {a}, a ∈ A is an injective function.

3. If A and B are sets where A or B is infinite then A ∪ B is infinite.

Proof:
Define f: A → A ∪ B as f(a) = a, a ∈ A

4. If A and B are sets where A (or B) is infinite and B ≠ φ (or A ≠ φ) then A × B is infinite.

Proof:
Choose an element $b_0 \in B$ (as B ≠ φ) and define f: A → A × B as
$$f(a) = (a, b_0)$$
Clearly f is an injective function.

Examples

(i) The set of integers Z is infinite.

Solution: N, the set of natural numbers is a subset of Z. Hence Z is infinite by prop. 1, 4.3.2.

(ii) The set of rational numbers Q is infinite.

Solution: N (or Z) is a subset of Q. Hence, Q is infinite by pro. 1, 4.3.2.

(iii) The set $N \times N$ is infinite.

Solution: N is infinite and product of two infinite sets is infinite.

(iv) The intersection of two infinite sets is not infinite.

Solution: (i) Let E = set of even integers

and O = set of odd integers.

Then $E \cap O = \phi$ which is a finite set

(ii) Let A = [0, 1] and B = [1, 2]

then $A \cap B = \{1\}$.

(v) Let A and B be infinite sets such that $B \subseteq A$. Is the set A − B necessarily infinite? Give example to support your assertion.

Solution: No, A − B need not be infinite

Let A = [0, 1] and B = [0, 1)

Then A − B = {1}.

(vi) The set of all strings in {a, b} of prime length.

Solution: The set of prime numbers is infinite. Hence the set of all strings in {a, b} of prime length is also infinite.

5.4 Recursive Functions

A large number of algorithms are structured, using the principle of recursion. Recursion is a powerful and elegant procedure, in which the main problem is decomposed into smaller problems, of the same type, which further subdivided into still smaller problems, that are then solved directly. This procedure is described as **divide and conquer technique**.

In this procedure, for solving each subproblem, a **recursive function**; i.e. a function that repeatedly calls itself, has to be employed.

An algorithm, that contains such a recursive function is called a recursive algorithm.

SOLVED EXAMPLES

Examples 1 : In n is a positive integer, finding n!.
Solution : $\quad n! = n(n-1)(n-2) \ldots 2.1 = n \cdot (n-1)!$
Hence from n!, we reduce the problem to finding $(n-1)!$.
Now, $\quad (n-1)! = (n-1)(n-2)!$
$\quad\quad\quad (n-2)! = (n-2)(n-3)!$
Counting this way, the problem reduces to 1!.
For example if n = 7, we have :

Problem	Decomposed problem
7!	7.6!
6!	6.5!
5!	5.4!
4!	4.3!
3!	3.2!
2!	2.1!
1!	1

Combining the subproblems we have :

Problem	Solution
1!	1
2!	2.1 = 2
3!	3.2! = 6
4!	4.3! = 24
5!	5.4! = 120
6!	6.5! = 720
7!	7.6! = 5040

The algorithm for n! is given below :
   Input : n, an integer ≥ 1
   Output : n!
1. Factorial (n)
2. begin
3. If n = 1, return to 1
4. return n × factorial (n – 1)
5. end.

Example 2 : Find the sum of the first n natural numbers.
Solution : Let $\quad S_n = 1 + 2 + \ldots + n$
$\quad\quad\quad\quad = (1 + 2 + \ldots + n_1) + n$
$\quad\quad\quad\quad = S_{n-1} + n \quad\quad\quad\quad\quad\quad\quad\quad\quad\quad (\because n \geq 2)$

The recursive function is :

$$S_n = S_{n-1} + n \quad \text{for } n \geq 2$$

For example, S_5 can be calculated follows :

$$S_1 = 1$$
$$S_2 = 1 + 2 = 3$$
$$S_3 = S_2 + 3 = 6$$
$$S_4 = S_3 + 4 = 10$$
$$S_5 = S_4 + 5 = 15$$

Decomposing the problem		Combining the subproblem	
Problem	Simplified problem	Problem	Solution
S_5	S_{4+5}	S_1	1
S_4	S_{3+4}	S_2	$S_{1+2} = 3$
S_3	S_{2+3}	S_3	$S_{2+3} = 6$
S_2	S_{1+2}	S_4	$S_4 = S_{3+4} = 10$
S_1	1	S_5	$S_5 = S_{4+5} = 15$

EXERCISE 5.2

1. Give an example to show that the cardinality of a set which is the intersection of two countably infinite sets may also be countably infinite.
2. Give an example to show that the cardinality of a set that is the intersection of two countably infinite sets may be finite.
3. Classify the following sets into finite, countably infinite or uncountably infinite.
   (i) Set of all types of trees in India.
   (ii) Set of all prime numbers.
4. State if the following sets are finite, denumerable or non-denumerable.
   (i) Class of all possible programs that can be written in any given programming language.
   (ii) Number of fish in the Pacific ocean.
   (iii) All possible books written in the English language.
   (iv) Set of real numbers between 0 and 1.
5. Classify the following sets as finite, denumerable or non-denumerable, giving reason
   (i) The set of all strings (words) in {a, b} of prime length.
   (ii) The set of all strings in {a, b} of length no greater than k.
   (iii) The set of all m × n matrices with entries from {0, 1, 2, ... k}.
   (iv) The set of all prepositional forms over the prepositional variables p, q, r and s.
   (v) The set of all points in the plane.
   (vi) The set of all points in the plane with positive integer co-ordinates.

6. Determine the cardinalities of the sets
   (a) $A = \{ n^7 \mid n \text{ is a positive integer} \}$
   (b) $B = \{ n^{109} \mid n \text{ is a positive integer} \}$
   (c) $A \cup B$
   (d) $A \cap B$.

7. Let N denote the set of all natural numbers. Let S denote the set of all finite subsets of N. What is the cardinality of the set S? Justify your answer.

8. Solve the following recurrence relations:
   (i) $a_r - 9a_{r-1} + 18a_{r-2} = 0$ with $a_0 = 1, a_1 = 4$
   (ii) $a_r - 2a_{r-1} + a_{r-2} = 2$ with $a_0 = 25, a_1 = 16$
   (iii) $S(k) - 4S(k-1) + 4S(k-2) = 3k + 2^k$ with $S(0) = 1, S(1) = 1$.
   (iv) $S(k) - 4S(k-1) - 11S(k-2) + 30S(k-3) = 0$
   with $S(0) = 0, S(1) = -35, S(2) = -85$

9. Find a closed form of the expression for the terms of the Fibonacci sequence.
   (**Hint:** Fibonacci sequence is given by 1, 1, 2, 3, 5, 8, 13, ...)

10. Solve the following difference equations using generating functions.
    (i) $S(k) + 3S(k-1) - 4S(k-2) = 0, k \geq 2$ with $S(0) = 3, S(1) = -2$.
    (ii) $G(k) - 7G(k-1) + 10G(k-2) = 0, k \geq 2$ with $G(0) = 1, G(1) = 3$.

11. Solve the recurrence relation:
    (i) $a_n = 2a_{n-1} + 3a_{n-2} + 5^n, n \geq 2$
       with $a_0 = -2, a_1 = 1$.
    (ii) $a_n + 6a_{n-1} + 12a_{n-2} + 8a_{n-3} = 2^n, n \geq 3$ with $a_0 = 0, a_1 = 0, a_2 = 2$.

ANSWERS - 5.2

8. (i) $a_r = \frac{2}{3}(3)^r + \left(\frac{1}{3}\right)6^r$
   (ii) $a_r = r^2 - 10r + 25$
   (iii) $S(k) = 12 + 3k + (k^2 + 7k + 22)2^{k-1}$
   (iv) $S(k) = 4(-3)^k + 2^k - 5^{k+1}$

9. $a_r = \left(\frac{1}{\sqrt{5}}\right)\left(\frac{1+\sqrt{5}}{2}\right)^r + \left(\frac{-1+\sqrt{5}}{\sqrt{5}}\right)\left(\frac{1-\sqrt{5}}{2}\right)^r$

10. (i) $S(k) = 2 + (-4)^k$ (ii) $G(k) = \frac{3}{2}(2^k) + 3(5^k)$

POINTS TO REMEMBER

- Let A and B be non-empty sets. A **function** f from A to B, denoted as f: A → B, is a relation from A to B such that for every a ∈ A, there exists a **unique** b ∈ B such that (a, b) ∈ f. If (a, b) ∈ f, we write f(a) = b.

- The set A is called as the **domain** of f, denoted **D(f)**. The set B is called as the **codomain**, and the set { f(a) | a ∈ A }, which is a subset of B, is called as the **range** of f, and denoted as **R(f)**. The element a is called an **argument** of the function f and f(a) is called the **value** of the function for the argument a.

- Let A and B be two sets. A partial function f with **domain A** and codomain B is any function from A' to B where A' ⊂ A. For any element x ∈ A − A', the value of f(x) is said to be undefined.

- Let f: A → B and g: C → D be functions. Then f and g are said to be equivalent or **identical** only if A = C, B = D and f(a) = g(a) for all a ∈ A.

    The function f: Z → Z given by f(x) = x and g: Z → Z^+ given by g(x) = x are not equivalent.

- Let f: A → B be a function.

    f is called a **surjective** (onto) function if f(A) = B, i.e. range of f is equal to the codomain of f.

    f is called an **injective** (one-to-one) function if for elements a, a' ∈ A, a ≠ a' implies f(a) ≠ f(a'), or equivalently if f(a) = f(a'), then a = a'.

    f is called bijection (one-to-one and onto) function if f is both surjective and injective.

- Let f: A → B be a bijection from A to B. The inverse of f denoted by f^{-1} is the function f^{-1}: B → A such that

    $f^{-1} \circ f = 1_A$ and
    $f \circ f^{-1} = 1_B$

- A set A is infinite if there exists an injection f: A → A such that f(A) is a proper subset of A. If no such injection exists, the set is finite.

Unit 3

Chapter 6: RECURRENCE RELATIONS

SYLLABUS:
- Recurrence Relations : Recurrence relation, Linear recurrence relations with constant coefficients, Homogeneous solutions, Particular solutions, Total solutions, Solutions by the method of generating functions.

OBJECTIVES:
- To generate functions from given sequences with initial conditions.

UTILITY:
- In modelling real life problems in terms of recurrence relations
- In development of software.

KEY CONCEPTS:
- Discrete numeric functions
- Generating functions
- Recurrence relations

6.0 Introduction

In the last chapter we have studied about functions which are binary relations that assign each element in the domain, a unique value in the range. When the domain is the set of natural numbers and the range is the set of real numbers, the functions are called discrete numeric functions. This special class of functions is useful in digital computation.

An alternative way to represent the numeric function is the generating function. With the help of generating functions, we can express infinite series in the closed form so that the mathematical operations can be performed easily on them. In the beginning of the chapter the numeric function and its alternative form i.e. the generating function are explained in detail.

In many discrete computation problems, the numeric functions are obtained in the form of a relation between its terms. The recursive formulae defining the numeric function are called recurrence relations. In this chapter, we will study the linear recurrence relations with constant coefficients.

6.1 Discrete Numeric Functions

In this section, we shall discuss about some functions which are useful in digital computations.

A function, whose domain is a set of natural numbers (including zero) and whose range is set of real numbers, is called a **discrete numeric function**, or briefly a **numeric function**.

If $a: \mathbf{N} \to \mathbf{R}$ is a discrete numeric function, then $a_0, a_1, a_2, \ldots, a_r, \ldots$ denote, the values of the function 'a' at $0, 1, 2, \ldots, r, \ldots$ i.e. $a(0) = a_0$, $a(1) = a_1$, $a(2) = a_2$, $\ldots$, $a(r) = a_r$, $\ldots$

The numeric function 'a' is written as
$$a = \{a_0, a_1, a_2, \ldots \ldots, a_r, \ldots \ldots\}$$

The numeric function often termed as **sequence**.

Discrete numeric functions can be represented in implicit form also. For example,
$$a_r = \begin{cases} 3r & , \ 0 \leq r \leq 5 \\ r+1 & , \ r \geq 6 \end{cases}$$

The above function can be written as
$$a = \{0, 3, 6, 9, 12, 15, 7, 8, 9, \ldots\}$$

Another example is $\quad b_r = 2r^2 + 3, \ r \geq 0$

For this numeric function, the expression is same for all the values of r, hence we can write
$$b = 2r^2 + 3$$

Now, consider the following example.

Example: In a process control system, a monitoring device measures the temperature inside a chemical reaction chamber once every 30 sec. Let a_r denote the rth reading in degrees centigrade. Determine an expression for a_r if it is known that the temperature rises from 100°C to 120°C at a constant rate in the first 300 sec. and stays at 120°C from then on.

Solution: Here, a_r denotes the rth reading and the temperature increases from 100°C to 120°C at constant rate for first 300 sec. Therefore, $a_0 = 100$, $a_1 = 102$, $a_2 = 104$, $\ldots$, $a_{10} = 120$ where the readings are taken at the interval of 30 sec.

Also since the temperature remains constant after 300 sec., hence
$$a_r = 120 \qquad r \geq 11$$

Therefore the discrete numeric function a_r can be defined as
$$a_r = \begin{cases} 100 + 2r & , \ 0 \leq r \leq 10 \\ 120 & , \ r \geq 11 \end{cases}$$

6.1.1 Operations on Numeric Functions

After defining the discrete numeric functions, now we shall study the different operations like addition, multiplication etc. on numeric functions.

Let a and b be two numeric functions. Then the sum of two numeric functions a and b is a numeric function c whose value at r is equal to the sum of the values of two numeric functions a and b at r. The sum of two functions is denoted by $c = a + b$, where, $c_r = a_r + b_r$ for given r.

The product of two numeric functions a and b is a numeric function d whose value at r is equal to the product of the values of two numeric functions at r. The product is denoted by $d = ab$, where $d_r = a_r b_r$ for any given r.

For example,

if $a_r = \begin{cases} 1, & 0 \leq r \leq 2 \\ 3r, & r \geq 3 \end{cases}$

and $b_r = \begin{cases} 2^r + 1, & 0 \leq r \leq 1 \\ r - 5, & r \geq 2 \end{cases}$

then the sum of a and b is

$c_r = a_r + b_r = \begin{cases} 2^r + 2, & 0 \leq r \leq 1 \\ -2, & r = 2 \\ 4r - 5, & r \geq 3 \end{cases}$

The product of a and b is

$d_r = a_r \, b_r = \begin{cases} 2^r + 1, & 0 \leq r \leq 1 \\ -3, & r = 2 \\ 3r^2 - 15r, & r \geq 3 \end{cases}$

Let a be the numeric function and α be any real number. Then αa is a numeric function whose value at r is equal to α times a_r. The function αa is called a scaled version of a with scaling factor α. For example, if $a = 3r^3 - 1$ and $\alpha = 10$, then $\alpha a = 10(3r^3 - 1)$.

For a numeric function a, |a| denotes a numeric function whose value at r is equal to a_r if a_r is non-negative and is equal to $-a_r$ if a_r is negative.

Thus if $a_r = (-1)^r \left(\dfrac{5}{7} r^3\right), \quad r \geq 0$

$|a| = \dfrac{5}{7} r^3, \quad r \geq 0$

The convolution of the numeric functions a and b is numeric function c denoted by $a * b$ where,

$c_r = a_0 b_r + a_1 b_{r-1} + a_2 b_{r-2} + \ldots + a_i b_{r-i} + \ldots + a_{r-1} b_1 + a_r b_0$

$= \sum_{i=0}^{r} a_i b_{r-i}$

For example, if $a_r = 5^r, \quad r \geq 0$
and $b_r = 7^r, \quad r \geq 0$
then $c = a * b$
where $c_r = \sum_{i=0}^{r} 5^i \, 7^{r-i}, \quad r \geq 0$

The forward difference of a numeric function a is a numeric function, denoted by Δa, whose value at r is equal to $a_{r+1} - a_r$. The backward difference of a is denoted by ∇a and is defined as

$$a_r = a_r - a_{r-1}, \quad r \geq 1$$

and $a_0 = 0$

If
$$a_r = \begin{cases} 1, & 0 \leq r \leq 2 \\ 3^r, & r \geq 3 \end{cases}$$

then the forward difference is

$$\Delta a_r = \begin{cases} 0, & 0 \leq r \leq 1 \\ 26, & r = 2 \\ 2 \times 3^r, & r \geq 3 \end{cases}$$

and the backward difference is

$$\nabla a_r = \begin{cases} 0, & r = 0 \\ 1, & r = 1 \\ 0, & r = 2 \\ 26, & r = 3 \\ 2 \times 3^{r-1}, & r \geq 4 \end{cases}$$

Let a be a numeric function and i be a positive integer, then $S^i a$ denotes a numeric function such that its value at r is zero for $r = 0, 1, 2, \ldots, i-1$ and is a_{r-i} for $r \geq i$.

Similarly $S^{-i} a$ denotes a numeric function such that its value at r is a_{r+i} for $r \geq 0$.

Now, if
$$a_r = \begin{cases} 1, & 0 \leq r \leq 10 \\ 2, & r \geq 11 \end{cases}$$

then the numeric function $s^5 a$ is given by

$$S^5 a_r = \begin{cases} 0, & 0 \leq r \leq 4 \\ 1, & 5 \leq r \leq 15 \\ 2, & r \geq 16 \end{cases}$$

and $S^{-7} a$ is given by

$$S^{-7} a_r = \begin{cases} 1, & 0 \leq r \leq 3 \\ 2, & r \geq 4 \end{cases}$$

The accumulated sum of a numeric function a is a numeric function whose value at r is $\sum_{i=0}^{r} a_i$.

For example, if $a_r = 3^r, \ r \geq 0$

then the accumulated sum of 'a' is given by $\sum_{i=0}^{r} (3)^i$

This is geometric series with (r + 1) terms and common ratio 3.

$$\therefore \text{ Accumulated Sum} = \sum_{i=0}^{r} (3)^i$$

$$= \frac{(3^{r+1} - 1)}{2}$$

Now we are in position to define asymptotic behaviour of a numeric function which shows how the values of the function varies for large values of r.

Suppose $a_r = 7r^3$, $r \geq 0$

and $b_r = \dfrac{9}{r}$, $r > 0$

It is clear from the definitions of a_r and b_r that as r increases, a_r increases but b_r decreases.

For comparing the asymptotic behaviour of the numeric functions, we use the term 'asymptotic dominance'. If a and b are numeric functions, we say that a asymptotically dominates b or b is asymptotically dominated by a, if there exist positive constants l and m such that

$$|b_r| \leq m\, a_r \quad , \quad r \geq l$$

If $a_r = 1 + 0.2\, r$, $r \geq 0$

and $b_r = (1.03)^{4r}$, $r \geq 0$

then b asymptotically dominates a because for $l = 9$ and $m = 1$,

$$|1 + 0.2\, r| \leq (1.03)^{4r} \quad , \quad r \geq 9$$

Following are the properties for asymptotic dominance.

For any numeric functions a and b if b is asymptotically dominated by a,

(i) |a| asymptotically dominates a.

(ii) For any constant α, αb is also asymptotically dominated by a.

(iii) For any integer i, $S^i b$ is asymptotically dominated by $S^i a$.

(iv) If both b and c are asymptotically dominated by a, then for any constants α and β, $\alpha b + \beta c$ is also asymptotically dominated by a.

(v) If c is asymptotically dominated by b and b is asymptotically dominated by a, then c is asymptotically dominated by a.

SOLVED EXAMPLES

Example 1: A ping pong ball is dropped to the floor from a height of 20 m. Suppose that the ball always rebounds to reach half of the height from which it falls.

(i) Determine the numeric function a, where a_r is the height, the ball reaches in the rth rebound.

(ii) If b_r denotes the loss in height during the rth rebound, express b_r in terms of a_r.

Solution: (i) Given a_r is the height, the ball reaches in r^{th} rebound. Therefore, in the 0th rebound, the height is 20 m from where the ball is dropped to the floor.

i.e. $a_0 = 20$

After 1st rebound, the ball reaches to half of the original height i.e. 10 m.

Hence $a_1 = 10$.

Since in each rebound, the ball reaches to half of its height, therefore,

$a_2 = 5$
$a_3 = 2.5$
$a_4 = 1.25$
....

Thus the numeric function is given by

$a = \{20, 10, 5, 2.5, 1.25 \ldots \ldots\}$

or it can be written as

$$a_r = \begin{cases} 20 & , r = 0 \\ \dfrac{a_{r-1}}{2} & , r \geq 1 \end{cases}$$

(ii) According to the problem, b_r is the loss in the height during the rth rebound, therefore, originally when the ball is about to fall (0th rebound), the loss in height is 0 m.

Hence $b_0 = 0$

After 1st rebound, the ball reaches to half of its original height (20 m). Hence the loss in height is 10 m.

Therefore, $b_1 = 10$

Similarly, we can see that

$b_2 = 15$
$b_3 = 17.5$
$b_4 = 18.75$ ......

Hence, the numeric function b is

$b = \{0, 10, 15, 17.5, 18.75, \ldots\}$

but $a = \{20, 10, 5, 2.5, 1.25, \ldots\}$

Therefore, in terms of a, the numeric function b can be expressed as

$b_r = a_0 - a_r, \quad r \geq 0$

Example 2: Ramesh deposits Rs. 200 in a saving account at an interest rate of 9 percent per year, compounded annually. If a_r denotes the amount in the account after r years, determine the numeric function a.

Solution: For the compound interest with principal amount P, rate r percent per year, the total amount after n years is

$$A = P\left(1 + \frac{r}{100}\right)^n$$

Here P = 200, r = 9, the number of years = r. Hence the amount deposited in the bank is

$$a_r = 200\left(1 + \frac{9}{100}\right)^r$$

therefore $a_r = 200(1.09)^r$

which is the required numeric function.

Example 3: If $a_r = \begin{cases} 0, & 0 \le r \le 2 \\ 5^r, & r \ge 3 \end{cases}$

and $b_r = \begin{cases} 3 + r, & 0 \le r \le 1 \\ 2^r, & r \ge 2 \end{cases}$

(i) Find c_r where $c_r = a_r + b_r$

(ii) Find d_r where $d_r = a_r b_r$

Solution: (i) For $a_r = \begin{cases} 0, & 0 \le r \le 2 \\ 5^r, & r \ge 3 \end{cases}$

the numeric function is

$$a = \{0, 0, 0, 5^3, 5^4, 5^5, \ldots\}$$

For $b_r = \begin{cases} 3 + r, & 0 \le r \le 1 \\ 2^r, & r \ge 2 \end{cases}$

the numeric function is

$$b = \{3, 4, 2^2, 2^3, 2^4, 2^5, \ldots\}$$

To find $c_r = a_r + b_r$, let c be a numeric function such that

$c_r = a_r + b_r$

Therefore, $c_r = \{0, 0, 0, 5^3, 5^4, 5^5, \ldots\} + \{3, 4, 2^2, 2^3, 2^4, 2^5, \ldots\}$

∴ $c_r = \{3, 4, 4, 5^3 + 2^3, 5^4 + 2^4, 5^5 + 2^5, \ldots\}$

or $c_r = \begin{cases} 3, & r = 0 \\ 4, & 1 \le r \le 2 \\ 5^r + 2^r, & r \ge 3 \end{cases}$

(ii) Since $d_r = a_r b_r$

where $a_r = \begin{cases} 0, & 0 \le r \le 2 \\ 5^r, & r \ge 3 \end{cases}$

i.e. $a = \{0, 0, 0, 5^3, 5^4, 5^5, \ldots\}$

and $\quad b_r = \begin{cases} 3+r, & 0 \le r \le 1 \\ 2^r, & r \ge 2 \end{cases}$

i.e. $\quad b = \{3, 4, 2^2, 2^3, 2^4, 2^5, \ldots\}$

therefore, $\quad d_r = \{0, 0, 0, 5^3\, 2^3, 5^4\, 2^4, 5^5\, 2^5, \ldots\}$

i.e. $\quad d_r = \begin{cases} 0, & 0 \le r \le 2 \\ 5^r \times 2^r, & r \ge 3 \end{cases}$

Example 4: Determine a ∗ b for the following numeric functions.

$$a_r = \begin{cases} 1, & 0 \le r \le 2 \\ 0, & r \ge 3 \end{cases} \text{ and } b_r = \begin{cases} r+1, & 0 \le r \le 2 \\ 0, & r \ge 3 \end{cases}$$

Solution: By definition of a_r, the numeric function a is given by

$$a = \{1, 1, 1, 0, 0, 0, 0, \ldots\}$$

Similarly, $\quad b = \{1, 2, 3, 0, 0, 0, 0, \ldots\}$

The convolution of a and b is a numeric function c such that

$$c = a * b$$

and $\quad c_r = \sum_{i=0}^{r} a_i\, b_{r-i}$

$c_r = a_0 b_r + a_1 b_{r-1} + a_2 b_{r-2} + \ldots + a_r b_0$

Thus $\quad c_0 = a_0 b_0 = 1$

$c_1 = a_0 b_1 + a_1 b_0 = 3$

$c_2 = a_0 b_2 + a_1 b_1 + a_2 b_0 = 6$

$c_3 = a_0 b_3 + a_1 b_2 + a_2 b_1 + a_3 b_0 = 5$

Similarly $\quad c_4 = 3$

$c_5 = 0$

$c_6 = 0.$

. . . .

Hence, the numeric function c is given by

$$c = \{1, 3, 6, 5, 3, 0, 0, 0, \ldots\}$$

i.e. $\quad c_r = \begin{cases} 1, & r = 0 \\ 3, & r = 1 \\ 6, & r = 2 \\ 5, & r = 3 \\ 3, & r = 4 \\ 0, & r \ge 5 \end{cases}$

Example 5: The numeric function a is defined as
$$a_r = \begin{cases} 2 & , 0 \leq r \leq 3 \\ 2^{-r} + 5 & , r \geq 4 \end{cases}$$

Determine (i) $S^2 a$, (ii) $S^{-2} a$, (iii) Δa, (iv) ∇a.

Solution: (i) For the numeric function a, the numeric function $S^i a$ is given by
$$(S^i a)_r = \begin{cases} 0 & , 0 \leq r \leq i-1 \\ a_{r-i} & , r \geq i \end{cases}$$

Hence for $i = 2$,
$$(S^2 a)_r = \begin{cases} 0 & , 0 \leq r \leq 1 \\ a_{r-2} & , r \geq 2 \end{cases}$$

According to the definition of a_r,
$$(S^2 a)_r = \begin{cases} 0 & , 0 \leq r \leq 1 \\ 2 & , 2 \leq r \leq 5 \\ 2^{-(r-2)} + 5 & , r \geq 6 \end{cases}$$

(ii) The numeric function $S^{-i} a$ is defined as
$$(S^{-i} a)_r = a_{r+i} \quad , r \geq 0$$

Thus for the numeric function $(S^{-2} a)$,
$$(S^{-2} a)_r = a_{r+2} \quad , r \geq 0$$

or
$$(S^{-2} a)_r = \begin{cases} 2 & , 0 \leq r \leq 1 \\ 2^{-(r+2)} + 5 & , r \geq 2 \end{cases}$$

(iii) The forward difference Δa is defined as
$$(\Delta a)_r = a_{r+1} - a_r \quad , r \geq 0$$

The numeric function Δa for the given function a is
$$(\Delta a)_r = \begin{cases} 0 & , 0 \leq r \leq 2 \\ 2^{-4} + 3 & , r = 3 \\ 2^{-(r+1)} - 2^{-(r)} & , r \geq 4 \end{cases}$$

(iv) The backward difference (Δa) is given by
$$(\nabla a)_r = a_r - a_{r-1} \quad , r \geq 1$$
$$(\nabla a)_0 = a_0 \quad , r = 0$$

Thus the numeric function (∇a) for the given function a is
$$(\nabla a)_r = \begin{cases} 2 & , r = 0 \\ 0 & , 1 \leq r \leq 3 \\ 2^{-4} + 5 & , r = 4 \\ 2^{-r} - 2^{-(r-1)} & , r \geq 5 \end{cases}$$

Chp 6 | 6.9

6.2 Generating Functions

In the previous section, we have studied the discrete numeric functions and the operations defined on them. In this section, we will be introduced to generate functions which are alternative representation of numeric functions.

For the numeric function,
$$a = \{a_0, a_1, a_2, \ldots, a_r, \ldots\}$$

We define an infinite series
$$a_0 + a_1 z + a_2 z^2 + a_3 z^3 + \ldots + a_r z^r + \ldots$$

which is called the **generating function** of the numeric function a. It is denoted by A (z).

Therefore,
$$A(z) = a_0 + a_1 z + a_2 z^2 + \ldots + a_r z^r + \ldots$$

$$= \sum_{r=0}^{\infty} (a_r z^r)$$

For example, if $a = \{4^0, 4^1, 4^2, 4^3, 4^4, \ldots 4^r, \ldots\}$

then, the generating function of a is
$$A(z) = 4^0 + 4z + 4^2 z^2 + 4^3 z^3 + \ldots + 4^r z^r + \ldots$$

In $A(z) = a_0 + a_1 z + a_2 z^2 + \ldots + a_r z^r + \ldots$

the term a_0 is called the constant term and the term $a_r z^r$ is the term of degree r. Note that A (z) generates its coefficients. If all the coefficients are zero from some point on, then A (z) is a polynomial. If $a_s = 0$ for $s \geq r + 1$, then A (z) is a polynomial of degree r.

The above infinite series can be written in the closed form as
$$A(z) = \frac{1}{1 - 4z}$$

Thus, we can say that using the generating functions, representation of numeric functions gives the possibility of expressing infinite series in the closed form so that the different operations can be performed conveniently on them.

Finite sequences can also be represented by generating functions.

Consider the numeric function $a_r = {}^nC_r$ for a fixed n. The generating function of a is
$$A(z) = {}^nC_0 + {}^nC_1 z + {}^nC_2 z^2 + \ldots + {}^nC_r z^r + \ldots + {}^nC_n z^n$$

Note that ${}^nC_r = 0$ for $r > n$.

$\therefore \quad A(z) = (1 + z)^n$

by application of binomial expansion.

Now, we define some operations on generating functions.

Let, $A(z) = a_0 + a_1 z + a_2 z^2 + \ldots + a_r z^r + \ldots$

and $B(z) = b_0 + b_1 z + b_2 z^2 + \ldots + b_r z^r + \ldots$

denote the generating functions.

Two generating functions are equal i.e. $A(z) = B(z)$
iff $a_r = b_r$ for each $r \geq 0$.
The sum of $A(z)$ and $B(z)$ is defined as

$$A(z) + B(z) = \sum_{r=0}^{\infty} (a_r + b_r) z^r$$

If k is any scalar then,

$$kA(z) = k(a_0 + a_1 z + a_2 z^2 + \ldots + a_r z^r + \ldots)$$

$$= k \sum_{r=0}^{\infty} a_r z^r$$

The product of $A(z)$ and $B(z)$ is given by

$$A(z) B(z) = a_0 b_0 + (a_0 b_1 + a_1 b_0) z + (a_0 b_2 + a_1 b_1 + a_2 b_0) z^2$$
$$+ \ldots + (a_0 b_r + a_1 b_{r-1} + \ldots + a_r b_0) z^r + \ldots$$

In the remaining section, we will see that the relation between the numeric functions correspond to the same type of relations between their generating functions. Let $A(z)$, $B(z)$, $C(z)$ be the generating functions of the numeric functions a, b and c. Let α be any scalar.
If $b = \alpha a$, then $B(z) = \alpha A(z)$.

Thus for $\quad b_r = 8 \times 9^r \quad , \quad r \geq 0$
$\quad\quad\quad\quad = 8 \times a_r \quad , \quad r \geq 0$
where $\quad a_r = 9^r \quad , \quad r \geq 0$
$\quad\quad\quad B(z) = 8 A(z)$
$\quad\quad\quad B(z) = 8 \left(\dfrac{1}{1-9z}\right) = \dfrac{8}{1-9z}$

It is obvious that corresponding to $c = a + b$, we have $C(z) = A(z) + B(z)$.

Thus if $\quad c_r = 3^r + 4^r \quad , r \geq 0$
then $\quad C(z) = \dfrac{1}{(1-3z)} + \dfrac{1}{(1-4z)}$
or $\quad C(z) = \dfrac{2-7z}{1-7z+12z^2}$

For $\quad b_r = \alpha^r a_r$
we have $\quad B(z) = \alpha^0 a_0 + \alpha a_1 z + \alpha^2 a_2 z^2 + \ldots + \alpha^r a_r z^r + \ldots$
or $\quad B(z) = a_0 + a_1 (\alpha z) + a_2 (\alpha^2 z^2) + \ldots + a_r (\alpha^r z^r) + \ldots$
$\therefore \quad B(z) = A(\alpha z)$

For example, if $\quad b_r = 3^r$
then $\quad B(z) = \dfrac{1}{1-3z}$

The generating function of $S^i a$ for any positive integer i is $z^i A(z)$ where $A(z)$ is the generating function of a.

Hence, if $\quad A(z) = \dfrac{z^4}{1-2z}$

we have, $\quad a_r = \begin{cases} 0, & 0 \le r \le 3 \\ 2^{r-4}, & r \ge 4 \end{cases}$

Also the generating function of $S^{-i}a$ is $z^{-i}\left[A(z) - a_0 - a_1 z - a_2 z^2 - \ldots - a_{i-1} z^{i-1}\right]$

For $b = \Delta a$, we have,

$$B(z) = \dfrac{1}{z}[A(z) - a_0] - A(z)$$

and for $b = \nabla a$, we have $B(z) = A(z) - z A(z)$

The generating function representation of numeric function is very useful in convolution of numeric functions.

If $c = a * b$ then $\quad C(z) = A(z) B(z)$

For example, if $\quad c = a * b$

where $\quad a_r = 3^r, \; b_r = 5^r, \; r \ge 0$

then $\quad C(z) = A(z) B(z)$

where $\quad A(z) = \dfrac{1}{1-3z}$

$\quad B(z) = \dfrac{1}{1-5z}$

∴ $\quad C(z) = \dfrac{1}{(1-3z)} \times \dfrac{1}{(1-5z)} = \dfrac{1}{2}\left[\dfrac{5}{1-5z} - \dfrac{3}{1-3z}\right]$

The closed form of the generating functions of some numeric functions are given in the table below.

Table 6.1

Numeric function	Generating function
$a_r = k\, a^r$	$A(z) = \dfrac{k}{1-az}$
$a_r = r$	$A(z) = \dfrac{z}{(1-z)^2}$
$a_r = b_r\, a^r$	$A(z) = \dfrac{abz}{(1-az)^2}$
$a_r = \dfrac{1}{r!}$	$A(z) = e^z$
$a_r = \begin{cases} {}^nC_r, & 0 \le r \le n \\ 0, & r > n \end{cases}$	$A(z) = (1+z)^n$

SOLVED EXAMPLES

Example 1: Determine the generating function of the numeric function a_r where

(i) $a_r = 3^r + 4^{r+1}$, $r \geq 0$

(ii) $a_r = 5$, $r \geq 0$

Solution: (i) Let $a_r = b_r + c_r$

where $b_r = 3^r$

and $c_r = 4^{r+1}$

Let $A(z)$, $B(z)$ and $C(z)$ be the generating functions of a, b and c.

For $b_r = 3^r$, the corresponding generating function is

$$B(z) = \frac{1}{1-3z}$$

For $c_r = 4^{r+1}$, $C(z) = \frac{4}{1-4z}$

∴ $A(z) = B(z) + C(z)$

$A(z) = \frac{1}{(1-3z)} + \frac{4}{(1-4z)}$

∴ $A(z) = \frac{(5-16z)}{(1-3z)(1-4z)}$

(ii) Given $a_r = 5$, $r \geq 0$

Therefore numeric function

$a = \{5, 5, 5, \ldots\}$

∴ Its generating function is

$A(z) = 5 + 5z + 5z^2 + 5z^3 + \ldots$

$= 5(1 + z + z^2 + z^3 + \ldots) = 5 \times \frac{1}{(1-z)}$

∴ $A(z) = \frac{5}{(1-z)}$

Example 2: Find the generating function of

$$a_r = \begin{cases} 0 & , \text{ r odd} \\ 2^{r+1} & , \text{ r even} \end{cases}$$

Solution: According to the problem, the numeric function

$a = \{2, 0, 2^3, 0, 2^4, 0, 2^5, \ldots\}$

This numeric function can be written as

$a_r = 2^r + (-2)^r$, $r \geq 0$

Its generating function is

$$A(z) = \frac{1}{(1-2z)} + \frac{1}{(1+2z)} = \frac{2}{(1-4z^2)}$$

Example 3: Determine the discrete numeric functions corresponding to the following generating functions

(i) $\dfrac{1}{(1+z)}$

(ii) $\dfrac{3-5z}{(1-2z-3z^2)}$

Solution: (i) Given the generating function

$$A(z) = \dfrac{1}{1+z} = \dfrac{1}{1-(-z)}$$

It is the sum of geometric progression whose first term is 1 and common ratio is $(-z)$.

$\therefore \quad A(z) = 1 - z + z^2 - z^3 + z^4 - \ldots$

Therefore, corresponding numeric function is

$$a_r = (-1)^r$$

(ii) Given $A(z) = \dfrac{3-5z}{(1-2z-3z^2)} = \dfrac{3-5z}{(1-3z)(1+z)}$

Here we use partial fraction method.

So let, $\dfrac{3-5z}{(1-3z)(1+z)} = \dfrac{A}{1-3z} + \dfrac{B}{1+z}$

which after simplification gives $A = 1$ and $B = 2$.

Therefore, $A(z) = \dfrac{3-5z}{(1-3z)(1+z)} = \dfrac{1}{(1-3z)} + \dfrac{2}{(1+z)}$

Corresponding to $\dfrac{1}{(1-3z)}$, the numeric function is 3^r and corresponding to $\dfrac{2}{1+z}$, the numeric function is $2(-1)^r$.

Therefore, the numeric function corresponding to the generating function $A(z)$ is

$$a_r = 3^r + 2(-1)^r, \quad r \geq 0$$

Example 4: Find the numeric functions corresponding to

(i) $\dfrac{2+3z-6z^2}{(1-2z)}$ (ii) $\dfrac{z^4}{(1-2z)}$

Solution: (i) The given generating function is

$$A(z) = \dfrac{2+3z-6z^2}{1-2z}$$

$\therefore \quad A(z) = 3z + \dfrac{2}{1-2z}$

which can be written as

$A(z) = B(z) + C(z)$

where $B(z) = 3z$

and $C(z) = \dfrac{2}{1-2z}$

For B (z), the numeric function is
$$b = \{0, 3, 0, 0, 0, \ldots\}$$
and for C (z),
$$c_r = 2 \times 2^r = 2^{r+1}$$
Therefore,
$$c = \{2, 2^2, 2^3, 2^4, \ldots\}$$
Hence the numeric function corresponding to A (z) is
$$a = b + c$$
$$a = \{0, 3, 0, 0, 0, \ldots\} + \{2, 2^2, 2^3, 2^4, \ldots\}$$
Thus,
$$a = \{2, 7, 2^3, 2^4, 2^5, 2^6, \ldots\}$$

or a can be written as
$$a_r = \begin{cases} 2, & r = 0 \\ 7, & r = 1 \\ 2^{r+1}, & r \geq 2 \end{cases}$$

(ii)
$$A(z) = \frac{z^4}{1 - 2z}$$

Now,
$$\frac{z^4}{1 - 2z} = -\frac{1}{2^4} - \frac{1}{2^3}z - \frac{1}{2^2}z^2 - \frac{1}{2}z^3 + \frac{1/16}{(1 - 2z)}$$

Therefore,
$$A(z) = B(z) + C(z) + D(z) + E(z) + F(z)$$

Hence the numeric function corresponding to A (z) is

$$A(z) = \left\{-\frac{1}{2^4}, -\frac{1}{2^3}, -\frac{1}{2^2}, -\frac{1}{2}, 0, 0, 0, \ldots\right\}$$
$$+ \{2^{-4} \times 2^0, 2^{-4} \times 2^1, 2^{-4} \times 2^2, 2^{-4} \times 2^3, 2^{-4} \times 2^4, 2^{-4} \times 2^5, \ldots\}$$

Therefore,
$$a = \{0, 0, 0, 0, 2^0, 2^1, 2^2, 2^3, \ldots\}$$

which can be written as
$$a_r = \begin{cases} 0, & 0 \leq r \leq 3 \\ 2^{r-4}, & r \geq 4 \end{cases}$$

Example 5: Define convolution of numeric function. Find the numeric function for $A(z) = \frac{2}{1 - 4z^2}$.

Solution: For convolution of numeric function, see page 6.3.

To find the numeric function for A(z), consider $A(z) = \frac{2}{1 - 4z^2} = \frac{2}{(1 - 2z)(1 + 2z)}$.

Using partial fraction, we get, $A(z) = \frac{1}{1 - 2z} + \frac{1}{1 + 2z}$

Corresponding to $\frac{1}{1 - 2z}$, the numeric function is 2^r and for $\frac{1}{1 + 2z}$, the numeric function is $(-2)^r$.

Therefore, the numeric function for A(z) is
$$a_r = 2^r + (-2)^r, \quad r \geq 0$$

EXERCISE - 6.1

1. An aircraft takes off after spending 10 minutes on the ground, climbs up at a uniform speed to a cruising altitude of 30,000 feet in 10 minutes, starts to descend uniformly after 110 minutes of flying time and lands 10 minutes later. If a_r denote the altitude of an aircraft, in thousands of feet, at the rth minute, determine the expression for the numeric function a_r.

2. Determine the numeric functions c and d if
   (i) $c_r = a_r + b_r$ (ii) $d_r = a_r b_r$

   Given $a_r = \begin{cases} 0, & 0 \leq r \leq 2 \\ 2^{-r} + 5, & r \geq 3 \end{cases}$

   and $b_r = \begin{cases} 3 - 2^r, & 0 \leq r \leq 1 \\ r + 2, & r \geq 2 \end{cases}$

3. Define the convolution of two numeric functions a and b. Find the convolution of the numeric functions a and b where $a_r = 9^r$ and $b_r = 3^r$.

4. If $a_r = 1$ for all r, find $c_r = a_r * b_r$

5. Determine the generating functions for the following numeric functions.
   (i) $a = \{0, 1, 2, 3, 4, \ldots\}$ (ii) $a = \{0, 3 \times 1 \times 2^1, 3 \times 2 \times 2^2, 3 \times 3 \times 2^3, 3 \times 4 \times 2^4, \ldots\}$

6. Find the discrete numeric functions for the following generating functions.
   (i) $A(z) = \dfrac{7z^2}{(1 - 2z)(1 + 3z)}$
   (ii) $A(z) = \dfrac{1}{(5 - 6z + z^2)}$

7. Explain: (a) Discrete numeric functions, (b) Generating functions.

8. Solve by method of generating functions:
   (i) $A(z) = \dfrac{1-z}{1 - 4z + z^2}$ (ii) $A(z) = \dfrac{z}{1 - 4z + z^2}$

ANSWERS 6.1

1. $a_r = \begin{cases} 30, & r = 0 \\ 20, & r = 1 \\ 5, & 2 \leq r \leq 5 \\ 0, & r \geq 6 \end{cases}$

2. (i) $c_r = \begin{cases} 3 - 2^r, & 0 \leq r \leq 1 \\ 4, & r = 2 \\ 2^{-r} + r + 7, & r \geq 3 \end{cases}$

(ii) $d_r = \begin{cases} 0 & , 0 \leq r \leq 2 \\ r \times 2^{-r} + 2^{-r+1} + 5r + 10 & , r \geq 3 \end{cases}$

3. Convolution $c = a * b$ where $c_r = \sum_{i=0}^{r} 9^i \, 3^{r-i} = \sum_{i=0}^{r} 3^{r+i}$

4. $c_r = 5$ for all r

5. (i) $A(z) = \dfrac{z}{(1-z)^2}$ (ii) $A(z) = \dfrac{6z}{(1-2z)^2}$

6. (i) $a_r = \begin{cases} -\dfrac{7}{6} - \dfrac{7}{30}(2^r + 4(-3)^r) & , r = 0 \\ -\dfrac{7}{30}(2^r + 4(-3)^r) & , r \geq 1 \end{cases}$

(ii) $a_r = \dfrac{1}{4} - \dfrac{1}{20}\left(\dfrac{1}{5}\right)^r \,, r \geq 0$

6.3 Recurrence Relations

In the previous sections, we have discussed about discrete numeric functions (sequences) and generating functions. In many discrete computation problems, it is easier to obtain the numeric function in the form of a relation between its terms. The recursive formula for defining the numeric function (or sequence) is called a **recurrence relation**.

If $a = \{a_0, a_1, a_2, ..., a_r, ...\}$ is a numeric function, then the recurrence relation for a is an equation relating a_r, for any r, to one or more a_i's (i < r). In other words, a recurrence relation on the numeric function 'a' is a formula that relates all the terms of 'a' to previous terms of 'a'. A recurrence relation is also called **difference equation**. To define the numeric function completely using the recurrence relation, the values of the numeric function at one or more points are required to initiate the computation. These given values of the function are called initial conditions. For example, consider the recurrence relation

$a_r = a_{r-1} + 3 \quad , \quad r \geq 1$ with $a_0 = 2$

Here
$a_1 = a_0 + 3 = 2 + 3 = 5$
$a_2 = a_1 + 3 = 5 + 3 = 8$
$a_3 = a_2 + 3 = 8 + 3 = 11$
$\vdots$

Thus the given recurrence relation recursively defines the numeric function

$a = \{2, 5, 8, 11, ...\}$

The condition $a_0 = 2$ is the initial condition.

Another example is "Fibonacci sequence of numbers". It is defined by the recurrence relation
$$a_r = a_{r-2} + a_{r-1}, \quad r \geq 2$$
with the initial conditions
$$a_0 = 1 \quad \text{and} \quad a_1 = 1$$
Here
$$a_2 = a_0 + a_1 = 2$$
$$a_3 = a_1 + a_2 = 3$$
$$a_4 = a_2 + a_3 = 5$$

Thus, the Fibonacci sequence is given by 1, 1, 2, 3, 5, 8, 13, ...

It is clear from above examples that according to the recurrence relation, we can carry out a step-by-step computation to determine a_r from a_{r-1}, a_{r-2}, ... for any r using given initial conditions. Thus the numeric function which is computed using recurrence relation is known as the **solution of the recurrence relation**.

6.3.1 Linear Recurrence Relations with Constant Coefficients

Most of the recurrence relations we come across are linear recurrence relations. Now, we define the linear recurrence relation with constant coefficients.

Suppose r and k are non-negative integers. A recurrence relation of the form

$$c_0 a_r + c_1 a_{r-1} + c_2 a_{r-2} + \ldots + c_k a_{r-k} = f(r) \text{ for } r \geq k \qquad \ldots (6.1)$$

where $c_0, c_1, c_2, \ldots, c_k$ are constant, is called a **linear recurrence relation with constant coefficient of order** k, provided c_0 and c_k are non-zero.

The relation $a_r - 2a_{r-1} = 2r$ is a first order linear recurrence relation with constant coefficients.

Similarly, $a_r + 2a_{r-3} = r^2$ is a third order linear recurrence relation.

But the relation $a_r^2 + a_{r-1} = 5$ is not a linear recurrence relation.

To solve the kth order linear recurrence relation with constant coefficients, we require k initial conditions to determine the numeric function uniquely. With fewer than k initial conditions, the numeric function computed is not unique.

Consider the second order linear relation $a_r + a_{r-1} + a_{r-2} = 4$ with only one initial condition $a_0 = 2$. The numeric functions which satisfy the given recurrence relation and initial condition are: (i) 2, 0, 2, 2, 0, 2, 2, 0, 2, 2, 0, ...

(ii) 2, 2, 0, 2, 2, 0, 2, 2, 0, 2, 2, ...

(iii) 2, 5, –3, 2, 5, –3, 2, 5, –3, ...

Thus, the numeric function described by the second order recurrence relation with only one initial condition is not unique.

6.3.2 Homogeneous Solutions

Each linear recurrence relation is associated with its homogeneous equation and the solution of homogeneous equation is called homogeneous solution of the given recurrence relation. Consider a kth order linear recurrence relation with constant coefficients.

$$c_0 a_r + c_1 a_{r-1} + c_2 a_{r-2} + \ldots + c_k a_{r-k} = f(r)$$

Homogeneous recurrence relation of the above recurrence relation is given by

$$c_0 a_r + c_1 a_{r-1} + c_2 a_{r-2} + \ldots + c_k a_{r-k} = 0$$

This means that for any linear recurrence relation, if $f(r) = 0$ (right hand side term zero), then the given equation is homogeneous recurrence relation.

For example, if the given recurrence relation is

$$a_r - 6a_{r-1} + 11a_{r-2} + 6a_{r-3} = 2r$$

then, its homogeneous recurrence equation is

$$a_r - 6a_{r-1} + 11a_{r-2} + 6a_{r-3} = 0$$

Now we describe the method to find the solution of homogeneous recurrence relation. For this, we first define the term **characteristic equation.**

The characteristic equation of the homogeneous k^{th} order linear recurrence relation

$$c_0 a_r + c_1 a_{r-1} + c_2 a_{r-2} + \ldots + c_k a_{r-k} = 0 \qquad \ldots (6.2)$$

is the kth degree polynomial equation

$$c_0 \alpha^k + c_1 \alpha^{k-1} + \ldots + c_k = 0 \qquad \ldots (6.3)$$

The above polynomial equation (6.3) in α is of degree k. Therefore, it has k roots, called **characteristic roots**. Suppose $\alpha_1, \alpha_2, \ldots \alpha_k$ are the roots of characteristic equation (6.3). If all the roots are distinct, then the solution of the homogeneous recurrence relation (6.2) is given by

$$a_r = A_1 \alpha_1^r + A_2 \alpha_2^r + \ldots + A_k \alpha_k^r$$

where, $A_1, A_2, \ldots A_k$ are constants which are to be determined by initial conditions.

If any characteristic root is repeated, say α_1, is repeated m times, then the term $A_1 \alpha_1^r$ is replaced by $\left(A_1 r^{m-1} + A_2 r^{m-2} + \ldots + A_{m-1} r + A_m\right) \alpha_1^r$

where the constants A_i's are to be calculated using initial conditions.

To understand the above procedure, consider the following examples.

Example 1: $a_r - 10a_{r-1} + 9a_{r-2} = 0$ with $a_0 = 3$ and $a_1 = 11$.

The characteristic equation is

$$\alpha^2 - 10\alpha + 9 = 0$$

$\Rightarrow \qquad (\alpha - 1)(\alpha - 9) = 0$

or $\qquad \alpha = 1, 9$

which are the characteristic roots of the equation.

Therefore, the solution of the given recurrence relation is
$$a_r = A_1 \, 1^r + A_2 \, 9^r \qquad \ldots (6.4)$$
where A_1, A_2 are constants.
To find A_1 and A_2, putting $r = 0$, we get
$$a_0 = A_1 + A_2$$
$$\Rightarrow \quad 3 = A_1 + A_2$$
Also putting $r = 1$ in equation (6.4), we get,
$$a_1 = A_1 + 9A_2$$
$$\Rightarrow \quad 11 = A_1 + 9A_2$$
On solving, we get, $A_1 = 2$ and $A_2 = 1$
Hence the homogeneous solution of the given recurrence relation is
$$a_r = 2(1)^r + (9)^r$$
or
$$a_r = 2 + 9^r$$

Example 2: Consider $a_r - 8a_{r-1} + 16a_{r-2} = 0$ where $a_2 = 16$ and $a_3 = 8$.
The characteristic equation is
$$\alpha^2 - 8\alpha + 16 = 0$$
$$\Rightarrow \quad (\alpha - 4)^2 = 0$$
$$\Rightarrow \quad \alpha = 4, 4$$
which is repeated twice.
Therefore the solution is
$$a_r = (A_1 r + A_2) \, 4^r$$
Now, given $a_2 = 16$ and $a_3 = 80$. So by putting $r = 2$ and $r = 3$ we get,
$$(2A_1 + A_2) \, 4^2 = 16$$
and
$$(3A_1 + A_2) \, 4^3 = 80$$
$$\Rightarrow \quad A_1 = \frac{1}{4}, \quad A_2 = \frac{1}{2}$$
Hence
$$a_r = \left(\frac{1}{4} r + \frac{1}{2}\right) 4^r$$
or
$$a_r = (r + 2) \, 4^{r-1}$$

Example 3: Solve the recurrence relations:
(i) $a_n = 2a_{n-1} - a_{n-2}$ with initial conditions $a_1 = 1.5$ and $a_2 = 3$.
(ii) $a_n = -3a_{n-1} - 2a_{n-2}$ with initial conditions $a_1 = -2, a_2 = 4$.

Solution: (i) $a_n = 2a_{n-1} - a_{n-2}$ with $a_1 = 1.5, a_2 = 3$. The characteristics equation is
$$\alpha^2 - 2\alpha + 1 = 0$$
$$\Rightarrow \quad (\alpha - 1)^2 = 0$$
$$\Rightarrow \quad \alpha = 1, 1 \text{ which is repeated twice}$$

Hence the solution is $a_r = (A_1 r + A_2) 1^r$
Given $a_1 = 1.5$ and $a_2 = 3$, so substitute $r = 1$ and $r = 2$, we get
$$(A_1 + A_2) 1 = 1.5$$
$$(2A_1 + A_2) 1^2 = 3$$
$\Rightarrow \quad A_1 = 1.5, \; A_2 = 0$
Hence, $a_r = (1.5\, r)$

(ii) $a_n = -3a_{n-1} - 2a_{n-2}$ with $a_1 = -2, a_2 = 4$.

The characteristic equation is
$$\alpha^2 + 3\alpha + 2 = 0$$
$$(\alpha + 1)(\alpha + 2) = 0$$
$\Rightarrow \quad \alpha = -1, -2$

The solution is $a_r = A_1 (-1)^r + A_2 (-2)^r$
Given: $a_1 = -2, a_2 = 4$ so substitute $r = 1, r = 2$.
So, $\quad -A_1 - 2A_2 = 2$
$\quad A_1 + 4A_2 = 4$
$\Rightarrow \quad A_1 = 0, \; A_2 = 1$
Hence, $a_r = (-2)^r$

6.3.3 Total Solutions

In the previous section, we have seen the method to find the homogeneous solution of the given homogeneous recurrence relation. A homogeneous recurrence relation is obtained by putting $f(r) = 0$ (Right hand side zero) in the given k^{th} order linear recurrence relation. The solution which satisfies the linear recurrence relation with $f(r)$ on right hand side is called the **particular solution.** There is no general procedure for determining the particular solution. It depends on the nature of $f(r)$. The homogeneous solution of the linear recurrence relation is denoted by $a_r^{(h)}$ and the particular solution is denoted by $a_r^{(p)}$. The addition of these two solutions is called a total solution of a given linear recurrence relation with the constant coefficients. Thus, the total solution a_r is given by

$$a_r = a_r^{(h)} + a_r^{(p)}$$

The homogeneous solution $a_r^{(h)}$ is found out by finding characteristic roots of the characteristic equation of corresponding homogeneous recurrence relation. However, there is no general procedure for determining the particular solution of the given recurrence relation. In some cases, the particular solution can be obtained by the method of inspection of $f(r)$.

For different functions $f(r)$ (right hand side of the recurrence relation), there are different forms of particular solutions. These forms are given in the following table 6.2.

Table 6.2: Particular Solutions for given Right Hand Sides

f (r) (Right hand side)	Form of particular solution
(i) A constant, d	A constant, P
(ii) A linear function, $d_0 + d_1 r$	A linear function $P_0 + P_1 r$
(iii) An nth degree polynomial $d_0 + d_1 r \, d_2 r^2 + \ldots + d_n r^n$	An nth degree polynomial $P_0 + P_1 r + P_2 r^2 + \ldots + P_n r^n$
(iv) An exponential function db^r, provided b is not the characteristic root.	An exponential function Pb^r
(v) An exponential function db^r where b is the characteristic root of the equation with multiplicity (m – 1).	An exponential function $Pr^{m-1} b^r$

Now, we give algorithm for solving non-homogeneous linear recurrence relation

$$c_0 a_r + c_1 a_{r-1} + c_2 a_{r-2} + \ldots + c_k a_{r-k} = f(r)$$

Algorithm:

(1) Write the associated homogeneous relation by putting f (r) = 0 and find the homogeneous solution $a_r^{(h)}$.

(2) According to the function f (r) (right hand side) given in the recurrence relation, choose the form of a particular solution with unknown coefficients which is most suited to the given recurrence relation.

(3) Substitute the form of a particular solution selected in the step 2 into the given recurrence relation. From the substitution, determine the unknown coefficients involved in the selected form of particular solution.

If all the known coefficients are evaluated then go to next step 4, otherwise go to back to the step 2 for choosing the form of a particular solution.

(4) Write the particular solution $a_r^{(p)}$ with the values evaluated in the step 3.

(5) Write the general solution of the given recurrence relation as the sum of homogeneous and particular solutions.

$$a_r = a_r^{(h)} + a_r^{(p)}$$

(6) If no initial conditions are given, then stop. Otherwise, for given k initial conditions, obtain k linear equations in k unknowns and solve the system to get a complete solution.

The above procedure can be understood by the following solved examples.

SOLVED EXAMPLES

Example 1: Solve $a_r - a_{r-1} - 6a_{r-2} = -30$ given $a_0 = 20$, $a_1 = -5$.

Solution: The corresponding homogeneous recurrence relation of the given recurrence relation is given by
$$a_r - a_{r-1} - 6a_{r-2} = 0$$
The characteristic equation is
$$\alpha^2 - \alpha - 6 = 0$$
$$\Rightarrow \quad \alpha = -2, 3$$
Therefore, the homogeneous solution of the given recurrence relation is
$$a_r^{(h)} = A_1(-2)^r + A_2(3)^r$$
To find the particular solution, we consider the term $f(r)$ (right hand side of the given equation). Since $f(r)$ is a constant, the particular solution will also be a constant P.

i.e. $a_r = P$ for all r.
$$\Rightarrow \quad a_{r-1} = a_{r-2} = P \text{ (constant)}$$
Substituting the values of a_r, a_{r-1}, and a_{r-2} in the given recurrence relation, we get,
$$P - P - 6P = -30$$
$$\therefore \quad P = 5$$
Hence, the particular solution is
$$a_r^{(p)} = 5$$
Thus the total solution or the general solution of the given recurrence relation is
$$a_r = a_r^{(h)} + a_r^{(p)}$$
$$\Rightarrow \quad a_r = A_1(-2)^r + A_2(3)^r + 5$$
To determine A_1 and A_2, we use the initial conditions. Putting $r = 0$ in the above equation we get,
$$a_0 = A_1 + A_2 + 5$$
Given, $a_0 = 20$
$$\Rightarrow \quad A_1 + A_2 = 15$$
Also using $a_1 = -5$, we get,
$$-2A_1 + 3A_2 = -10$$
which on solution gives $A_1 = 11$, $A_2 = 4$.
Hence the complete solution is
$$a_r = 11(-2)^r + 4(3)^r + 5$$

Example 2: Solve $a_r - 7a_{r-1} + 10a_{r-2} = 6 + 8r$ with $a_0 = 1$, $a_1 = 2$.

Solution: The corresponding homogeneous equation is
$$a_r - 7a_{r-1} + 10a_{r-2} = 0$$

Thus the characteristic equation is
$$\alpha^2 - 7\alpha + 10 = 0$$
$$\Rightarrow \alpha = 2, 5$$

The homogeneous solution is $a_r^{(h)} = A_1 \, 2^r + A_2 \, 5^r$

For particular solution, since f (r) (right hand side) is a linear polynomial, therefore, the particular solution will be of the form $(P_0 + P_1 r)$.

i.e.
$$a_r = P_0 + P_1 r$$
$$a_{r-1} = P_0 + P_1 (r - 1)$$
$$a_{r-2} = P_0 + P_1 (r - 2)$$

Substituting these values in the given recurrence relation, we get,
$$(P_0 + P_1 r) - 7\{P_0 + P_1 (r - 1)\} + 10\{P_0 + P_1 (r - 2)\} = 6 + 8r$$
$$\Rightarrow (4P_0 - 13P_1) + (4P_1) r = 6 + 8r$$

On comparing the coefficients of polynomials, we get,
$$4P_0 - 13P_1 = 6$$
and
$$4P_1 = 8$$
which on solving give, $P_0 = 8$ and $P_1 = 2$

Hence, the particular solution is $a_r^{(p)} = 8 + 2r$

Thus the general solution is
$$a_r = a_r^{(h)} + a_r^{(p)}$$
$$\Rightarrow a_r = A_1 \, 2^r + A_2 \, 5^r + 8 + 2r$$

Using the initial conditions $a_0 = 1$ and $a_1 = 2$, we get,
$$A_1 = -9 \text{ and } A_2 = 2$$

Therefore, $a_r = -9 \, (2)^r + 2 \, (5)^r + 8 + 2r$

Example 3: Find the general solution of $a_r + 5a_{r-1} + 6a_{r-2} = 3r^2$.

Solution: The characteristic equation of the corresponding homogeneous equation is
$$\alpha^2 + 5\alpha + 6 = 0$$
$$\Rightarrow \alpha = -2, -3$$

Thus, the homogeneous solution is
$$a_r^{(h)} = A_1 \, (-2)^r + A_2 \, (-3)^r$$

For a particular solution, since f (r) (right hand side) of the given recurrence relation is a quadratic polynomial, the form of the particular solution will be $P_0 + P_1 r + P_2 r^2$.

i.e.
$$a_r = P_0 + P_1 r + P_2 r^2$$
$$a_{r-1} = P_0 + P_1 (r - 1) + P_2 (r - 1)^2$$
$$a_{r-2} = P_0 + P_1 (r - 2) + P_2 (r - 2)^2$$

Substituting in the given recurrence relation, we get,
$$(P_0 + P_1 r + P_2 r^2) + 5\{P_0 + P_1 (r - 1) + P_2 (r - 1)^2\} + 6\{P_0 + P_1 (r - 2) + P_2 (r - 2)^2\} = 3r^2$$

Equating the coefficients of powers of r, we get,
$$12 P_2 = 3$$
$$-12 P_1 + 12 P_2 = 0$$
$$12 P_0 - 17 P_1 + 29 P_2 = 0$$

Solving, we get, $P_0 = \dfrac{115}{288}$, $P_1 = \dfrac{17}{24}$, $P_2 = \dfrac{1}{4}$

The particular solution is
$$a_r^{(p)} = \dfrac{115}{288} + \dfrac{17}{24} r + \dfrac{1}{4} r^2$$

Thus the solution is
$$a_r = A_1 (-2)^r + A_2 (-3)^r + \dfrac{115}{288} + \dfrac{17}{24} r + \dfrac{1}{4} r^2$$

Example 4: Solve: $a_r + a_{r-1} = 3r \, 2^r$

Solution: The characteristic equation is
$$\alpha + 1 = 0$$
$$\therefore \quad \alpha = -1$$

So, homogeneous solution is
$$a_r^{(h)} = A_1 (-1)^r$$

Here, the form of the particular solution is $(P_0 + P_1 r) 2^r$

Substituting in the given recurrence relation, we get,
$$(P_0 + P_1 r) 2^r + \{P_0 + P_1 (r-1)\} 2^{r-1} = 3r \, 2^r$$

which simplifies to
$$\dfrac{3}{2} P_1 r \, 2^r + \left(-\dfrac{1}{2} P_1 + \dfrac{3}{2} P_0\right) 2^r = 3r \, 2^r$$

Comparing the two sides, we obtain the equations
$$\dfrac{3}{2} P_1 = 3$$

and
$$-\dfrac{1}{2} P_1 + \dfrac{3}{2} P_0 = 0$$

Thus, $P_0 = \dfrac{2}{3}$, $P_1 = 2$

The particular solution is $a_r^{(p)} = \left(\dfrac{2}{3} + 2r\right) 2^r$

Hence the general solution is $a_r = A_1 (-1)^r + \left(\dfrac{2}{3} + 2r\right) 2^r$

Example 5: Find the general solution of

$$a_r - 3a_{r-1} - 4a_{r-2} = 4^r$$

Solution: The characteristic equation is

$$\alpha^2 - 3\alpha - 4 = 0$$

$$\Rightarrow \alpha = -1, 4$$

The homogeneous solution is

$$a_r^{(h)} = A_1 (-1)^r + A_2 \, 4^r$$

Now, consider the form of particular solution. Here $f(r)$ is 4^r, but the form of particular solution is not $P4^r$ because 4 is the characteristic root also. Since the characteristic root 4 is repeated only once, the form of the particular solution is $Pr4^r$.

Substitute $a_r = Pr4^r$ in the given recurrence relation, we get,

$$Pr4^r - 3P(r-1)4^{r-1} - 4P(r-2)4^{r-2} = 4^r$$

$$\Rightarrow Pr4^r - \frac{3}{4} P(r-1) 4^r - \frac{4}{4^2} P(r-2) 4^r = 4^r$$

Compare the coefficients of 4^r,

$$\frac{3P}{4} + \frac{2P}{4} = 1$$

$$\therefore P = \frac{4}{5} = 0.8$$

Therefore, $a_r^{(p)} = 0.8 \, r \, 4^r$

and the general solution is $a_r = A_1 (-1)^r + A_2 \, 4^r + 0.8 \, r \, 4^r$

Example 6: Solve: $a_r - 4a_{r-1} + 4a_{r-2} = (r+1) 2^r$

Solution: The characteristic equation is

$$\alpha^2 - 4\alpha + 4 = 0$$

$$\Rightarrow (\alpha - 2)^2 = 2$$

$$\Rightarrow \alpha = 2, 2$$

So the homogeneous solution is

$$a_r^{(h)} = (A_1 + A_2 \, r) 2^r$$

For particular solution, $f(r)$ is of the form $(r+1) 2^r$ and 2 is the characteristic root with multiplicity 2, therefore, the particular solution will be of the form $(P_0 + P_1 r) r^2 2^r$.

Substitute $a_r = (P_0 + P_1 r) r^2 2^r$

into the given recurrence relation we get,

$$(P_0 + P_1 r) r^2 2^r - 4 \left[\{P_0 + P_1 (r-1)\} (r-1)^2 2^{r-1} \right] + 4 \left[\{P_0 + P_1 (r-2)\} (r-2)^2 2^{r-2} \right] = (r+1) 2^r$$

On simplification, we get,

$$6P_1 r \cdot 2^r = r \cdot 2^r$$

and $\quad (-6P_1 + 2P_0) 2^r = 2^r$

which gives $\quad P_1 = \dfrac{1}{6}, \; P_0 = 1$

Hence, the particular solution is

$$a_r^{(p)} = \left(1 + \dfrac{1}{6}r\right) r^2 \, 2^r$$

Thus the complete solution is $\; a_r = (A_1 + A_2 r) 2^r + \left(1 + \dfrac{1}{6}r\right) r^2 \, 2^r$

Example 7: Solve $a_n = 2a_{n-1} + 3a_{n-2} + 5^n, n \geq 2$ with $a_0 = -2, a_1 = 1$.

Solution: The characteristic equation is

$$\alpha^2 - 2\alpha - 3 = 0$$

$\Rightarrow \quad (\alpha - 3)(\alpha + 1) = 0$

or $\quad \alpha = 3, -1$

So, the homogeneous solution is

$$a_n^{(h)} = A_1 \, 3^n + A_2 (-1)^n$$

For particular solution, $f(n)$ is of the form 5^n.

Therefore, the form of the particular solution is $P5^n$.

Substituting in the given recurrence relation, we get

$$P5^n - 2P5^{n-1} - 3P \, 5^{n-2} = 5^n$$

$\Rightarrow \quad P - \dfrac{2P}{5} - \dfrac{3P}{25} = 1 \; \Rightarrow \; P = \dfrac{25}{12}$

∴ The particular solution is

$$a_n^{(P)} = \dfrac{25}{12} 5^n$$

∴ The complete solution is

$$a_n = A_1 \, 3^n + A_2 (-1)^n + \dfrac{25}{12} 5^n$$

Using the initial conditions $a_0 = -2, a_1 = 1$, we get

$$A_1 = \dfrac{-27}{8}, \; A_2 = \dfrac{-17}{24}$$

∴ $\quad a_n = \dfrac{-27}{8} (3)^n - \dfrac{17}{24} (-1)^n + \dfrac{25}{12} (5)^n$

Example 8: Solve: $a_n + 6a_{n-1} + 12a_{n-2} + 8a_{n-3} = 2^n$ with $n \geq 3, a_0 = 0, a_1 = 0, a_2 = 2$.

Solution: The characteristic equation is

$$\alpha^3 + 6\alpha^2 + 12\alpha + 8 = 0$$

$\Rightarrow \quad (\alpha + 2)^3 = 0$

$\therefore \qquad \alpha = -2, -2, -2$

where $\alpha = -2$ is the root with multiplicity 3.

Hence, the homogeneous solution is

$$a_n^{(h)} = (A_1 n^2 + A_2 n + A_3)(-2)^n$$

The particular solution will be of the form $P(2^n)$.

Substituting in the given recurrence relation, we get

$$P2^n + 6P \, 2^{n-1} + 12P \, 2^{n-2} + 8P \, 2^{n-3} = 2^n$$

$$\Rightarrow P + 3P + 3P + P = 1 \Rightarrow P = \frac{1}{8}$$

$\therefore \qquad a_n^{(P)} = \frac{1}{8}(2^n) = 2^{n-3}$

Total solution is $\qquad a_n = (A_1 n^2 + A_2 n + A_3)(-2)^n + 2^{n-3}$

Using the initial conditions $a_0 = 0$, $a_1 = 0$ and $a_2 = 2$, we get,

$$A_1 = 0, \quad A_2 = \frac{1}{4}, \quad A_3 = -\frac{1}{8}.$$

$\therefore \qquad a_n = \left(\frac{1}{4}n - \frac{1}{8}\right)(-2)^n + 2^{n-3}$

Example 9: Solve: $a_r - 5a_{r-1} + 6a_{r-2} = 2^r + r$, $r \geq 2$ with $a_0 = 1$, $a_1 = 1$.

Solution: Characteristic equation is

$$\alpha^2 - 5\alpha + 6 = 0 \Rightarrow (\alpha - 2)(\alpha - 3) = 0$$

$\therefore \quad \alpha = 2, 3$ are characteristic roots.

$\therefore \quad$ Homogeneous solution is $a_r^{(h)} = A_1 2^r + A_2 3^r$.

The particular solution will be of the form $P_1 r \, 2^r + (P_2 + P_3 r)$. (Here R.H.S. of given equation is $2^r + r$ and 2 is the characteristic root also.) Substituting in given equation

$$(P_1 r \, 2^r + P_2 + P_3 r) - 5(P_1(r-1) 2^{r-1} + P_2 + P_3(r-1))$$

$$+ 6(P_1(r-2) 2^{r-2} + P_2 + P_3(r-2)) = 2^r + r$$

$$\therefore \ 2^r \left[P_1 r - \frac{5}{2} P_1 (r-1) + \frac{3}{2} P_1 (r-2)\right] + 2P_2 + 2P_3 r - 7P_3 = 2^r + r$$

$$\Rightarrow 2^r \left[-\frac{1}{2} P_1\right] + r(2P_3) + (2P_2 - 7P_3) = 2^r + r$$

On comparing the coefficients, we get

$$-\frac{P_1}{2} = 1, \quad 2P_3 = 1, \quad 2P_2 - 7P_3 = 0$$

$\Rightarrow \quad P_1 = -2, \quad P_3 = \dfrac{1}{2}, \quad P_2 = \dfrac{7}{4}$

$\therefore \quad a_r^{(P)} = -2r\, 2^r + \dfrac{1}{2} + \dfrac{7}{4} r$

Total solution is $\quad a_r = a_r^{(h)} + a_r^{(P)}$

$\Rightarrow \quad a_r = A_1 2^r + A_2 3^r - 2r\, 2^r + \dfrac{1}{2} + \dfrac{7}{4} r$

Using boundary conditions $a_0 = 1$, $a_1 = 1$, we get

$$A_1 = -\dfrac{5}{4}, \quad A_2 = \dfrac{7}{4}$$

$\therefore \quad a_r = -\dfrac{5}{4} 2^r + \dfrac{7}{4} 3^r - 2r\, 2^r + \dfrac{1}{2} + \dfrac{7}{4} r$

$\quad a_r = 2^r\left(-\dfrac{5}{4} - 2r\right) + \dfrac{7}{4}(3^r + r) + \dfrac{1}{2}$

6.3.4 Solution of Recurrence Relation by the Method of Generating Functions

Recurrence relations can also be solved by using the generating functions. For this, we directly determine the generating function of the numeric function from the given recurrence relation. Once the generating function is determined, an expression for the value of the numeric function can easily be obtained. Closed form expression for some generating functions and their numeric functions (sequences) are given in the following table 6.3.

Table 6.3: Numeric Functions for the Closed Form Expression of Generating Functions

Generating Functions	Numeric Functions
$A(z) = \dfrac{1}{1-az}$	A^r
$A(z) = \dfrac{1}{(1-z)^2}$	$(r+1)$
$A(z) = \dfrac{1}{(1-az)^2}$	$(r+1)a^r$
$A(z) = \dfrac{z}{(1-z)^2}$	R
$A(z) = \dfrac{az}{(1-az)^2}$	ra^r
$A(z) = e^z$	$\dfrac{1}{n!}$
$A(z) = (1+z)^n$	$\begin{cases} {}^nC_r, & 0 \le r \le n \\ 0, & r > n \end{cases}$

SOLVED EXAMPLES

Example 1 : Solve $a_r - 3a_{r-1} = 2$, $r \geq 1$ with $a_0 = 1$ using the generating functions.

Solution: Given recurrence relation is
$$a_r - 3a_{r-1} = 2$$
Multiplying both sides by z^r, we obtain
$$a_r z^r - 3a_{r-1} z^r = 2z^r$$
Since $r \geq 1$, summing for all r, we get,
$$\sum_{r=1}^{\infty} a_r z^r - 3 \sum_{r=1}^{\infty} a_{r-1} z^r = 2 \sum_{r=1}^{\infty} z^r$$

Consider the first term,
$$\sum_{r=1}^{\infty} a_r z^r = a_1 z + a_2 z^2 + a_3 z^3 + \ldots$$

Since the generating function
$$A(z) = a_0 + a_1 z + a_2 z^2 + a_3 z^3 + \ldots$$

$\Rightarrow$
$$\sum_{r=1}^{\infty} a_r z^r = A(z) - a_0$$

For second term,
$$\sum_{r=1}^{\infty} a_{r-1} z^r = z \sum_{r=1}^{\infty} a_{r-1} z^{r-1}$$
$$= z A(z)$$

Also the third term gives
$$\sum_{r=1}^{\infty} z^r = \frac{z}{(1-z)}$$

Hence we obtain
$$[A(z) - a_0] - 3z A(z) = \frac{2z}{1-z} \quad \text{or} \quad (1-3z) A(z) = \frac{2z}{1-z} + a_0$$

But, $a_0 = 1$

$\Rightarrow \qquad (1-3z) A(z) = \dfrac{2z}{1-z} + 1$

$\Rightarrow \qquad (1-3z) A(z) = \dfrac{1+z}{1-z}$

or $\qquad A(z) = \dfrac{1+z}{(1-z)(1-3z)} = \dfrac{2}{(1-3z)} - \dfrac{1}{(1-z)}$

Consequently we have, $\qquad a_r = 2(3)^r - (1)^r$, $r \geq 0$
which is the solution of the given recurrence relation.

Example 2: Solve $a_r - 2a_{r-1} - 3a_{r-2} = 0$, $r \geq 2$ with $a_0 = 3$, $a_1 = 1$ using generating functions.

Solution: Multiply both the sides of the given recurrence relation by z^r, we get,

$$a_r z^r - 2a_{r-1} z^r - 3a_{r-2} z^r = 0$$

Since $r \geq 2$, summing for all r, we have,

$$\sum_{r=2}^{\infty} a_r z^r - 2 \sum_{r=2}^{\infty} a_{r-1} z^r - 3 \sum_{r=2}^{\infty} a_{r-2} z^r = 0 \quad \ldots (1)$$

Now,
$$\sum_{r=2}^{\infty} a_r z^r = A(z) - a_0 - a_1 z$$

$$\sum_{r=2}^{\infty} a_{r-1} z^r = z \sum_{r=2}^{\infty} a_{r-1} z^{r-1}$$
$$= z [A(z) - a_0]$$

and
$$\sum_{r=2}^{\infty} a_{r-2} z^r = z^2 \sum_{r=2}^{\infty} a_{r-2} z^{r-2}$$
$$= z^2 A(z)$$

Substituting these values in (1), we get,

$$[A(z) - a_0 - a_1 z] - 2\{z [A(z) - a_0]\} - 3z^2 A(z) = 0$$

Given $a_0 = 3$, $a_1 = 1$

$$\Rightarrow \quad A(z)(1 - 2z - 3z^2) = 3 - 5z$$

$$\Rightarrow \quad A(z) = \frac{3-5z}{(1-2z-3z^2)} = \frac{3-5z}{(1-3z)(1+z)}$$

Using partial fractions, we get, $A(z) = \dfrac{1}{(1-3z)} + \dfrac{2}{(1+z)}$

Hence, $a_r = 3^r + 2(-1)^r$

EXERCISE - 6.2

1. Solve the following recurrence relations:
   (i) $a_r - 9a_{r-1} + 18a_{r-2} = 0$ with $a_0 = 1$, $a_1 = 4$
   (ii) $a_r - 2a_{r-1} + a_{r-2} = 2$ with $a_0 = 25$, $a_1 = 16$
   (iii) $S(k) - 4S(k-1) + 4S(k-2) = 3k + 2^k$ with $S(0) = 1$, $S(1) = 1$.
   (iv) $S(k) - 4S(k-1) - 11S(k-2) + 30S(k-3) = 0$
   with $S(0) = 0$, $S(1) = -35$, $S(2) = -85$

2. Find a closed form of the expression for the terms of the Fibonacci sequence.
   (**Hint:** Fibonacci sequence is given by 1, 1, 2, 3, 5, 8, 13, ...)

3. Solve the following difference equations using generating functions.

(i) $S(k) + 3S(k-1) - 4S(k-2) = 0$, $k \geq 2$ with $S(0) = 3$, $S(1) = -2$.

(ii) $G(k) - 7G(k-1) + 10G(k-2) = 0$, $k \geq 2$ with $G(0) = 1$, $G(1) = 3$.

4. Solve the recurrence relation:

(i) $a_n = 2a_{n-1} + 3a_{n-2} + 5^n$, $n \geq 2$
with $a_0 = -2$, $a_1 = 1$.

(ii) $a_n + 6a_{n-1} + 12a_{n-2} + 8a_{n-3} = 2^n$, $n \geq 3$ with $a_0 = 0$, $a_1 = 0$, $a_2 = 2$.

ANSWERS - 6.2

1. (i) $a_r = \frac{2}{3}(3)^r + \left(\frac{1}{3}\right)6^r$

   (ii) $a_r = r^2 - 10r + 25$

   (iii) $S(k) = 12 + 3k + (k^2 + 7k + 22)2^{k-1}$

   (iv) $S(k) = 4(-3)^k + 2^k - 5^{k+1}$

2. $a_r = \left(\frac{1}{\sqrt{5}}\right)\left(\frac{1+\sqrt{5}}{2}\right)^r + \left(\frac{-1+\sqrt{5}}{\sqrt{5}}\right)\left(\frac{1-\sqrt{5}}{2}\right)^r$

3. (i) $S(k) = 2 + (-4)^k$

   (ii) $G(k) = \frac{3}{2}(2^k) + 3(5^k)$

POINTS TO REMEMBER
• A function, whose domain is a set of natural numbers (including zero) and whose range is set of real numbers, is called a **discrete numeric function**, or briefly a **numeric function**.
• Let a and b be two numeric functions. Then the sum of two numeric functions a and b is a numeric function c whose value at r is equal to the sum of the values of two numeric functions a and b at r. The sum of two functions is denoted by $c = a + b$, where, $c_r = a_r + b_r$ for given r.
• The product of two numeric functions a and b is a numeric function d whose value at r is equal to the product of the values of two numeric functions at r. The product is denoted by $d = ab$, where $d_r = a_r b_r$ for any given r.
• The recursive formula for defining the numeric function (or sequence) is called a **recurrence relation**.
• Suppose r and k are non-negative integers. A recurrence relation of the form $c_0 a_r + c_1 a_{r-1} + c_2 a_{r-2} + \ldots + c_k a_{r-k} = f(r)$ for $r \geq k$ ... (6.1) where $c_0, c_1, c_2, \ldots, c_k$ are constant, is called a **linear recurrence relation with constant coefficient of order** k, provided c_0 and c_k are non-zero.

Chapter 7: ANALYSIS OF ALGORITHMS

SYLLABUS:
- Analysis of algorithms : Introduction, Largest number algorithm, Sorting algorithms : Bubble sort, Divide and Conquer algorithms : Binary search algorithm, Strassens matrix multiplication, Time complexity of algorithms, complexity of problems, Tractable and Intractable problems.

OBJECTIVES:
- To understand the basic concepts in designing the algorithms.
- To learn the complexity of problems.

UTILITY:
- In sorting the data using bubble sort and binary search technique.

KEY CONCEPTS:
- Pseudocode.
- Design techniques.
- Time complexity.
- Tractable and Interactable problems.

7.0 Introduction

Algorithm plays an important role in both science and computing.

The word algorithm, named for the ninth century Persian mathematician al-Khowarizmi, refers to a set of rules for carrying out calculations manually or on a machine. Thus, algorithms can be considered as the procedural solutions to the problems.

In computer science, problems like sorting, searching, string processing, graph colouring, numerical computations and many more have attracted the attention from researchers and scientists. Various algorithms are developed to solve these problems which are of practical importance.

For a specific problem, we can design an algorithm in many ways. The effectiveness of an algorithm depends upon various factors like time complexity and space complexity, which are essential to study in analysis of algorithms. Also, the complexity of the problem which leads to algorithms optimality is an important factor for designing the algorithm.

In this chapter, we will study some of the algorithms like Bubble sort, binary search algorithm and strassens matrix multiplication.

The time complexity and tractable and intractable problems will also be discussed here.

7.1 Algorithm

An algorithm is a well-defined sequence of instructions to solve a given problem. It is a procedural solutions to the problems. i.e. these are specific instructions for getting answers.

For example, consider the problem of finding the greatest common divisor of two positive integers m, n denoted by gcd (m, n), the simplest algorithm is

(i) Find prime factors of m.

(ii) Find prime factors of n.

(ii) Identify all common factors in two prime expansions found in steps (i) and (ii).

If p is a common factor occurring p_i times in expansion of m and p_j times in expansion of n then it should be repeated min (p_i, p_j) times.

(iv) Compute the product of all the common factors and return it as the greatest common divisor of given numbers.

If m = 80 and n = 120, then prime factorization of m and n are

$$m = 2^4 \times 5$$
$$n = 2^3 \times 3 \times 5$$

Hence gcd (80, 120) = $2^3 \times 5$ = 40

However, much more efficient algorithm for calculating greatest common divisors exists, called **Euclid's algorithm** (third century B.C.) which is based on applying repeatedly

$$gcd (m, n) = gcd (n, m \bmod n)$$

until m mod n becomes zero.

Here m mod n is the remainder 'r' when m is divided by n.

The steps involve in Euclid's algorithm are :

(i) If n = 0, then return the value of m as greatest common divisor of given members and stop, otherwise go to step (ii).

(ii) Divide m by n and assign the value of the remainder to r.

(iii) Assign the value of n to m and the value of r to n.

(iv) Go to step (i).

In above example,

$$gcd (120, 80) = gcd (80, 40)$$
$$= gcd (40, 0)$$
$$= 40$$

In above example, for finding the greatest common divisor of 80 and 120, input numbers are 80 and 120 and output is 40. Also the algorithm stops in finite number of steps as the second number in the pair gets smaller with each iteration and it cannot become negative. For next iteration, the new value of n is m mod n (remainder) which is always smaller than n. When second number in pair becomes 0, algorithm stops.

From the above example it is clear that an algorithm has input, output and it terminates after some finite number of steps. Also each instruction should be clear and the operation must be feasible. This shows that, all algorithms must satisfy the following criteria :

(i) **Input :** The quantities supplied externally (zero or more).
(ii) **Output :** Quantities produced (atleast one).
(iii) **Definiteness :** Every instruction should be clear and unambiguous.
(iv) **Finiteness :** In all cases, the algorithm must terminate after finite number of steps.
(v) **Effectiveness :** Each operation must be feasible.

An input to an algorithm specifies an **instance** of the problem which an algorithm is solving. It is important to specify the range of instances. It may happen that algorithm may work correctly for a majority of inputs but crash on some boundary value. A correct algorithm is that which works correctly for all legitimate inputs most of the time.

In the example, of Euclid's algorithm, beginning instance is (120, 80). After dividing 120 by 80 the another instance is (80, 40) for the same problem. Also the output of this example is 40, which is the second criterion that the algorithm produces atleast one output.

According to criteria three and five, each operation must be definite and feasible and criterion four requires the termination of algorithm in finite number of steps.

Algorithms which are definite and effective are also called computational procedure.

After defining the algorithm and specifying its criteria, we will move to the development of the algorithm which is explained in the next article.

7.2 Development of Algorithm

As we know, an algorithm consists of a well defined sequence of instructions to solve a given problem. The steps involve in complete development of an algorithm to solve a problem are given below :

- Statement of the problem.
- Developing a model.
- Designing the algorithm.
- Correctness of algorithm.
- Analyzing the complexity of the algorithm.
- Implementation of algorithm.

We will briefly discuss each of these steps involved in development of algorithm.

7.2.1 Statement of the Problem

Before designing an algorithm, it is necessary to understand the given problem completely. A proper statement of the problem should be carefully written otherwise it will result in garbage in and garbage out (GIGO) situation. The problem statement can be defined in macro terms. Then on repeated trials by superimposing the requirements of the problem, the macro statements can be refined to a problem statement.

7.2.2 Development of Model

After understanding the problem and writing its statement, the next step is to develop a model for it. As we know, a model is an abstraction of reality and it represents a reality in understandable form. The model representation may be in the form of a equation, matrix, graph, sequence of logic, objective function with set of constraints etc.

For example, to find the shortest route from a given source to destination, a road map of the city defines the model.

As an another example, to forecast the production of any unit, the objective function together with constraints gives the idea of the model.

7.2.3 Design of Algorithm

As defined earlier, an algorithm is a sequence of well defined steps for solving a problem. For many problems, algorithm design is an iterative process which continues till each step is clear with feasible operation. In some problems, main problem is subdivided into a number of meaningful subproblems, each subproblem is subdivided again to further smaller subproblems and this continuous till a well defined set of steps are obtained for the main problem. In the process of design the algorithm, the focus should be given to the objective of the problem and accordingly each and every step is to be added into the algorithm so that the entire algorithm contains a less number of steps (if possible), takes less time for its execution and requires less computer primary memory for storing the input and the intermediate results of the algorithm.

There are various design techniques that have proven to be useful and that have often yielded good algorithms. Dynamic programming, Divide and Conquer, Greedy method, Back Tracking, Branch and Bound are some of the techniques for algorithm formation and they have applications in a variety of areas. It is not true that, each of these general techniques will be necessarily applicable to every problem. Algorithm design techniques make it possible to classify algorithms according to an underlying design idea.

Once we have designed an algorithm, we need to specify it in some manner. There are many ways to do this. Word description (in step by step form), graphical representation and pseudocode presentation are most widely used for specifying the algorithms.

The word description form of algorithm using a natural language is always appealing but surprisingly it is difficult. We must make sure that the resulting instructions are definite.

Graphical representation called flow charts is another way to specify the algorithm. It is the method of expressing an algorithm by a collection of connected geometric shapes containing description of the algorithm's step. This method works well only if the algorithm is small and simple.

A **pseudocode** is a mixture of natural language and programming language that mostly resembles C or Pascal. It is usually more precise than a natural language. In writting the pseudocode, usually the declaration of scalar quantities (integer, real or Boolean) is omitted. In case where it matters like recursive functions and procedures, all variables used are implicitly understood to be local variables, unless the context make it clear otherwise. For simplification, the **begin** and **end** statements are avoided. The statements such as **if, while** or **for**, as well as that of declaration such as **procedure, function** or **record** is shown by indenting the statements affected. The statement **return** makes the dynamic end of a procedure or a function and in case of function, it also supplies the value of function. The type of parameters in **procedure** and **function** and also the result returned by function are not declared usually. Arrow ← is used for assignment operation and two slashes // are used for comments.

The pseudocode for Euclid's algorithm defined in article 7.1 is given below :

Algorithm Euclid (m, n)

// Compute gcd (m, n) using Euclid's algorithm

// Input : Two positive integers m and n

// Output : Greatest common divisor of m and n

while $n \neq 0$ **do**

    r ← m mod n

    m ← n

    n ← r

return m

7.2.4 Correctness of the Algorithm

Once an algorithm has been specified, the correctness of its steps have to be checked. Generally, the different modules of an algorithm contains many steps, branching and loops. For correctness, every module should work as per the expected results by giving a set of predetermined input.

In other words, the algorithm should yield a required result for every legitimate input in a finite amount of time.

For example, correctness of Euclid's algorithm for finding gcd of any two positive numbers stems from the correctness of the equality

$$\gcd(m, n) = \gcd(n, m \bmod n)$$

and the algorithm terminates in some finite steps. As explained in article 7.1, the second number in pair becomes smaller on every iteration and the algorithm stops when it becomes zero.

A proof of correctness is quite easy for some algorithm and it can be complex for others. For proving correctness, mathematical induction is a common technique as an algorithm's iterations provide a sequence of steps needed for the induction process.

It is worth mentioning that although tracing the algorithm's performance for a few inputs can be worthwhile activity, it cannot prove the algorithm's correctness conclusively. To show that an algorithm is incorrect, it is sufficient to show that for one instance of its input, algorithm fails. If algorithm found to be incorrect, we have to redesign it and again check its correctness. It is advisable to do calculations manually for a few iterations and comparing the intermediate results with that of known results.

7.2.5 Analysis of Algorithm

After checking the correctness of the algorithm, the most important part is its efficiency. There are two types of algorithm efficiency, time efficiency and space efficiency. **Time efficiency** means how fast an algorithm runs. **Space efficiency** is related to the memory space needed for the algorithm. This indicates that the performance of the algorithm is based on computing time and storage requirement. These are referred as **time complexity** and **space complexity** of the algorithm. These terms are discussed in detail in the next article 7.3 of this chapter.

Another required characteristic of an algorithm is **simplicity**. As we know, simpler algorithms are easier to understand and easier to program and therefore the resulting program usually contain fewer errors. Sometimes simpler algorithms are more efficient than complicated alterative algorithms but it is not always true.

7.2.6 Implementation

Once the algorithm's performance is analyzed on the basis of time and space complexity, it has to be converted into set of codes (program) which can be executed on a computer. The computer program should be written in a particular computer language in which the algorithm is to be implemented. The decision of choosing a programming language is important as it has a great impact on program productivity. Sometimes, the transition from an algorithm to a program may be done incorrectly or inefficiently. Therefore, the validity of program must be established by testing. Testing and debugging of the program should be done thoroughly while implementing the algorithm.

A working program provides an additional opportunity in allowing an empirical analysis of the underlying algorithm. The analysis is based on timing the program on several inputs and them analyzing the results obtained.

As we have seen above, the whole process of development of the algorithm depends upon its design, performance and its implementation. If any one of the factor does not give satisfied result then we have to rework for better efficient algorithm as a good algorithm is a result of repeated effort and rework.

In our next section, as mentioned earlier, we will outline a general frame work for analyzing the efficiency of algorithms.

7.3 Efficiency of Algorithms

As we know, the performance of an algorithm depends upon two important factors. How fast the algorithm run and how much space it requires to store. The first one is related to time and the second one is related to space and they are referred as time complexity and space complexity of the algorithm.

These factors play an important role in analyzing the algorithm. Sometimes, for a given problem, there may be several suitable algorithms available and to choose the best one, we usually compare algorithms on the basis of their execution time and storage capacity. Now a days, with technological advancement, the speed and memory size of computer have increased by many orders of magnitude. The amount of extra space required by an algorithm is therefore not of much concern and to analyze the algorithm efficiency, we concentrate only on time complexity.

7.3.1 Time Complexity

Time complexity is related to measuring an algorithm's running time. This is done by counting the number of times the algorithm's basic operation is executed on inputs of size n. The basic operation is the most important operation of the algorithm which is usually in the algorithm's innermost loop and it contributes for most of the total running time.

If C_{op} is an execution time of an algorithm's basic operation on a given computer and C(n) is the number of times this operation executed in the algorithm, then the estimate of running time T(n) of a program implementing this algorithm on the computer is given by

$$T(n) \sim C_{op} C(n)$$

This expression clearly shows that the running time T(n) depends upon the input size n. If the input size n is small, then the difference in running time does not really distinguishes efficient algorithms from inefficient algorithms. When n becomes large then the difference in algorithms efficiencies become both clear and important from running time point of view.

For large values of n, it is the function's order of growth that plays an important role for estimating the running time of the algorithm. The following table 7.1 shows values of the functions for different values of n.

Table 7.1

n	Function	$\log_2 n$	$n \log_2 n$	n^2	n^3	2^n	n!
1		0	0	1	1	2	1
2		1	2	4	8	4	2
4		2	8	16	64	16	24
8		3	24	64	512	256	40320
16		4	64	256	4096	65, 536	2.09×10^{13}
32		5	160	1024	32, 768	4, 294, 967, 296	3.71×10^{41}

It is evident from the table 7.1 that the function growing the slowest among these is the logarithmic function. The exponential function 2^n and factorial function n! grow so fast that their values become astronomically large even for small values of n. Sometimes both the functions are referred as "exponential-growth functions". As an example for the function 2^n, if n = 40 then number of steps needed is 1.09×10^{12}. If a computer is performing one billion steps per second, this would require about 18.3 minutes. If n = 50, then the same algorithm would run for about 13 days on this computer and for n =60, around 310.56 years will take to execute this algorithm. Thus, we may say that the algorithms with exponential number of steps execution have less practical utility and it is limited to n ≤ 40. In other words, algorithms that require an exponential number of operations are practical for solving only problems of very small sizes.

In the next section, we will define asymptotic notations which are used for comparing and ranking of algorithms. Algorithm which is asymptotically superior performs better on all sufficiently large instances.

7.3.2 Asymptotic Notations

As discussed above, the efficiency analysis frame work concentrates on the order of growth of an algorithm's basic operation which in turn depends upon the input size n. To compare and rank the orders of growth, three **asymptotic notations** are used, namely, O (big Oh), Ω (omega) and Θ (theta). These notations are called asymptotic because they deal with behaviour of the functions in the limit, that is, for sufficiently large values of its parameters. Usually an asymptotic superior algorithm is very often preferable even on instances of moderate size.

The formal definitions for asymptotic notations are given below :

O-notation :

A function t(n) is said to be in O(g(n)) iff there exist some positive constant c and some non-negative integer n_0 such that

$$t(n) \leq c\, g(n) \text{ for all } n \geq n_0$$

In other words, t(n) is bounded above by some constant multiple of g(n) for all large n.

For example, consider the function t(n) = 4n + 2.

$$t(n) = 4n + 2 \leq 4n + n \quad (n \geq 2)$$
$$= 5n = c\, g(n)$$

Hence, $\quad t(n) = 4n + 2 \leq 5n = c\, g(n),\ n \geq 2$

Here c = 5, n_0 = 2 and g(n) = n.

Therefore, we say that 4n + 2 = O(n).

Or, $\qquad$ 4n + 2 $\in$ O(n)

Also, $\qquad$ 4n + 2 $\leq$ 5n $\leq$ $5n^2$ (n $\geq$ 2)

Hence, $\qquad$ 4n + 2 = $O(n^2)$ (by taking c= 5, n_0 = 2)

Similarly, we have

$$5n^2 + 6n + 2 = O(n^2)$$

as $\qquad 5n^2 + 6n + 2 \leq 7n^2$ for $n \geq 4$

But $\qquad 5n^2 + 6n + 2 \neq O(n)$

for any positive constant c and for all n $\geq$ n_0.

Thus, we can say n = $O(n^2)$

$$5n + 3 = O(n^2), \qquad \frac{1}{2}n(n-1) = O(n^2)$$

but $\qquad n^3 \neq O(n^2), \qquad n^4 + n + 1 \neq O(n^2)$

Indeed, we can say that $O(g(n))$ is the set of all functions with a smaller or same order of growth as $g(n)$ (to within a constant multiple).

We consider $O(1)$ as constant computing time. $O(n)$ is called linear, $O(n^2)$ as quadratic, $O(n^3)$ as cubic and $O(2^n)$ as exponential. If an algorithm takes time $O(\log n)$, it is faster for sufficiently large n than time taken as $O(n)$. Similarly $O(n \log n)$ is better than $O(n^2)$.

Ω-notation :

A function $t(n)$ is said to be in $\Omega(g(n))$ iff there exist some positive constant c and some non-negative integer n_0 such that $t_n \geq c\, g(n)$ for all $n \geq n_0$ or $t(n)$ is bounded below by some positive constant multiple of $g(n)$ for all large n.

As an example the function $t(n) = 4n + 2 \geq 4n$ for all $n \geq 0$.

Hence $4n + 2 = \Omega(n)$ or we say $4n + 2 \in \Omega(n)$.

Here, $c = 4$ and $n_0 = 0$.

Similarly, $\quad 5n^2 + 6n + 2 = \Omega(n^2)$

Also $\quad 7n^2 + 2n + 3 = \Omega(n),\ n^3 = \Omega(n^2),\ 100n + 5 \neq \Omega(n^2)$

Thus, $\Omega(g(n))$ is the set of all functions with a large or same order of growth as $g(n)$ (to within a constant multiple).

Θ-notation :

A function $t(n)$ is said to in $\Theta(g(n))$, iff there exist some positive constant c_1 and c_2 and some non-negative integer n_0 such that

$$c_1\, g(n) \leq t(n) \leq c_2\, g(n) \text{ for all } n \geq n_0$$

i.e. the function $t(n)$ is bounded both above and below by some positive constant multiples of $g(n)$ for all large n.

Consider $\quad t(n) = \dfrac{1}{2} n(n-1) = \dfrac{1}{2} n^2 - \dfrac{1}{2} n \leq \dfrac{1}{2} n^2$ for all $n \geq 0$

Also $\quad \dfrac{1}{2} n(n-1) = \dfrac{1}{2} n^2 - \dfrac{1}{2} n \geq \dfrac{1}{2} n^2 - \left(\dfrac{1}{2} n\right)\left(\dfrac{1}{2} n\right) = \dfrac{1}{4} n^2$

$\Rightarrow \quad \dfrac{1}{2} n(n-1) \geq \dfrac{1}{4} n^2$ for all $n \geq 2$

$\Rightarrow \quad \dfrac{1}{4} n^2 \leq \dfrac{1}{2} n(n-1) \leq \dfrac{1}{2} n^2$.

Hence, $\quad \dfrac{1}{2} n(n-1) = \Theta(n^2)$

Here $c_1 = \dfrac{1}{4},\ c_2 = \dfrac{1}{2}$ and $n_0 = 2$.

As an another example,

$$3n + 2 \leq 4n \text{ and } 3n + 2 \geq 3n$$

$\Rightarrow \qquad 3n \leq 3n + 2 \leq 4n, \quad n \geq 2$

$$3n + 2 = \Theta(n)$$

A very useful property of asymptotic notations is given below without proof.

If $t_1(n) = O(g_1(n))$ and $t_2(n) = O(g_2(n))$ then $t_1(n) + t_2(n) = O(\max(g_1(n), g_2(n)))$

Similar property holds for Ω and Θ notations also.

The formal definitions of asymptotic notations, which are described above are useful for proving their abstract properties, however they are rarely used for comparing the growth of order of two specific functions. The method which is based on computing the limit of ratio of two functions is much more convenient to use.

Consider $\lim\limits_{n \to \infty} \dfrac{t(n)}{g(n)} = \begin{cases} 0 & \Rightarrow t(n) \text{ has a smaller order of growth than } g(n) \\ c > 0 & \Rightarrow t(n) \text{ has same order of growth as } g(n) \\ \infty & \Rightarrow t(n) \text{ has a larger order of growth as } g(n) \end{cases}$

The first two cases meant that

$$t(n) = O(g(n))$$

The last two cases mean that

$$t(n) = \Omega(g(n))$$

and the second case mean that

$$t(n) = \Theta(g(n))$$

For example, consider the growth of functions.

$$t(n) = \frac{1}{2} n(n-1) \text{ and } g(n) = n^2$$

then
$$\lim_{n \to \infty} \frac{t(n)}{g(n)} = \lim_{n \to \infty} \frac{\frac{1}{2} n(n-1)}{n^2} = \frac{1}{2} \lim_{n \to \infty} \frac{n^2 - n}{n^2}$$

Using L'Hospital's rule,

$$\lim_{n \to \infty} \frac{t(n)}{g(n)} = \frac{1}{2} \lim_{n \to \infty} \frac{2n-1}{2n} = \frac{1}{2} \lim_{n \to \infty} \left(1 - \frac{1}{2n}\right) = \frac{1}{2}$$

Since limit is a positive constant $\frac{1}{2} > 0$.

$\Rightarrow$ Both the functions have the same order of growth.

$\Rightarrow$ $\frac{1}{2}n(n-1) = \Theta(n^2)$

$\Rightarrow$ $t(n) = \Theta(g(n))$

Now we will discuss about worst-case, best-case and average case efficiencies of the algorithm.

7.3.3 Worst-Case, Best-Case and Average-Case Efficiencies

As we have seen in the article 7.3.1 that the running time T(n) of the program depends upon c(n), the number of times, the basic operation is executed and which is a function of a parameter indicating the size n of the input. In many algorithms, the running time does not depend only on an input size but also on the specifics of a particular input, i.e. the time taken by an algorithm, can vary considerably between two different instances of the same size. This gives rise to the terms worst-case, best-case and average-case efficiency of an algorithm.

The **worst-case efficiency** of an algorithm is defined as its efficiency for the worst-case input size. It means it is an input of size n for which the algorithm runs the longest among all possible inputs of that size n. To find the worst-case efficiency of the algorithm, we have to consider that instance of size n on which the algorithm requires the maximum time. For analyzing worst-case efficiency, we have to see what kind of inputs yield the largest value of the basic operation's count c(n) among all possible inputs of size n and then compute worst-case value $c_{worst}(n)$. This analysis provides an important information about an algorithm's efficiency by bounding its running time from above, i.e. for any instance of size n, running time will not exceed $c_{worst}(n)$. Worst-case analysis is important an algorithm whose response time is critical.

The **best-case efficiency** of an algorithm is defined as its efficiency for the best-case input of size n. This means that it is an input of size n for which the algorithm runs the fastest among all possible inputs of that size n. To analyze the best-case efficiency, we have to determine the kind of inputs for which the basic operation's count c(n) will be the smallest among all possible inputs of size n. For the best-case, c(n) is denoted by $c_{best}(n)$.

Sometimes, neither the worst-case nor the best-case analysis yield the necessary information about an algorithm's behaviour on a given input. In this situation, we consider the **average-case efficiency** of the algorithm which is harder to find than its best and worst-case. To find the average-case efficiency, all instances of size n are divided into several classes so that for each instance of the class, the number of times the algorithm's basic operation is executed is the same. Then a probability distribution of inputs is obtained or assumed so that the expected value of the basic operation's count c(n) can be found. The average-case analysis is to be applied when an algorithm is to be used many times on many different instances, that is, when it is important to know the average execution time on instances of size n, we need to find average-case efficiency of the algorithm.

In next few sections, we will study some basic algorithms like largest number algorithm, bubble sort algorithm etc.

7.4 Largest Number Algorithm

This algorithm finds the largest number in a given set of n numbers. Consider a list of n numbers and it is required to find the value of the largest number in given list.

Here the given list of n numbers is taken in the form of array A[0], A[1], ..., A[n – 1] and the largest number in the list is denoted as "maxval". Initially, A[0] is taken as maxval. This element is compared with the next element in the array A[1]. If A[1] is greater than maxval then A[1] is taken as maxval. In this way, all the numbers in the list are compared and the new value is assigned to maxval if any number in the list is found to be greater than the value of maxval at that time.

The pseudocode of above algorithm is given below :

Algorithm : MaxElement (A[0... n – 1])
//   Determines the value of largest element in a given array
//   Input : Array A [0 ... n – 1] of real numbers
//   Output : The value of the largest element in A
     maxval ← A[0]
for i ← 1 to n – 1 **do**
    if A[i] > maxval
       maxval ← A[i]
return maxval.

In above algorithm, the number of elements n in the array gives the input size and two operations are executed inside "for" loop. One is comparison of A[i] with maxval and second is the assignment of A[i] to maxval. Since the comparison is executed on each repetition of the loop, while assignment may not be there every time, we consider the comparison as the algorithm's basic operation. Also, the number of comparisons will be the same for all array's of size n.

If c(n) denotes the number of times the comparison is executed then since algorithm makes one comparison on each execution of the loop, we get

$$c(n) = \sum_{i=1}^{n-1} 1 = n - 1 \in \Theta(n)$$

In the next section, we present sorting algorithm, which helps us in rearranging the data in some order.

7.5 Sorting Algorithms

The sorting problem has an important place in computer science as it has many data processing applications.

Sorting means rearranging the items in the given list according to some order (ascending/descending). It can be sorting the list of numbers, characters from an alphabet character string etc. and the most important of it is the sorting the records. They may be the reocrds maintained by the school about their students, libraries about their holdings (books, journals etc.) and companies about their employees. In case of records, a piece of information is required to perform the sort.

For example, the students record can be sort in alphabetical order of their names or it can be sort by the roll numbers assigned to them by the college or sorting can be done using the marks obtained by the students. This special information is called a **key**. This word is commonly used even when lists items are not records. Sorting the keys of the records in a file can be in ascending or descending order. For example, in case of item file, the records are to be sorted as per the ascending order of the item code, but the records in the order file of an order processing system are to be sorted as per the descending order of the delivery dates of the orders.

There are many different sorting algorithms like bubble sort, heap sort, quick sort etc. which are developed by computer scientists. Some algorithms are better than others, but there is no algorithm that would be the best solution in all situations. Some of the sorting algorithms are simple but relatively slow while others are faster but more complex. Here, we will describe the Bubble sort algorithm to sort an array of n numbers in ascending order. With small changes, the algorithm can be used for sorting in descending order also.

7.5.1 Bubble Sort Algorithm

This algorithm compares adjacent elements of the list and exchange them if they are out of order. By doing it repeatedly, we finish "bubbling up" the largest element to the last position on the list. The next iteration (pass) bubbles-up the second last position and so on until, after (n – 1) iterations, the whole list is sorted.

If there are total n number of keys represented as an array A[1], A[2], ..., A[n] then in the first iteration, bubble sort algorithm pushes the highest key to n^{th} position by comparing the two adjacent keys.

If A[j + 1] < A[j] then it interchanges (swaps) the values at two positions so that they are in the ascending order.

In the next iteration, it pushes the second highest key to the $(n - 1)^{th}$ position. This process continuous for (n – 1) iterations. At the end, all the keys are in ascending order.

The pseudocode of this algorithm is given below :

Algorithm : Bubble sort (A[1 ... n)].

// Sorts a given array by bubble sort.

// Input : An array A[1 · n] of orderable elements.

// Output : Array A[1 .. n] sorted in ascending order.

For i ← 1 to n – 1 **do**

    for j ← 1 to n – i **do**

        if A[j + 1] < A[j] swap A[j] and A[j + 1]

Here swaping (interchanging) of two values) can be done using a third variable called "temp". First the value of A[j + 1] will be sorted in "temp" and A[j] value will be assigned to A[j + 1], then temp value will be assigned to A[j].

In above algorithm, the input size is given by the number of keys n. The algorithm's basic operation is the key comparison A[j + 1] < A[j]. The number of times this is done depends upon only on the array's size and given by the following sum :

$$c(n) = \sum_{i=1}^{n-1} \sum_{j=1}^{n-i} 1$$

$$= \sum_{i=1}^{n-1} (n - i) = \sum_{i=1}^{n-1} n - \sum_{j=1}^{n-1} i$$

$$= n(n - 1) - \frac{(n - 1)n}{2}$$

$$= \frac{n(n - 1)}{2}$$

$\Rightarrow$ $c(n) = \Theta(n^2)$

However, the number of key swaps depends on the input.

For example, consider an array of 4 keys shown in table 7.2.

Table 7.2

Key	1	2	3	4
Key value	77	65	105	20

To sort the keys in ascending order the bubble sort algorithm is applied in the following manner.

Here n = 4.

First iteration i = 1,

j = 1	77	↔	65		105	20
	65		77		105	20
j = 2	65		77	↔	105	20
	65		77		105	20
j = 3	65		77		105 ↔	20
	65		77		20	105

Second iteration i = 2,

j = 1	65	↔	77		20	105
	65		77		20	105
j = 2	65		77	↔	20	105
	65		20		77	105

Third iteration i = 3,

j = 1	65	↔	20		77	105
	20		65		77	105

The sorted array is 20 65 77 105.

The next section describes the divide and conquer technique which is used to design important algorithms like binary search and matrix multiplication algorithms.

7.6 Divide-and-Conquer Technique

The technique for designing the algorithm which consists of decomposing the instances into a number of smaller subinstances, solving successively and independently each of these subinstances and then combining the subsolutions of these subinstances to obtain the solution of the original instance is called divide-and-conquer technique. It is probably the best known general algorithm design technique.

Suppose a function is to be computed on n inputs. Then according to divide-and-conquer method, the input n is splitted into k distinct subsets, 1 < k ≤ n, yielding k subproblems. These subproblems are solved and a combine solutions of these subproblems give the solution of the original problem. If the subproblems are still relatively large, then the divide-and-conquer strategy can be reapplied. Often the subproblems resulting from divide-and-conquer design are of the same type as the original problem. Smaller and smaller subproblems of the some kind are generated until eventually subproblems that are small enough to be solved without splitting are produced.

For example, consider the problem of computing the sum of n numbers $a_0, a_1, ..., a_{n-1}$. If n > 1, we can divide the problem into two instances of the same problem : To compute the sum of first $\lfloor n/2 \rfloor$ numbers $\lfloor x \rfloor$ denotes the greatest integer not greater than x and to compute the sum of remaining numbers. After computing each of these two sums, we add their values to get the sum of $a_0, a_1, ..., a_{n-1}$.

Hence, $\quad a_0 + a_1 + ... a_{n-1} = (a_0 + a_1 + ... + a_{\lfloor n/2 \rfloor})$

$$+ (a_{\lfloor n/2 \rfloor + 1} + ... a_{n-1})$$

This method of computing the sum is not an efficient one. Thus not every divide-and-conquer algorithm is necessarily more efficient than their counterpart. But this technique is ideally suited for parallel computations, in which each subproblem can be solved simultaneously by its own processor.

In above example, problem's instance size n is subdivided into two subinstances of size n/2.

This typical case is depicted in the following Fig. 7.1.

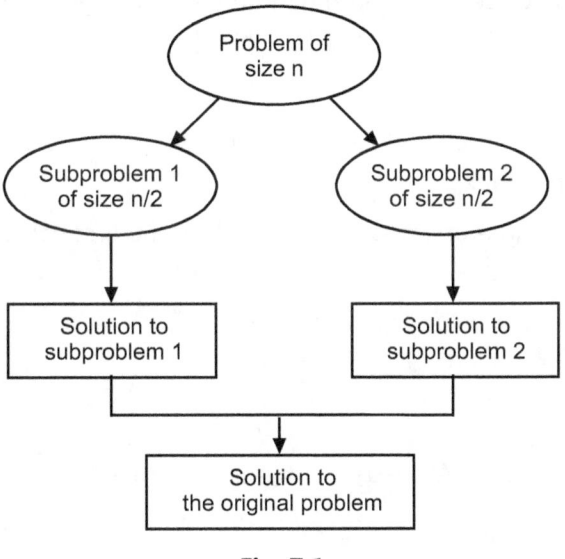

Fig. 7.1

More generally, an instance of size n is divided into b instances of size n/b, with 'a' of them needed to be solved where a and b are constants and a ≥ 1 and b > 1. If we assume that size n is a power of b, we get the recurrence relation for running time T(n) as

$$T(n) = a\,T(n/b) + f(n)$$

where, f(n) is a function that accounts for the time spent on dividing the problem into smaller ones and combining their solutions. The above equation is called general divide-and-conquer recurrence.

For the problem of summation described above a = b = 2 and f(n) = 1.

The divide-and-conquer technique is used to design binary search algorithm which is described in the next section.

7.6.1 Binary Search Algorithm

Binary search algorithm is an efficient algorithm for searching an item in a sorted array. It compares the search key K with the array's middle element A[m]. If they match, the algorithm stops; otherwise the same operation is repeated recursively for the first half of an array if K < A[m] and for the second half if K > A[m]. The algorithm is described below in more explicit manner.

Let A[i], 1 ≤ i ≤ n be the list of elements that are sorted in non-decreasing order. It is required to determine whether an item K is present in the list or not. If K is not present then algorithm will return the value 0. If l and h denote the lowest and highest index of the array then the middle index m of the array is m = $\lfloor (l + h)/2 \rfloor$.

Initially l = 1 and h = n.

The search K is compared by middle value A[m]. If K = A[m] then search is stopped and the algorithm returns the index m.

If K < A[m] then the same operation is repeated for the first half of array. In this case the new value of index h is m − 1.

If K > A[m], then the new value of l becomes m + 1.

$$K$$
$$\updownarrow$$

A[1] ………… A[m − 1]   A[m]   A[m + 1] ……… A[n]

If K < A[m], l = 1, h = m − 1   If K > A[m], l = m + 1, h = n

The pseudocode for binary search algorithm is as follows :

Algorithm : Binary search (A[1 .. n], k)

//   Input : An array A[1 .. n] sorted in ascending order and a search key K.
//   Output : An index of the array's element that is equal to K or 0 if there is no such
//   element.

$l \leftarrow 1, h \leftarrow n$

while $l \leq h$ **do**

    $m \leftarrow \lfloor (l + h)/2 \rfloor$

    if $K = A[m]$ **return** m

    else if $K < A[m]$

        $h \leftarrow m - 1$

    else $l \leftarrow m + 1$

return 0

For example, consider an array of 13 numbers and the search key K = 79.

| 5 | 15 | 27 | 30 | 40 | 52 | 63 | 79 | 85 | 89 | 91 | 95 | 97 |

The iterations of the algorithm are described below.

Index	1	2	3	4	5	6	7	8	9	10	11	12	13
Value	5	15	27	30	40	52	63	79	85	89	91	95	97
First Iteration	l = 1						m = 7						h = 13
Second iteration								l = 8		m = 10			h = 13
Third iteration								l = 8, m = 8	h = 9				

Here when m = 8, A[m] = 79.

Hence search is performed in three iteration.

As we have seen in above example, first we find the mid-point of array (m = 7) and the search key k = 79 is compared with A[m] = 63. Since K > A[7], the search is shifted to second half (right to the middle) of the array and then search key K = 79 is compared with the value of the mid item of second half of original array. Continue this way, in third iteration, we get our search key k = 79 = A[8]. Thus divide-and-conquer technique is used to divide the problem into smaller subproblems and then find the solution of original problem. The same technique is used to multiply two matrices known as strassen's matrix multiplication which is explained in the next article.

7.6.2 Strassen's Matrix Multiplication

Using divide-and-conquer technique, the algorithm for matrix multiplcation can be improvised by using less number of multiplications.

As we all know, if A and B are two matrices of order n × n then their product matrix C = AB is also an n × n matrix whose elements are computed as the scalar products of the rows of matrix A and columns of matrix B. The $(i, j)^{th}$ element of c is formed by taking the element in the ith row of A and j^{th} column of B and then multiplying the corresponding elements and adding, we get

$$C[i, j] = \sum_{1 \leq k \leq n} A[i, k] \; B[k, j]$$

where, i = 1, 2, ..., n

j = 1, 2, ..., n

$$C[i, j] = A[i, 1] \; B[1, j] + A[i, 2] \; B[2, j] + \ldots + A[i, n] \; B[n, j]$$

The pseudocode for matrix multiplication is given below :

Algorithm : Matrix multiplication (A[1 . . n, 1 . . n], B[1 . . n, 1 . . n].

// Multiplies two n × n matrices A and B.

// Input : Two n × n matrices A and B.

// Output : Matrix C = AB.

for i ← 1 to n **do**

    for j ← 1 to n **do**

      C [i, j] ← 0 · 0

      for k ← 1 to n **do**

        C[i, j] ← C[i, j] + A[i, k] * B[i, k]

return C.

Here the input size is n which is the order of the matrices. In the algorithm's innermost loop, two operations addition and multiplication are performed. Both the operations are performed exactly once in the loop. We consider multiplication as basic operation as it takes more time to compute than the addition. Let M(n) denotes the total number of multiplications executed by the algorithm. Since there is only one multiplication executed on each repetition of the algorithm's innermost loop, which is governed by variable. k (for k = 1 to n), the number of multiplications in inner loop for specific values of i and j is given by

$$\sum_{k=1}^{n} 1$$

Thus the total number of multiplications M(n) executed by algorithm is

$$M(n) = \sum_{i=1}^{n} \sum_{j=1}^{n} \sum_{k=1}^{n} 1 = \sum_{i=1}^{n} \sum_{j=1}^{n} (n) = \sum_{i=1}^{n} n^2$$

$$\Rightarrow \quad M(n) = n^3$$

The running time estimated is

$$T(n) = C_m M(n) = C_m n^3$$

$$\Rightarrow \quad T(n) \in \Theta(n^3)$$

To get more accurate running time, we can consider the additions also, which gives

$$T(n) = C_m M(n) + C_a A(n) = C_m n^3 + C_a n^2$$

where, C_a is the time for one addition and C_m is the time taken for one multiplication.

If we have two matrices A and B of order 2×2 then total number of multiplications are 8 as $M(n) = n^3$ and here $n = 2$. Also the number of additions are four.

In 1969, **V. Strassen** published the improved algorithm for matrix multiplication that uses only 7 multiplications for 2×2 matrices, consider two matrices A and B of order 2×2.

$$A = \begin{bmatrix} a_{11} & a_{12} \\ a_{21} & a_{22} \end{bmatrix} \text{ and } B = \begin{bmatrix} b_{11} & b_{12} \\ b_{21} & b_{22} \end{bmatrix}$$

then

$$C = AB = \begin{bmatrix} c_{11} & c_{12} \\ c_{21} & c_{22} \end{bmatrix}$$

$$= \begin{bmatrix} a_{11}b_{11} + a_{12}b_{21} & a_{11}b_{12} + a_{12}b_{22} \\ a_{21}b_{11} + a_{22}b_{21} & a_{21}b_{12} + a_{22}b_{22} \end{bmatrix}$$

Strassen represented these values as

$$C = AB = \begin{bmatrix} m_1 + m_4 - m_5 + m_7 & m_3 + m_5 \\ m_2 + m_4 & m_1 + m_3 - m_2 + m_6 \end{bmatrix}$$

where,

$$m_1 = (a_{11} + a_{22})(b_{11} + b_{22})$$
$$m_2 = (a_{21} + a_{22}) b_{11}$$
$$m_3 = a_{11}(b_{12} - b_{22})$$
$$m_4 = a_{22}(b_{21} - b_{11})$$
$$m_5 = (a_{11} + a_{12}) b_{22}$$
$$m_6 = (a_{21} - a_{11})(b_{11} + b_{12})$$
$$m_7 = (a_{12} - a_{22})(b_{21} + b_{22})$$

As mentioned above, to multiply two 2 × 2 matrices, Strassen's algorithm uses only seven multiplcations and 18 additions/subtractions.

Now consider the problem of multiplying two matrices A and B of order n × n.

where n is a power of 2, that is there exits a non-negative integer k such that $n = 2^k$. If n is not a power of two, then sufficient rows and columns of zeros should be added to both A and B, so that the resulting dimensions are power of 2.

As explained in the beginning of this article, the number of multiplications required here are n^3. Using divide-and-conquer technique, the two matrices A and B and their product C = AB can be divided into four square submatrices, each submatrix having dimensions $\frac{n}{2} \times \frac{n}{2}$.

$$\begin{bmatrix} A_{11} & A_{12} \\ A_{21} & A_{22} \end{bmatrix} \begin{bmatrix} B_{11} & B_{12} \\ B_{21} & B_{22} \end{bmatrix} = \begin{bmatrix} C_{11} & C_{12} \\ C_{21} & C_{22} \end{bmatrix}$$

$\Rightarrow$
$$C_{11} = A_{11} B_{11} + A_{12} B_{21}$$
$$C_{12} = A_{11} B_{12} + A_{12} B_{22}$$
$$C_{21} = A_{21} B_{11} + A_{22} B_{21}$$
$$C_{22} = A_{21} B_{12} + A_{22} B_{22}$$

Or using Strassen's formulae

$$C_{11} = M_1 + M_4 - M_5 + M_7$$
$$C_{12} = M_3 + M_5$$
$$C_{21} = M_2 + M_4$$
$$C_{22} = M_1 + M_3 - M_2 + M_6$$

where, $M_1, M_2, M_3, M_4, M_5, M_6$ and M_7 are found using Strassen's formulae with the numbers replaced by the corresponding submatrices. Here seven products of $\frac{n}{2} \times \frac{n}{2}$ matrices are computed in one iteration. If the same method is applied recursively then we call the algorithm as **Strassen's algorithm for matrix multiplication**.

To count the number of multiplications M(n) in Strassen's algorithm, since in each iteration the order n of the matrix reduces to n/2 and there are seven multiplications, we have

$$M(n) = 7M(n/2) \text{ for } n > 1, \; M(1) = 1$$

Since $n = 2^k$

$$M(2^k) = 7M(2^{k-1})$$
$$= 7 \times 7M(2^{k-2}) = 7^2 M(2^{k-2}) \ldots\ldots$$
$$= 7^k M(2^{k-k})$$

$\Rightarrow \quad M(n) = M(2^k) = 7^k$

but $\quad n = 2^k \Rightarrow k = \log_2 n$

$\Rightarrow \quad M(n) = 7^{\log_2 n} = n^{\log_2 7} \sim n^{2.807}$

$\Rightarrow \quad T(n) \in \Theta(n^{2.807})$

which is smaller than n^3 required by algorithm given in the beginning.

If we consider the number of additions also, then since Strassen's algorithm needs to multiply seven matrices of order n/2 and 18 additions of matrices of order n/2, we get

$$T(n) = 7T(n/2) + 18(n/2)^2$$

After Strassen, computer scientists invented many algorithms which are in $O(n^\alpha)$ for smaller value of α. The fastest algorithm so far is that of Coopersmith and Winograd with its efficiency in $O(n^{2.376})$. However, these algorithms have less practical utility as they are complex in nature and having large multiplicative constants.

As we have seen in last few sections that the efficiency of bubble sort algorithm is $\Theta(n^2)$ and that of Strassen's algorithm for matrix multiplication is $\Theta(n^{2.807})$. This means these algorithms can be solve in polynomial time. This leads to definition of tractable and intractable problems which are described in the following section.

7.7 Tractable and Intractable Problems

In the study of computational complexity of problems, the main concern is whether a given problem can be solved in polynomial time by some algorithm. According to the computing time taken by the best algorithm for the solution, the problems are clustered into two groups. The first group consists of problems whose solution times are bounded by polynomials of small degree. The bubble sort which is $\Theta(n^2)$ and Strassen's algorithm for matrix multiplication which is $\Theta(n^{2.807})$ are some of the examples, which we have studied for this class of problems.

The second group consists of problems whose best known algorithms are non-polynomial. Travelling salesman and knapsack problems are some of the famous problems in computer science, which have the complexities $O(n^2 2^n)$ and $O(2^{n/2})$ i.e. the problems are solved in non-polynomial time. In quest to develop efficient algorithms, no one has been able to develop the algorithm, which gives solution in polynomial time for these problems.

Problems that can be solved in polynomial time are called **tractable** and problems that cannot be solved in polynomial time are called **intractable** problem. We say that an algorithm solves a problem in polynomial time if its worst case time efficiency is $O(p(n))$ where, $p(n)$ is a polynomial in n (input size of the problem). That is to say, the worst case efficiency of algorithm is bounded above by a polynomial function of its input size n. Algorithms with the worst case time complexity $2n$, $3n^3 + 4n$, $5n + n^{10}$, $n\lg n$ are all polynomial time algorithms. Algorithms with 2^n, $2^{\sqrt{n}}$, $n!$ as worst case efficiency are non-polynomial time algorithms. Note that $n\lg n$ is not a polynomial in n but $n\lg n < n^2$ that is, it is bounded by a polynomial is n, which means the algorithm with time complexity $n\lg n$ is polynomial time algorithm.

An intractable problem is impossible to solve with a polynomial-time algorithm. Intractability is a property of the problem. For a problem to be intractable, there must be no polynomial time algorithm that can solve it. For any problem, if we obtain a non-polynomial time algorithm, then it does not mean that problem is intractable. There may be some other algorithms for the problem which are polynomial time algorithms. Hence the problem is not intractable because it can be solved in polynomial time.

Polynomial time algorithms are usually better than algorithms that are not polynomial time because the computing time is less for polynomial time algorithms for even large size problems.

SOLVED EXAMPLES

Example 7.1 : Write the algorithm to obtain the sum of first n natural numbers. What is the basic operation in the algorithm and how many times it is executed. What is efficiency class of this algorithm ?

Solution : The algorithm for finding the sum of n natural numbers is given below :

Algorithm sum (n)

//   Input : A positive integer n
//   Output : Sum of n numbers

s ← 0

for i ← 1 to n **do**

    s ← s + i

return s

Here basic operation is addition.

If c(n) is number of times addition is executed then

$$c(n) = \sum_{i=1}^{n} 1 = n \in \Theta(n)$$

Hence, the efficiency class is $\Theta(n)$.

Example 7.2 : Write the algorithm for addition of two matrices of order m × n. What is efficiency of the algorithm ?

Solution : Given A and B two matrices of order m × n.

Let C = A + B, which is a matrix of order m × n.

where,   C [i, j] = A [i, j] + B [i, j]

The algorithm for addition of matrices A and B is given below :

Algorithm Matrix addition (A [1 ... m, 1 ... n], B [1 ... m, 1 ... n)]

//   Adds two matrices A and B

//   Input : Two matrices A and B of order m × n

//   Output : Matrix C = A + B

for i ← 1 to m **do**

    for j ← 1 to n **do**

        C [i, j] = A [i, j] + B [i, j]

return C

Here the number of times the addition is executed.

$$c(n) = \sum_{i=1}^{n} \sum_{j=1}^{n} 1 = \sum_{i=1}^{m} n = mn$$

⇒   Time complexity $T(n) \in \Theta(mn)$.

Example 7.3 : Explain the algorithm for computing factorial function F(n) = n! for an arbitrary non-negative integer n.

Solution : The factorial function F(n) = n! is defined as

$$F(n) = n! = n(n-1)(n-2)\ldots 1, \quad F(0) = 0! = 1$$

This equation can be written in the form of recurrence relation.

$$F(n) = n F(n-1)$$

Using this recursive definition for F(n), we can write the algorithm for computing F(n) = n!

Algorithm : F(n) = n!

// Compute n! recursively.

// Input : A non-negative integer n.

// Output : n!.

If n = 0 **return** 1.

else return F(n − 1) ∗ n.

This algorithm is called **recursive algorithm** as it uses recursive function F(n). The basic operation of this algorithm is multiplication. Let M(n) be the number of executions of this basic operation multiplication. Since F(n) = F(n − 1) ∗ n for n > 0.

The number of multiplications M(n) is given by

$$M(n) = \underbrace{M(n-1)}_{\text{to compute } F(n-1)} + \underbrace{1}_{\text{to multiply } F(n-1) \text{ by } n}, \quad n > 0 \text{ and } M(0) = 0$$

Here, to compute F(n − 1), we use M(n − 1) multiplications and one multiplication is needed to multiply the result by n.

Also, M(n − 1) = M(n − 2) + 1, M(n − 2) = M(n − 3) + 1 and so on, we have

$$\begin{aligned} M(n) &= M(n-1) + 1 \\ &= [M(n-2) + 1] + 1 = M(n-2) + 2 \\ &= [M(n-3) + 1] + 2 = M(n-3) + 3 \\ &\quad \ldots\ldots\ldots \\ &= M(n-n) + n \\ &= M(0) + n \end{aligned}$$

$\Rightarrow \qquad M(n) = n$

Therefore, time complexity of this algorithm

$$T(n) \in \Theta(n)$$

Example 7.4 : The Fibonacci sequence is defined as

0, 1, 1, 2, 3, 5, 8, 13, 21, 34 ……

write the algorithm to obtain n^{th} term of Fibonacci sequence.

Solution : The Fibonacci sequence 0, 1, 1, 2, 3, 5, 8, 13, 21, 34 ... can be defined recursively as follows :

$$F(n) = F(n-1) + F(n-2), \ n > 1$$

with two initial conditions

$$F(n) = 0, \ F(1) = 1$$

The iterative algorithm for Fibonacci sequence is given below :

Algorithm : Fib(n).

// Computes the nth Fibonacci number iteratively.

// Input : A non-negative integer n.

// Output : The nth Fibonacci number.

$F[0] \leftarrow 0, \ F[1] \leftarrow 1$

for i $\leftarrow$ 2 **to** n **do**

$F[i] \leftarrow F[i-1] + F[i-2]$

return F[n].

This algorithm makes (n − 1) addition. Hence, it is linear as a function of n and only exponential as a function of the number of bits b in n's binary representation.

Example 7.5 : Use binary search algorithm to search the key k = 27 in the following array of numbers.

| 10 | 13 | 27 | 54 | 69 | 75 | 82 | 91 | 102 | 107 | 111 |

Solution : Here the array contains 11 numbers and the search key k = 27.

Index	1	2	3	4	5	6	7	8	9	10	11
Key value	10	13	27	54	69	75	82	91	102	107	111

Initially, $l = 1, \ h = 11 \Rightarrow m = \lfloor(l + h)/2\rfloor = 6$.

Hence the middle point is 6.

The given item k = 27 is compared with A[6] = 75.

Since 27 < 75 i.e. k < A[6], the search will be shifted to first half of array (between A[1] to A[5]). Hence, $l = 1, \ h = 5 \Rightarrow m = \lfloor(1 + 5)/2\rfloor = 3$. In second iteration, key k = 27 is compared with A[m] = A[3] = 27.

Since k = 27 = A[3], the search is stopped and the return value of the algorithm is A[3] = 27.

The above iterations are summarized in the following table :

Index	1	2	3	4	5	6	7	8	9	10	11
Key value	10	13	27	54	69	75	82	91	102	107	111
First iteration	$l = 1$					$m = 6$					$h = 11$
Second iteration	$l = 1$		$m = 3$		$h = 5$						

when m = 3, A[3] = 27 and the search is completed.

Example 7.6 : Search the key k = 84 in the following array using binary search algorithm.

5	11	23	56	65	72	84	91	98	105

Solution : Here total number of elements in the array are 10 and the search key is k = 84.

Index	1	2	3	4	5	6	7	8	9	10
Value	5	11	23	56	65	72	84	91	98	105

Initially $l = 1$, $h = 10$, $m = \lfloor (l + h)/2 \rfloor = \lfloor (1 + 10)/2 \rfloor = 5$.

The middle index is m = 5.

The search key k = 84 will be compared with A[m] = A[5] = 65.

Since 84 > 65, the search is shifted to right of the middle index m = 6 (between A[6] to A[10]).

For second iteration, $l = 6$, $h = 10$.

$\Rightarrow \qquad m = \lfloor (6 + 10)/2 \rfloor = 8$

Here, $\qquad A[m] = A[8] = 91$.

The search key k = 84 < 91. Therefore, the search is now shifted to left of index 8 (between A[6] to A[7]).

For third iteration, $l = 6$, $h = 7$,

$\qquad m = \lfloor (6 + 7)/2 \rfloor = 6$

with $\qquad A[m] = A[6] = 72$

The search key k = 84 is compared with A[6] but 84 > 72. Therefore, the search is shifted to right of index 6 (between A[7] to A[7]).

For fourth iteration, $l = 7$, $h = 7$, $m = \lfloor (7 + 7)/2 \rfloor = 7$ and A[m] = A[7] = 84.

Again search key k = 84 is compared with A[7] = 84.

Since k = 84 = A[7], search is completed and the return value of the index is 7.

Index	1	2	3	4	5	6	7	8	9	10
Value	5	11	23	56	65	72	84	91	98	105
First iteration	l = 1				m = 5					h = 10
Second iteration						l = 6		m = 8		h = 10
Third iteration						l = 6 m = 6	h = 7			
Fourth iteration							l = 7 h = 7 m = 7			

Example 7.7 : Sort the following array in ascending order using bubble sort algorithm.

| 42 | 69 | 35 | 78 | 53 |

Solution : Here the array contains 5 elements. To sort the array in ascending order using bubble sort, the values A[j] and A[j + 1] are compared and if A[j] > A[j + 1] then the values of A[j] and A[j + 1] are swapped. In the first iteration, the highest value goes to the last position A[5]. In the second iteration, the second highest value goes to second last position A[4] and so on.

The iterations for bubble sort algorithm are given below :

First iteration i = 1,

```
j = 1    42  ↔  69      35      78      53
         42      69      35      78      53
j = 2    42      69  ↔  35      78      53
         42      35      69      78      53
j = 3    42      35      69  ↔  78      53
         42      35      69      78      53
j = 4    42      35      69      78  ↔  53
         42      35      69      53      78
```

Second iteration i = 2,

```
j = 1    42  ↔  35      69      53      78
         35      42      69      53      78
j = 2    35      42  ↔  69      53      78
         35      42      69      53      78
j = 3    35      42      69  ↔  53      78
         35      42      53      69      78
```

Third iteration i = 3,

	j = 1	35	↔	42		53	69	78
		35		42		53	69	78
	j = 2	35		42	↔	53	69	78
		35		42		53	69	78

Fourth iteration i = 4,

| | j = 1 | 35 | ↔ | 42 | 53 | 69 | 78 |
| | | 35 | | 42 | 53 | 69 | 78 |

The sorted array in ascending order is

      35   42   53   69   78

EXERCISE

1. Explain the steps involving in development of algorithm.
2. Explain briefly the term "design of a algorithm".
3. Write short notes on time complexity of algorithm.
4. What are tractable and intractable problems ? Explain.
5. Discuss the method of divide-and-conquer.
5. Write the recursive algorithm for Fibonacci sequence.
6. Discuss the time complexity of bubble sort algorithm.
7. Write an algorithm for matrix multiplication for n × n matrices. Explain Divide-and-conquer technique for its improved version.
8. Search the item k = 95 in the following array using binary search algorithm.

Key	0	1	2	3	4	5	6	7	8	9	10
Key value	70	82	93	95	99	111	121	141	160	170	173

9. Use bubble sort technique to sort the following keys in ascending order :

Key	1	2	3	4	5	6
Key value	60	55	95	80	23	65

❑❑❑

Unit 4

Chapter 8: GRAPH THEORY

SYLLABUS:
- Basic Terminology, Multi Graphs and Weighted Graphs, Paths and Circuits, Dijkestra's Shortest Path Algorithms, Hamiltonian and Eulerian Paths and Circuits, Factors of a Graph, Planer Graph.

OBJECTIVES:
- Introducing the basic concepts in graph theory, study of properties and operations.
- Visualize various physical problems in terms of graphs.

UTILITY:
- Applicable in solving real life problems such as travelling salesman problem, Odd party problem, three utility problems.
- Finding the shortest path in any given network.

KEY CONCEPTS:
- Complete graph
- Bipartite graph
- Connected graph
- Eulerian and Hamiltonian graphs and circuits.
- Isomorphism of graphs.

8.0 Introduction

During the last four decades, graph theory has emerged as one of the important branch of Mathematics. Now-a-days, it is considered as a powerful tool to solve the large complex systems. The simplicity of the graph theory finds its applications in different fields like Computer Science, Chemistry, Operations research, economics, linguistics etc. In addition, graph theory has proved useful in the study of problems arising in other branches of Mathematics such as group theory and matrix theory.

The theory of graph originated from the famous königsberg seven bridges problem which was solved by great Swiss Mathematician **Euler** in the year 1736. After hundred years,

DISCRETE STRUCTURE AND GRAPH THEORY (NMU) — GRAPH THEORY

Kirchhoff developed the theory of trees (special type of graphs) for its application in the study of electrical networks. In recent times, the graph theory is widely used in various engineering applications such as network analysis, data structures, artificial intelligence, compiler writing, computer graphics etc.

In this chapter, first we introduce some of the basic terminology of graph theory and then we study some important graphs and operations on the graphs.

8.1 Basic Terminology of a Graph

A graph is simply a collection of points, called **'vertices'**, and a collection of lines, called **'edges'**, each of which joins either a pair of points or a single point to itself.

Mathematically, a graph G is an ordered pair (V, E) where V is the set of vertices and E is the set of edges. Each edge e_{ij} is associated with an unordered pair of vertices (v_i, v_j). The vertices v_i and v_j are called **end vertices** or **terminal vertices** of the edge e_{ij} or simply the, edge e. For example, consider the graph G_1 shown in Fig. 8.1. It has four vertices namely v_1, v_2, v_3 and v_4 and five edges e_1, e_2, e_3, e_4 and e_5. The end vertices of the edge e_1 are v_1 and v_2 i.e. $e_1 = (v_1, v_2)$.

Similarly $e_2 = (v_2, v_3)$, $e_3 = (v_3, v_4)$, $e_4 = (v_4, v_1)$ and $e_5 = (v_1, v_3)$. In short, we can represent G_1 as $G_1 = (V_1, E_1)$ where $V_1 = \{v_1, v_2, v_3, v_4\}$ and $E_1 = \{e_1, e_2, e_3, e_4, e_5\}$.

A vertex is also referred to as a **node, a junction or a point**. Other terms used for an edge are **a line**, an **element** or **an arc**.

Following are various examples of the graphs given in Fig. 8.1.

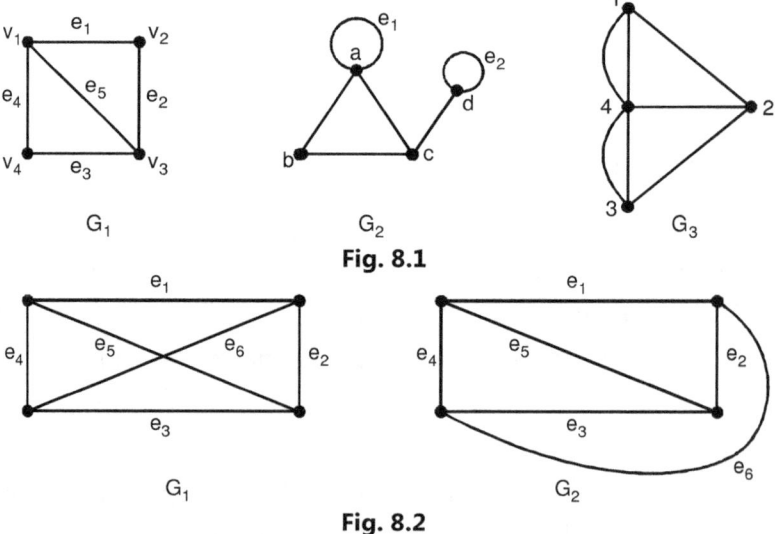

Fig. 8.1

Fig. 8.2

The representation of the graph is not unique. It is immaterial whether the edges are drawn as straight lines or curves. What is important is the incidence between the vertices and edges. For example, the graphs G_1 and G_2 in Fig. 8.2 represent the same graph.

8.1.1 Self loops and Parallel Edges

If the end vertices v_i and v_j of any edge e_{ij} are same, then the edge e_{ij} is called as **self loop** or simply a **loop**. In Fig. 8.3, the edge $e_4 = (v_3, v_3)$ is a self loop.

If there are more than one edges associated with a given pair of vertices then those edges are called **parallel edges** or **multiple edges**. In Fig. 8.3, $e_1 = (v_1, v_2)$ and $e_2 = (v_1, v_2)$ are parallel edges. Similarly, e_6 and e_7 are also parallel edges.

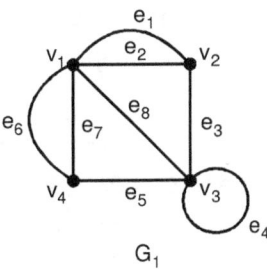

Fig. 8.3

8.1.2 Simple and Multiple Graphs

A graph that has neither self loops nor parallel edges is called a **simple graph**, otherwise, it is called a **multiple graph**.

In the following Fig. 8.4, G_1 is a simple graph but G_2 is not.

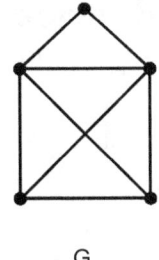
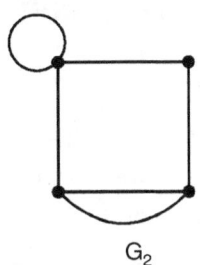

Fig. 8.4

8.1.3 Weighted Graph

Let G be a graph with vertex set V and edge set E. If each edge or each vertex or both are associated with some positive real numbers then the graph is called a **weighted graph**. For example, a graph representing a system of pipelines in which the weights assigned indicate the amount of some commodity transferred through the pipe is a weighted graph. Similarly, a graph of city streets may be assigned weights according to the length of each street or according to the traffic density on each street. Fig. 8.5 shows a weighted graph where weights are assigned to each edge.

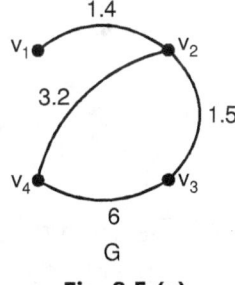

Fig. 8.5 (a)

8.1.4 Finite and Infinite Graphs

> A graph with finite number of vertices as well as finite number of edges is called a **finite graph**, otherwise, it is an infinite graph.

Graph G in Fig. 8.5 is a finite graph.

In most of the theory and applications, the graphs are taken as finite graphs. In the following sections and chapters, we are dealing with finite graphs only.

8.1.5 Labelled Graphs

A graph G = (V, E) is called a labeled graph if its edges are labeled with some name or data. For example, graph shown in Fig. 8.5 (b) is a labeled graph.

Here, $G = \{\{v_1, v_2, v_3, v_4\}, \{e_1, e_2, e_3, e_4, e_5\}\}$
where $V = \{v_1, v_2, v_3, v_4\}$ and $E = \{e_1, e_2, e_3, e_4, e_5\}$

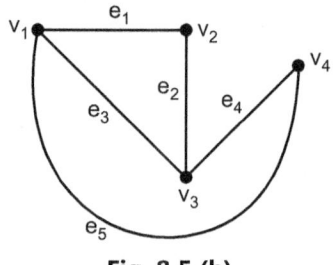

Fig. 8.5 (b)

8.2 Adjacency and Incidence

Let us define the relation between the vertices and edges in the graph.

Two vertices v_1 and v_2 of a graph G are said to be **adjacent** to each other if they are the end vertices of the same edge. In other words, if two vertices are joined directly by at least one edge then there vertices are called **adjacent vertices**.

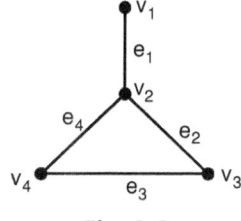

Fig. 8.6

In Fig. 8.6, v_1 and v_2 are adjacent vertices but v_1 and v_4 are not.

For incidence, if the vertex v_i is the end vertex of an edge $e_{ij} = (v_i, v_j)$ then the edge e_{ij} is said to be incident on v_i. Similarly, e_{ij} is said to be incident on v_j. In Fig. 8.6, e_1 is incident on v_1 and v_2.

Two non-parallel edges are said to be **adjacent** if they are incident on a common vertex. For example, e_1 and e_2 are adjacent. Similarly, e_3 and e_4 are also adjacent edges.

8.2.1 Degree of a vertex

The number of edges incident on a vertex v_i with self loop counted twice, is called the degree of the vertex v_i. It is denoted by $d(v_i)$. In the following Fig. 8.7, $d(v_1) = 3$, $d(v_2) = 3$, $d(v_3) = 1$, $d(v_4) = 3$, $d(v_5) = 4$, $d(v_6) = 0$.

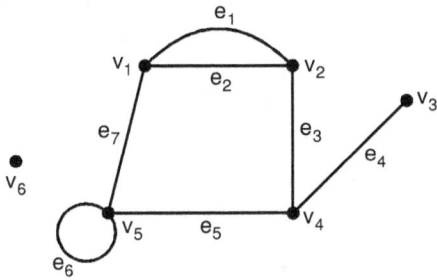

Fig. 8.7

8.2.2 Isolated Vertex and Pendant Vertex

A vertex with degree **zero** is called an **isolated vertex**. More formally, a vertex having no incident edge is an isolated vertex. A vertex of **degree 1** is called a **pendant vertex**. In Fig. 8.7, v_6 is an isolated vertex and v_3 is a pendant vertex.

8.2.3 Handshaking Lemma

Consider a graph G with e number of edges and n number of vertices. Since each edge contributes two degrees, the sum of the degrees of all vertices in G is twice the number of edges in G. i.e.

$$\sum_{n=1}^{n} d(v_i) = 2e \qquad \ldots (8.1)$$

This is called **handshaking lemma**. The result is so named because it implies that if several people shake hands, the total number of hands shaken must be even, precisely, because two hands are involved in one handshake.

From the equation (8.1), we shall derive the following interesting result.

Theorem 8.2.1: The number of vertices of odd degree in a graph is always even.

Proof:

Let G be a graph with e edges and n number of vertices.

Then by handshaking lemma,

$$\sum_{i=1}^{n} = d(v_i) = 2e = \text{even number}$$

Now, the total degree of all the vertices can be expressed as the sum of degrees of even degree vertices and odd degree vertices.

$$\Rightarrow \quad \sum d(v_j) + \sum d(v_k) = \sum_{i=1}^{n} d(v_i)$$

(even degree vertices) + (odd degree vertices)

$$\Rightarrow \quad \sum d(v_j) + \sum d(v_k) = 2e = \text{an even number}$$

(even degree vertices)   (odd degree vertices)

But the sum of degrees of even degree vertices is always even i.e. $\sum d(v_j)$ is even and 2e is always an even number.

Therefore, the sum of degrees of odd degree vertices should be even.

$$\Rightarrow \quad \sum d(v_k) = \text{an even number.}$$

odd degree vertices

This shows that the sum of the degrees of odd vertices is an even number and which is possible only when the number of odd degree vertices is even.

8.3 Matrix Representation of Graphs

A graph can also be represented by a matrix. Matrix representation of the graph is very convenient and useful for computer calculations. Two important ways are used for matrix representation of a graph; namely using (i) Adjacent matrix and (ii) Incident matrix.

8.3.1 Adjacency Matrix

The adjacency matrix of a graph G with n vertices and no parallel edges is a symmetric binary matrix $A(G) = [a_{ij}]$ or order $n \times n$ where,

a_{ij} = 1, if there is an edge between vertices v_i and v_j
(v_i and v_j are adjacent)
= 0, if v_i and v_j are not adjacent.

From the definition, it is clear that elements along principle diagonal of A(G) are all zeros if and only if the graph has no self loops. A self loop at vertex v_i corresponds to $a_{ij} = 1$.

Also if the graph has no self loops and no parallel edges, then the degree of a vertex is equal to the number of ones in the corresponding row or column vector of A(G).

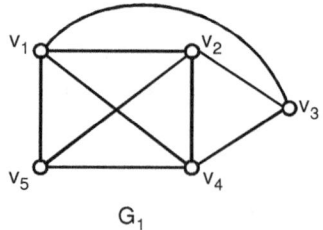

Fig. 8.8

Consider the graph G_1 shows in Fig. 8.8 which is without self loop.
Its adjacent matrix is

$$A(G_1) = \begin{array}{c} \\ v_1 \\ v_2 \\ v_3 \\ v_4 \\ v_5 \end{array} \begin{array}{c} \begin{array}{ccccc} v_1 & v_2 & v_3 & v_4 & v_5 \end{array} \\ \left[\begin{array}{ccccc} 0 & 1 & 1 & 1 & 1 \\ 1 & 0 & 1 & 1 & 1 \\ 1 & 1 & 0 & 1 & 0 \\ 1 & 1 & 1 & 0 & 1 \\ 1 & 1 & 0 & 1 & 0 \end{array} \right] \end{array}$$

Another graph G_2 and its adjacency matrix are shown below.

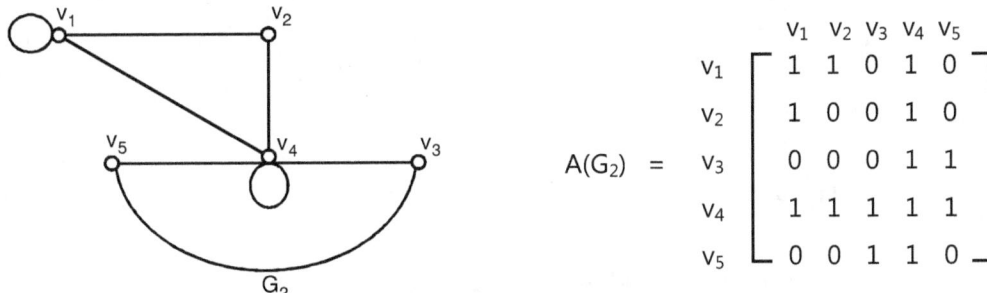

$$A(G_2) = \begin{array}{c} \\ v_1 \\ v_2 \\ v_3 \\ v_4 \\ v_5 \end{array} \begin{array}{c} \begin{array}{ccccc} v_1 & v_2 & v_3 & v_4 & v_5 \end{array} \\ \left[\begin{array}{ccccc} 1 & 1 & 0 & 1 & 0 \\ 1 & 0 & 0 & 1 & 0 \\ 0 & 0 & 0 & 1 & 1 \\ 1 & 1 & 1 & 1 & 1 \\ 0 & 0 & 1 & 1 & 0 \end{array} \right] \end{array}$$

Fig. 8.9

The adjacency matrix for the multigraph G with n vertices is an n × n matrix. $A(G) = [a_{ij}]$, where the elements a_{ij} are defined as

a_{ij} = N, if one or more edges are there between vertices v_i and v_j and N is the number of edges between v_i and v_j

= 0, otherwise

The multigraph G and its adjacency A(G) are shown in Fig. 8.10

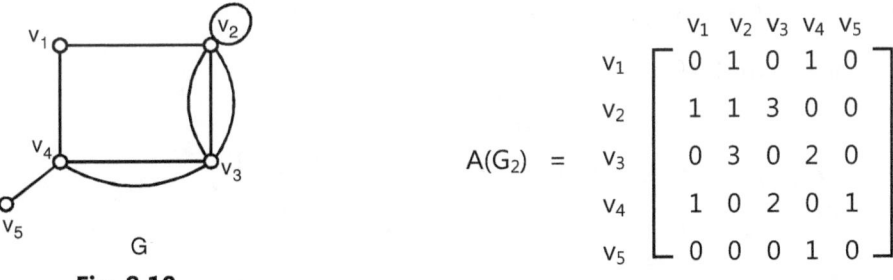

$$A(G_2) = \begin{array}{c} \\ v_1 \\ v_2 \\ v_3 \\ v_4 \\ v_5 \end{array} \begin{array}{c} \begin{array}{ccccc} v_1 & v_2 & v_3 & v_4 & v_5 \end{array} \\ \left[\begin{array}{ccccc} 0 & 1 & 0 & 1 & 0 \\ 1 & 1 & 3 & 0 & 0 \\ 0 & 3 & 0 & 2 & 0 \\ 1 & 0 & 2 & 0 & 1 \\ 0 & 0 & 0 & 1 & 0 \end{array} \right] \end{array}$$

Fig. 8.10

8.3.2 Incidence Matrix

Given a graph G with n vertices, e edges and no self loops. The incidence matrix $X(G) = [x_{ij}]$ of the graph G is an $n \times e$ matrix where,

$$x_{ij} = 1; \text{ if } j^{th} \text{ edge } e_j \text{ is incident on } i^{th} \text{ vertex } v_i$$
$$= 0; \text{ otherwise}$$

Here n rows correspond to n vertices and e columns correspond to e edges.

The graph G and its incidence matrix are given below in Fig. 8.11.

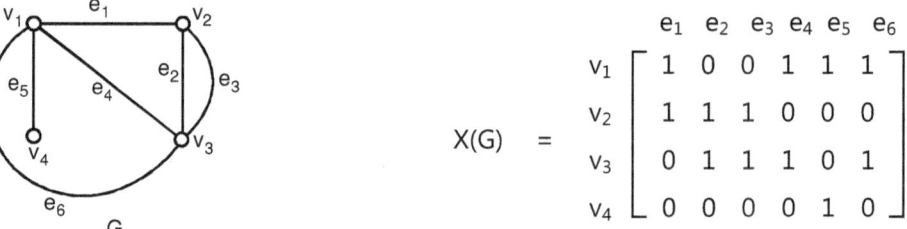

$$X(G) = \begin{array}{c} \\ v_1 \\ v_2 \\ v_3 \\ v_4 \end{array} \begin{array}{c} e_1 \; e_2 \; e_3 \; e_4 \; e_5 \; e_6 \\ \begin{bmatrix} 1 & 0 & 0 & 1 & 1 & 1 \\ 1 & 1 & 1 & 0 & 0 & 0 \\ 0 & 1 & 1 & 1 & 0 & 1 \\ 0 & 0 & 0 & 0 & 1 & 0 \end{bmatrix} \end{array}$$

Fig. 8.11

It is observed that, since every edge is incident on two vertices, each column of X(G) has exactly two ones. Thus, the number of ones in each row represents the degree of the corresponding vertex if the graph has no self loops. The row with all elements zero, represent the isolated vertex. If the graph has self loop for the edge e_i, then the corresponding column of e_i in the incidence matrix will contain only single one. This is evident from the following example, consider the graph G with self loop defined in Fig. 8.12.

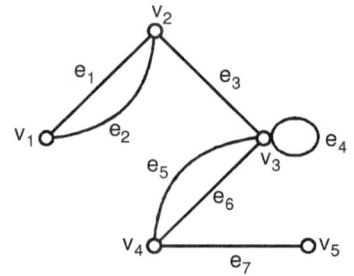

Fig. 8.12

Its incidence matrix X(G) is given by

$$X(G) = \begin{array}{c} \\ v_1 \\ v_2 \\ v_3 \\ v_4 \\ v_5 \end{array} \begin{array}{c} e_1 \; e_2 \; e_3 \; e_4 \; e_5 \; e_6 \; e_7 \\ \begin{bmatrix} 1 & 1 & 0 & 0 & 0 & 0 & 0 \\ 1 & 1 & 1 & 0 & 0 & 0 & 0 \\ 0 & 0 & 1 & 1 & 1 & 1 & 0 \\ 0 & 0 & 0 & 0 & 1 & 1 & 1 \\ 0 & 0 & 0 & 0 & 0 & 0 & 1 \end{bmatrix} \end{array}$$

Adjacency matrix of a diagraph:

Adjacency matrix of a directed graph is defined in a similar fashion as it is defined for undirected graph in section 8.3.1. Let G be a directed graph with n vertices with no parallel edges. The adjacency matrix $A(D) = [a_{ij}]$ of the digraph is then defined as an $n \times n$ matrix containing zeros and ones with

$$a_{ij} = 1; \text{ if there is an edge directed from } v_i \text{ to } v_j$$
$$= 0; \text{ otherwise}$$

Adjacency matrix is also called connection matrix (in network flow) or transition matrix. The directed graph D and its adjacency matrix are given below.

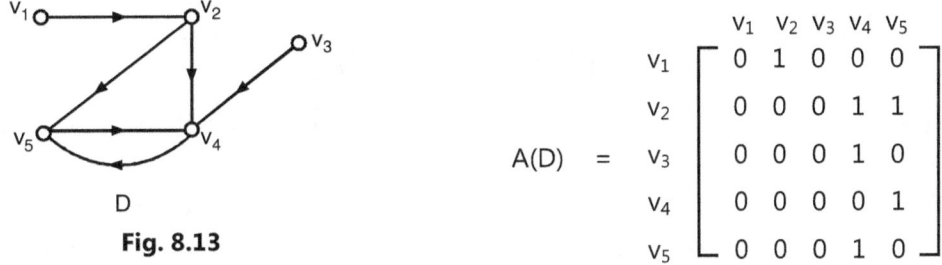

Fig. 8.13

The adjacency matrix is used as a tool to investigate the various properties such as connectedness of a diagraph by means of a digital computer.

Incidence matrix of a digraph:

The incidence matrix of a diagraph with n vertices, e edges and no self loops is a matrix $X(G) = [x_{ij}]$ or order $n \times n$, whose rows correspond to vertices and columns correspond to edges such that

$$x_{ij} = 1; \text{ if } j^{th} \text{ edge } e_j \text{ is incident out of } i^{th} \text{ vertex } v_i$$
$$= -1; \text{ if } j^{th} \text{ edge } e_j \text{ is incident into } i^{th} \text{ vertex } v_i$$
$$= 0; \text{ if } j^{th} \text{ edge } e_j \text{ is not incident on } i^{th} \text{ vertex } v_i$$

A graph D and its incidence matrix are shown in Fig. 8.14.

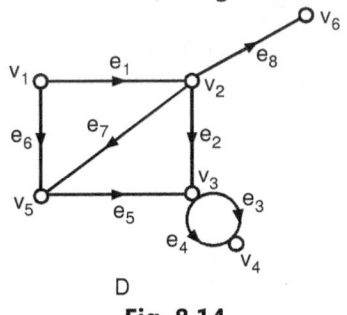

Fig. 8.14

$$X(G) = \begin{array}{c} \\ v_1 \\ v_2 \\ v_3 \\ v_4 \\ v_5 \\ v_6 \end{array} \begin{bmatrix} e_1 & e_2 & e_3 & e_4 & e_5 & e_6 & e_7 & e_8 \\ 1 & 0 & 0 & 0 & 0 & 1 & 0 & 0 \\ -1 & 1 & 0 & 0 & 0 & 0 & 1 & 1 \\ 0 & -1 & 1 & 1 & -1 & 0 & 0 & 0 \\ 0 & 0 & -1 & -1 & 0 & 0 & 0 & 0 \\ 0 & 0 & 0 & 0 & 1 & -1 & -1 & 0 \\ 0 & 0 & 0 & 0 & 0 & 0 & 0 & -1 \end{bmatrix}$$

It is observed that, in the incident matrix for digraph the number of ones in any row shows the out degree of the corresponding vertex. Similarly, the number of negative one's shows the in degree of the vertex.

SOLVED EXAMPLES

Example 1: Show that the maximum degree of any vertex in a simple graph with n vertices is $(n-1)$.

Solution: Let G be a simple graph on n vertices. Consider any vertex v of G.

Since the graph is simple (i.e. without self loops and parallel edges), the vertex v can be adjacent to at most remaining $(n-1)$ vertices. Hence, the degree of the vertex v can be at the most $(n-1)$. Hence maximum degree of any vertex in a simple graph with n vertices is $(n-1)$.

Example 2: Show that the maximum number of edges in a simple graph with n vertices is $\dfrac{n(n-1)}{2}$.

Solution: Let G be a simple graph with n vertices. By handshaking lemma,

$$\sum_{i=1}^{n} d(v_i) = 2e \text{ where, e is the number of edges in the graph G.}$$

$\Rightarrow d(v_1) + d(v_2) + \ldots + d(v_n) = 2e$

We know that the maximum degree of each vertex in the graph G can be at the most $(n-1)$. Therefore, above equation reduces to

$$\underbrace{(n-1) + (n-1) + \ldots + (n-1)}_{n \text{ times}} = 2e$$

$\Rightarrow \quad n(n-1) = 2e$

$\Rightarrow \quad e = \dfrac{n(n-1)}{2}$

Hence, the maximum number of edges in any simple graph with n vertices is $\frac{n(n-1)}{2}$.

Example 3: How many nodes are necessary to construct a graph with exactly 6 edges in which each node is of degree 2.

Solution: Suppose there are n vertices (nodes) in the graph with 6 edges. Also, given the degree of each vertex is 2. Therefore, by handshaking lemma,

$$\sum_{i=1}^{n} d(v_i) = 2e = 2 \times 6$$

$\Rightarrow \quad d(v_1) + d(v_2) + \ldots + d(v_n) = 2 \times 6 = 12$

$\Rightarrow \quad \underbrace{2 + 2 + \ldots + 2}_{n \text{ times}} = 12$

$\Rightarrow \quad 2n = 12$

$\Rightarrow \quad n = 6$

Hence, 6 nodes are required to construct a graph with 6 edges in which each node is of degree 2.

Example 4: Determine the number of edges in a graph with 6 nodes, 2 of degree 4 and 4 of degree 2. Draw two such graphs.

Solution: Suppose the graph with 6 vertices has e number of edges. Therefore, by handshaking lemma,

$$\sum_{i=1}^{6} d(v_i) = 2e$$

$\Rightarrow \quad d(v_1) + d(v_2) + d(v_3) + d(v_4) + d(v_5) + d(v_6) = 2e$

Now, given 2 vertices are of degree 4 and 4 vertices are of degree 2.
Hence, from the above equation

$(4 + 4) + (2 + 2 + 2 + 2) = 2e$

$\Rightarrow \quad 16 = 2e$

$\Rightarrow \quad e = 8$

Hence the number of edges in a graph with 6 vertices with given conditions is 8.
Two such graphs are shown below in Fig. 8.15.

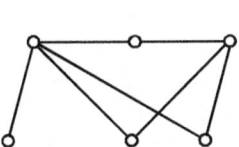 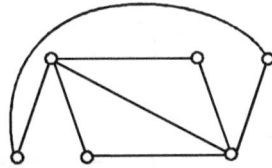

Fig. 8.15

Example 5: Is it possible to construct a graph with 12 nodes such that 2 of the nodes have degree 3 and the remaining nodes have degree 4.

Solution: Suppose it is possible to construct a graph with 12 nodes out of which 2 of them are having degree 3 and remaining vertices are having degree 4.

Hence, by handshaking lemma,

$$\sum_{i=1}^{12} d(v_i) = 2e$$

where e is the number of edges.

According to given conditions,

$$(2 \times 3) + (10 \times 4) = 2e$$
$$\Rightarrow 6 + 40 = 2e$$
$$\Rightarrow 46 = 2e$$
$$\Rightarrow e = 23$$

It is possible to construct a graph with 23 edges and 12 nodes which satisfy given conditions.

Example 6: A man is supposed to bring a dog, a sheep and a bag of cabbage across a river on a row boat. The boat is very small and he can carry only one of these items on the boat at a time. Furthermore, he cannot leave the dog alone with the sheep nor the sheep alone with the cabbage. Construct the graph and determine all possible ways for the man to transport all items across the river.

Solution: Suppose 'M' denotes for man, 'S' for sheep, 'D' for dog and 'C' for cabbage.

In the beginning, suppose all the items are with man on one side of a river keeping in mind that sheep can eat the cabbage and the dog can eat the sheep, all the possible ways for the man to transport all items across the river are as follows:

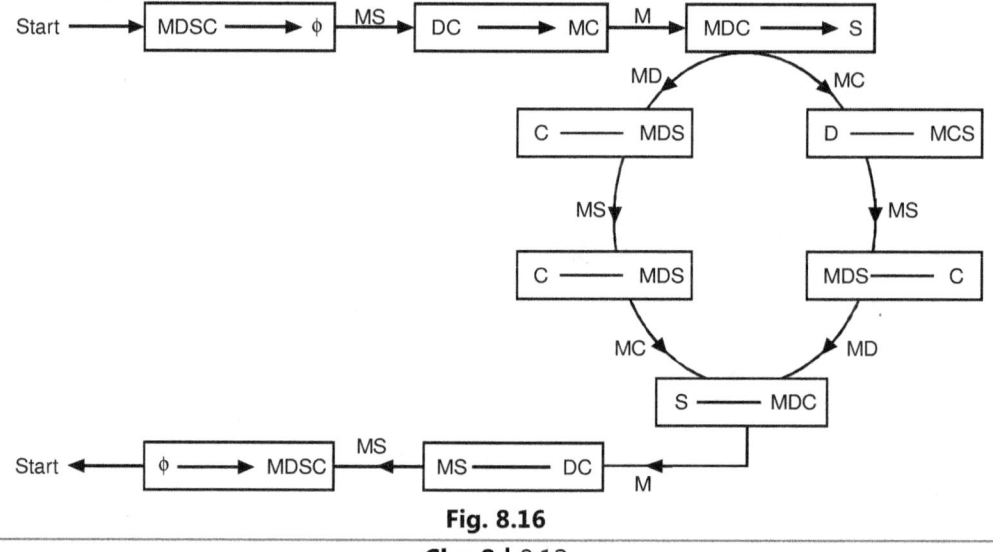

Fig. 8.16

Example 7: An odd fellow wishes to have an odd party that is attended by an odd number of odd people, each of whom is acquainted with an odd number of other odd people at the party. Can this odd situation occur?

Solution: Represent each person in a party (except host) by a vertex – and each pair of acquaintances by an edge. Then the odd party can be represented by a graph with odd number of vertices such that the degree of each vertex is odd. But this is the contradiction to theorem 8.2.1 which says that number of odd vertices in any graph is always even.

Hence the odd party is impossible.

Example 8: Is it possible to draw a simple graph with 4 vertices and 7 edges? Justify.

Solution: In the simple graph with n vertices, the maximum number of edges will be $\frac{n(n-1)}{2}$. Hence, a simple graph with 4 vertices will have at the most $\frac{4 \times 3}{2} = 6$ edges. Therefore, the simple graph with 4 vertices can not have 7 edges. Hence such a graph does not exist.

Example 9: Find the adjacency matrix of the following graphs:

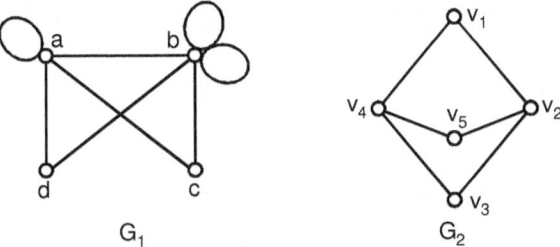

Fig. 8.17

Solution: The adjacency matrices for the graphs G_1 and G_2 are given below.

$$A(G_1) = \begin{array}{c c} & \begin{array}{cccc} a & b & c & d \end{array} \\ \begin{array}{c} a \\ b \\ c \\ d \end{array} & \left[\begin{array}{cccc} 1 & 1 & 1 & 1 \\ 1 & 2 & 1 & 0 \\ 1 & 1 & 0 & 0 \\ 1 & 1 & 0 & 0 \end{array} \right] \end{array}$$

v_1 v_2 v_3 v_4 v_5

$$A(G_2) = \begin{matrix} v_1 \\ v_2 \\ v_3 \\ v_4 \\ v_5 \end{matrix} \begin{bmatrix} 0 & 1 & 0 & 1 & 0 \\ 1 & 0 & 1 & 0 & 1 \\ 0 & 1 & 0 & 1 & 0 \\ 1 & 0 & 1 & 0 & 1 \\ 0 & 1 & 0 & 1 & 0 \end{bmatrix}$$

Example 10: Draw the graph corresponding to each adjacency matrix.

$$\text{(i)} \quad \begin{matrix} v_1 \\ v_2 \\ v_3 \\ v_4 \\ v_5 \end{matrix} \begin{matrix} v_1 & v_2 & v_3 & v_4 & v_5 \\ \begin{bmatrix} 0 & 1 & 1 & 0 & 0 \\ 1 & 0 & 1 & 0 & 0 \\ 1 & 1 & 0 & 1 & 0 \\ 0 & 0 & 1 & 0 & 1 \\ 0 & 0 & 0 & 1 & 1 \end{bmatrix} \end{matrix}$$

$$\text{(ii)} \quad \begin{matrix} a \\ b \\ c \\ d \end{matrix} \begin{matrix} a & b & c & d \\ \begin{bmatrix} 1 & 0 & 0 & 1 \\ 0 & 0 & 2 & 1 \\ 0 & 2 & 0 & 0 \\ 1 & 1 & 0 & 1 \end{bmatrix} \end{matrix}$$

Solution: (i) The graph represented by adjacency matrix (i) is shown below.

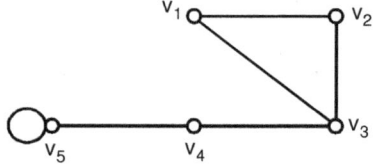

Fig. 8.18

(ii) The graph G with adjacency matrix (ii) is given by

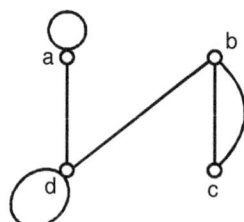

Fig. 8.19

Example 11: Determine the incidence matrix of the following graphs.

(a)

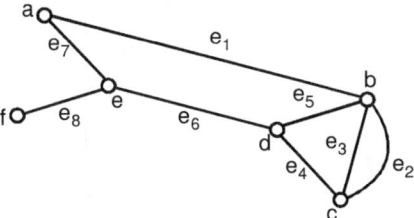

Fig. 8.20 (a)

(b)

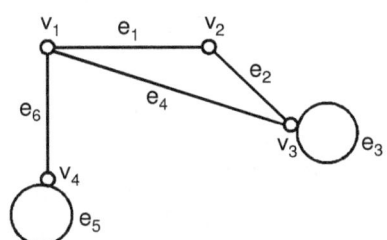

Fig. 8.20 (b)

Solution: (a) The incidence matrix for the graph shown in Fig. 8.20 (a) is as follows:

$$X(G) = \begin{array}{c} \\ a \\ b \\ c \\ d \\ e \\ f \end{array} \begin{bmatrix} e_1 & e_2 & e_3 & e_4 & e_5 & e_6 & e_7 & e_8 \\ 1 & 0 & 0 & 0 & 0 & 0 & 1 & 0 \\ 1 & 1 & 1 & 0 & 1 & 0 & 0 & 0 \\ 0 & 1 & 1 & 1 & 0 & 0 & 0 & 0 \\ 0 & 0 & 0 & 1 & 1 & 1 & 0 & 0 \\ 0 & 0 & 0 & 0 & 0 & 1 & 1 & 1 \\ 0 & 0 & 0 & 0 & 0 & 0 & 0 & 1 \end{bmatrix}$$

(b) The graph G in (b) has following incidence matrix.

$$X(G) = \begin{array}{c} \\ v_1 \\ v_2 \\ v_3 \\ v_4 \end{array} \begin{bmatrix} e_1 & e_2 & e_3 & e_4 & e_5 & e_6 \\ 1 & 0 & 0 & 1 & 0 & 1 \\ 1 & 1 & 0 & 0 & 0 & 0 \\ 0 & 1 & 1 & 1 & 0 & 0 \\ 0 & 0 & 0 & 0 & 1 & 1 \end{bmatrix}$$

Example 12: Draw the graph for following incidence matrix.

$$\begin{array}{c} \\ a \\ b \\ c \\ d \\ e \end{array} \begin{array}{c} e_1 \ e_2 \ e_3 \ e_4 \ e_5 \ e_6 \\ \begin{bmatrix} 0 & 1 & 0 & 0 & 1 & 1 \\ 0 & 1 & 1 & 0 & 1 & 0 \\ 0 & 0 & 0 & 1 & 0 & 1 \\ 1 & 0 & 0 & 0 & 0 & 0 \\ 1 & 0 & 0 & 1 & 0 & 0 \end{bmatrix} \end{array}$$

Solution: The corresponding graph has the vertices and six edges shown below.

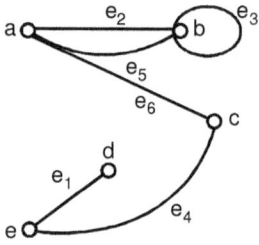

Fig. 8.21

Example 13: How many simple labeled graphs with n vertices are there?

Solution: We know that a simple graph with n vertices has maximum possible number of edges $\frac{n(n-1)}{2}$.

To construct a simple graph with e number of edges with n vertices, can be done in $\binom{\frac{n(n-1)}{2}}{e}$ ways i.e. $^{n(n-1)/2}C_e$ ways. The number of edges e can vary from zero to $\frac{n(n-1)}{2}$.

Hence the total number of ways to construct such type of graphs is given by

$$\binom{\frac{n(n-1)}{2}}{0} + \binom{\frac{n(n-1)}{2}}{1} + \binom{\frac{n(n-1)}{2}}{2} + \ldots + \binom{\frac{n(n-1)}{2}}{\frac{n(n-1)}{2}}$$

which is equal to $2^{\frac{n(n-1)}{2}}$ because $\binom{k}{0} + \binom{k}{1} + \binom{k}{2} + \ldots \binom{k}{k} = 2^k$.

8.4 Some Important and Useful Graphs

After defining the basic terminology, now we are in position to define some important and useful graphs.

> **(a) Directed graphs or Digraphs:** A **directed graph** or **digraph D** is an ordered pair (V, A) where V is a non empty set of elements called vertices and A is the set of ordered pair of elements called directed edges or arcs. In other words, we can say that if the each edge of the graph G has a direction then the graph is called **directed graph** or **digraph**.

In Fig. 8.22, we have a digraph D = (V, A) in which the vertex set V = $\{v_1, v_2, v_3, v_4\}$ and the directed edge set A = $\{e_1, e_2, e_3, e_4, e_5, e_6, e_7\}$. The edges are given by $e_1 = (v_1, v_3)$, $e_2 = (v_3, v_3)$, $e_3 = (v_2, v_3)$, $e_4 = (v_1, v_2)$, $e_5 = (v_1, v_2)$, $e_6 = (v_4, v_2)$, $e_7 = (v_2, v_4)$.

In Fig. 8.22, the vertices v_1 and v_2 are joined by more than one arc with the same directions. Such arcs are called **multiple arcs**. The arcs e_6 and e_7 are not multiple arcs because their directions are different though their end vertices are same.

The self loop for the digraph is defined exactly in the same way as defined for undirected graph in 8.1.1. In Fig. 8.22, the arc e_2 is a self loop.

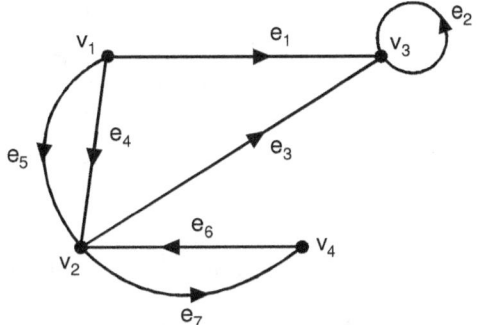

Fig. 8.22

Digraphs without loops and multiple arcs are known as **simple digraphs**.

Incidence

Let u be any vertex of the digraph D = (V, A). An arc 'a' in D is said to be incident into the vertex u if it is of the form (v, u) for some v ∈ V. Similarly, 'a' is said to be incident out of the vertex u if it is of the form (u, v) for some v ∈ V. For example, e_1 is incident into the vertex v_3 and incident out of the vertex v_1 in Fig. 8.22.

Indegree and Outdegree

> The indegree of a vertex u of digraph D is defined as the **number of arcs which are incident into u** and is denoted by $\overrightarrow{d(u)}$. Similarly, the **outdegree of** a vertex u is defined as the **number of arcs which are incident out of u** and is denoted by $\overleftarrow{d(u)}$.

As shown in Fig. 8.22, indegree of different vertices are

$$\overrightarrow{d(v_1)} = 0, \quad \overrightarrow{d(v_2)} = 3, \quad \overrightarrow{d(v_3)} = 3, \quad \overrightarrow{d(v_4)} = 1,$$

The outdegree of vertices are

$$\overleftarrow{d(v_1)} = 3, \quad \overleftarrow{d(v_2)} = 2, \quad \overleftarrow{d(v_3)} = 1, \quad \overleftarrow{d(v_4)} = 1$$

Underlying Graph of a Digraph

The underlying graph of a digraph D is obtained by neglecting the directions of the arcs. For example, D_2 is a underlying graph of D_1 in Fig. 8.23.

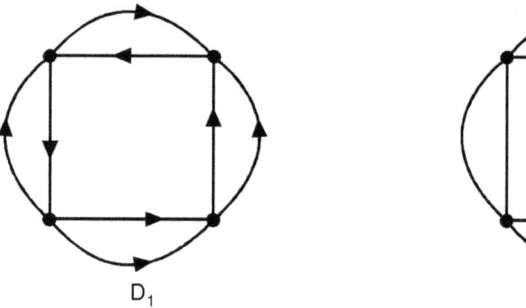

Fig. 8.23

Here D_1 is a simple digraph but its underlying graph D_2 is not a simple graph.

(b) Null Graph: If the edge set of any graph with n vertices is an empty set, then the graph is known as **null graph**. It is denoted by N_n. Following are the examples of null graph on 3 vertices and 4 vertices respectively.

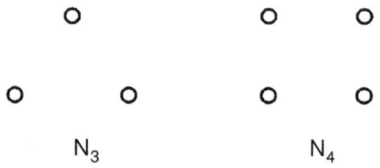

Fig. 8.24

(c) Complete Graph: Let G be a simple graph on n vertices. If the degree of each vertex is (n – 1), then the graph G is called a **complete graph**. More generally, if every pair of vertices is adjacent in any simple graph, then the graph is said to be a **complete graph**. Complete graph on n vertices is denoted by K_n. Complete graph on two, three, four and five vertices are shown in the following Fig. 8.25.

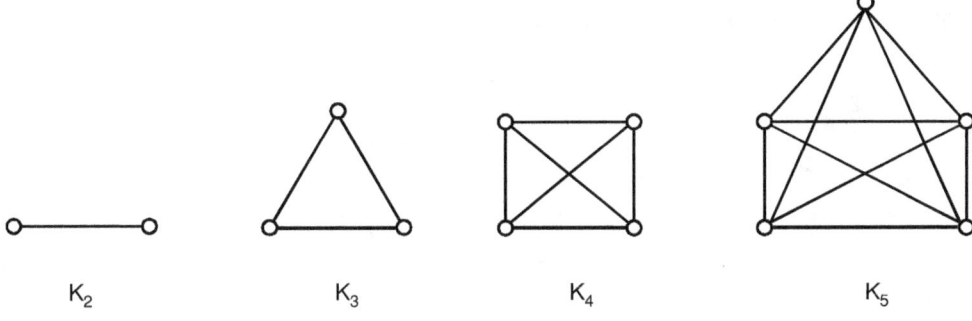

K₂ K₃ K₄ K₅

Fig. 8.25

In a complete graph K_n, the number of edges are $\frac{n(n-1)}{2}$.

(d) Regular Graph: If the **degree of each vertex is same** say 'r' in any graph G, then the graph G is said to be a **regular graph of degree r.**

The regular graph of degree r is also called r-regular graph. For example, the regular graph of degree 2 is also called 2-regular graph.

For example, the Peterson graph shown in Fig. 8.26 (a) is a regular graph of degree 3.

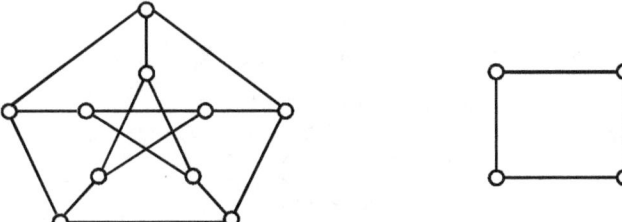

(a) Regular Graph of Degree 3   (b) Regular Graph of Degree 2

Fig. 8.26

Complete graph K_n is also a regular graph of degree (n − 1). But every regular graph need not be a complete graph. For example, Fig. 8.26 (b) is a regular graph of degree 2 but it is not a complete graph.

(e) Bipartite Graph: Let G be a graph with vertex set V and edge set E, then G is called a **bipartite graph** if its vertex set V can be partitioned into two disjoint subsets say V_1 and V_2 such that $V_1 \cup V_2 = V$ and $V_1 \cap V_2 = \phi$ and also each edge of G joins a vertex of V_1 to a vertex of V_2.

Following graphs shown in Fig. 8.27 are bipartite graphs.

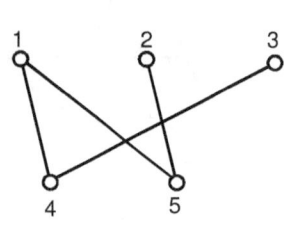 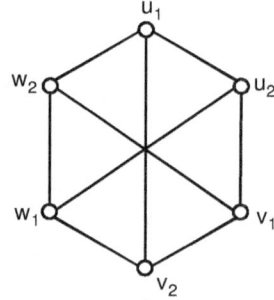 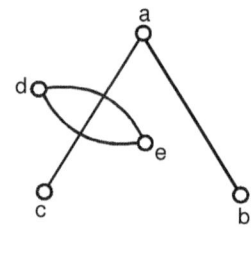

$V_1 = \{1, 2, 3\}$ $V_1 = \{u_1, v_1, w_1\}$ $V_1 = \{a, d\}$
$V_2 = \{4, 5\}$ $V_2 = \{u_2, v_2, w_2\}$ $V_2 = \{b, c, e\}$

Fig. 8.27

In bipartite graph, the vertices of V_1 should **not** be joined. Similarly, vertices of V_2 also should **not** be joined by edges. A bipartite graph cannot have a self loop.

> **(f) Complete Bipartite Graph:** A bipartite graph is called a **complete bipartite graph** if **each** vertex of V_1 is joined to every vertex of V_2 by a unique edge.

A complete bipartite graph is denoted by $K_{m,n}$ if the number of vertices in V_1 is m and that in V_2 is n.

Total number of edges in any complete bipartite graph $K_{m,n}$ is given by (mn).

Following are some examples of complete bipartite graphs.

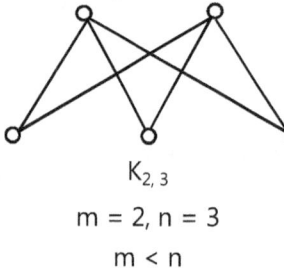 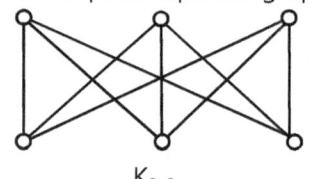 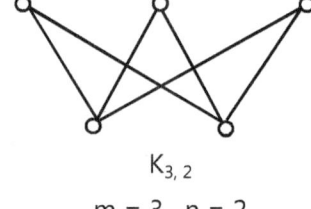

$K_{2,3}$ $K_{3,3}$ $K_{3,2}$
m = 2, n = 3   m = 3, n = 3   m = 3, n = 2
m < n   m = n   m > n

Fig. 8.28 (a)

The graph $K_{1,n}$ is known as **star**. A star $K_{1,5}$ shown in Fig. 8.28 (b).

Every complete bipartite graph is regular if m = n, $K_{3,3}$ is a regular graph of degree 3 shown in Fig. 8.28 (a).

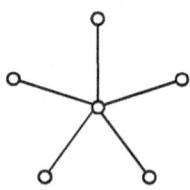

Fig. 8.28 (b)

8.5 Linked Represented of Graphs

Many practical problems which involve large graphs are solved using digital computer. Various methods are available to store the graph in a computer. Sequential representation using adjacency matrix, edge listing, link representation is some of the methods used for this purpose. The link representation which is also called adjacency structure for storing the graph in computer is described in this section.

In this method, the graph is represented by a linear array. After assigning the vertex, in any order, the number 1, 2, ... n, we represent each vertex k by a linear array, whose first element is a vertex k and whose remaining elements are the vertices that are immediate successor of k, that is, the vertices which have a directed path of length one from k (In an undirected graph these are the adjacent vertices to vertex k).

For example, consider the digraph as shown in Fig. 8.29.

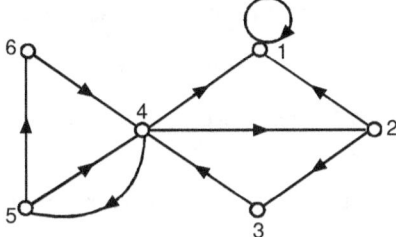

Fig. 8.29

The vertices and their adjacent vertices are as follows:

```
1 : 1
2 : 1, 3
3 : 4
4 : 1, 2, 5
5 : 4, 6
6 : 4
```

The above adjacency can be represented as

G = [1: 1;   2: 1, 3;   3: 4;   4: 1, 2, 5;   5: 4, 6;   6: 4]

This is called link representation of the graph G.

The link representation of a graph G stores the graph in the memory of computer by using its adjacency lists and will contain two files namely (i) vertex file and (ii) edge file. The vertex file will contain the list of vertices of G, usually maintained by a linked list and the edge file will contain all the edges of G. Each record of the edge file will correspond to a vertex in an adjacency list and hence, indirectly, to an edge of the graph G.

SOLVED EXAMPLES

Example 1: Determine which of the graphs given in following Fig. 8.30 are Bipartite graphs.

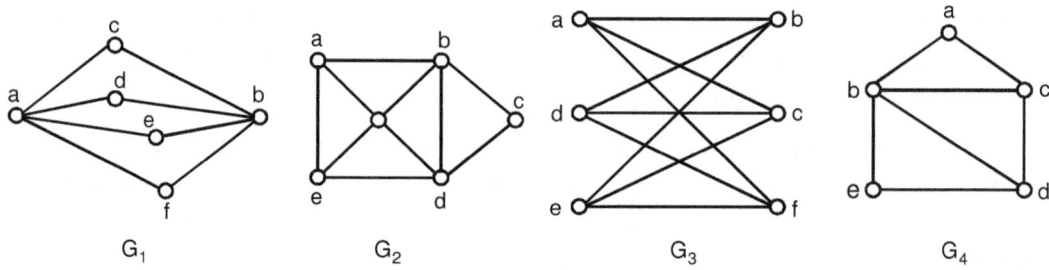

Fig. 8.30

Solution: Consider G_1, this is a bipartite graph because we can divide its vertex set V = {a, b, c, d, e, f} into two sets of vertices V = {a, b} and V_2 = {c, d, e, f} such that $V_1 \cup V_2$ = V, $V_1 \cap V_2$ = ϕ also edges of G_1 join the vertices from V_1 to V_2.

For G_2, it is not a bipartite graph because we cannot partition its vertex set into two parts satisfying the conditions for bipartite graphs.

Consider G_3, it is a bipartite graph because its vertex set V can be partitioned into two subsets V_1 and V_1 where V_1 = {a, d, e}, V_2 = {b, c, f} such that $V_1 \cup V_2$ = V and $V_1 \cap V_2$ = ϕ. Also edges of G_3, join the vertices of V_1 to vertices of V_2. In fact, G_3 is a complete bipartite graph because each vertex of V_1 is joined to each vertex of V_2. G_4 is not a bipartite graph.

Example 2: Draw a complete bipartite graph which is not a regular graph.

Solution: A complete bipartite graph $k_{m, n}$ is not a regular graph if m ≠ n. For example, $k_{2, 3}$ shown in Fig. 8.31 is not a regular graph.

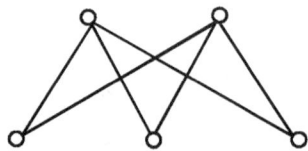

Fig. 8.31

Example 3: How many edges has each of the following graphs: (i) k_{10} (ii) $k_{5, 7}$.

Solution: (i) k_{10} is a complete graph on 10 vertices and will have $\frac{10 \times 9}{2}$ = 45 edges.

(ii) $k_{5, 7}$ is a complete bipartite graph and will have 5 × 7 = 35 edges.

Example 4: Draw a graph which is regular of degree 3 (other than k_4 and $k_{3,3}$).

Solution: The Peterson graph is a regular graph of degree 3 which is shown in Fig. 8.32.

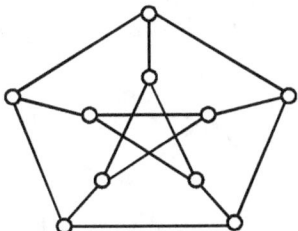

Fig. 8.32

Example 5: Draw the directed graph whose adjacency matrix is given below.

$$A(D) = \begin{array}{c} \\ a \\ b \\ c \\ d \\ e \\ f \end{array} \begin{array}{cccccc} a & b & c & d & e & f \\ \left[\begin{array}{cccccc} 0 & 0 & 1 & 0 & 0 & 0 \\ 0 & 0 & 0 & 0 & 1 & 0 \\ 0 & 0 & 0 & 1 & 0 & 0 \\ 0 & 0 & 0 & 1 & 1 & 0 \\ 0 & 0 & 0 & 0 & 1 & 1 \\ 0 & 1 & 0 & 0 & 0 & 1 \end{array}\right] \end{array}$$

Solution: The directed graph with six vertices with adjacency matrix given above is as follows.

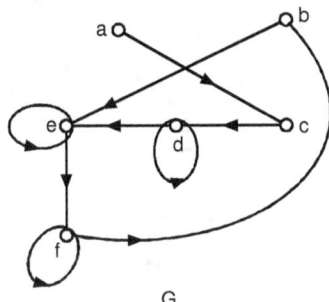

G

Fig. 8.33

Example 6: Draw the directed graph with incidence matrix shown below.

	e_1	e_2	e_3	e_4	e_5	e_6	e_7	e_8	e_9
a	−1	−1	0	1	1	0	0	0	0
b	1	0	1	0	0	0	−1	0	0
c	0	1	−1	0	0	−1	0	0	1
d	0	0	0	−1	0	1	1	1	0
e	0	0	0	0	−1	0	0	−1	−1

Solution: The directed graph with five vertices and 9 edges with given incidence matrix is as follows:

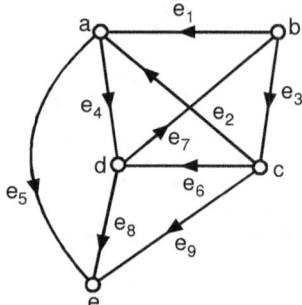

Fig. 8.34

Example 7: Find the adjacency matrix, incidence matrix and linked representation for the graph shown in the following Fig. 8.35.

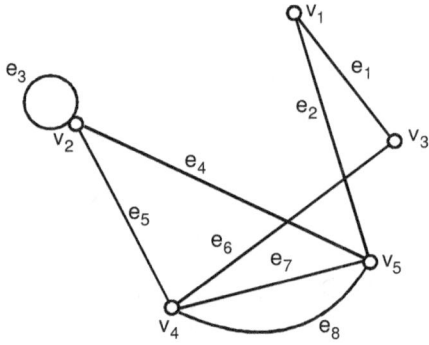

Fig. 8.35

Solution: Since the graph has five vertices, its adjacency matrix will contain five rows and five columns. It is given by

$$A(G) = \begin{array}{c} \\ v_1 \\ v_2 \\ v_3 \\ v_4 \\ v_5 \end{array} \begin{array}{c} \begin{array}{ccccc} v_1 & v_2 & v_3 & v_4 & v_5 \end{array} \\ \left[\begin{array}{ccccc} 0 & 0 & 1 & 0 & 1 \\ 0 & 1 & 0 & 1 & 1 \\ 1 & 0 & 0 & 1 & 0 \\ 0 & 1 & 1 & 0 & 2 \\ 1 & 1 & 0 & 2 & 0 \end{array} \right] \end{array}$$

The given graph has five vertices and eight edges therefore its incidence matrix will be 5×8 matrix given by

$$X(G) = \begin{array}{c} \\ V_1 \\ V_2 \\ V_3 \\ V_4 \\ V_5 \end{array} \begin{array}{c} \begin{array}{cccccccc} e_1 & e_2 & e_3 & e_4 & e_5 & e_6 & e_7 & e_8 \end{array} \\ \left[\begin{array}{cccccccc} 1 & 1 & 0 & 0 & 0 & 0 & 0 & 0 \\ 0 & 0 & 1 & 1 & 1 & 0 & 0 & 0 \\ 1 & 0 & 0 & 0 & 0 & 1 & 0 & 0 \\ 0 & 0 & 0 & 0 & 1 & 1 & 1 & 1 \\ 0 & 1 & 0 & 1 & 0 & 0 & 1 & 1 \end{array} \right] \end{array}$$

The adjacency structure of vertices is give by

V_1 : V_3, V_5
V_2 : V_2, V_4, V_5
V_3 : V_1, V_4
V_4 : V_2, V_3, V_5
V_5 : V_1, V_2, V_4

Hence the linked representation of given graph is

[V_1: V_3, V_5; V_2: V_2, V_4, V_5; V_3: V_1, V_4; V_4: V_2, V_3, V_5; V_5: V_1, V_2, V_4]

8.6 Isomorphism

In geometry, two figures are thought of as equivalent (and called congruent) if they have identical behaviour in terms of geometric properties. Likewise, two graphs are thought of as equivalent (called **isomorphic**) if they have identical behaviour in terms of graph-theoretic properties. The problem of graph isomorphism arises in many field, such as chemistry, switching theory, information retrieval etc. Now we define isomorphism of graph as follows:

Two graphs $G_1 (V_1, E_1)$ and $G' (V', E')$ are said to be isomorphic to each other if there is a one-one correspondence between their vertices and between their edges such that the incidence relationship is preserved. In other words, suppose that edge e is incident on vertices v_1 and v_2 of G, then the corresponding edge e' in G' must be incident on the vertices v_1' and v_2' that corresponds to v_1 and v_2.

In particular, adjacency between vertices is preserved. More generally two graphs G_1 and G_2 are isomorphic if we can find the bijections $f_V: V_1 \rightarrow V_2$ and $f_e: E_1 \rightarrow E_2$ such that if $e \in E_1$, given by e = (a, b) where a and b are vertices in V_1 then $f_e (e) = (f_V (a), f_V (b))$, where $f_V (a)$ and $f_V (b)$ are vertices in V_2.

Isomorphic graphs are denoted by $G_1 \cong G_2$.

In following Fig. 8.36, G_1 is isomorphic to G_2.

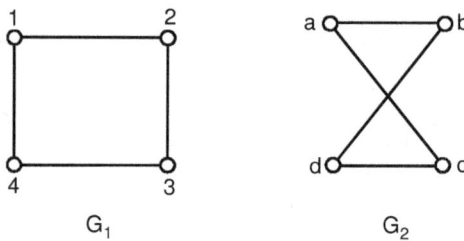

Fig. 8.36

The one-one correspondence between the vertices are

$1 \to a$

$2 \to b$

$3 \to d$

$4 \to c$

It is immediately apparent by definition of isomorphism that two isomorphic graphs must have

1. The same number of vertices.
2. The same number of edges.
3. An equal number of vertices with a given degree.

However, these conditions are by no means sufficient. For instance, the two graphs shown in Fig. 8.37, satisfy all the three conditions given above, yet they are not isomorphic.

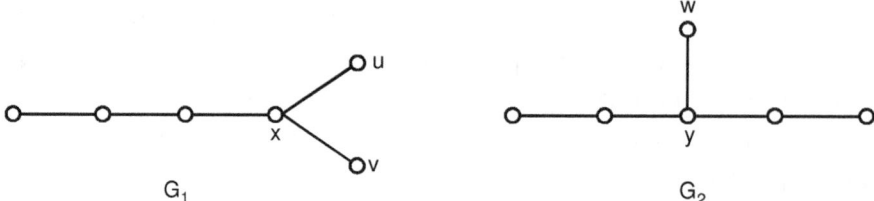

Fig. 8.37

In Fig. 8.37, the graph G_1 has a vertex x of degree 3 which is adjacent to two pendant vertices u and v and one vertex of degree 2. But in G_2, the vertex y of degree 3 is adjacent to only one pendant vertex y and two vertices of degree 2. Hence, adjacency is not preserved. Therefore $G_1 \not\cong G_2$.

SOLVED EXAMPLES

Example 1: Show that following graph are isomorphic.

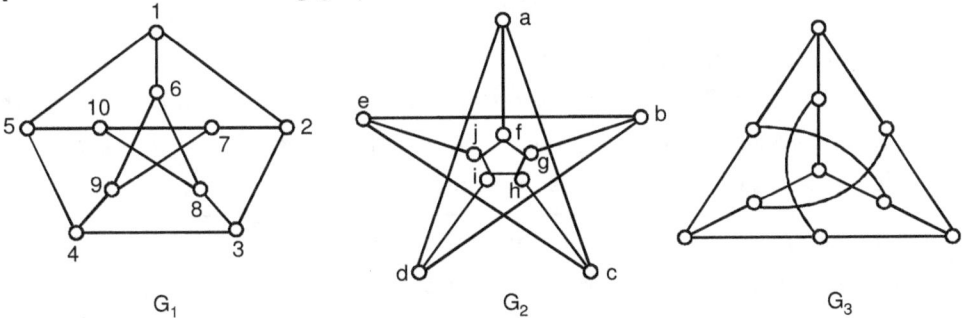

Fig. 8.38

Solution: Consider the given graphs G_1 and G_2. Here both the graphs contain 10 vertices and 15 edges. The number of vertices of degree 3 is 10 in both the graphs. Also the adjacency is preserved. Hence, both the graphs are isomorphic.

Isomorphism is given by

$$\begin{aligned} 1 &\to f \\ 2 &\to g \\ 3 &\to h \\ 4 &\to i \\ 5 &\to j \\ 6 &\to a \\ 7 &\to b \\ 8 &\to c \\ 9 &\to d \\ 10 &\to e \end{aligned}$$

In the similar way, we can show that G_2 and G_3 are also isomorphic.

Example 2: Determine whether following graphs are isomorphic or not.

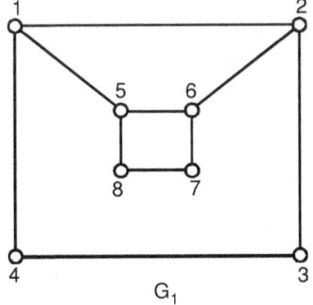

Fig. 8.39

Solution: Here both the graphs G_1 and G_2 contain 8 vertices and 10 edges. The number of vertices of degree 2 in both the graphs is four. Also the number of vertices of degree 3 in both the graphs is 4.

For adjacency, consider the vertex 1 of degree 3 in G_1. It is adjacent to two vertices of degree 3 and 1 vertex of degree 2. But in G_2 there does not exist any vertex of degree 3 which is adjacent to two vertices of degree 3 and 1 vertex of degree 2. Hence, adjacency is not preserved. Hence, given graphs are not isomorphic.

Example 3: Draw all non-isomorphic graphs on 2 and 3 vertices.

Solution: All non-isomorphic graphs on 2 vertices are

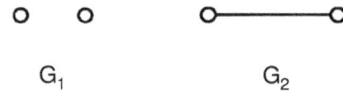

Fig. 8.40

All non-isomorphic graphs on 3 vertices are as follows:

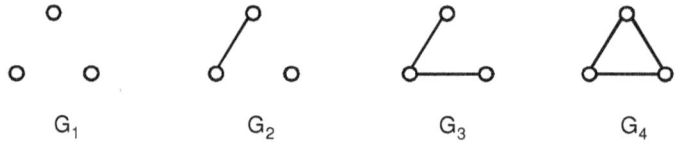

Fig. 8.41

Example 4: Find whether following pairs of graphs shown in Fig. 8.42, 8.43 and 8.44 and 8.45 are isomorphic or not.

(i)

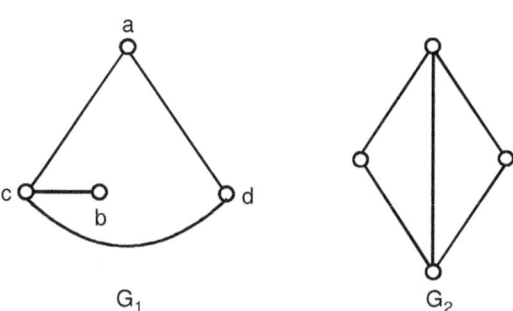

Fig. 8.42

Solution: Here G_1 and G_2 both have 4 vertices but G_1 has 4 edges and G_2 has 5 edges. Hence G_1 is not isomorphic to G_2.

(ii)

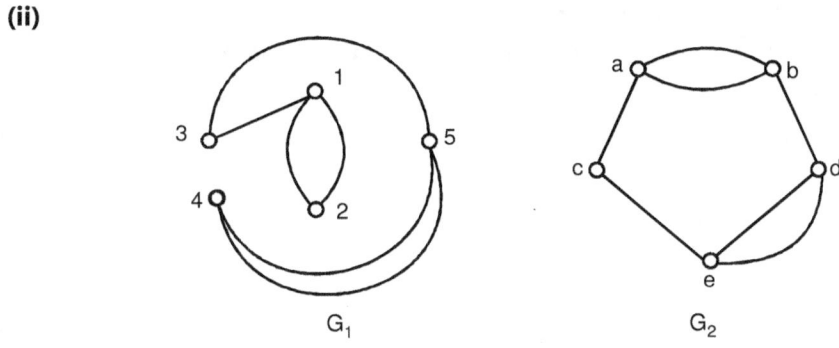

Fig. 8.43

Solution: Here again G_1 and G_2 both have 5 vertices but G_1 has 6 edges while G_2 has 7 edges. Hence $G_1 \not\cong G_2$.

(iii)

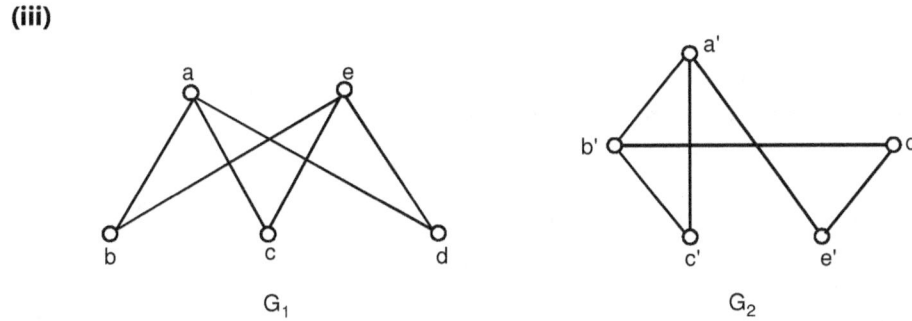

Fig. 8.44

Solution: G_1 and G_2 both have 5 vertices and 6 edges.

In G_1, the vertex 'a' of degree 3 is adjacent to 3 vertices of degree 2. But in G_2, both the vertices a' and b' of degree 3 are **not** adjacent to 3 vertices of degree 2. Hence, 'a' in G_1 can not be mapped to either a' or b' in G_2. Hence, bijection between vertices does not exist. Hence G_1 is not isomorphic to G_2.

(iv)

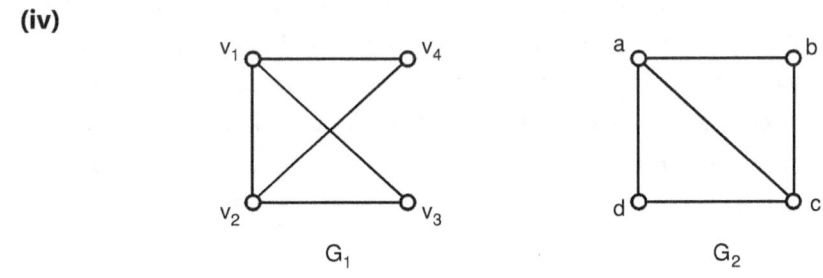

Fig. 8.45

Solution: Here both the graphs have 4 vertices and 5 edges.
In G_1 and G_2 both, there are 2 vertices of degree 2 and 2 vertices of degree 3.
Also the adjacency is preserved. The one-one correspondence between vertices is given by

$$v_1 \to a$$
$$v_2 \to c$$
$$v_3 \to d$$
$$v_4 \to b$$

Hence $G_1 \cong G_2$.

Example 5: Find whether k_6 and $k_{3,3}$ are isomorphic or not?
Solution: k_6 and $k_{3,3}$ both contain 6 vertices. But k_6, the complete graph on 6 vertices has $\frac{6 \times 5}{2} = 15$ edges while $k_{3,3}$, the complete bipartite graph has $3 \times 3 = 9$ edges. Hence, k_6 is **not** isomorphic to $k_{3,3}$.

Example 6: Which of the graphs shown in Fig. 8.46 are isomorphic.

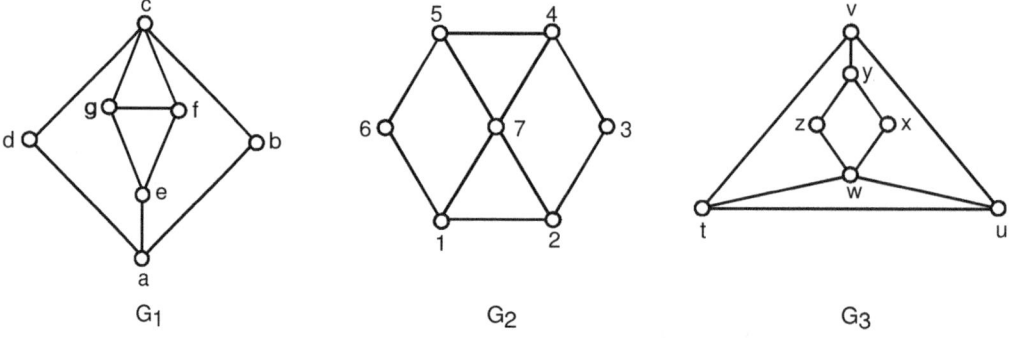

Fig. 8.46

Solution: Note first that each of the graphs is simple, connected and has 7 vertices and 11 edges. Furthermore, each has one vertex of degree 4, four vertices of degree 3 and two vertices of degree 2. Now, consider the graph G_1. In this graph, the vertex C of degree 4 is adjacent to 2 vertices of degree 3, while in G_2, the vertex 7 of degree 4 is adjacent to four-vertices of degree 3. Hence, G_1 and G_2 are not isomorphic. Graphs G_1 and G_3 are isomorphic because adjacency is preserved. An isomorphism is defined by the following vertex bijection: $a \to y$, $b \to x$, $c \to w$, $d \to z$, $e \to v$, $f \to t$, $g \to u$. Hence $G_1 \cong G_3$ since, $G_1 \cong G_2$ and $G_1 \cong G_3$, therefore $G_2 \cong G_3$.

Hence, in the given Fig. 8.46 only G_1 and G_3 are isomorphic.

Example 7: Are the graphs drawn below isomorphic? Why?

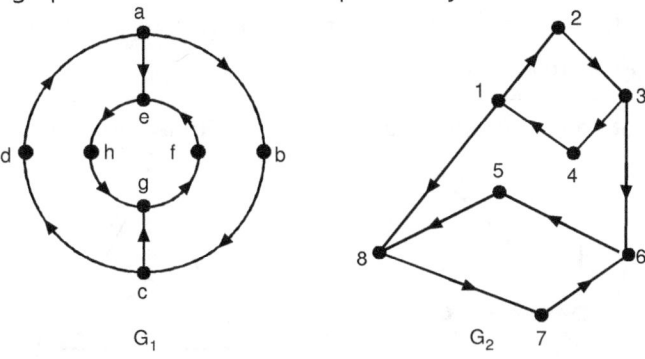

Fig. 8.47

Solution: Here both the graphs G_1 and G_2 have same number of vertices 8 and same number of edges 10. Furthermore, each has 4 vertices of degree 2 and 4 vertices of degree 3. Also the adjacency is preserved. The one-one correspondence between the vertices is given by

$$a \to 1$$
$$b \to 2$$
$$c \to 3$$
$$d \to 4$$
$$e \to 8$$
$$f \to 5$$
$$g \to 6$$
$$h \to 7$$

Hence G_1 and G_2 are isomorphic graphs.

Example 8: State and justify whether the following graphs are isomorphic or not?

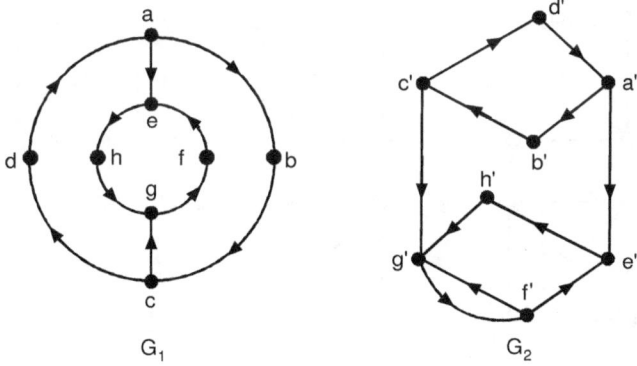

Fig. 8.48

Solution: Consider the graphs G_1 and G_2, both the graphs have same number of vertices 8, but the number of edges are not same in both the graphs. G_1 has 12 edges while G_2 has 11 edges. Therefore graphs are not isomorphic.

Example 9: Show that pairs of graphs are isomorphic / not isomorphic.

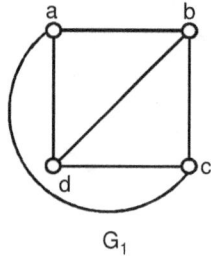
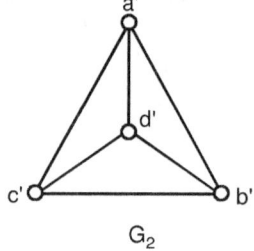

Fig. 8.49

Solution: Here both the graphs G_1 and G_2 have same number of vertices 4 and same number of edges 6. Also each vertex is of degree 3 and adjacency is preserved in both the graphs. The one-one correspondence between the vertices is given by

$$a \to a'$$
$$b \to b'$$
$$c \to c'$$
$$d \to d'$$

Hence, G_1 and G_2 are isomorphic graphs.

Here both the graphs are K_4 (the complete graph on 4 vertices).

Example 10: Find all non-isomorphic connected graphs with four vertices.

Solution: All non-isomorphic connected graphs with four vertices are

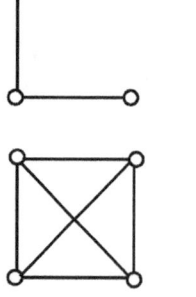
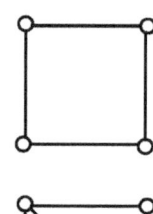
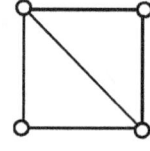
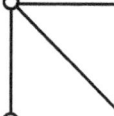

Fig. 8.50

Example 11: Determine whether the following graphs G = (V, E) and G* = (V*, E*) are isomorphic or not.

G = ({a, b, c, d}, {(a, b), (a, d), (b, d), (c, d), (c, b), (d, c)})
G* = ({1, 2, 3, 4}, {(1, 2), (2, 3), (3, 1), (3, 4), (4, 1), (4, 2)})

Solution: The graphs G and G* are given by

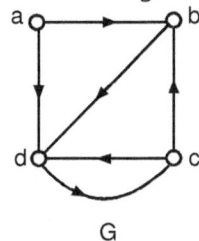 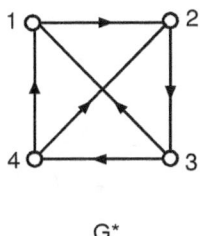

Fig. 8.51

Here G and G* have same number of vertices and same number of edges but they are not isomorphic because indegree of vertex d in G is 3 and outdegree of d in G is 1 and there does not exist any vertex in G* which has indegree 3 and outdegree 1. Therefore, G and G* are not isomorphic.

Example 12: State whether the given graphs are isomorphic or not.

(i)

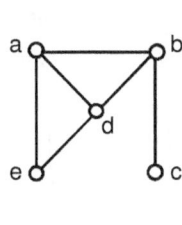 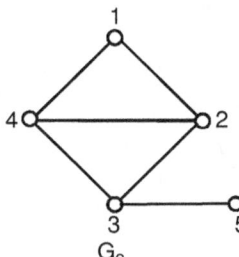

Fig. 8.52

(ii)

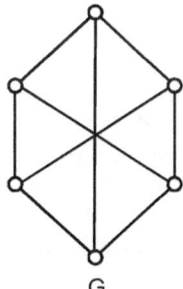 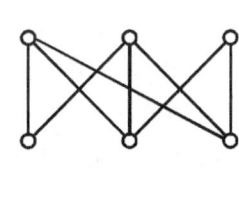

Fig. 8.53

Solution: (i) Here the graphs G_1 and G_2 have 5 vertices and six edges. Both the graphs have one vertex of degree 1, one vertex of degree 2 and three vertices of degree 3. Also the adjacency is preserved. Hence, both the graphs are isomorphic.

Isomorphism is given by

$$c \to 5$$
$$b \to 3$$
$$d \to 2$$
$$e \to 1$$
$$a \to 4$$

(ii) Here G_1 and G_2, both have six vertices but G_1 has 9 edges and G_2 has eight edges, therefore, G_1 and G_2 are non-isomorphic graphs.

8.7 New Graphs From Old Ones

In this section, we derive new graphs from old graphs.

(a) Subgraph: Let $G = (V, E)$ be any given graph. Then the graph $G' = (V', E')$ is called a **subgraph** of G if $V' \subseteq V$ and $E' \subseteq E$. In Fig. 8.54, H_1, H_2 and H_4 subgraphs of G but H_3 is not a subgraph of G because it contains the edge e which is not there in the graph G.

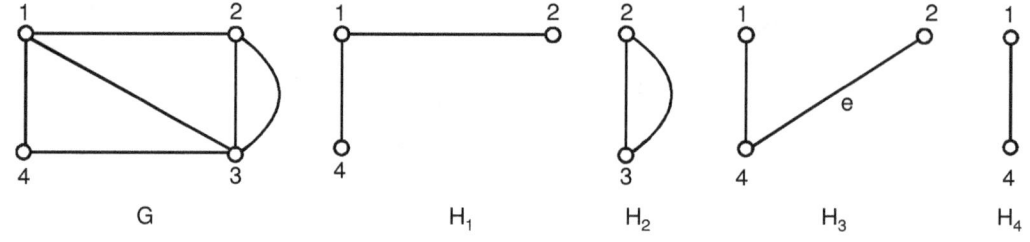

Fig. 8.54

Properties:
1. Each graph is a subgraph of itself.
2. A single vertex of a graph G is a subgraph of G.
3. A single edge together with its end vertices is also a subgraph of a graph G.
4. A subgraph of a subgraph of a graph G is a subgraph of G.

(b) Edge Disjoint Subgraphs: Two subgraphs H_1 and H_2 of the graph G are said to be **edge disjoint subgraphs** of a graph G if there is **no edge** common between H_1 and H_2 (but may have vertex common).

In Fig. 8.54, H_1 and H_2 are edge disjoint subgraphs of graph G.

(c) Vertex Disjoint Subgraphs: Two subgraphs H_1 and H_2 are said to be **vertex disjoint subgraphs** of a graph G if there is **no vertex** common between them (i.e. they do not have common edges also).

For example, in Fig. 8.54, H_2 and H_4 are vertex disjoint subgraphs of G but H_1 and H_2 are not.

(d) Spanning Subgraph: Let G = (V, E) be any graph. Then G' is said to be the **spanning subgraph** of the graph G if its vertex set V' is **equal to** the vertex set V of G.

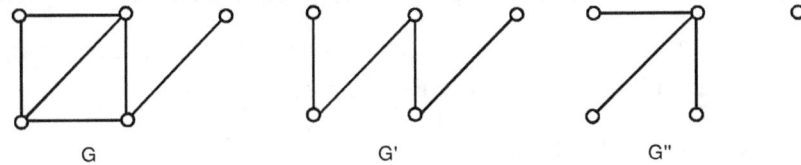

Fig. 8.55

In Fig. 8.55, G' and G" are spanning subgraphs of the graph G.

(e) Null Subgraph: A subgraph H of a graph G is called a null subgraph if its vertex set is same as the vertex set of G and its edge set is empty set. i.e. it does not contain any edges. A null subgraph is constructed from a graph G by deleting all the edges of G.

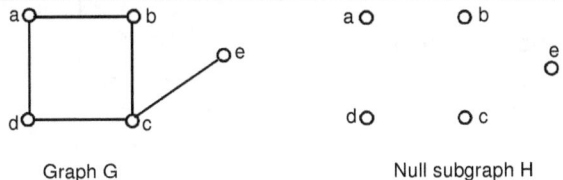

Fig. 8.56

(f) Factors of a Graph: A **k-factor** of a graph is defined to be a spanning subgraph of the graph with the degree of each of its **vertex** being **k**.

For example, for the graph in Fig. 8.57 (a), its 1-factor graph is shown in Fig. 8.57 (b) and its 2-factor graph is shown in Fig. 8.57 (c).

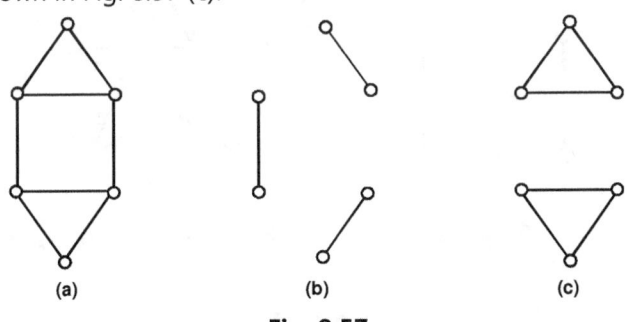

Fig. 8.57

A graph might have many different k-factors or might not have any k-factor at all for some k. Fig. 8.58 shows a graph which does not have any 1 factor graph.

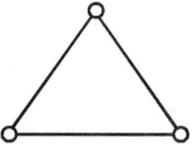

Fig. 8.58

(g) Complement of a Graph: Let G be a simple graph. Then the **complement of G** denoted by $\bar{G}$ is the graph whose vertex set is the same as the vertex set of G and in which two vertices are adjacent if and only if they are **not** adjacent in G.

A graph and its complement are shown in Fig. 8.59.

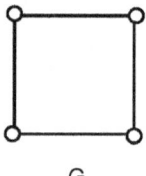 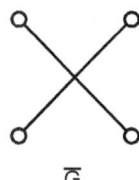

G $\bar{G}$

Fig. 8.59

Complement of a complete graph is a null graph and vice versa.

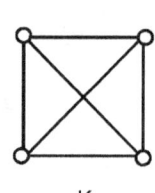

K_4 $\bar{K}_4 = N_4$

Fig. 8.60

A graph is said to be self complementary if it is isomorphic to its complement.

A graph G and its self complementary graph are shown in Fig. 8.61.

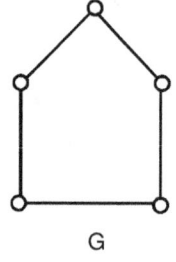 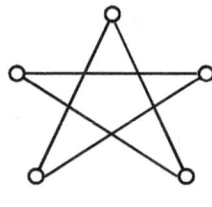

G G'
Graph G Self Complementary Graph of G

$G \cong G'$

Fig. 8.61

SOLVED EXAMPLES

Example 1: What is the complement of complete bipartite graph $K_{3,2}$. Is it a regular graph?

Solution: The graph $K_{3,2}$ is given by

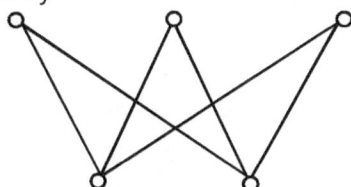

Fig. 8.62

It's complement is given by

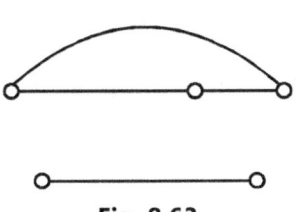

Fig. 8.63

It is not a regular graph.

Example 2: Is the graph H shown in Fig. 8.64 is a subgraph of a graph G in Fig. 8.64. Is it a spanning subgraph of G?

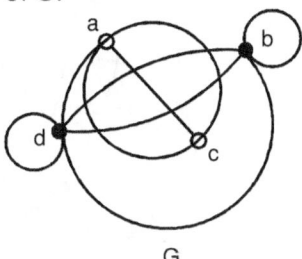
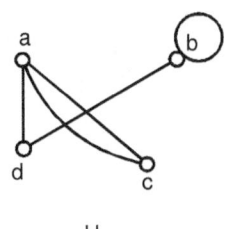

G   H

Fig. 8.64

Solution: Yes, H is a subgraph of G because its vertex set and edge set are subsets of vertex and edge sets of G. Also H contains all the vertices of G, hence, H is a spanning subgraph of G.

Example 3: Which of the subgraphs of G are vertex disjoint and edge disjoint subgraphs.

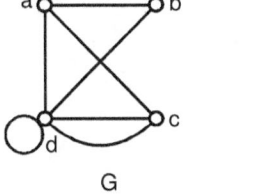
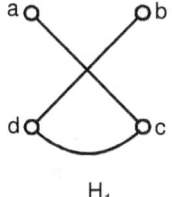
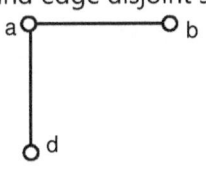

G H_1 H_2

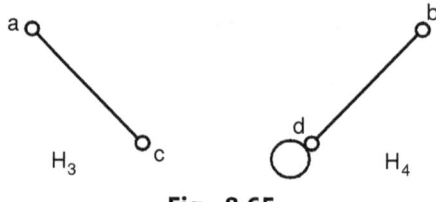

Fig. 8.65

Solution: Consider H_1 and H_2, both have common vertices. Hence they are **not** vertex disjoint subgraphs. In fact, they are edge disjoint subgraphs because edges are not common to them. Consider (H_1, H_3) and (H_1, H_4), they are neither edge disjoint nor-vertex disjoint subgraphs. The vertex disjoint subgraphs are H_3 and H_4. For H_2 and H_3, they are edge disjoint subgraphs.

Example 4: Find the complement of the following graph in Fig. 8.66. Is it self complementary?

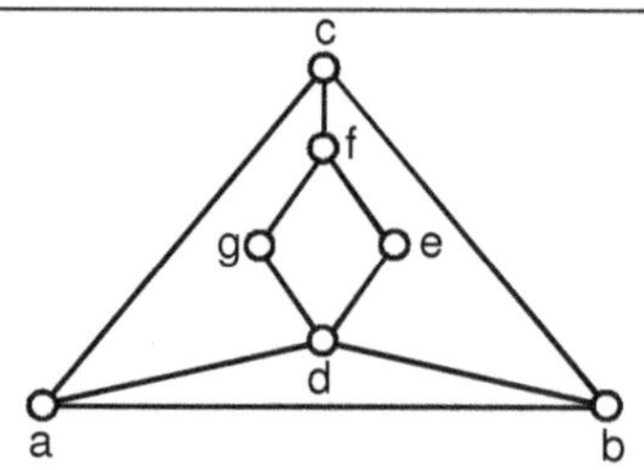

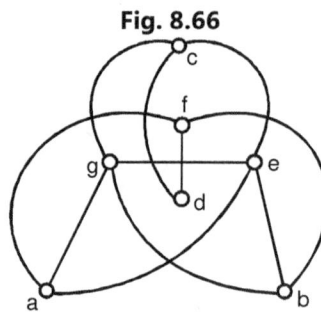

Fig. 8.66

Solution: The complement of the given graph is shown in Fig. 8.67.

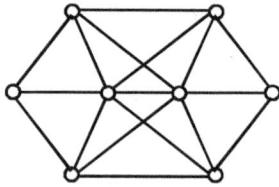

Fig. 8.67

The graph G is **not** self complementary because it is not isomorphic to its complement $\overline{G}$.

Example 5: Find 1-factor graph of the following graph in Fig. 8.68. Find its 2-factor graph also, if possible.

Fig. 8.68

Solution: 1-factor graph of the graph G in Fig. 8.69 is as follows:

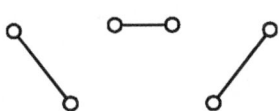

Fig. 8.69

2-factor graph of the graph G is

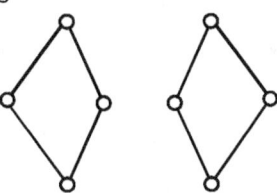

Fig. 8.70

Example 6: For the following graphs, determine whether H = H(V', E') is a subgraph of G, where

(i) V' = {A, B, F}, E' = [{A, B}, {A, F}]

(ii) V' = {B, C, D}, E' = [{B, C}, {B, D}]

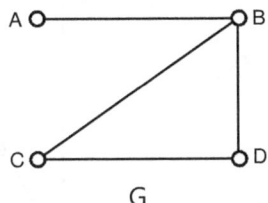

Fig. 8.71 (a)

Solution: (i) No, H is not a subgraph of G because vertex set V' of H contains the vertex F which does not belong to the graph G. Hence, H is not a subgraph of G.

(ii) Yes, all the vertices and edges of H belong to the graph G also. Hence, H is a subgraph of G.

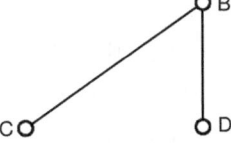

Fig. 8.71 (b)

8.8 Operations on Graphs

In previous sections, we have defined graphs in terms of set of vertices and set of edges. Now we define some standard set theoretical operations like union, intersection etc. on the graphs.

(a) Union of Two Graphs: Let $G_1 = (V_1, E_1)$ and $G_2 = (V_2, E_2)$ be any two given graphs. The union of these two graphs is denoted by $G_1 \cup G_2$ and it is a graph whose vertex set is $V_1 \cup V_2$ and edge set is $E_1 \cup E_2$.

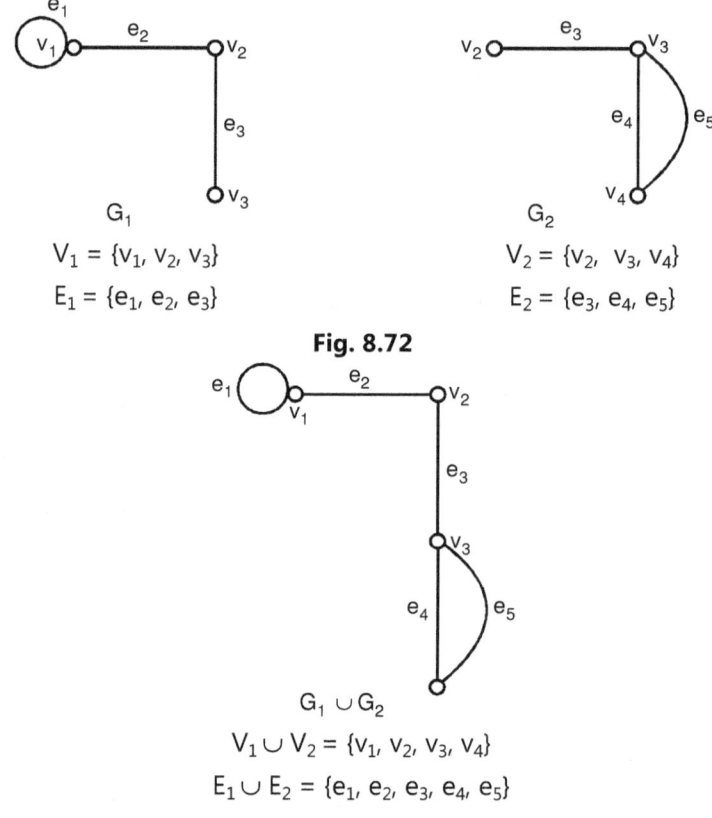

$V_1 = \{v_1, v_2, v_3\}$ $V_2 = \{v_2, v_3, v_4\}$

$E_1 = \{e_1, e_2, e_3\}$ $E_2 = \{e_3, e_4, e_5\}$

Fig. 8.72

$V_1 \cup V_2 = \{v_1, v_2, v_3, v_4\}$

$E_1 \cup E_2 = \{e_1, e_2, e_3, e_4, e_5\}$

Fig. 8.73

G_1, G_2 are given in Fig. 8.72 and their union $G_1 \cup G_2$ is shown in Fig. 8.73. For any graph G, $G \cup G = G$.

(b) Intersection of Two Graphs: The intersection of two graphs $G_1 (V_1, E_1)$ and $G_2 (V_2, E_2)$ is a graph whose vertex set is $V_1 \cap V_2$ and edge set is $E_1 \cap E_2$. It is denoted by $G_1 \cap G_2$. Consider the graphs G_1 and G_2 shown in Fig. 8.72. Their intersection $G_1 \cap G_2$ is shown in the following Fig. 8.74.

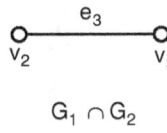

$G_1 \cap G_2$

Fig. 8.74

If G_1 and G_2 are edge disjoint graphs then $G_1 \cap G_2$ is a null graph.

If G_1 and G_2 are vertex disjoint graphs then $G_1 \cap G_2$ is an empty set. For any graph G, $G \cap G = G$.

(c) **Ring Sum of Two Graphs:** The ring sum of two graphs $G_1 (V_1, E_1)$ and $G_2 (V_2, E_2)$ is a graph consisting of the vertex set $V_1 \cup V_2$ and of edges that either in G_1 or G_2 but **not** in both. Ring sum is denoted by $G_1 \oplus G_2$.

In the following Fig. 8.75, the ring sum of two graphs is shown where G_1 and G_2 are the graphs given in Fig. 8.75.

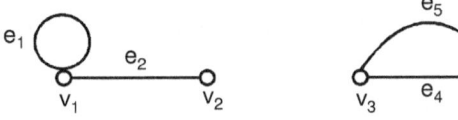

$G_1 \oplus G_2$

Fig. 8.75

For any graph G, $G \oplus G$ = a null graph.

(d) **Removal of an Edge:** Let G (V, E) be any graph. Let $e \in E$. Then the graph (G – e) can be obtained by removing the edge e from the graph.

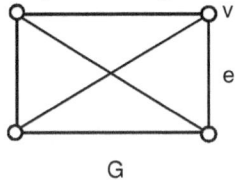
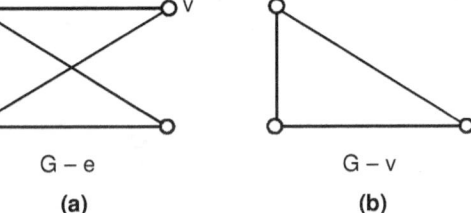

G   G – e   G – v

(a)   (b)

Fig. 8.76

In Fig. 8.76 for the graph G, the graph (G – e) is shown in Fig. 8.76 (a).

It is important to note that removal of any edge e from the graph G does **not** mean the removal of its **end vertices**.

(e) **Removal of a Vertex:** Let G (V, E) by any graph. Let $v \in V$. The graph (G – v) can be obtained by removing the vertex v from the graph G. Removal of v means, removal of all these edges also which are incident on v.

For the graph G in Fig. 8.76, the (G – v) is given in Fig. 8.76 (b).

SOLVED EXAMPLES

Example 1: What is the union of (i) two null graphs N_3 and N_4, (ii) two complete graphs k_2 and k_3.

Solution: (i) Union of two null graphs N_3 and N_4 is a null graph on seven vertices N_7.

(ii) Union of two complete graphs k_2 and k_3 is a complete graph k_3 as shown in Fig. 8.77.

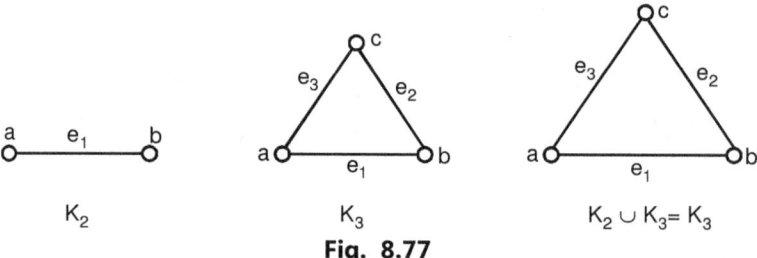

Fig. 8.77

Example 2: What is the intersection of two complete graphs k_3 and k_4?

Solution: k_3 and k_4 are given by

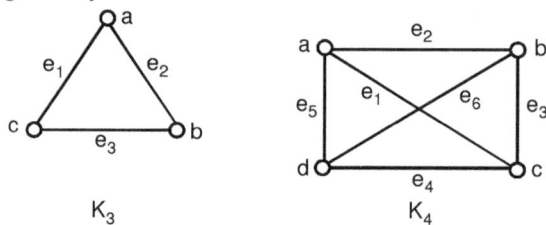

Fig. 8.78

The intersection of k_3 and k_4 is k_3.

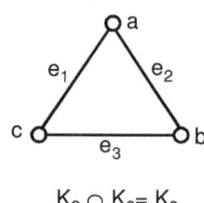

$K_2 \cap K_3 = K_3$

Fig. 8.79

Example 3: Draw the graphs (i) G − v, (ii) G − e, where the graph G is shown in Fig. 8.80.

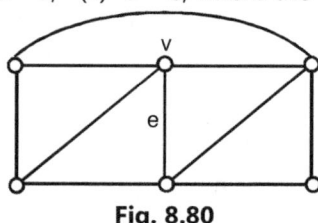

Fig. 8.80

Solution: The graph G – v, after deleting the vertex v from the graph G is shown below:

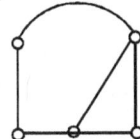

Fig. 8.81

The graph (G – e), after deleting the edge e from G is given by

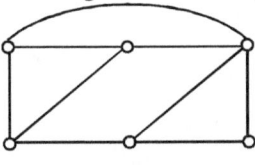

Fig. 8.82

EXERCISE - 7.1

1. Define the following graphs and give an example of each.
   - (i) Bipartite graph
   - (ii) Spanning subgraph
   - (iii) Complement of a graph
   - (iv) Subgraph
   - (v) Complete graph
   - (vi) Weighted graph.
   - (vii) Multiple graphs.
   - (viii) Complete Bipartite graph.
   - (ix) Factors of a graph
   - (x) Null subgraph

2. Define isomorphism of graphs. Are the graphs shown in the following figure isomorphic? Justify your answer.

   (i)

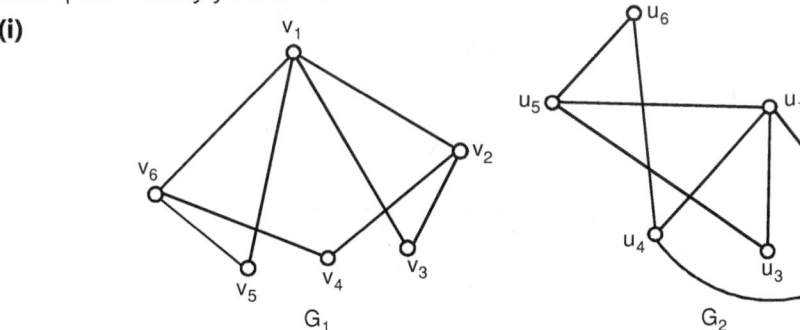

Fig. 8.83 (a)

(ii)

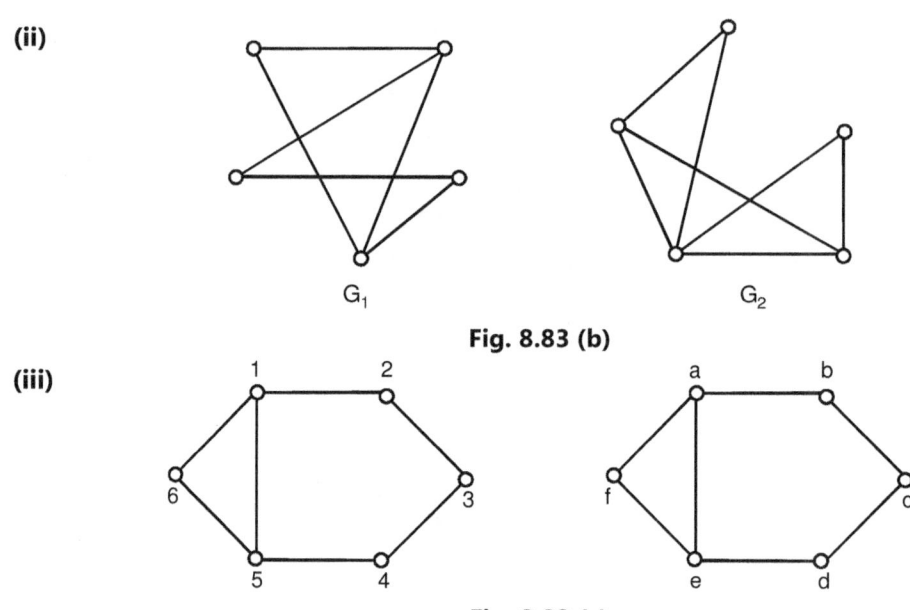

Fig. 8.83 (b)

(iii)

Fig. 8.83 (c)

3. Is there exist a regular graph of degree 5 on 9 vertices?
4. Find union and intersection of following graphs.

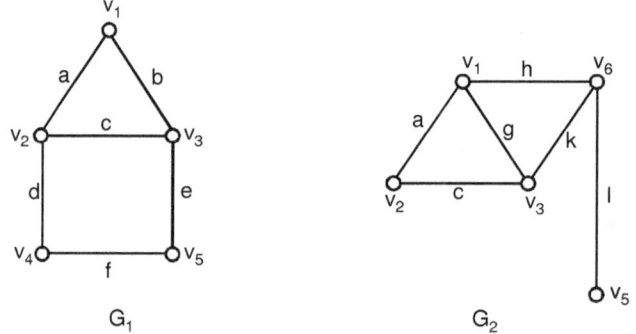

Fig. 8.84

5. Find (G – v) and (G – e) from the following graph.

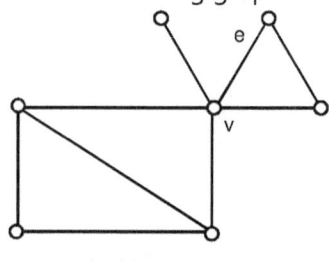

Fig. 8.85

6. Show that the number of edges in a complete graph K_n is $\frac{n(n-1)}{2}$.
7. Three married couples on a journey came to a river where they find a boat which cannot carry more than two persons at a time. The crossing of the river is complicated by the fact that the husbands are all very jealous and will not permit their wives to be left without them in a company where there are other men present. Construct a graph to show how it is possible.
8. Draw a graph with 4 nodes and 7 edges.
9. Draw all simple graphs on 4 nodes.
10. Draw a simple graph with 6 nodes all of degree 2 or greater and with at least 2 nodes of degree 3.
11. Check for isomorphism.

    (i)

    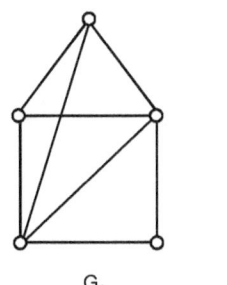

    Fig. 8.86

    (ii)

    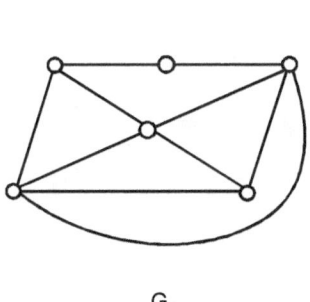 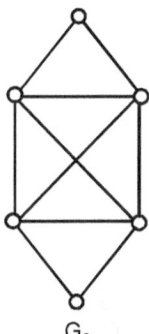

    Fig. 8.87

12. State handshaking lemma. How many nodes are necessary to construct a graph with exactly 8 edges in which each node is of degree 2.

ANSWERS - 8.1

2. (i) Yes, $v_1 \to u_1$, $v_2 \to u_4$, $v_3 \to u_2$, $v_4 \to u_6$, $v_5 \to u_3$, $v_6 \to u_5$.
   (ii) No, graph G_1 has 6 edges and G_2 has 7 edges.
   (iii) No, vertex 3 of degree 2 in G_1 is adjacent to two vertices of degree 2. But in G_2, there does not exist any vertex of degree 2 fulfilling this condition. Hence, adjacency is not preserved.

3. No, the total degree of the graph = $5 \times 9 = 45$ which is not an even number.

4. $G_1 \cup G_2 =$

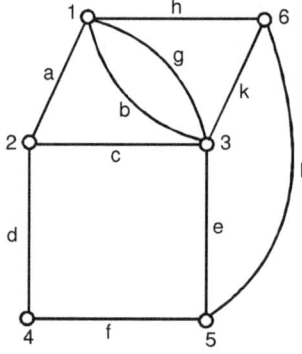

Fig. 8.88

$G_1 \cap G_2$

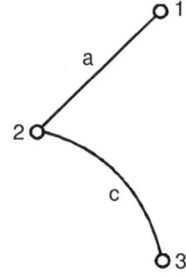

Fig. 8.89

5. G − v   G − e

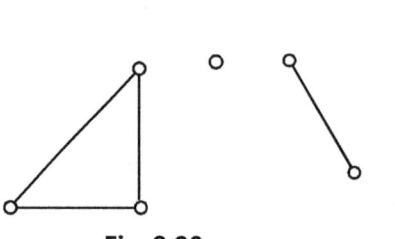 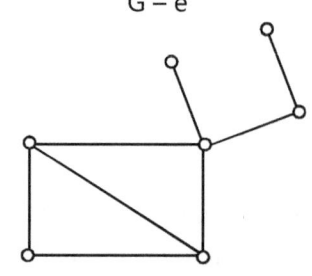

Fig. 8.90   Fig. 8.91

7. Suppose 3 couple be denoted by (h_1, w_1), (h_1, w_2) and (h_3, w_3). The possible way to cross the river is shown as follows:

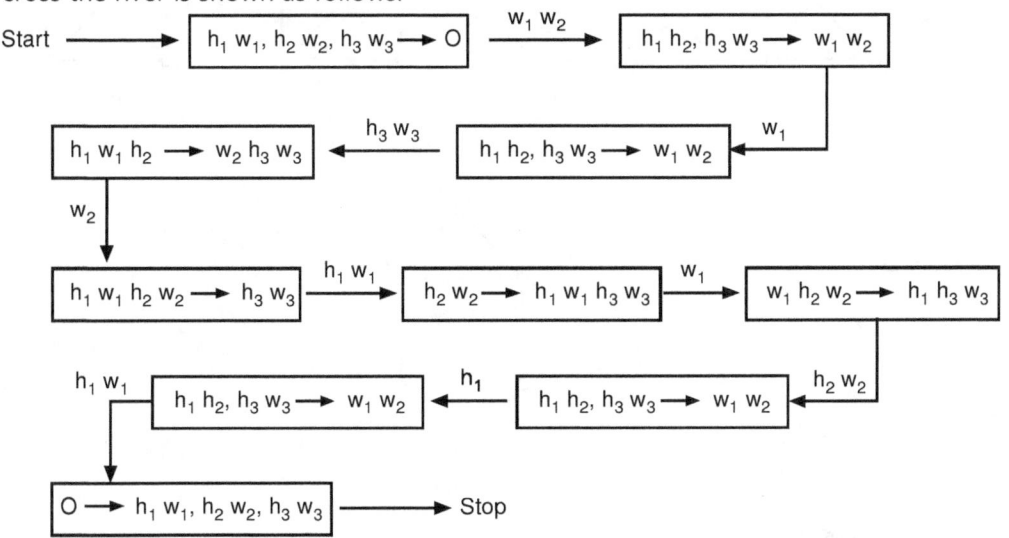

8.

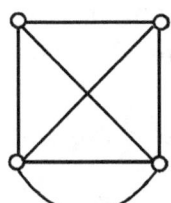

Fig. 8.92

9. Each simple graph with 4 nodes is isomorphic to one of the following:

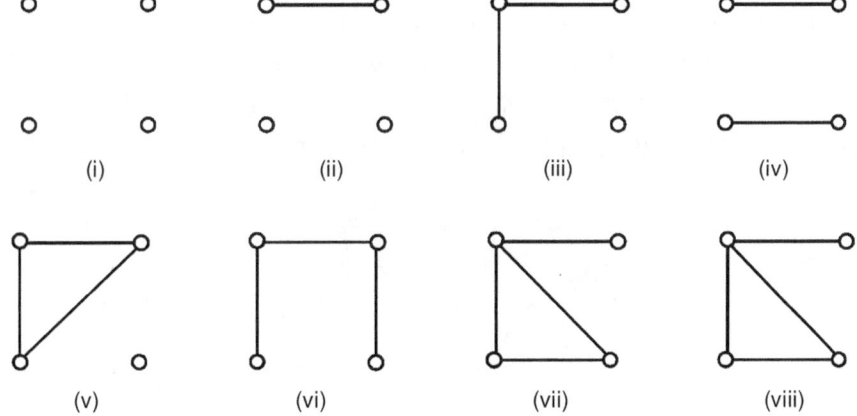

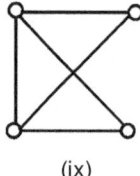 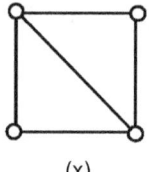 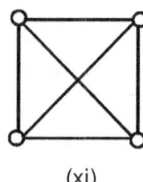 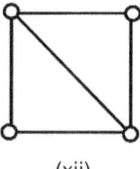

(ix) (x) (xi) (xii)

Fig. 8.93

10.

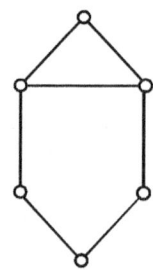

Fig. 8.94

8.9 Paths and Circuits

In this chapter, we will introduce the concept of paths, circuits, Euler graphs, Hamiltonian graphs which deal mainly with the nature of connectivity in graphs. Planarity of the graphs is also discussed in detail.

The solutions of some practical problems like Konigsberg bridge problem, three utilities problem are also described here.

Before defining Euler's and Hamiltonian graphs, first we will give a formal definition of a path and a circuit and discuss some related concepts.

Let $G = (V, E)$ be any graph and let v_0 and v_n be any two vertices in V. A **path P of length n** from v_0 to v_n is a sequence of vertices and edges of the form $(v_0, e_1, v_1, e_2, \ldots e_n, v_n)$ where each e_j is an edge between v_{j-1} and v_j. The vertices v_0 and v_n are called the **end points** of the path and the other vertices $v_1, v_2, \ldots v_{n-1}$ are called its **interior vertices**.

Following are same paths in the graph G shown in Fig. 8.95.

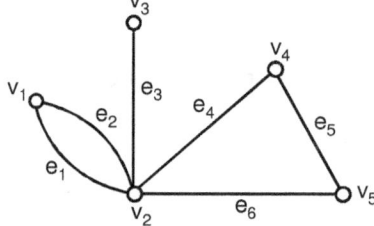

Fig. 8.95

Path I   → $v_1\ e_2\ v_2\ e_4\ v_4$
Path II   → $v_4\ e_4\ v_2\ e_2\ v_1\ e_1\ v_2\ e_3\ v_3$
Path III → $v_3\ e_3\ v_2\ e_2\ v_1\ e_1\ v_2\ e_3\ v_3$

In a simple graph with no loops and parallel edges, a path may be described by giving only the sequence of vertices traversed in the path. For example, in the following Fig. 8.96 the path $(v_5\ e_4\ v_1\ e_1\ v_2\ e_2\ v_3)$ can be written as $(v_5\ v_1\ v_2\ v_3)$ also.

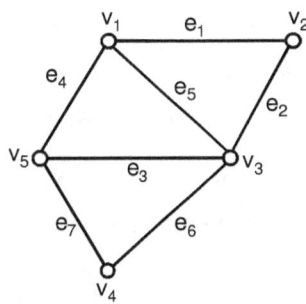

Fig. 8.96

8.9.1 Simple Path

A path in a graph G is called a **simple path** if the edges do **not** repeat in the path.

In Fig. 8.95, path I, and path II are simple paths but path III is not a simple path because the edge e_3 is repeated twice.

8.9.2 Elementary Path

A path is said to be an **elementary** path if vertices do **not** repeat in the path.

For example, the path I in Fig. 8.95 is an elementary path but path II is not.

8.9.3 Circuit

Suppose that $C = (v_0, e_1, v_1 \ldots v_n)$ is a path in a graph G. If $v_0 = v_n$ i.e. if the end vertices of the path are **same** then the path C is called a circuit.

In the following Fig. 8.97 $C_1 = (v_1, e_1, v_2, e_2, v_1)$, $C_2 = (v_3, e_4, v_1, e_1, v_2, e_3, v_3)$ are some examples of circuits.

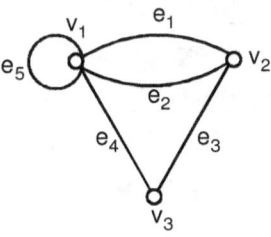

Fig. 8.97

8.9.4 Simple and Elementary Circuit

> A circuit in the graph G is said to be a **simple circuit** if it does not include the same **edge** twice.

> A circuit is said to be an **elementary circuit** if it does not meet the same **vertex** twice (except for first and last vertex).

Consider the graph G shown in Fig. 8.98. The simple circuit in G is (v_1 e_1 v_3 e_3 v_2 e_2 v_1) which is also an elementary circuit in G.

The circuit (v_1 e_2 v_2 e_6 v_4 e_7 v_5 e_8 v_3 e_4 v_4 e_5 v_1) is a simple circuit but it is not an elementary circuit because v_4 is repeated twice in the circuit.

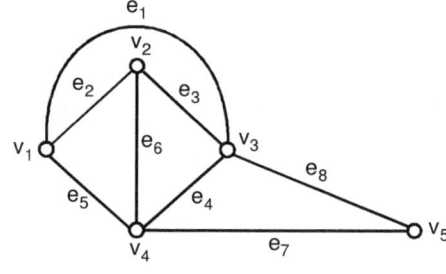

Fig. 8.98

Number of edges in any circuit is called the length of the circuit.

Paths and circuits have been defined in a similar way for the directed graph also.

Now, we give a very important result which has a great significance in the vector space associated with the graph G.

Theorem 8.9.1: The ring sum of two circuits in a graph G is either a circuit or an edge disjoint union of circuits.

8.10 Connected and Disconnected Graphs

Now, we define connected and disconnected graphs in terms of paths.

> A graph is said to be a **connected graph** if there exists a **path** between every pair of vertices, otherwise the graph is **disconnected**.

It follows that disconnected graph consists of two or more parts called **components**, each of which is a connected graph and there is **no path** between two vertices if they belong to **different components**.

A connected graph has only one component.

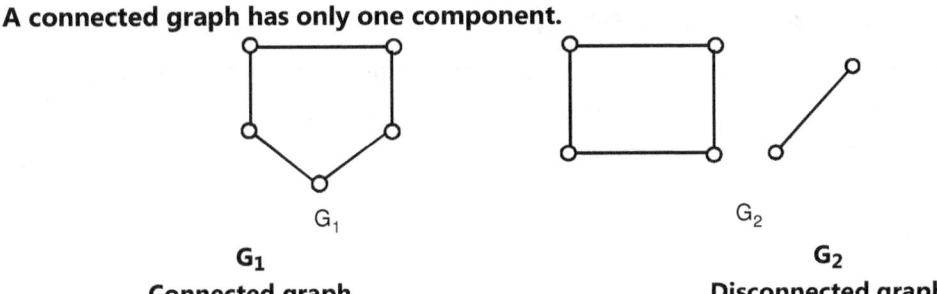

        G_1 G_2
Connected graph   **Disconnected graph**

Fig. 8.99

In Fig. 8.99, G_1 is a connected graph and G_2 is disconnected graph which has two components.

In a similar way, we can define a connected digraph also.

A directed graph or digraph is said to be **strongly connected** if for every pair of vertices a and b in the digraph, there is a path from a to b as well as a path from b to a.

A digraph is **weakly connected** if it is not strongly connected and its underlying graph is connected. Digraph which is neither strongly connected nor weakly connected is known as disconnected digraph.

As shown in Fig. 8.100, D_1 is strongly connected; D_2 is weakly connected diagraph because there does not exist any path from v_1 to v_5, also its underlying graph is connected as shown in Fig. 8.101.

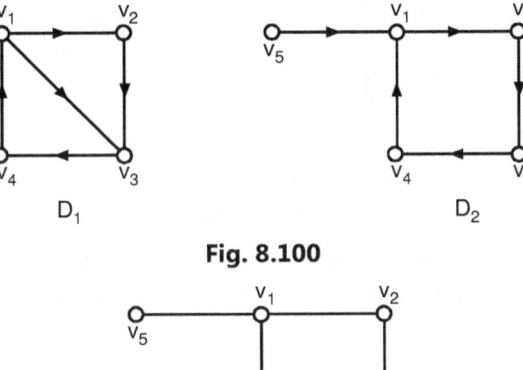

Fig. 8.100

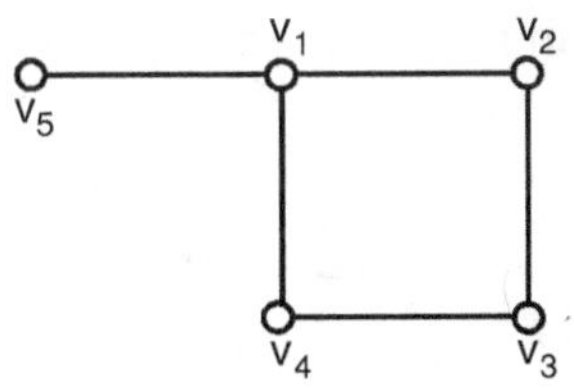

Fig. 8.101
(Underlying graph of D_2)

8.11 Edge and Vertex Connectivity

In this section, we will see how the removal of edges and vertices disconnects the graph. Also we will define the terms edge connectivity and vertex connectivity which are useful in construction of communication network.

8.11.1 Edge Connectivity

In a **connected graph** G, a **cut-set** is a **minimal set** of edges whose removal disconnects the graph and increases the components of the graph by **one**.

In other words, a cutset in a connected graph G is a set of edges whose removal from G leaves G disconnected provided removal of **no** proper subset of these edges disconnects G.

For instance, in Fig. 8.102 $\{e_1, e_4, e_8\}$ is a cut set whereas $\{e_1, e_4, e_8, e_9\}$ is **not** a cut set because its subset $\{e_1, e_4, e_8\}$ is also a cut set.

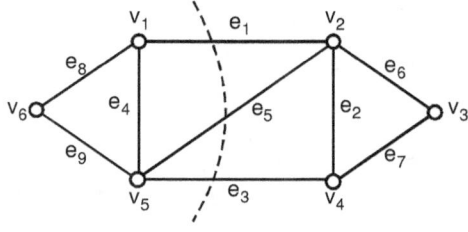

Fig. 8.102

Other cutsets in the graph are $\{e_6, e_7\}$, $\{e_8, e_9\}$, $\{e_1, e_3, e_5\}$ etc.

For the cutset $\{e_1, e_3, e_5\}$, the above graph G will have 2 components, namely G_1 and G_2 as given in Fig. 8.103.

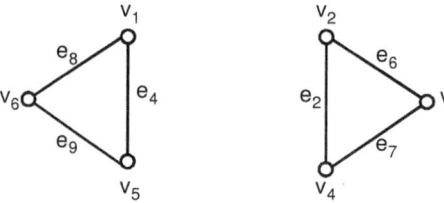

Fig. 8.103

Hence, if S is a cutset then (G − S) has exactly two components.

If the cutset of the connected graph contains only **one edge** then that edge is called an **isthmus** or **bridge** i.e. removal of an isthmus (edge) disconnects the graph. e is an isthmus in the graph given in Fig. 8.104.

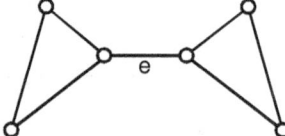

Fig. 8.104

The number of edges in a smallest cutset of a connected simple graph G is called an **edge connectivity** of the graph G and it is denoted by λ (G). In other words, λ(G) is the smallest number of edges in G whose removal disconnects G. In Fig. 8.103, λ (G) = 2. For Fig. 8.104, λ (G) = 1.

8.11.2 Vertex Connectivity

The vertex connectivity K (G) of a simple connected graph G is defined as the **smallest number of vertices whose removal disconnects the graph.**

For instance, k (G) = 2 in the following Fig. 8.105.

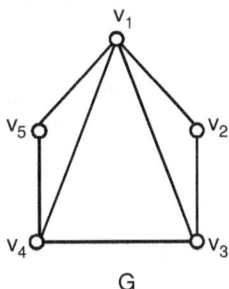

Fig. 8.105

If we remove the vertices v_1 and v_4 then the above graph G will be disconnected as shown below in Fig. 8.106.

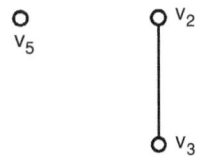

Fig. 8.106

A graph is said to be **k-connected** if its vertex connectivity is k.

A graph is said to be a **separable graph** if its vertex connectivity is **one**. In a separable graph, a vertex whose removal disconnects the graph is said to be a **cut vertex** or a **cut point**.

In Fig. 8.107, v is a cut point.

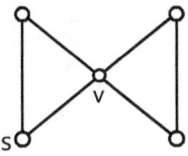

Fig. 8.107

The above defined terms; edge connectivity and vertex connectivity are related to the minimum degree of a vertex in the graph. This relation is given by

$$k(G) \leq \lambda(G) \leq \delta \qquad \ldots (8.12.1)$$

where, $k(G)$ is the vertex connectivity of G,

$\lambda(G)$ is the edge connectivity of G, and

δ is the minimum degree of a vertex in the graph G.

The edge connectivity $\lambda(G)$ is also related to the number of edges and vertices in the given graph and which is given by

$$\lambda(G) \leq \left\lfloor \frac{2e}{n} \right\rfloor \qquad \ldots (8.12.2)$$

where, e is the number of edges and n is the number of vertices in the graph G.

SOLVED EXAMPLES

Example 1: Find the edge connectivity for the complete graph K_5.

Solution: For complete graph K_5, the number of vertices is 5 and the degree of each vertex is 4 as shown in following Fig. 8.108. If we remove all four edges incident on any vertex, then the graph will become disconnected.

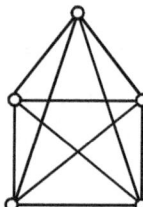

Fig. 8.108

Hence it edge connectivity $\lambda(G) = 4$.

Example 2: Find $k(G)$, $\lambda(G)$ for $K_{4,3}$ the complete bipartite graph.

Solution: The complete bipartite graph $K_{4,3}$ is given by,

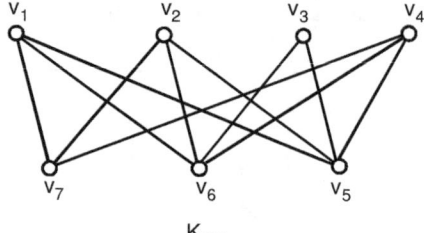

$K_{4,3}$

Fig. 8.109

To make the graph disconnected, the smallest cutset should contain 3 edges. Hence its edge connectivity λ (G) = 3.

If we remove v_5, v_6, v_7 vertices then the graph will be disconnected. Hence its vertex connectivity k (G) = 3.

Example 3: Find the edge connectivity of the following graph.

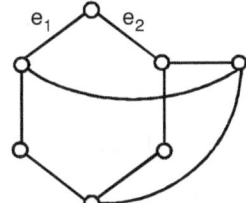

Fig. 8.110

Solution: In the given graph, total number of edges e = 9 and total number of vertices n = 7.

By the result (8.12.2), the edge connectivity $\leq \left\lceil \dfrac{2e}{n} \right\rceil$

$\Rightarrow$ The edge connectivity $\leq \left\lceil \dfrac{18}{7} \right\rceil = 2$.

From the graph, it is clear that the edge connectivity = 2.
(Remove two edges e_1 and e_2, the graph becomes disconnected)

Example 4: Suppose that we have 6 houses and enough wire to establish telephone links between 10 pair of houses. How should this be done so as to make it possible for any two houses to communicate and so as to minimize the danger of disrupted communications due to several lines?

Solution: Represent the houses by nodes and wires by edges. Given that there are 6 houses i.e. 6 nodes and 10 edges in the graph.

According to the problem, we have to find the minimum number of edges where removal of disconnects the graph i.e. we have to find the edge connectivity of the graph. From the result (8.12.2) edge connectivity is less than or equal to $\left\lceil \dfrac{2 \times 10}{6} \right\rceil = 3$.

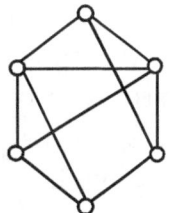

Fig. 8.111

i.e. the degree of each vertex should be at least 3 in the graph which has 6 vertices and 10 edges. The following graph satisfies all the above conditions and has edge connectivity 3.

Example 5: For a given graph G, find
  (i) all simple paths from A to C,
  (ii) all cycle,
  (iii) subgraph H of G generated by H = {B, C, X, Y}

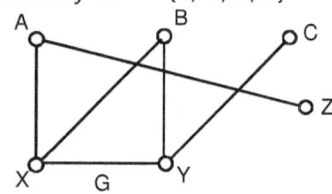

Fig. 8.112 (a)

Solution: (i) Simple paths from A to C are
  (a) AXYC
  (b) AXBYC
  (ii) Cycle in G is XYBX.
  (iii) Subgraphs H_1, H_2, H_3 generated by the vertices B, C, X, Y are given by

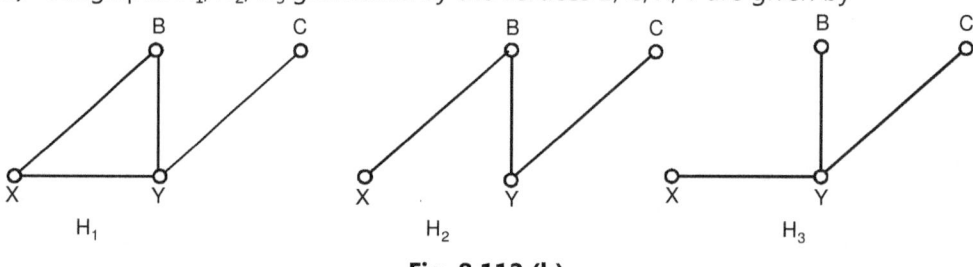

Fig. 8.112 (b)

8.12 Shortest Path Algorithm

A large number of optimization problems are mathematically equivalent to finding the shortest paths in a graph. For example, given a railway network connecting several cities, it is required to find shortest route between two cities.

In this case, we represent the railway network by the graph in which vertices represent the cities and the edges represent the railway routes. The weight of the edge is the distance between two cities. Then the given problem of finding the shortest route between two cities reduces to finding the shortest distance between two vertices.

We now give an algorithm for solving the shortest path problem. The algorithm was found by Dijkstra in 1959 and is known as Dijkstra's shortest path algorithm. This algorithm gives the shortest length of the path from the vertex 'a' to the vertex 'z' but it does not give the actual path for the shortest distance from the vertex a to the vertex z.

DISCRETE STRUCTURE AND GRAPH THEORY (NMU) — GRAPH THEORY

Dijkstra's Algorithm to find the shortest path from the vertex a to the vertex z.

Let G = (V, E) be a simple graph. Let a and z be any two vertices of the graph. Suppose L (x) denotes the label of the vertex z which represents the **length of the shortest path** from the vertex a to the vertex (z). w_{ij} denotes the weight of the edge e_{ij} = (v_i, v_j).

Step 1: Let P = φ where P is the set of those vertices which have permanent labels and T = {all vertices of the graph G}

Set L (a) = 0, L (x) = ∞ ∀ x ∈ T and x ≠ a

Step 2: Select the vertex v in T which has the smallest label. This label is called the permanent label of v.

Also set P = P ∪ { v } and T = T − { v }. If v = z, then L (z) is the length of the shortest path from the vertex a to z and stop.

Step 3: If v ≠ z, then revise the labels of vertices of T i.e. **the vertices which do not have permanent lables**. The new lable of a vertex x in T is given by

L (x) = min {old L (x), L (v) + w (v, x)}

where w (v, x) is the weight of the edge joining the vertex v and x.

If there is no direct edge joining v and x then take w (v, x) = ∞.

Step 4: Repeat steps 2 and 3 until z gets the permanent lable.

SOLVED EXAMPLES

Example 1: Determine a shortest path between the vertices a and z as shown in the graph below. The numbers associated with the edges are the distances between vertices.

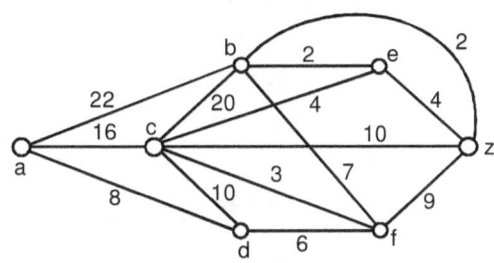

Fig. 8.113

Solution: Dijkstra's Algorithm to find the shortest path from a to z is as follows:

1. P = φ, T = {a, b, c, d, e, f, z}

   L (a) = 0, L (x) = ∞, ∀ x = T   x ≠ a

2. $v = a$

   $P = \{a\}$ $\qquad T = \{b, c, d, e, f, z\}$

   $\qquad\qquad\qquad L(b) = \min\{\text{old } L(b), L(a) + w(a, b)\}$

   $\qquad\qquad\qquad L(b) = \min\{\infty, 0 + 22\}$

   $\qquad\qquad\qquad L(b) = 22$

   Similarly, $\quad L(c) = 16$

   $\qquad\qquad\qquad L(d) = 8$

   $\qquad\qquad\qquad L(e) = \infty$

   $\qquad\qquad\qquad L(f) = \infty$

   $\qquad\qquad\qquad L(z) = \infty$

3. $v = d$; the permanent label of d is 8

   $\qquad\qquad P = \{a, d\}, T = \{b, c, e, f, z\}$

   $\qquad\qquad L(b) = \min\{\text{old } L(b), L(d) + w(b, d)\}$

   $\qquad\qquad\qquad = \min\{22, 8 + \infty\} = 22$

   $\qquad\qquad L(c) = \min\{16, 8 + 10\} = 16$

   $\qquad\qquad L(e) = \min\{\infty, 8 + \infty\} = \infty$

   $\qquad\qquad L(f) = \min\{\infty, 8 + 6\} = 14$

   $\qquad\qquad L(z) = \min\{\infty, 8 + \infty\} = \infty.$

4. $v = f$, the permanent label of f is 14.

   $\qquad\qquad P = \{a, d, f\}, T = \{b, c, e, z\}$

   $\qquad\qquad L(b) = \min\{22, 14 + 7\} = 21$

   $\qquad\qquad L(c) = \min\{16, 14 + 3\} = 16$

   $\qquad\qquad L(e) = \min\{\infty, 14 + \infty\} = \infty$

   $\qquad\qquad L(z) = \min\{\infty, 14 + 9\} = 23$

5. $v = c$, the permanent label of c is 16.

   $P = \{a, d, f, c\}, \quad T = \{b, e, z\}$

   $\qquad\qquad L(b) = \min\{21, 16 + 20\} = 21$

   $\qquad\qquad L(e) = \min\{\infty, 16 + 4\} = 20$

   $\qquad\qquad L(z) = \min\{23, 16 + 10\} = 23$

6. $v = e$, the permanent label of e is 20,

   $\qquad\qquad P = \{a, d, f, c, e\}, T = \{b, z\}$

   $\qquad\qquad L(b) = \min\{21, 20 + 2\} = 21$

   $\qquad\qquad L(z) = \min\{23, 20 + 4\} = 23$

$$L(f) = \min\{\infty, 0 + \infty\} = \infty$$
$$L(g) = \min\{\infty, 0 + \infty\} = \infty$$
Similarly $L(h) = \infty$, $L(i) = \infty$, $L(z) = \infty$

7. $v = b$, the permanent label of b is 21.
$$P = \{a, d, f, c, e, b\}, \ T = \{z\}$$
$$L(z) = \min\{23, 21 + 2\} = 23.$$

Now the permanent label of z is 23. Hence, the length of the shortest path from the vertex a to the vertex z is **23**.

The shortest path is adfz shown in the following figure.

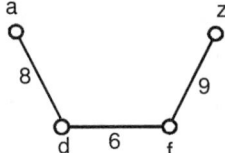

Fig. 8.114

Example 2: Apply Dijkstra's shortest path algorithm to obtain the shortest path between vertices a and z in the figure shown below.

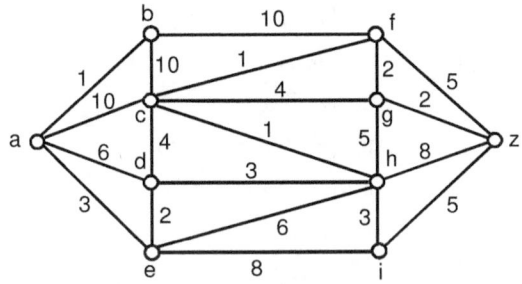

Fig. 8.115 (a)

Solution: The steps of Dijkstra's algorithm to find the shortest path from a to z are shown as follows.

1. $P = \phi$, $\quad T = \{a, b, c, d, e, f, g, h, i, z\}$
   $L(a) = 0, \quad L(x) = \infty \ \forall x \in T, x \neq a$
2. $v = a$, the permanent label of a is 0
   $P = \{a\}, \quad T = \{b, c, d, e, f, g, h, i, z\}$
   $L(b) = \min\{\infty, 0 + 1\} = 1$
   $L(c) = \min\{\infty, 0 + 10\} = 10$

$$L(d) = \min\{\infty, 0 + 6\} = 6$$
$$L(e) = \min\{\infty, 0 + 3\} = 3$$
$$L(f) = \min(\infty, 0 + \infty) = \infty$$
$$L(g) = \min(\infty, 0 + \infty) = \infty$$

Similarly, $L(h) = \infty$, $L(z) = \infty$

3. $v = b$ the permanent label of b is 1.

$P = \{a, b\}$ $T = \{c, d, e, f, g, h, i, z\}$.
$$L(c) = \min\{10, 1 + 10\} = 10$$
$$L(d) = \min\{6, 1 + \infty\} = 6$$
$$L(e) = \min\{3, 1 + \infty\} = 3$$
$$L(f) = \min\{\infty, 1 + 10\} = 11$$
$$L(g) = \min\{\infty, 1 + \infty\} = \infty$$
$$L(h) = \infty,\ L(i) = \infty,\ L(z) = \infty.$$

4. $v = e$, the permanent label of e is 3.

$P = \{a, b, e\}$, $T = \{c, d, f, g, h, i, z\}$
$$L(c) = \min\{10, 3 + \infty\} = 10$$
$$L(d) = \min\{6, 3 + 2\} = 5$$
$$L(f) = \min\{11, 3 + \infty\} = 11$$
$$L(g) = \min\{\infty, 3 + \infty\} = \infty$$
$$L(h) = \min\{\infty, 3 + 6\} = 9$$
$$L(i) = \min\{\infty, 3 + 8\} = 11$$
$$L(z) = \min\{\infty, 3 + \infty\} = \infty$$

5. $v = d$, the permanent label of d is 5.

$P = \{a, b, e, d\}$, $T = \{c, f, g, h, i, z\}$
$$L(c) = \min\{10, 5 + 4\} = 9$$
$$L(f) = \min\{11, 5 + \infty\} = 11$$
$$L(g) = \min\{\infty, 5 + \infty\} = \infty$$
$$L(h) = \min\{9, 5 + 3\} = 8$$
$$L(i) = \min\{11, 5 + \infty\} = 11$$
$$L(z) = \min\{\infty, 5 + \infty\} = \infty$$

6. $v = h$ the permanent label of h is 8.

$P = \{a, b, e, d, h\}$, $T = \{c, f, g, i, z\}$
$$L(c) = \min\{9, 8, + 1\} = 9$$

$$L(f) = \min\{11, 8 + \infty\} = 11$$
$$L(g) = \min\{\infty, 8 + 5\} = 13$$
$$L(i) = \min\{11, 8 + 3\} = 11$$
$$L(z) = \min\{\infty, 8 + 8\} = 16$$

7. $v = c$, the permanent label of C is 9.
   $P = \{a, b, e, d, h, c\}$, $\quad T = \{f, g, i, z\}$
   $$L(f) = \min\{11, 9 + 1\} = 10$$
   $$L(g) = \min\{13, 9 + 4\} = 13$$
   $$L(i) = \min\{11, 9 + \infty\} = 11$$
   $$L(z) = \min\{16, 9 + \infty\} = 16$$

8. $v = f$, the permanent label of f is 10.
   $P = \{a, b, e, d, h, c, f\}$, $T = \{g, i, z\}$
   $$L(g) = \min\{13, 10 + 2\} = 12$$
   $$L(i) = \min\{11, 10 + \infty\} = 11$$
   $$L(z) = \min\{16, 10 + 5\} = 15$$

9. $v = i$, the permanent level of i is 11.
   $P = \{a, b, e, d, h, i, f, i\}$, $\quad T = \{g, z\}$
   $$L(g) = \min\{12, 11 + \infty\} = 12$$
   $$L(z) = \min\{15, 11 + 5\} = 15.$$
   $v = g$, the permanent label of g is 12.
   $P = \{a, b, e, d, h, c, f, i, g\}$, $\quad T = \{z\}$
   $$L(z) = \min\{15, 12 + 2\} = 14$$
   $v = z$, the permanent label of z is 14.

Hence, the length of shortest path from a to z is 14.

The shortest path is a e d c f g z which is shown in the following figure.

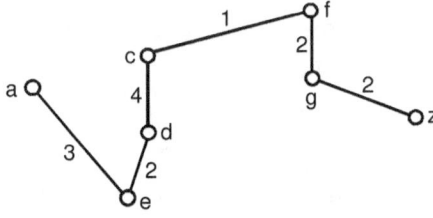

Fig. 8.115 (b)

Example 3: The graph in Fig. 8.116 shows the communication channels and the communication time delays in the channels among eight communication centres. The centres are represented by vertices, the channels are represented by edges, and the communication time delay in minutes in each channel is represented by the weight of the edge. Suppose that at 3.00 p.m. communication centre 'a' broadcasts through all it channels the news that someone has found a way to build a better mouse trap. Other communication centres will then broadcast this news through their channels as soon as they receive it. For the communication centres b, c, d, e, f, g and h, determine the earliest time each receives the news.

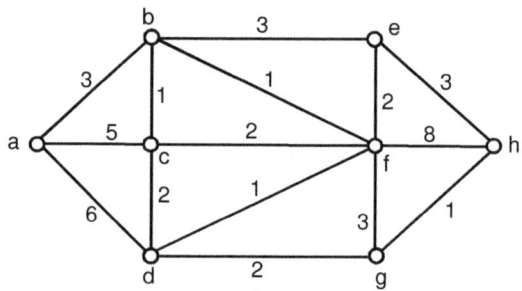

Fig. 8.116

Solution: In this problem, we have to find a shortest path from the communication centre 'a' to each centre b, c, d, e, f, g and h, which can be done by using Dijkstra's shortest path algorithm.

1. $P = \phi$, $T = \{a, b, c, d, e, f, g, h\}$
   $L(a) = 0$, $L(x) = \infty, \forall x \in T, x \neq a$

2. $v = a$, the permanent label of a is 0.
   $P = \{a\}$, $T = \{b, c, d, e, f, g, h\}$
   $L(b) = \min\{\infty, 0 + 3\} = 3$
   $L(c) = \min\{\infty, 0 + 5\} = 5$
   $L(d) = \min\{\infty, 0 + 6\} = 6$
   $L(e) = \min\{\infty, 0 + \infty\} = \infty$

   Similarly $L(f) = \infty$, $L(g) = \infty$, $L(h) = \infty$.

3. $v = b$, the permanent label of b is 3.
   $P = \{a, b\}$, $T = \{c, d, e, f, g, h\}$
   $L(c) = \min\{5, 3 + 1\} = 4$
   $L(d) = \min\{6, 3 + \infty\} = 6$
   $L(e) = \min\{\infty, 3 + 3\} = 6$

$L(f) = \min\{\infty, 3+1\} = 4$

$L(g) = \min\{\infty, 3+\infty\} = \infty$

$L(h) = \min\{\infty, 3+\infty\} = \infty$

4. $v = c$, the permanent label of c is 4.

   $P = \{a, b, c\}$, $\quad T = \{d, e, f, g, h\}$

   $L(d) = \min\{6, 4+2\} = 6$

   $L(e) = \min\{6, 4+\infty\} = 6$

   $L(f) = \min\{4, 4+2\} = 4$

   $L(g) = \min\{\infty, 4+\infty\} = \infty$

   $L(h) = \min\{\infty, 4+\infty\} = \infty$

5. $v = f$, the permanent label of f is 4.

   $P = \{a, b, c, f\}$, $\quad T = \{d, e, g, h\}$

   $L(d) = \min\{6, 4+1\} = 5$

   $L(e) = \min\{6, 4+2\} = 6$

   $L(g) = \min\{\infty, 4+4\} = 8$

   $L(h) = \min\{\infty, 4+8\} = 12$

6. $v = d$, the permanent label of d is 5.

   $P = \{a, b, c, f, d\}$ $\quad T = \{e, g, h\}$

   $L(e) = \min\{6, 5+\infty\} = 6$

   $L(g) = \min\{8, 5+2\} = 7$

   $L(h) = \min\{12, 5+\infty\} = 12$

7. $v = e$, the permanent label of e is 6.

   $P = \{a, b, c, f, d, e\}$ $\quad T = \{g, h\}$

   $L(g) = \min\{7, 6+\infty\} = 7$

   $L(h) = \min\{12, 6+3\} = 9$

8. $v = g$, the permanent label of g = 7

   $P = \{a, b, c, f, d, e, g,\}$, $\quad T = \{h\}$

   $L(h) = \min\{9, 7+1\} = 8$

9. $v = h$, the permanent label of g is 8.

   $P = \{a, b, c, f, d, e, g, h\}$ $\quad T = \phi$.

Hence according to Dijkstra's shortest path algorithm

   b will receive the news after 3 minutes

   c will receive the news after 4 minutes

f will receive the news after 4 minutes
d will receive the news after 5 minutes
e will receive the news after 6 minutes
g will receive the news after 7 minutes
h will receive the news after 8 minutes.

Example 4: Apply Dijkstra's shortest path algorithm to find the shortest path between vertices a and z in the figures below.

(i)

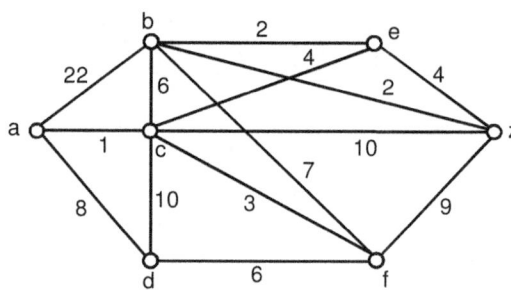

Fig. 8.117 (a)

(ii)

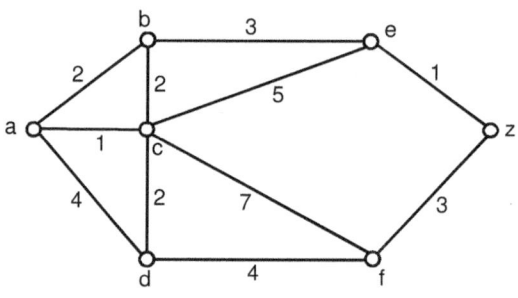

Fig. 8.117 (b)

Solution: (i) The steps involved in Dijkstra's Algorithm to find the shortest path from a to z are as follows:

1. $P = \phi$, $T = \{a, b, c, d, e, f, z\}$
        $L(a) = 0$, $L(x) = \infty$ $\forall x \in T, x \neq a$

2. $V = a$, the permanent label of a is 0.
        $P = \{a\}$, $T = \{b, c, d, e, f, z\}$
                       $L(b) = \min(\infty, 0 + 22) = 22$
                       $L(c) = \min(\infty, 0 + 1) = 1$

$$L(d) = \min(\infty, 0+8) = 8$$
$$L(e) = \min(\infty, 0+\infty) = \infty$$
$$L(f) = \min(\infty, 0+\infty) = \infty$$
$$L(z) = \min(\infty, 0+\infty) = \infty$$

3. $V = c$, the permanent label of c is 1.
    $P = \{a, c\}$, $T = \{b, d, e, f, z\}$
    $$L(b) = \min(22, 1+6) = 7$$
    $$L(d) = \min(8, 1+10) = 8$$
    $$L(e) = \min(\infty, 1+4) = 5$$
    $$L(f) = \min(\infty, 1+3) = 4$$
    $$L(z) = \min(\infty, 1+10) = 11$$

4. $V = f$, the permanent label of $f = 4$.
    $P = \{a, c, f\}$, $T = \{b, d, e, z\}$
    $$L(b) = \min(22, 4+7) = 11$$
    $$L(d) = \min(8, 4+6) = 8$$
    $$L(e) = \min(5, 4+\infty) = 5$$
    $$L(z) = \min(11, 4+9) = 11$$

5. $V = e$, the permanent label of $e = 5$.
    $P = \{a, c, f, e\}$, $T = \{b, d, z\}$
    $$L(b) = \min(11, 5+2) = 7$$
    $$L(d) = \min(8, 5+\infty) = 8$$
    $$L(z) = \min(11, 5+4) = 9$$

6. $V = b$, the permanent label of $b = 7$.
    $P = \{a, c, f, e, b\}$, $T = \{d, z\}$
    $$L(d) = \min(8, 7+\infty) = 8$$
    $$L(z) = \min(9, 7+2) = 9$$

7. $V = d$, the permanent label of $d = 8$.
    $$P = \{a, c, f, e, b, d\}, \quad T = \{z\}$$
    $$L(z) = \min(9, 8+\infty) = 9$$

∴ The permanent label of $z = 9$.

Hence the length of shortest path from a to z is 9.

The shortest path is acez.

(ii) According to Dijkstra's Algorithm, the shortest path from a to z can be calculated as follows:

1. $P = \phi$, $\quad\quad T = \{a, b, c, d, e, f, z\}$
   $L(a) = 0$, $L(x) = \infty \quad \forall x \in T, x \neq a$

2. $V = a$, the permanent label of $a = 0$.
   $P = \{a\}$, $\quad\quad T = \{b, c, d, e, f, z\}$
   $L(b) = \min(\infty, 0 + 2) = 2$
   $L(c) = \min(\infty, 0 + 1) = 1$
   $L(d) = \min(\infty, 0 + 4) = 4$
   $L(e) = \min(\infty, 0 + \infty) = \infty$
   $L(f) = \min(\infty, 0 + \infty) = \infty$
   $L(z) = \min(\infty, 0 + \infty) = \infty$

3. $V = c$, the permanent label of $c = 1$.
   $P = \{a, c\}$, $\quad\quad T = \{b, d, e, f, z\}$
   $L(b) = \min(2, 1 + 2) = 2$
   $L(d) = \min(4, 1 + 2) = 3$
   $L(e) = \min(\infty, 1 + 5) = 6$
   $L(f) = \min(\infty, 1 + 7) = 8$
   $L(z) = \min(\infty, 1 + \infty) = \infty$

4. $V = b$, the permanent label of $b = 2$.
   $P = \{a, c, b\}$, $\quad\quad T = \{d, e, f, z\}$
   $L(d) = \min(3, 2 + \infty) = 3$
   $L(e) = \min(6, 2 + 3) = 5$
   $L(f) = \min(8, 2 + \infty) = 8$
   $L(z) = \min(\infty, 2 + \infty) = \infty$

5. $V = d$, the permanent label of $d = 3$,
   $P = \{a, c, b, d\}$, $\quad\quad T = \{e, f, z\}$
   $L(e) = \min(5, 3 + \infty) = 5$
   $L(f) = \min(8, 3 + 4) = 7$
   $L(z) = \min(\infty, 3 + \infty) = \infty$

6. $V = e$, the permanent label of $e = 5$,
   $P = \{a, c, b, d, e\}$, $\quad\quad T = \{f, z\}$
   $L(f) = \min(7, 5 + \infty) = 7$
   $L(z) = \min(\infty, 5 + 1) = 6$

7. $V = z$, the permanent label of $z = 6$.
   Hence the length of the shortest path from a to z is 6. This shortest path is abez.

Example 5: For the following graph in Fig. 8.118 (a), find the shortest path using Dijkstra's Algorithm.

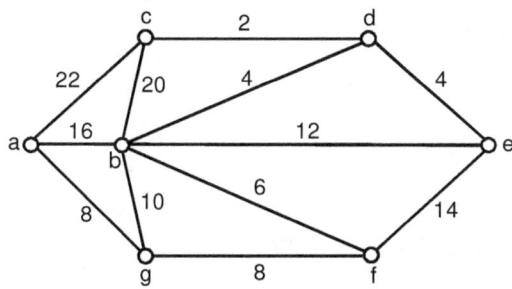

Fig. 8.118 (a)

Solution: According to the algorithm, the shortest path from a to e can be calculated as follows:

(1) P = $\emptyset$ T = {a, b, c, d, e, f, g}

L (a) = 0,   L(x) = ∞ $\forall$ x $\in$ T, x $\neq$ a

(2) V = a, the permanent label of a = 0.

P = {a},   T = {b, c, d, e, f, g}

L (b) = min (∞, 0 + 16) = 16

L (c) = min (∞, 0 + 22) = 22

L (d) = min (∞, 0 + ∞) = ∞

L (e) = min (∞, 0 + ∞) = ∞

L (f) = min (∞, 0 + ∞) = ∞

L (g) = min (∞, 0 + 8) = 8

(3) V = g, the permanent label of g = 8.

P = {a, g},   T = {b, c, d, e, f}

L (b) = min (16, 8 + 10) = 16

L (c) = min (22, 8 + ∞) = 22

L (d) = min (∞, 8 + ∞) = ∞

L (e) = min (∞, 8 + ∞) = ∞

L (f) = min (∞, 8 + 8) = 16

(4) V = b, the permanent label of b is 16.

P = {a, g, b},   T = {c, d, e, f}

L (c) = min (22, 16 + 20) = 22

L (d) = min (∞, 16 + 4) = 20

$$L(e) = \min(\infty, 16 + 12) = 28$$
$$L(f) = \min(16, 16 + 6) = 16$$

(5) V = f, the permanent label of f is 16.

P = {a, g, b, f}, T = {c, d, e}
$$L(c) = \min(22, 16 + \infty) = 22$$
$$L(d) = \min(20, 16 + \infty) = 20$$
$$L(e) = \min(28, 16 + 14) = 28$$

(6) V = d, the permanent label of d is 20.

P = {a, g, b, f, d}, T = {c, e}
$$L(c) = \min(22, 20 + 2) = 22$$
$$L(e) = \min(28, 20 + 4) = 24$$

(7) V = c, the permanent label of c is 22.

P = {a, g, b, f, d, c}, T = {e}
$$L(e) = \min(24, 22 + \infty)$$
$$= 24$$

(8) V = e, the permanent label of e is 24.

Hence, the length of shortest path from a to e is 24.

The shortest path from a to e is abde which is shown below.

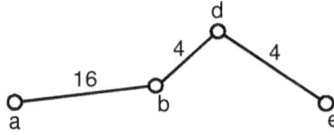

Fig. 8.118 (b)

8.13 Eulerian Path and Eulerian Circuit

Now, we are in a position to define an eulerian path and an eulerian circuit which has many practical applications.

A path is called an **Eulerian Path** if every edge of the graph G appears exactly once in the path.

Similarly, the circuit which contains every edge of the graph G exactly once is called an **Eulerian Circuit**. A graph which has an Eulerian circuit is called an **Eulerian Graph**.

For example in Fig. 8.119, G_1 has an eulerian path e_1 e_2 e_3 e_4 e_5 but G_2 does not have an eulerian path. Similarly, G_3 contains an eulerian circuit 1 2 3 4 5 1 but G_4 does not.

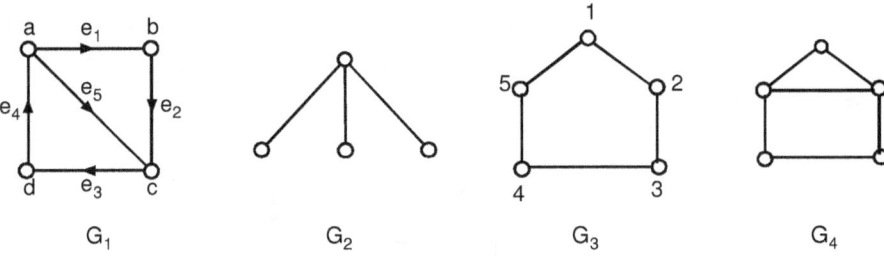

Fig. 8.119

A graph which has an eulerian path may not have an eulerian circuit. For instance, G_1 has an eulerian path but it does not have an eulerian circuit.

The existence of eulerian paths or circuits in a graph is related to the degree of vertices as given below:

Theorem 8.13.1: A graph possesses an eulerian path if and only if it is connected and has either zero or two vertices of odd degrees.

Theorem 8.13.2: A graph possesses an eulerian circuit if and only if it is connected and its vertices are all of even degrees.

Theorem 8.13.3: A directed graph possesses an eulerian circuit if it is connected and the incoming degree of every vertex is equal to its outgoing vertex.

For example, in the Fig. 8.120, the incoming degree of each vertex is equal to the outgoing degree of each vertex. Hence, the diagraph has an eulerian circuit $v_1 v_2 v_3 v_4 v_5 v_3 v_1$.

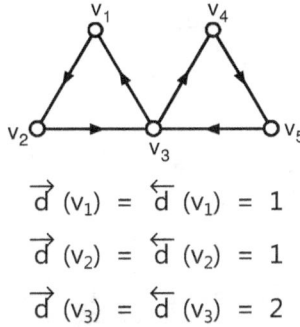

$\vec{d}(v_1) = \overleftarrow{d}(v_1) = 1$

$\vec{d}(v_2) = \overleftarrow{d}(v_2) = 1$

$\vec{d}(v_3) = \overleftarrow{d}(v_3) = 2$

Fig. 8.120

We shall now give the solution of famous Königsberg seven bridges problem which was solved by Swiss Mathematician Leonhard Euler in 1736, Euler presented the paper with the solution of seven bridges problem which is considered as the birth mark of graph theory. The problem is depicted in Fig. 8.121.

Two islands C and D formed by Pregel river in Königsberg (then the capital of East Prussia but now renamed Kaliningrad and in West Soviet Russia) were connected to each other and to the banks A and B with seven bridges as shown in Fig. 8.121. The problem was to start at any of the four land areas of the city A, B, C or D, walk over each of the seven bridges exactly once and return to the starting point.

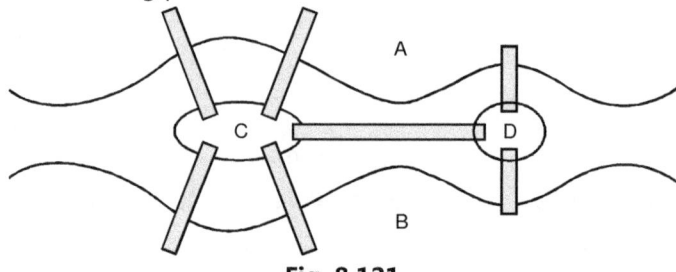

Fig. 8.121

Euler represented this situation by means of graph as shown in Fig. 8.122 and proved that the solution to this problem does not exist.

In above Fig. 8.122, vertices present the land areas and the edges present the bridges of the problem. According to the problem, we have to walk through all the edges and come back to the original vertex. That is it is required to find an eulerian circuit in a graph. As the degree of each vertex is not even, hence by **Theorem** 8.13.2, there does not exist any eulerian circuit in the graph.

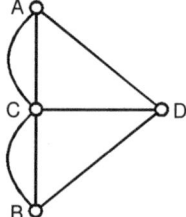

Fig. 8.122

Hence, it is not possible to walk through all seven bridges exactly once and come back to original position. Therefore, there is **no** solution to Konigsberg bridge problem.

SOLVED EXAMPLES

Example 1: Find out the eulerian circuit in the following graph. Also find an euler path from the vertex 'a' to the vertex 'b'.

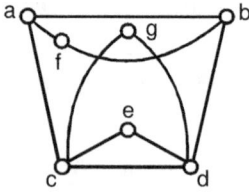

Fig. 8.123

Solution: In the above graph, the degree of the vertex a is 3 which is not an even number. Hence by Theorem 8.13.2, the graph does not have an eulerian circuit.

Also the given graph has exactly two vertices a and b of odd degrees. Hence by Theorem 8.13.1, the graph has an eulerian path. It is given by a c e d c g d b f a b.

Example 2: Draw a graph which has an eulerian circuit and has a cut vertex also.

Solution: A graph which has an eulerian circuit and cut vertex both is shown in the following Fig. 8.124.

Here, the eulerian circuit is a v c d v f a and the cut vertex is 'v'.

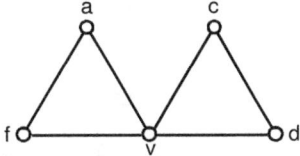

Fig. 8.124

Example 3: Draw a graph which contains an eulerian path but does not contain an eulerian circuit.

Solution: Consider a graph shown in Fig. 8.125.

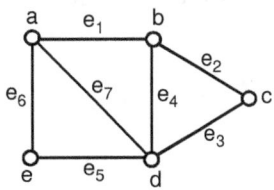

Fig. 8.125

The above graph has an eulerian path a e_1 e_2 e_3 e_5 e_6 e_7 e_4 b.

But it is does not contain an eulerian circuit because the degree of each vertex is not even.

Example 4: For what values of n does K_n, the complete graph on n nodes, have an Euler circuit? For which it has an Euler path?

Solution: In K_n, each vertex is joined to remaining (n − 1) vertices i.e. the degree of each vertex is (n − 1). If n is odd then the degree of each vertex will be even. Hence, by Theorem 8.13.2, the complete graph K_n will contain an Euler circuit.

For an Euler path, the graph should have either zero or exactly two vertices of odd degree. Exactly two vertices of odd degree is possible only in K_2 given in Fig. 8.126.

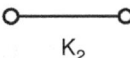

K_2

Fig. 8.126

Also, zero vertices of odd degree are possible in K_n when n is odd. Hence K_2 and all complete graphs K_n when n is odd have an Euler path.

Example 5: Find under what conditions $K_{m,n}$ the complete bipartite graph will have an eulerian circuit.

Solution: In complete bipartite graph $K_{m,n}$ consider the following cases:

(i) When $m = n$ and both m and n are even, then degree of each vertex is even and hence the graph $K_{m,n}$ will contain an eulerian circuit. For example, $K_{2,2}$, $K_{4,4}$ etc.

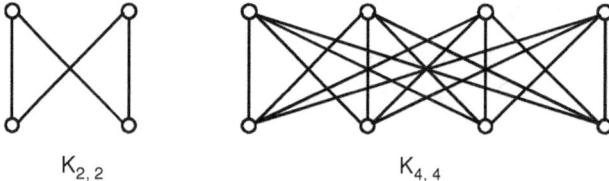

Fig. 8.127

(ii) If $m = n$ and both are odd, then the degree of each vertex is odd. Hence, the graph will **not** contain an eulerian circuit.

For example, $K_{3,3}$ etc.

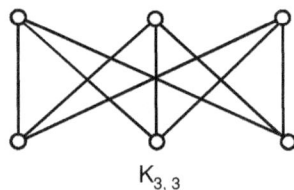

Fig. 8.128

(iii) If $m \neq n$ and both m and n are even, then the graph has an eulerian circuit. For instance, $K_{2,4}$ has an eulerian circuit.

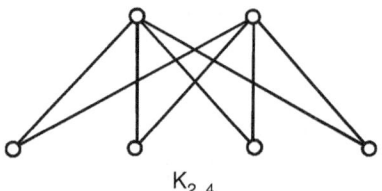

Fig. 8.129

(iv) If $m \neq n$ and either m is odd, n is odd or both are odd, then the graph will **not** possess an eulerian circuit. $K_{2,3}$, $K_{3,5}$ are the examples of graphs which do not possess an eulerian circuit.

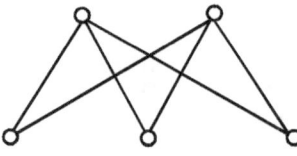

Fig. 8.130

Example 6: Consider the graph G shown in Fig. 8.131. The edges in the graph can be partitioned into two edge disjoint paths. Show one such partition.

Does the graph G possess an eulerian circuit? What is the minimum number of edges that can be added to the graph G so that the resultant graph will have an eulerian circuit?

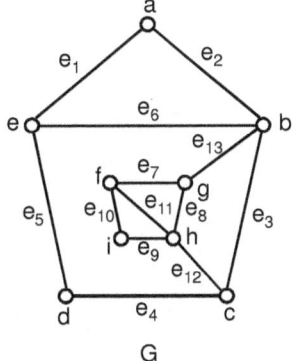

Fig. 8.131

Solution: The two edge disjoint paths in the graph G are

$g\ e_8\ e_{12}\ e_4\ e_5\ e_1\ e_2\ e_6$ and $c\ e_3\ e_{13}\ e_7\ e_{10}\ e_9\ e_{11}\ f$.

The above graph does not possess an eulerian circuit because the degree of vertices c, e, f and g are odd.

The graph will contain an eulerian circuit if we make odd degree vertices as even degree vertices by introducing the edges between them.

Join the vertices e and f by an edge and the vertices g and c by an edge so that the degree of each vertex becomes even and the graph will contain an eulerian circuit. The resultant graph is shown in Fig. 8.132.

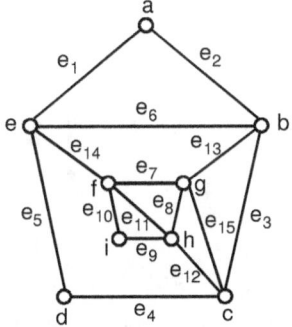

Fig. 8.132

An eulerian circuit in the resultant graph in Fig. 8.132 is $f\ e_{14}\ e_1\ e_2\ e_6\ e_5\ e_4\ e_3\ e_{13}\ e_{15}\ e_{12}\ e_9\ e_{10}\ e_{11}\ e_8\ e_7\ f$.

Example 7: Determine whether Eulerian Path and Eulerian circuit exist in the graphs G_1 and G_2 shown in Fig. 8.133.

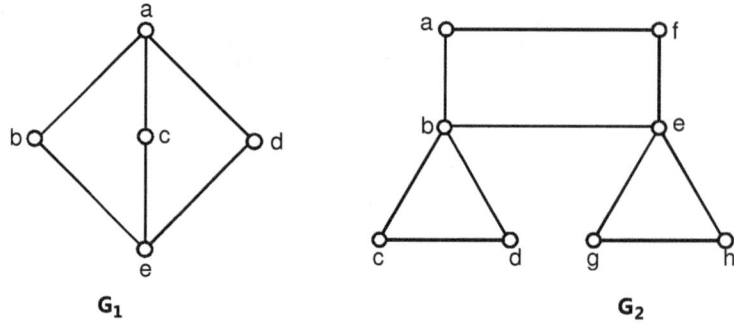

Fig. 8.133

Solution: If the path/circuit contains each edge of the graph exactly once then it is called an Eulerian path/circuit.

In G_1, there are exactly two vertices of odd degree, hence by Theorem 8.13.1, the graph G_1 contains an Eulerian path. It is given by a d e b a c e. Also, since the degree of each vertex is not even, the graph G_1 will not contain an Eulerian circuit.

In G_2, the degree of each vertex is even and hence by Theorem 8.13.2 the graph will contain an Eulerian circuit. It is given by a f e h g e b d c b a. Since the graph has an Eulerian circuit it will contain an Eulerian path also which will be given by a f e h g e b d c b a.

Example 8: Which of the following graphs possess Euler's path or circuit?

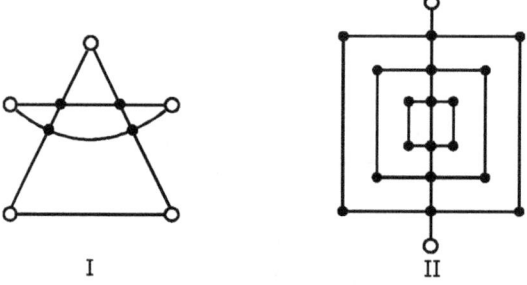

Fig. 8.134

Solution: In the graph (I), each vertex is of even degree. Hence it possesses an Euler's circuit. Graph (II) is connected graph and it has exactly 2 vertices of odd degree. Hence this graph possess an Euler's path.

8.14 Hamiltonian Path and Hamiltonian Circuit

In the last section, we have introduced the terms eulerian path and eulerian circuit in a connected graph. In a similar way, we will now define Hamiltonian path and Hamiltonian circuit in a connected graph which gives the solution to the famous game "all around the world" invented by Sir William Hamiltonian in 1859.

A circuit in a connected graph G is called a **Hamiltonian Circuit** if it contains every **vertex of G exactly once** (except the first and the last vertex).

Similarly a path in a connected graph G is a **Hamiltonian Path** if it contains every **vertex of G exactly once**. A graph which has a Hamiltonian circuit is called a **Hamiltonian graph**.

For example, for the graph G_1 in Fig. 8.135, the Hamiltonian circuit is given by (1 2 3 4 1)

A graph that contains the Hamiltonian path may not contain a Hamiltonian cycle. In Fig. 8.135, G_2 has a Hamiltonian path b a c but it does **not** contain any Hamiltonian circuit.

Now we present the famous "all around the world" problem.

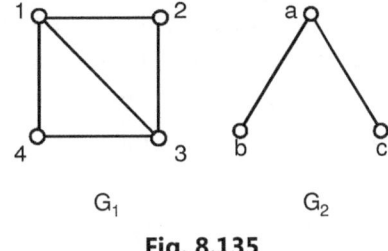

Fig. 8.135

All Around The World:

This problem was first posed by Irish Mathematician, Sir William Hamiltonian. He made a regular dodecahedron from wood with 20 vertices and 30 edges as shown in Fig. 8.136 in which each of 20 vertices were marked with the name of a city. The puzzle was to start from any city and find a route along the edge of the dodecahedron that passes through each city exactly once and return to the city of origin. That is, it was required to find a Hamiltonian circuit in the graph of dodecahedron.

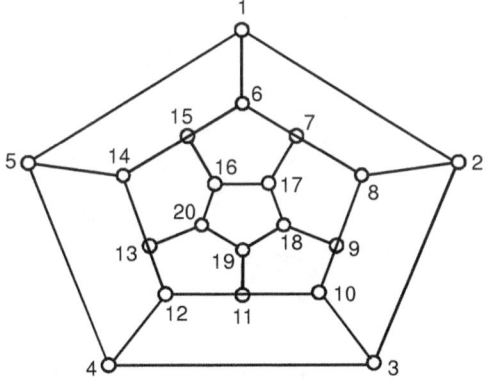

Fig. 8.136

One such route (Hamiltonian circuit) is 1 2 8 9 10 3 4 5 14 15 16 20 13 12 11 19 18 17 7 6 1. Obviously not every connected graph has a Hamiltonian circuit. For example, the graph in the following Fig. 8.137 does not have any Hamiltonian circuit.

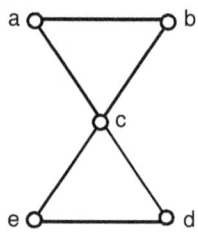

Fig. 8.137

A necessary and sufficient condition for a connected graph to have a Hamiltonian circuit is still unknown. However, there are some results which give sufficient conditions (not necessary) for a Hamiltonian circuit and Hamiltonian path.

We present now general conditions that are sufficient to guarantee for existence of a Hamiltonian path and a Hamiltonian circuit in a connected graph G.

Theorem 8.14.1:

> Let G be a simple connected graph on n vertices. If the sum of the degree for each pair of vertices in G is (n – 1) or large, then there exists a Hamiltonian path in G.
>
> For example, in Fig. 8.137, total number of vertices n = 5 and the degree sum of every pair of vertices is 4 or greater than 4. Hence, there exists a Hamiltonian path in G which is given by a b c e d.
>
> It is easy to see that the condition in the Theorem 8.14.1 is a **sufficient** condition but **not** a necessary condition for the existence of a Hamiltonian path in a graph. For instance, let G be a graph on 6 vertices given by Fig. 8.138.
>
>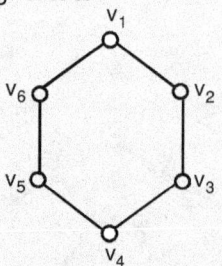
>
> **Fig. 8.138**
>
> Here the graph G has a Hamiltonian path $v_1\ v_2\ v_3\ v_4\ v_5\ v_6$ but the degree sum of any pair of vertices = 4 ≥ (6 – 1) = (n – 1)
>
> The next theorem which was proved by Dirac in 1952 gives a **sufficient** condition for existence of a Hamiltonian circuit in a simple connected graph.

Theorem 8.14.2:

If G = (V, E) is a simple connected graph on n vertices and if the degree of **each** vertex v is greater than or equal to $\frac{n}{2}$ i.e. $d(v) \geq n/2 \ \forall \ v \in V$ then G will contain a Hamiltonian circuit.

For example, consider the graph G with 6 vertices given in Fig. 8.139. In G, the degree of each vertex is greater than or equal to 3. Hence by above theorem 8.14.2, the graph has a Hamiltonian circuit which is given by $v_1 v_2 v_3 v_4 v_5 v_6 v_1$.

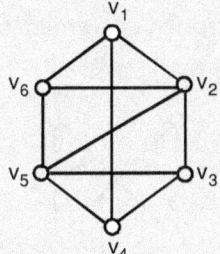

Fig. 8.139

The condition given in theorem 8.14.2 is only a sufficient condition for a given graph to have a Hamiltonian circuit. For instance, the graph G with 8 vertices in Fig. 8.140 has a Hamiltonian circuit 1 2 3 4 5 6 7 8 1 but degree of each vertex $d(v) = 2 \geq 8/2 = 4$.

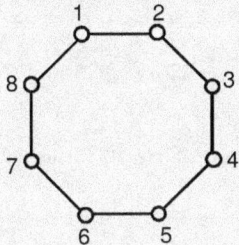

Fig. 8.140

Now, we give some necessary condition for a graph to have a Hamiltonian circuit.

Theorem 8.14.3:

Let G be a connected simple graph. If G has a Hamiltonian circuit then for **every** proper non-empty subset S of V(G), the components in the graph (G − S) is less than or equal to the number of vertices in S.

With the help of above necessary condition, we will show that the complete bipartite graph $K_{m, n}$ does not have a Hamiltonian circuit if $m \neq n$. In fact it has a Hamiltonian circuit when m = n.

Consider the complete bipartite graph $K_{m,n}$ when $m \neq n$.

Let (V_1, V_2) be a partition of the vertex set of $K_{m,n}$ where $|V_1| = m$, and $|V_2| = n$ and $m < n$. The graph $K_{m,n} - V_1$ is a null graph on n vertices and hence it is a disconnected graph with n components.

Therefore, the number of components in $K_{m,n} - V_1 = n \leq |V_1| = m$ which is contradiction to $m < n$. Hence by theorem 8.14.3, $K_{m,n}$ does not contain a Hamiltonian circuit when $m \neq n$.

Consider the complete bipartite graph $K_{m,n}$ when $m = n = 2$ i.e. $K_{2,2}$. It is shown in Fig. 8.141.

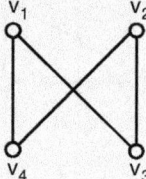

Fig. 8.141

Here the total number of vertices = 4 and the degree of each vertex v is d(v) = 2 which satisfies the condition for theorem 8.5.3.

i.e. $\quad d(v) = 2 \geq \dfrac{4}{2}$

$\Rightarrow d(v) = 2 \geq 2$

Hence $K_{2,2}$ has a Hamiltonian circuit.

In general, we can say that $K_{m,n}$ has a Hamiltonian circuit (and also has a Hamiltonian path) if **m = n**.

8.15 Travelling Salesman Problem

In the previous section, we have studied the theorems for hamiltonian graphs. One of the problems related to Hamiltonian circuit is "Travelling Salesman Problem" which is stated below.

A salesman is required to visit a number of cities during a trip. Given the distances between the cities, in what order should he travel so as to visit every city precisely once and return home with the minimum distance travelled?

The above problem can be represented by a weighted graph, in which vertices represent the cities and the roads between the cities represent the edges. The weight of each edge is the distance between the two cities. Thus the travelling salesman problem reduces to find the Hamiltonian circuit in the given graph with minimum weight.

For example, consider the following weighted graph.

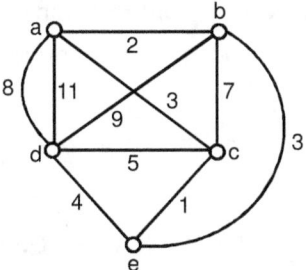

Fig. 8.142

There are several Hamiltonian circuits starting from a
  (i)   abceda with weight 22
  (ii) abecda with weight 21
  (iii) acebda with weight 26 and so on.

The minimum Hamiltonian circuit is abecda.

If the graph is k_n(complete graph on n vertices) then the problem can be solved, theoretically by listing all possible $\frac{(n-1)!}{2}$ Hamiltonian circuits and picking the one which has the least weight. However, for a large value of n, this is highly inefficient algorithm.

In fact, no efficient algorithm is available to find the solution of travelling salesman problem. There are methods available that give a route very close to the shortest one but do not guarantee the shortest path. One such method is nearest-neighbour method which gives good results to the salesman problem.

8.15.1 Nearest-Neighbour Method

In this method, we start the Hamiltonian circuit with any arbitrary vertex and find the vertex which is nearest to it. Continuing this way and coming back to the starting vertex by travelling through all the vertices exactly once, we get the Hamiltonian circuit.

> The nearest-neighbour method is described below:
> (1) Start with any arbitrary vertex (say v_1) and choose the vertex closest to the starting vertex to form an initial path of one edge. Construct this path by selecting different vertices as described in step (2).

(2) Let v_n denote the latest vertex that was added to the path. Select the vertex v_{n+1} closest to v_n from all vertices that are not in the path and add this vertex to the path.

(3) Repeat step (2) till all the vertices of the graph G are included in the path.

(4) Lastly form a circuit by adding the edge connecting the starting vertex and the last vertex added.

The circuit obtained using the nearest-neighbour method will be the required Hamiltonian circuit.

SOLVED EXAMPLES

Example 1: Use nearest-neighbour method to find out Hamiltonian circuit for the graph shown in Fig. 8.143

(a) Starting at vertex a.
(b) Starting at vertex d.
(c) Determine the minimum Hamiltonian circuit.

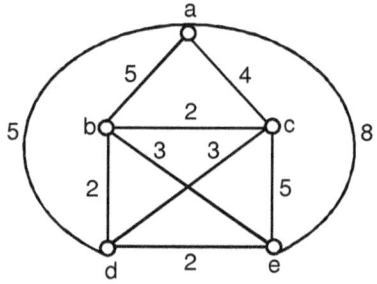

Fig. 8.143

Solution: (a) Start with vertex a. There are 4 adjacent vertices to a namely b, c, d and e but nearest neighbour is c (weight of the edge ac is 4 which is minimum).

(i)   Path = {a, c}

(ii) There are three vertices adjacent to c, namely b, d and e (except a). The nearest neighbour is b.

                     Path = {a, c, b}

(iii)   Path = {a, c, b, d}

(iv)   Path = {a, c, b, d, e}

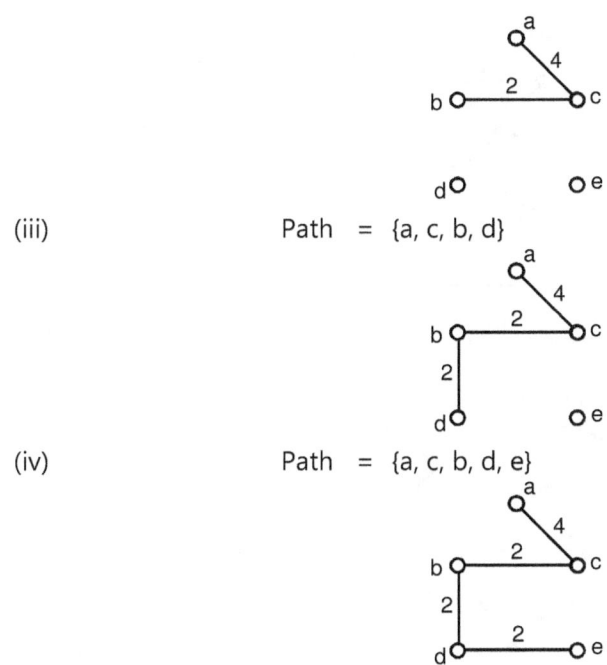

(v) Since all the vertices are traversed, to complete the Hamiltonian circuit, we have to reach back to the vertex a from e.

Hamiltonian circuit = {a, c, b, d, e, a}

The weight of Hamiltonian circuit = 18.

Fig. 8.144

(b) To find the Hamiltonian circuit starting from d, consider the starting vertex d. Since both the vertices b and e are nearest to d (at a distance 2), we can choose any one of them. Let the vertex e be chosen.

(i)   Path = {d, e}

(ii)   Path = {d, e, b}

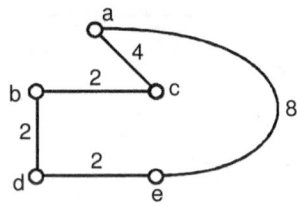

(iii) Path = {d, e, b, c}

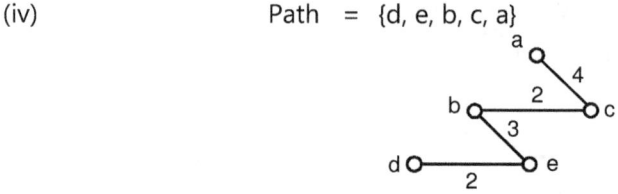

(iv) Path = {d, e, b, c, a}

(v) Hamiltonian circuit = {d, e, b, c, a, d}

Fig. 8.145

Weight = 16.

(c) The minimum Hamiltonian circuit is debcad with weight 16.

Example 2: Use nearest-neighbour method to find the Hamiltonian circuit starting from a in the following graph. Find its weight.

Fig. 8.146

Solution: (i) Path = {a, f}

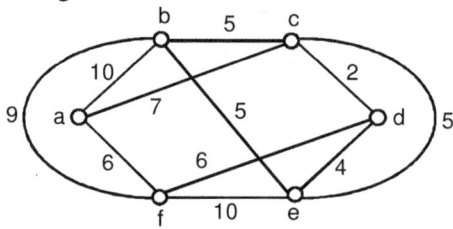

(ii) Path = {a, f, d}

(iii)   Path = {a, f, d, c}

(iv)   Path = {a, f, d, c, e}

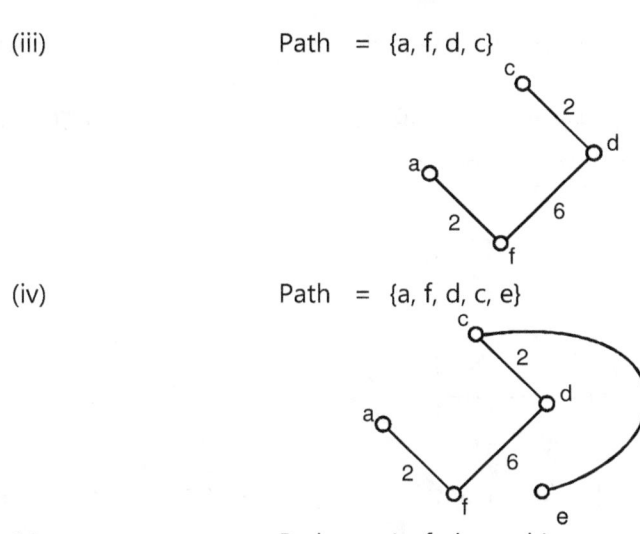

(v)   Path = {a, f, d, c, e, b}

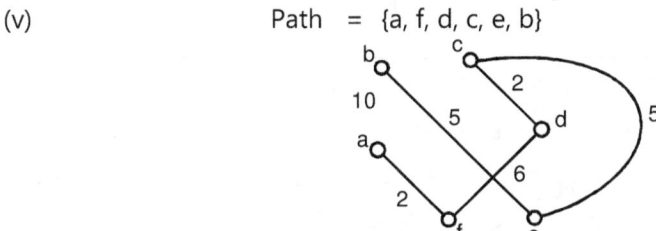

(vi) Hamiltonian circuit = {a, f, d, c, e, b, a}.

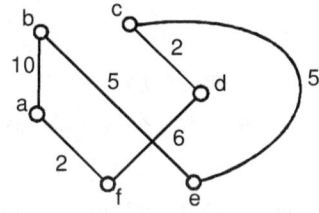

Fig. 8.147

Weight of the Hamiltonian circuit = 34.

Example 3: Show that the complete graph K_n ($n \geq 3$) has a Hamiltonian circuit. What is the length of that circuit? How many Hamiltonian circuits exist in K_n?

Solution: The complete graph K_n ($n \geq 3$) has n vertices and the degree of each vertex is $(n-1)$.

We know that when $n \geq 3$, $n - 1 \geq \dfrac{n}{2}$

$\Rightarrow \quad d(v) \geq \dfrac{n}{2} \quad \forall \ v \in V(K_n)$

Therefore the theorem 8.14.2 is satisfied. Hence, the complete graph on n vertices has a Hamiltonian circuit.

For example, consider K_4 as shown in Fig. 8.148, the Hamiltonian circuit is a b c d a. The length of the Hamiltonian circuit is the number of edges in the circuit. For K_4, the Hamiltonian circuit will contain 4 edges.

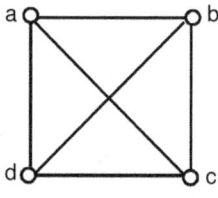

Fig. 8.148

Hence in K_n, the length of the Hamiltonian circuit is n. There are $\frac{(n-1)!}{2}$ Hamiltonian circuits in the complete graph K_n.

Example 4: Find a Hamiltonian path and a Hamiltonian circuit in $K_{4,3}$.

Solution: The complete bipartite graph $K_{4,3}$ is given by

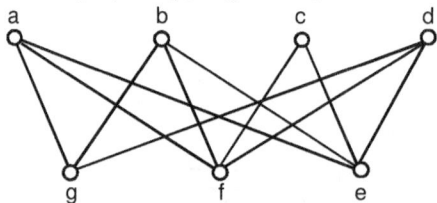

Fig. 8.149

Here the total number of vertices in the graph $K_{4,3}$ is 7. Also the degree sum of any pair of vertices $\geq (7-1)$.

Hence by theorem 8.14.1, the graph $K_{4,3}$ has a Hamiltonian path. It is given by a g b f c e d. Also, the graph $K_{4,3}$ does not contain a Hamiltonian circuit because $m \neq n$.

Example 5: Is the following graph contains a Hamiltonian circuit? If yes, find the Hamiltonian circuit.

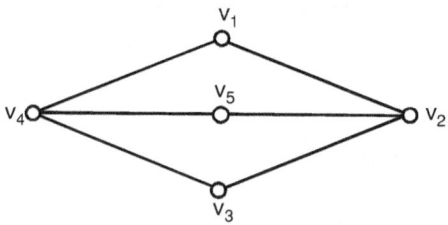

Fig. 8.150

Solution: Since there are five vertices, a Hamiltonian circuit must have five edges. Suppose that we could eliminate edges from the graph to produce a Hamiltonian circuit. We would have to eliminate one edge incident on v_2 and one edge incident on v_4, since each vertex in a Hamiltonian circuit has degree 2. But this leaves four edges - **not** enough for a Hamiltonian circuit. Therefore, the graph does not contain a Hamiltonian circuit.

Example 6: Consider the problem of scheduling seven examinations in seven days so that two examinations given by the same instructor are not scheduled on consecutive days. If no instructor gives more than four examinations, show that it is always possible to schedule the examination.

Solution: Let G be a graph with seven vertices corresponding to the seven Examinations. There is an edge between two vertices if and only if two vertices correspond to two examinations given by **different** instructors.

First we will show that degree of each vertex is **at least** 3. Suppose not i.e. there exists a vertex v of degree less than 3. This means that at the most only two vertices will have an edge with the vertex v i.e. the remaining 4 vertices will have **no** edge with v. Now, these 4 vertices together with the vertex v correspond to 5 different examinations given by the same instructor which is a contradiction to the assumption that no instructor gives more than 4 examinations.

Hence, the degree of each vertex is at least 3 and therefore the degree sum of any pair of vertices is at least 6 which is greater than or equal to $(7 - 1) = 6$.

Hence, by theorem 8.14.1, the graph will have a Hamiltonian path. This shows that, it is possible to schedule the examination under given condition.

Example 7: (i) Give an example of a graph that has both an Eulerian circuit and Hamiltonian circuit.

(ii) Give an example of a graph that has an Eulerian circuit but no Hamiltonian circuit.

(iii) Give an example of a graph that has Hamiltonian circuit but no Eulerian circuit.

(iv) Give an example of a graph that has neither Hamiltonian circuit nor Eulerian circuit.

Solution: (i) Graph with Eulerian circuit and Hamiltonian circuit is as shown in Fig. 8.151.

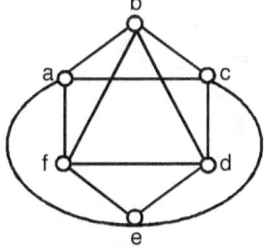

Fig. 8.151

Eulerian circuit b c e d c a f d b f e a b
Hamiltonian circuit b c d e f a b

(ii) Graph with Eulerian circuit but no Hamiltonian circuit.

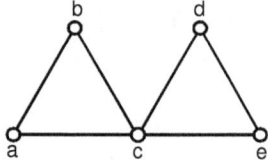

Fig. 8.152

Eulerian circuit a b c d e c a
No Hamiltonian circuit.

(iii) Graph with Hamiltonian circuit but not Eulerian circuit.

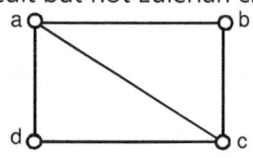

Fig. 8.153

Hamiltonian circuit a b c d a
No Eulerian circuit.

(iv) Graph with neither Hamiltonian nor Eulerian circuit.

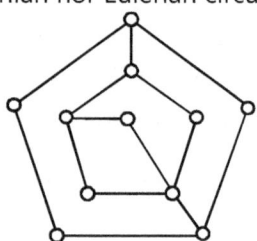

Fig. 8.154

Example 8: Show that any Hamiltonian circuit in the graph shown in Fig. 8.155 that contains the edge x must also contain the edge y.

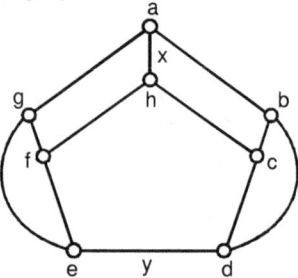

Fig. 8.155

Solution: A Hamiltonian circuit contains each vertex of the graph exactly once. Consider the Hamiltonian circuit either starting from the vertex a and containing the edge x = (a, h). At h, if we take the path h c b d then to cover all the vertices in the circuit, we have to cross the edge y = (d, e) to traverse through the remaining vertices e, f and g.

Similarly, if the circuit starts from the vertex h or any other vertex from the graph and contains the edge x, then to traverse through all the vertices of the graph we have to travel through the edge y.

Hence, any Hamiltonian circuit in the graph that contains the edge x must contain the edge y.

Example 9: (i) Is there a Hamiltonian path in a complete bipartite graph $K_{4,4}$ and $K_{4,5}$?
(ii) Is there a Hamiltonian circuit in the graphs shown in G_1 and G_2 in Fig. 8.156.

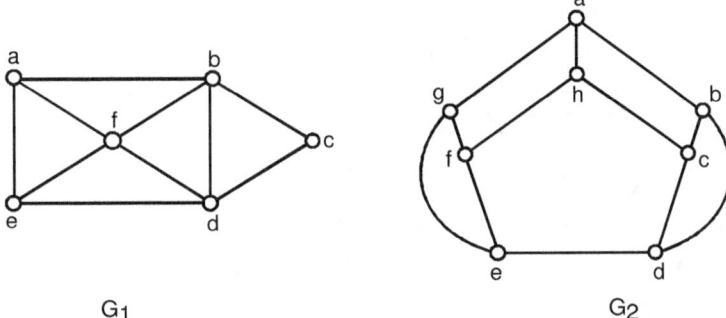

Fig. 8.156

Solution: (i) In $K_{4,4}$ the number of vertices are 8 and the degree of each vertex is 4.

Hence the degree sum of any pair of vertices in $K_{4,4}$ is 4 + 4 = 8.

Hence by Theorem 8.14.1

Degree sum (4 + 4) > (8 − 1) = (n − 1)

⇒ 8 > 7

Hence, $K_{4,4}$ contains a Hamiltonian path.

Similarly in $K_{4,5}$ there are 9 vertices and there are 4 vertices of degree 5 and 5 vertices of degree 4.

Hence, the degree sum of pair of vertices

$(4 + 4) = 8 > (9 − 1) = n − 1$

or $(4 + 5) = 9 > (9 − 1) = (n − 1)$

$(5 + 5) = 10 > (9 − 1)$

Hence by Theorem 8.14.1, the graph $K_{4,5}$ has a Hamiltonian path.

(ii) In G_1, the Hamiltonian path is a b c d f e.

A Hamiltonian circuit is a b c d f e a.

In G_2, the Hamiltonian path is a b d c h f e g

The Hamiltonian circuit is a b d c h f e g a.

Example 10: (i) Is there a Hamiltonian circuit in a complete bipartite graph $K_{4,4}$, $K_{4,5}$ and $K_{4,6}$?

(ii) Is there a Hamiltonian circuit in the graph shown in Fig. 8.157? What about a Hamiltonian path?

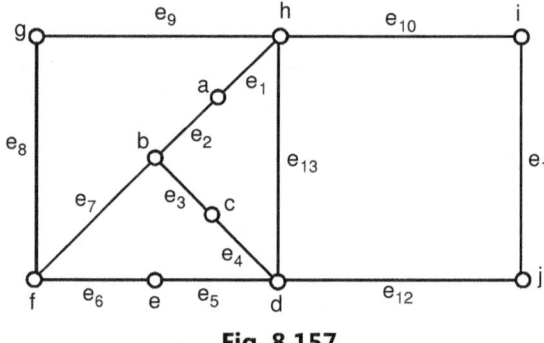

Fig. 8.157

Solution: (i) We know that in the complete bipartite graph $K_{m,n}$ if m = n, the Hamiltonian circuit exists, and if m ≠ n, the Hamiltonian circuit does not exist.

Hence in $K_{4,4}$, the Hamiltonian circuit exists.

In $K_{4,5}$ and $K_{4,6}$, the Hamiltonian circuit does not exist.

(ii) We know that for any Hamiltonian circuit, all the vertices of the graph should be traversed exactly **once**. Each vertex in the **circuit** must have degree exactly 2 because if the vertex has degree more than 2 in the circuit, it means that the vertex is traversed more than once in the circuit. Hence we have to remove additional edges, if any, keeping in mind the connectedness of the graph.

Consider the vertex f of degree 3, if we remove e_6 or e_8, the vertices g and e will become of degree 1 which is not allowed for the circuit.

Hence remove the edge e_7 so that the vertex f becomes of degree 2. This implies b also becomes of degree 2. To make the vertex d of degree 2, we have to remove 2 edges incident on d. Remove the edge e_{13}. Now we cannot remove the edges e_4, e_5 or e_{12} otherwise the vertices c, e or j will become of degree 1. Hence it is not possible to make the vertex d of degree 2 by removing the edges. Therefore, the graph does not have a Hamiltonian circuit.

The Hamiltonian path is given by c b a h i j d e f g.

Example 11: Show that the graph shown in Fig. 8.158 has no Hamiltonian circuit.

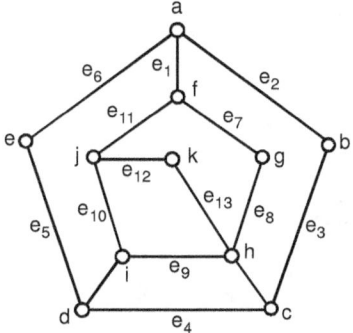

Fig. 8.158

Solution: For a Hamiltonian circuit, each vertex should have degree exactly 2 in the circuit. Hence we have to remove the additional edges.

Consider the vertex a of degree 3. Edges e_2 and e_6 incident on a can not be removed since they are incident on vertices b and e of degree 2 also. Hence we have to remove the edge e_1.

Similarly, consider the vertex d of degree 3, with the same argument we cannot remove the edge e_5. Remove the edge e_{15}.

Consider the vertex c of degree 3, to maintain the connectivity of the graph, we have to retain the edges e_4 and e_3. This means we can remove the edge e_{14} only to make the vertex c of degree 2. But this is not possible because otherwise the graph will become disconnected. Hence the given graph has no Hamiltonian circuit.

Example 12: Does $K_{1,3}$ have an Eulerian circuit? A Hamiltonian circuit?

Solution: The complete bipartite graph $K_{1,3}$ is shown below.

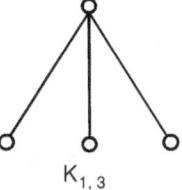

$K_{1,3}$

Fig. 8.159

The above graph does not have even degree vertices. Therefore it does not contain an Eulerian circuit. Also $K_{m,n}$ will have a Hamiltonian circuit, if $m = n$. Hence $K_{1,3}$ will not have a Hamiltonian circuit.

Example 13: Determine which of the graphs G_1 and G_2 represent Eulerian circuit, Eulerian path, Hamiltonian circuit, Hamiltonian path. Justify your answer.

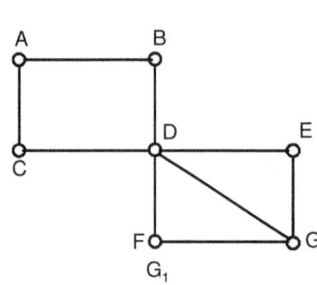
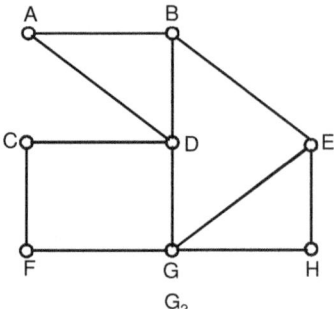

Fig. 8.160

Solution: For the graph G_1,

(i) There is no Eulerian circuit because degree of each vertex is not even.

(ii) There exists an Eulerian path in G_1 because G_1 contains exactly two vertices of odd degree. It is given by GEDBACDFGD.

(iii) No Hamiltonian circuit. To cover all the vertices exactly once, the vertex D has to traverse twice.

(iv) G_1 has Hamiltonian path EGFDBAC.

For the graph G_2,

(i) No Eulerian circuit because degree of each vertex is not even.

(ii) There is an Eulerian path BADCFGHEGDBE.

(iii) It has Hamiltonian path and circuit both. It is ABEHGFCDA.

Example 14: Draw the graphs formed by the vertices and edges of a tetrahedron, a cube and an octahedron. Find a Hamiltonian cycle in each graph.

Solution: Tetrahedron has four vertices, six edges and four triangular faces. It is shown in Fig. 8.160 (a).

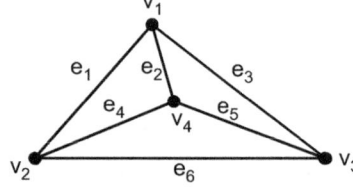

Fig. 8.160 (a)

The Hamiltonian circuit in tetrahedron given by Fig. 8.160 (a) is $v_1 v_2 v_3 v_4 v_1$.

The octahedron called a platonic solid has eight triangular faces with 6 vertices and 12 edges. It is shown in Fig. 8.160 (b).

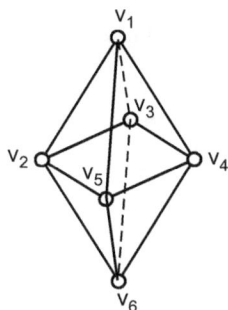

Fig. 8.160 (b)

The Hamiltonian circuit in octahedron shown in Fig. 8.160 (b) is given by $v_1 \, v_2 \, v_3 \, v_4 \, v_6 \, v_5 \, v_1$.

The cube is shown in Fig. 8.160 (c).

It has Hamiltonian circuit given by $v_1 \, v_2 \, v_3 \, v_4 \, v_5 \, v_8 \, v_7 \, v_6 \, v_1$.

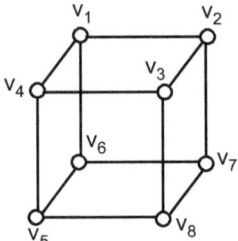

Fig. 8.160 (c)

8.16 Planar Graph

In this last section of the chapter, we study drawing of a graph in a plane without its edges crossing over, which is useful in many fields like technology of printed circuits, design of large scale integrated circuits etc.

> A graph is said to be a **planar graph** if it can be drawn on the plane **with no intersecting edges** i.e. a graph is a planar graph if it is drawn on a plane such that no edges cross each other.

For instance, the graph shown in Fig. 8.161 is a planar graph.

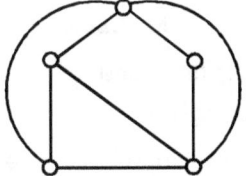

Fig. 8.161

A graph which is non planar in one representation may become a planar graph after redrawing it.

Consider a graph G_1 in Fig. 8.162 which appears a non planar graph because its edges e_5 and e_6 are seemed to be crossing each other.

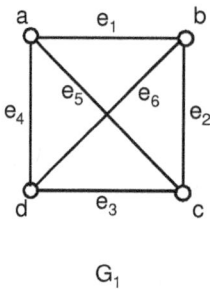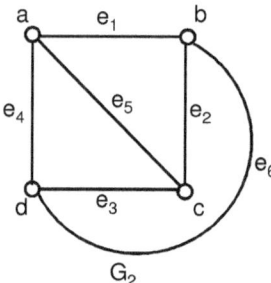

Fig. 8.162

The graph G_1 in the above Fig. 8.162 can be redrawn as G_2 given in Fig. 8.162. The graph G_2 is indeed a **planar graph**.

8.16.1 Regions:

A planar representation of a graph divides the plane into regions (also called **windows, faces** and **meshes**). **A region is characterized by the set of edges forming its boundary.**

Fig. 8.163 shows different regions of the graph G which are marked by 1, 2, 3, 4, 5 and 6.

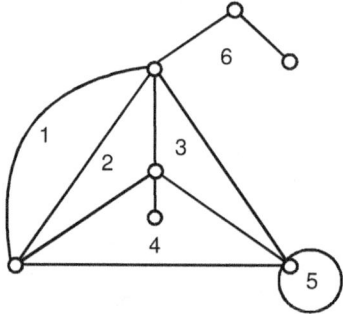

Fig. 8.163

A region is said to be finite if its **area** is finite and it is said to be infinite if its **area** is infinite. A planar graph has exactly **one infinite region**.

In Fig. 8.163, the regions 1, 2, 3 and 4 are finite but the region 6 is an infinite region.

8.16.2 Euler's Formula

Since a planar graph may have different planar representations, the number of regions resulting from each representation is the same. The number of regions in any planar representation depends upon the number of vertices and the number of edges in the graph. The relation between edges, vertices and faces of any graph is given by Euler's formula.

Theorem 8.16.1:

For any connected planar graph,

$$v - e + r = 2 \qquad \ldots (8.16.1)$$

where v, e, r are the total number of vertices, edges and regions in the graph respectively. For instant, consider the graph G with 12 vertices and 15 edges as shown in Fig. 8.164.

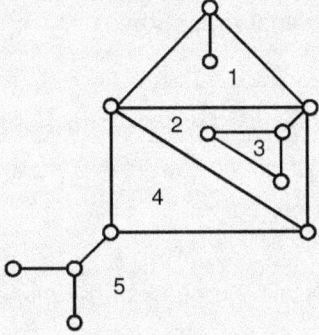

Fig. 8.164

According to Euler's formula, the graph G should have $r = 2 - v + e$ faces i.e. $r = 2 - 12 + 15 = 5$ faces. These 5 regions are shown in the given Fig. 8.164.

Proof of Euler's theorem:

Proof:

Let G be any connected planar graph with v vertices, e edges and r number of faces. Since G is connected, two cases arise: (i) G is a tree, (ii) G is not a tree. We will prove Euler's theorem for both the cases

Case I: If G is a tree then G contains $(v - 1)$ number of edges and has only one unbounded face so that $r = 1$.

Therefore,
$$v - e + r = v - (v - 1) + 1 = 2$$

$\Rightarrow \qquad v - e + r = 2$

Thus, theorem 8.16.1 holds if G is a tree.

Case II: Suppose G is not a tree. Then G contains cycles. We will prove the result by induction on the number of edges $e \geq 0$. If $e = 0$ then $v = 1$ and $r = 1$.

$$\Rightarrow \quad v - e + r = 1 - 0 + 1 = 2$$

For induction step, suppose theorem 8.13.1 is true for $(e - 1)$ number of edges. From the graph G, remove the edge e' which forms the cycle in G. The graph $(G - e')$ is connected and has $(e - 1)$ number of edges and $(r - 1)$ number of faces.

Now, by induction $v - (e - 1) + (r - 1) = 2$.

i.e. $\quad v - e + r = 2$

Now, we give some results which are based on Euler's formula.

Corollary 8.16.1:

If G (V, E) is a simple connected planar graph, then

$$\boxed{e \leq 3v - 6} \quad \ldots (8.16.2)$$

where e is the total number of edges and v is the total number of vertices in the graph G.

Proof: Since the graph is a simple planar graph, therefore each region of the planar graph is bounded by at least three or more edges.

Hence the total number of edges $e \geq 3r$.

Also, each edge is included in at least 2 regions of the planar graph G, therefore

$$2e \geq 3r$$

or $\quad \dfrac{2e}{3} \geq r \quad \ldots (8.16.3)$

Substitute this value of r in Euler's formula, we get

$$v - e + \dfrac{2e}{3} \geq 2$$

or $\quad 3v - 6 \geq e$.

The most important application to this corollary (8.16.1) is to show that the complete graph K_5 on 5 vertices are **non planar**. K_5 is known as **Kuratowski's First Graph**.

In K_5, the number of vertices $v = 5$

The number of edges $e = 10$

According to (8.16.2)

$\Rightarrow \quad 3v - 6 \geq e$

$\Rightarrow \quad 3(5) - 6 \geq 10$

$\Rightarrow \quad 9 \geq 10$

which is impossible.

Hence, K_5 is non-planar.

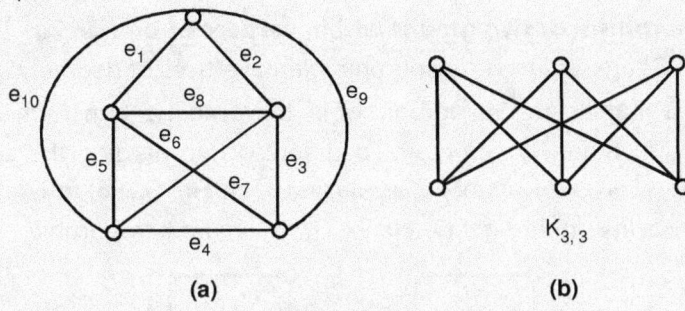

Fig. 8.165

As shown above in Fig. 8.165 (a) it is **not** possible to draw the edges e_6 and e_7 without crossing.

Hence, K_5 is non-planar.

Algebraically, we can show that in K_5, the crossing of edges cannot be avoided. K_5 is shown in Fig. 8.165 (a).

The inequality 8.16.2 is only a **necessary** condition but it is **not** a sufficient condition for the planarity of a graph. In other words, every simple planar graph must satisfy the condition (8.16.2), but the converse need not be true. That is the satisfaction of the inequality 8.16.2 does not guarantee for planarity of a graph.

For example, $K_{3,3}$ **Kuratowski's second** graph given in Fig. 8.165 (b) satisfies (8.16.2) because e = 9, v = 6. Hence $3v - 6 \geq e$, yet the graph $K_{3,3}$ is a **non planar graph**.

To prove the non planarity of $K_{3,3}$ we use the additional fact that no regions in the graph K_{33} is bounded with fewer than 4 edges. Hence, if this graph were planar, we would have

$$2e \geq 4r$$

or

$$\frac{e}{2} \geq r$$

Hence, according to Euler's formula

$$v - e + \frac{e}{2} \geq 2$$

$$\Rightarrow \quad 2v - 4 \geq e \qquad \ldots (8.16.4)$$

In $K_{3,3}$ inequality (8.16.2) becomes

$$(2 \times 6) - 4 \geq 9$$

$$\Rightarrow \quad 8 \geq 9$$

which is impossible. Hence $K_{3,3}$ is not a planar graph.

Kuratowski gave a necessary and sufficient condition for a graph to be planar in 1930.

Before we present a necessary and sufficient condition for planarity of a graph, we will define the new term **isomorphism of two graphs within vertices of degree 2.**

Two graphs G_1 and G_2 are said to be isomorphic within vertices of degree 2 (or homeomorphic) if they are isomorphic or if they can be transformed to isomorphic graphs by repeated insertion of vertices of degree 2 or by merging the edges which have exactly one common vertex of degree 2 as illustrated in Fig. 8.166. In Fig. 8.166, in G_1, the vertex v of degree 2 is inserted to get G_2. Hence G_1, G_2 are homeomorphic.

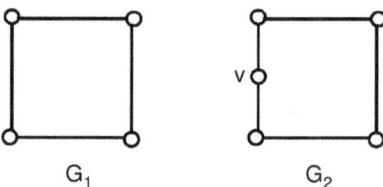

Insertion of a Vertex v

Fig. 8.166

In Fig. 8.167, in the graph G_3, two edges e_1 and e_2 are merged to get the graph G_4. Therefore, G_3 and G_4 are homeomorphic.

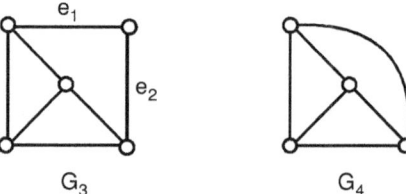

Fig. 8.167: Merging of Edges e_1 or e_2

Theorem 8.16.2 (Kuratowski Theorem):

> A graph is a planar graph if and only if it does not contain any subgraph that is isomorphic to within vertices of degree 2 to either K_5 or $K_{3,3}$.
>
> Consider the following graph G in Fig. 8.168.
>
>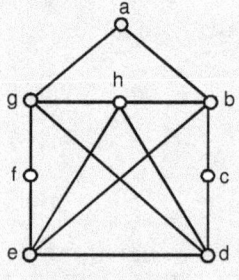
>
> **Fig. 8.168**

Merge the edges which are incident on the vertices a, c and f. After merging the graph is shown in Fig. 8.169 (a) which is isomorphic to K_5 as shown in Fig. 8.169 (b).

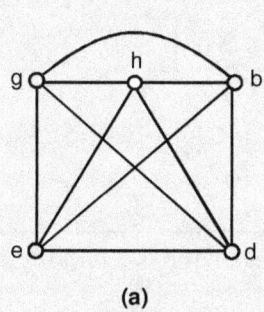
(a)

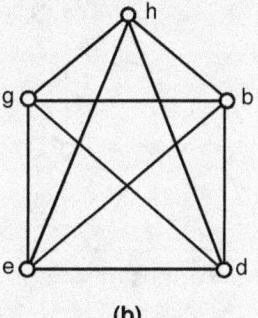
(b)

Fig. 8.169

Hence, the given graph G is non planar according to theorem 8.13.2.

SOLVED EXAMPLES

Example 1: By drawing the graph, show that following graphs are planar graphs.

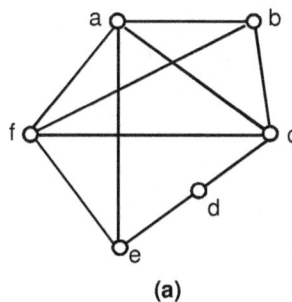
(a)

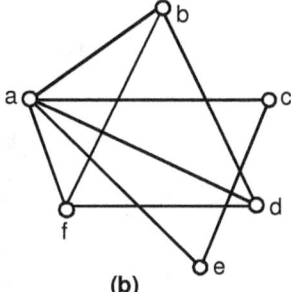
(b)

Fig. 8.170

Solution: The graph shown in Fig. 8.170 (a) can be redrawn as planar graph as follows:

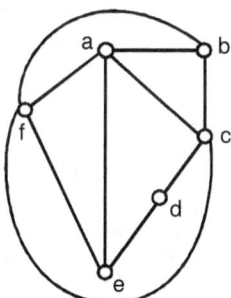

Fig. 8.171

The planar representation of the graph in Fig. 8.170 (b) is shown below:

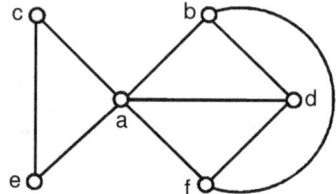

Fig. 8.172

Example 2: How many edges must a planar graph have if it has 7 regions and 5 modes. Draw one such graph.

Solution: According to Euler's formula, in a planar graph $v - e + r = 2$.

where v, e, r are the number of vertices, edges and faces in a planar graph.

Here $v = 5$, $r = 7$, $e = ?$

Since the graph is a planar graph, therefore $5 - e + 7 = 2$

$$\Rightarrow e = 10$$

Hence, the given graph must have 10 edges. This graph is shown below in Fig. 8.173.

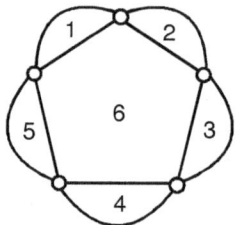

Fig. 8.173

Example 3: Determine the number of regions defined by a connected planar graph with 6 nodes and 10 edges. Draw a simple and a non simple graph.

Solution: Given $v = 6$, $e = 10$.

Hence by Euler's formula for a planar graph

$$v - e + r = 2 \quad \text{where, r is the number of faces.}$$
$$\Rightarrow 6 - 10 + r = 2$$
$$\Rightarrow r = 6$$

Hence the graph should have 6 faces.

Simple and a multiple graphs with $v = 6$, $e = 10$ and $r = 6$ are shown below.

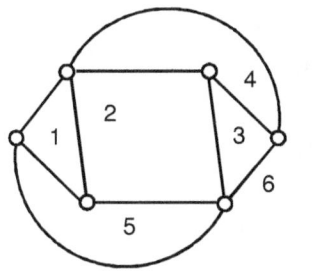

Simple Graph   **Multiple Graph**

Fig. 8.174

Example 4: A connected planar graph has nine vertices having degrees 2, 2, 2, 3, 3, 3, 4, 4 and 5.
How many edges are there? How many faces are there?

Solution: By Handshaking lemma

$$2e = \sum_{i=1}^{n} d(v_i) = \text{total degree}$$

where e is the number of edges

$$\Rightarrow \quad 2e = 2+2+2+3+3+3+4+4+5$$
$$2e = 28 \Rightarrow e = 14$$

Now, by Euler's formula

$$v - e + r = 2$$
$$\Rightarrow \quad 9 - 14 + r = 2$$
$$\Rightarrow \quad r = 7$$

Hence, there are 14 edges and 7 faces in the graph.

Example 5: Show that a simple planar graph has a vertex of degree 5 or less.

Solution: Let $G = (V, E)$ be a simple planar graph, where $|V| = v$, $|E| = e$.
If the number of vertices is less than or equal to 6, then there exists a vertex of degree 5 or less in the graph.
Suppose $|V| > 6$ and there is no vertex of degree ≤ 5.
Hence, by Handshaking lemma

$$2e = \sum_{i=1}^{v} d(v_i) \geq 6v$$

$$\Rightarrow \quad 2e \geq 6v$$

Therefore, by corollary 8.16.1,

$$e \le (3v - 6)$$
$$\Rightarrow \quad 2e \le 2(3v - 6)$$
$$\Rightarrow \quad 2e \le 6v - 12$$
$$\Rightarrow \quad 6v \le 2e \le 6v - 12$$
$$\Rightarrow \quad 6v \le 6v - 12$$
$$\Rightarrow \quad 0 \le -12$$

which is impossible.

Hence in a simple planar graph, there exists a vertex of degree 5 or less.

Example 6: Three utility problem: There are three homes H_1, H_2 and H_3, each to be connected to each of the three utilities: Water (W), Gas (G) and Electricity (E) by means of conduits. Is it possible to make such connections without any crossovers of the conduits?

Solution: The problem can be represented by a graph shown in Fig. 8.175, the conduits are shown as edges while the houses and utility supply centres are vertices.

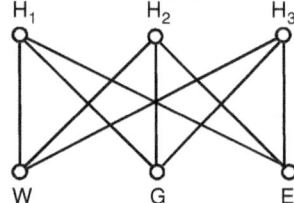

Fig. 8.175

The above graph is a complete bipartite graph $K_{3,3}$ which is a non-planar graph. Hence it is not possible to draw edges without crossing over.

Therefore it is **not** possible to make the connection without any crossovers of the conduits.

Example 7: Which of the following graphs are planar?

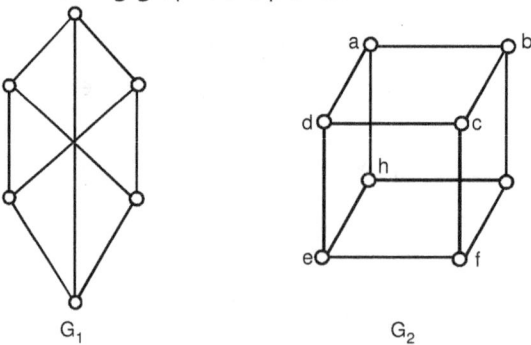

Fig. 8.176

Solution: The graph G_1 can be drawn as follows:

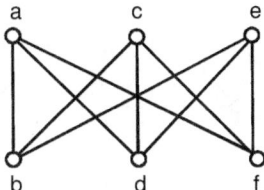

Fig. 8.177

The above graph is a Kuratowski's second graph $K_{3,3}$ which is non-planar. Hence, the given graph G_1 is non-planar.

Consider G_2, it can be redrawn as follows:

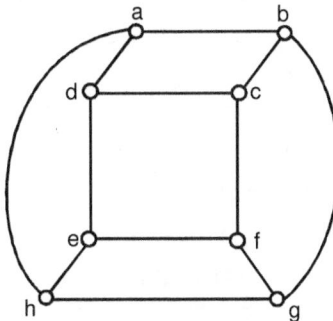

Fig. 8.178

The above graph is a planar graph because edges do not cross each other. Hence, the given graph G_2 is a planar graph.

Example 8: Draw a planar representation of each graph if possible.

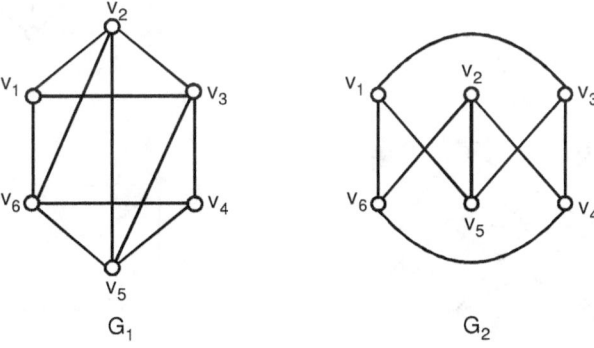

Fig. 8.179

Solution: The planar representation of G_1 is shown in Fig. 8.180.

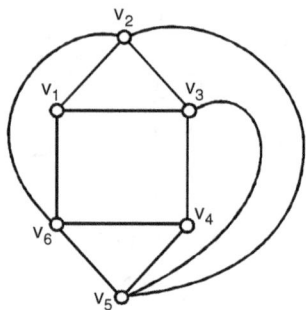

Fig. 8.180

The planar representation of G_2 is shown as follows:

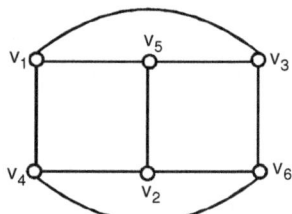

Fig. 8.181

Example 9: Determine which of the graphs of Fig. 8.182 represents Eulerian circuit, Hamiltonian circuit, Bipartite graph and planar graph. Justify your answer in each case.

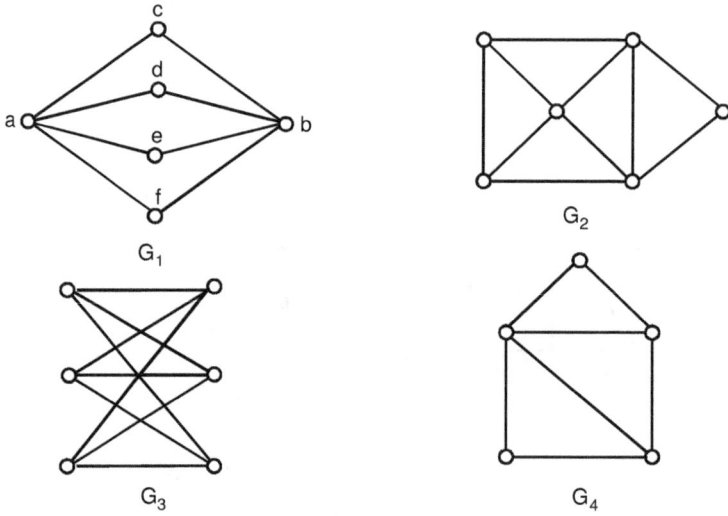

Fig. 8.182

Solution: G_1 is a bipartite graph in which the set of vertices V can be partitioned into two sets V_1 and V_2, where V_1 = {a, b} and V_2 = {c, d, e, f}

Such that $V_1 \cup V_2$ = V and $V_1 \cap V_2 = \emptyset$ also each edge of G is from V_1 to V_2. The other representation of the graph is

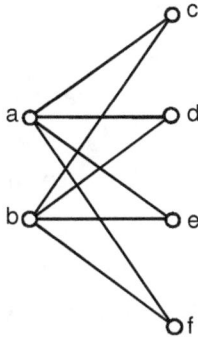

Fig. 8.183

Also, it is a complete bipartite graph $K_{2,3}$. Also the degree of each vertex in G_1 is even hence it contains an Eulerian circuit a c b d a e b f a. G_1 does not contain any Hamiltonian circuit.

It is a planar graph since no two edges are intersecting each other.

Consider G_2

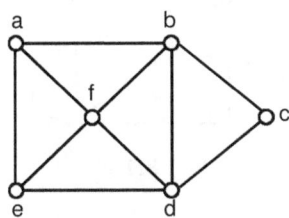

Fig. 8.184

It is not a bipartite graph because we cannot partition its vertex set into two parts V_1 and V_2 not having edges among themselves.

It contains a Hamiltonian circuit a b c d f e a.

Since the degree of each vertex is not even hence it does not contain an Eulerian circuit. But it contains an Eulerian path because there exists exactly two vertices of odd degree. An Eulerian path is a b c d f b d e f a e.

It is a planar graph because edge crossing is not there in the graph G_2.

Consider G_3

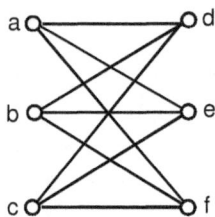

Fig. 8.185

It is a bipartite graph. Divide its vertex set V = {a, b, c, d, e, f} into two parts V_1 and V_2 such that V_1 = {a, b, c}, V_2 = {d, e, f} and each edge in G_3 is from V_1 to V_2.

In fact, it is a complete bipartite $K_{3,3}$ graph because each vertex in V_1 is joined to each vertex of V_2.

Since the degree of each vertex is not even, it does not have an Eulerian circuit.

As we know $K_{m,n}$ has a Hamiltonian circuit if m = n. Hence G_3 = $K_{3,3}$ has a Hamiltonian circuit given by a d b e c f a.

$K_{3,3}$ is known as Kuratowski's second graph which is given by planar graph.

Consider G_4

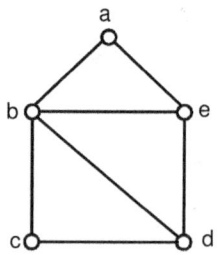

Fig. 8.186

It is not a bipartite graph.

Degree of each vertex is not even ⇒ there is no Eulerian circuit.

But it has an Eulerian path because it contains exactly two vertices d and e of odd degree. An Eulerian path is d b a e b c d e.

It contains a Hamiltonian circuit a b c d e a.

It is a planar graph.

Example 10: Show that in a connected planar linear graph with 6 vertices and 12 edges, each of the regions is bounded by 3 edges.

Solution: According to Euler's theorem for planar graph, v − e + r = 2, where v is the number of vertices, e is the total number of edges and r is the number of regions in the given graph.

Here, v = 6 and e = 12.
Therefore, we have
$$6 - 12 + r = 2$$
$$r = 8$$
Hence, the given graph contains 8 regions. If each region is bounded by 3 edges then
$$2e = 3r$$
i.e. $2 \times 12 = 3 \times 8$
$24 = 24$, which is true.

Hence, each region of the given graph is bounded by 3 edges.

Example 11: Identify whether the graphs given are planar or not.

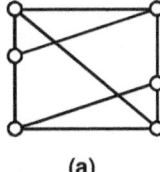 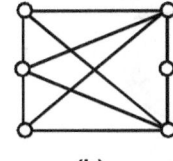 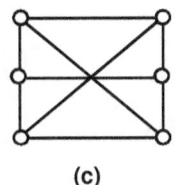 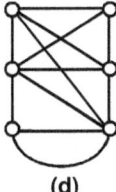

(a) (b) (c) (d)

Fig. 8.187

Solution: (a) The graph shown in Fig. 8.187 (a) is planar. Its planar graph is

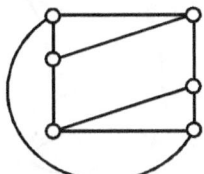

Fig. 8.188

(b) The planar graph of Fig. 8.187 (b) is as follows:

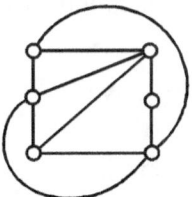

Fig. 8.189

(c) The graph shown in Fig. 8.187 (c) is non-planar because it is Kuratowski's graph $k_{3,3}$, which is non-planar.

The graph shown in Fig. 8.187 (c) can be redrawn as follows:

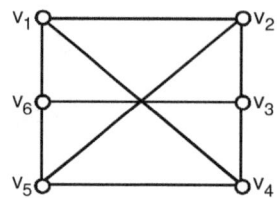 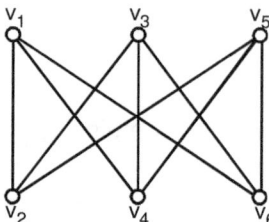

Fig. 8.190

(d) The graph shown in Fig. 8.187 (d) is planar as shown below:

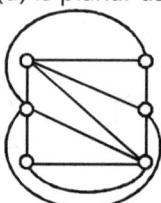

Fig. 8.191

EXERCISE - 8.2

1. Find the edge connectivity of the graph shown in Fig. 8.192.

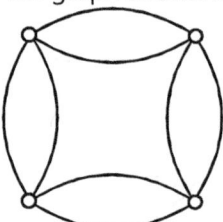

Fig. 8.192

2. Determine the maximal edge connectivity of a connected graph with 5 nodes and 8 edges. Draw a graph in which the connectivity is met and one in which it is not.

3. Define a connected graph.

   In the following graph in Fig. 8.193, what will happen if we remove the vertices v_1 and v_2? Draw the graph after removal.

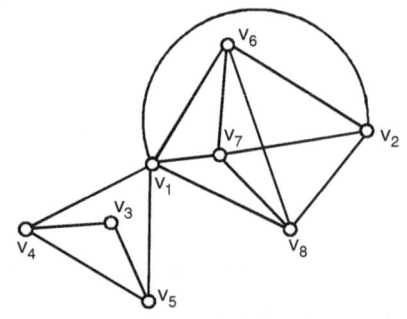

Fig. 8.193

4. Explain edge connectivity and vertex connectivity with examples. What is the relation between them?
5. Is the graph given in Fig. 8.193 is a separable graph? Justify your answer.
6. Define Isthmus. Find whether any edge in the graph G in Fig. 8.194 is an isthmus or not.

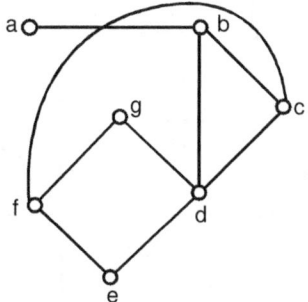

Fig. 8.194

7. Write Dijkstra's shortest path algorithm to obtain a shortest path between two vertices in the graph.
8. Apply shortest path algorithm to determine a shortest path between a and z in the graphs shown below:

(i)

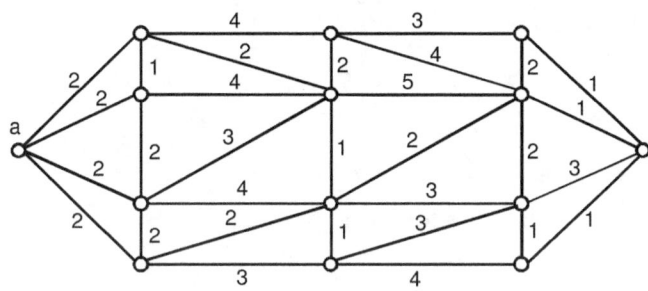

Fig. 8.195

(ii)

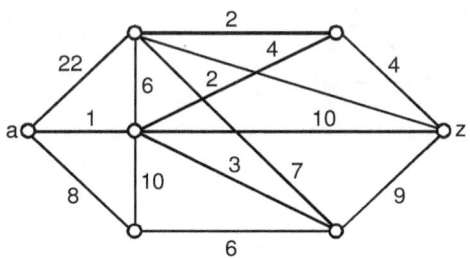

Fig. 8.196

(iii)

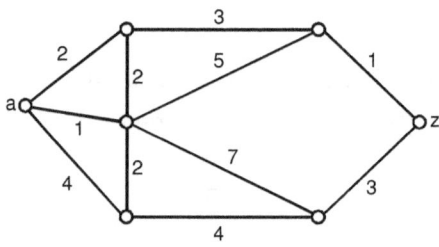

Fig. 8.197

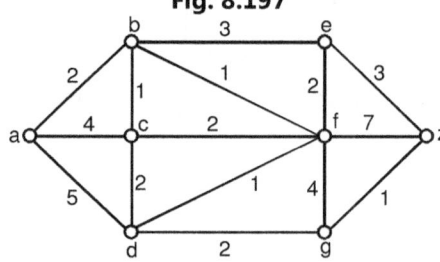

Fig. 8.198

9. Show that none of the following graphs contains a Hamiltonian circuit.

(i)   (ii)

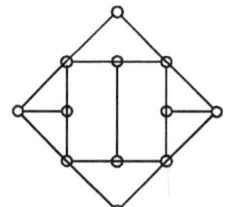 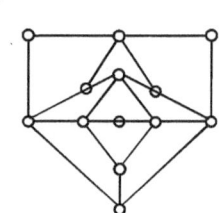

Fig. 8.199

10. Find an Eulerian circuit in the following graphs:

(i)   (ii)

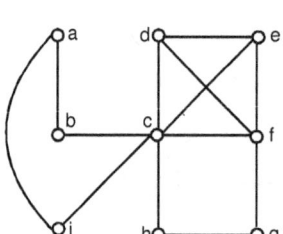 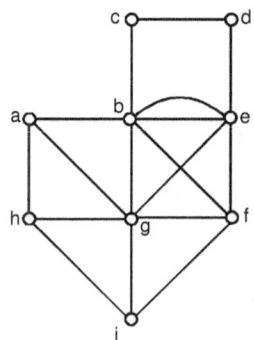

Fig. 8.200

11. Define the following terms:
    (i) Eulerian graph
    (ii) Hamiltonian graph
    (iii) Eulerian path
    (iv) Planar graph
    (v) Hamiltonian circuit

12. Determine whether following has a Hamiltonian circuit or not:

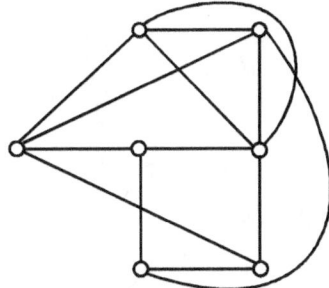

Fig. 8.201

13. State Euler's formula for a planar graph.
    Draw 2 non-isomorphic simple planar graphs with 6 nodes and 9 edges.

14. Draw a simple planar graph with 6 nodes and 11 edges.

15. Consider the graph as shown in Fig. 8.202. Find all the subgraphs when each vertex is deleted. Does any subgraph have any cut points?

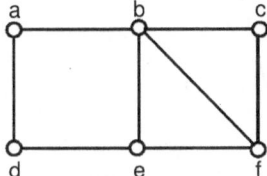

Fig. 8.202

16. Discuss with example relationship between complete bipartite graph and hamiltonian path.

17. Define planar graph. Let G be a connected planar graph with p vertices and q edges where $p \geq 3$ then show that $q \leq 3p - 6$.

18. Define and derive Euler's formula for the planar graph.

ANSWERS 8.2

1. Edge connectivity 4
2. Maximal edge connectivity $= \left\lceil \dfrac{16}{5} \right\rceil = 3$

   When the edge connectivity is met

   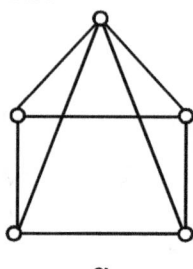

   α
   Fig. 8.203

   When the edge connectivity is not met

   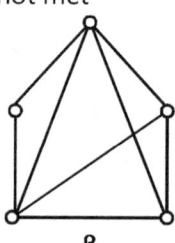

   β
   Fig. 8.204

3. The graph will become disconnected and it will have 2 components.

   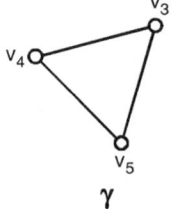

   γ   φ
   Fig. 8.205

5. Yes it is a separable graph.
   Removal of v_1 disconnects the graph.
6. The edge (a, b) is an isthmus.
8. (i) Shortest path is 8. (ii) Shortest path for a to z is 9. (iii) Shortest path is 6.
10. (i) a b c d e d f e c f g h c i a
    The vertex a has degree 3, hence no Eulerian circuit.
12. No Hamiltonian circuit.

13.

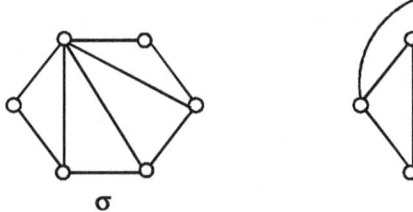

Fig. 8.206

14.

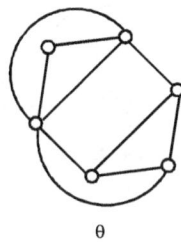

Fig. 8.207

15. All subgraphs of the given graph when each vertex is deleted are shown below:

   (i) when a is deleted:

   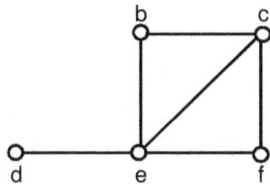

   Fig. 8.208

   e is a cut point.

   (ii) when b is deleted:

   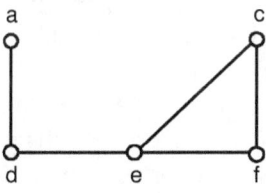

   Fig. 8.209

   e is a cut point.

(iii) when c is deleted:

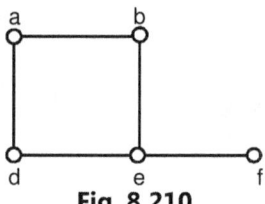

Fig. 8.210

e is a cut point.

(iv) when d is deleted

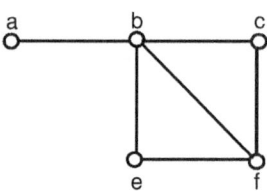

Fig. 8.211

b is a cut point.

(v) when e is deleted:

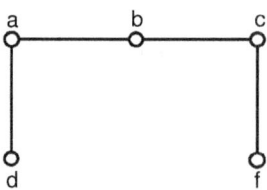

Fig. 8.212

Now, b is a cut point.

(vi) when f is deleted:

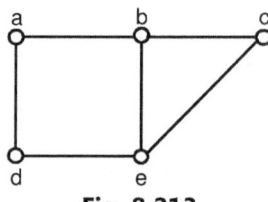

Fig. 8.213

No cut point is there.

POINTS TO REMEMBER

- A graph that has neither self loops nor parallel edges is called a **simple graph**, otherwise, it is called a **multiple graph**.
- Let G be a graph with vertex set V and edge set E. If each edge or each vertex or both are associated with some positive real numbers then the graph is called a **weighted graph**.
- A graph with finite number of vertices as well as finite number of edges is called a **finite graph**, otherwise, it is an infinite graph.
- A graph G = (V, E) is called a labeled graph if its edges are labeled with some name or data.

- Two vertices v_1 and v_2 of a graph G are said to be **adjacent** to each other if they are the end vertices of the same edge.
- The number of edges incident on a vertex v_i with self loop counted twice, is called the degree of the vertex v_i. It is denoted by $d(v_i)$.
- A vertex with degree zero is called an isolated vertex. More formally, a vertex having no incident edge is an isolated vertex. A vertex of degree 1 is called a pendant vertex.
- Consider a graph G with e number of edges and n number of vertices. Since each edge contributes two degrees, the sum of the degrees of all vertices in G is twice the number of edges in G. i.e.

$$\sum_{n=1}^{n} d(v_i) = 2e \qquad \ldots (8.1)$$

This is called **handshaking lemma**.
- Given a graph G with n vertices, e edges and no self loops. The incidence matrix $X(G) = [x_{ij}]$ of the graph G is an $n \times e$ matrix where,

$$x_{ij} = 1; \text{ if } j^{th} \text{ edge } e_j \text{ is incident on } i^{th} \text{ vertex } v_i = 0; \text{ otherwise}$$

Here n rows correspond to n vertices and e columns correspond to e edges.
- **Directed graphs or Digraphs:** A **directed graph** or **digraph D** is an ordered pair (V, A) where V is a non empty set of elements called vertices and A is the set of ordered pair of elements called directed edges or arcs. In other words, we can say that if the each edge of the graph G has a direction then the graph is called **directed graph** or **digraph**.
- The indegree of a vertex u of digraph D is defined as the **number of arcs which are incident into u** and is denoted by $\overrightarrow{d(u)}$. Similarly, the **outdegree of** a vertex u is defined as the **number of arcs which are incident out of u** and is denoted by $\overleftarrow{d(u)}$
- **Null Graph:** If the edge set of any graph with n vertices is an empty set, then the graph is known as **null graph**. It is denoted by N_n.
- **Complete Graph:** Let G be a simple graph on n vertices. If the degree of each vertex is (n – 1), then the graph G is called a **complete graph**. More generally, if every pair of vertices is adjacent in any simple graph, then the graph is said to be a **complete graph**.
- **Bipartite Graph:** Let G be a graph with vertex set V and edge set E, then G is called a **bipartite graph** if its vertex set V can be partitioned into two disjoint subsets say V_1 and V_2 such that $V_1 \cup V_2 = V$ and $V_1 \cap V_2 = \emptyset$ and also each edge of G joins a vertex of V_1 to a vertex of V_2.
- **Subgraph:** Let G = (V, E) be any given graph. Then the graph G' = (V', E') is called a **subgraph** of G if $V' \subseteq V$ and $E' \subseteq E$. In Fig. 8.54, H_1, H_2 and H_4 subgraphs of G but H_3

is not a subgraph of G because it contains the edge e which is not there in the graph G.
- **Edge Disjoint Subgraphs:** Two subgraphs H_1 and H_2 of the graph G are said to be **edge disjoint subgraphs** of a graph G if there is **no edge** common between H_1 and H_2 (but may have vertex common).
- **Vertex Disjoint Subgraphs:** Two subgraphs H_1 and H_2 are said to be **vertex disjoint subgraphs** of a graph G if there is **no vertex** common between them (i.e. they do not have common edges also).
- **Spanning Subgraph:** Let G = (V, E) be any graph. Then G' is said to be the **spanning subgraph** of the graph G if its vertex set V' is **equal to** the vertex set V of G.
- **Null Subgraph:** A subgraph H of a graph G is called a null subgraph if its vertex set is same as the vertex set of G and its edge set is empty set. i.e. it does not contain any edges. A null subgraph is constructed from a graph G by deleting all the edges of G.
- **Complement of a Graph:** Let G be a simple graph. Then the **complement of G** denoted by $\overline{G}$ is the graph whose vertex set is the same as the vertex set of G and in which two vertices are adjacent if and only if they are **not** adjacent in G.
- **A graph is said to be self complementary if it is isomorphic to its complement.**
- A path in a graph G is called a **simple path** if the edges do **not** repeat in the path.
- A path is said to be an **elementary** path if vertices do **not** repeat in the path.
- A circuit in the graph G is said to be a **simple circuit** if it does not include the same **edge** twice.
- A circuit is said to be an **elementary circuit** if it does not meet the same **vertex** twice (except for first and last vertex).
- A graph is said to be a **connected graph** if there exists a **path** between every pair of vertices, otherwise the graph is **disconnected**.
- **The vertex connectivity K (G)** of a simple connected graph G is defined as the **smallest number of vertices whose removal disconnects the graph.**
- A path is called an **Eulerian Path** if every edge of the graph G appears exactly once in the path.
- A circuit in a connected graph G is called a **Hamiltonian Circuit** if it contains every **vertex of G exactly once** (except the first and the last vertex).
- A graph is said to be a **planar graph** if it can be drawn on the plane **with no intersecting edges** i.e. a graph is a planar graph if it is drawn on a plane such that no edges cross each other.
- A planar representation of a graph divides the plane into regions (also called **windows**, **faces** and **meshes**). **A region is characterized by the set of edges forming its boundary.**

Unit 4

Chapter 9: TREES

SYLLABUS:
- Trees, rooted trees, path length in rooted trees, prefix codes, binary search trees, spanning trees and cut set, minimal spanning trees, Kruskal's and Prim's algorithms for minimal spanning tree.

OBJECTIVES:
- To study various properties of trees.
- Concept of binary search trees and spanning trees.
- Algorithm to find optimal binary tree.

UTILITY:
- Applications in solving problems in telecommunication, and transport networks.
- In sorting the data using binary search techniques.

KEY CONCEPTS:
- Binary search tree
- Optimal tree
- Spanning tree
- Fundamental cutset

9.0 Introduction

Trees are special type of connected graphs which appear as natural inverted trees. Trees were discovered by Kirchhoff in 1847 while investigating the electrical networks. In nineteenth century, Sir Arthur Cayley used trees to study the structure of hydrocarbons. Now-a-days, trees play an important role in many fields like computer science, chemistry, operations, research etc. In computer science, trees are useful in organizing and relating data in data base and analysis of algorithms. Trees also arise in theoretical problems such as the optimal time for sorting etc.

9.1 Definition and Properties of Trees

A "tree" is a simple connected graph without any circuits.

(Fig. 9.1 shows trees with one, two, three and four vertices.)

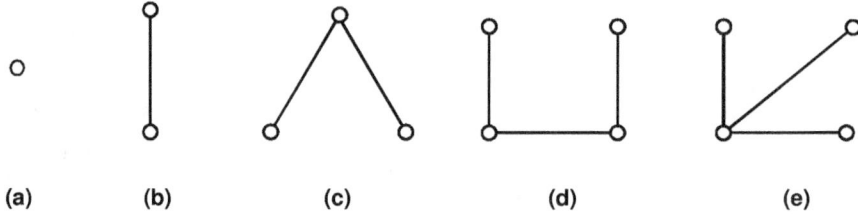

(a) (b) (c) (d) (e)

Fig. 9.1

The graph in Fig. 9.2 however is not a tree because it contains a cycle abca. Observe that if we remove the edge cb, we get a graph which is a tree.

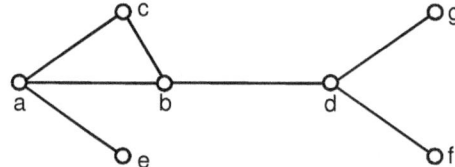

Fig. 9.2

Trees appear in numerous instances. The genealogy of a family is often represented by means of a tree (called a family tree). A river with its tributaries and subtributaries (sub tributaries) can be represented by a tree. The sorting of mail according to zip code is also done according to tree called **decision tree**.

It is shown in Fig. 9.3.

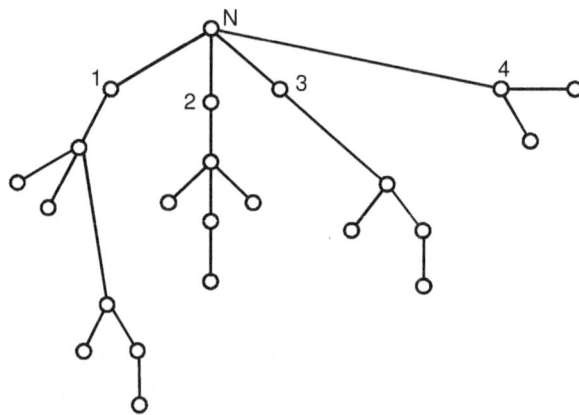

Fig. 9.3

A collection of disjoint trees is known as a **forest**. A vertex of degree 1 in a tree is called a **leaf** or a **terminal node** and a vertex of degree greater than one is called a **branch node** or an **internal node**. For example in the following Fig. 9.4, the vertices a, h, i etc. are leaves and vertices b, c, d, e are branch nodes.

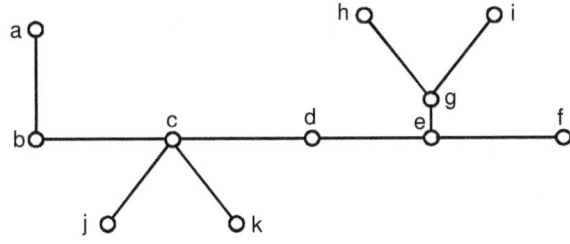

Fig. 9.4

A tree which is defined as non-cyclic connected graph, can be defined in terms of number of edges and vertices in the given graph.

Theorem 9.1.1

G is a tree if and only if there exists a **unique** path between every pair of vertices of G.
Proof:
We note first that existence of a path between every pair of vertices assures that the graph G is connected. Moreover, the graph G cannot contain a circuit if these paths are unique, since the existence of a circuit implies that there are two paths between a certain pair of vertices. Thus, we conclude that a graph in which there is a unique path between every pair of vertices is a tree. Conversely, if the graph G is a tree, it is connected and hence, there must be at least one path between every pair of vertices in G. Now suppose that there are two distinct paths between vertices a and b of G. The union of these two paths will contain a circuit and then, G cannot be a tree which is a contradiction. Therefore if G is a tree then it has a unique path between every pair of vertices of G.

Theorem 9.1.2

G is a tree if and only if G is connected and has exactly (n − 1) edges, where n is the number of vertices in G.

Proof:

Given G is a connected graph with the total number of edges e = (n – 1).

For tree, it is suffices to prove that it is non cyclic.

Suppose G contains a circuit C.

Let p denote the number of vertices in the circuit C which is equal to the number of edges in C also.

By the connectivity of G, we can say that every vertex of G that is not in C must be connected to the vertices in C.

Now each edge of G that is not in C can connect only one additional vertex to the vertices in C.

There are (n – p) vertices of G which are not in the circuit C.

Thus G must contain at least (n – p) edges that are not in C.

Hence, the total number of edges e in G is given by e · p + (n – p) = n which is a contradiction to the hypothesis that e = n – 1.

It follows that G does not contain a circuit and is, therefore a tree.

Conversely, if G is a tree then by definition it is connected and non cyclic.

We have to prove that the number of edges in G are e = (n – 1).

We will prove this result by induction on n.

For n = 1 the result is obvious.

Let n > 1, consider G – e', for any edge e' of G.

Since a tree is a circuitless graph hence, G – e' is a disconnected graph with two components G_1 and G_2.

Now G_1 and G_2 are connected and contain no cycles since they are both subgraphs of G which is non cyclic.

Let G_i contains v_i vertices and e_i edges. for i = 1, 2.

-][pBy induction

$$e_i = n_i - 1, \quad i = 1, 2$$

Therefore, the number of edges in G is given by

$$e = e_1 + e_2 + 1$$

$\Rightarrow \qquad e = (n_1 - 1) + (n_2 - 1) + 1$

$\Rightarrow \qquad e = n_1 + n_2 - 1$

$\Rightarrow \qquad e = n - 1$

Hence a tree contains (n – 1) number of edges.

The results of the preceding theorems can be summarized by saying that the following are equivalent definitions of a tree.

That is, a graph G with n vertices is called a tree, if
G is connected and a circuitless graph.
(ii) G is connected and has (n – 1) edges.
(iii) G is circuitless and has (n – 1) edges.
(iv) There is exactly one path between every pair of vertices in G.

9.2 Centre of a Tree

As we have seen in the previous section that each of the tree has several pendant vertices. Consider the following tree shown in Fig. 9.5. It has 5 pendant vertices.

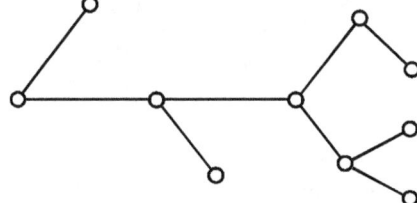

Fig. 9.5

For pendant vertices, we have an important result which says that **in any tree, there are at least two pendant vertices.** The reason is that in a tree of n vertices, we have (n – 1) edges and hence the total degree 2 (n – 1) has to be divided among n vertices. Since no vertex can be zero degree, we must have at least two vertices of degree one in a tree.

9.2.1 Eccentricity of a Vertex

We know that the distance between two vertices in a connected graph is a length of the shortest path between them.

The **eccentricity** E(v) of a vertex v in a graph G is the distance from v to the vertex farthest from v in G. i.e.

$$E(v) = \max d(v_i, v)$$

In the following Fig. 9.6.

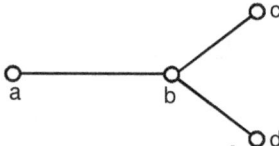

Fig. 9.6

E(a) = 2, E(b) = 1, E(c) = 2, E(d) = 2

A vertex with the **minimum eccentricity** is called a **centre** of G. In the above Fig. 9.6 the vertex b is the centre of that tree.

Every tree has either one or two centres. Consider the following tree in Fig. 9.7.

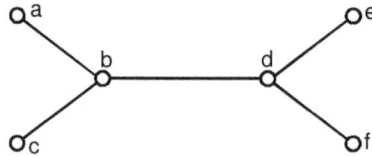

Fig. 9.7

Here   E(a) = E(c) = E(e) = E(f) = 3
and   E(b) = E(d) = 2

Hence this tree has 2 **centres** b and d.

9.2.2 Cut Points

As we have defined earlier, the cut points or cut vertices are those vertices whose removal disconnects the graph. **In any tree, all the vertices except pendant vertices (degree 1) are cut vertices.** For instance, in the following tree shown in Fig. 9.8, c, d, g are cut points.

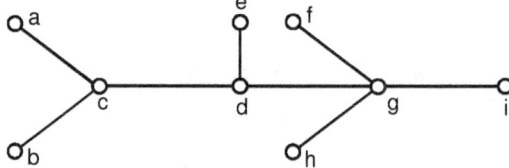

Fig. 9.8

SOLVED EXAMPLES

Example 1: Draw all non-isomorphic trees on 5 vertices.

Solution: All non-isomorphic trees on 5 vertices are shown below.

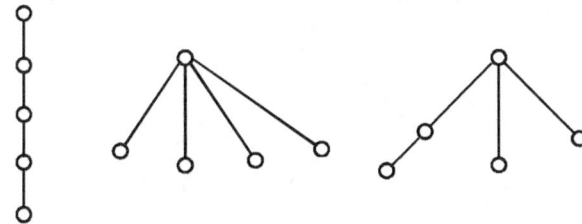

Fig. 9.9

Example 2: Draw a tree with 6 nodes, exactly 3 of which have degree 1.

Solution: A tree with 6 vertices which contains 3 pendant vertices is given by

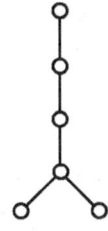

Fig. 9.10

Example 3: Show that it is possible to draw a tree with 10 vertices which has vertices either of degree 1 or of degree 3. Draw the tree. Is it possible to draw the same type of tree with 11 vertices ?

Solution: Given the tree has 10 vertices. Therefore it has 9 edges. Suppose there are x number of vertices of degree 1 and y number of vertices of degree 3 in the tree.

Hence, $x + y = 10$.

Also, by Handshaking lemma ... (1)

$$2e = \sum_{i=1}^{n} d(v_i)$$

$\Rightarrow \quad 2 \times 9 = x + 3y$

$\Rightarrow \quad 18 = x + 3y$ ... (2)

Solving equations (1) and (2) simultaneously, we get,

$x = 6$ and $y = 4$

That is there exist 6 vertices of degree 1 and 4 vertices of degree 3 in the tree of 10 vertices. One such tree is shown below.

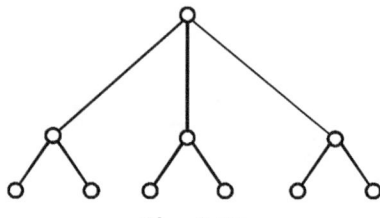

Fig. 9.11

For the second part, consider a tree with 11 vertices and 10 edges which has x vertices of degree 1 and y vertices of degree 3.

Hence $x + y = 11$

Also, by Handshaking lemma $2 \cdot 10 = x + 3y$

By above equations, we get

$x = \dfrac{13}{2}$ and $y = \dfrac{9}{2}$ which is impossible.

Therefore, it is not possible to draw a tree with 11 vertices which has vertices of degree 1 or 3.

Example 4: Is it possible to draw a tree with five vertices having degrees 1, 1, 2, 2, 4 ?

Solution: Since the tree has 5 vertices hence, it has 4 edges. Now given the vertices of tree are having degrees 1, 1, 2, 2, 4 i.e. the total degree of the tree = 10.

By Handshaking lemma $2e = \sum_{i=1}^{5} d(v_i)$

where e is the number of edges in the graph.

$\Rightarrow 2e = 10$

$\Rightarrow e = 5$

which is a contradiction to the statement that the tree has 4 edges. Hence the tree with given degrees of vertices does not exist.

Example 5: Which trees are complete bipartite graphs ?

Solution: Suppose T is a tree which is a complete bipartite graph. Let $T = k_{m, n}$ then the total number of vertices in T is (m + n). Hence the tree T contains (m + n − 1) number of edges. But the graph $k_{m, n}$ has (mn) number of edges.

Therefore $\qquad m + n - 1 = mn$

$\Rightarrow (m - 1)(1 - n) = 0$

$\Rightarrow m = 1$ or $n = 1$

This means T is either $k_{1,n}$ or $k_{m,1}$ i.e. T is a star.

Example 6: Find the centre of the following tree in Fig. 9.12.

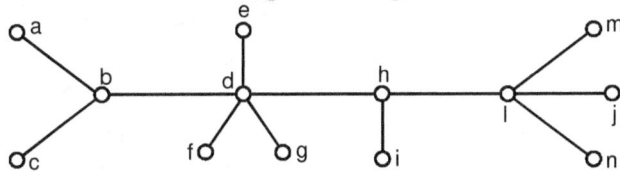

Fig. 9.12

Solution: The centre of the tree is a vertex with minimum eccentricity where eccentricity of the vertex is the distance of it from the farthest vertex.

The eccentricity of the different vertices of the tree in Fig. 9.12 are given as follows.

e (a) = 5, e (b) = 4, e (c) = 5, e (d) = 3, e (e) = 4, e (f) = 4, e (g) = 4, e (h) = 3, e (i) = 4
e (l) = 4, e (m) = 5, e (n) = 5, e (j) = 5.

The vertices with minimum eccentricity are d and h. Hence d and h are the **centres** of the tree.

9.3 Rooted and Binary Trees

Many of the applications of graph theory, particularly in computer science, use a certain kind of tree, called a rooted tree. These trees are used as models for the structures of file directories. Some of the other important uses of rooted trees include the representation and sorting of data, the representation of algebraic expressions etc.

A tree in which one vertex (called the root) is distinguished from all the other vertices is known as **rooted tree**. Trees without any root are called **free trees** or **simply trees**. A vertex of degree one which is not a root is called a leaf or external node and all the vertices (including the roots) that are not leaves are called interior nodes. For instance in Fig. 9.13 a vertex v is a root for all the trees shown.

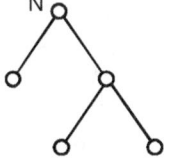 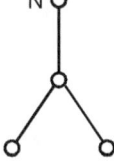 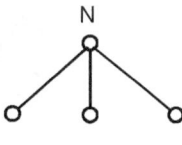

Fig. 9.13

The other example of rooted tree is sorting of mail according to the zip code. Consider the Fig. 9.13. The point N from where all the mail goes out is distinguished from the rest of the vertices. Hence N can be considered as the root of the tree.

A rooted tree is often used to specify hierarchical relationships. A example of such a tree, which is an organization chart of a corporation is given in the following Fig. 9.14.

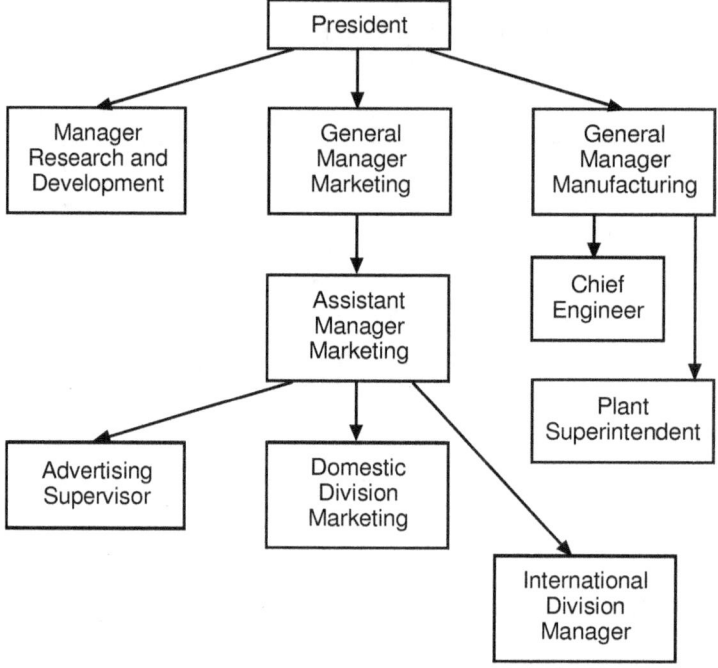

Fig. 9.14

A directed tree (a tree with directions) is called a **rooted tree** if there is exactly one vertex whose incoming degree is **zero** and all other vertices have incoming degree **one**. The vertex with incoming degree 0 is known as the **root** of the tree. In Fig. 9.15 the vertex a is the root of the directed tree.

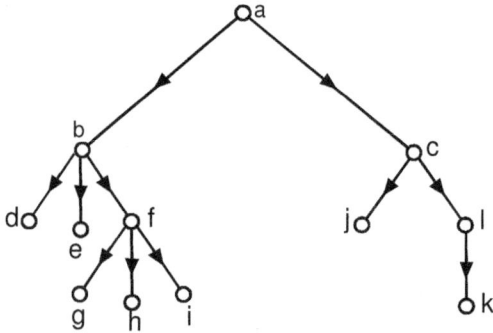

Fig. 9.15

In a directed rooted tree, a vertex whose outgoing degree is 0 is called a *leaf* and a vertex whose outgoing degree is non zero is called a **branch node** or an **internal node**. In Fig. 9.15 the vertices b, c and f are branch nodes and the vertices d, e, g are leaves.

Now we are in position to define the level of a vertex in a rooted tree.

A vertex x in a rooted tree is said to be at **level n** if there is a path of length n from the root to the vertex x. The **height** of the tree is the maximum of the levels of its vertices. Height of the tree is also called the **depth** of the tree. In the following Fig. 9.16, b is at level 1 and g is at level 3. The height of the tree is 3.

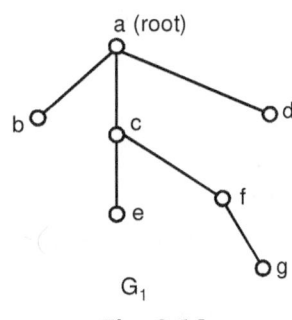

Fig. 9.16

In a rooted tree, if the level of a vertex y in greater than the level of the vertex x, then we say **y is below x**. If y is below x and there is an edge from x to y, then we say y is the **son** of x. Also, x is said to be the **father** of y. Two vertices are said to be **brothers** if they are sons of the same vertex. If $P = (x, v_1, v_2, ..., v_{n-1}, y)$ is a path from x to y, then y is called a **descendant** of x. Also, x is said to be an ancestor of y. These terms clearly indicate that family trees are indeed rooted trees. To understand these terms, consider rooted tree G_1 in Fig. 9.16. The vertex e is below the vertex c. Hence e is the son of c or c is the father of e. Also e and f are the sons of c. Therefore the vertices e and f are brothers. Also, the vertices c and g are connected by the sequence of edges and g is below c. Therefore, g is a descendant of c or we can say c is an ancestor of g.

The degree of a tree is the maximum degree of the nodes in the tree. In Fig. 9.16, the degree of the tree is 3.

A **forest** is a set of disjoint trees. If we remove the root of a tree, we get a forest i.e. set of disjoint trees.

In another words, if the root and corresponding edges connecting the nodes (sons) to the root are deleted from a tree, we obtain a set of disjoint trees. This set of disjoint trees is called a **forest**.

"We present now the definitions of subtree and m-ary tree in a rotated tree".

In a rooted tree T, a vertex x, together with all its descendants, is called the **subtree of T rooted at x.** Following Fig. 9.17 shows the rooted tree T, and its subtree T' rooted at b.

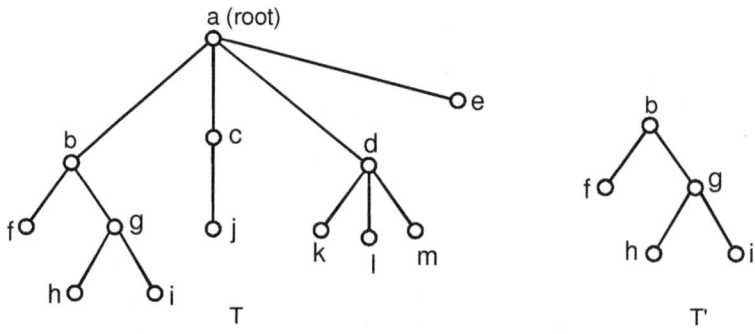

Fig. 9.17

| A rooted tree in which every interior node has atmost m sons is called an m-ary tree. |

An m-ary tree is said to be **regular m-ary tree** or **full m-ary tree** if every branch node has **exactly** m sons. For example, in the following Fig. 9.18 G_1 is a 2 - ary tree or binary tree but it is not a regular binary tree. G_2 is a regular 3 - ary tree or a ternary tree.

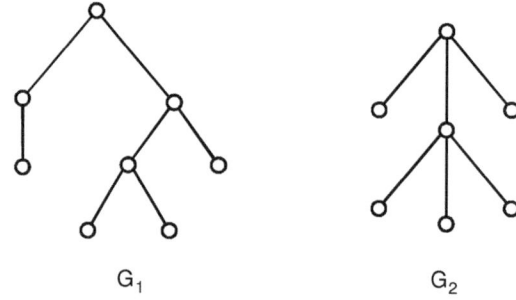

Fig. 9.18

In a regular m-ary tree, the relation between the interior nodes and the total number of nodes is given by following theorem.

Theorem 9.3.1

| A regular m-ary tree with i interior nodes has (mi + 1) nodes at all. |

Proof:

Suppose the given regular m-ary tree has n number of vertices, out of which there are i interior vertices.

Clearly, the number of leaves or sons in the tree is t = (n – i).

Since the given graph is a regular m-ary tree hence each of the i interior nodes has m sons and thus the regular m-ary tree will have total (mi) sons.

But root is not a son.

Therefore the given tree has a total of (mi + 1) number of vertice(s).
Hence $n = mi + 1$

9.3.1 Binary Trees

Binary trees form an important class of rooted trees. They are extensively used in the sorting procedure, binary identification problems and variable length binary codes. As mentioned earlier, in binary tree, every internal vertex has atmost 2 sons. The vertex to the left of the root is called its left child and the vertex to the right of the root is called its right child. Vertex having left child or right child or both is called parent of both the children. Two vertices having the same parent are called siblings. A vertex with no children is a leaf. In binary three no vertex or node can have more than two subtrees. The subtree whose root is the left child of some vertex is called the left subtree of that vertex. Simiarly, if the root of the subtree is the right child of the vertex, then the subtree is the right subtree of the vertex. A binary tree is a full or regular binary tree if each internal vertex has **exactly** 2 sons i.e. in a full binary tree these is exactly one vertex of degree 2 and each of the remaining vertices is of degree one or three. The vertex of degree two serves as a root. Fig. 9.19 shows a regular binary tree with root a.

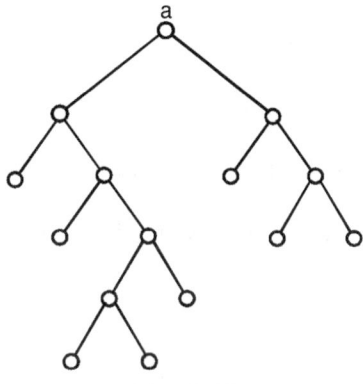

Fig. 9.19

9.3.2 Binary Tree Traversal

Traversing means processing all the nodes of the tree. A binary tree traversal requires that each node of the tree to be processed once and only once in a predetermined sequence. Depth-first Breadth-first are two general methods for traversing the binary tree. These are described below.

Depth-First Traversal:

In this method, the processing proceeds vertically from the root through one child to the most distant descendent of that first child before processing a second child. In other words, we process all of the descendents of a child before going to the next child. There are three standard methods for this, namely preorder traversal, post order traversal and in order traversal.

In the **pre order traversal** the root node is processed first, followed by the left subtree and then the right subtree.

In the **post order** traversal, it processes first the left-subtree then the right subtree and then, in last the root of the tree.

The **inorder traversal** processes the left subtree, then the root and finally the right subtree. The meaning of prefix "in" is that the root is processed in between the subtrees.

The above three standard traversals are shown in the following Fig. 9.20.

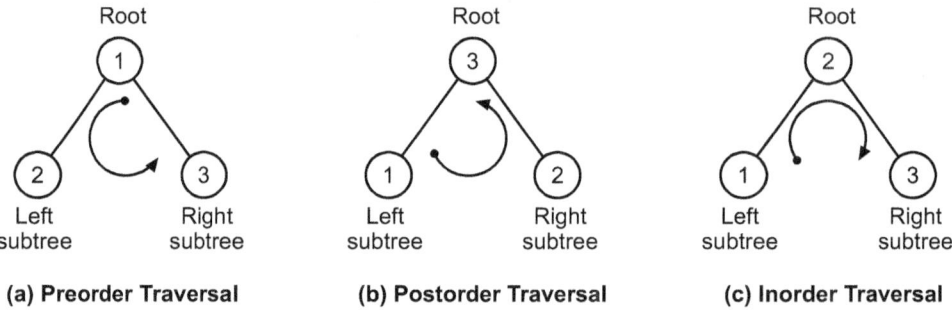

Fig. 9.20: Binary tree traversal

To understand the concept of preorder, postorder and inorder traversal, consider the following binary tree in Fig. 9.21.

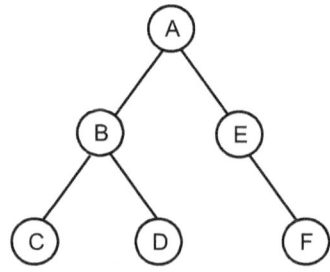

Fig. 9.21

The preorder, postorder and inorder traversals of the above tree are given by

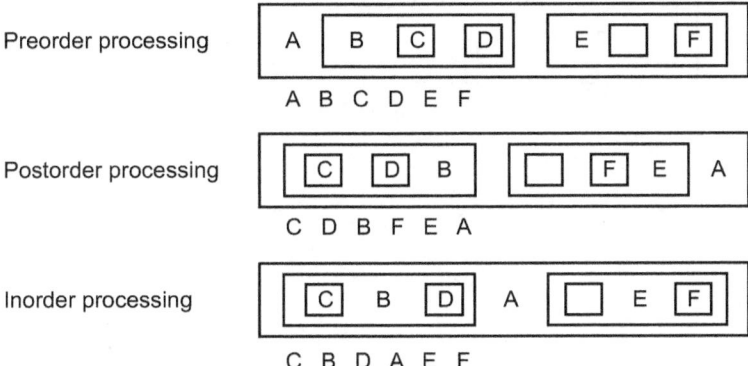

Breadth-First Traversal:

In breadth-first traversal, the processing proceeds horizontally from the root of all of its children, then to its children's children and so on until all the nodes have been processed. In other words, each level completely processed before the next level is started.

For the binary tree shown in Fig. 9.22 the Breadth-first process is shown below.

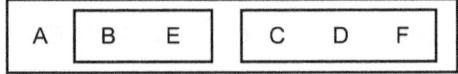

Fig. 9.22

Hence ABECDF will be the processing order for breadth-first traversal.

After defining binary tree traversal techniques, we now move to one of the important application of binary tree, an expression tree, which we define in next section.

9.3.3 Binary Expression Tree

Algebraic expression can be conveniently expressed by its expression tree. An expression tree is a binary tree with the following properties:

(i) Each leaf is an operand.

(ii) The root and interval nodes are operators.

(iii) Subtrees are sub expressions, with the root being an operator.

Here we consider only standard arithmetic operators +, –, *, /. An expression having operator can be decomposed into.

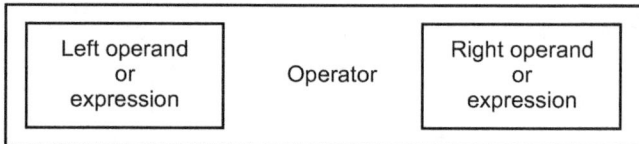

Fig. 9.23

For example, the expression (a + (b × c)) − (d × (e × f)) can be represented as the tree shown in Fig. 9.24.

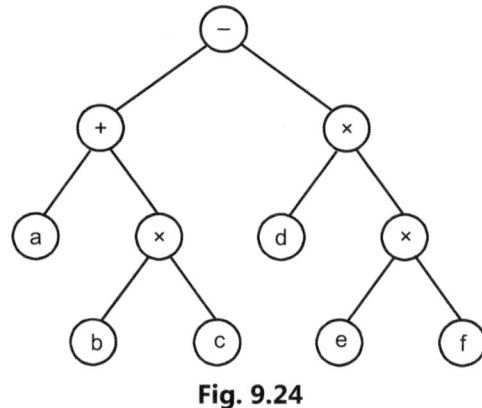

Fig. 9.24

9.3.4 Conversion of General Tree to Binary Tree

As we know that for general tree, each node can have as many children as it is necessary to satisfy its requirements. For certain applications, it is required to process general trees. It is considerably easier to represent binary trees in programs than it is to represent general trees. In this section, the method to convert general tree to binary tree is explained.

Consider the tree shown in Fig. 9.25 (a). To convert it into a binary tree, we first identify the branch from the parent to its first or leftmost child. These branches from each parent become left pointers in the binary tree. They are shown in Fig. 9.25 (b). Then we connect sibling, starting with the leftmost or first child, using a branch for each sibling to its right sibling. These branches are shown in Fig. 9.25 (c) and they are the right pointers in the binary tree. Now, remove all unneeded branches from the parent to its children. The resulting binary tree is shown in Fig. 9.25 (d). This binary tree is thus obtained by connecting together all siblings of a node and deleting all links from a node to its children except for the link to its leftmost or first child. This binary tree is formed using leftmost or first-child-next-right-sibling relationship.

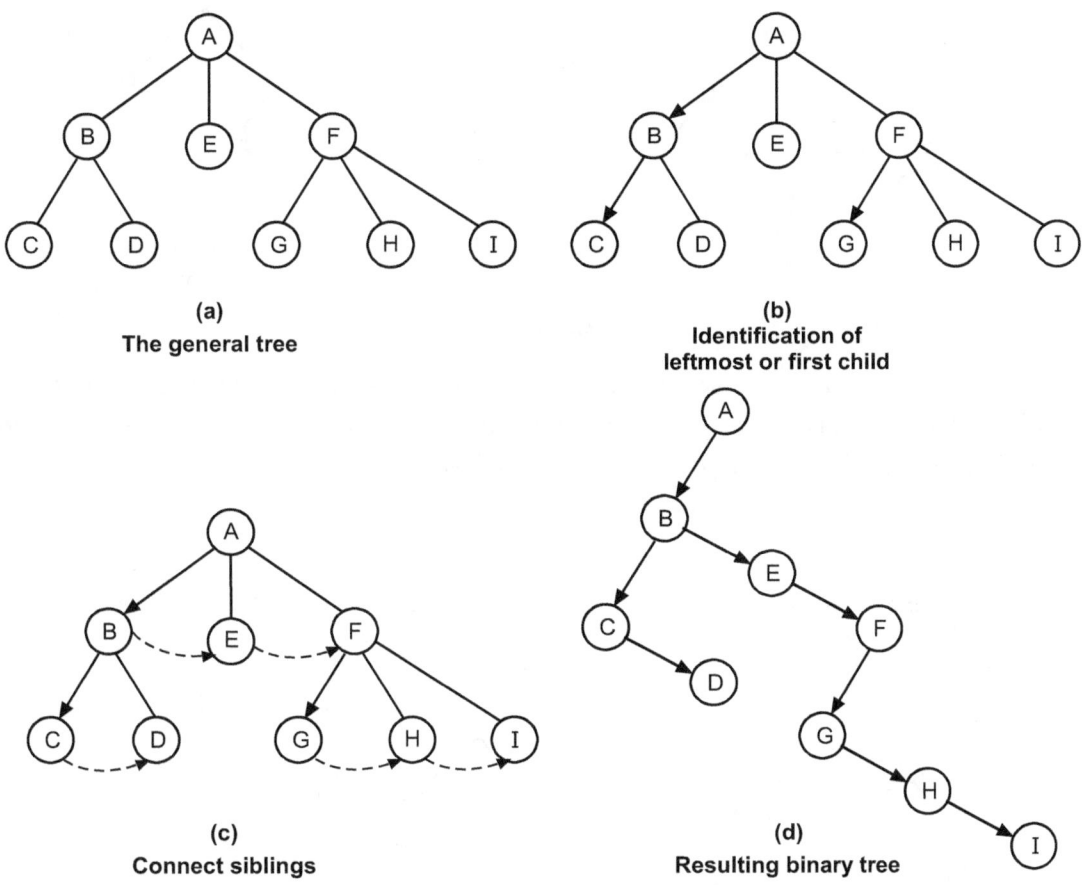

Fig. 9.25

9.3.5 Full Binary Tree

Let T be a binary tree with height greater than zero and with root 'a'. Deleting the root 'a' and its two incident edges produces two disjoint binary trees, whose roots are level 1 vertices of T. These disjoint binary trees are called **left subtree** and **right subtree** of the root 'a'. The roots of these subtrees are called the left son and the right son of 'a' and the edges which are deleted are called left branch and right branch of 'a' respectively. Consider the binary tree with the root 'a' in Fig. 9.26. T_1 is the left subtree with root 'b' and T_2 is the right subtree with root 'c' of T respectively. e_1 is the left branch and e_2 is the right branch of T.

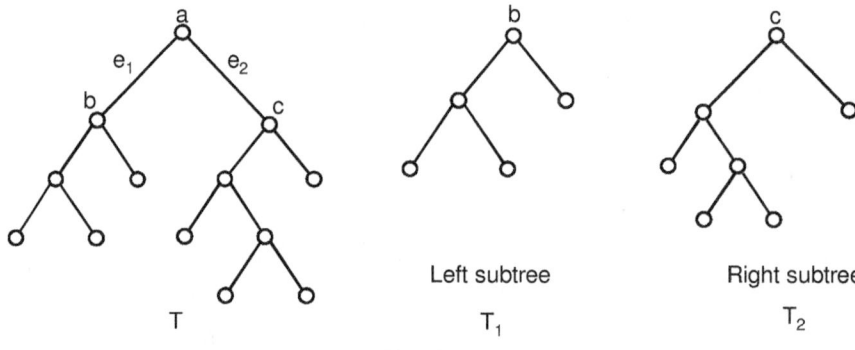

Fig. 9.26

We now define a very important characteristic of a binary tree called its balance. The **balance factor** of a binary tree is the difference in height between its left and right subtrees. If HL and HR are the heights of left and right subtrees respectively then the balance factor B of the tree is given by

$$B = H_L - H_R$$

Consider the binary tree and its left and right subtree shown in Fig. 9.27.

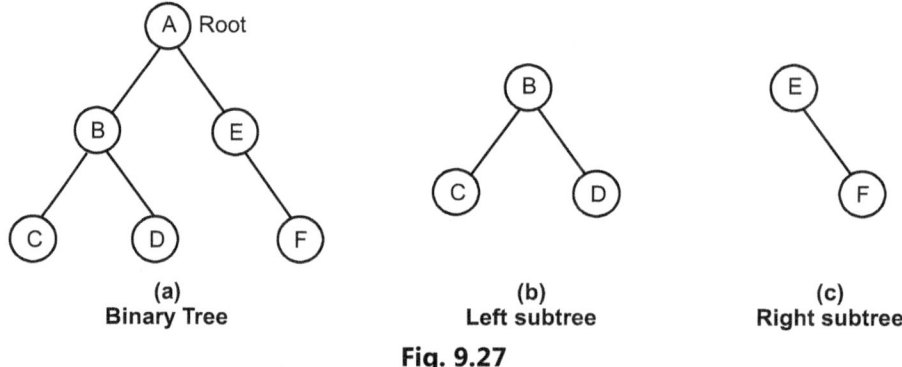

Fig. 9.27

The balance factor of binary tree (a) is 0. A three is balanced if its balance factor is zero and its subtrees are also balanced.

In the next section traversing of binary trees using depth-first and breadth-first methods is explained.

The simplest example of a full binary tree is a single elimination tournament. In the graph of single elimination tournament which is a full binary tree, the contestants are represented by leaves and the winners by the internal nodes. Eventually, there is a single winner at the root. If the number of contestants is not a power of 2, then some contestants receive byes. The following Fig. 9.28 shows a single elimination tournament with 8 contestants.

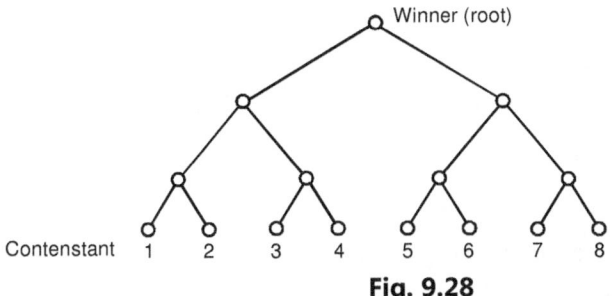
Fig. 9.28

SOLVED EXAMPLES

Example 1: Draw all rooted tree with four nodes.

Solution: Each rooted tree with four vertices rooted at 'a' will be isomorphic to one of the following:

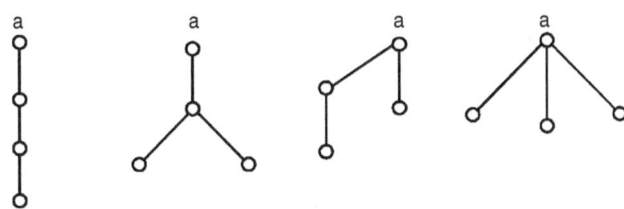
Fig. 9.29

Example 2: Draw all full binary trees with 7 nodes.

Solution: Each full binary tree will be isomorphic to one of the following:

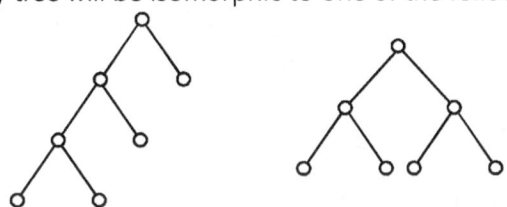
Fig. 9.30

Example 3: Consider the rooted tree shown in Fig. 9.31.

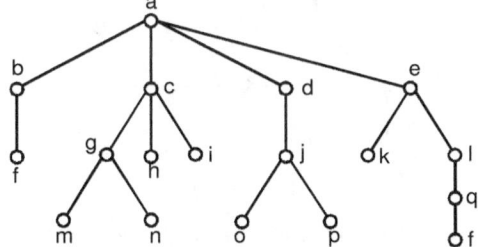
Fig. 9.31

(i) Find the father of c and of h.
(ii) Find the ancestors of f and of j.
(iii) Find the sons of d and of e.
(iv) Find the descendants of d.
(v) How many terminal vertices are there ?
(vi) How many internal vertices are there ?
(vii) Draw the subtree rooted at e.

Solution: (i) The father of c is a and the father of h is c.
(ii) The ancestors of f are b and a. Also the ancestors of j are d and a.
(iii) The son of d is j and the sons of e are k and l.
(iv) The descendant of d are j, o and p.
(v) There are 9 terminal vertices.
(vi) There are 9 internal vertices.
(vii) The subtree rooted at e is shown below:

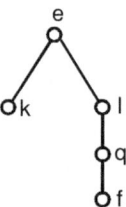

Fig. 9.32

Example 4: For the following rooted tree, draw the diagram with the root v at the top and find out whether it is a full m-ary tree for some 'm' or not.

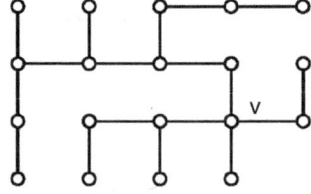

Fig. 9.33

Solution: With the root v at the top, the given rooted tree can be drawn as shown in Fig. 9.34.

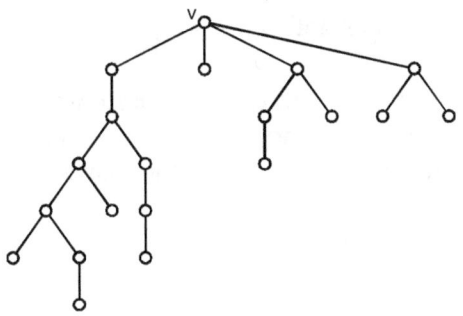

Fig. 9.34

It is a 4-ary tree (because its one internal node v has 4 sons) but it is *not* a full 4-ary tree because each internal node does not have 4 sons exactly.

Example 5: What is the total number of nodes in a full binary tree with 20 leaves ?

Solution: Let n represent the total number of nodes in a full binary tree. Then numbers of internal nodes $i = (n - 20)$.

Also, by theorem 9.3.1, the total number of nodes in a full m-ary tree is given by $n = mi + 1$.

In full binary tree $m = 2$.

$\Rightarrow n = 2i + 1$
$\Rightarrow n = 2(n - 20) + 1$
$\Rightarrow n = 2n - 40 + 1$
$\Rightarrow n = 39$

Hence a full binary tree with 20 leaves has total 39 nodes.

Example 6: Does there exist a ternary tree with exactly 21 nodes ?

Solution: Here the given tree is a ternary tree $\Rightarrow m = 3$, also $n = 21$.

Hence, according to theorem 9.3.1,

$n = mi + 1$
$\Rightarrow 21 = 3i + 1$
$\Rightarrow 20 = 3i$

The solution to the above equation is not an integer. Thus there does not exist any ternary tree with 21 nodes.

Example 7: If there are 60 contestants in a single elimination tournament, how many matches are played ?

Solution: A single elimination tournament can be represented by a full binary tree, in which contestant represent terminal vertices and winners, the internal vertices. According to the problem, there are 60 contestants (leaves). Let i be the number of internal vertices. Hence the total number of vertices

$$n = 60 + i.$$

Now, by theorem 9.3.1

$$(60 + i) = 2i + 1$$
$$\Rightarrow \quad i = 59$$

Hence 59 matches are played in the tournament.

Example 8: A telephone network is established among 100 people. Information received by the first person is passed along to the 99 others as follows; the first person calls exactly 3 people, and each of these people calls 3 others, and so on until there are no others to call. If each call takes 5 minutes, how long does it take for a message to be relayed from the first person to receive the message to everyone else ? How many people make no calls ?

Solution: The given situation can be represented by a tree with a total of 100 nodes, where each node represents a person in the telephone network. Also, since each person calls exactly 3 people, hence each node has 3 sons. Therefore, the given tree is a full ternary tree. If there are i internal nodes then according to theorem 9.3.1.

$$100 = 3i + 1$$
$$\Rightarrow \quad i = 33$$

i.e. there are 33 interior nodes and thus there are 100 − 33 = 67 terminal nodes (leaves). Therefore 67 persons do not make any call. Now, the first person which is serving as the root will send the message to exactly 3 persons. Also each call takes 5 minutes. Hence after 5 minutes, 1 + 3 = 4 people have received the message. Each of these 3 people will call again 3 people. After 10 minutes, the total number of persons getting the message is 1 + 3 + 9 = 13. Continuing in this way, after 15 minutes 1 + 3 + 9 + 27 = 40 and after 20 minutes 1 + 3 + 9 + 27 + 81 = 121 persons could get the message. But we have only 100 nodes. Thus it takes 20 minutes for the message to be relayed to everyone.

Example 9: Show that the total number of vertices in a full binary tree is always odd.

Solution: We know that in a full binary tree, there is exactly one vertex of degree even (root) and the remaining (n − 1) vertices are of odd degrees. We know that the number of vertices of odd degree in any graph is always even. Thus (n − 1) is even. Hence n is odd.

Example 10: Find the number of leaves in a full binary tree with n vertices.

Solution: In a full binary tree, the number of internal nodes i is given by

$$n = 2i + 1$$

$$\Rightarrow i = \left(\frac{n-1}{2}\right)$$

Hence the number of leaves $t = (n - i)$

$$t = n - \left(\frac{n-1}{2}\right)$$

$$t = \frac{n+1}{2}$$

Hence a full binary tree contains $\left(\frac{n+1}{2}\right)$ number of leaves.

Example 11: 19 lamps are to be connected to a single electrical outlet, using extension chords, each of which has 4 outlets. Find the number of extension chords needed and draw the corresponding tree.

Solution: Represent lamps by the leaves and the extension chords by the branch nodes of the tree. Since there are 19 lamps to be connected and each extension chords has 4 outlets, this means the tree has 19 leaves and each branch node has 4 sons. Hence the tree is a full 4-ary (quaternary) tree with 19 leaves.

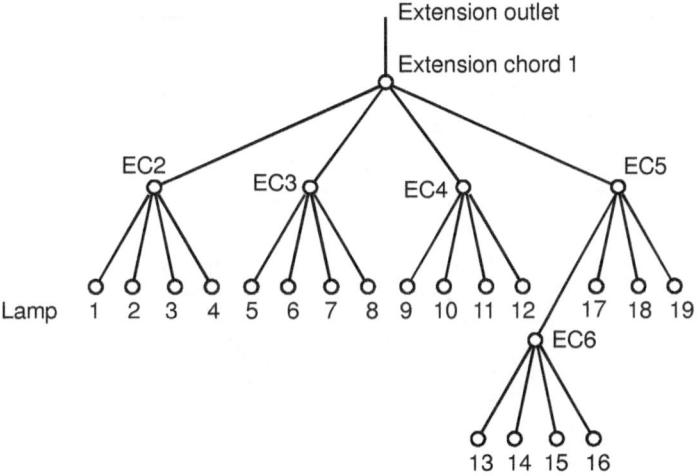

Fig. 9.35

Now, by theorem 9.3.1, total number of vertices in a full 4-ary tree n = 4i + 1, where i is the number of branch nodes.

But   n = 19 + i

Hence   19 + i = 4i + 1

$\Rightarrow i = 6$

Hence, 6 extension chords are required to connect 19 lamps with a single outlet. The required tree is shown below in Fig. 9.35.

Example 12: Consider the tree as shown in Fig. 9.36 (i) Which of the vertices are cut points? (ii) Find all the vertices at level three, if the vertex picked as a root is U and W.

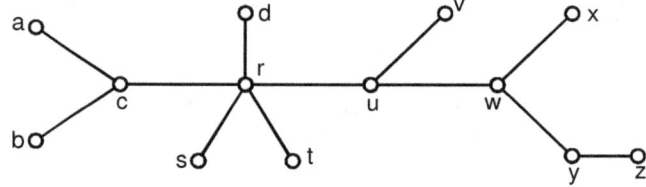

Fig. 9.36

Solution: (i) We know that every vertex of degree more than one is a cut point in a tree, hence in the given tree, c, r, u, w, y are cut points.

(ii) Consider the given tree with root as U. Since the level of the vertex is its distance from the root, the vertices of level 3 are a, b and z.

If we take w as a root of the tree in Fig. 9.36 then, the vertices of level 3 are d, s, t, c.

Example 13: Find the preorder, postorder and inorder traversal of the following tree:

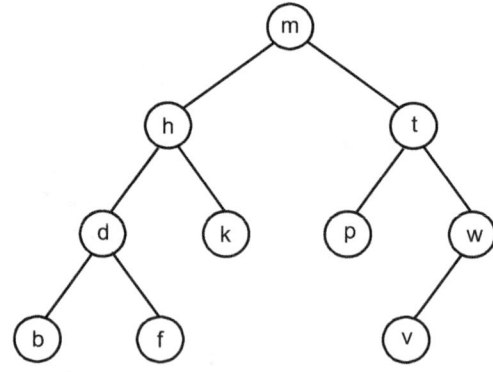

Fig. 9.37

Solution: The preorder, postorder and inorder traversals are as follows:

Preorder traversal:

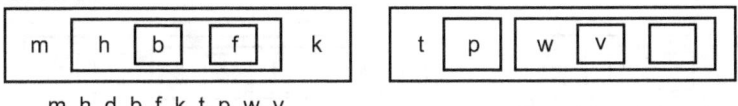

m h d b f k t p w v

Postorder traversal:

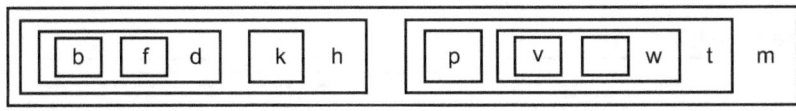

b f d k h p v w t m

Inorder traversal:

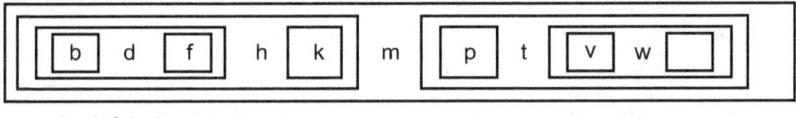

b d f h k m p t v w

Example 14: Determine the preorder, post order and inorder traversal of the binary tree shown in Fig. 9.38.

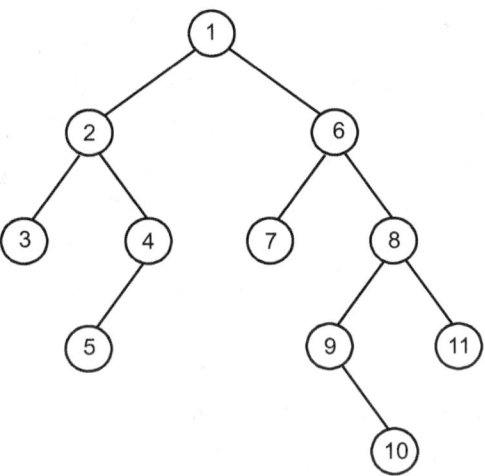

Fig. 9.38

Solution: The preorder, postorder and inorder traversals for the given tree are given below.

Preorder:

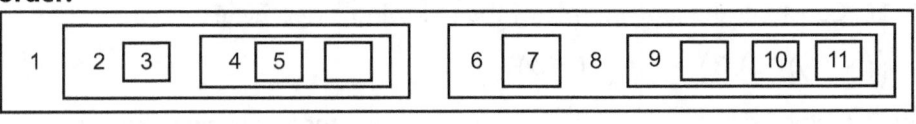

1 2 3 4 5 6 7 8 9 10 11

Postorder traversal:

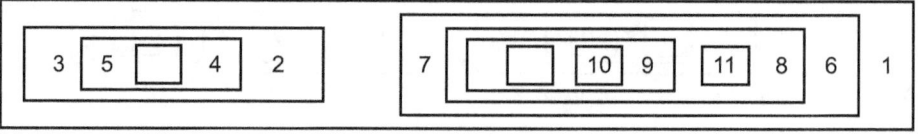

3 5 4 2 7 10 9 11 8 6 1

Inorder traversal:

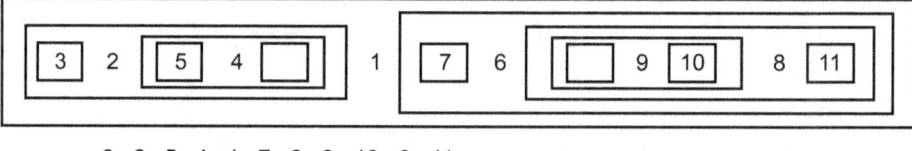

3 2 5 4 1 7 6 9 10 8 11

Example 15: Write and evaluate the expression tree shown below.

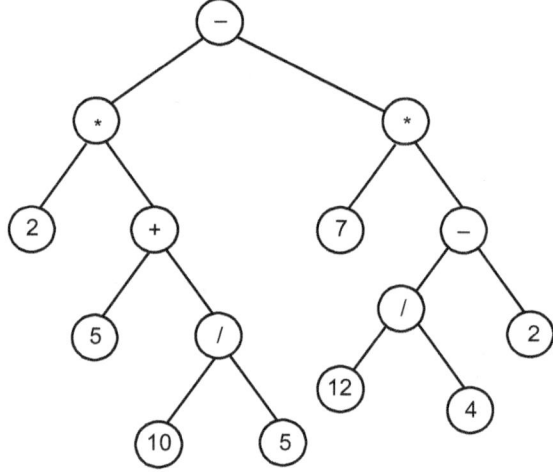

Fig. 9.39

Solution: The algebraic expression given by the expression tree is as follows:

$$\Big(\big((2) * ((5) + ((10)/(5)))\big)\big((7) * (((12)/(4)) - 2)\big)\Big)$$

It's value is $(14) - (7) = 7$.

Example 16: Construct the labeled tree of the following algebraic expression:

$$\big(((x + y) * z)/3\big) + \big(19 + (x * x)\big)$$

Solution: The expression tree for the given algebraic expression is given below:

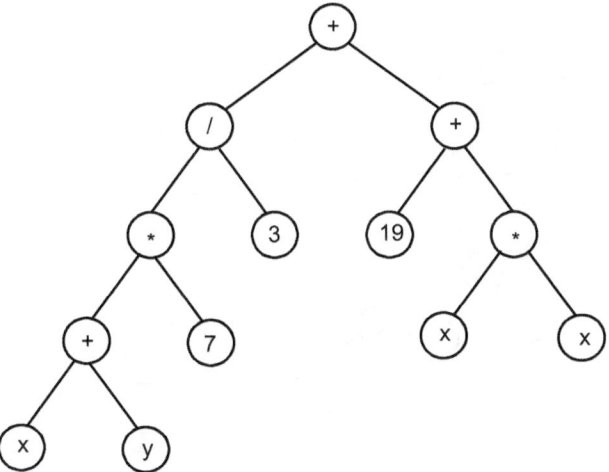

Fig. 9.40

Example 17: Convert the following tree into binary tree:

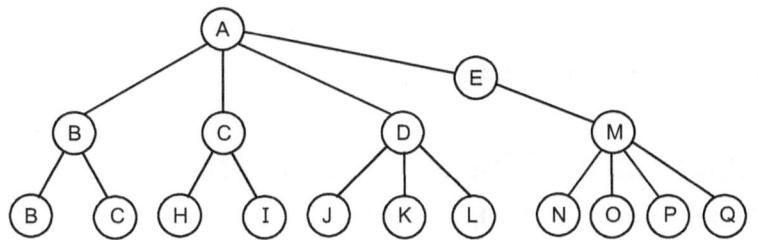

Fig. 9.41

Solution: The steps involve in convert the given tree into a binary tree are as follows:

(i)

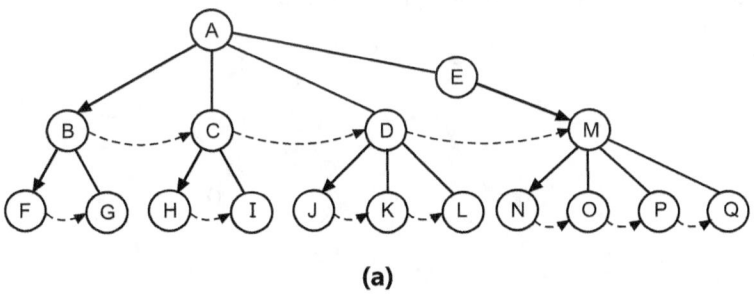

(a)

(ii)

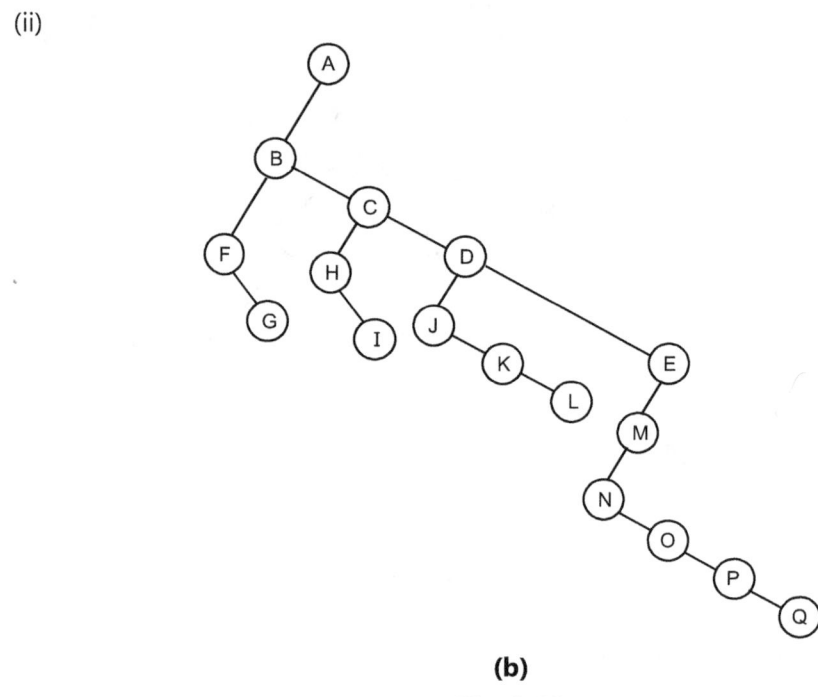

(b)

Fig. 9.42

The binary tree is shown in Fig. 9.42 (b).

9.4 Prefix Codes and Binary Search Trees

A set of sequences is said to be a **prefix code** if *no* sequences in the set is a prefix of another sequence in the set. For example, the set {01, 10, 11, 000, 001} is a prefix code. The set {1, 00, 01, 000, 0001} is **not** a prefix code because the sequence 00 is a prefix of the sequence 0001. To obtain a prefix code, we use a full binary tree described in section 9.3.1. For a given full binary tree, we label the two branches incident from each internal node with 0 and 1. For the left branch, we assign 0 and for the right branch we assign 1.

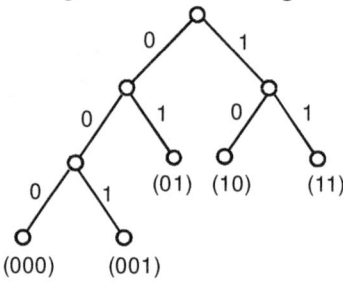

Fig. 9.43

Assign to each leaf of sequence of 0's and 1's which is the sequence of labels of the edges in the path from the root to that leaf. For example, Fig. 9.43 shows a full binary tree and the sequences assigned to its leaves.

Prefix code for the above Fig. 9.43 is {000, 001, 01, 10, 11}. It is clear that the set of sequences assigned to the leaves in any full binary tree is a prefix code.

9.4.1 Optimal tree

Let T be any full binary tree and let $w_1, w_2 \ldots w_t$ be the weights of the terminal vertices (leaves). Then, the weight W of the binary tree is given by

$$W(T) = \sum_{i=1}^{t} w_i \ell_i$$

where ℓ_i is the length of the path of the leaf i from the root of the tree. The full binary tree is called an **optimal tree** if its weight is **minimum**.

For instance, suppose 3, 4 and 5 are the weights of the leaves in a full binary tree. Fig. 9.44 shows two such binary trees T_1 and T_2.

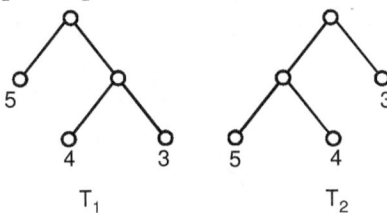

Fig. 9.44

The weight $w(T_1)$ of the tree T_1 in Fig. 9.44 is

$w(T_1)$ = $3 \times 2 + 4 \times 2 + 5 \times 1$

= $6 + 8 + 5$

= 19

while the weight $w(T_2)$ of the tree t_2 in Fig. 9.44 is

$w(T_2)$ = $3 \times 1 + 4 \times 2 + 5 \times 2$

= $3 + 8 + 10$

= 21

Here $w(T_1) < w(T_2)$.

Thus T_1 is an optimal tree for the weights 3, 4 and 5.

Optimal trees are used in constructing variable length binary codes, where the letters of the alphabet (A, B, C ...... Z) are represented by binary digits. Since different letters have different frequencies of occurrence (frequencies are interpreted as weights W_1, W_2 ...... W_{26}), a binary tree with minimum weighted path length (optimal tree) corresponds to a binary code of minimum cost.

9.4.2 Huffman Algorithm to find an optimal tree

Let w_1, w_2, ... w_t be the weights of the leaves and it is required to construct an optimal binary tree. The following algorithm gives the required optimal binary tree.

Step 1: Arrange the weights in increasing order.

Step 2: Consider two leaves with the minimum weights w_1 and w_2. Replace these two leaves and their father by a leaf and assign to this new leaf the weight $w_1 + w_2$.

Step 3: Repeat the step 2 for the weights ($w_1 + w_2$), w_3, w_4 ... w_t until no weight remains.

Step 4: The tree obtained in this way is an optimal tree for given weights, and stop.

9.4.3 Optimal Prefix Code

A binary prefix code obtained from a optimal tree is called an **optimal prefix code**. For example, consider an optimal tree for the weights 2, 6, 7 and 9 in Fig. 9.45.

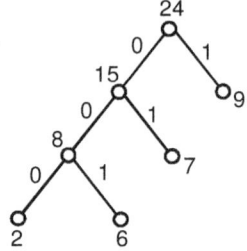

Fig. 9.45

The optimal prefix code for the weights 2, 6, 7 and 9 is given by

{000, 001, 01, 1}

9.4.4 Binary Search Tree

Now we formulate the problem of searching for an item in an ordered list which arise many a time in our daily life. To find a person's telephone number in a telephone directory, to find the record of an employee in a company are some of the examples of a searching problem.

Consider the problem of searching an item x in the ordered list $k_1, k_2 \ldots k_n$ where $k_1, k_2 \ldots k_n$ are given items called **keys**. Assume $k_1 < k_2 < k_3 \ldots < k_n$. Our problem is to find whether the given item x is equal to one of the keys or whether x falls between k_i and k_{i+1} for some i. For this, we define a search tree for the keys $k_1, k_2 \ldots k_n$ to be a full binary tree with n branch nodes are labelled $k_1, k_2 \ldots k_n$ and the leaves are labelled $k_0, k_1, k_2 \ldots k_n$. For the branch node with the label k_i, its left subtree contains only vertices with labels $< k_i$ and its right subtree contains only vertices with labels $\cdot$ k_i. It is convenient to take the middle of the key from k_1, $k_2 \ldots k_n$ as a root of the tree. The search tree constructed in this way is known as **binary search** tree.

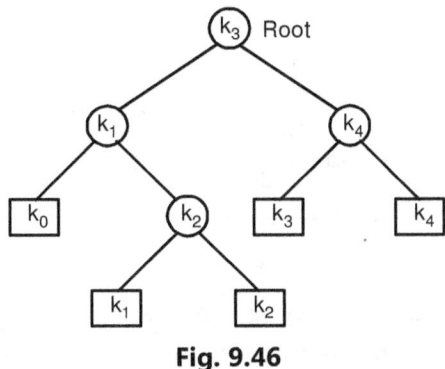

Fig. 9.46

In the search procedure, we compare a given item x with the label of the root of the tree. If x is equal to the label of the root, the search is completed. If x is less than the label of the root then we shall compare x with the **left son** of the root, and if x is larger than the label of the root, we shall compare x with the **right son** of the root. Such comparisons continue for successive branch nodes until either x matches a key or a leaf is reached. Clearly, if a leaf labelled k_j is reached, it means that x is larger than the key k_j but less than the key k_{j+1}. If the leaf k_0 is reached, it means that x is less than k_1 and if the leaf k_n is reached, it indicates that x is larger than k_n.

For example, consider the keys k_1, k_2, k_3 and k_4 where $k_1 < k_2 < k_3 < k_4$ we construct a binary search tree with the branch nodes k_1, k_2, k_3 and k_4 and with the terminal nodes k_0, k_1, k_2, k_3 and k_4. With k_3 as a root, the binary search tree for the given keys is shown in Fig. 9.46 where circles denote the branch vertices and boxes denote the leaves.

Now, suppose the keys k_1, k_2, k_3, k_4 represent the items CD, EH, GI and PR respectively and the item x = DD is to be searched in the given keys. The search steps according to Fig. 9.46 will be as follows:

Step 1: Compare DD with k_3 = GI.

Step 2: Since DD is less than GI, go to left son of k_3 and compare DD with k_1 = CD.

Step 3: Since DD is larger than CD, go to right son of k_1 and compare DD with k_2 = EH.

Step 4: Since DD is less than EH, go to left son of k_2. In this way, the leaf labelled k_1 = CD is reached.

Thus, we conclude that our given item DD is larger than k_1 = CD and less than k_2 = EH.

Hence a binary search tree is a binary tree in which all items in the left subtree are less than the root, all items in the right subtree are greater than or equal to the root and each subtree is itself a binary search tree. Fig. 9.47 shows a binary search tree for key item k.

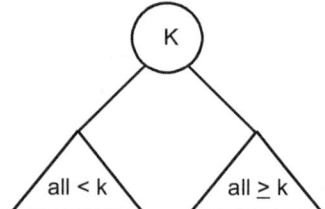

Fig. 9.47: Binary search tree

In binary search tree, any item can be inserted or deleted.

To insert a given item 'k' in a given binary search tree, first compare the item k with the root node. If the item k > root node, proceed to the right child and it becomes the root node for the right subtree. If item k < root node, proceed to the left child. Now, if item k is greater than the node, then the item k is inserted as the right child and if item k is less than the node, then the item k is inserted as the left-child.

To explain the procedure, consider the example of inserting in order the integers 20, 3, 10, 22, 15, 35, 9, 2. The resulting binary search tree is given in Fig. 9.48.

For deleting any item k from the binary search tree, we have to consider the number of children of the deleted node (k). If deleted node (k) has no children, then replace the node with null. If deleted node (k) has only one child, then replace the value of deleted node with the only child.

If deleted node has two children, then replace the deleted node with the node that is closest in the value to the deleted node. To find the closest value, we move once to the left and then to the right as far as possible. This node is called immediate predecessor. Now replace the value of deleted node with immediate predecessor and then delete the replaced node by using previous cases. In another words, we find the largest node in the deleted node's left subtree as an immediate predecessor.

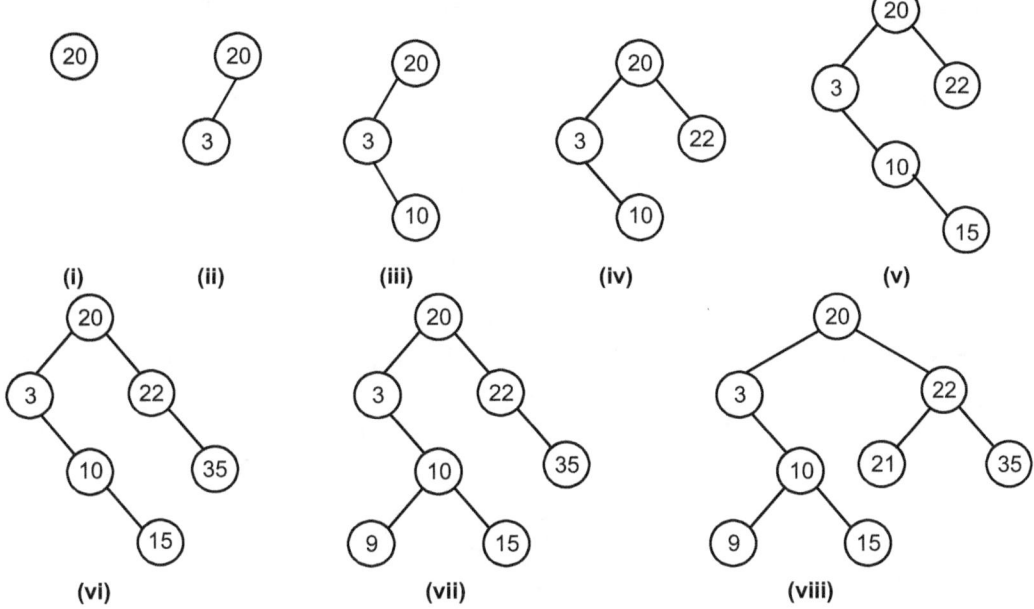

Fig. 9.48

To understand the above procedure, consider the following binary search tree in Fig. 9.49.

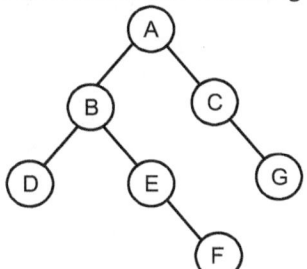

Fig. 9.49

After deleting the node D, the binary search tree will be

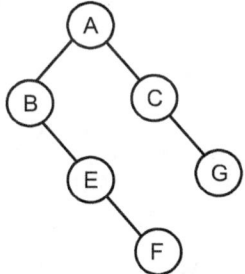

Fig. 9.50

If we delete the node C which has one child, the binary search tree after deletion of C is

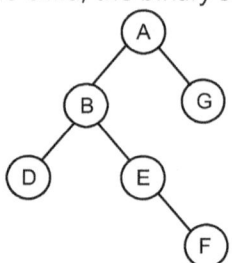

Fig. 9.51

The binary search tree obtained after deletion of root A which has two children is given by

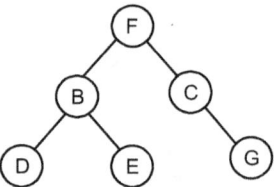

Fig. 9.52

SOLVED EXAMPLES

Example 1: Obtain the prefix code of the following full binary tree in Fig. 9.53.

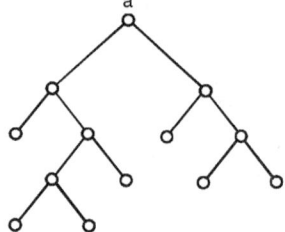

Fig. 9.53

Solution: Given 'a' is the root of the full binary tree. Assign 0 to the left son and 1 to the right son of each branch node of the tree.

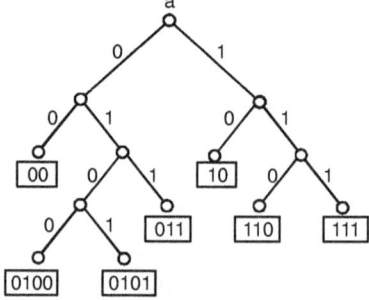

Fig. 9.54

The code words for the leaves obtained in this way are shown in the boxes. Hence, the prefix code for the given tree is {00, 10, 011, 110, 111, 0100, 0101}.

Example 2: Construct an optimal tree for the weights 8, 9, 10, 11, 13, 15, 22. Find the weight of the optimal tree.

Solution: The construction of an optimal tree for the weights 8, 9, 10, 11, 13, 15 and 22 is shown below.

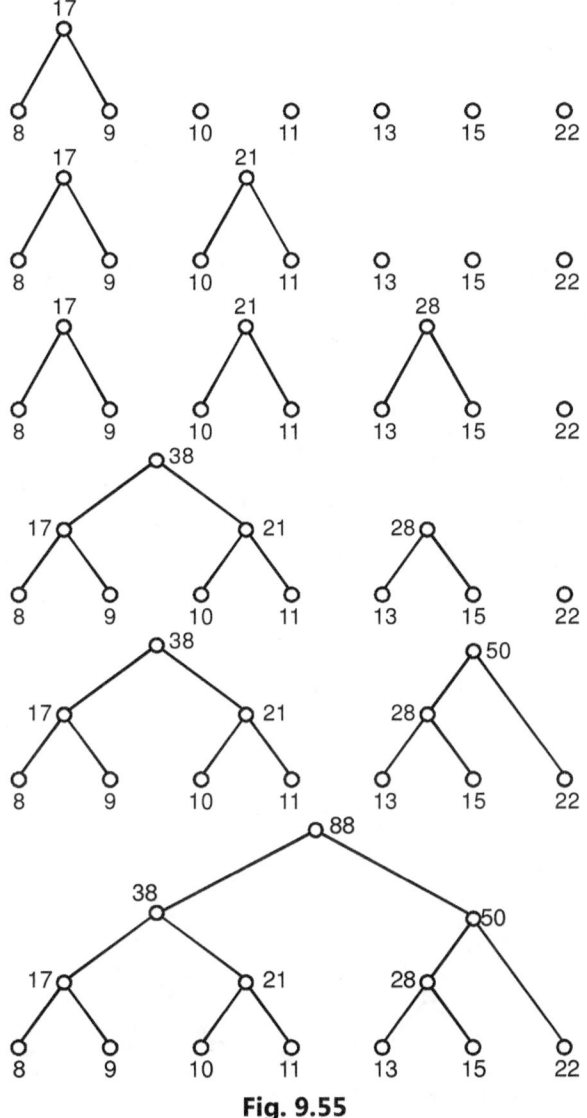

Fig. 9.55

The weight of the tree = $8 \times 3 + 9 \times 3 + 10 \times 3 + 11 \times 3 + 13 \times 3 + 15 \times 3 + 22 \times 2 = 242$.

DISCRETE STRUCTURE AND GRAPH THEORY (NMU) — TREES

Example 3: For each of the following sets of weights construct an optimal binary prefix code. For each weight in the set give the corresponding code word:

(i) 1, 2, 3, 4, 5, 6, 9, 10, 12

(ii) 10, 11, 14, 16, 18, 21.

(iii) 5, 7, 8, 15, 35, 40.

Solution: Optimal binary prefix code for data 1, 2, 3, 4, 5, 6, 9, 10, 12 is as shown below.

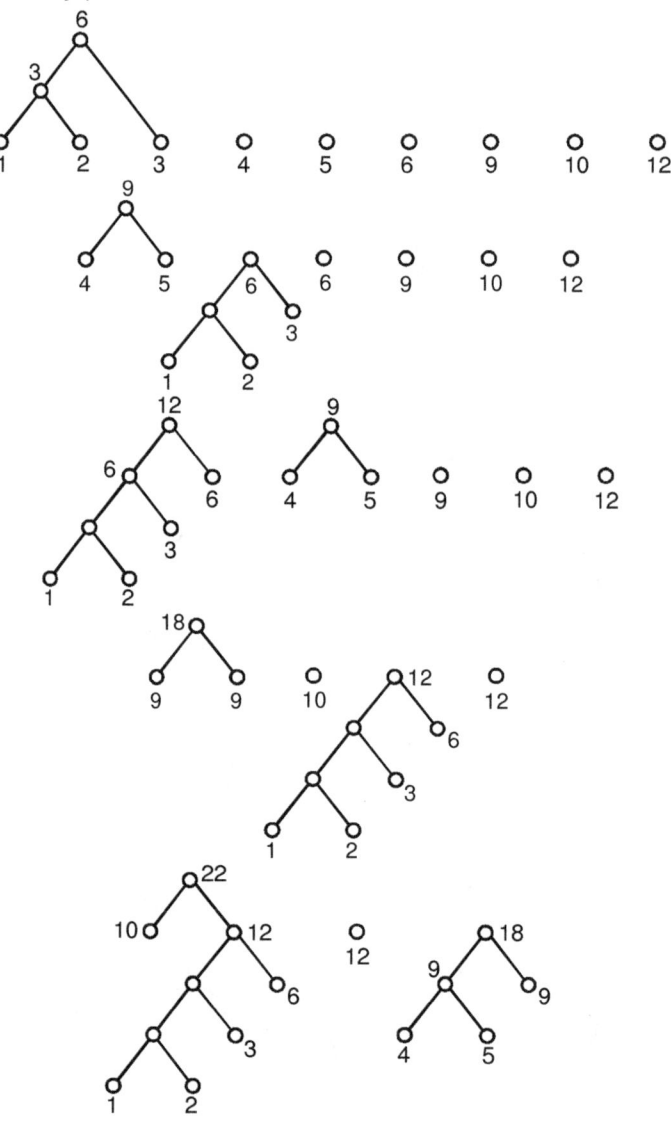

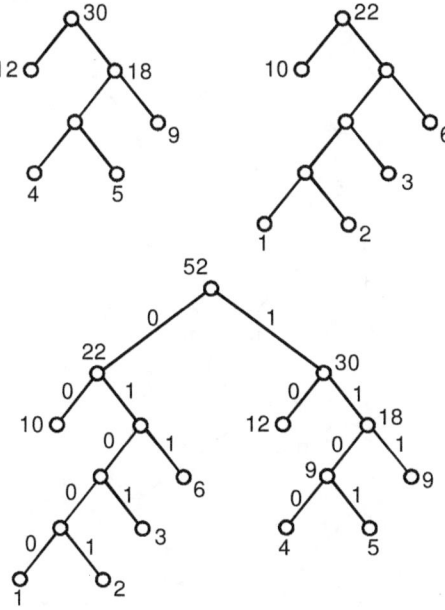

Fig. 9.56

The code words for the leaves are

    1 → 01000
    2 → 01001
    3 → 0101
    4 → 1100
    5 → 1101
    6 → 011
    9 → 111
    10 → 00
    12 → 10

(ii) The optimal binary prefix code for 10, 11, 14, 16, 18, 21 is given as follows:

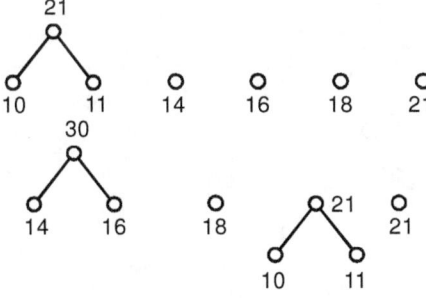

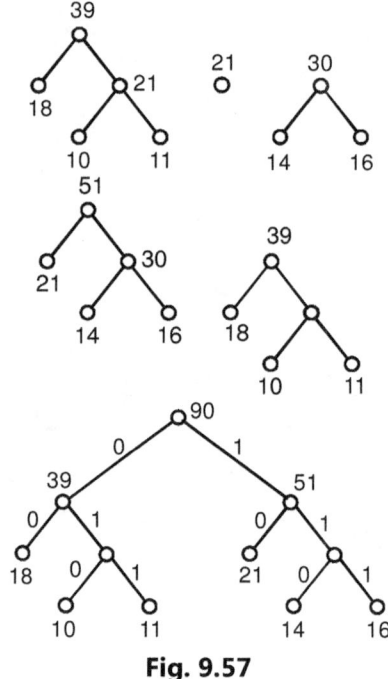

Fig. 9.57

The code words for leaves are

    18 → 00

    10 → 010

    11 → 011

    21 → 10

    14 → 110

    16 → 111

(iii) For the weight 5, 7, 8, 15, 35, 40, the optimal binary prefix code is given by following tree:

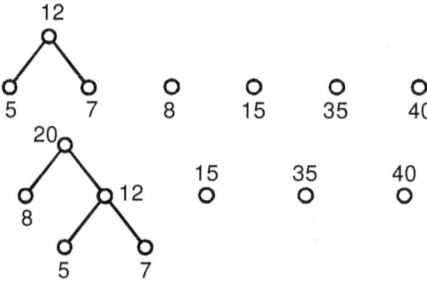

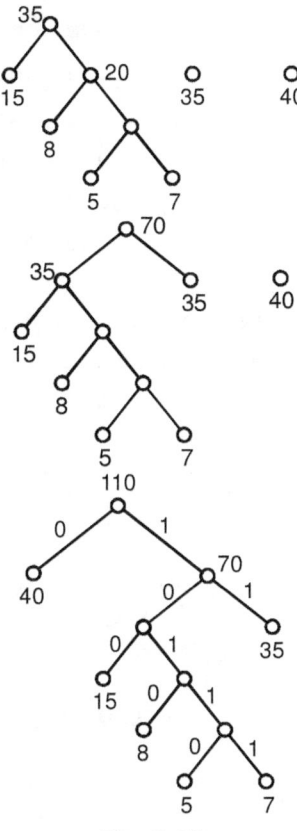

Fig. 9.58

The code words are

    40 → 0

    15 → 100

    8 → 1010

    5 → 10110

    7 → 10111

    35 → 11

Example 4: For the following sets of weights, construct optimal binary prefix code. For each weight in the set, give the corresponding code words: 8, 9, 12, 14, 16, 19.

Solution: Optimal binary prefix code for weights 8, 9, 12, 14, 16, 19 is as shown in following figure:

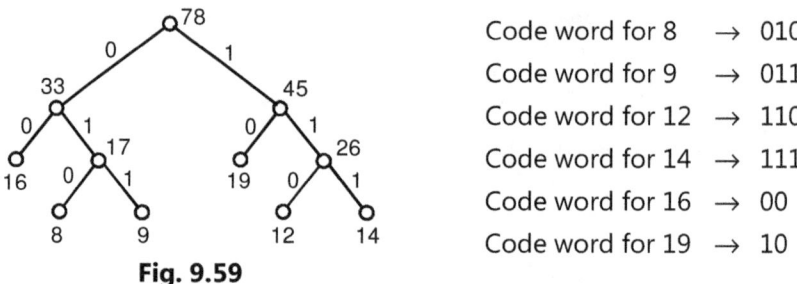

Code word for 8	→	010
Code word for 9	→	011
Code word for 12	→	110
Code word for 14	→	111
Code word for 16	→	00
Code word for 19	→	10

Fig. 9.59

Example 5: A secondary storage media contains information of files with different formats. The frequency of different types of files is as follows:

Exe (20), bin (75), bat (20), jpeg (85), dat (51), doc (32), sys (26), c (19), cpp (25), bmp (30), avi (24), prj (29), lst (35), zip (37).

Construct the Huffman code for this.

Solution: (i)

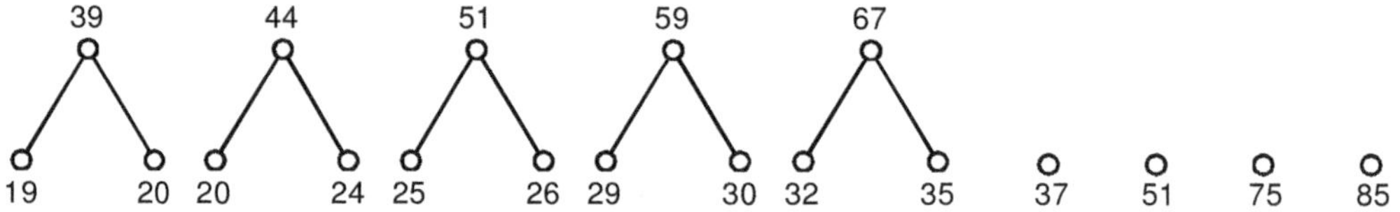

Fig. 9.60

(ii)

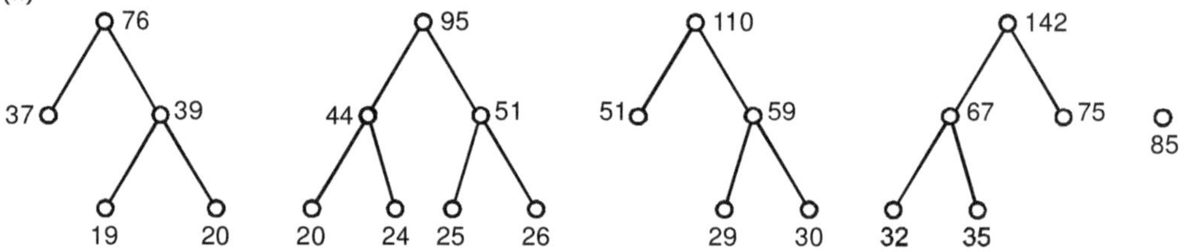

Fig. 9.61

(iii)

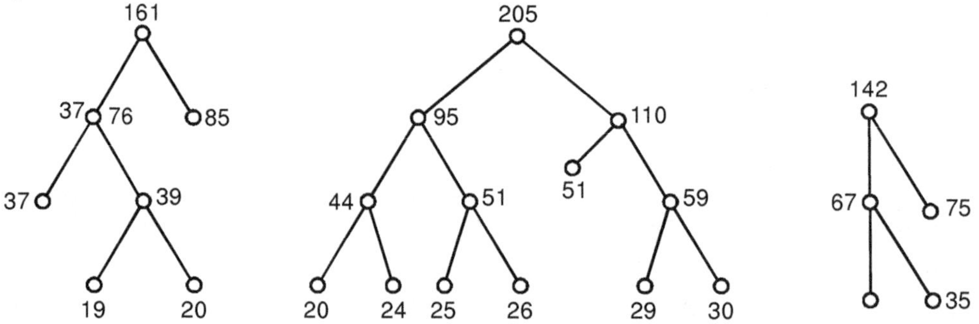

Fig. 9.62

(iv)

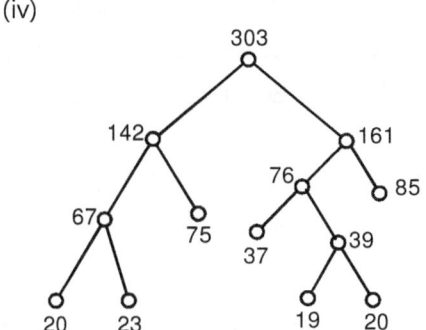
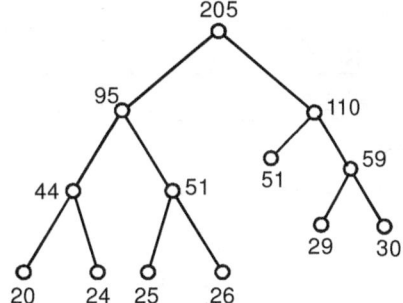

Fig. 9.63

(v) The optimal tree is

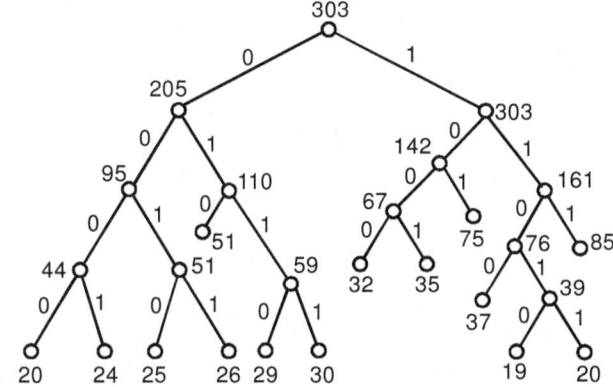

Fig. 9.64

The Huffman code for frequency

20 → 0000
24 → 0001
25 → 0010
26 → 0011
51 → 010
29 → 0110
30 → 0111
32 → 1000
35 → 1001
75 → 101
37 → 1100
19 → 11010
20 → 11011
85 → 111

Example 6: Suppose data items A, B, C, D, E, F, G occur with the following probability distribution:

Data item	A	B	C	D	E	F	G
Probability	10	30	05	15	20	15	05

Construct a Huffman code for the data. What is the minimum weighted path length ?

Solution: The steps involved in constructing the Huffman code for the given data are as follows:

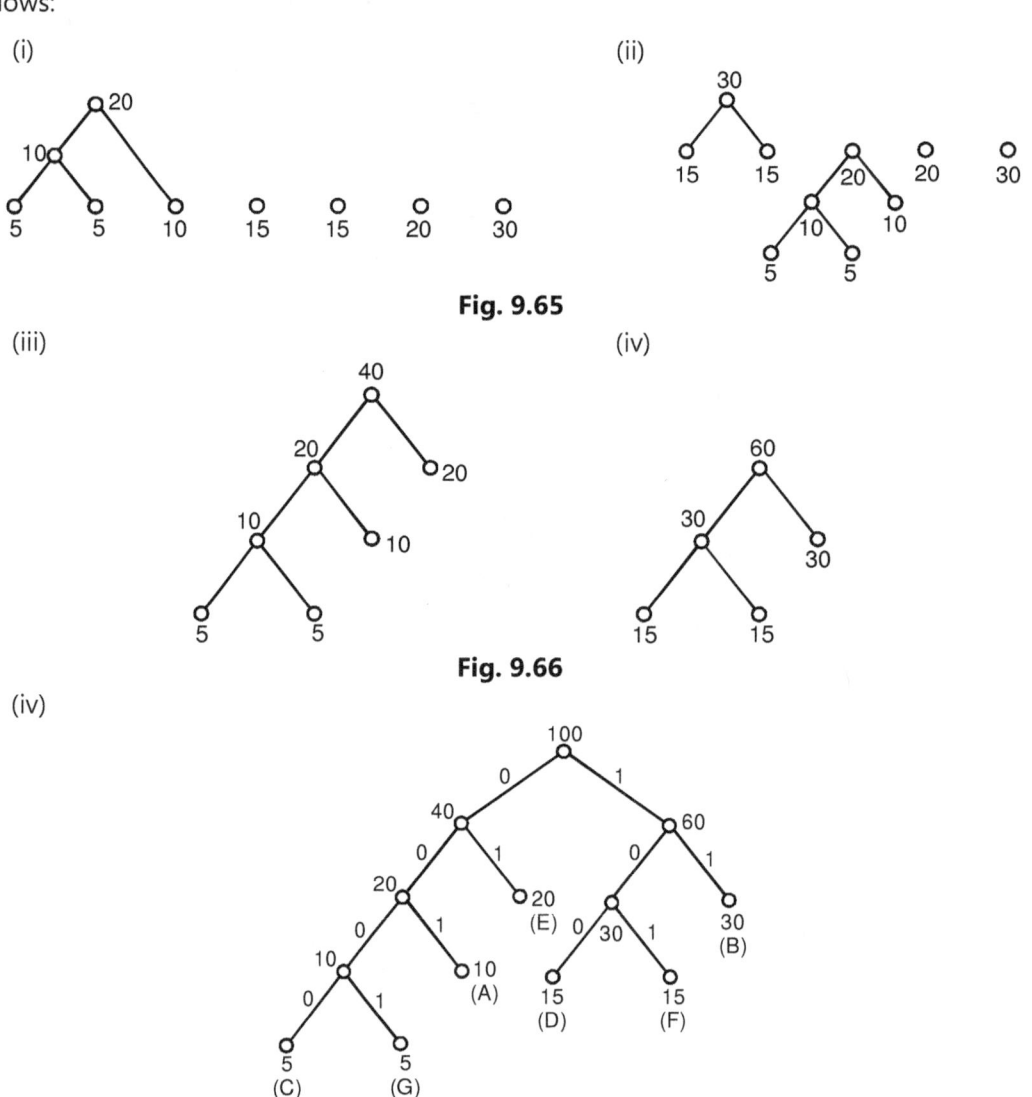

Fig. 9.65

Fig. 9.66

Fig. 9.67

The Huffman code for the given data is

$05 \to 0000$ and 0001

$10 \to 001$

$15 \to 100$ and 101

$20 \to 01$

$30 \to 11$

The minimum weight of the tree is

$2(5 \times 4) + 10 \times 3 + 20 \times 2 + 2(15 \times 3) + 30 \times 2 = 260$

The minimum weight path length for the vertices in optimal tree is

A $\to 3$

B $\to 2$

C and G $\to 4$

D and F $\to 3$

E $\to 2$

Example 7: State whether the given set is a prefix code. Justify {000, 001, 01,10, 11}

Solution: The given set which contains 5 elements will be a prefix code if we can construct a full binary tree with five leaves.

Let n be the total number of vertices and i be the total number of interior vertices in a full binary tree with five leaves.

then, $n = i + 5 \Rightarrow i = n - 5$

Also, $n = 2(n-5) + 1 \Rightarrow n = 9$

Therefore, $i = 4$

Hence, the full binary tree with five leaves will have total a vertices and 4 interior nodes. One such full binary tree is

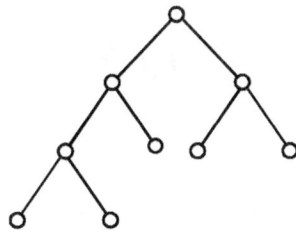

Fig. 9.68

Now assign 0 to the left branch and 1 to the right branch we get

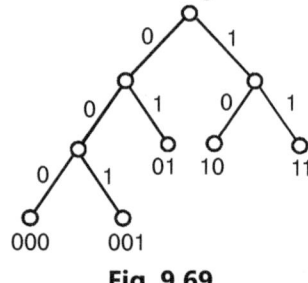

Fig. 9.69

Since we can construct the full binary tree with leaves as prefix codes. The given set is in prefix code.

Example 8: A binary search tree generated by inserting integers in order 50, 15, 62, 5, 20, 58, 91, 3, 8, 37, 60, 24. Determine the number of nodes in left and right.

Solution: The steps involved in drawing the resultant binary search tree in Fig. 9.70.

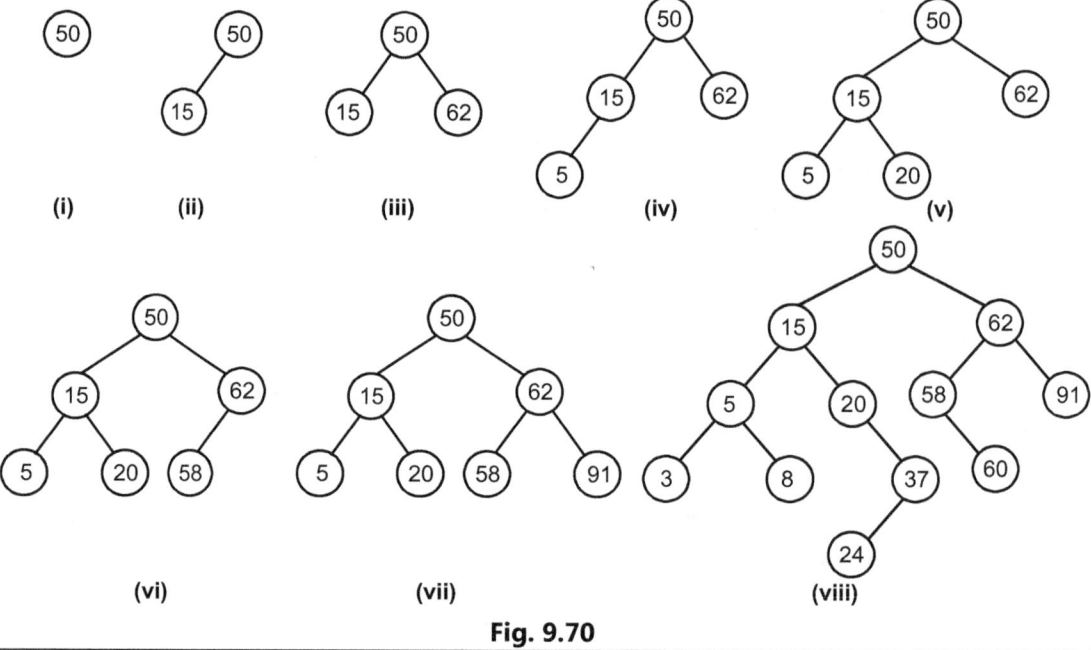

Fig. 9.70

9.5 Spanning Trees

In this section, we study the definition of spanning tree and the algorithms to find a minimum spanning tree in a connected graph.

Let G be any connected graph. A **spanning subgraph** of G which is a tree is called a **spanning tree** of G. i.e. a subgraph of G, which is a tree and contains all the vertices of G is called a spanning tree of G.

It is obvious that there can be many spanning trees for a given connected graph. For instance, consider the graph G in Fig. 9.71, two spanning trees of G are T_1 and T_2.

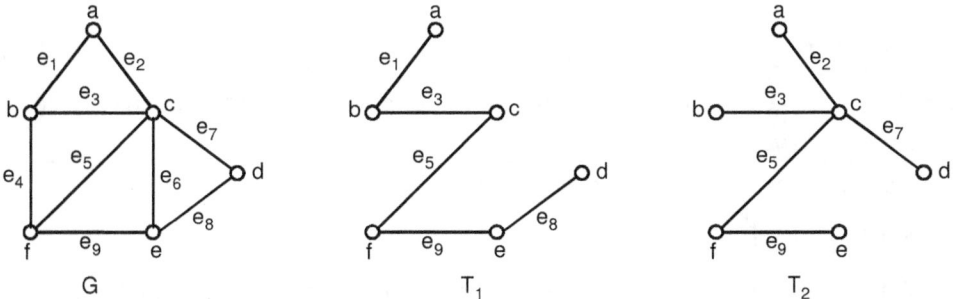

Fig. 9.71

Consider the spanning tree T_1 of G in Fig. 9.71. The edges of spanning tree T_1 are called **branches** of T_1. The edges of G which are **not** in T_1 are called **chords** of T_1. For example, the branches of T_1 are e_1, e_3, e_5, e_8 and e_9 and the chords of T_1 are e_2, e_4, e_6 and e_7. Similarly for the spanning tree T_2 of G in Fig. 9.51 the branches of T_2 are e_2, e_3, e_5, e_7 and e_9 and the chords of T_2 are e_1, e_4, e_6 and e_8. This shows that branches and chords corresponding to different spanning trees are different.

Suppose the connected graph G contains v number of vertices and e number of edges. Therefore, its spanning tree will contain same number of vertices v and (v – 1) number of edges. Hence, there are total (v – 1) branches in any spanning tree of G. Thus, the number of chords will be given by e – (v – 1) = e – v + 1.

9.5.1 Minimum Spanning Tree

A spanning tree of a **weighted connected** graph G is called a **minimum spanning tree** if its weight is minimum. Minimum spanning trees are useful in building a network of roads or railway lines connecting a numbers of cities. Suppose there are n cities $v_1, v_2 ... v_n$ and suppose the cost c_{ij} of constructing a direct link between the cities v_i and v_j are known. The connector problem is to design a network that connects all the n stations such that the total cost of construction is **least**. This problem can be represented by a weighted connected graph as follows.

Represent each city as a vertex of a weighted graph G and the cost c_{ij} of building the road as the weight of the edge (v_i, v_j). Then the connector problem reduces to find a spanning tree with the minimum weight in a weighted connected graph G.

Two algorithms, Prim's algorithm and Kruskal's algorithm are discussed here to find the minimum spanning tree.

9.5.2 Prim's Algorithm

Let G = (V, E) be a connected weighted graph. Construct a minimal spanning tree T for G inductively as follows:
Step 1: Take a vertex v_0 in the graph G. Set T = $\{\{v_0\}\ \emptyset\}$
Step 2: Find the edge $e_1 = (v_0, v_1)$ in E such that its one end vertex v_0 is in T and its weight is minimum. Adjoin the vertex v_1 and the edge e_1 to T i.e. T = $\{\{v_0, v_1\}, \{e_1\}\}$.
Step 3: Choose the next edge $e_i = (v_i, v_j)$ in such a way that its one end vertex v_i is in T and the other end vertex v_j is not in T (i.e. e_i should not form the circuit with the edges in T) and the weight of the edge e_i is as small as possible. Adjoin the edge e_i and vertex v_j to T.
Step 4: Repeat the step 3 until T contains all the vertices of G. The set T will give the minimum spanning tree of the graph G.

Another algorithm due to Kruskal (1956) is described here to find a minimum spanning tree in a weighted connected graph G.

9.5.3 Kruskal Algorithm

Let G = (V, E) be a weighted connected graph.
Step 1: Pick up an edge e_i of G such that its weight w (e_i) is minimum.

Step 2 : If edges $e_1, e_2 \ldots\ldots e_k$ have been chosen, then pick an edge e_{k+1} such that
   (i) $e_{k+1} \cdot e_i$ for any i = 1, 2 $\cdot$ k.
   (ii) The edges $e_1, e_2 \ldots\ldots e_k, e_{k+1}$ do not form the circuit.
   (iii) The weight w (e_{k+1}) is as small as possible subject to condition (ii).

Step 3: Stop, when (step 2) cannot be implemented.

Few examples which show the working of Prim's and Kruskal's algorithms (for minimal spanning tree) are illustrated here.

SOLVED EXAMPLES

Example 1: Find all the spanning trees for the following graph.

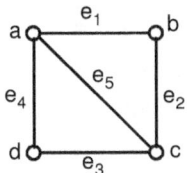

Fig. 9.72 (a)

Solution: Following are the different spanning trees of the given graph.

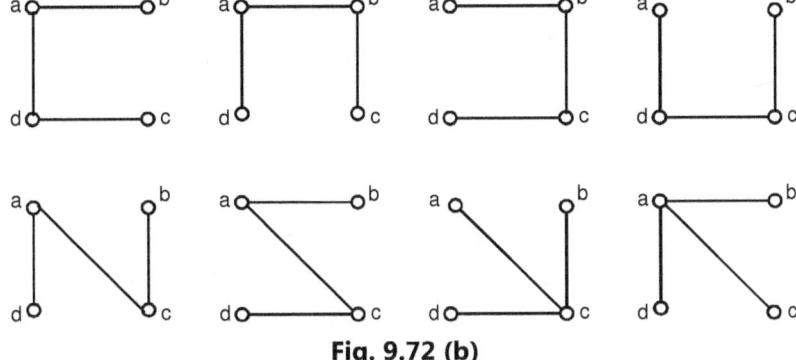

Fig. 9.72 (b)

Example 2: Find the minimal spanning tree for the following graph by using Prim's algorithm.

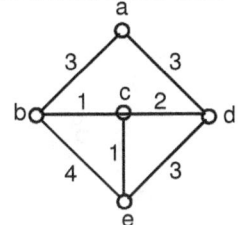

Fig. 9.73 (a)

Solution: Starting from the vertex a, the minimum spanning tree of the given graph can be obtained by using Prim's algorithm as follows:

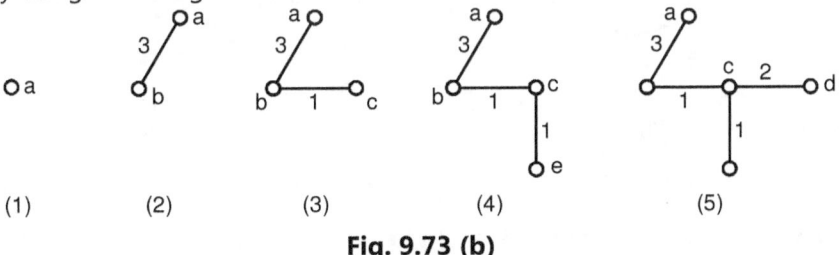

Fig. 9.73 (b)

The graph T obtained in step 5 is a minimum spanning tree.
Its weight is 7.

Example 3: Use Prim's algorithm to construct a minimal spanning tree for the weighted graph in Fig. 9.74 starting from the vertex a. Repeat the process starting from the vertex b. Verify that both trees have the same weight.

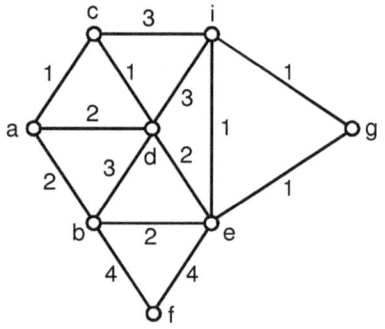

Fig. 9.74

Solution: With the help of Prim's algorithm, the minimum spanning tree of the graph in Fig. 9.75, starting from a is given as follows:

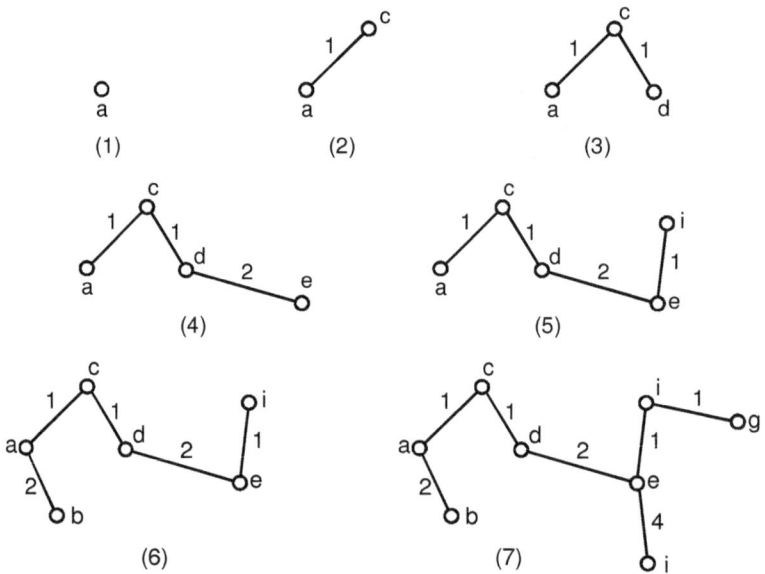

Fig. 9.75

The total weight of the minimum spanning tree is 12.

Now, use the same procedure, starting from the vertex b.

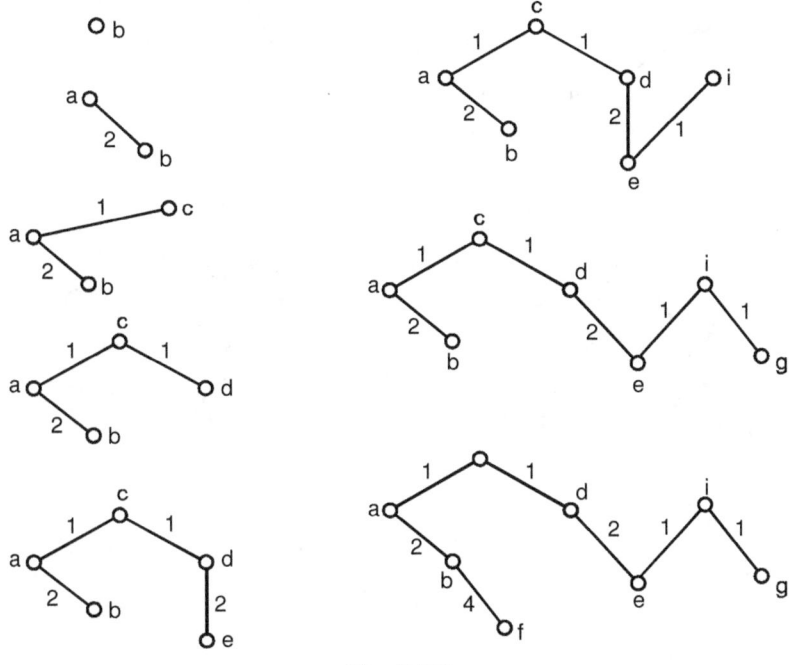

Fig. 9.76

The total weight of the above minimum spanning tree is also 12. Hence both the trees obtained in Fig. 9.75 and Fig. 9.76 have the same weight.

Example 4: Use Kruskal algorithm to find a minimum spanning tree for the graph shown in Fig. 9.77.

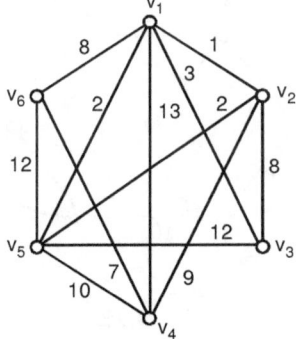

Fig. 9.77

Solution: The minimum spanning tree by using Kruskal's algorithm is given in following steps:

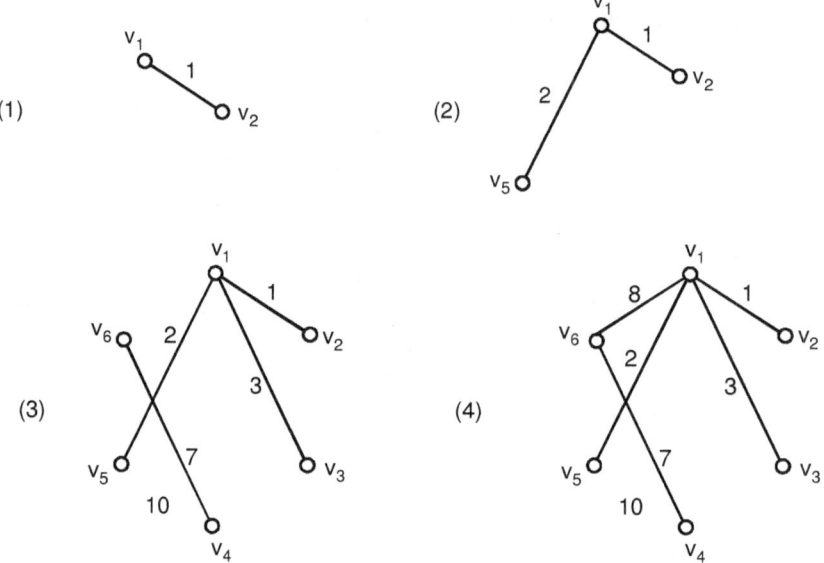

Fig. 9.78

Now at this stage we cannot take any edge from G because otherwise edges will form a circuit. Hence the graph in Fig. 9.78 is a minimal spanning tree.

Example 5: Determine a minimum spanning tree for the graph shown below.

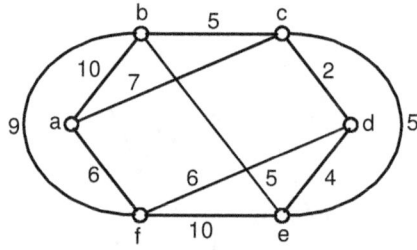

Fig. 9.79

Solution: Using Prim's algorithm we obtain a minimum spanning tree for the given graph as follows:

(1) o a

(2) a o
    6
    o f

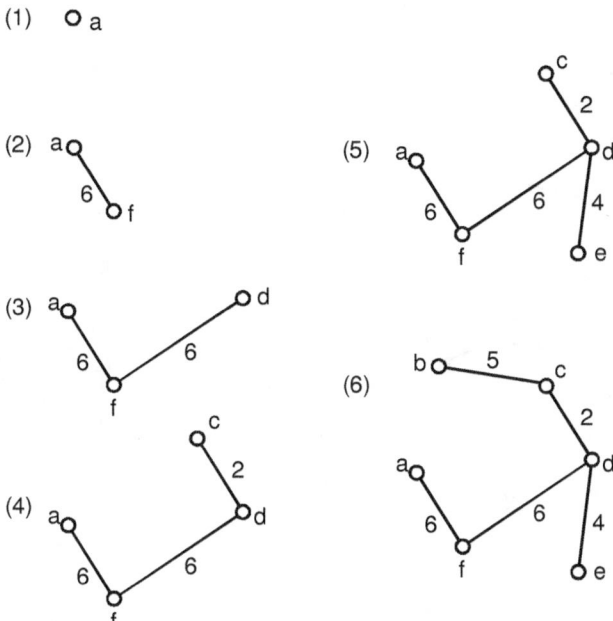

Fig. 9.80

The above tree T is a minimum spanning tree for the given graph.
Its weight is 23.

Example 6: Find the minimum spanning tree for Fig. 9.81.

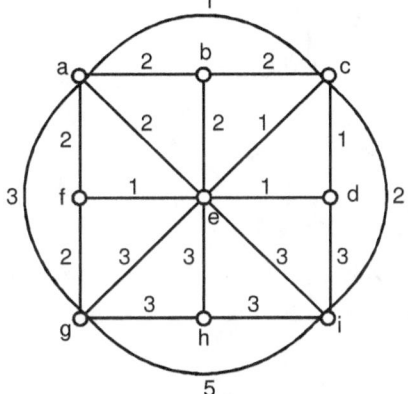

Fig. 9.81

Solution: With the help of Prim's algorithm, the minimum spanning tree of the graph shown in Fig. 9.82 can be obtained as follows:

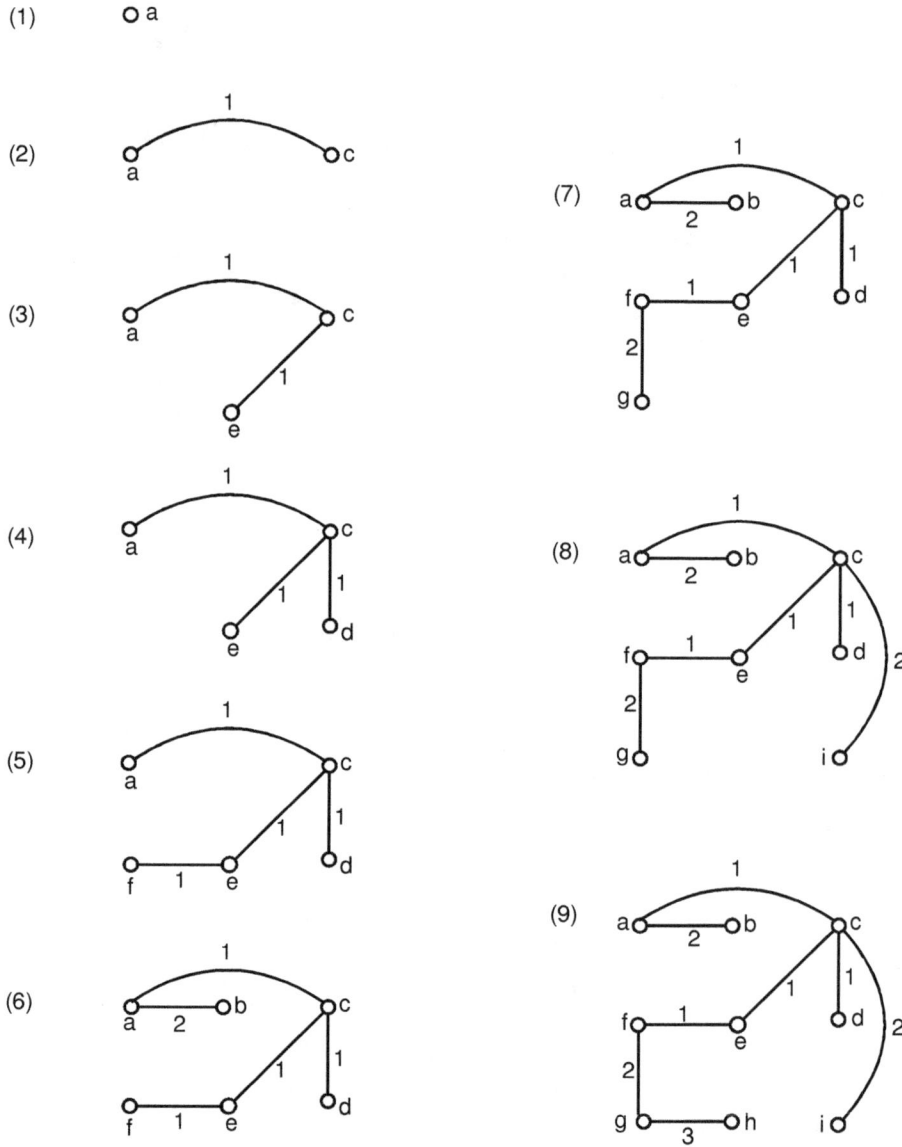

Fig. 9.82

The graph T shown in Fig. 9.82 is a minimum spanning tree. Its weight is 13.

Example 7: Obtain the minimum spanning tree for the graph shown in Fig. 9.83. Obtain the total cost of minimum spanning tree.

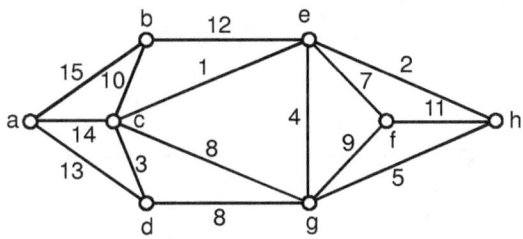

Fig. 9.83

Solution: Using *Kruskal* algorithm, the minimum spanning tree is obtained as follows:

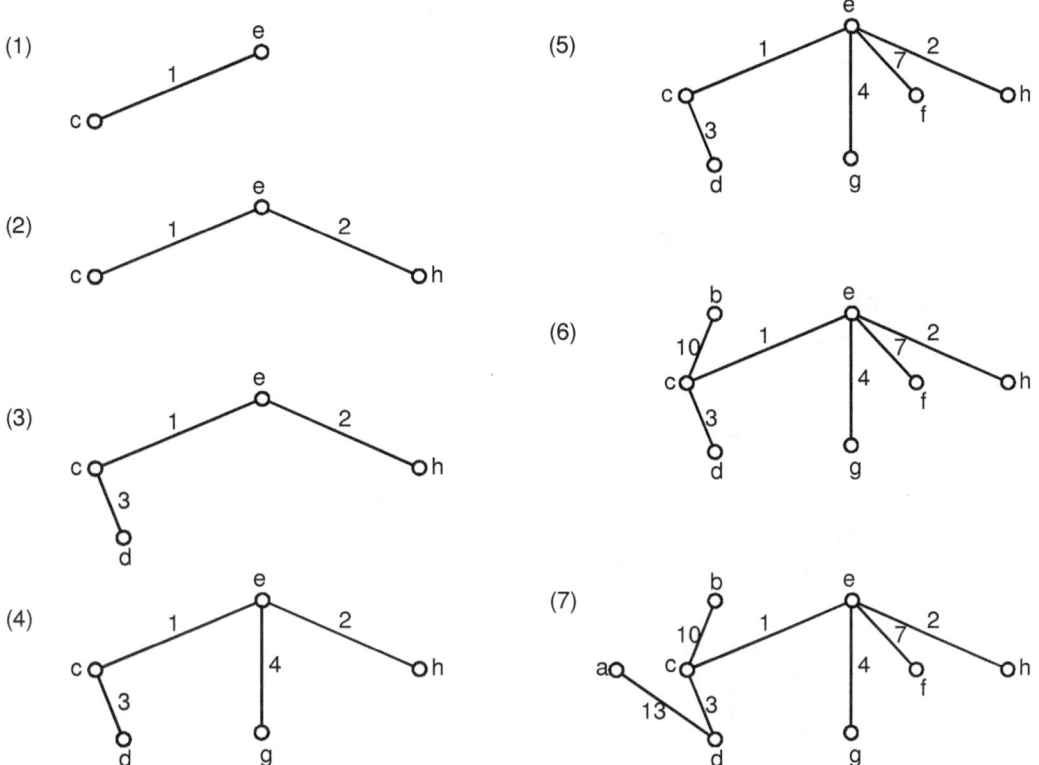

Fig. 9.84

The graph T is a minimum spanning tree of the given graph. Its total cost is 40.

Example 8: Give the stepwise construction of minimum spanning tree for the following graph using Kruskal's algorithm.

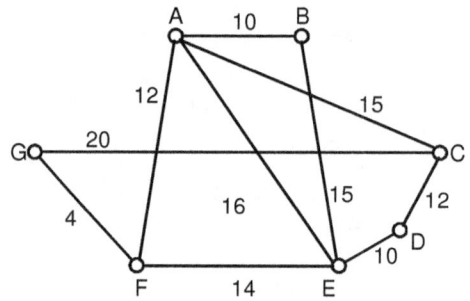

Fig. 9.85

Solution: Using Kruskal's algorithm, the minimum spanning tree can be obtained as follows:

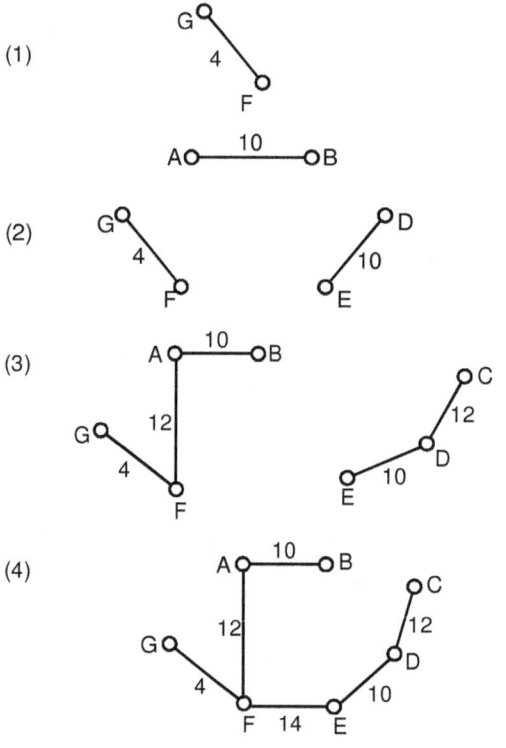

Fig. 9.86

Example 9: Use Kauskal's algorithm to find minimum spanning tree for the graph shown in following Fig. 9.87.

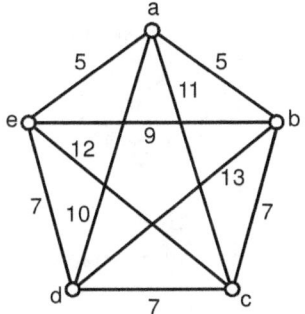

Fig. 9.87

Solution: The minimum spanning tree by using Krushal's algorithm is as follows:

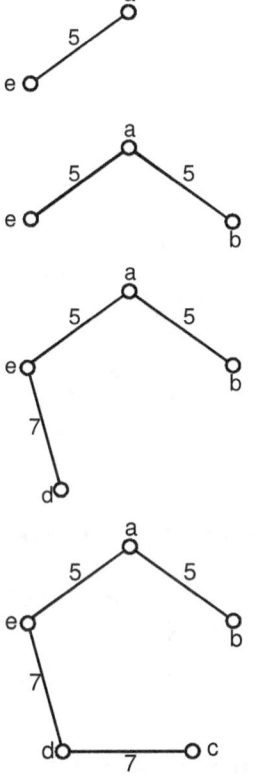

Fig. 9.88

The above tree T is a minimum spanning tree for the given graph. Its weight is 24.

Example 10: Use Prim's algorithm to find the minimum spanning tree for graph given below.

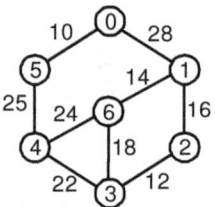

Fig. 9.89

Solution: Using Prim's algorithm, the minimum spanning tree can be obtained as shown in following steps:

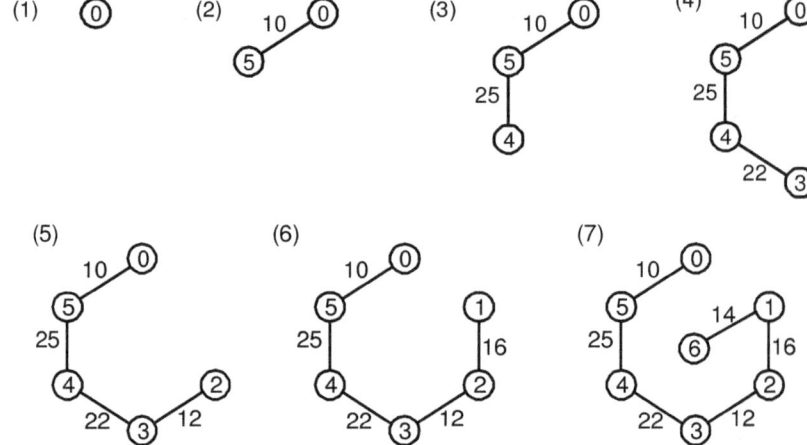

Fig. 9.90

The tree T is a minimum spanning tree with weight 99.

9.6 Fundamental Circuits and Fundamental Cut Sets

In this section, we describe the inter relationship between spanning trees, cycles and cut sets. Let G be a connected graph and let T be a spanning tree of G. Consider a **chord** of T i.e. an edge e of G which is not in T. Then T + e contains a unique circuit called **fundamental circuit** of G with respect to T. A fundamental circuit in a graph G is always with respect to a spanning tree of G. For different spanning trees of the graph G, the fundamental circuits will be different. For example, in Fig. 9.91, T_1 and T_2 are two spanning trees of a connected graph G.

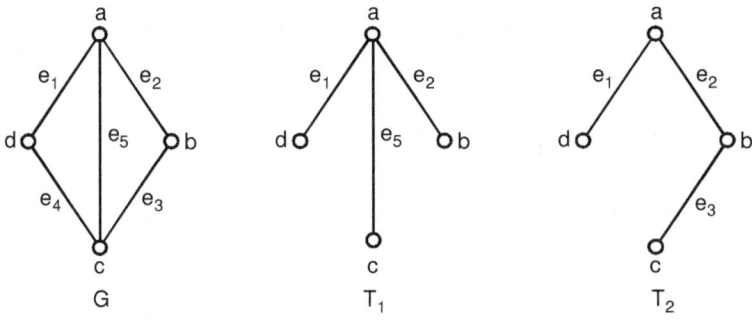

Fig. 9.91

For T_1, the edge e_3 and e_4 of G are chords. If the chord e_3 is added to T_1, then we obtain a circuit $\{e_2, e_5, e_3\}$. This is a fundamental circuit corresponding to e_3. Similarly corresponding to e_4, the fundamental circuit of G in T_1 is $\{e_1, e_5, e_4\}$.

Now consider the spanning tree T_2 of G. The chords of T_2 are e_4 and e_5. For e_4, the fundamental circuit is $\{e_1, e_2, e_3, e_4\}$ and for e_5, $\{e_2, e_3, e_5\}$ is a fundamental circuit. From above, it is clear that different spanning trees have different fundamental circuits. The number of fundamental circuit in any spanning tree is equal to the number of chords of that spanning tree. Hence, if the connected graph G has v number of vertices and e number of edges then the spanning tree T has (v − 1) branches and (e − v + 1) number of chords. Thus, there will be **(e − v + 1)** number of fundamental circuits in G with respect to the spanning tree T.

Fundamental Cut set

We have already discussed about cut sets in a connected graph in chapter 7. The cut sets related to the spanning tree of a connected graph are defined below.

Let T be the spanning tree of the connected graph G. Since the removal of any branch from a spanning tree breaks the spanning tree into two trees, we say that corresponding to a branch in a spanning tree, there is a division of the vertices in the graph into two subsets corresponding to the vertices in the two trees. It follows that for every branch in a spanning tree there is a corresponding cut set called fundamental cut set. The set of all fundamental cut sets of the graph G with respect to the spanning tree T is called a fundamental system of cut set. For example, for the following graph G shown in Fig. 9.92. The removal of the branch e_1 from the spanning tree T (Fig. 9.92) divides the vertices of T into two subsets {a, f, d} and {b, c}. Hence corresponding to the branch e_1, the fundamental cut set of G with respect to T is $\{e_1, e_3, e_6\}$. That is, by removing e_1, e_3, e_6 edges from the graph G, the graph will become disconnected and will have two components with vertex set {a, f, d} and {b, c} respectively.

Similarly, for the branches e_2, e_4 and e_5, the fundamental cut sets are $\{e_2, e_3, e_6\}$, $\{e_4, e_3\}$ and $\{e_5, e_6, e_3\}$.

From the above discussion, it is clear that each fundamental cut set contains **exactly one branch** of the spanning tree.

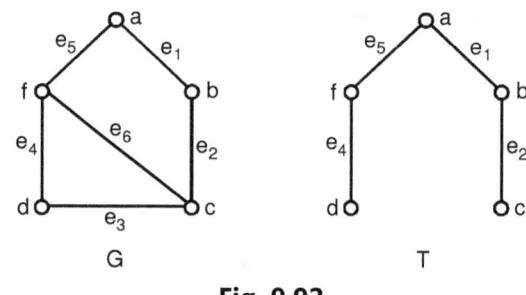

Fig. 9.92

The number of fundamental cut sets is equal to the number of branches in the spanning tree. If the connected graph G has v number of vertices and e number of edges, then the spanning tree has (v – 1) branches which is the same as the number of fundamental cut sets.

Now we present a close relationship between the fundamental circuits and the fundamental cut sets relative to a spanning tree.

Theorem 9.6.1

A cut-set and any spanning tree must have at least one edge in common.

Proof:

Suppose there is a cut set that has no common edge with a spanning tree.

Then, the removal of the cut set will leave the spanning tree intact.

This means that the removal of the cut set will not separate the graph into two components, which is in contradiction to the definition of a cut set.

Hence, there must be at least one edge common between the cut set and the spanning tree of the graph.

Theorem 9.6.2

A circuit and the complement of any spanning tree must have at least one edge in common.

Proof:

We know that the complement of a graph G is a graph whose vertex set is same as the vertex set of G and which contains the edges which are **not** in G.

Thus, the complement of a spanning tree will contain the edges which are not in the spanning tree.

> If there is a circuit that has no common edge with the complement of a spanning tree, the circuit should be contained in the spanning tree.
> However, this is impossible as a tree cannot contain a circuit.
> Hence, a circuit and the complement of the spanning tree must have at least one edge in common.

Theorem 9.6.3

> For a given spanning tree, let $D = \{e_1, e_2, e_3 \ldots e_k\}$ be a fundamental cut-set in which e_1 is a branch and $e_2, e_3 \ldots e_k$ are chords of the spanning tree. Then, e_1 is contained in the fundamental circuits corresponding to e_i for $i = 2, 3 \ldots k$. Moreover, e_1 is not contained in any other fundamental circuits.

Proof:

> Let C be the fundamental circuit corresponding to the chord e_2.
> Since D also contains e_2, hence, e_2 is common in both C and D.
> Now, C contains branches of the spanning tree and the chord e_2 and D contains the chords $e_2, e_3 \ldots e_k$ and the branch e_1.
> Also, every circuit has an even number of edges in common with every cut-set.
> Therefore C and D will have an even number of edges in common and e_1 is the only **other** edge that can possibly be in both C and D.
> Thus, e_1 must be contained in C.
> Similarly, it can be shown that e_1 is contained in the fundamental circuits of $e_3, e_4 \ldots e_k$.
> Also, e_1 is not contained in any other fundamental circuit.
> To prove this, suppose C' is a fundamental circuit corresponding to a chord not in D. C' cannot contain e_1, because otherwise, C' and D will have e_1 as the only edge in common.

SOLVED EXAMPLES

Example 1: How many fundamental cut sets and fundamental circuits are there in a graph G (with respect to any spanning tree) with 8 vertices and 11 edges ?

Solution: Since the graph G contains 8 vertices, hence, its spanning tree T will contain 7 branches. We know that corresponding to each branch of the spanning tree T, there exists a unique fundamental cut set. Hence, there are 7 fundamental cut-sets of G with respect to T.

Also, the given graph has 11 edges. Thus, the total number of chords is 11 – 7 = 4. Since corresponding to each chord, there is a unique fundamental circuit, hence, there are 8 fundamental circuits in G with respect to T.

Example 2: Find the fundamental circuits of the following graph G with respect to the given spanning tree T shown below.

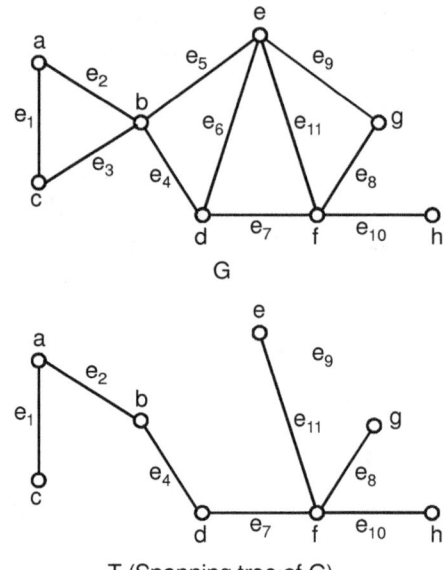

T (Spanning tree of G)

Fig. 9.93

Solution: The branches of T are $e_1, e_2, e_4, e_7, e_8, e_{10}$ and e_{11}. The chords of G are e_3, e_5, e_6 and e_9. Hence, there will be four fundamental circuits. Corresponding to e_3, the fundamental circuit is $\{e_1, e_2, e_3\}$.

Corresponding to the chords e_5, e_6 and e_9 the fundamental circuits are

$\{e_4, e_7, e_{11}, e_5\}$, $\{e_7, e_{11}, e_6\}$ and $\{e_{11}, e_8, e_9\}$ respectively.

Example 3: Find the fundamental cut-sets of the following graph G with respect to the given spanning tree T.

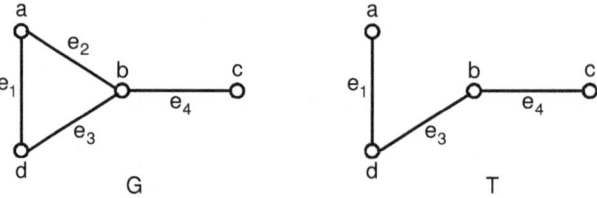

Fig. 9.94

Solution: Corresponding to each branch of the spanning tree, there exists a unique fundamental cut set. Here the spanning tree T has 3 branches e_1, e_3, e_4. Hence the graph G has 3 fundamental cut-sets with respect to T.

For e_1, $\{e_1, e_2\}$ is a fundamental cut-set.

For e_3 and e_4, $\{e_2, e_3\}$ and $\{e_4\}$ are fundamental cut sets respectively.

Example 4: Find the fundamental system of cut set for the graph G shown in Fig. 9.95 with respect to the spanning tree T.

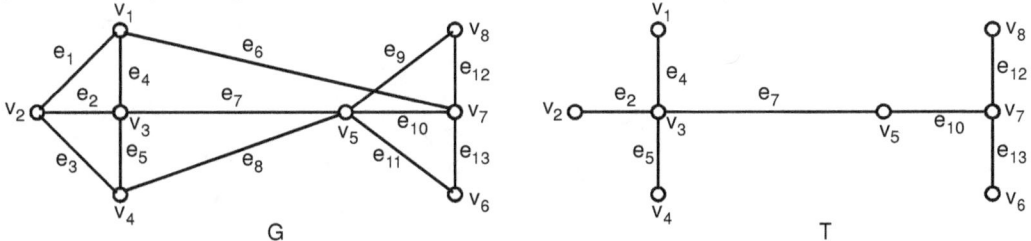

Fig. 9.95

Solution: Here the spanning tree has 7 branches and corresponding to each branch there is a fundamental cut set. Hence there are 7 fundamental cut-set of G with respect to T. Different fundamental cut, sets are given below:

Branch name	Fundamental cut set
e_2	$\to \{e_2, e_1, e_3\}$
e_4	$\to \{e_4, e_1, e_6\}$
e_5	$\to \{e_5, e_3, e_8\}$
e_7	$\to \{e_7, e_6, e_8\}$
e_{10}	$\to \{e_{10}, e_6, e_9, e_{11}\}$
e_{12}	$\to \{e_{12}, e_9\}$
e_{13}	$\to \{e_{13}, e_{11}\}$

Example 5: Determine all possible spanning tress of the given graph shown in Fig. 9.96. Consider any spanning tree, find its fundamental system of cut-sets.

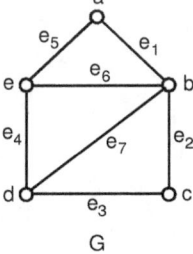

Fig. 9.96 (a)

Solution: All possible spanning tree are shown as follows:

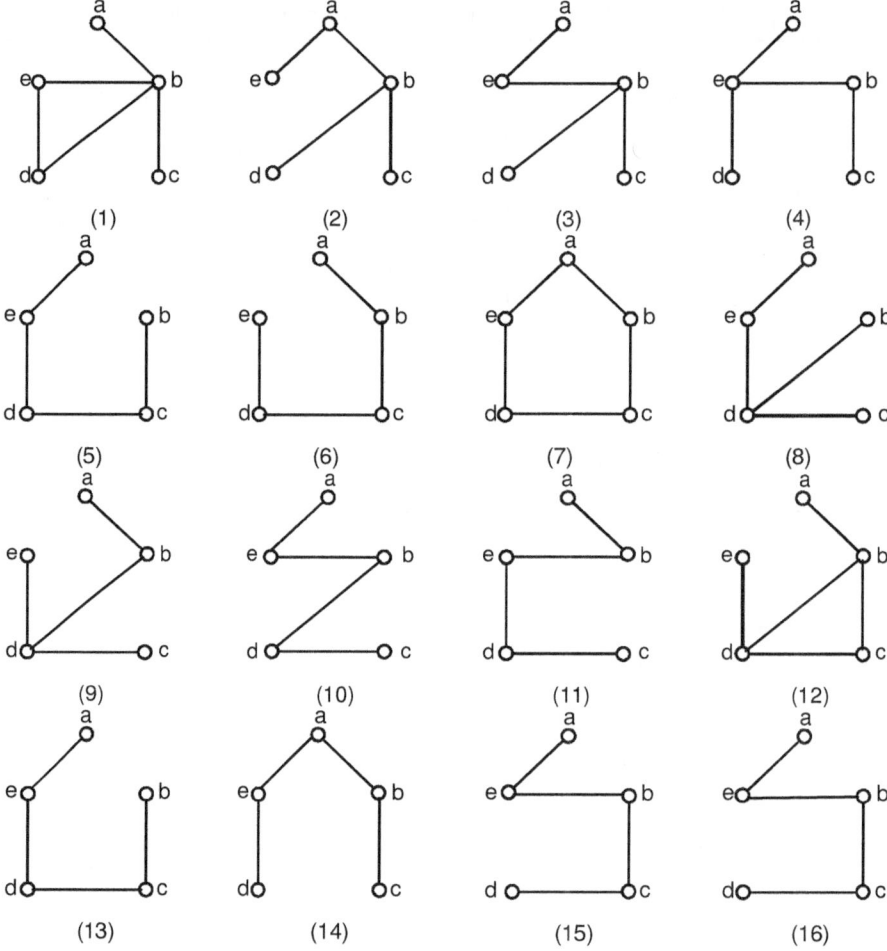

Fig. 9.96 (b)

Now, consider the following spanning tree T of the graph G in Fig. 9.97. The fundamental cut-sets with respect to T are as follows:

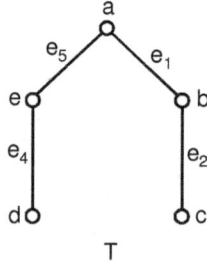

T

Fig. 9.97

Branch	Fundamental cut-set
$e_1 \to$	$\{e_1, e_3, e_6, e_7\}$
$e_2 \to$	$\{e_2, e_3\}$
$e_4 \to$	$\{e_4, e_3, e_7\}$
$e_5 \to$	$\{e_5, e_6, e_7, e_3\}$

Example 6: Determine all possible cut-sets of the graph G in a Fig. 9.98. Construct a spanning tree of the graph G and find its fundamental system of cut-sets.

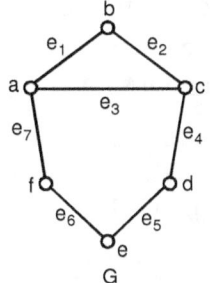

Fig. 9.98

Solution: A cut-set is a set of minimum number of edges where removal disconnects the graph. Following are the possible cut-sets of G –

(1) $\{e_1, e_2\}$, (2) $\{e_2, e_3, e_4\}$, (3) $\{e_4, e_5\}$ (4) $\{e_5, e_6\}$, (5) $\{e_6, e_7\}$, (6) $\{e_7, e_3, e_1\}$, (7) $\{e_2, e_3, e_5\}$, (8) $\{e_1, e_3, e_5\}$, (9) $\{e_2, e_3, e_6\}$, (10) $\{e_1, e_3, e_6\}$, (11) $\{e_4, e_6\}$, (12) $\{e_7, e_4\}$, (13) $\{e_7, e_5\}$, (14) $\{e_2, e_3, e_7\}$, (15) $\{e_1, e_3, e_4\}$.

Now consider the following spanning tree in Fig. 9.99.

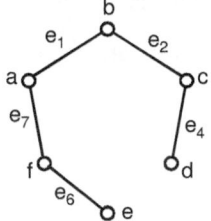

Fig. 9.99

The fundamental cut-sets are

Branch	Fundamental cut-set
$e_1 \to$	$\{e_1, e_3, e_5\}$
$e_2 \to$	$\{e_2, e_3, e_5\}$
$e_4 \to$	$\{e_4, e_5\}$
$e_6 \to$	$\{e_6, e_5\}$
$e_7 \to$	$\{e_7, e_5\}$

Example 7: Prove that the complement of a spanning tree does not contain a cut-set and that the complement of a cut-set does not contain a spanning tree.

Solution: Suppose the complement of a spanning tree contains a cut-set. This means, the spanning tree does not contain the cut-set. Hence there is no edge common between the cut-set and the spanning tree. But this is the contradiction to the theorem 9.6.1 that there is at least one edge common between a cut-set and the spanning tree. Therefore the complement of a spanning tree does not contain a cut-set.

For the second part, again assume that the complement of a cut-set contains the edges of spanning tree. This means there is no edge common to the cut-set and the spanning tree, which is the contradiction to the theorem 9.6.1. Hence the complement of a cut-set does not contain a spanning tree.

Example 8: Draw the fundamental cut-sets and union of edge disjoint fundamental cut-sets of the graph G with respect to spanning trees T_1 and T_2 given below.

Fig. 9.100

Solution: The fundamental cut-sets with respect to the spanning tree T_1 are as follows:

Branch		Fundamental cut-set
e_1	→	$\{e_1, e_2\}$
e_3	→	$\{e_2, e_3, e_4\}$
e_5	→	$\{e_4, e_5\}$

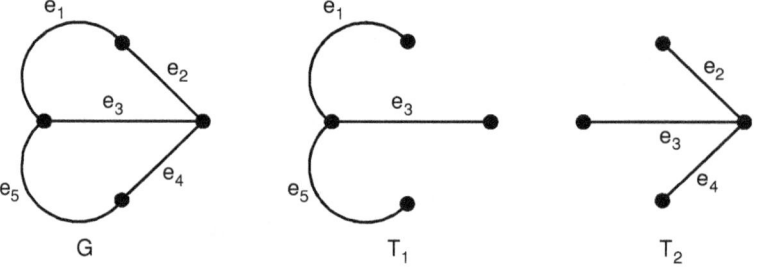

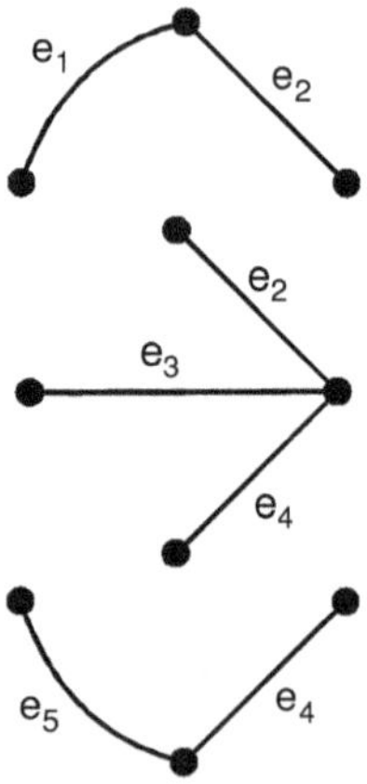

Fig. 9.101 (a)

For the spanning tree T_2,

Branch		Fundamental cut-set
e_1	→	$\{e_1, e_2\}$
e_3	→	$\{e_1, e_3, e_5\}$
e_4	→	$\{e_4, e_5\}$

The union of edges disjoint fundamental cut-sets is $\{e_1, e_2, e_4, e_5\}$

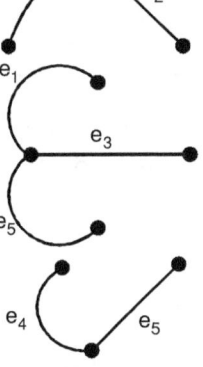

Fig. 9.101 (b)

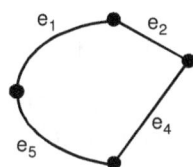

Fig. 9.101 (c)

Example 9: For the figure shown, give fundamental circuit.

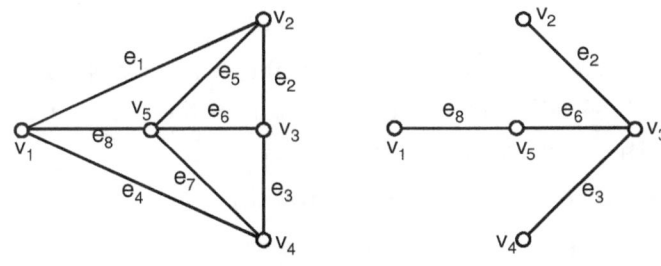

Fig. 9.102

Solution: Since there are four chords e_1, e_4, e_5, e_7, there will be four fundamental circuits corresponding to each chord.

Chord	Fundamental Circuit
e_1	$\{e_1, e_2, e_6, e_8\}$
e_4	$\{e_4, e_8, e_6, e_3\}$
e_5	$\{e_5, e_2, e_6\}$
e_7	$\{e_7, e_3, e_6\}$

Example 10: For the graph drawn in Fig. 9.103 (a) and spanning tree in Fig. 9.103 (b), determine fundamental system of cut sets and fundamental circuits.

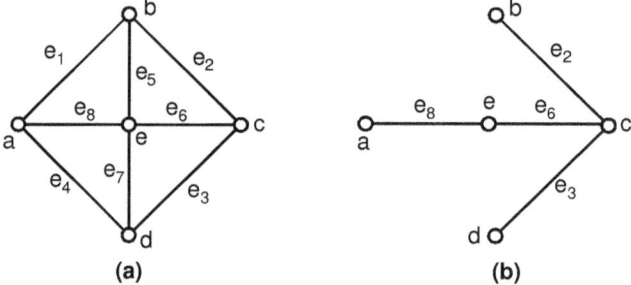

Fig. 9.103

Solution: Since there are 4 branches in the spanning tree (b), therefore there will be four fundamental cut sets corresponding to each branch.

Branch	Fundamental cutset
e_2	$\rightarrow \{e_1, e_5, e_2\}$
e_3	$\rightarrow \{e_4, e_7, e_3\}$
e_6	$\rightarrow \{e_1, e_5, e_7, e_4, e_6\}$
e_8	$\rightarrow \{e_1, e_4, e_8\}$

Since the spanning tree contains 4 branches, the remaining 4 edges in the graph are chords, namely e1, e4, e5, e7. Corresponding to each of the chord, there is a circuit called fundamental circuit. They are given as follows:

Chord	Fundamental circuit
e_1	$\rightarrow \{e_1, e_2, e_6, e_8\}$
e_4	$\rightarrow \{e_4, e_8, e_6, e_3\}$
e_5	$\rightarrow \{e_5, e_2, e_6\}$
e_7	$\rightarrow \{e_7, e_6, e_3\}$

EXERCISE - 9.1

1. Draw all non isomorphic trees with 4 and 6 vertices.
2. Draw a tree with 16 vertices which has either degree 1 or degree 3. Can you draw such a tree with 15 vertices.
3. Is it possible to draw a tree with six vertices having degrees 1, 1, 1, 1, 3, 3. If yes, draw the tree.
4. (a) Define – (i) Rooted tree, (ii) m-ary tree, (iii) full binary tree, (iv) level of vertex the rooted tree, (v) Subtree and regular tree, (iv) Regular m-ary tree with example.
   (b) Find the cut points of the following tree. Also find the level of each vertex.

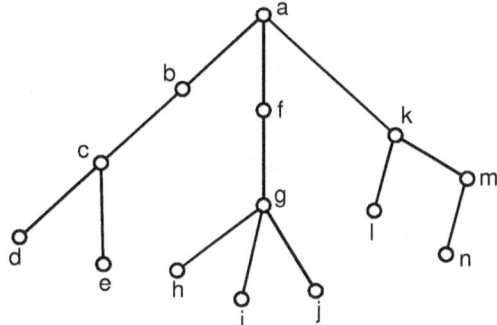

Fig. 9.104

5. Define the height of the tree. Find the height of the tree shown in Fig. 9.104 in the above problem 4.
6. Draw a full binary tree with 5 terminal vertices and 4 internal vertices.
7. (a) Explain the following terms in a rooted tree –
   (i) son (ii) parent (iii) subtree (iv) ancestor (v) descendant.
   (b) Answer the following questions for the tree in Fig. 9.89.
      (i) Find the parents of f and of i.
      (ii) Find the ancestors of c and d.
      (iii) Find the descendant of e and of d.
      (iv) Draw the subtree rooted at c.

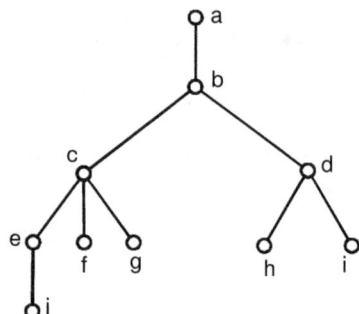

Fig. 9.105

8. Find whether the following tree is a full m-ary tree for some m or not. Find the height of the tree. Redraw the tree with the root 'v' on the top.

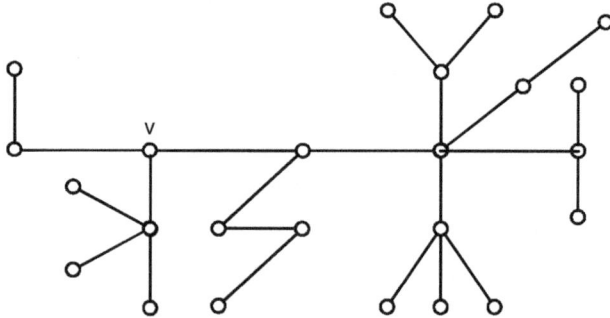

Fig. 9.106

9. Determine the total number of nodes on a full binary tree with 5 interior nodes.
10. Determine the number of leaves on a full 4-ary tree with 20 interior nodes.
11. Is there a full 4-ary tree with 100 nodes ?
12. Define an optimal binary prefix code.
13. For the following set of weights, construct an optimal binary prefix code. For each weight in the set, give the corresponding code word.
    (i) 2, 3, 5, 7, 9, 13.
    (ii) 8, 9, 10, 11, 13, 15, 22.
14. Define a spanning tree in a connected graph. When is it called minimum spanning tree.
15. Write an algorithm to find a minimum spanning tree in a weighted connected graph.
16. Obtain the minimum spanning tree for the following graphs. Find the total cost of the minimum spanning tree.

(i)

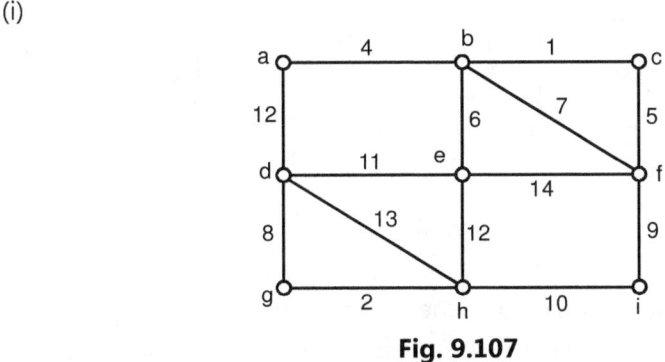

Fig. 9.107

(ii)

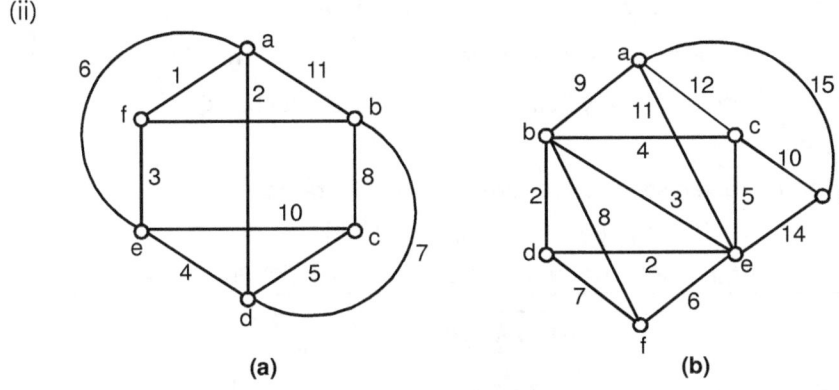

Fig. 9.108

17. Define the terms cut-set, fundamental system of cut-sets and fundamental circuits.

18. Determine all possible cut-sets of the following graph shown in Fig. 9.109. Construct a spanning tree of the graph G and find its fundamental system of cut-sets.

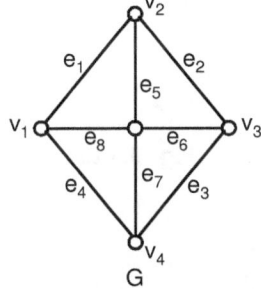

Fig. 9.109

19. Find the fundamental system of cut-set for the following graph G with respect to the spanning tree T given in Fig. 9.110.

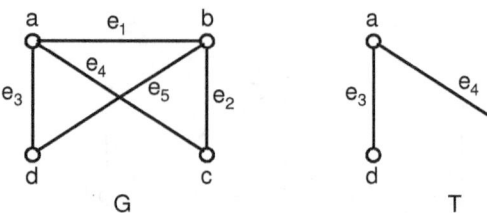

Fig. 9.110

20. For a given spanning tree, let C = {e_1, e_2, e_3, ... e_k} be a fundamental circuit in which e_1 is a chord and e_2, e_3 ... e_k are branches of the spanning tree. Prove that, e_1 is contained in the fundamental cut-sets corresponding to e_i for i = 2, 3, ... k. Moreover e_1 is not contained in any other fundamental cut-set.

21. Prove that a regular m-ary tree with i-interior nodes has ($m_i + 1$) nodes at all.

22. Write a short note on "Binary Search tree and its applications".

23. Define prefix code.

    Justify whether given set of codes are prefix codes or not.
    (i) {000, 001, 01, 10, 11}, (ii) {1, 00, 01, 000, 0001}.

24. Define: (i) Forest, (ii) Height of tree, (iii) Ordered tree, (iv) Properties of tree.

ANSWERS - 9.1

1. Non-isomorphic trees on 6 vertices are:

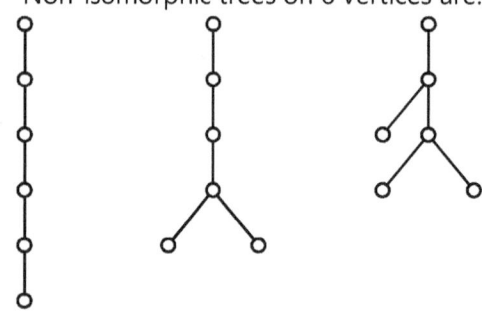

Fig. 9.111

Non-isomorphic trees on 4 vertices are:

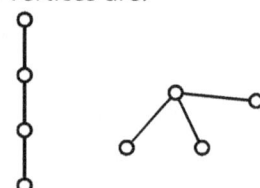

Fig. 9.112

2. Tree with 16 vertices of degree 1 or 3.

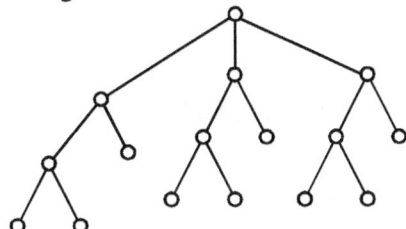

Fig. 9.113

It is not possible to draw a tree with 15 nodes which has degree 1 or 3.

3. Yes.

Fig. 9.114

4. The vertices of degree other than one are cut vertices. Levels of vertices of T are given below:

$$l(b) = l(f) = l(k) = 1$$
$$l(c) = l(g) = l(l) = l(m) = 2$$
$$l(d) = l(e) = l(h) = l(i) = l(j) = l(n) = 3.$$

5. height = 3

6.

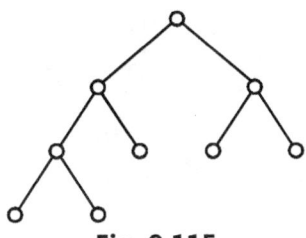

Fig. 9.115

7. (i) c and d
   (ii) a and b
   (iii) f and (h, i)
   (iv) The subtree rooted at c is

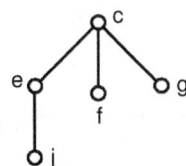

Fig. 9.116

8. No, it is not a full m-ary tree. Height 3.
9. 11
10. 61
11. No, the integer solution to the equation 100 = 4i + 1 does not exist.
13. (i)   Code word for 2 · 0000
         Code word for 3 · 0001
         Code word for 5 · 001
         Code word for 7 · 10
         Code word for 9 · 11
         Code word for 13 · 01

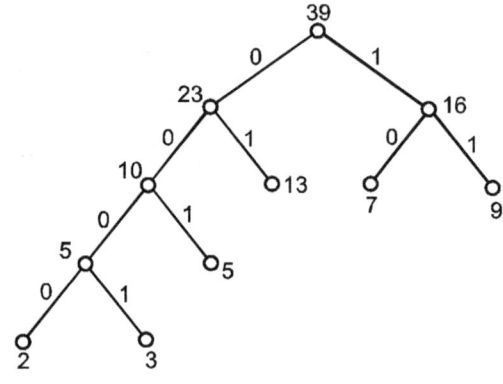

Fig. 9.117

(ii)

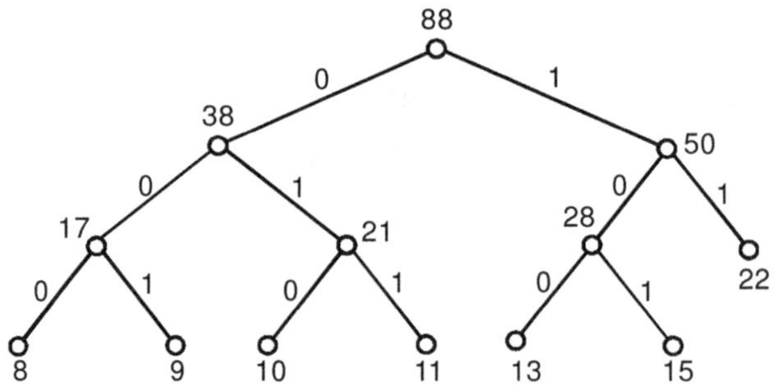

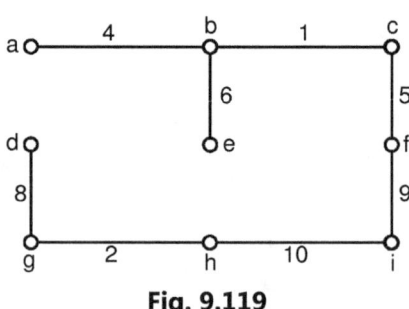

Fig. 9.118

The prefix code for the weights 8, 9, 10, 11, 13, 15 and 22 is given by {000, 001, 010, 011, 100, 101, 11}

16. (i)

Fig. 9.119

Weight = 48

(ii)

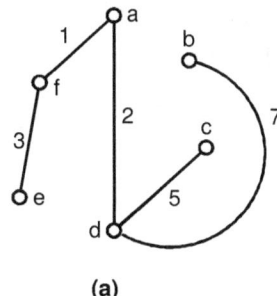 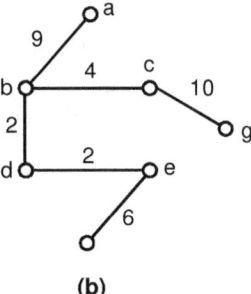

(a)   (b)

Fig. 9.120

Weight = 18

18. All possible cut-sets are $\{e_1, e_4, e_8\}$, $\{e_1, e_2, e_5\}$, $\{e_2, e_3, e_6\}$, $\{e_3, e_4, e_7\}$, $\{e_5, e_6, e_7, e_8\}$, $\{e_4, e_8, e_5, e_2\}$, $\{e_1, e_5, e_6, e_3\}$, $\{e_4, e_6, e_7, e_2\}$, $\{e_1, e_8, e_7, e_3\}$ $\{e_1, e_8, e_7, e_6, e_2\}$, $\{e_2, e_5, e_8, e_7, e_3\}$, $\{e_4, e_8, e_5, e_6, e_3\}$, $\{e_1, e_5, e_6, e_7, e_4\}$

19. $\{e_5, e_3\}$, $\{e_4, e_1, e_5\}$, $\{e_1, e_5, e_2\}$.

POINTS TO REMEMBER

- A "tree" is a simple connected graph without any circuits.
- The eccentricity E(v) of a vertex v in a graph G is the distance from v to the vertex farthest from v in G. i.e.

$$E(v) = \max d(v_i, v)$$

- A tree in which one vertex (called the root) is distinguished from all the other vertices is known as rooted tree. Trees without any root are called free trees or simply trees.
- A forest is a set of disjoint trees.
- A rooted tree in which every interior node has atmost m sons is called an m-ary tree.
- Let T be any full binary tree and let $w_1, w_2 \ldots\ldots w_t$ be the weights of the terminal vertices (leaves). Then, the weight W of the binary tree is given by

$$W(T) = \sum_{i=1}^{t} w_i \, l_i$$

> where l_i is the length of the path of the leaf i from the root of the tree. The full binary tree is called an optimal tree if its weight is minimum.
> - Let G be any connected graph. A spanning subgraph of G which is a tree is called a spanning tree of G. i.e. a subgraph of G, which is a tree and contains all the vertices of G is called a spanning tree of G.

Unit 5

Chapter 10: GROUPS AND RINGS

SYLLABUS:

- Algebraic Systems : Semi groups, Subsemigroup Monoid, Submonoid, Groups, Abelian group, Subgroups, Isomorphism, Subsemigroup, Automorphism, Homomorphism Ring, Integral domain, Field, Ring.

OBJECTIVES:

- Study of algebraic structures, groups, rings and fields.

UTILITY:

- Used in design of computer hardware.
- Development of softwares such as finite state machines.

KEY CONCEPTS:

- Group
- Ring
- Integral domain
- Field
- Polynomial ring

10.0 Introduction

In this chapter, we study sets with additional structure, induced by one or more binary operations on the elements of the set. These discrete structures are called as algebraic systems as they obey a set of rules or axioms which are similar to the rules of addition and multiplication of numbers in elementary algebra. In fact many of these structures are prototype models of mathematical systems, with which we are familiar.

We first introduce a general algebraic system and discuss its properties. We then concentrate our attention on some special algebraic systems such as semigroups, groups, rings and fields.

An important application of groups is in coding theory where techniques are developed for detecting and correcting errors in transmitted data. The section on codes discusses some of these techniques in detail.

Besides coding theory, algebraic systems are also widely applied in the design of computer hardware and development of software especially formal language theory and finite state machines.

10.1 Algebraic System

Let us first define an operation on the elements of a set, such that the resulting element is also an element of the set.

10.1.1 Definition

An n-ary operation on a non-empty set A is a function $f: A^n \rightarrow A$, A^n being the product set of A.

Observe the following properties that a binary operation must satisfy.

(i) The n-ary operation must be defined for each n-tuple $(a_1, a_2, ..., a_n) \in A$.

(ii) Since f is a function, only one element of A should be assigned to each n-tuple of A^n.

If n = 1, f is called **unary,**

if n = 2, f is called **binary,**

if n = 3, f is called **ternary** and so on.

Let us consider the following examples.

Examples:

(i) The function $f: Z \rightarrow Z$, where

$$f(x) = -x, \text{ is unary,}$$

(ii) $f: Z \times Z \rightarrow Z$, defined as

$$f(x, y) = x + y, \text{ is binary,}$$

(iii) f: $Z \times Z \times Z \to Z$, defined as

$f(x, y, z)$ = y; if $x \neq 0$

= z; otherwise,

is ternary.

We now proceed to define an algebraic system.

10.1.2 Definition

An algebraic system is an ordered pair (A, F) where
(i) A is a set of elements, called as the **carrier** of the algebra.
(ii) F is a finite set of m-ary operations on the carrier, m being a variable.

In the notation for an algebraic system, the carrier set A is first specified, followed by the elements of F, which are actually listed, viz (A, f_1) or (A, f_1, f_2) etc.

Examples:

(i) Let E = {0, 2, 4, ...}. Then E with the binary operation of addition + represents an algebraic system (E, +).

(ii) The set of integers Z with the two binary operations of addition + and multiplication × is an algebraic system, and is denoted as (Z, +, ×).

(iii) The set of real numbers R, with a single unary operation minus − and two binary operations of addition and multiplication is an algebraic system denoted by (R, −, +, ×).

(iv) For a fixed integer n > 0, let M_n (R) denote the set of all n × n matrices. Then under the binary operation of matrix addition, M_n (R) forms an algebraic system (M_n (R), +).

Similarly, under matrix multiplication, (M_n (**R**), ×) is another algebraic system.

(v) Let P(A) denote the power set of a non-empty set A. Then P(A) together with the set operations of union, intersection and complementation forms an algebraic system (P(A), ∪, −).

(vi) Let E = {a, b} be a set of symbols, called as the **alphabets**. A **word** over E is a finite string of symbols a, b, with possible repetitions, e.g. a, aa, abab, etc. Given two words x and y. We can form a new word xy by simply just opposing the symbols of x with those of y in the order xy. For example, if x = aa, y = aba, then xy = aaaba, whereas yx = abaaa. This operation is called as **concatenation**. If E^* denotes the set of all words over E, then concatenation is a binary operation on E^*.

In what follows, we will deal with algebraic systems, having only binary operations.

10.2 Properties of Binary Operations

10.2.1 Definition

A binary operation * on A is said to be **commutative** if $a * b = b * a$, for all elements $a, b \in A$.

Examples:
(i) The binary operation of addition on the set of integers is commutative, but the operation of subtraction on the set of integers is not commutative.
(ii) The binary operation of multiplication on the set of integers is commutative.

10.2.2 Definition

A binary operation * on A is said to be **associative** if
$$a * (b * c) = (a * b) * c, \text{ for all elements, } a, b, c \in A.$$

Examples:
(i) The binary operation of addition on the set of integers is associative, whereas the binary operation of subtraction is not associative.
(ii) The binary operation of multiplication on the set of integers is associative.

10.2.3 Definition

A binary operation * on A is said to satisfy the **idempotent** property if $a * a = a$, for all $a \in A$.

Example:
(i) Let L be a lattice with the operators $\wedge$ (meet) and $\vee$ (join). Then $\wedge$ and $\vee$ are binary operations and we know that
$$a \vee a = a,$$
$$a \wedge a = a, \text{ for all } a \in A.$$
Hence both $\wedge$ and $\vee$ satisfy the idempotent property.

10.2.4 Tables of Binary Operations

If $A = \{a_1, a_2, ..., a_n\}$ is a finite set, we can define a binary operation on A, by means of a table, is shown below. The entry in the i-th row and j-th column denotes the element $a_i * a_j$.

*	a_1	a_2	a_j	A_n
a_1				
a_2				
a_i			$a_i * a_j$	
a_n				

Example:

Let A = {0, 1} and let × denote multiplication. Then we have the binary table

×	0	1
0	0	0
1	0	1

SOLVED EXAMPLES

Example 1: For each of the following, determine whether * is a binary operation:
  (i) R is the set of real numbers and a * b = ab.
  (ii) Z^+ is the set of positive integers and a * b = a / b.
  (iii) On Z^+ where a * b = a − b.
  (iv) On R, where a * b = min {a, b}.
  (v) On R, where a * b = a × |b|.
  (vi) On Z, where a * b = a^b.

Solution:
  (i) Yes, since f: $R^2 \to R$ defined as f(a, b) = ab is a function, with a b ∈ **R**.
  (ii) No, since (a, b) ∈ $Z^+ \times Z^+$ does not imply that a * b = a / b ∈ Z
      (1, 2) ∈ $Z^+ \times Z^+$, but 1/2 ∉ Z^+.
  (iii) No, since (1, 2) ∈ $Z^+ \times Z^+$ but
      1 − 2 = −1 ∉ Z^+
  (iv) Yes, since * is a function, with min {a, b} ∈ **R**.
  (v) Yes, since * is a function, with a × |b| ∈ **R**.
  (vi) No, since 2 * (−1) = 2^{-1} = $\frac{1}{2}$ ∉ Z.

Example 2: For each of the following, determine whether the binary operation * is commutative or associative:
  (i) N is the set of natural numbers and a * b = a + b + 2, for a, b ∈ N.

(ii) On N, where a * b = max (a, b).
(iii) On N, where a * b = min (a, b).
(iv) On N, where a * b = min (a, b + 2)
(v) On R, where a * b = ab + 2b.
(vi) On R, where a * b = ab / 3.
(vii) On the set of non-zero real numbers, a * b = a / b.
(viii) On R, a * b = a^b.

Solution:

(i) * is commutative since a * b = a + b + 2 and b * a = b + a + 2. Hence both are equal.

$$a * (b * c) = a * (b + c + 2)$$
$$= a + (b + c + 2) + 2 = a + b + c + 4.$$
$$(a * b) * c = (a + b + 2) * c$$
$$= (a + b + 2) + c + 2$$
$$= a + b + c + 4$$

Hence * is associative.

(ii) a * b = max (a, b) = max (b, a) = b * a. Hence * is commutative.

Let a, b, c ∈ N. Consider b * c.

b * c = max {b, c}.

∴ b * c = b ; if b ≥ c
or = c ; if c ≥ b

Let us suppose {b, c} = b, so that
b * c = b.

Then a * (b * c) = max {a, b}
= a ; if a ≥ b
or = b ; if b ≥ a

If a ≥ b, then a * (b * c) = a

Then a * b = max {a, b} = a.

Hence (a * b) * c = max {a, c} = a; since a ≥ b and b ≥ c.

Hence if a ≥ b ≥ c, then (a * b) * c = a * (b * c).

Similarly, one can prove (a * b) * c = a * (b * c), for other cases.

Hence * is associative.

(iii) * is commutative as well as associative. Proof is similar to (ii).

(iv) * is not commutative since

$$2 * 3 = \min(2, 5) = 2, \text{ whereas,}$$
$$3 * 2 = \min(3, 4) = 3.$$

* is also not associative since

$$4 * (3 * 1) = 4 * 3 = 4, \text{ while}$$
$$(4 * 3) * 1 = 4 * 1 = 3.$$

(v) * is not commutative since

$$2 * 3 = 6 + 6 = 12, \text{ while}$$
$$3 * 2 = 6 + 4 = 10$$

Clearly * is also not associative.

(vi) * is commutative and associative.

(vii) * is not commutative; and * is also not associative since a * (b * c)

$$= a * (b/c) = a/b/c = ac/b; \text{ whereas}$$
$$(a * b) * c = (a/b) * c = a/b/c = \frac{a}{bc}$$

(viii) * is not commutative since $a^b \neq b^a$.

* is also not associative since,

$$(a * b) * c = (a^b)^c = a^{bc}$$

whereas $\quad a * (b * c) = a^{b^c}$

Example 3: Let (A, *) be an algebraic system where * is a binary operation such that for any a, b, ∈ A, $\quad$ a * b = a.

(i) Show that * is an associative operation.

(ii) Can * ever be a commutative operation ?

Solution:

(i) a * (b * c) = a * b = a. (a * b) * c
$$= a * c = a.$$

Hence * is associative.

(ii) * is commutative only if a * b = b * a, i.e. a = b, for all a, b ∈ A. This is possible if A is the singleton set {a} and a * a = a, i.e. * is an idempotent operation on A.

Example 4: Let (A, *) be an algebraic system such that for all a, b, c, d ∈ A,

$$a * a = a,$$
$$(a * b) * (c * d) = (a * c) * (b * d)$$

Show that $\quad a * (b * c) = (a * b) * (a * c)$

Chp 10 | 10.7

Solution: Since
$$a * a = a,$$
$$a * (b * c) = (a * a) * (b * c)$$
$$= (a * b) * (a * c) \qquad \text{(by the second condition)}$$

Example 5: Let $(A, *)$ be an algebraic system such that for all $a, b \in A$,
$$(a * b) * a = a$$
$$(a * b) * b = (b * a) * a.$$

(i) Show that $a * (a * b) = a * b$, for all $a, b, \in A$
(ii) Show that $a * a = (a * b) * (a * b)$, for all $a, b \in A$.
(iii) Show that $a * a = b * b$, for all a, b.
(iv) Show that $a * b = b * a$ iff $a = b$.
(v) Let $(A, *)$ satisfy the additional condition $a * b = (a * b) * b$, for all $a, b \in A$. Show that $*$ is idempotent and commutative.

Solution:

(i) $\quad a * (a * b) = ((a * b) * a) * (a * b),$
since $\quad a = (a * b) * a,$ (by the first condition)
Now let $\quad c = a * b.$
Then R.H.S. $= (c * a) * c = c$ again by the first condition.
Hence $a * (a * b) = a * b$

(ii) $\quad a * a = ((a * b) * a) * a$
$\qquad = (c * a) * a, \text{ putting } a * b = c$
$\qquad = (a * c) * c$
$\qquad = (a * (a * b)) * (a * b)$
$\qquad = (a * b) * (a * b) \qquad \text{(by (i))}$

(iii) $\quad a * a = (a * b) * (a * b) \qquad \text{(by (ii))}$
$\qquad = c * c, \quad \text{where} \quad a * b = c$
$\qquad = (c * b) * (c * b) \qquad \text{(by (ii))}$
$\qquad = ((a * b) * b) * ((a * b) * b)$
$\qquad = ((b * a) * a) * ((b * a) * a)$
$\qquad = (b * a) * (b * a) \;\Big\}\qquad \text{(by (ii))}$
$\qquad = b * b$

(iv) If $a = b,\; a * b = b * a.$
Conversely, let $a * b = b * a.$
Then $\quad a = (a * b) * a = (b * a) * a$
$\qquad = (a * b) * b \qquad \text{(by given condition)}$

	= (b * a) * b		
	= b	(by given condition)	
(v)	a * a = (a * a) * a	(by given condition)	
	= a, since (a * b) * a = a for all a, b ∈ A.		

To show * is commutative

$$a * b = (a * b) * b$$
$$= (b * a) * a$$
$$= b * a \quad \text{(by given condition.)}$$

Hence * is commutative.

Example 6: The following table, of a binary operation * is given. Is * commutative?

*	a	b	c
a	b	c	a
b	c	b	a
c	a	b	c

Solution: From the table we observe the following:

$$a * b = c, \quad b * a = c$$
$$a * c = a, \quad c * a = a$$
$$b * c = a, \quad c * b = b, \text{ and } a \neq b.$$

Hence * is not commutative.

Example 7: Consider the binary operation * defined on the set A = {a, b, c, d} by the following table:

*	A	b	c	d
a	a	c	b	d
b	d	a	b	c
c	c	d	a	a
d	d	b	a	c

Find

(i) c * d and d * c

(ii) b * d and d * b

(iii) a * (b * c) and (a * b) * c

(iv) Is * commutative, associative?

Solution:

(i) $c * d = a$, $\quad d * c = a$

(ii) $b * d = c$, $\quad d * b = b$

(iii) $b * c = b$, $\quad a * (b * c) = a * b = c$

$\qquad a * b = c$. Hence $(a * b) * c = c * c = a$

(iv) $*$ is not commutative, since $b * d \neq d * b$.

$*$ is also not associative, since $a * (b * c) \neq (a * b) * c$.

We shall now study some special algebraic systems.

Example 8: Consider the following table for a binary operation $*$ on the set $\{a, b, c, d\}$.

*	a	b	c	d
a	a	b	c	d
b	b	d	a	a
c	c	a	b	d
d	d	a	b	c

(i) Is $*$ associative ?

(ii) Find the identity element e.

(iii) What is the inverse of b ?

Solution: (i) $*$ is not associative.

Consider $\qquad (b * c) * d = a * d = d$

However, $\qquad b * (c * d) = b * d = a$

(ii) Notice that the first column and first row contains the ordered sequence of elements $\{a, b, c, d\}$. Hence a is the identity element (i.e. a is left identity as well as right identity).

(iii) Since $b * c = a = c * b$ and also $b * d = a = d * b$, b has two inverse i.e. both c and d are inverse of b.

10.3 Semigroups

Let $(A, *)$ be an algebraic system, with a binary operation $*$ on A. Then $(A, *)$ is called a **semigroup** if $*$ is associative, i.e.

$$a * (b * c) = (a * b) * c, \text{ for all } a, b, c \in A.$$

The semigroup is further said to be commutative if $*$ is commutative.

Examples:
   (i) $(Z, +)$ is a commutative semigroup.
   (ii) $(Z, \times)$ is a commutative semigroup.
   (iii) For a non-empty set A, $(P(A), \cup)$ is a commutative semigroup and so is $(P(A), \cap)$.
   (iv) $(Z, -)$ is not a semigroup, since subtraction is not associative.

10.3.1 Definitions

(i) An element e in $(A, *)$ is called as **left identity** element if for each element $x \in A$, $e * x = x$.
(ii) e is called a **right** identity if $x * e = x$, for all $x \in A$.

A semigroup can have more than one left (or right) identity, as seen from the following example.

Example: The algebraic system $(A, *)$ whose table is given below is a semigroup.

*	a	b	c
a	a	b	c
b	a	c	b
c	a	b	c

Since the rows for both the elements a and c are equal to [a b c] it follows that both a and c are left identities. However there is no right identity since none of the columns are equal to [a b c].

10.3.2 Definition

An element e in a semigroup $(A, *)$ is called an **identity** element if $a * e = e * a = a$, for all $a \in A$, i.e. e is both a left identity and right identity. It is clear that e is unique.

Examples:
   (i) The semigroup $(Z, +)$ has the identity element which is the number 0.
   (ii) The semigroup $(Z, \times)$ has the identity element which is the number 1.
   (iii) The semigroup $(N, +)$ has no identity element, where the set N is the set of natural numbers, excluding 0.

10.3.3 Definition

A **monoid** is a semigroup $(A, *)$ that has an identity element.

Examples:

(i) Let $E = \{0, 2, 4, 6, ...\}$. Then $(E, +)$ is a monoid, with the number 0 as the identity element.

(ii) Let E^* be the set of all words over the alphabet set $E = \{a, b\}$. Let concatenation be the binary operation. The empty word Λ is the identity for E^*. Hence E^* under concatenation is a monoid.

10.3.4 Definition

Let $(A, *)$ be an algebraic system, and let B be a subset of A. Then B is said to be closed under $*$, if for any elements b, c ∈ B, b $*$ c is also in B.

10.3.5 Definition

Let $(A, *)$ be a semigroup and let B be a non-empty set of A, such that B is closed under $*$. Then $(B, *)$ is itself a semigroup and is called a **sub semigroup** of $(A, *)$.

10.3.6 Definitions

Let $(A, *)$ be a monoid, and let B be a non-empty subset of A. Then $(B, *)$ is called a **submonoid** of $(A, *)$ if

(i) B is closed under $*$.

(ii) The identity element e ∈ B.

Example:

Let $E = \{0, 2, 4, 6, ...\}$. Then $(E, +)$ is a submonoid of $(Z, +)$.

The concepts of semigroups and monoids are used in finite state machines.

10.3.7 Definitions

Let $(A, *)$ be a monoid with identity element e. Let B be a non-empty subset of A. Then the monoid generated by B, denoted by $< B >$ is defined as follows:

(i) e ∈ $< B >$, and if b ∈ B, then b also is in $< B >$, that is B ⊆ $< B >$.

(ii) $< B >$ is closed under $*$.

(iii) The only elements of $< B >$ are those obtained from steps (i) and (ii).

Examples:

1. Find the smallest submonoid of $(Z, +)$ generated by the set $\{-4, 6\}$.

Solution: Let B = {– 4, 6}. Then < B > is obtained as follows:
(i) 0, 6, – 4 ∈ < B >.
(ii) If x, y ∈ < B >, then x + y ∈ < B >.
(iii) < B > contains only the elements obtained from steps (i) and (ii).

Hence   < B > = {0, 6, – 4, 2, – 2, 4, 8, – 6, 10, ...}
              = {, ... – 6, – 4, – 2, 0, 2, 4, 6, 8, 10, ...}
              = set of even integers.

(ii) Let E = {a, b} and B = {aa, bbb}.
Find the submonoid of E* generated by B.
            < B > = {∧, aa, bbb, aabbb, bbbaa, aaaa, bbbbbb, ...}.

(iii) Let A = {a, b, c, d} and let C(A) denote the set of all functions on A. Let f: A → A be defined by the following diagram.

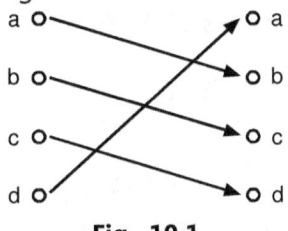

Fig. 10.1

Find the submonoid of (C(A), o), where o denotes composition of functions, generated by f.

Solution: The identity element is 1_A. Consider fof = f^2 which is defined by the following diagram.

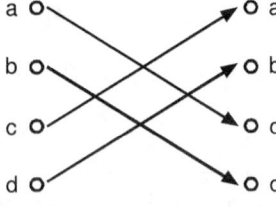

Fig. 10.2

fofof = f^3 is defined as

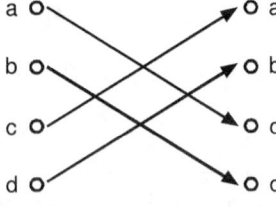

Fig. 10.3

f^4 is defined as

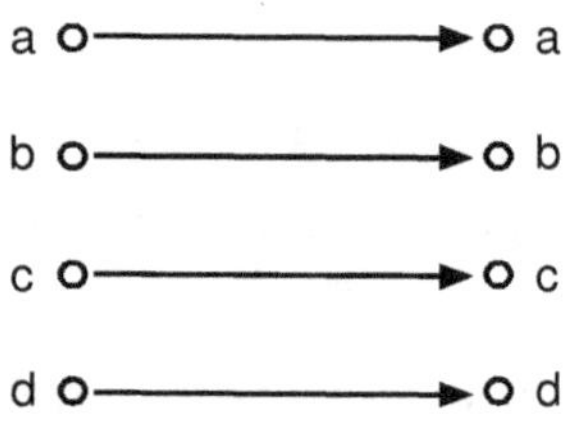

```
a o────────▶o a
b o────────▶o b
c o────────▶o c
d o────────▶o d
```

Fig. 10.4

$$\therefore \quad f^4 = 1_A$$

Hence the submonoid generated by f is the set $\{1_A, f, f^2, f^3\}$.

SOLVED EXAMPLES

Example 1: Show that the set of integers of the form 3m + 1 is closed under multiplication. Is this set a submonoid of (Z, ×) ?

Solution: Let $B = \{n \in Z \mid n = 3m + 1\}$.

Let r, s ∈ B, then r = 3m + 1 and s = 3n + 1 for m, n ∈ Z.

then
$$rs = (3m + 1)(3n + 1)$$
$$= 9mn + 3n + 3m + 1$$
$$= 3(m + n + 3mn) + 1$$
$$= 3t + 1, \text{ where } t = m + n + 3mn.$$

Hence B is closed under ×.

Since the identity element 1 can be written as 1 = 3·0 + 1, 1 ∈ B. Hence B is a submonoid of (Z, ×).

Example 2: (i) Determine the submonoid of (Z, +) generated by 6 and 9.

(ii) Submonoid of (Z, +) generated by – 3 and 5.

Solution: (i) Let S = {6, 9}

then < S > = {0, 6, 9, 12, 15, 18, 21, 24, ...}

(ii) Let S = {– 3, 5}.

then < S > = {0, –3, 5, 2, –1, –2, 4, 7, – 4, 1, 3, ...}
= {, ... –3, –2, –1, 0, 1, 2, 3, ...}
= Z

Example 3: Let A = {a, b}. Which of the following tables define a semigroup of A? Monoid on A?

(i)

*	a	B
a	a	b
b	a	a

(ii)

*	a	b
a	a	b
b	b	b

(iii)

*	a	B
a	b	a
b	a	b

(iv)

*	a	b
a	a	b
b	b	a

Solution: (i) * is not associative. Consider b * (a * b) = b * b = a. On the other hand (b * a) * b = a * b = b. Therefore (A, *) is not a semigroup and hence not a monoid.

(ii)
$$a * (b * b) = a * b = b$$
$$(a * b) * b = b * b = b$$
$$a * (a * b) = a * b = b$$
$$(a * a) * b = a * b = b$$
$$a * (b * a) = a * b = b$$
$$(a * b) * a = b * a = b$$

Similarly * is associative for the remaining combinations.

The identity element is a. Hence (A, *) is not only a semigroup, but it is also a monoid.

(iii)
$$a * (a * b) = a * a = b$$
$$(a * a) * b = b * b = b$$

Similarly checking for other combinations, one can show that * is associative. The identity element is b. Hence (A, *) is not only a semigroup, but it is also a monoid.

(iv)
$$a * (b * a) = a * b = b$$
$$(a * b) * a = b * a = b$$

Similarly one can verify that * is associative for other combinations as well.

Hence (A, *) is a semigroup. Note that a * b = b = b * a, and a * a = a.

Hence the identity element is a.

Hence (A, *) is also a monoid.

Example 4: Let A = {a, b}. Write the operation table for the semigroup (P(A), ∪).

Solution: P(A) = {φ, A, {a}, {b}}.

Table:

∪	φ	A	{a}	{b}
φ	φ	A	{a}	{b}
A	A	A	A	A
{a}	{a}	A	{a}	A
{b}	{b}	A	A	{b}

Example 5: Prove that the intersection of two subsemigroups of a semigroup (S, ∗) is a subsemigroup of (S, ∗).

Solution: Let S_1, S_2 be subsemigroups of S. We have only to show that $S_1 \cap S_2$ is closed under ∗. Let x, y ∈ $S_1 \cap S_2$. Then x, y ∈ S_1 and x, y ∈ S_2. Since S_1 and S_2 are subsemigroups, x ∗ y ∈ S_1 and x ∗ y ∈ S_2 which means that x ∗ y ∈ $S_1 \cap S_2$. Hence $S_1 \cap S_2$ is closed under ∗. Therefore ($S_1 \cap S_2$, ∗) is a subsemigroup.

Example 6: Prove that the intersection of two submonoids of a monoid (S, ∗) is a submonoid of (S, ∗).

Solution: Let S_1 and S_2 be submonoids of S. Then by the above example ($S_1 \cap S_2$, ∗) is a subsemigroup. We have only to prove the identity element is in $S_1 \cap S_2$ which is obvious. Hence ($S_1 \cap S_2$, ∗) is a submonoid.

Example 7: Show that the set of all idempotents in a commutative monoid S is a submonoid of S.

Solution: Recall an element x ∈ S is called an idempotent if x ∗ x = x. Let T be the set of all idempotents in S. Then e ∈ T since e ∗ e = e. We have only to prove that T is closed under ∗. For x, y ∈ T consider (x ∗ y) ∗ (x ∗ y).

$$\begin{aligned}
&= ((x * y) * x) * y &&\text{(by associativity of ∗)}\\
&= (y * (x * x)) * y &&\text{(using both commutativity and associativity)}\\
&= (y * x) * y\\
&= x * (y * y)\\
&= x * y
\end{aligned}$$

We have thus shown that x ∗ y is an idempotent element, and hence x ∗ y ∈ T. T is therefore closed under ∗ and is hence a submonoid of S.

Example 8: Let Z_n denote the set of integers {0, 1, 2,..., n – 1}. Let ⊙ be binary operation on Z_n such that

a ⊙ b = the remainder of ab divided by n.

(i) Construct the table for the operation ⊙ for n = 4.
(ii) Show that $(Z_n, ⊙)$ is a semigroup for any n.

Solution: (i) $Z_4 = \{0, 1, 2, 3\}$.

Table

⊙	0	1	2	3
0	0	0	0	0
1	0	1	2	3
2	0	2	0	2
3	0	3	2	1

(ii) Let $a ⊙ b = r$, where

$ab = pn + r$ ... (1)

Then $(a ⊙ b) ⊙ c = r ⊙ c$

$= s$, where $rc = qn + s$ ... (2)

Let $b ⊙ c = t$, where $bc = ln + t$ ... (3)

$a ⊙ (b ⊙ c) = a ⊙ t = k$, where $at = mn + k$ ... (4)

We have to prove $s = k$.

Now $a(bc) = aln + at = aln + mn + k$ ... (5)

Also $(ab)c = (pn + r)c = pnc + rc$

$= pnc + qn + s$ ... (6)

Now since equations (5) and (6) are equal, it follows that $k = s$.

Hence $(a ⊙ b) ⊙ c = a ⊙ (b ⊙ c)$.

Hence $(Z_n, ⊙)$ is a semigroup for any n.

Example 9: Let $(A, *)$ be a semigroup. Let a be an element in A. Consider a binary operation $*$ on A such that for every $x, y \in A$, $x * y = x * a * y$.
Show that $*$ is an associative operation.

Solution:
$(x * y) * z = (x * a * y) * z$
$= x * a * y * a * z$

Now $x * (y * z) = x * (y * a * z)$

Hence $(x * y) * z = x * (y * z)$

therefore $*$ is an associative operation.

Example 10: Let $(\{a, b\}, *)$ be a semigroup where
$$a * a = b.$$ Show that
(i) $a * b = b * a$
(ii) $b * b = b.$

Solution: (i) $a * b = a * (a * a) = (a * a) * a$ (as $*$ is associative)
$$= b * a$$

(ii) Since $(A, *)$ is closed under $*$, $a * b = a$ or $a * b = b$.

Let us first assume $a * b = a$.

Then by associativity property of $*$,
$$a * (a * b) = (a * a) * b$$
$\Rightarrow \quad a * a = b * b$
$\Rightarrow \quad b = b * b$

Next assume $a * b = b$.

Then $\quad a * (a * b) = (a * a) * b$
$\Rightarrow \quad a * b = b * b$
$\Rightarrow \quad b = b * b$

Hence in either case $b * b = b$.

Hence the result is proved.

Example 10: Consider the algebraic system $(Q, *)$, where Q is set of rational numbers and $*$ is binary operation defined by $a * b = a + b - ab$, $\forall\, a, b \in Q$.

Determine whether $*$ is associative.

Solution: Let $a, b, c \in Q$.

Consider $(a * b) * c$. Let $a * b = p$.

Then $\quad p = a + b - ab.$ Now $(a * b) * c$
$$= p * c = p + c - pc$$
$$= (a + b - ab + c) - (a + b - ab) c \quad \ldots (1)$$

Now, $\quad a * (b * c) = a * q$ (say)
$$= a + q - aq, \text{ (where } q = b + c - bc)$$
$$= (a + b + c - bc) - a(b + c - bc)$$
$$= a + b + c - bc - ab - ac + abc \quad \ldots (2)$$

Since equations (1) and (2) are equal, it follows that $*$ is associative.

10.4 Groups

A **group** (G, *) is a monoid, with identity e, such that for every element a ∈ G there exists an element a^{-1} ∈ G, called as the inverse of a, such that $a * a^{-1} = a^{-1} * a = e$.

Thus a group is a set G together with a binary operation * on G such that

(i) (a * b) * c = a * (b * c), for all a, b, c ∈ G

(i.e. * is **Associative**)

(ii) There is a unique element e in G such that a * e = e * a, for a ∈ G.

(**Identity** element)

(iii) For each a ∈ G, there exists an element a^{-1} ∈ G, such that $a * a^{-1} = a^{-1} * a = e$.

(**Inverse** element)

10.4.1 Definition

A group (G, *) is called an **Abelian** group if a * b = b * a, for all a, b ∈ G.

Examples:

(i) The set of all integers Z with the operation of addition is a group. The identity element is the number 0 and for every n ∈ Z, its inverse is (– n).

(ii) The set $Q^* = Q - \{0\}$ of non-zero rational numbers is a group under multiplication. The identity element is the number 1 and inverse of each element p/q ∈ Q^* is q/p.

(iii) The set of all **non zero** real numbers under the operation of multiplication is a group, with the number 1 as the identity element; and inverse of each number a is 1/a.

The next is a very important example of a group.

(iv) Let n be any positive integer (n > 0). For elements x, y ∈ Z, define a relation ≡ on them as x ≡ y or x = y (mod n) if x – y is divisible by n. The relation is an equivalence relation and for each element x ∈ Z, we obtain the corresponding equivalence class [x].

There are in all n distinct equivalence classes. Let Z_n denote the set of all equivalence classes; Z_n is called as a set of **residue classes modulo n**, where [x] = [y] implies x = y (mod n).

For any two elements [x], [y] ∈ Z_n define [x] + [y] = [x + y]. One can easily see that + is both associative and commutative. The identity element is [0], and for each [x] ∈ Z_m, its inverse is [m – x], since [x] + [m – x} = [x + m – x] = [m] = [0]. Thus (Z_m, +) is an abelian group.

(v) If p is a prime number, then $Z_p - \{0\} = Z_p^*$ is a multiplicative abelian group where the multiplication · is defined naturally as

$$[x] \cdot [y] = [x \cdot y].$$

However, for a non-prime number Z_m^* is not a group. Consider $Z_4^* = \{[1], [2], [3]\}$. Z_4 is not a group since $[2] \cdot [2] = [4] = [0] \notin Z_4^*$. Hence Z_4^* is not closed under ·, and therefore it is not a group.

We give below the group tables for Z_3 and Z_4 under +.

+	[0]	[1]	[2]
[0]	[0]	[1]	[2]
[1]	[1]	[2]	[0]
[2]	[2]	[0]	[1]

(Z_3, +)

+	[0]	[1]	[2]	[3]
[0]	[0]	[1]	[2]	[3]
[1]	[1]	[2]	[3]	[0]
[2]	[2]	[3]	[0]	[2]
[3]	[3]	[0]	[1]	[2]

(Z_4, +)

(iv) Let A = {a, b, c} and let F denote the set of functions from A to A, which are given below.

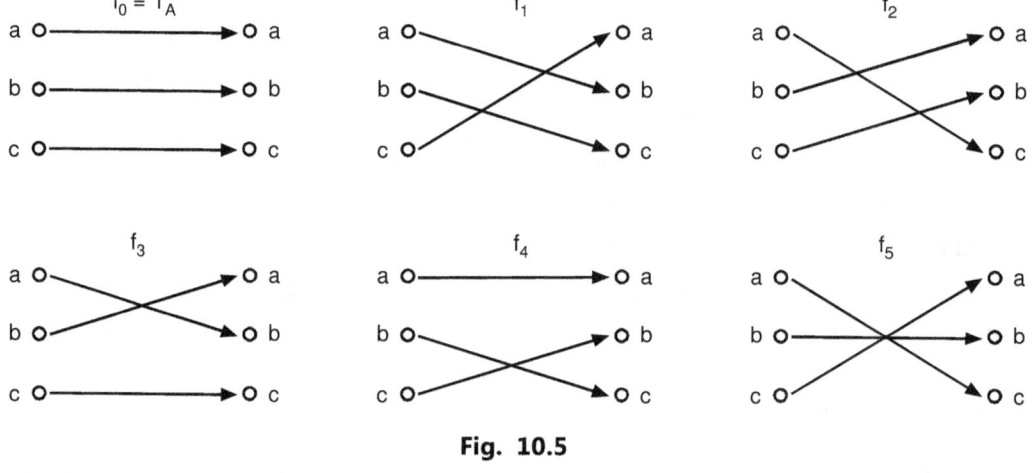

Fig. 10.5

The set (F, ·), where · denotes composition forms, a group. The group table is given below.

·	f_0	f_1	f_2	f_3	f_4	f_5
f_0	f_0	f_1	f_2	f_3	f_4	f_5
f_1	f_1	f_2	f_0	f_5	f_3	f_4
f_2	f_2	f_0	f_1	f_4	f_5	f_3
f_3	f_3	f_4	f_5	f_0	f_1	f_2
f_4	f_4	f_5	f_3	f_2	f_0	f_1
f_5	f_5	f_3	f_4	f_1	f_2	f_0

This group is non-abelian, since $f_1 \cdot f_3 = f_5$ and $f_3 \cdot f_1 = f_4$.

(vii) **The Permutation Group (Group of Symmetries of a triangle):** Consider an equilateral triangle (Fig. 10.6) with vertices 1, 2, 3. Since the triangle is determined by its vertices, a symmetry of the triangle is a **permutation** of the vertices. We describe the various symmetries of this triangle.

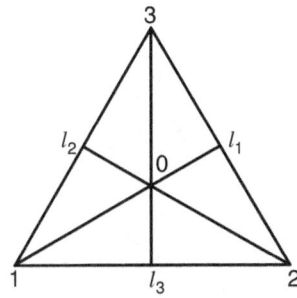
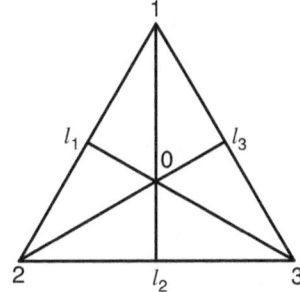

Fig. 10.6   **Fig. 10.7**

$f_0 = \begin{pmatrix} 1 & 2 & 3 \\ 1 & 2 & 3 \end{pmatrix}$ is the identity permutation, that keeps the vertices undisturbed.

Next consider the anti-clockwise rotation f_2 of the triangle about 0 through 120°. (Fig. 10.7). Then

$$f_1 = \begin{pmatrix} 1 & 2 & 3 \\ 2 & 3 & 1 \end{pmatrix}$$

Next obtain an anti-clockwise rotation f_3 about 0 through 240°, which is the permutation

$$f_2 = \begin{pmatrix} 1 & 2 & 3 \\ 3 & 1 & 2 \end{pmatrix}$$

Finally, there is an anti-clockwise rotation about 360° which is the same as f_1.

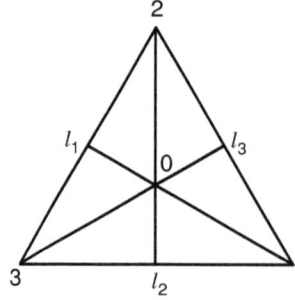 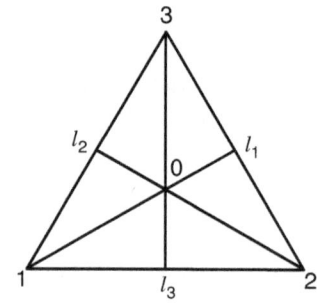

Fig. 10.8 Fig. 10.9

We also obtain three additional symmetries of the triangle g_1, g_2 and g_3 by reflecting about the lines l_1, l_2 and l_3 respectively. We denote these reflections by the following permutations.

$$g_1 = \begin{pmatrix} 1 & 2 & 3 \\ 1 & 3 & 2 \end{pmatrix}, \quad g_2 = \begin{pmatrix} 1 & 2 & 3 \\ 3 & 2 & 1 \end{pmatrix}$$

$$g_3 = \begin{pmatrix} 1 & 2 & 3 \\ 2 & 1 & 3 \end{pmatrix}$$

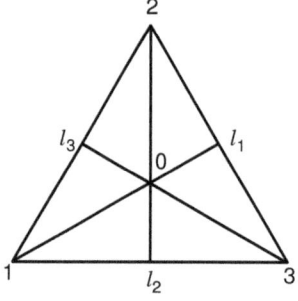 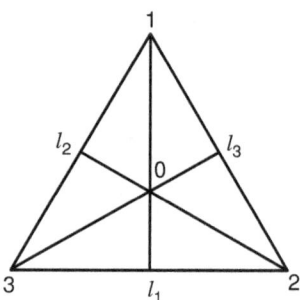

Fig. 10.10 Fig. 10.11

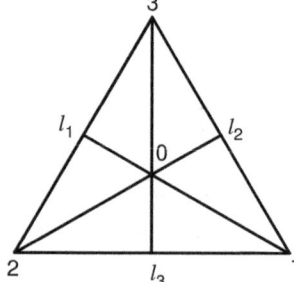

Fig. 10.12

We denote the set of all these permutations by $S_3 = \{f_0, f_1, f_2, g_1, g_2, g_3\}$. S_3 is a non-abelian group of order 6, under composition $\cdot$, with f_1 as the identity element.

$\cdot$	f_0	f_1	f_2	g_1	g_2	g_3
f_0	f_0	f_1	f_2	g_1	g_2	g_3
f_1	f_1	f_2	f_0	g_3	g_1	g_2
f_2	f_2	f_0	f_1	g_2	g_3	g_1
g_1	g_1	g_2	g_3	f_0	f_1	f_2
g_2	g_2	g_3	g_1	f_2	f_0	f_1
g_3	g_3	g_1	g_2	f_1	f_2	f_0

Group table of S_3

(viii) If $(G, *)$ and $(G', *')$ are groups then $(G \times G', \cdot)$ is a group with group operation defined by

$$(a_1, b_1) \cdot (a_2, b_2) = (a_1 * a_2, b_1 *' b_2),$$ called as the **product** group.

The following is an example of a product group.

Let $G = G' = Z_2$. For simplicity of notation, let us denote the equivalence class [0] by $\bar{0}$ and [1] by $\bar{1}$. Then the multiplication table for the product group $Z_2 \times Z_2$ is given below.

$\cdot$	$(\bar{0}, \bar{0})$	$(\bar{1}, \bar{0})$	$(\bar{0}, \bar{1})$	$(\bar{1}, \bar{1})$
$(\bar{0}, \bar{0})$	$(\bar{0}, \bar{0})$	$(\bar{1}, \bar{0})$	$(\bar{0}, \bar{1})$	$(\bar{1}, \bar{1})$
$(\bar{1}, \bar{0})$	$(\bar{1}, \bar{0})$	$(\bar{0}, \bar{0})$	$(\bar{1}, \bar{1})$	$(\bar{0}, \bar{1})$
$(\bar{0}, \bar{1})$	$(\bar{0}, \bar{1})$	$(\bar{1}, \bar{1})$	$(\bar{0}, \bar{0})$	$(\bar{1}, \bar{0})$
$(\bar{1}, \bar{1})$	$(\bar{1}, \bar{1})$	$(\bar{0}, \bar{1})$	$(\bar{1}, \bar{0})$	$(\bar{0}, \bar{0})$

10.4.2 Definition

Let $(G, *)$ be a group. The order of G is the cardinality of G, denoted by $|G|$.

Examples:

(i) The group $(Z, +)$ is of infinite order.

(ii) The group $(Z_m, +)$ is of finite order viz. m.

10.4.3 Definition

Let (G, *) be a group. Let a ∈ G. The order of a is the **smallest** positive integer n such that $a * a * \ldots * a = a^n = e$. If no such value of n exists for a, then a is said to be of infinite order.

Examples:
  (i) In (Z, +), every number n ≠ 0 is of infinite order.
  (ii) In (Z_4, +), order of [1] is 4, order of [2] is 2, order of [3] is 4.

10.5 Basic Properties of a Group

1. Uniqueness of Identity and Inverse

Let (G, *) be a group, then

Identity element e of G is unique.

(ii) Every element x ∈ G has a unique inverse x^{-1} in G.

Proof:

Suppose there exists an element e' is G, with the same property as x.

Then $x * e' * e' * x = x$, for all x ∈ G.

In particular, for x = e, we have $e * e' = e' * e = e'$. But since e is also an identity,

$$e * e' = e^1 * e = e.$$

Hence e = e'.

Let an element y ∈ G, such that for all x ∈ G, $x * y = y * x = e$ premultiplying by x^{-1}, we have $x^{-1} * (x * y) = x^{-1} * (y * x) = x^{-1} * e = x^{-1}$.

Using the associativity of *, we have $(x^{-1} * x) * y = x^{-1}$ which implies $y = x^{-1}$.

Cancellation Laws:

10.5.1 Theorem

(i) **Left cancellation law:** For a ∈ G, $a * x = a * y$ implies x = y ; and

(ii) **Right cancellation law:** For a ∈ G, $x * a = y * a$ implies x = y.

  Proof: Left as an exercise.

10.6 Cyclic Group

A group (G, *) is said to be a cyclic group if there exists an element a ∈ G such that every element of G can be written as some power of a, viz a^k, for some integer k. By a^k, we mean $a * a * a \ldots * a$ (k times). We then say that G is generated by a or a is a generator of G.

A cyclic group is abelian, since for any two elements $a^r, a^s \in G$, $a^r * a^s = a^{r+s} = a^{s+r} = a^s * a^r$.

Examples:
  (i) The group $(Z_2, +)$ is cyclic generated by the equivalence class [1].
  In general, the group $(Z_m, +)$ is a cyclic group of order m, generated by [1].
  (ii) Let S be the unit circle and let ρ_0 be a rotation of the circle through an angle $2\pi/n$. Then the set of rotations $\{\rho_0, \rho_0^2, \rho_0^3, ..., \rho_n^n\}$ forms a cyclic group of order n, under the operation composition of functions.

The following theorem is significant, as it describes, completely, the structure of finite cyclic groups.

10.6.1 Theorem

Let G be a cyclic group of order n. Then n is the smallest positive integer such that $a^n = e$, where a is a generator of G.
Proof:
Consider the subset $\{a, a^2, ...\}$ of G. Since G is finite, the power of a must terminate at some stage.   Hence there exists positive integers r and s such that $a^r = a^s$.   Assume $r > s$. Then $a^{(r-s)} = e$.   Since there exists atleast (at least) one element with this property, choose m least such that $a^m = e$.   Now $m \leq n$, since otherwise order of g is greater than n.   We shall show m = n.   Suppose m < n.   Then for any k such that $m < k \leq n$, by division algorithm $k = pm + q$, where $0 \leq q < m$.   Then $a^k = a^{pm+q} = (a^p)^m * a^q = a^q$.   Since $q < m$, $a^q \in \{a, a^2, ..., a^m\}$.   Since a is a generator for G, this means $G \subset \{a, a^2, ..., a^m\}$, which is absurd.   Hence m < n and therefore m = n.

10.7 Subgroups

Subgroups are subsets of a group G, which inherit the group structure of G.

10.7.1 Definition

Let H be a non-empty subset of a group G. Then H is said to be a **subgroup** of (G, *) if H is itself a group under *.

The singleton set {e} is a subgroup of G.

The following theorem gives necessary and sufficient conditions for a subset to be a subgroup.

10.7.2 Theorem

A non-empty subset H of (G, *) is a subgroup iff

a, b ∈ H implies a * b ∈ H, i.e. H is closed under *.

(ii) a ∈ H implies a^{-1} ∈ H.

Proof:

Let H be a subgroup of G, then (i) and (ii) are satisfied.

Conversely, let conditions (i) and (ii) hold.

We have to show that H satisfies the group axioms.

For a, b, c ∈ H, a * (b * c) = (a * b) * c holds for G and hence for H.

Hence the associative law holds for H.

Also by condition (ii) every element in H has an inverse in H.

It remains to show that the identity element e ∈ H.

Now by condition (ii) a ∈ H implies a^{-1} ∈ H.

Hence a * a^{-1} = a^{-1} * a = e ∈ H, by condition (i).

Thus the theorem is proved.

For a finite group however, condition (ii) becomes redundant as proved in the following theorem.

10.7.3 Theorem

If H is a non-empty finite subset of a group G and H is closed under multiplication, then H is a subgroup of G.

Proof:

It is enough to show by Theorem 8.9.12 that whenever a ∈ H, a^{-1} ∈ H.

Suppose a ∈ H, then $a^2, a^3, \ldots, a^m$ ∈ H, as H is closed under *.

This means that the infinite set $\{a, a^2, ..., a^m, ...\}$ is a subset of H, which is finite.

This is possible only if the elements are repeated.

Hence for some s, t, s > t, $a^s = a^t$.

By cancellation law, this implies $a^{s-t} = e$.

Hence e ∈ H.

Since s–t–1 ≥ 0, a^{s-t-1} ∈ H and $a^{-1} = a^{s-t-1}$, as $a * a^{s-t-1} = a^{s-t} = e$.

Thus a^{-1} ∈ H, it is proved.

Examples:
(i) For a positive integer n, let H = nZ = {nx | x ∈ Z}. Then (H, +) is a subgroup of (Z, +).
(ii) Let H = {[0], [4]} in (Z_8, +). H is then a subgroup of Z_8.
(iii) Let G be the group of all 2 × 2 matrices $\begin{pmatrix} a & b \\ c & d \end{pmatrix}$ with ad − bc ≠ 0, under matrix multiplication. Let H = $\left\{ \begin{pmatrix} a & b \\ c & d \end{pmatrix}, ad \neq 0 \right\}$. H is then a subgroup of G.
(iv) Let G be the group of all non-zero complex numbers a + ib (a, b real) under multiplication. Let H = {a + ib | $a^2 + b^2 = 1$}. Then H is a subgroup of G.

10.8 Cosets

In this section, we shall see that a subgroup H defines an equivalence relation on a group G, so that G is partitioned into equivalence classes called as cosets.

10.8.1 Definition

Let (G, *) be a group and let H be a subgroup of G. For a, b ∈ G, we say a is congruent to b modulo H, written as a + b mod H, if $a * b^{-1}$ ∈ H. One can easily see that the congruence relation is an equivalence relation on G. It therefore partitions G into equivalence classes called as **cosets** of H. The set of these equivalence classes is also called as the **quotient** set of G by H.

10.8.2 Definition

Let H be a subgroup of a group (G, *). For a ∈ G, define
$$Ha = \{ h * a \mid h \in H \}.$$ Then Ha is called a **right coset** of H in G.

> Similarly, $aH = \{ a * h \mid h \in H \}$ is called a left coset of H in G.
>
> a is called as the representative element of the coset aH or Ha. If $a \in H$, then $Ha = aH = H$.

Again one can easily show that the cosets are precisely the equivalence classes formed through the congruence relation.

Hence the right cosets of H in G partition G into disjoint subsets. Likewise, the left cosets of H in G yield a partition of G into disjoint subsets.

The concept of cosets as equivalence classes leads to the following theorem, known as Lagrange's theorem, which gives an important relationship between a group and its subgroup.

10.8.3 Theorem (Lagrange)

> The order of a subgroup of a finite order divides the order of the group.
>
> **Proof:**
>
> Let (G, *) be a finite group of order n and let H be a subgroup of G of order m.
>
> Consider a right coset Ha $a \in G$. If $a \in H$, then Ha = H, which means that number of elements in Ha is the same as the order of H, which means that m/n.
>
> Next let $a \in G$ but $a \notin H$.
>
> Then for any two distinct elements $h_1, h_2 \in H$, $h_1 * a \neq h_2 * a$.
>
> Hence distinct elements in Ha correspond to distinct elements in H and vice versa.
>
> This means that each right (left) coset contains exactly m elements.
>
> Since the right (left) cosets partition G into disjoint subsets, each containing m elements, it follows that since order of G is n, we must have n/m cosets.
>
> This proves that m divides n.

10.8.4 Remarks

From Lagrange's theorem, we deduce the following:

(i) Any group of prime order has only the trivial group {e} as its proper subgroup.

(ii) Consider the permutation group $(S_3, 0)$ described in article 10.6.2, (Example vii) S_3 has subgroups of order 3 and order 2.

Finding these subgroups is left as an exercise.

10.9 Normal Sub-groups

We have seen that a subgroup H of G induces an equivalence relation on G, so that G can be partitioned into equivalence classes. Our aim now, is to impose a group structure on the set of equivalence classes, so as to form the quotient group. For this, we must first define the product of two equivalence classes, so that this product is compatible with the group operation on G.

Let H be a subgroup of G, and let Ha, Hb be right cosets of H in G. We want to define Ha * Hb.

A natural way, that suggests itself is Ha * Hb = Hab. However, this definition makes sense only if Ha = aH. Then for $h_1, h_2 \in H$, $(h_1 * a) * (h_2 * b) = h_1 * h_3 * a * b \in$ Hab.

Hence subgroups in which the right and left cosets are one and the same form an important class of subgroups called as normal subgroups. More formally, we have the following definition of a normal subgroup.

10.9.1 Definition

A subgroup H of G is said to be a **normal** subgroup of G if for every $a \in G$, aH = Ha.

Examples:
   (i) A subgroup of an abelian group is normal. For example, nZ is normal in Z (n > 0).
   (ii) Consider the symmetric group $(S_3, 0)$, described in article 10.6.2 (Ex. vii). Then H = $\{f_0, g_2\}$ is a subgroup of S_3. But H is not normal in S_3. Consider f_1 H = $\{f_1, g_1\}$. But Hf_1 = $\{f_1, g_3\}$ since $f_1 H \neq H f_1$, it follows that H is not normal in S_3.

However consider K = $\{f_0, f_1, f_2\}$. Note that $f_2 = f_1^2$, so that K = $\{f_0, f_1, f_1^2\}$. One can show that every right coset of K in G is equal to a left coset of K is G and vice versa. Hence k is normal in G.

10.10 Quotient group

Let N be a normal subgroup of G. Then G/N is the set of cosets of N in G.

For two coset elements g_1 N, g_2 N $\in$ G/N define an operation * on G/N as g_1 N * g_2 N = (g_1*g_2) N. Note that the operation * on G/N is induced by the operation * in G. (We use the same symbol for both the operations).

With this operation, G/N is a group, with identity element eN. The inverse of each element g_1 N is naturally g_1^{-1} N. The other group axioms, one can easily verify.

10.11 Homomorphism of Groups

While discussing quotient group, we have implicitly related elements of G and G/H by associating g with g = gH.

In other words, we have defined a function $\phi: G \to G/H$ where

$$\phi(g) = gH.$$

Note that $\phi(g_1 * g_2) = \phi(g_1) *' \phi(g_2)$.

A function characterised by this property is defined below.

10.11.1 Definition

Let $(G, *)$ and $(G', *')$ be two semigroups, then a function $\phi: (G, *) \to (G', *')$ is called a homomorphism of G and G' if for every $a, b \in G$, $\phi(a * b) = \phi(a) *' \phi(b)$.

In particular if G and G' are groups, then ϕ is called a group homomorphism.

We have the following theorem which shows that under a group homomorphism, identity is mapped onto identity, and inverse onto inverse.

10.11.2 Theorem

Let ϕ be a homomorphism of G into G', where G and G' are groups. Then
  (i) $\phi(e) = e'$ is the identity element of G'.
  (ii) $\phi(g^{-1}) = \phi(g)^{-1}$, for all $g \in G$.

Proof:

For any $g \in G$.
$\phi(g) *' e' = \phi(g) *' \phi(e)$
$= \phi(g * e) = \phi(e * g) = \phi(g)$.
Similarly one can prove $e' *' \phi(g) = \phi(g)$.
Hence e' is the identity element of G'.
(ii) For any $g \in G$, $\phi(g) *' \phi(g^{-1})$
$= \phi(g * g^{-1}) = \phi(e) = e'$.
Similarly one can prove $\phi(g^{-1}) *' \phi(g) = e'$.
Hence $\phi(g^{-1}) = (\phi(g))^{-1}$

10.11.3 Definition

> Let $\phi: G \to G'$ be a homomorphism of semigroups (or groups). Then ϕ is called an **isomorphism** if ϕ is one-one and onto (i.e. injective as well as surjective).
> If $G' = G$, then ϕ is called an automorphism.

Examples:

The homomorphism $\phi: Z \to Z$ such that $\phi(n) = -n$ is an automorphism of the group $(Z, +)$.

(i) Define $\phi: Z \to Z_m$, where $\phi(n) = [n]$. Then ϕ is a homomorphism of groups $(Z, +)$ and $(Z_m, +)$.

(ii) The mapping $\pi: Z \to Z |_{mZ}$, where $\pi(n) = $ coset $n + mZ$ is a homomorphism.

(iii) The following example plays an important role in the transmission of information in coded form, in coding theory.

Consider $\phi: Z_2 \times Z_2 \to Z_2 \times Z_2 \times Z_2$ given by $\phi(a, b) = (a, b, a + b)$.

Note that $\phi(0, 0) = (0, 0, 0)$, $\phi(1, 0) = (1, 0, 1)$, $\phi(0, 1) = (0, 1, 1)$, $\phi(1, 1) = (1, 1, 0)$. Clearly ϕ is one-one and onto. Hence ϕ is an isomorphism.

(iv) Let $Z_5^* = Z_5 - \{0\}$. Then Z_5^* is a group under multiplication.

Consider the group $(Z_4, +)$ and define a mapping $\phi: (Z_4, +) \to (Z_5^*, \times)$ as $\phi([0]) = [1]$, $\phi([1]) = [2]$, $\phi([3]) = [3]$, $\phi([2]) = [4]$.

Obviously, ϕ is one-one and onto mapping. One can also verify that ϕ is a homomorphism, by the following method:

Consider the group tables of $(Z_4, +)$ and $(Z_5^*, \times)$.

$(Z_4, +)$

+	[0]	[1]	[2]	[3]
[0]	[0]	[1]	[2]	[3]
[1]	[1]	[2]	[3]	[0]
[2]	[2]	[3]	[0]	[1]
[3]	[3]	[0]	[1]	[2]

$(Z_5^*, \times)$

×	[1]	[2]	[3]	[4]
[1]	[1]	[2]	[3]	[4]
[2]	[2]	[4]	[1]	[3]
[3]	[3]	[1]	[4]	[2]
[4]	[4]	[3]	[2]	[1]

In $(Z_4, +)$ replace [0] by [1], [1] by [2], [2] by [4] and rewrite the table as

+	[1]	[2]	[4]	[3]
[1]	[1]	[2]	[4]	[3]
[2]	[2]	[4]	[3]	[1]
[4]	[4]	[3]	[1]	[2]
[3]	[3]	[1]	[2]	[4]

Then change + to × and rearrange the rows and columns, so that we obtain

×	[1]	[2]	[3]	[4]
[1]	[1]	[2]	[3]	[4]
[2]	[2]	[4]	[1]	[3]
[4]	[3]	[1]	[4]	[2]
[3]	[4]	[3]	[2]	[1]

This table is same as $(Z_5^*, \times)$. Hence it follows that $(Z_5^*, \times)$ is isomorphic to $(Z_4, +)$.

(v) Let (A, *) be the semigroup whose table of operation is given below.

*	a	b	c	d
a	a	b	c	d
b	b	a	a	c
c	b	d	d	c
d	a	b	c	d

Then the function f: A → A given by

$$f(a) = d$$
$$f(b) = c$$
$$f(c) = b$$
$$f(d) = a.$$

is an automorphism of (A, *). f is one-one and onto and one can verify that for any elements x, y ∈ A, f(x * y) = f(x) * f(y).

For example f(a * b) = f(b) = c by definition of f, and also f(a) * f(b) = d * c = c.

Hence f(a * b) = f(a) * f(b).

SOLVED EXAMPLES

Example 1: In each of the following determine whether the set together with the binary operation is a group. If it is a group, determine if it is abelian, specify the identity and inverse of an element a.

    (i)   Z, where * is ordinary multiplication.

    (ii)   Z, where * is subtraction.

    (iii)   Q, the set of all rational numbers under the operation of addition.

    (iv)   Q, the set of all rational numbers under the operation of multiplication.

    (v)   R, under the operation of multiplication.

Solution: (i) (Z, *) is not a group since the inverses of elements of Z do not exist in Z.

    (ii)   * is not associative, hence (Z, *) is not a group.

    (iii)   (Q, +) is an abelian group, with 0 as the identity element.

(iv) $(Q, \times)$ is not a group since the element 0 does not possess an inverse.

(v) $(R, \times)$ is not a group, since the element 0 does not possess an inverse.

Example 2: Let A = {a, b, c, d} be a group under the operation $*$ defined in the table given below. Find the identity element of the group and find the inverse of each element in the group. Solve the equation $b * x = d$.

*	a	b	c	d
a	c	d	a	b
b	d	a	b	c
c	a	b	c	d
d	b	c	d	a

Solution: Identity element is c, since $a * c = c * a = a$, $b * c = c * b = b$, $c * c = c$, $d * c = c * d = d$.

Since $a * a = c$ a is the inverse of itself. $b * d = c = d * b$. Hence inverse of b is d, and inverse of d is b. Since $b * a = d$, $x = a$.

Example 3: Solve the following equations in $(Z_{12}, +)$

(i) $[5] + x = [2]$, (ii) $[7] + x = [5]$.

Solution: $Z_{12} = \{[0], [1], [2], ..., [11]\}$ identity element is the equivalence class $[0]$.

(i) $\quad\quad\quad\quad [5] + x = [2]$

$\Rightarrow \quad\quad\quad [5] + x = [14]$, since for any element $[y] \in Z_{12} > [y] = [y + 12]$

$\therefore \quad\quad\quad\quad x = [14] - [5] = [9]$

(ii) $\quad\quad\quad [7] + x = [5]$

$\Rightarrow \quad\quad\quad [7] + x = [17]$

$\Rightarrow \quad\quad\quad\quad x = [17 - 7] = [10]$

Example 4: Find the order and inverse of each element in $(Z_{12}, +)$.

Solution: The following table gives the elements and their inverses.

Element	Inverse
[0]	[0]
[1]	[11]
[2]	[10]
[3]	[9]
[4]	[8]
[5]	[7]
[6]	[6]

The following table gives the elements and their orders.

Element	Order of the element
[0]	1
[1]	12
[2]	6
[3]	4
[4]	3
[5]	12
[6]	2
[7]	12
[8]	3
[9]	4
[10]	6
[11]	12

Example 5: Let $(A, *)$ be a monoid such that for every x in A, $x * x = e$, where e is the identity element. Show that $(A, *)$ is an abelian group.

Solution: Since $x * x = e$, for all $x \in A$, every element is its own in inverse in A. Hence $(A, *)$ is a group. Let $a, b \in A$.

Consider $(a * b) * (b * a) = a * (b * b) * a = a * e * a = a * a = e$.

Similarly, $(b * a) * (a * b) = e$.

Hence $b * a$ is the inverse of $a * b$. Since a group has unique inverse, it follows that
$$a * b = b * a.$$

Example 6: Let $(A, *)$ be a group. Show that $(A, *)$ is an abelian group if and only if $a^2 * b^2 = (a * b)^2$.

Solutison: Let $(A, *)$ be an abelian group. Then $a * b = b * a$, for all $a, b \in A$.

Hence
$$\begin{align} a^2 * b^2 &= (a * a) * (b * b) \\ &= a * (a * b) * b && (\text{$*$ is associative}) \\ &= a * (b * a) * b && (\text{$*$ is commutative}) \\ &= (a * b) * (a * b) \\ &= (a * b)^2 \end{align}$$

Conversely, let $a^2 * b^2 = (a * b)^2$.

To show A is abelian we have
$$a * (a * b) * b = (a * b) * (a * b)$$
$$= a * (b * a) * b \qquad \ldots (1)$$

premultiply (1) by a^{-1} and postmultiply by b^{-1}. Then
$$(a^{-1} * a) * (a * b) * (b * b^{-1}) = (a^{-1} * a) * (b * a) * (b * b^{-1})$$
$$\Rightarrow e * (a * b) * e = e * (b * a) * e$$
$$\Rightarrow a * b = b * a, \quad \text{for all } a, b \in A.$$

Hence (A, *) is an abelian group.

Example 7: Let G be a finite group with identity e, and let a be an arbitrary element of G. Prove that there exists a non-negative integer n such that $a^n = e$.

Solution: Let $|G| = m$, and $a \in G$. Consider $a, a^2, a^3, \ldots, a^m, a^{m+1}$. There are $m + 1$ elements. But since $|G| = m$, this means that $a^{m+1} = a^k$ ($1 \le k \le m$).

Hence it follows that $a^{m+1-k} = e$. Putting $n = m + 1 - k$, we obtain $a^n = e$.

Example 8: Let $(Z^+, \cdot)$ denote the group of positive integers under multiplication $\cdot$, and let $H = \{3^k \mid k \in Z\}$. Is H a subgroup of $(Z^+, \cdot)$?

Solution: First we have to show H is closed under $\cdot$. Let $3^{k_1}, 3^{k_2} \in H$.

Then $3^{k_1} \cdot 3^{k_2} = 3^{k_1 + k_2} \in H$. Hence H is closed under $\cdot$.

Next let $3^{k_1} \in H$. Then by definition 3^{-k_1} is also in H. Hence H is a subgroup of $(Z^+, \cdot)$.

Example 9: Let G be an abelian group with identity e and let $H = \{x \mid x^2 = e\}$. Show that H is a subgroup of G.

Solution: Let $x, y \in H$, then $x^2 = e, y^2 = e$. Consider $(xy)^2 = (xy)(yx) = x^2 y^2 = e$ using the fact that G is abelian. Hence H is closed under the group operation. By definition of H, every element x of H is its own inverse. Hence H is a subgroup.

Example 10: Let G be a group with identity e. Show that the function $f: G \to G$ defined by $f(a) = e$, for all $a \in G$, is a homomorphism.

Solution: We have to show that for all $a, b \in G$, $f(a * b) = f(a) * f(b)$.

Now $\quad f(a * b) = e.$
Also $\quad f(a) * f(b) = e * e = e.$

Hence f is a homomorphism.

Example 11: Let G be a group. Show that the function $f: G \to G$, defined by $f(a) = a^2$ is a homomorphism iff G is abelian.

Solution: Let G be abelian, and let a, b ∈ G.
Then
$$f(ab) = (ab)^2 = abab$$
$$= aabb = a^2 b^2 = f(a) \cdot f(b).$$
Hence if G is abelian, f is a homomorphism.
Conversely, let f be a homomorphism. We have to show G is abelian.
Let a, b ∈ G.
$$f(ab) = f(a) \, f(b)$$
$$(ab)^2 = a^2 b^2$$
$$\Rightarrow \quad abab = aabb. \text{ Premultiply this equation by } a^{-1} \text{ and } b^{-1}.$$
Then $\quad a^{-1} ababb^{-1} = a^{-1} aabbb^{-1}$
$$\Rightarrow \quad ebae = eabe$$
$$\Rightarrow \quad ba = ab, \text{ i.e. G is abelian.}$$

Example 12: Let G = {e, a, a², a³, a⁴, a⁵} be a group under the operation of $a^i \, a^j = a^r$, where i + j = r (mod 6). Prove that G and Z_6 are isomorphic.

Solution: $\quad Z_6 = \{[0], [1], [2], [3], [4], [5]\}$,
Define f: G → Z_6 as follows
$$e \to [0]$$
$$[1] \to [a]$$
$$[2] \to [a^2]$$
$$[3] \to [a^3]$$
$$[4] \to [a^4]$$
$$[5] \to [a^5].$$
∴ $f([i] + [j]) = a^r$, where i + j = r (mod 6)
f is clearly an isomorphism.

Example 13: Find the subgroup of (Z_4, +) generated by [2]. Subgroup generated by [3] ?
Solution: Subgroup H_1 = {[2], [0]}.
$$H_2 = \{[3], [2], [1], [0]\} = Z_4$$

Example 14: Find the right cosets of {[0], [3], [6], [9]} of (Z_{12}, +).
Solution: H = {[0], [3], [6], [9]}
We obtain the following distinct right cosets
$$H_0 = \{[0], [3], [6], [9]\}$$
$$H_1 = \{[1], [4], [7], [10]\}$$

$$H_2 = \{[3], [6], [9], [0]\}$$
$$H_3 = \{[5], [8], [11], [2]\}$$
$$H_4 = \{[6], [9], [0], [3]\}$$
$$H_6 = \{[8], [11], [2], [5]\}$$
$$H_7 = \{[9], [0], [3], [6]\}$$
$$H_8 = \{[11], [2], [5], [8]\}$$

Example 15: The set $H = \{f_0, f_1, f_2\}$ is a subgroup of $(S_3, 0)$. Find the left coset of H. (Refer to article 10.6.2, Ex. vii).

Solution:
$$f_0 = \begin{pmatrix} 1 & 2 & 3 \\ 1 & 2 & 3 \end{pmatrix}, \quad f_1 = \begin{pmatrix} 1 & 2 & 3 \\ 2 & 3 & 1 \end{pmatrix},$$

$$f_2 = \begin{pmatrix} 1 & 2 & 3 \\ 3 & 1 & 2 \end{pmatrix}, \quad g_1 = \begin{pmatrix} 1 & 2 & 3 \\ 1 & 3 & 2 \end{pmatrix}, \quad g_2 = \begin{pmatrix} 1 & 2 & 3 \\ 3 & 2 & 1 \end{pmatrix}$$

$$g_3 = \begin{pmatrix} 1 & 2 & 3 \\ 2 & 1 & 3 \end{pmatrix}$$

$$g_1 H = \{g_1, g_2, g_3\}$$
$$g_2 H = \{g_2, g_3, g_1\}$$
$$g_3 H = \{g_3, g_1, g_2\}$$

Example 16: Find the subgroups of
(i) Z_8 (ii) $Z_2 \times Z_2$

Solution: (i) The group table for Z_8 under addition is given below:

+	$\bar{0}$	$\bar{1}$	$\bar{2}$	$\bar{3}$	$\bar{4}$	$\bar{5}$	$\bar{6}$	$\bar{7}$
$\bar{0}$	$\bar{0}$	$\bar{1}$	$\bar{2}$	$\bar{3}$	$\bar{4}$	$\bar{5}$	$\bar{6}$	$\bar{7}$
$\bar{1}$	$\bar{1}$	$\bar{2}$	$\bar{3}$	$\bar{4}$	$\bar{5}$	$\bar{6}$	$\bar{7}$	$\bar{0}$
$\bar{2}$	$\bar{2}$	$\bar{3}$	$\bar{4}$	$\bar{5}$	$\bar{6}$	$\bar{7}$	$\bar{0}$	$\bar{1}$
$\bar{3}$	$\bar{3}$	$\bar{4}$	$\bar{5}$	$\bar{6}$	$\bar{7}$	$\bar{0}$	$\bar{1}$	$\bar{2}$
$\bar{4}$	$\bar{4}$	$\bar{5}$	$\bar{6}$	$\bar{7}$	$\bar{0}$	$\bar{1}$	$\bar{2}$	$\bar{3}$
$\bar{5}$	$\bar{5}$	$\bar{6}$	$\bar{7}$	$\bar{0}$	$\bar{1}$	$\bar{2}$	$\bar{3}$	$\bar{4}$
$\bar{6}$	$\bar{6}$	$\bar{7}$	$\bar{0}$	$\bar{1}$	$\bar{2}$	$\bar{3}$	$\bar{4}$	$\bar{5}$
$\bar{7}$	$\bar{7}$	$\bar{0}$	$\bar{1}$	$\bar{2}$	$\bar{3}$	$\bar{4}$	$\bar{5}$	$\bar{6}$

The following are the subgroups of $(Z_8, +)$

$$H_1 = \{\bar{0}, \bar{2}, \bar{4}, \bar{6}\} \text{ and}$$

$$H_2 = \{\bar{0}, \bar{4}\}$$

H_1 and H_2 are closed under group operation. (cf. Theorem 10.7.3).

(ii) The group table for $(Z_2 \times Z_2, +)$ is given below:

+	$(\bar{0},\bar{0})$	$(\bar{1},\bar{0})$	$(\bar{0},\bar{1})$	$(\bar{1},\bar{1})$
$(\bar{0},\bar{0})$	$(\bar{0},\bar{0})$	$(\bar{1},\bar{0})$	$(\bar{0},\bar{1})$	$(\bar{1},\bar{1})$
$(\bar{1},\bar{0})$	$(\bar{1},\bar{0})$	$(\bar{0},\bar{0})$	$(\bar{1},\bar{1})$	$(\bar{0},\bar{1})$
$(\bar{0},\bar{1})$	$(\bar{0},\bar{1})$	$(\bar{1},\bar{1})$	$(\bar{0},\bar{0})$	$(\bar{1},\bar{0})$
$(\bar{1},\bar{1})$	$(\bar{1},\bar{1})$	$(\bar{0},\bar{1})$	$(\bar{1},\bar{0})$	$(\bar{0},\bar{0})$

The following are subgroups of $Z_2 \times Z_2$

$$H_1 = \{(\bar{0},\bar{0}), (\bar{0},\bar{1})\}$$

$$H_2 = \{(\bar{0},\bar{0}), (\bar{1},\bar{0})\}$$

$$H_3 = \{(\bar{0},\bar{0}), (\bar{1},\bar{1})\}$$

One can verify that H_1, H_2, H_3 are all closed under group operation. (cf. Theorem 10.7.3).

Example 17: Let G be a group; for a fixed element G, let $G_x = \{a \in G: ax = xa\}$. Show that G_x is a subgroup of G for all $x \in G$.

Solution: One of the conditions for G_x to be a subgroup is that G_x should be closed under multiplication. Let $a, b \in G_x$, we have to prove that $ab \in G_x$. Now $ax = xa$, $bx = xb$.

∴ $\quad\quad\quad\quad (ab) x = a (bx)$

$\quad\quad\quad\quad\quad\quad\quad = a (xb) = (ax) (b) = (xa) (b)$

$\quad\quad\quad\quad\quad\quad\quad = x (ab)$.

Also it is clear that $e \in G_x$. It only remains to show that $x^{-1} \in G_x$. For this consider
$e = a \Rightarrow x^{-1} (xa) = a \Rightarrow x^{-1} (ax) = a \Rightarrow (x^{-1}a) (xx^{-1}) = ax^{-1}$.

i.e. $\quad\quad\quad (x^{-1}a) (e) = x^{-1}a = ax^{-1}$

Hence, G_x is a subgroup of G.

Example 18: G is a group and there exists two relatively prime positive integers m and n such that $a^m b^m = b^m a^m$ and $a^n b^n = b^n a^n$ for all $a, b \in G$. Prove that G is abelian.

Solution: Since m and n are relatively prime, there exist integers p, q such that $mp + nq = 1$.
First we shall show that, $\forall\ a, b \in G$.

$$(a^m b^n)^{pm} = (b^n a^m)^{pm}\ \text{and}$$

Similarly, $(a^m b^n)^{2n} = (b^n a^m)^{2n}$

Note that:
$$(a^m b^n)^{pm} = a^m (b^n a^m)(b^n a^m) \ldots (b^n a^m) b^n \quad (pm - 1)\ \text{times}$$
$$= a^m (b^n a^m)^{pm-1} \cdot b^n$$
$$= a^m (b^n a^m)^{pm} (b^n a^m)^{-1} \cdot b^n$$
$$= a^m (b^m a^m)^{pm} a^{-m} b^{-n} \cdot b^n$$
$$= (b^n a^m)^{pm} a^m a^{-m} \quad (\because a^m b^m = b^m a^m,\ \forall\ a, b \in G).$$

Similarly, $(a^m b^n)^{qn} = (b^n a^m)^{qn}$

$\therefore$
$$a^m b^n = (a^m b^n)^{pm + qn}$$
$$= (a^m b^n)^{pm} (a^m b^n)^{qn}$$
$$= (b^n a^m)^{pm} (b^n a^m)^{qn}$$
$$= (b^n a^m)^{pm + qn} = b^n a^m,\ \forall\ a, b \in G$$

Now consider,
$$ab = a^{pm + qn} b^{pm + qn}$$
$$= a^{pm} \cdot a^{qn} \cdot b^{pm} \cdot b^{qn} = a^{pm}$$
$$= a^{pm} (a^q)^n (b^p)^m b^{qn}$$
$$= a^{pm} b^{pm} a^{qn} b^{qn}$$
$$= b^{pm} a^{pm} b^{qn} a^{qn}$$
$$= b^{pm} b^{qn} a^{pm} a^{qn}$$
$$= (b)^{pm + qn} (a)^{pm + qn}$$
$$= b^1 a^1 = ba$$

Example 19: Show that {1, 2, 3} under multiplication modulo 4 is not a group but that {1, 2, 3, 4} under multiplication modulo 5 is a group.

Solution: Let, $G_1 = \{1, 2, 3\}$. Multiplication Table for G_1 is

X_4	1	2	3
1	1	2	3
2	2	0	2
3	3	2	1

$0 \notin G_1$, closure property is not satisfied, hence G_1 is not a group.

Let $G_2 = \{1, 2, 3, 4\}$

Multiplication Table for G_2 is

X_5	1	2	3	4
1	1	2	3	4
2	2	4	1	3
3	3	1	4	2
4	4	3	2	1

G_2 is closed under multiplication. Multiplication is associative.

For example, $2 \times (3 \times 4) = 2 \times 2 = 4$ and $(2 \times 3) \times 4 = 1 \times 4 = 4$.

The rows and columns when interchanged yield the same elements, so that G_2 is commutative. From table the inverses of 1, 2, 3, 4 are 1, 3, 2, 4 respectively. Hence, G_2 is an abelian group under X_5.

Example 20: Show that $(A, +)$ is a group where $A = \{\ldots -4a, -3a, -2a, 0, a, 2a, 3a, 4a, \ldots\}$.

Solution: $A = \{na \mid n \in Z\}$

(i) $+$ is associative

$$(x + y) + z = (n_1 + n_2)a + n_3 a$$
$$= (n_1 + n_2 + n_3)a$$
$$x + (y + z) = n_1 a + (n_1 a + n_3 a)$$
$$= (n_1 + n_2 + n_3)a$$

(ii) $\quad x + 0 = na + 0 = na = x$

(iii) If $x = na$, $-x = -na$.

$$x + (-x) = (n - n)a = 0a = 0$$

Hence $(A, +)$ is a group.

Example 21: Let G be the set of all non-zero real numbers and let $a * b = \dfrac{ab}{2}$. Show that $(G, *)$ is an abelian group.

Solution: (i) $*$ is associative, since

$$(a * b) * c = \left(\dfrac{ab}{2}\right) * c = \dfrac{abc}{4}$$

$$a * (b * c) = a * \left(\dfrac{bc}{2}\right) = \dfrac{abc}{4}$$

(ii) $e = 2$ since $a * 2 = \dfrac{2a}{2} = a = 2 * a$.

(iii) For each $a \in G$, $a^{-1} = \dfrac{4}{a}$, because $a * a^{-1} = a * \left(\dfrac{4}{a}\right)$

$$= \dfrac{4a}{2a} = 2$$

$$a^{-1} * a = \left(\dfrac{4}{a}\right) * a = \dfrac{4a}{2a} = 2$$

(iv) $\quad a * b = \dfrac{ab}{2} = b * a$, i.e. $*$ is commutative.

Hence, $(G, *)$ is an Abelian group.

Example 22: Consider an algebraic system $(Q, *)$, where Q is set of rational numbers and $*$ is binary operation defined by $a * b = a + b - ab$; $\forall\ a, b \in Q$. Determine whether $(Q, *)$ is a group.

Solution: We have shown that $\forall$ is associative (Refer Ex. 10, Page 10.17). Suppose $(Q, *)$ is a group, let us find the identity element e.

Let $a \neq 1 \in Q$. Then $a * e = a \Rightarrow a + e - ae = a \Rightarrow a(1 - a) = 0 \Rightarrow e = 0$.

Hence the number 0 must be the identity element if $(Q, *)$ where to be a group. Let '1'' be inverse of 1. Then $1 * 1' = 0 \Rightarrow 1 + 1' - 1 \cdot 1' = 0 \Rightarrow 1 + 1' - 1' = 0 \Rightarrow 1 = 0$ observed. Hence the number 1 has no inverse in $(Q, *)$. Hence, $(Q, *)$ is not a group. If we remove 1 from Q, i.e. consider $Q = Q - \{1\}$, then $(Q, *)$ becomes a group with identity element 0 and inverse of every element a, given by $\dfrac{a}{1-a}$.

10.12 Rings, Integral Domains and Fields

10.12.1 Rings

So for we have discussed groups which are algebraic structures with a single binary operation. We now turn our attention to algebraic structures, with two binary operations, called **rings.** We shall denote these binary operations by + and · respectively. In analogy with numbers, + is called addition and · multiplication.

10.12.2 Definition

An algebraic structure $(R, +, \cdot)$ is called a ring if
  (i) $(R, +)$ is an abelian group.
  (ii) Associativity of multiplication holds: $a \cdot (b \cdot c) = (a \cdot b) * c$.

(iii) The left distributive law
$$a \cdot (b + c) = a \cdot b + a \cdot c,$$ and the right distributive law
$$(b + c) \cdot a = b \cdot a + c \cdot a$$ are satisfied by + and $\cdot$.

10.12.3 Definition

A ring R is said to be commutative ring if $a \cdot b = b \cdot a$, for all $a, b \in R$.

10.12.4 Definition

A ring R is said to be a ring with **unit** element if there exists an element, denoted by the symbol 1 such that $a \cdot 1 = 1 \cdot a = a$, for all $a \in R$.

Examples:

(i) $(Z, +, \cdot)$ is a ring, where Z is the set of integers, + and $\cdot$ are the usual addition and multiplication respectively. It is a commutative ring with unit element, the integer 1.

(ii) Z_m, the set of integers modulo m is a commutative ring with unit element (1) under addition and multiplication (modulo m).

(iii) The set of even integers including 0, under addition and multiplication is a commutative ring with no unit element.

(iv) The set of m × m matrices over the real numbers, is a non-commutative ring but with unit element (the identity matrix), under matrix addition and multiplication.

(v) Other common examples are the set of rational, real and complex numbers, which however form a special class of rings called as fields.

For a ring R, we shall denote the additive identity by 0 and the multiplicative unit element by 1.

10.12.5 Basic Properties

If R is a ring with identity 0 and unit element 1, then following are true, for all elements $a, b \in R$.

(i) $a \cdot 0 = 0 \cdot a = 0$.

(ii) $a \cdot (-b) = (-a) \cdot b = -(a \cdot b)$.

(iii) $(-a) \cdot (-b) = a \cdot b$

(iv) unit element is unique

(v) $(-1) \cdot a = -a$
(vi) $(-1) \cdot (-1) = 1$.

Proof:

(i) $a \cdot 0 = a \cdot (0 + 0) = a \cdot 0 + a \cdot 0$ by left distributive law. Hence it follows by cancellation law, $a \cdot 0 = 0$.

(ii) Consider $a \cdot (-b) + a * b = a \cdot (-b + b)$ (left distributive law)
$$= a \cdot 0 = 0$$
Hence by uniqueness of inverse, it follows that
$$a \cdot (-b) = -(a \cdot b)$$
One can prove similarly that
$$(-a) \cdot b = -(a \cdot b)$$

(iii) $(-a) \cdot (-b) = -((-a) \cdot (b))$
$= a \cdot b$. Since $-(-a) = a$.

(iv) Suppose there exists another element $1'$ with the same property of 1, then $1 \cdot 1' = 1' \cdot 1 = 1$, since $1'$ is unit element. Since 1 is also a unit element, $1 \cdot 1' = 1' \cdot 1 = 1'$.

This implies $1 = 1'$, i.e. unit element, if it exists, is unique.

(v) and (vi) follow from (ii) and (iii) respectively.

The above theorem tells us that we can freely compute with negative and 0, as we do in the case of numbers.

Subring: Analogous to the concept of subgroup of a group, we introduce that of a subring in a ring.

10.12.6 Definition

A subset $R \subseteq S$, where $(S_1 +, \cdot)$ is a ring, is called a subring of S if $(R, +, \cdot)$ is a ring with the operations + and $\cdot$ restricted to elements of R.

Examples: (i) The ring of even integers is a subring of the ring of integers. More generally for any positive integer n, the set
$$nZ = \{ nm \mid m \in Z \} \text{ is a subring of } Z.$$

(ii) The set of rationals is a subring of the ring of real numbers.

10.12.7 Ring Homomorphism

Let $(R, +, \cdot)$ and $(S, +', \cdot')$ be rings. A mapping $\phi: R \to S$ is called a **ring homomorphism,** if for any $a, b \in R$.

(i) $\phi(a + b) = \phi(a) +' \phi(b)$

(ii) $\phi(a * b) = \phi(a) *' \phi(b)$.

If ϕ is one-one and onto, it is called as a ring **isomorphism.**

One can easily verify that $\phi(0) = 0'$ and $\phi(-a) = -\phi(a)$, for every $a \in R$.

10.12.8 Definition

Let $(R, +, \times)$ and $(S, +', \psi')$ be rings, with identities 0 and $0'$ respectively. Let $f: R \to S$ be a ring homomorphism. Then **kernel** of f is defined as the set $\{x \in R \mid f(x) = 0'\}$.

We denote kernel of f as ker (f) or ker f.

Example:

Let $R = \left\{ \begin{bmatrix} a & b \\ b & a \end{bmatrix} : a, b \in Z \right\}$. f is the mapping that takes $\begin{bmatrix} a & b \\ b & a \end{bmatrix}$ to $a - b$.

(i) Show that if is a homomorphism.

(ii) Determine the kernel of f.

Solution:

(i) $f\left(\begin{bmatrix} a & b \\ b & a \end{bmatrix} + \begin{bmatrix} c & d \\ d & c \end{bmatrix} \right) = f\left(\begin{bmatrix} a+c & b+d \\ b+d & a+c \end{bmatrix} \right)$

$= (a + c) - (b + d)$

$= (a - b) + (c - d)$

$= f\left(\begin{bmatrix} a & b \\ b & a \end{bmatrix} \right) + f\left(\begin{bmatrix} c & d \\ d & c \end{bmatrix} \right)$

Also $f\left(\begin{bmatrix} a & b \\ b & a \end{bmatrix} \cdot \begin{bmatrix} c & d \\ d & c \end{bmatrix} \right) = f\left(\begin{bmatrix} ac+bd & ad+bc \\ bc+ad & bd+ac \end{bmatrix} \right)$

$= (ac + bd) - (ad + bc)$

$= (ac - bc) + (bd - ad)$

$= (a - b)(c - d)$

$$= f\left(\begin{bmatrix} a & b \\ b & a \end{bmatrix}\right) \cdot f\left(\begin{bmatrix} c & d \\ d & c \end{bmatrix}\right)$$

(ii) $\quad \ker(f) = \left\{ \begin{bmatrix} a & b \\ b & a \end{bmatrix} ; a - b = 0 \right\}$

i.e. $\left\{ \begin{bmatrix} a & a \\ a & a \end{bmatrix} ; a \in Z \right\}$.

Examples:

(i) The mapping $\phi : Z \to Z_n$ defined by $m \to [m]$, is a ring homomorphism.

Similar to the concept of a normal subgroup in groups, we have the concept of an **ideal** in ring R.

10.12.9 Definition

A non-empty set I of a ring R is called an **ideal** in R if

(i) I is a subgroup of R, under addition.

(ii) For every $a \in I$, $a \cdot x = x \cdot a$, for all $x \in R$.

Examples:

(i) If Z is the set of integers, then the set nZ is an ideal in the ring $(Z, +, \cdot)$.

For an ideal I in R, the quotient group R/I becomes a ring in a natural way.

For elements $x + I$, $y + I$ in R/I, we define $(x + I) \cdot (y + I) = xy + I$, $x, y \in R$.

The routine verification of the various ring axioms, is left as an exercise. The ring R/I is called the **quotient ring** of R.

The mapping $\phi: R \to R/I$ defined as $\phi(x) = x + I$ is a ring homomorphism, details to be worked out as an exercise.

10.12.10 Zero Divisors

Let R be a commutative ring. Then $a \neq 0 \in R$ is called a zero divisor if there exists $b \neq 0 \in R$, such that $a * b = 0$.

Examples:

(i) [2] is a zero divisor in $(Z_4, +, \cdot)$, since [2], [2] = [2·2] = [4] = 0.

(ii) In the quotient ring $Z/6Z$, $(2 + 6Z)(3 + 6Z) = 0 + 6Z$.

Hence $2 + 6Z$ and $3 + 6Z$ are zero divisors.

10.12.11 Integral Domains and Fields

Definition:

Let R be a commutative ring. Then R is called an **integral domain** if it has no zero divisors.

10.12.12 Definition

Let R be a commutative ring with unit element. If every non-zero element has a multiplicative inverse, then R is called a field. A field is an integral domain, since if a, b ∈ R, then a · b = 0 implies $(a^{-1} \cdot a) \cdot (b \cdot b^{-1}) = (a^{-1} \cdot 0) \cdot b^{-1} = 0$ which further implies $1 \cdot 1 = 0$, which is not true, since $1 \cdot 1 = 1$.

Examples:

The ring of rational numbers, the ring of real numbers are standard examples of fields, as each non-zero element possesses its multiplicative inverse.

A field is an integral domain. However, not every integral domain is a field. The following theorem tells us which of them are fields.

10.12.13 Theorem

A finite integral domain is a field.

Proof:

Let D be a finite integral domain.

We must show that D possesses the unit element 1 and for every $a \neq 0$ in D, $a^{-1} \in D$.

Since D is finite, let $x_1, x_2, ..., x_n$ be distinct elements of D.

Let $a \neq 0 \in D$.

Then the elements $a \cdot x_1, a \cdot x_2, ..., a \cdot x_n$ are all in D.

We claim that these elements are all distinct.

Suppose not, then $a \cdot x_i = a \cdot x_j$, for $x_i, x_j \in D$.

This means that $a * (x_i - x_j) = 0$.

Since D is an integral domain, this implies $x_i - x_j = 0$, i.e. $x_i = x_j$.

Hence our claim is valid.

Since D contains exactly n elements, we must have $a = a \cdot x_k$ for some $x_k \in D$.

We prove what x_k is the unit element of D. Let $y \in D$.

Then $y = a \cdot x_i$, for some $x_i \in D$. Hence $y \cdot x_k$

$$= (a \cdot x_i) \cdot x_k = x_i * (a \cdot x_k)$$
$$= x_i \cdot a = y.$$

Hence we have shown that D contains a unit element $1 = x_k$.

Since $1 \in D$, $1 = a * x_j$, for some x_j, for any $a \neq 0 \in D$.

Hence every non-zero element has a multiplicative inverse in D.

This completes the proof.

Examples:

Example 1: For any prime p, Z_p is a field.

Example 2: Find the multiplicative inverse of each non-zero element in $(Z_7, +, \cdot)$.

Solution: (1) Table is

×	[1]	[2]	[3]	[4]	[5]	[6]
[1]	[1]	[2]	[3]	[4]	[5]	[6]
[2]	[2]	[4]	[6]	[1]	[3]	[5]
[3]	[3]	[6]	[2]	[5]	[1]	[4]
[4]	[4]	[1]	[5]	[2]	[6]	[3]
[5]	[5]	[3]	[1]	[6]	[4]	[2]
[6]	[6]	[5]	[4]	[3]	[2]	[1]

(2) The elements and their inverses are given below.

Element	Inverse
[1]	[1]
[2]	[4]
[3]	[5]
[4]	[2]
[5]	[3]
[6]	[6]

Example 3: Show that $S = \{a + b\sqrt{2} \; ; a, b \in Z\}$ for the operations $+, \times$ is an integral domain but not a field.

Solution: We have

$$(a + b\sqrt{2}) + (c + d\sqrt{2}) = (a + c) + (b + d)\sqrt{2}$$
$$(a + b\sqrt{2})(c + d\sqrt{2}) = (ac + 2bd) + (bc + ad)\sqrt{2}$$

Clearly S is a commutative ring with unit element 1.

We have to prove S is an integral domain.

Let $(a + b\sqrt{2})(c + d\sqrt{2}) = 0$

This implies

$$ac + 2bd = 0 \qquad \ldots (1)$$

and

$$bc + ad = 0 \qquad \ldots (2)$$

Suppose $a = 0$; then $bd = bc = 0$.

∴ either $b = 0$ or both $d = c = 0$.

Hence, if $a = 0$, $a + b\sqrt{2} = 0$

or $c + d\sqrt{2} = 0$

Assume $a \neq 0$. Multiplying (1) by d gives

$$acd + 2bd^2 = 0 \qquad \ldots (3)$$

From (2), $ad = -bc$

Hence, substituting this in equation (3), we have

$$-bc^2 + 2bd^2 = 0$$

$\Rightarrow \qquad b(2d^2 - c^2) = 0$

∴ $b = 0$ or $c^2 = 2d^2$, i.e. $c = \sqrt{2}\, d$.

Since c is an integer, $c^2 = 2d^2$ is true only if $c = d = 0$.

Hence, if $c^2 \neq 2d^2$, $b = 0$. But $b = 0$ implies $a = 0$.

Hence, in any case either $a + b\sqrt{2} = 0$ or $c + d\sqrt{2} = 0$.

Hence, S is an integral domain.

To show that S is not a field consider the element $2 + \sqrt{2}$. It's multiplicative inverse does not exist in S, for $(2 + \sqrt{2})(c + d\sqrt{2}) = 1$

$\Rightarrow 2c + 2d = 1 \Rightarrow c + d = \dfrac{1}{2}$

Absurd, since $c, d \in Z$.

Example 4: If R is a ring such that $a^2 = a$, $\forall\ a \in R$, prove that

(i) $a + a = 0$, $\forall\ a \in R$.

(ii) R is a commutative ring.

Solution: (i) Let $b = -a$, i.e. inverse of a.

We have to prove $a = b$.

Consider, $a - b = (a - b)(a - b)$

i.e. $a - b = a^2 - ba - ab + b^2$

$= a - ba - ab + b$

$$= (a + b) - ba - ab$$
$$= 0 - ba - ab = -ba - ab \quad \ldots (1)$$

Now, $\quad 0 = a + b = (a + b)(a + b)$
$$= a^2 + ba + ab + b^2$$
$$= a + ba + ab + b$$
$$= (a + b) + ba + ab$$
$$= 0 + ba + ab \quad \ldots (2)$$

∴ $\quad ba + ab = 0$

Hence, $a - b = 0$, i.e. $a = b$.

(ii) We have to prove that R is commutative. For any elements $a, b \in R$,
$$a + b = (a + b)(a + b)$$
$$= a^2 + ba + ab + b^2$$
$$= a + ba + ab + b$$

∴ $\quad ba + ab = 0$

or $\quad ab = -ba$

By (1) every element is its own inverse. Hence, $-ba = ba$.

∴ $ab = ba$, i.e. R is commutative.

EXERCISE - 10.1

1. For each of the following, determine whether the binary operation is associative or commutative.
   (i) on **R**, where $a * b = a\sqrt{b}$
   (ii) on Z^+, where $a * b = ab + 1$
   (iii) on a lattice A, where $a * b = a \vee b$
   (iv) on the set of all $n \times n$ Boolean matrices, under matrix addition.
   (v) on the set of all prime numbers, under multiplication.

2. In each of the following, complete the table, so that the binary operation * is associative.
   (i)

*	a	b	c	d
a	a	b	c	d
b	b	a	d	c
c	c	d	a	b
d	–	–	–	–

(ii)

*	a	b	c	d
a	a	b	c	d
b	b	a	c	d
c	–	–	–	–
d	d	c	c	d

3. Let A be a set with n elements.
   (i) How many binary operations can be defined on A ?
   (ii) How many commutative binary operations can be defined on A ?
4. Let A = {a, b, c}. For each of the binary operation * defined on A, by the corresponding tables, determine whether * is associative or commutative. Determine also whether * has a right or left identity.

   (i)

*	a	b	c
a	b	c	a
b	c	a	b
c	a	b	c

   (ii)

*	a	b	c
a	a	b	c
b	b	b	a
c	a	c	b

5. Let G be a group with identity e. Show that if $x^2 = x$ for some x in G, then x = e.
6. Let G be a group. Show by mathematical induction that if ab = ba, then $(ab)^n = a^n b^n$ for $n \in Z^+$.
7. Let G be a group of integers under the operation of addition and let H = {3k | k ∈ Z}. Is H a subgroup of G ?
8. Let G be a group and let $H = \{x \mid x \in G \text{ and } xy = yx \text{ for all } y \in G\}$. Prove that H is a subgroup of G.
9. If H and K are subgroups of a group G, then show that H ∩ K is also a subgroup. Is H ∪ K a subgroup ?
10. Prove that the function f(x) = |x| is a homomorphism from the group G of non-zero real numbers under multiplication to the group G^e of positive real numbers under multiplication.
11. Is the set {{0}, {3}, {5}} a subgroup in $(Z_6, +)$?
12. Find the subgroup of $(Z_{12}, +)$ generated by the set {[6], [9]}.
13. Find the left cosets of the subgroup {[0], [3], [6], [9]} of $(Z_{12}, +)$.
14. Which elements of $(Z_{12}, +)$ generate a proper cyclic subgroup ?

15. Show that the set H = {0, 4, 8} is a subgroup of $(Z_{12}, +)$. Find its left cosets.
16. Show that if (G, *) is a cyclic group, then every subgroup of (G, *) is cyclic.
17. Let (G, *) be a group of prime order p. Show that G is a cyclic group. Deduce that the groups (G, *) and $(Z_p, +)$ are isomorphic.
18. Which of the following are rings ?
    (i) The set Q^* of positive rational numbers under addition and multiplication.
    (ii) Let p be a prime, and let Q_p be the set of rational numbers of the form $\{x : x = m \mid p^n ..., m \in Z\}$ under addition and multiplication.
    (iii) The subset {[0], [2], [4]} of $(Z_6, +)$.
19. Find all the subgroups of (i) Z_8, (ii) $Z_2 \times Z_2$.
20. Show that in the ring $(Z_6, +)$ both S = {[0], [2], [4]} and T = {[0], [3]} are subrings.
21. Write the operation tables for $(Z_2^2, +, \times)$. Is Z_2^2 a ring, integral domain, field ?
22. Show that the following rings are not isomorphic
    (i) $(3Z, +, \times)$ and $(4Z, +, \times)$.
    (ii) $(Z_2 \times Z_2, +, \cdot)$ and $(Z_4, +, \cdot)$.
23. Prove that $Z_2 \times Z_3$ is a commutative ring with unity. Find all zero divisors of $Z_2 \times Z_3$.
24. We are given the ring ({a, b, c, d}, +, ·) whose operations are given below:

+	a	b	c	d		·	a	b	c	d
a	a	b	c	d		a	a	a	a	a
b	b	c	d	a		b	a	c	a	c
c	c	d	a	b		c	a	a	a	a
d	d	a	b	c		d	a	c	a	a

Is it a commutative ring ? Does it have an identity ? What is the zero of this ring ? Find the additive inverse of each of its elements.

25. Prove that the ring $(Z_5, +, \cdot)$ is a field. Is $(Z_6, + \cdot)$ a field ?
26. Prove that the set of numbers of the form $a + b\sqrt{2}$, where a, b are rational numbers, is a field.
27. Prove that the four matrices
    $\begin{bmatrix} 1 & 0 \\ 0 & 1 \end{bmatrix}, \begin{bmatrix} 0 & 0 \\ 0 & 0 \end{bmatrix}, \begin{bmatrix} 1 & 1 \\ 1 & 0 \end{bmatrix}, \begin{bmatrix} 0 & 1 \\ 1 & 1 \end{bmatrix}$ form a field, where the entries $0, 1 \in Z_2$.
28. Let R = {0°, 60°, 120°, 180°, 240°, 300°} and * = binary operation so that for a and b in R, a * b is overall angular rotation corresponding to successive rotations by a and then by b. Show that (R, *) is group.

29. Let Z_n be the set of integers {0, 1, 2, ..., n – 1}. Let ⊕ be a binary operation on Z_n such that $a \oplus b = \begin{cases} a + b; & \text{if } a + b < n \\ a + b - n; & \text{if } a + b \geq n \end{cases}$

    Let ⊙ be a binary operation on Z_n such that a ⊙ b = the remainder of and divided by n. Show that (Z_n, ⊕) is abelian group and (Z_n, ⊕, ⊙) is a ring.

30. Define homomorphism and normal subgroups with example.

31. Define with example (with respect to group).
    - (i) Isomorphism and Homomorphism
    - (ii) Automorphism.
    - (iii) Group
    - (iv) Permutation group
    - (v) Subgroup
    - (vi) Normal subgroup
    - (vii) Algebraic system with two binary operations

32. Define congruence classes with respect to groups. Define Abelian group. Show that <Z_6, +> is Abelian group.

33. Define Abelian group, subgroup, power subgroup and normal subgroup with example.

34. Define subgroup of a group. Z is a group of integers under addition, H is the subset of Z consisting of all multiples of a positive integer m, that is
    H = {..., – 3m, – 2m, – m, 0, n, 2m, 3m, ... }. Show that H is a subgroup of Z.

35. Let R = {0°, 60°, 120°, 180°, 240°, 300°} and ∗ binary operation so that for a and b in R, a ∗ b is overall angular rotation corresponding to successive rotations by a and then by b. Show that (R, ∗) is a group.

36. Show that G = {1, 5, 7, 11} is a group under multiplication modulo 12.

37. Show that the set of cube roots of unity forms a group under multiplication.

POINTS TO REMEMBER

- An n-ary operation on a non-empty set A is a function f: $A^n \to A$, A^n being the product set of A.
- An algebraic system is an ordered pair (A, F) where
  (i) A is a set of elements, called as the **carrier** of the algebra.
  (ii) F is a finite set of m-ary operations on the carrier, m being a variable.
- A binary operation ∗ on A is said to be **commutative** if a ∗ b = b ∗ a, for all elements a, b ∈ A
- A binary operation ∗ on A is said to be **associative** if
  a ∗ (b ∗ c) = (a ∗ b) ∗ c, for all elements, a, b, c ∈ A.

- A binary operation * on A is said to satisfy the **idempotent** property if a * a = a, for all a ∈ A.
- Let (A, *) be an algebraic system, with a binary operation * on A. Then (A, *) is called a **semigroup** if * is associative, i.e.
  a * (b * c) = (a * b) * c, for all a, b, c ∈ A.
- An element e in (A, *) is called as **left identity** element if for each element x ∈ A, e * x = x.
- e is called a **right** identity if x * e = x, for all x ∈ A.
- An element e in a semigroup (A, *) is called an **identity** element if a * e = e * a = a, for all a ∈ A, i.e. e is both a left identity and right identity. It is clear that e is unique.
- Let (A, *) be a monoid, and let B be a non-empty subset of A. Then (B, *) is called a **submonoid** of (A, *) if
  (i) B is closed under *.
  (ii) The identity element e ∈ B.
- Let (A, *) be a monoid with identity element e. Let B be a non-empty subset of A. Then the monoid generated by B, denoted by < B > is defined as follows:
  (i) e ∈ < B >, and if b ∈ B, then b also is in < B >, that is B ⊆ < B >.
  (ii) < B > is closed under *.
  (iii) The only elements of < B > are those obtained from steps (i) and (ii).
- A group (G, *) is called an **Abelian** group if a * b = b * a, for all a, b ∈ G.
- Let (G, *) be a group. The order of G is the cardinality of G, denoted by |G|.
- Let (G, *) be a group. Let a ∈ G. The order of a is the **smallest** positive integer n such that a * a * ... * a = a^n = e. If no such value of n exists for a, then a is said to be of infinite order.
- A group (G, *) is said to be a cyclic group if there exists an element a ∈ G such that every element of G can be written as some power of a, viz a^k, for some integer k. By a^k, we mean a * a * a ... * a (k times). We then say that G is generated by a or a is a generator of G.
- Let H be a non-empty subset of a group G. Then H is said to be a **subgroup** of (G, *) if H is itself a group under *.
- Let H be a subgroup of a group (G, *). For a ∈ G, define
  $Ha = \{ h * a \mid h \in H \}$. Then Ha is called a **right coset** of H in G.
  Similarly, $aH = \{ a * h \mid h \in H \}$ is called a left coset of H in G. a is called as the representative element of the coset aH or Ha. If a ∈ H, then Ha = aH = H.

- A subgroup H of G is said to be a **normal** subgroup of G if for every a ∈ G, aH = Ha.
- Let (G, *) and (G', *') be two semigroups, then a function φ : (G, *) → G', *') is called a homomorphism of G and G' if for every a, b ∈ G, φ (a * b) = φ(a) *' φ(b). In particular if G and G' are groups, then φ is called a group homomorphism.
- Let φ: G → G' be a homomorphism of semigroups (or groups). Then φ is called an **isomorphism** if φ is one-one and onto (i.e. injective as well as surjective).
  If G' = G, then φ is called an automorphism.
- An algebraic structure (R, +, ·) is called a ring if
  (i) (R, +) is an abelian group.
  (ii) Associativity of multiplication holds: a · (b · c) = (a · b) * c.
  (iii) The left distributive law
      a · (b + c)   = a · b + a · c, and the right distributive law
      (b + c) · a   = b · a + c · a are satisfied by + and ·.
- A ring R is said to be commutative ring if a · b = b · a, for all a, b ∈ R.
- A ring R is said to be a ring with **unit** element if there exists an element, denoted by the symbol 1 such that a · 1 = 1 · a = a, for all a ∈ R.
- A subset R ⊆ S, where (S_1 +, ·) is a ring, is called a subring of S if (R, +, ·) is a ring with the operations + and · restricted to elements of R.
- Let (R, +, ·) and (S, +', ·') be rings. A mapping φ: R → S is called a **ring homomorphism,** if for any a, b ∈ R.
  (i) φ (a + b) = φ (a) +' φ(b)
  (ii) φ (a * b) = φ (a) *' φ(b).
  If φ is one-one and onto, it is called as a ring **isomorphism.** One can easily verify that φ(0) = 0' and φ(–a) = – φ(a), for every a ∈ R.
- Let (R, +, ×) and (S, +', ψ') be rings, with identities 0 and 0' respectively. Let f: R → S be a ring homomorphism. Then **kernel** of f is defined as the set {x ∈ R | f(x) = 0'}.
  We denote kernel of f as ker (f) or ker f.
- A non-empty set I of a ring R is called an **ideal** in R if
  (i) I is a subgroup of R, under addition.
  (ii) For every a ∈ I, a · x = x · a, for all x ∈ R.
- Let R be a commutative ring with unit element. If every non-zero element has a multiplicative inverse, then R is called a field. A field is an integral domain, since if a, b ∈ R, then a · b = 0 implies (a^{-1} · a) · (b · b^{-1}) = (a^{-1} · 0) · b^{-1} = 0 which further implies 1 · 1 = 0, which is not true, since 1 · 1 = 1.

Chapter 11: BOOLEAN ALGEBRAS

SYLLABUS:
- Lattice and Algebraic Systems, Principle of Duality, Basic Properties of Lattice, Distributive and Complemented Lattices, Boolean Algebras, Boolean Functions, Boolean Expression, Numbers System and Interconversion of Number Systems.

OBJECTIVES:
- To study the Axioms of Boolean Algebra and derive basic theorems from these axioms.
- To understand Boolean Expressions and learn to convert them into Normal forms.

UTILITY:
- In the design of logic gates and switching circuits.

KEY CONCEPTS:
- Boolean Algebra.
- Boolean Expression.
- Disjunctive Normal Form.
- Conjunctive Normal Form.

11.0 Introduction

In 1854, the English mathematician George Boole proposed that algebraic methods should be applied to Logic, by pointing out a close analogy between the algebraic symbols and the logical operators. He suggested that in this way, logical propositions can be expressed as algebraic expressions. George Booles' original discovery lead to the development of 'Algebra of Logic' or 'Boolean Algebra' as we know it today. Later Researchers extended the work of George Boole and found many practical applications, such as in the design of electronic devices, digital computers etc.

11.1 Boolean Algebra

The concept of partial order relation and the theory of Lattice has already been discussed in detail in the chapter 10. In what follows, we will define Boolean Algebra (axiomatically) and discuss the various properties. We will find on the way, that Boolean Algebra, infact, is a special type of lattice, with certain properties already known to us.

11.1.1 Definition

A Boolean algebra is a non-empty set B, with two binary operations $\wedge$ (meet) and $\vee$ (join) together with a unary operation $-$ (complementation), two universal bounds 0 (least element), 1 (greatest element), satisfying the following conditions :

11.1.1 Axioms of Boolean Algebra

(i) Commutative laws : $\quad x \vee y = y \vee x$

$x \wedge y = y \wedge x, \quad \forall\, x, y \in B$

(ii) Distributive laws : $\quad x \wedge (y \vee z) = (x \wedge y) \vee (x \wedge z)$

$x \vee (y \wedge z) = (x \vee y) \wedge (x \vee z), \quad \forall\, x, y, z \in B$

(iii) Identity laws : $\quad x \vee 0 = x, \quad \forall\, x \in B$

$x \wedge 1 = x, \quad \forall\, x \in B$

(iv) Complement laws : $\quad x \vee \bar{x} = 1, \quad \forall\, x \in B$

$x \wedge \bar{x} = 0, \quad \forall\, x \in B$

(v) $0 \neq 1$.

Generally, a Boolean algebra is denoted as $< B, \wedge, \vee, -, 0, 1 >$.

Examples :

1. **Example from Set Theory :** Consider a non-empty set A and set P(A) denote the power set of A. Then $< P(A), \cap, \cup, -, \phi, A >$ is a Boolean algebra.

2. **Example from Propositional Logic :** Let A denote the set of statements $\{p, q, r, ...\}$ with logical connectives $\vee$ (disjunction), $\wedge$ (conjugation) and $-$ (negation). Let T and F denote tautology and contradiction. Then $< A, \wedge, \vee, -, F, T >$ is a Boolean algebra.

3. **Example from Number Theory :** Let D denote the set of all positive, integral powers of the number '30', i.e. D = $\{1, 2, 3, 5, 6, 10, 15, 30\}$. Define $\forall\, x, y \in D, x \wedge y = $ gcd $\{x, y\}$, i.e. greatest common divisor of $\{x, y\}$ and $x \vee y = $ lcm$\{x, y\}$, i.e. least common multiple of $\{x, y\}$. For any $x \in D$, $\bar{x} = 30/x$. If $x = 6$, $\bar{x} = 30/6 = 5$. $\therefore x \wedge y = $ gcd $\{5, 6\} = 1$ & $x \vee y = $ lcm $\{5, 6\} = 30$. Hence the '0' of D is 1 and the element '1' of D is 30. It can be shown by verifying the axioms that $< D, \vee, \wedge, -, 1, 30 >$ is indeed a Boolean algebra.

11.1.2 Properties of Boolean Algebra

Theorem 1 (Uniqueness of complement) : If x and y are element of B such that $x \vee y = 1$ and $x \wedge y = 0$, then $y = \bar{x}$, (or $\bar{y} = x$).

Proof :

$$y = y \vee 0 = y \vee (x \wedge \bar{x})$$
$$= (y \vee x) \wedge (y \vee \bar{x})$$
$$= 1 \wedge (y \vee \bar{x})$$
$$= y \vee \bar{x}$$

Similarly,
$$\bar{x} = \bar{x} \vee 0$$
$$= \bar{x} \vee (x \wedge y)$$
$$= (\bar{x} \vee x) \wedge (\bar{x} \vee y)$$
$$= 1 \wedge (\bar{x} \vee y) = \bar{x} \vee y = y \vee \bar{x}$$

We have therefore proved that $\bar{x} = y \vee \bar{x}$ i.e. complement of element x is unique.

The property of uniqueness of complement coupled with the property of distributivity, leads to the following definition of Boolean algebra, as a special case of lattice (See chapter 10).

Definition : A Boolean algebra is a lattice, with universal bounds 0 and 1 ($0 \neq 1$), which is both complemented and distributive.

Theorem 2 (Idempotent law) : If $x \in B$, then $x \wedge x = x$ and $x \vee x = x$.

Proof :
$$x = x \wedge 1$$
$$= x \wedge (x \vee \bar{x})$$
$$= (x \wedge x) \vee (x \wedge \bar{x})$$
$$= (x \wedge x) \vee 0$$
$$= x \wedge x$$

Also
$$x = x \vee 0$$
$$= x \vee (x \wedge \bar{x})$$
$$= (x \vee x) \wedge (x \vee \bar{x})$$
$$= (x \vee x) \wedge 1$$
$$= x \vee x$$

Theorem 3 (Law of Involution) : For any $x \in B$, $\bar{\bar{x}} = x$.

Proof : Complement of $\bar{x}$ is x. Hence by uniqueness of complement $\bar{\bar{x}} = x$.

Dual statement : In the course of discussing the axioms of a Boolean algebra or studying the basic properties, we come across 'dual' statements, for example $x \wedge y = y \wedge x$ and $x \vee y = y \vee x$, $x \vee \bar{x} = 1$ and $x \wedge \bar{x} = 0$. This leads to the observation that one statement can be obtained from the other, by replacing $\wedge$ by $\vee$, $\vee$ by $\wedge$, 1 by 0 and 0 by 1. We shall now discuss this property of duality.

Definition : The dual of any proposition in Boolean algebra is the proposition obtained by substituting $\vee$ for $\wedge$, $\wedge$ for $\vee$, 0 for 1, 1 for 0, in the original proposition.

Example : 1. If the given proposition is $(x \vee y) \wedge (x \vee z) = x \vee (y \wedge z)$, its dual is
$$(x \wedge y) \vee (x \wedge z) = x \wedge (y \vee z)$$

2. Dual of the proposition $x \vee (y \wedge 1) = x \vee y$ is the proposition $x \wedge (y \vee 0) = x \wedge y$

Definition (Principle of duality) : If any proposition is derived, using the axioms of Boolean algebra, then the dual proposition too is derived.

The duality principle is a very convenient tool to establish the properties of Boolean algebra.

Theorem 4 : For any $x \in B$, $x \wedge 0 = 0$ and $x \vee 1 = 1$.

Proof : $x \wedge 0 = (x \wedge 0) \vee 0 = (x \wedge 0) \vee (x \wedge \bar{x}) = x \wedge (0 \vee \bar{x}) = x \wedge \bar{x} = 0$.

It follows by duality principle that $x \vee 1 = 1$.

Theorem 5 (Absorption law) : For example, $x, y \in B$, $x \wedge (x \vee y) = x$, $x \vee (x \wedge y) = x$.

Proof : $x \wedge (x \vee y) = (x \vee 0) \wedge (x \vee y) = x \vee (0 \wedge y) = x \vee 0 = x$

By duality principle $x \vee (x \wedge y) = x$.

Theorem 6 (Cancellation law) : For elements $x, y, z \in B$, if $x \wedge y = x \wedge z$ and $\bar{x} \wedge y = \bar{x} \wedge z$, then $y = z$.

Proof :
$$\begin{aligned}
y &= y \wedge 1 = y \wedge (x \vee \bar{x}) \\
&= (y \wedge x) \vee (y \wedge \bar{x}) \\
&= (x \wedge y) \vee (\bar{x} \wedge y) \\
&= (x \wedge z) \vee (\bar{x} \wedge z) \\
&= (x \vee \bar{x}) \wedge z \\
&= 1 \wedge z = z
\end{aligned}$$

Theorem 7 (Associative laws) : For elements $x, y, z \in B$.

$$x \vee (y \vee z) = (x \vee y) \vee z$$

and

$$x \wedge (y \wedge z) = (x \wedge y) \wedge z$$

Proof : We will first show that for any $x \in B$,

$$x \wedge [x \vee (y \vee z)] = x \wedge [(x \vee y) \vee z]$$

and

$$\overline{x} \wedge [x \vee (y \vee z)] = \overline{x} \wedge [(x \vee y) \vee z]$$

Then, using the "cancellation law" theorem, the associative laws will be established.

Now, $\quad x \wedge [x \vee (y \vee z)] = x$, by absorption law

Also, $\quad x \wedge [(x \vee y) \vee z] = (x \wedge (x \vee y)) \vee (x \wedge z)$

$$= x \vee (x \wedge z)$$

$$= x, \text{ by absorption law}$$

Next, $\quad \overline{x} \wedge [x \vee (y \vee z)] = (\overline{x} \wedge x) \vee (\overline{x} \wedge (y \vee z))$

$$= 0 \vee (\overline{x} \wedge (y \vee z))$$

$$= \overline{x} \wedge (y \vee z)$$

Also, $\quad \overline{x} \wedge [(x \vee y) \vee z] = (\overline{x} \wedge (x \vee y)) \vee (\overline{x} \wedge z)$

$$= (\overline{x} \wedge x) \vee (\overline{x} \wedge y) \vee (\overline{x} \wedge z)$$

$$= 0 \vee (\overline{x} \wedge y) \vee (\overline{x} \wedge z)$$

$$= (\overline{x} \wedge y) \vee (\overline{x} \wedge z)$$

$$= \overline{x} \wedge (y \vee z)$$

Hence, applying the cancellation property, we have

$$x \vee (y \vee z) = (x \vee y) \vee z$$

By duality principle, it follows that

$$x \wedge (y \wedge z) = (x \wedge y) \wedge z$$

Theorem 8 (De Morgan's laws) :

$$\overline{(x \vee y)} = \overline{x} \wedge \overline{y} \quad \text{and} \quad \overline{(x \wedge y)} = \overline{x} \vee \overline{y}.$$

Proof : We use the uniqueness of complement property to prove the laws.

$$(x \vee y) \wedge (\bar{x} \wedge \bar{y}) = (x \wedge (\bar{x} \wedge \bar{y})) \vee (y \wedge (\bar{x} \wedge \bar{y}))$$
$$= [(x \wedge \bar{x}) \wedge \bar{y}] \vee [(y \wedge \bar{y}) \wedge \bar{x}]$$
$$= (0 \wedge \bar{y}) \vee (0 \wedge \bar{x})$$
$$= 0 \vee 0 = 0$$

Also
$$(x \vee y) \vee (\bar{x} \wedge \bar{y}) = ((x \vee y) \vee \bar{x}) \wedge ((x \vee y) \vee \bar{y})$$
$$= ((x \vee \bar{x}) \vee y) \wedge (x \vee (y \vee \bar{y}))$$
$$= (1 \vee y) \wedge (x \vee 1)$$
$$= 1 \wedge 1 = 1$$

Hence the element $\bar{x} \wedge \bar{y}$ satisfies the properties of complement of $x \vee y$, therefore by uniqueness of complement $\overline{x \vee y} = \bar{x} \wedge \bar{y}$.

The dual result $\overline{x \wedge y} = \bar{x} \vee \bar{y}$ is established, using the principle of duality.

Theorem 9 : For elements $x, y \in B$, $x \wedge \bar{y} = 0$ if and only if $x \wedge y = x$.

Proof : Let $x \wedge \bar{y} = 0$.
$$x = x \wedge 1 = x \wedge (y \vee \bar{y})$$
$$= (x \wedge y) \vee (x \wedge \bar{y})$$
$$= (x \wedge y) \vee 0$$
$$= x \wedge y$$

Conversely, let $x \wedge y = x$. This implies
$$x \wedge \bar{y} = (x \wedge y) \wedge \bar{y} = x \wedge (y \wedge \bar{y}) = x \wedge 0 = 0.$$

SOLVED EXAMPLES

Example 1 : Prove that $(\bar{x} \wedge \bar{y}) \vee (x \vee y) = 1$.

Proof :
$$(\bar{x} \wedge \bar{y}) \vee (x \vee y) = (\bar{x} \vee (x \vee y)) \wedge (\bar{y} \vee (x \vee y))$$
$$= [(\bar{x} \vee x) \vee y] \wedge [(\bar{y} \vee y) \vee x]$$
$$= (1 \vee y) \wedge (1 \vee x)$$
$$= 1 \wedge 1 = 1$$

Example 2 : Prove that $(x \wedge \bar{y}) \wedge (x \wedge y) = 0$.

Proof :
$$\begin{aligned}
(x \wedge \bar{y}) \wedge (x \wedge y) &= (\bar{x} \vee y) \wedge (x \wedge \bar{y}) \\
&= ((\bar{x} \wedge x) \wedge \bar{y}) \vee (y \wedge x) \wedge \bar{y}) \\
&= (0 \wedge \bar{y}) \vee (y \wedge \bar{y}) \wedge x) \\
&= 0 \vee (0 \wedge x) \\
&= 0 \vee 0 = 0
\end{aligned}$$

Example 3 : Prove that $\overline{(x \wedge y)} \vee (x \wedge \bar{y} \wedge z) = (\overline{x \vee y})$.

Proof :"
$$\begin{aligned}
\overline{(x \wedge y)} \vee (x \wedge \bar{y} \wedge z) &= (\overline{x \vee y}) \vee (x \wedge \bar{y} \wedge z) \\
&= (x \vee \bar{y} \vee x) \wedge (x \vee \bar{y} \vee y) \wedge (x \vee \bar{y} \vee z) \\
&= (x \vee x \vee \bar{y}) \wedge (x \vee \bar{y}) \wedge (x \vee \bar{y} \vee z) \\
&= (x \vee \bar{y}) \wedge (x \vee \bar{y} \vee z) \\
&= x \vee \bar{y} \quad \text{(by absorption law)}
\end{aligned}$$

Example 4 : Prove that $(x \vee y) \wedge (y \vee z) \wedge \bar{z} = y \wedge \bar{z}$.

Proof :
$$\begin{aligned}
(x \vee y) \wedge (y \vee z) \wedge \bar{z} &= (x \vee y) \wedge (z \vee y) \wedge \bar{z} \\
&= ((x \wedge z) \vee y) \wedge \bar{z} \\
&= ((x \wedge z) \wedge \bar{z}) \vee (y \wedge \bar{z}) \\
&= (x \wedge (z \wedge \bar{z})) \vee (y \wedge \bar{z}) \\
&= (x \wedge 0) \vee (y \wedge \bar{z}) \\
&= 0 \vee (y \wedge \bar{z}) \\
&= y \wedge \bar{z}
\end{aligned}$$

11.1.3 Boolean Expression

Boolean expression is of considerable importance in the design of switching circuits.

Definition : Let $x_1, x_2, ..., x_n$ be Boolean variables, which assume values from the Boolean set B. The expression obtained by applying the operations, $\wedge, \vee, -$, a finite number of times on the Boolean variables, is called a Boolean expression. It is usually denoted by $E(x_1, x_2, ..., x_n)$.

Examples :

1. $E(x_1, x_2, x_3) = (x_1 \wedge x_2 \wedge x_3) \vee (\overline{x_1} \wedge x_3)$

2. $E(x_1, x_2) = (x_1 \vee x_2) \wedge x_1 \wedge \overline{x_2}$.

Boolean function : A Boolean expression $E(x_1, x_2, \ldots, x_k)$ defines a function $f : B^k \to B$, where $f(b_1, b_2, \ldots, b_k) = E(b_1, b_2, \ldots, b_k)$, replacing x_i by b_i ($1 \leq i \leq k$), in the Boolean expression.

SOLVED EXAMPLES

Example 1 : Let $B = \{0, 1\}$, the 2-element Boolean set. Consider $E(x_1, x_2) = (x_1 \wedge x_2) \vee \overline{x}$. Then the Boolean function $f : B^2 \to B$ is defined by the following input-output table.

x_1	x_2	$(x_1 \wedge x_2) \vee \overline{x_1} = f(x_1, x_2)$
1	0	0
0	1	1
0	0	1
1	1	1

Example 2 : Let the Boolean expression $E(x_1, x_2, x_3) = (x_1 \vee \overline{x_2}) \wedge x_3$, over $B = \{0, 1\}$. The input/output table for the Boolean function $f(x_1, x_2, x_3)$ is

x_1	x_2	x_3	$\overline{x_2}$	$(x_1 \vee \overline{x_2})$	$f(x_1, x_2, x_3)$
1	1	1	0	1	1
1	1	0	0	1	0
1	0	1	1	1	1
1	0	0	1	1	0
0	1	1	0	0	0
0	1	0	0	0	0
0	0	1	1	1	1
0	0	0	1	1	0

The above examples illustrate the fact that if the underlying Boolean set is of cardinality 2, the number of distinct functions from B^k to B is 2^{2^k}; for $k = 2$, the pair of variables (x_1, x_2)

has 4 choices, whereas for k = 3, the triple (x_1, x_2, x_3) has 2^3 = 8 choices. There are only 2 possible values 0 or 1, which a function $f(x_1, x_2)$ or $f(x_1, x_2, x_3)$ can assume. Hence, the number of distinct functions will be $2 \times 2 \times 2 \times 2 = 2^4$ for $f(x_1, x_2)$. In the case of $f(x_1, x_2, x_3)$, the number of such distinct functions will be $2 \times 2 \times 2 \times \ldots 2$ (8 times) = 2^8.

11.1.4 Normal or Canonical forms of Boolean Expression

We first define some basic concepts.

Literal : A literal is a Boolean variable x_i or its complement $\overline{x_i}$.

Minterm : A Boolean expression $y_1 \wedge y_2 \wedge \ldots \wedge y_k$ is called a minterm if each y_i is a literal, i.e. $y_i = x_i$ or $\overline{x_i}$, but both x_i and $\overline{x_i}$ should not appear in the expression.

For example, $y = x_1 \wedge \overline{x_2}$ is a minterm, but $y = x_1 \wedge \overline{x_1}$ is not a minterm.

A minterm is also referred to as a **fundamental product**.

Maxterm : A Boolean expression $y = y_1 \vee y_2 \vee \ldots \vee y_k$ is called a maxterm, if each y_i is a literal, i.e. $y = x_i$ or $\overline{x_i}$, provided that both x_i and $\overline{x_i}$ do not appear in the expression.

For example, $y = x_1 \vee \overline{x_2}$ is a maxterm but $y = x_1 \vee \overline{x_1}$ is not a maxterm.

A maxterm is also referred to as a **fundamental sum**.

Disjunctive normal form (Definition) : It is also referred to as sum-of-products form.

Definition : A Boolean expression $E(x_1, x_2, \ldots, x_n)$ in n variables is said to be in disjunctive normal form, if it is the disjunction (join) of two or more.

Minterms, none of which is included in another.

Example : 1. $E(x_1, x_2) = (x_1 \wedge x_2) \vee (\overline{x_1} \wedge x_2)$

2. $E(x_1, x_2, x_3) = (x_1 \wedge \overline{x_2}) \wedge (x_1 \wedge x_3) \vee (x_2 \wedge x_3)$

Conjunctive normal form (Definition) : It is also referred to as product-of-sums form.

Definition : A Boolean expression $E(x_1, x_2, \ldots, x_n)$ in n variables is said to be in conjunctive. Normal form, if it is the conjunction (meet) of two or more maxterms, none of which is included in another.

Example : 1. $E(x_1, x_2) = (x_1 \vee x_2) \wedge (\overline{x}_1 \vee x_2)$

2. $E(x_1, x_2, x_3) = (x_1 \vee \overline{x_2} \vee x_3) \wedge (x_1 \vee \overline{x_3})$

Any Boolean expression is expressible in the normal form. This is usually done by using the laws of Boolean algebra.

SOLVED EXAMPLES

Example 1 : Express $(x_1 \wedge (\bar{x}_2 \vee x_3)) \vee \bar{x}_3$ in both Dnf as well as Cnf.

Solution :
$$(x \wedge (y' \vee z)) \vee z' = (x \wedge y') \vee (x \wedge z) \vee z' - \text{Dnf}$$
$$(x \wedge (y' \vee z)) \vee z' = (x \vee z') \wedge (y' \vee z \vee z')$$
$$= (x \vee z') \wedge (y' \vee 1)$$
$$= (x \vee z') \wedge y' \quad - \text{Cnf}$$

Example 2 : Express $E(x_1, x_2, x_3) = (\bar{x}_1 \wedge x_3) \vee (x_2 \wedge \bar{x}_3) \vee (x_2 \vee x_3)$ in the canonical forms.

Solution : Disjunctive normal form : The first two terms $\bar{x}_1 \wedge x_3$, $x_2 \wedge \bar{x}_3$ are minterms. We can express the third term $x_2 \vee x_3$ as

$$(x_2 \wedge 1) \vee (x_3 \wedge 1) = (x_2 \wedge (x_1 \vee \bar{x}_1)) \vee (x_3 \wedge (x_1 \vee \bar{x}_1))$$
$$= (x_2 \wedge x_1) \vee (x_2 \wedge \bar{x}_1) \vee (x_3 \wedge x_1) \vee (x_3 \wedge \bar{x}_1)$$

Hence, $E(x_1, x_2, x_3) = (\bar{x}_1 \wedge x_3) \vee (x_2 \wedge \bar{x}_3) \vee (x_2 \wedge x_1) \vee (x_2 \wedge \bar{x}_1) \vee (x_3 \wedge x_1)$

which is dnf.

Conjunctive normal form :

$$(\bar{x}_1 \wedge x_3) \vee (x_2 \wedge \bar{x}_3) = [(\bar{x}_1 \wedge x_3) \vee x_2] \wedge [(\bar{x} \wedge x_3) \vee \bar{x}_3]$$
$$= (\bar{x}_1 \vee x_2) \wedge (x_3 \vee x_2) \wedge (\bar{x}_1 \vee \bar{x}_3) \wedge (x_3 \vee \bar{x}_3)$$
$$= (\bar{x}_1 \vee x_2) \wedge (x_3 \vee x_2) \wedge (\bar{x}_1 \vee \bar{x}_3) \wedge 1$$
$$= (\bar{x}_1 \vee x_2) \wedge (x_3 \vee x_2) \wedge (\bar{x}_1 \vee \bar{x}_3)$$

Hence, $[(\bar{x}_1 \vee x_2) \wedge (x_3 \vee x_2) \wedge (\bar{x}_1 \vee \bar{x}_3)] \vee (x_2 \vee x_3)$

$$= (\bar{x}_1 \vee x_2 \vee x_3) \wedge (x_2 \vee x_3) \wedge (\bar{x}_1 \vee \bar{x}_3 \vee x_3 \vee x_2)$$
$$= (\bar{x}_1 \vee x_2 \vee x_3) \wedge (x_2 \vee x_3) \wedge (\bar{x}_1 \vee 1 \vee x_2)$$
$$= (\bar{x}_1 \vee x_2 \vee x_3) \wedge (x_2 \vee x_3) \wedge 1$$
$$= (\bar{x}_1 \vee x_2 \vee x_3) \wedge (x_2 \vee x_3) = \text{cnf}.$$

Complete (full) disjunctive normal form :

Definition : If each min term in the disjunctive normal form, contains the literals of all the variables, then it is said to be complete or full.

Complete (full) conjunctive normal form.

Definition : If each maxterm in the Conjunctive, Normal form contains the literals of all the variables, then it is said to be complete or full.

Example : 1. $E(x_1, x_2, x_3) = (x_1 \wedge x_2 \wedge x_3) \vee (\overline{x_1} \wedge x_2 \wedge \overline{x_3})$ is in full dnf.

2. $E(x_1, x_2, x_3) = (x_1 \vee \overline{x_2} \vee x_3) \wedge (\overline{x_1} \vee x_2 \vee \overline{x_3}) \wedge (x_1 \vee x_2 \vee x_3)$

is in full cnf

Truth table method to find full dnf or full cnf.

Example 1 : Express $E(x_1, x_2, x_3) = (x_1 \wedge x_2) \vee (\overline{x_1} \wedge x_3) \vee (x_2 \wedge x_3)$ in full dnf and full cnf.

Solution : Consider the truth table (input/output) of the function $f(x_1, x_2, x_3)$.

x_1	x_2	x_3	$f(x_1, x_2, x_3)$
0	1	0	0
0	0	1	1
0	1	1	1
0	0	0	0
1	1	0	1
1	0	1	0
1	1	1	1
1	0	0	0

Select the rows, which has the entry 1 in the column of $f(x_1, x_2, x_3)$. Corresponding to each entry consider the minterm $y = y_1 \wedge y_2 \wedge y_3$ where,

$$y_i = x_i \text{ if } x_i \text{ takes the value 1}$$

$$= \overline{x_1} \text{ if } x_i \text{ takes the value 0.}$$

In this manner, corresponding to the value 1, which $f(x_1, x_2, x_3)$ assumes, we have the minterms as $\overline{x_1} \wedge \overline{x_2} \wedge x_3$, $\overline{x_1} \wedge x_2 \wedge x_3$, $x_1 \wedge x_2 \wedge \overline{x_3}$, $x_1 \wedge x_2 \wedge x_3$ in the second, third, fifth and seventh rows respectively.

Then
$$E(x_1, x_2, x_3) = (\overline{x_1} \wedge \overline{x_2} \wedge x_3) \vee (\overline{x_1} \wedge x_2 \wedge x_3)$$
$$\vee (x_1 \wedge x_2 \wedge \overline{x_3}) \vee (x_1 \wedge x_2 \wedge x_3),$$

which is in full dnf.

Likewise, corresponding to the entry 0 in the column of $f(x_1, x_2, x_3)$, we have the maxterms $x_1 \vee \bar{x}_2 \vee x_3$, $x_1 \vee \bar{x}_2 \vee \bar{x}_3$, $\bar{x}_1 \vee x_2 \vee \bar{x}_3$, $\bar{x}_1 \vee x_2 \vee x_3$.

Then $\quad E(x_1, x_2, x_3) = (x_1 \vee \bar{x}_2 \vee x_3) \wedge (x_1 \vee x_2 \vee x_3)$

$\qquad \wedge (\bar{x}_1 \vee x_2 \vee \bar{x}_3) \wedge (\bar{x}_1 \vee x_2 \vee x_3)$ is in full cnf.

SOLVD EXAMPLES

Example 1 : Prove that $(x \wedge y') \vee y = x \vee y$.

Solution : $\quad (x \wedge y') \vee y = (x \wedge y') \vee (y \wedge (x \vee x'))$

$\qquad = (x \wedge y') \vee (y \wedge x) \vee (y \wedge x')$

$\qquad = [(x \wedge y') \vee (x \wedge y)] \vee [(x \wedge y) \vee (x' \wedge y)]$

(Using idempotent and commutative laws)

$\qquad = (x \wedge (y' \vee y)) \vee ((x \vee x') \wedge y)$

$\qquad = (x \wedge 1) \vee (1 \wedge y)$

$\qquad = x \vee y$

Example 2 : Prove that : $(x \vee (y \wedge z)) \wedge (\bar{y} \vee x) \wedge (\bar{y} \vee \bar{z}) = x \wedge (\bar{y} \vee \bar{z})$

Solution : $\quad$ L.H.S. $= (x \vee y) \wedge (x \vee z) \wedge (x \vee \bar{y}) \wedge (\bar{y} \vee \bar{z})$

$\qquad = (x \vee y) \wedge (x \vee \bar{y}) \wedge (x \vee z) \wedge (\bar{y} \vee \bar{z})$

$\qquad = (x \vee (y \wedge \bar{y})) \wedge (x \vee z) \wedge (\bar{y} \vee \bar{z})$

$\qquad = (x \vee 0) \wedge (x \vee z) \wedge (\bar{y} \vee \bar{z})$

$\qquad = x \wedge (\bar{y} \vee \bar{z}) \qquad (x \wedge (x \vee z) = x$ by absorption law)

Example 3 : Prove that $(x \wedge y) \vee (\bar{x} \wedge z) \vee (y \wedge z) = (x \wedge y) \vee (\bar{x} \wedge z)$.

Solution : $\quad$ L.H.S. $= (x \wedge y) \vee (\bar{x} \wedge z) \vee [(x \vee \bar{x}) \wedge (y \wedge z)]$

$\qquad (\because x \vee \bar{x} = 1 \quad 1 \wedge (y \wedge z) = y \wedge z)$

$\qquad = (x \wedge y) \vee (\bar{x} \wedge z) \vee (x \wedge y \wedge z) \vee (\bar{x} \wedge y \wedge z)$

$\qquad = (x \wedge y) \vee (x \wedge y \wedge z) \vee (\bar{x} \wedge z) \vee (\bar{x} \wedge y \wedge z)$

$\qquad = (x \wedge (y \vee (y \wedge z)) \vee \bar{x} \wedge (z \vee (y \wedge z))$

$\qquad = (x \wedge y) \vee (\bar{x} \wedge z)$

$\qquad (y \vee (y \wedge z) = y$ and $z \vee (y \wedge z) = z$, by absorption law)

Example 4 : Prove that : $x \wedge (\bar{x} \vee y) = (\bar{x} \wedge y) \vee x \vee y$.

Solution : L.H.S. $= (x \wedge \bar{x}) \vee (x \wedge y) = 0 \vee (x \wedge y) = x \wedge y$

$$\begin{aligned}
\text{R.H.S.} = (\bar{x} \wedge y) \vee x \vee y &= [(\bar{x} \vee x) \wedge (y \vee x)] \vee y \\
&= [1 \wedge (y \vee x)] \vee y \\
&= (y \vee x) \vee y \\
&= (y \vee y) \vee x \\
&= y \vee x \\
&= x \vee y
\end{aligned}$$

Example 5 : Simplify $(x \vee y) \wedge (\bar{x} \vee \bar{y})$.

Solution :
$$\begin{aligned}
(x \vee y) \wedge (\bar{x} \vee \bar{y}) &= [(x \vee y) \wedge \bar{x}] \vee [(x \vee y) \wedge \bar{y}] \\
&= [(x \wedge \bar{x}) \vee (y \wedge \bar{x})] \vee [(x \wedge \bar{y}) \vee (y \wedge \bar{y})] \\
&= (0 \vee (y \wedge \bar{x})) \vee ((x \wedge \bar{y}) \vee 0) \\
&= (y \wedge \bar{x}) \vee (x \wedge \bar{y})
\end{aligned}$$

Example 6 : Simplify the Boolean expression $x \vee (y \wedge (x \vee y)) \vee (x \wedge (\bar{x} \vee y))$

Solution : $x \vee (y \wedge (x \vee y)) \vee (x \wedge (\bar{x} \vee y))$

$$\begin{aligned}
&= x \vee (y \wedge x) \vee y \vee (x \wedge \bar{x}) \vee (x \wedge y) \\
&= (x \vee y) \vee 0 \vee (x \wedge y) \\
&= (x \vee y)
\end{aligned}$$

Example 7 : Represent the Boolean expression $(x \vee y) \wedge (\bar{x} \vee \bar{y})$ in disjunctive normal form.

Solution :
$$\begin{aligned}
(x \vee y) \wedge (\bar{x} \vee \bar{y}) &= (x \wedge (\bar{x} \vee \bar{y})) \vee (y \wedge (\bar{x} \vee \bar{y})) \\
&= (x \wedge \bar{x}) \vee (x \wedge \bar{y}) \vee (y \wedge \bar{x}) \vee (y \wedge \bar{y}) \\
&= 0 \vee (x \wedge \bar{y}) \vee (y \wedge \bar{x}) \vee 0 \\
&= (x \wedge \bar{y}) \vee (\bar{x} \wedge y)
\end{aligned}$$

which is in dnf.

Example 8 : Represent the Boolean expression $\overline{(x \wedge y)} \wedge (x \vee z)$ in full disjunctive normal form.

Solution :
$$\overline{(x \wedge y)} \wedge (x \vee z) = (\overline{\overline{x}} \vee \overline{y}) \wedge (x \vee z)$$
$$= (x \vee \overline{y}) \wedge (x \vee z)$$
$$= x \vee (\overline{y} \wedge z)$$
$$= (x \wedge 1 \wedge 1) \vee (\overline{y} \wedge z \wedge 1)$$
$$= (x \wedge (y \vee \overline{y}) \wedge (z \vee \overline{z}) \vee (\overline{y} \wedge z \wedge (x \vee \overline{x}))$$
$$= ((x \wedge y) \vee (x \wedge \overline{y})) \wedge (z \vee \overline{z}) \vee (\overline{y} \wedge z \wedge x) \vee (\overline{y} \wedge z \wedge \overline{x})$$
$$= (x \wedge y \wedge z) \vee (x \wedge y \wedge \overline{z}) \vee (x \wedge \overline{y} \wedge z)$$
$$\vee (x \wedge \overline{y} \wedge \overline{z}) \vee (\overline{x} \wedge \overline{y} \wedge z)$$

11.1.5 Application of Boolean Algebra to Switching Theory

A simple switch is a two-state device, it is either closed (on) or open (off). If the switch is closed, it allows the current to flow, hence a value 1 is assigned to the switch in the closed state, similarly, if it is open, no current flows, hence a value 0 is assigned to the switch in the open state. Hence we can apply the theory of Boolean Algebra to switching theory. As a matter of convention, the algebraic symbols +; , − are used in place to ∨, ∧, − respectively. Hence instead of $x_1 \vee x_2$, we will write $x_1 + x_2$ and the product $x_1 \cdot x_2$ instead of $x_1 \wedge x_2$.

The following are the Boolean operations on the states of switches.

1. **Boolean Sum (Parallel switches) :**

Boolean Table		
x_1	x_2	$x_1 + x_2$
0	0	0
1	0	1
0	1	1
1	1	1

Diagram of circuit

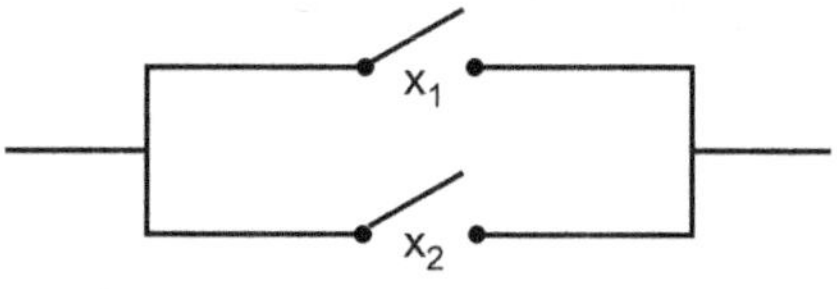

Fig. 1.1

2. **Boolean Product (Switches in Series) :**

Boolean Table		
x_1	x_2	$x_1 x_2$
0	0	0
1	0	0
0	1	0
1	1	1

Diagram of circuit

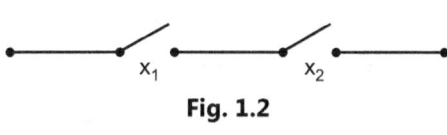

Fig. 1.2

3. **Boolean Complementation ($\bar{x}$) :**

Table	
x	$\bar{x}$
1	0
0	1

Diagram

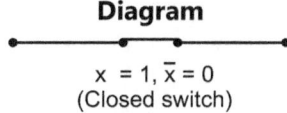

$x = 1, \bar{x} = 0$
(Closed switch)
Fig. 1.3 (a)

Closed switch

$x = 1, \bar{x} = 0$

(Closed switch)

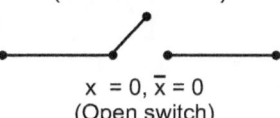

$x = 0, \bar{x} = 0$
(Open switch)
Fig. 1.3 (b)

$x = 0 \quad \bar{x} = 1$
(Open switch)

A complex circuit can be represented by an appropriate Boolean expression.

Example 1 : Consider the following circuit :

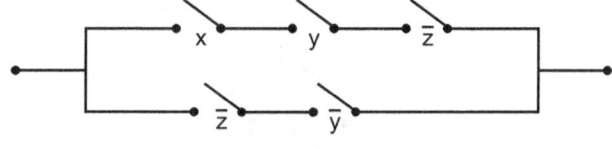

Fig. 1.4

The Boolean expression for the circuit is $xy\bar{z} + \bar{y}\bar{z}$.

The above circuit can be replaced by a more simple circuit by simplying the corresponding Boolean expression :

$$xy\bar{z} + \bar{y}\bar{z} = (xy + \bar{y}) \cdot \bar{z}$$

Now, $\quad xy + \bar{y} = (x + \bar{y})(y + \bar{y})$ as

$(x + \bar{y})(y + \bar{y}) = xy + \bar{y}y + x\bar{y} + \bar{y} = xy + 0 + (x+1) = xy + \bar{y}$

Hence, $\quad (xy + \bar{y})\bar{z} = (x + \bar{y})(y + \bar{y})\bar{z} = (x + \bar{y})\bar{z}$

Hence the simplified circuit is :

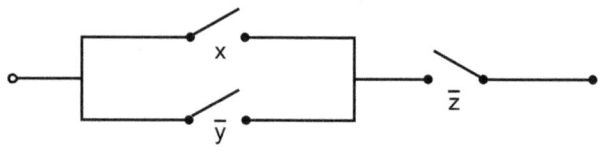

Fig. 1.5

Note that the five switches in the original circuit has been minimized to three switches in the equivalent circuit.

Example 2 : Write the Boolean expression corresponding to the following circuit.

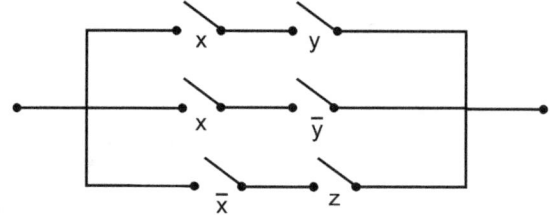

Fig. 1.6

Simplify the expression and draw the corresponding circuit diagram.

Solution : Expression $xy + x\bar{y} + \bar{x}z$

$$= x(y + \bar{y}) + \bar{x}z$$

$$= x \cdot 1 + \bar{x}z = x(1 + z) + \bar{x}z$$

$$= x(x + \bar{x} + z) + \bar{x}z$$

$$= x^2 + 0 + xz + \bar{x}z$$

$$= x + (x + \bar{x})z = x + z$$

The corresponding circuit is

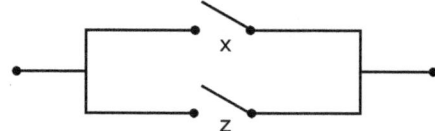

Fig. 1.7

11.1.6 Logic Circuits and Logic Gates

A digital computer consists of numerous electronic circuits, which in turn are composed of elementary circuits, performing logical operations. These elementary circuits are called as logic gates. The processing of information (input signals) is done by these logic gates, which operate on one or more inputs to produce an output. Each input and output can take either the value 1 (high voltage) or the value 0 (low voltage).

The following are the basic types of logic gates :

1. **OR-GATE** : Output $f(x_1, x_2) = (x_1 + x_2)(x_1 \vee x_2)$.

Table

Input		Output
x_1	x_2	$f(x_1, x_2) = x_1 + x_2$
0	0	0
0	1	1
1	0	1
1	1	1

Diagram

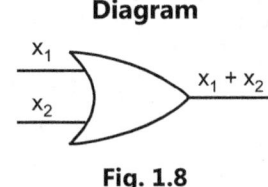

Fig. 1.8

2. **AND-GATE** : $f(x_1, x_2) = x_1 \cdot x_2 \; (x_1 \wedge x_2)$

Table

Input		Output
x_1	x_2	$f(x_1, x_2) = x_1 x_2$
0	0	0
0	1	1
1	0	1
1	1	1

Diagram

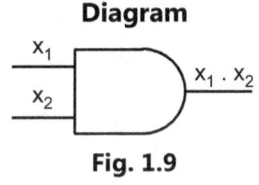

Fig. 1.9

3. **NOT-GATE (Inverter)** : $f(x_1) = \bar{x}_1$:

Table

Input	Output
x_1	$f(x_1) = \bar{x}_1$
1	0
0	1

Diagram

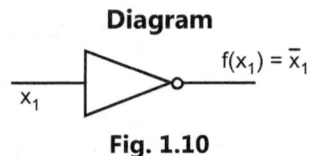

Fig. 1.10

4. **NOR-GATE** : $f(x_1, x_2) = \overline{x_1 + x_2}$:

Table

Input		Output
x_1	x_2	$f(x_1, x_2) = \overline{x_1 + x_2}$
0	0	1
0	1	0
1	0	0
0	0	1

Diagram

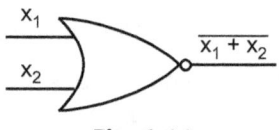

Fig. 1.11

5. **NAND-GATE** : $f(x_1, x_2) = \overline{x_1} \cdot \overline{x_2}$:

Table

Input		Output
x_1	x_2	$f(x_1, x_2) = \overline{x_1} \cdot \overline{x_2}$
0	0	1
1	0	1
0	1	1
1	1	0

Diagram

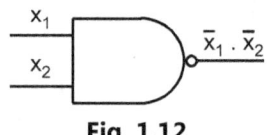

Fig. 1.12

6. **XOR-GATE** : $f(x_1, x_2) = x_1 \overline{x_2} + \overline{x_1} x_2$:

Table

Input		Output
x_1	x_2	$f(x_1, x_2) = x_1\overline{x_2} + \overline{x_1}x_2$
0	0	0
0	1	1
1	0	1
1	1	0

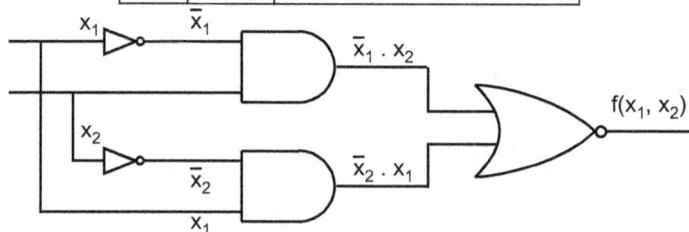

Fig. 1.13

7. **XNOR-GATE :** $f(x_1, x_2) = (\bar{x}_1 + x_2)(x_1 + \bar{x}_2)$:

Table		
Input		Output
x_1	x_2	$f(x_1, x_2) = (\bar{x}_1 + x_2)(x_1 + \bar{x}_2)$
0	0	1
0	1	0
1	0	0
1	1	1

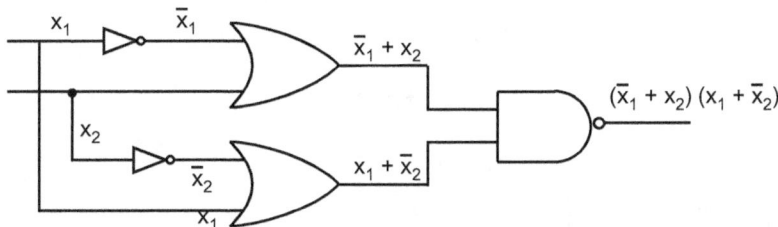

Fig. 1.14

SOLVED EXAMPLES

Example 1 : Draw the gate diagram corresponding to the input function

$$f(x_1, x_2, x_3) = x_1 x_2 + \bar{x}_1 x_2 x_3$$

Solution : The gate diagram for $f(x_1, x_2, x_3)$ is :

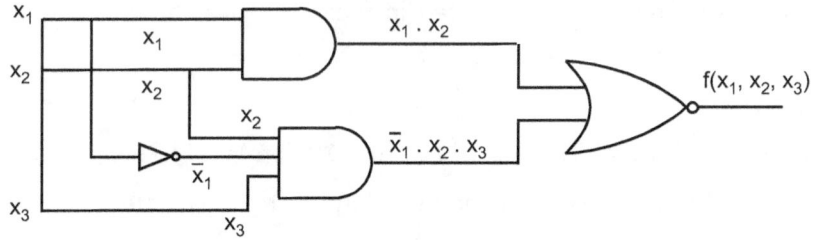

Fig. 1.15

Example 2 : Draw the logic gate diagram, given the following input/output table :

Input			Output
x_1	x_2	x_3	$f(x_1, x_2, x_3)$
1	1	1	1
1	1	0	0
1	0	1	0
1	0	0	1
0	1	1	0
0	1	0	1
0	0	1	0
0	0	0	0

Solution : Expressing $f(x_1, x_2, x_3)$ in dnf, we have :

$$f(x_1, x_2, x_3) = x_1 x_2 x_3 + x_1 \bar{x}_2 \bar{x}_3 + \bar{x}_1 x_2 \bar{x}_3$$

$$= x_1 x_2 x_3 + \bar{x}_2 \bar{x}_3 (x_1 + \bar{x}_1)$$

$$= x_1 x_2 x_3 + \bar{x}_2 \bar{x}_3$$

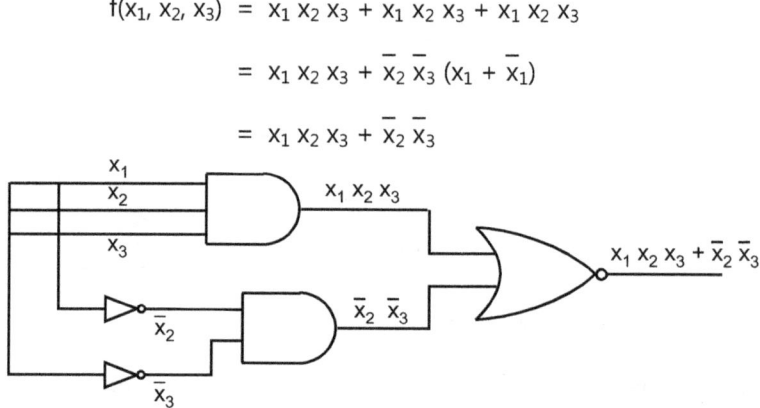

Fig. 1.16 : Logic gate diagram

11.1.7 Binary Addition by Logic Gates

Any non-negative integer is represented in binary form as a sequence (of 0'n or 1's) $a_n\ a_{n-1}\ a_{n-2}\ \ldots\ a_0$.

For example :

0 = 0000, 1 = 0001, 2= 0010, 7 = 0111, 10 = 1010, 14= 1110 etc.

The process of addition of binary numbers is done, using logic gates.

The result of adding two bits (binary digits) consists of a sum s and a carry digit c. For example, 1 + 1 yields the sum s = 0 and carry c = 1. 0 + 1 = 1 yields s = 1 and carry c = 0.

The table below describes this process.

x	y	binary sum	s	c
0	0	0	0	0
1	0	1	1	0
0	1	1	1	0
1	1	10	0	1

Hence binary sum $s = x \oplus y = (x + y)(\overline{xy})$ $(x \oplus y = x\overline{y} + \overline{x}y = (x+y)(\overline{xy}))$.

The logic gate shown below, represents this operation.

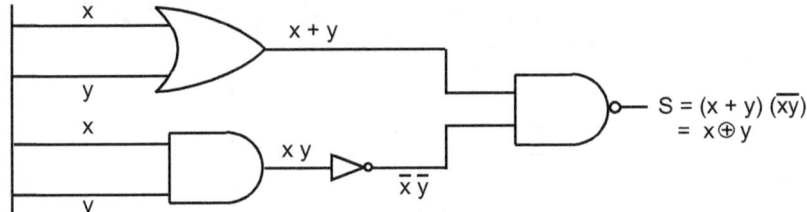

Fig. 1.17

This network is called as half adder. A half adder has only two terminals, hence cannot add 3-bits.

A full adder is a logic circuit that can carry out the operation of addition of 3 bits.
The following table describes this operation.

x	y	z	sum = s	carry = c
0	0	0	0	0
0	0	1	1	0
0	1	0	1	0
1	0	0	1	0
1	0	1	0	1
1	1	0	0	1
0	1	1	0	1
1	1	1	1	1

Expressing s as dnf, we have,

$$s = \overline{x}\,\overline{y}z + \overline{x}y\overline{z} + x\overline{y}\,\overline{z} + xyz$$

The logic circuit for sum s is shown below :

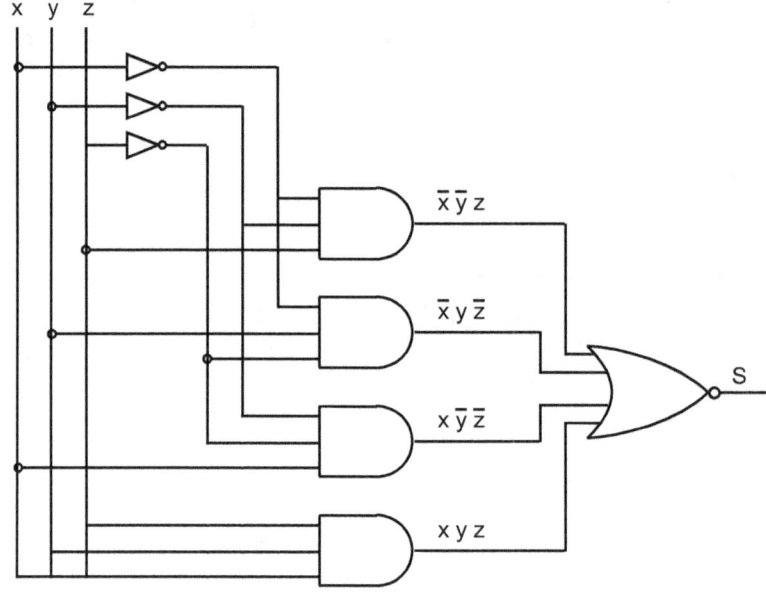

Fig. 1.18

Similarly express carry as dnf.

$$c = x\bar{y}z + xy\bar{z} + \bar{x}yz + xyz$$
$$= (x\bar{y}z + xyz) + (xy\bar{z} + xyz) + (\bar{x}yz + xyz)$$
$$= xz(\bar{y} + y) + xy(\bar{z} + z) + (\bar{x} + x)yz$$
$$= xz + xy + yz$$

Logic circuit for c is shown below.

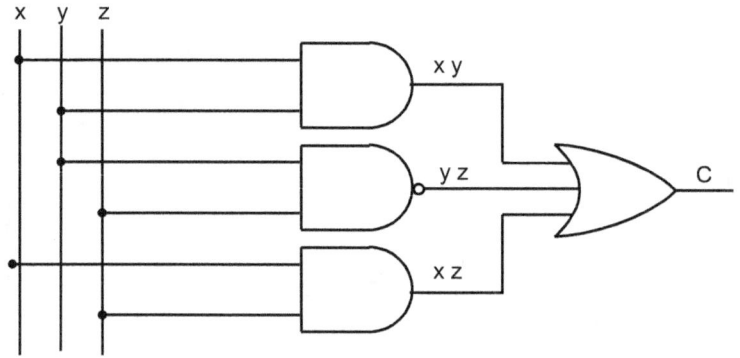

Fig. 1.19

11.1.8 Number Systems

Representation of a number in the decimal system : A positive integer N is represented as a string of decimal digits 0 to 9, with base as 10.

For example, the number N = 2347 is expressible as $2 \times 10^3 + 3 \times 10^2 + 4 \times 10^1 + 7 \times 10^0$. The powers of 10, read from right to left, are called as the place values of the digits. A fractional number M, is represented by a string of decimal digits, together with a decimal point, using negative powers of 10.

For example, 0.7285 is expressed as

$$7 \times 10^{-1} + 2 \times 10^{-2} + 8 \times 10^{-3} + 5 \times 10^{-4} = \frac{7}{10} + \frac{2}{100} + \frac{8}{1000} + \frac{5}{10000} = 0.7285$$

Representation of a number in the binary system :

In the binary system, the base is 2, and any binary integer is a string of binary digits 0 and 1.

For example, the binary number 1110 is expressible as

$1 \times 2^3 + 1 \times 2^2 + 1 \times 2^1 + 0 \times 2^0 = 8 + 4 + 2 + 0 = 14$ in the decimal system.

Similarly, the fractional part of a binary number are the negative powers of 2.

For example,

$$0.1011 = 1 \times 2^{-1} + 0 \times 2^{-2} + 1 \times 2^{-3} + 1 \times 2^{-4}$$
$$= 0.5000 + 0.1250 + 0.0625 = 0.6875$$

in the decimal system.

The following table given the conversion of some decimal integers into binary integers.

Decimal number	Binary number
0	0
1	1
2	10
3	11
4	100
5	101
6	110
7	111
8	1000
9	1001
10	1010
11	1011
12	1100
13	1101
14	1110
15	1111

SOLVED EXAMPLES

Example 1 : Convert each binary number to its decimal form : (i) 1100111, (ii) 1110.1011.

Solution : (1) $1100111 = 1 \times 2^6 + 1 \times 2^5 + 0 \times 2^4 + 0 \times 2^3 + 1 \times 2^2 + 1 \times 2^1 + 1 \times 2^0$

$= 64 + 32 + 0 + 0 + 4 + 2 + 1 = 103$

(ii) $\quad 1110 = 1 \times 2^3 + 1 \times 2^2 + 1 \times 2^1 + 0 \times 2^0 = 14$

$0.1011 = 1 \times 2^{-1} + 2 \times 2^{-2} + 1 \times 2^{-3} + 1 \times 2^{-4}$

$= \dfrac{1}{2} + \dfrac{1}{8} + \dfrac{1}{16} = 0.6875$

Hence $\quad 1110.1011 = 14.6875$ in decimal system.

Example 2 : Convert the decimal number 567.12465 into binary form.

Solution : Consider the integer part i.e. 567. Divide 567 by 2 successively, noting the reminders.

	Remainder
2) 567	
2) 283	1
2) 141	1
2) 70	1
2) 35	0
2) 17	1
2) 8	1
2) 4	0
2) 2	0
2) 1	0

The remainders taken in the reverse order gives the binary equivalent of 567, i.e. 1000110111.

For the fractional part 0.12465, multiply successively by 2, noting the integral part of the product.

$$\begin{array}{r}0.12465\\ \times\,2\\ \hline 0.24930\\ \times\,2\\ \hline 0.49860\\ \times\,2\\ \hline 0.99720\\ \times\,2\\ \hline 1.99440\\ \times\,2\\ \hline 1.98880\\ \times\,2\\ \hline 1.97760\\ \times\,2\\ \hline 1.95520\\ \times\,2\\ \hline 1.91040\\ \times\,2\\ \hline 1.82080\end{array}$$

and so on.

Containing in this manner, depending on the number of places required.

0.12465 is equivalent to the binary number 0.000111111.

EXERCISE

1. Show that in a Boolean algebra $x = y$ if and only if $(x \wedge \bar{y}) \vee (\bar{x} \wedge y) = 0$.

2. Show that in a Boolean algebra :
   (i) $x \vee y = y \Leftrightarrow x \wedge y = x$
   (ii) $\bar{x} \vee y = 1 \Leftrightarrow x \wedge \bar{y} = 0$.

3. In a Boolean algebra, the partial order $\leq$ on elements x, y is defined as $x \leq y$ if $x \wedge y = x$. Show that for any elements x, y, $x \leq y$ if and only if $\bar{y} \leq \bar{x}$.

4. For elements x, y, z in a Boolean algebra, establish the following identities.

   (i) $(x \wedge y) \vee (x \wedge \bar{y}) = x$.

   (ii) $(x \wedge y \wedge z) \vee (y \wedge z) = y \wedge z$.

   (iii) If $x \leq y$, then $x \vee (y \wedge z) = y \wedge (x \vee z)$.

5. In a Boolean algebra, prove that :

   (i) $\bar{x} \vee (x \wedge y) = \bar{x} \vee y$.

   (ii) $\overline{(x \vee y)} \vee \overline{(x \vee \bar{y})} = \bar{x}$

   (iii) $\overline{(\bar{x} \vee y))} \wedge (x \vee \bar{y}) = (x \wedge y) \vee (\bar{x} \wedge \bar{y})$

   (iv) $(x \wedge y) \wedge \bar{x} \wedge \bar{y} = 0$

   (v) $x \vee \overline{((\bar{y} \vee x) \wedge y)} = 1$

6. Let B be the set of divisions of 45. For all x, y ∈ B, define :

   $x \vee y$ = least common multiple of x and y

   $x \wedge y$ = highest common factor of x and y.

   $\bar{x} = 45/x$

   Is $< B, \wedge, \vee, - >$ a Boolean algebra ?

7. Express each of the following Boolean expressions in disjunctive form :

   (i) $(\bar{x_1} \wedge x_2) \vee (x_1 \wedge \bar{x_2})$

   (ii) $x_2 \wedge \overline{(\bar{x_1} \vee (x_1 \wedge x_3))}$

   (iii) $[(x \vee \bar{x_2}) \vee \overline{(x_2 \vee x_3)}] + (x_2 \wedge x_3)$

   (iv) $(\bar{x_1} \vee x_2 \vee x_3) \wedge (\bar{x_1} \vee x_2 \vee \bar{x_3})$

   (v) $(x_1 \wedge \bar{x_2}) \vee (x_1 \wedge x_3) \vee \bar{x_1}$

8. Express each of the following expressions in conjunctive normal form :

   (i) $(x_1 \wedge x_2) \vee (\bar{x_1} \wedge \bar{x_3})$

   (ii) $(x_1 \wedge \bar{x_2}) \vee (\bar{x_1} \wedge \bar{x_3})$

   (iii) $(\bar{x_1} \wedge x_2) \vee (x_1 \wedge x_3)$

   (iv) $(x_1 \wedge x_2) \vee (\bar{x_1} \wedge x_2) \vee (\bar{x_1} \wedge \bar{x_2})$

   (v) $(x_1 \wedge \bar{x_2} \wedge x_3) \vee (\bar{x_1} \wedge x_2 \wedge \bar{x_3})$

9. Simplifies the following Boolean expressions :

   (i) $\overline{[x_1 \vee (x_2 \wedge (\overline{x_1 \vee x_3}))]}$

   (ii) $\overline{(\overline{x_1 \wedge x_2}) \vee (x_1 \wedge \overline{x_2})}$

   (iii) $(x_1 \vee x_2) \wedge (x_1 \vee x_3) \wedge \overline{(\overline{x_1} \wedge \overline{x_2})}$

   (iv) $(x_1 \vee (x_2 \wedge x_3)) \wedge x_3) \vee (x_1 \vee x_2) \wedge (x_1 \vee x_3)$

   (v) $(x_1 \wedge \overline{x_2} \wedge x_3) \vee (x_1 \wedge \overline{x_2} \wedge \overline{x_3}) \vee (\overline{x_1} \wedge \overline{x_2} \wedge x_3) \vee (\overline{x_1} \wedge \overline{x_2} \wedge \overline{x_3})$

10. Draw the circuit diagram corresponding to the following Boolean expressions :

    (i) $(x_1 + x_2) x_3 + \overline{x_2}$

    (ii) $(x_1 + x_2)(x_1 + x_3)$

    Simplify the expression and draw the simplified circuit diagram.

11. Find the Boolean expression corresponding to the following circuit :

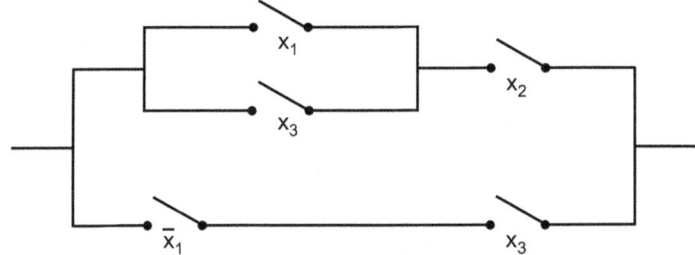

Fig. 1.20

12. Draw the logic gate corresponding to the following Boolean expression :

    (i) $x_1 x_2 \overline{x_3} + x_1 \overline{x_2} x_3 + \overline{x_1} x_2 x_3$

    (ii) $\overline{(x_1 + x_2)} (\overline{x_1} + x_2 x_3)$

13. Write the Boolean expression corresponding to the following logic gate :

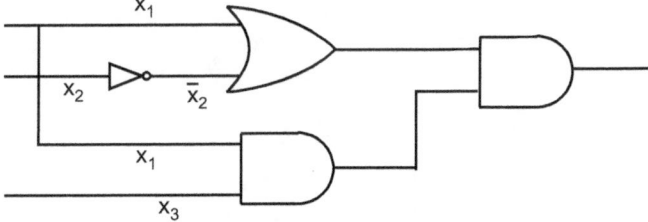

Fig. 1.21

14. Draw the logic gate diagram for the Boolean function $f(x_1, x_2, x_3) = (x_1 + x_2)\overline{x_3} + x_1$.
15. Convert each binary number to its decimal equivalent :
    (i) 10110100, (ii) 1110110111.
16. Convert (i) 111.011, (ii) 1011.1011 to its decimal equivalent.
17. Convert (i) 3127, (ii) 569 to binary form.
18. Convert to its binary equivalent (i) 124.675, (ii) 37.2450.

❏❏❏

Discrete Structure and Graph Theory
MARCH 2015

Instructions to Candidates :
1. Do not write anything on question paper except Seat No.
2. Graph or diagram should be drawn with the black ink pen being used for writing paper or black HB pencil.
3. Students should note, no supplement will be provided.
4. Solve any two sub questions out of three sub questions for each unit.
5. Assume suitable data whenever necessary.
6. Draw neat diagrams whenever necessary.

UNIT-I

1. (a) (i) A room has 3 sockets. From a collection of 10 bulbs out of which 6 are not good. A person select 3 bulbs and put into socket then find probability that : **(4)**
   (1) He get light from all the three bulbs.
   (2) He get light from atleast one.
   (ii) Explain proposition and proposition connectives. **(4)**

(b) (i) Explain permutation and combination with suitable example. **(4)**
   (ii) If $P(A) = \frac{1}{2}$, $P(B) = \frac{1}{3}$ and $P(A \cup B) = \frac{2}{3}$ then show that, A and B are independent events. **(4)**

(c) (i) Among integers between 1 to 300. Find how many are not divisible by 3 nor by 5. **(4)**
   (ii) Explain mathematical induction principle with suitable example. **(4)**

UNIT-II

2. (a) (i) Explain pigeonhole principle with suitable example. **(4)**
   (ii) Explain properties of binary relation. **(4)**

(b) Explain equivalence relation with suitable example. Also explain equivalence class with its properties and example. **(8)**

(c) Define function. Explain conditions for function with suitable example. Explain types of functions with example of each. **(8)**

UNIT-III

3. (a) (i) Explain merge sort algorithm with an example. **(4)**
   (ii) Explain total solution with suitable example. **(4)**

(b) Find homogeneous solution of following difference equation. **(8)**
   (1) $a_r + 6a_{r-1} + 12a_{r-2} + 8a_{r-3} = 0$.
   (2) $4a_r - 20a_{r-1} + 17a_{r-2} - 4a_{r-3} = 0$.

(c) Explain time complexity of an algorithm. (8)
Find time complexity of a bubble sort algorithm with an example.
Also explain tractable and intractable problems with an example.

UNIT-IV

4. (a) (i) Explain Huffman's algorithm for optical binary tree with an example. (4)
   (ii) Explain isomorphic graph and homomorphic graph. (4)
(b) Determine the shortest path from vertex a to z using Dijkstra's algorithm. (8)

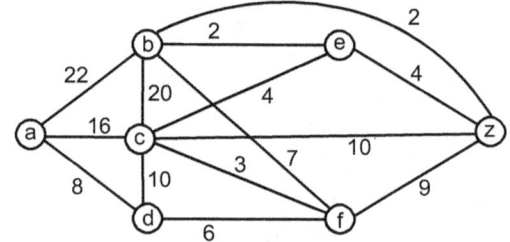

(c) (i) Explain fundamental circuit and fundamental cutset with suitable example. (4)
   (ii) Explain binary tree and rooted tree with example. (4)

UNIT-V

5. (a) Convert the following : (8)
   (i) $(1248.56)_8 = (\ )_{10}$
   (ii) $(1110010.1110)_2 = (\ )_8$
   (iii) $(45.15)_{10} = (\ )_2$
   (iv) $(252.65)_{10} = (\ )_{16}$
(b) Explain and prove the properties of an algebraic system defined by lattice. (8)
   (i) Explain group with suitable example. (4)
(c) (ii) Explain isomorphism and automorphism with an example. (4)

www.ingramcontent.com/pod-product-compliance
Lightning Source LLC
Chambersburg PA
CBHW081141290426
44108CB00018B/2403